Canonical Collections of the Early Middle Ages (ca. 400–1140)

HISTORY OF MEDIEVAL CANON LAW

Edited by Wilfried Hartmann and Kenneth Pennington

Canonical Collections of the Early Middle Ages (ca. 400–1140): A Bibliographical Guide to the Manuscripts and Literature

Papal Letters in the Early Middle Ages

The History of Western Canon Law to 1000

The History of Byzantine and Eastern Canon Law to 1500

The History of Canon Law in the Age of Reform, 1000–1140

The History of Medieval Canon Law in the Classical Period, 1140–1234

The History of Medieval Canon Law, 1234–1300

Doctrines of Canon Law, 1100–1298

The History of Medieval Canon Law in the Late Middle Ages

The History of Courts and Procedure in Medieval Canon Law

A Guide to Medieval Canon Law Jurists and Collections, 1140–1500

Lotte Kéry

Canonical Collections of the Early Middle Ages

(ca. 400–1140)

A Bibliographical Guide to the Manuscripts and Literature

The Catholic University of America Press • Washington, D.C.

Printed in the United States of America

The paper used in this publication meets the minimum requirements of the American National Standards for Information Science—Permanence of Paper for Printed Library materials, ANSI Z39.48-1984.

Library of Congress Cataloging-in-Publication Data
Kéry, Lotte.
Canonical collections of the early Middle Ages (ca. 400–1140) : a bibliographical guide to the manuscripts and literature / Lotte Kéry.
p. cm. — (History of medieval canon law ; 1)
Includes indexes.
1. Canon law—Sources—Bibliography. 2. Law, Medieval—Sources—Bibliography. I. Title. II Series. LAW
016.2629—dc21
98-23184
ISBN 978-0-8132-2190-0 (alk. paper)

Contents

Foreword

The present volume contains a bibliographical survey of the chronological and systematic canonical collections in the Latin West from the beginnings of Christianity to Gratian's Decretum (ca. 1140). Dr. Kéry not only has compiled a catalogue of early medieval canonistic manuscripts, but has included valuable information about them. For each collection she has described its type and contents, the time and place of compilation, and,when possible, its author. Full bibliographies have been provided for each collection, arranged in chronological order. Scholars will find her work particularly useful since she has also noted where scholars have differed and where their opinions may be found. Special attention has been paid to the numerous recensions of the collections. She has given a separate entry for important recensions and has lists of fragments and abbreviated forms of the collections.

The arrangement of the collections is divided into three large chronological periods, Early Medieval, Carolingian, and Gregorian Reform. Within each of these sections the organization is chronological and geographical as far as the collections can be either dated or placed within a certain region. In parts two and three the numerous smaller collections have been placed at the end of the sections, separated from the more influential collections. For some collections, especially those with a small number of manuscripts, time and place of compilation can be established only within the most broad and general limits. Consequently, the indices are the easiest guide to a particular collection. When seeking a certain manuscript in the indices, users will note that the names of the cities in which the manuscripts now reside are given in the language of the country and have not been subjected to the vagaries of past English practice.

Not all collections with canonical materials have been included in this volume. Alongside the most important and most widely circulated collections, Dr. Kéry has considered only those collections that were produced specifically for ecclesiastical use. Very small collections that contain few canonical texts and circulated in only one manuscript have been omitted. Bishops' capitularies and Roman legal texts often established norms for ecclesiastical institutions. However, because penitentials, capitularies, and secular legal texts belong to different genres, she has not listed these sources.

For the most important manuscripts she has provided bibliographical guidance. Although absolute completeness was not the goal of the bibliographies for the collections and the manuscripts, the most important studies for each have been listed. Most of the literature, particularly the most significant, has been checked personally. However, although secondary literature has been exploited, we have had to rely on it for the information that we give on dating, provenance, and other details of the manuscripts.

This thorough and complete listing and bibliography will permit the authors of individual chapters in our History of Medieval Canon Law to dispense with similar lists. The exception will be the chapters in the volume devoted to the canon law of the Eastern Churches where citations to manuscripts and editions will be given. We are planning to publish a revised edition of this volume at a future time.

Published separately from the volumes of the History of Medieval Canon Law devoted to the early Middle Ages we hope that this volume will serve as a 'vademecum' for scholars working in the archives. It will provide them with the latest information about canonical collections before Gratian. With its indices of manuscripts, libraries, and collections, scholars will be able to easily discover whether the manuscripts that they find are new discoveries or already recorded in the literature.

This volume rests, as all scholarly work does, on the work of many scholars, without whose labors it would never have been written. For the canonical collections of the early Middle Ages and the Carolingian period, Hubert Mordek's articles and books have been invaluable. Other chapters in the early volumes of this History that have not yet been published were mined as well for information about various collections: the chapters of Horst Fuhrmann, Antonio García y García, Jörg Müller, Rudolf Pokorny, Roger Reynolds, Gerhard Schmitz have all been helpful.

In particular we must thank Rudolf Pokorny (Venice) who has thoroughly read various stages of this work. With his superb critical eye, he has helped us to avoid errors and lapses of all sorts. In the last stages of the work, he has also given us valuable suggestions about its final organization. Martin Brett (Cambridge) has also generously shared his notes on the manuscripts of Ivo's Panormia, the Tripartita, and the Collectio Lanfranci with us. In the last stages of the work, Linda Fowler-Magerl provided valuable additional information about the collections in Part III. Further, we must thank Martina Schmid (University of Regensburg) for helping us to translate the work into English. We also wish to thank Jochen Böder and Clemens Radl for their work in compiling the indices.

This work would never have been completed without the dedication of Lotte Kéry to this project. She has worked on this volume for many years on both sides of the Atlantic. The editors are grateful for her long hours of work, forbearance with our requests for changes, and patience for bringing a long and difficult piece of research to a successful conclusion. This project would not have been possible without the financial support of several institutions and foundations. The National Endowment for the Humanities gave the editors a grant that permitted them to launch the project and that supported it for six years. The Werner Reimers Stiftung granted us and our collaborators the opportunity to meet under ideal circumstances at their conference center in Bad Homburg in 1990 and 1992. This particular volume, as well as others that will appear, were not even a part of the original project but emerged from our collaborative discussions in pleasant and beautiful surroundings. We would particularly like to thank the Gerda Henkel Stiftung (Düsseldorf) for supporting the project in general financially and for providing a special stipend for Dr. Kéry. The University of Regensburg also helped to support Dr. Kéry during this period. The Alexander-von-Humboldt Stiftung's Transcoop grant enabled Dr. Kéry and the editors to travel across the Atlantic several times to work on this volume together. Finally, we must thank Syracuse University and Vice-President for Research, Dr. Ben Ware, for funding our project.

Wilfried Hartmann
Kenneth Pennington
Syracuse, New York, August 1997

Abbreviations

Abh. Abhandlungen

ACO Acta Conciliorum Oecumenicorum

AfD Archiv für Diplomatik

AHC Annuarium historiae conciliorum

AHDE Anuario de Historia del Derecho Español

AHP Archivum historiae pontificum

AKKR Archiv für katholisches Kirchenrecht

AnTh Annales Theologici: Rivista di teologia del Centro Accademico Romano della Santa Croce, Roma

Archiv Archiv der Gesellschaft für ältere deutsche Geschichtskunde zur Beförderung einer Gesammtausgabe der Quellenschriften deutscher Geschichten des Mittelalters, ed. G. H. Pertz

BDHI Bibliothek des Deutschen Historischen Instituts in Rom

BEC Bibliothèque de l'Ecole des Chartes

BGPhMA Beiträge zur Geschichte der Philosophie und Theologie des Mittelalters

Bibl. mun. Bibliothèque municipale

BIDR Bullettino dell'Istituto di diritto romano, Milano

BIHR Bulletin of the Institute of Historical Research

BISIAM Bollettino dell'Istituto storico italiano per il medio evo e Archivio Muratori (Roma)

BMCL Bulletin of Medieval Canon Law

BN Bibliothèque Nationale (Paris)

BSBS Bollettino storico-bibliografico subalpino: Organo della Deputazione di storia patria, Torino

CCL	Corpus Christianorum, Series Latina
CCM	Cahiers de civilisation médiévale
CLA	Codices latini antiquiores, cf. below 'Short titles'
CSEL	Corpus scriptorum ecclesiasticorum latinorum
DA	Deutsches Archiv für Erforschung des Mittelalters
DACL	Dictionnaire d'archéologie chrétienne et de liturgie
DBI	Dizionario biografico degli Italiani
DDC	Dictionnaire de droit canonique
DHEE	Diccionário Histórico Eclesiastico de España
DHGE	Dictionnaire d'histoire et de géographie ecclésiastiques
DissA	Dissertation Abstracts
DThC	Dictionnaire de Théologie Catholique
ECelt	Etudes Celtiques
EHR	English Historical Review
EL	Ephemerides liturgicae
EOMIA	Ecclesiae Occidentalis Monumenta Iuris Antiquissima
Erg.bd	Ergänzungsband
FMSt	Frühmittelalterliche Studien
HJb	Historisches Jahrbuch
HLF	Histoire littéraire de la France
HRG	Handwörterbuch zur Deutschen Rechtsgeschichte
HS	Hispania sacra, Revista de historica ecclesiástica
IMU	Italia medioevale e umanistica
IRMAE	Ius Romanum Medii Aevi
JBOeB	Jahrbuch der österreichischen Byzantinistik
JEH	Journal of Ecclesiastical History
JE JK JL	Jaffé, Regesta pontificum romanorum . . . ed. secundam curaverunt S. Loewenfeld (JL: an. 882–1198), F. Kaltenbrunner (JK: an. 64?–599), P. Ewald (JE: an. 590–882) (Leipzig 1885)
JMH	Journal of Medieval History
JTS	Journal of Theological Studies
Kl.	Klasse
LMA	Lexikon des Mittelalters
LThK	Lexikon für Theologie und Kirche
MEFR	Mélanges de l'Ecole française de Rome: Moyen âge—Temps modernes
MGH	Monumenta Germaniae Historica
MIC	Monumenta Iuris Canonici
PL	Jacques Paul Migne, Patrologiae cursus completus, Series latina

MIÖG	Mitteilungen des Instituts für Österreichische Geschichtsforschung
MLJ	Mittellateinisches Jahrbuch
MM	Miscellanea mediaevalia
MS	Mediaeval Studies (Toronto)
NA	Neues Archiv
Nachr.	Nachrichten
NCE	New Catholic Encyclopedia
NDB	Neue Deutsche Biographie
N.F.	Neue Folge
Novarien	Associazione di Storia Ecclesiastica di Novara
ÖAKR	Österreichisches Archiv für Kirchenrecht
OOeHB	Oberösterreichische Heimatblätter
PerDer	Persona y derecho
Prov.	Provenance
QuadS	Quaderni Storici
QF	Quellen und Forschungen aus italienischen Archiven und Bibliotheken
QM	Quaderni medievali
RB	Revue Bénédictine
RDC	Revue de droit canonique
RE	Realencyklopädie für protestantische Theologie und Kirche
REAug	Recherches Augustiniennes
REDC	Revista española de derecho canonico
Rep. font.	Repertorium fontium historiae medii aevi
repr.	reprint, reprinted
RH	Revue Historique
RHD	Revue historique de droit français et étranger
RHE	Revue d'histoire ecclésiastique
RHF	Recueil des Historiens des Gaules et de la France
RhV	Rheinische Vierteljahrsblätter
RQ	Römische Quartalschrift
RSCI	Rivista di storia della Chiesa in Italia
RSDI	Rivista di storia del diritto Italiano
RTAM	Recherches de théologie ancienne et médiévale
SB Munich	Sitzungsberichte der Bayerischen Akademie der Wissenschaften (Munich), phil.-hist. Klasse
SB Vienna	Sitzungsberichte der kaiserlichen Akademie der Wissenschaften, Wien, phil.-hist. Klasse (Vienna)
ScrCiv	Scrittura e civiltà

Script.	Scriptorium
SDHI	Studia et Documenta Historiae et Iuris
SE	Sacris erudiri
SG	Studia Gratiana
SGreg	Studi Gregoriani
SM	Studi Medievali, ser. 3
SMGBOZ	Studien und Mitteilungen zur Geschichte des Benediktinerordens und seiner Zweige
St.	Saint, Sankt
ThPh	Theologie und Philosophie
TRE	Theologische Realenzyklopädie
TRG	Tijdschrift voor Rechtsgeschiedenis
ZKG	Zeitschrift für Kirchengeschichte
ZKR	Zeitschrift für Kirchenrecht
ZKTh	Zeitschrift für Katholische Theologie
ZRG	Zeitschrift der Savigny-Stiftung für Rechtsgeschichte
Kan. Abt.	Kanonistische Abteilung
Germ. Abt.	Germanistische Abteilung
ZSKG	Zeitschrift für Schweizerische Kirchengeschichte

Short Titles

ACO = E. Schwartz (ed.), *Acta conciliorum oecumenicorum* 1–3, 4.2 (Strasbourg, Berlin, Leipzig 1914–1940); 4.1 ed. J. Straub (Berlin 1971)

Amelli, *Spicilegium Casinense* = A. Amelli, *Spicilegium Casinense complectens analecta sacra et profana e codd. Casinensibus aliarumque bibliothecarum collecta atque edita cura et studio Archicoenobii montis Casini* (Monte Cassino 1888)

Andrieu, *Ordines Romani* = M. Andrieu, *Les Ordines Romani du haut moyen âge,* 1–5 (Spicilegium Sacrum Lovaniense 11, 1931; 23, 1948; 24, 1951; 28, 1956; 29, 1961)

Autenrieth, 'Bernold von Konstanz' = J. Autenrieth, 'Bernold von Konstanz und die erweiterte 74-Titel-Sammlung', DA 14 (1958) 375–394

Autenrieth, *Domschule* = J. Autenrieth, *Die Domschule von Konstanz zur Zeit des Investiturstreits* (Forschungen zur Kirchen- und Geistesgeschichte N.F. 3; Stuttgart 1956)

Ballerini, *De antiquis . . . collectionibus et collectoribus* = P. and G. Ballerini, *De antiquis tum editis, tum ineditis collectionibus et collectoribus canonum ad Gratianum usque tractatus in quatuor partes distributus* (Appendix ad sancti Leonis Magni opera III, Venice 1757) i–cccxx (repr. Migne PL 56.11–354B, excerpt in Migne PL 140.497–504)

Bardenhewer, *Literatur* = O. Bardenhewer, *Geschichte der altkirchlichen Literatur* 1–5 (Freiburg im Breisgau ^{2}1913–1932; repr. Darmstadt 1962)

Becker, *Catalogi* = G. Becker, *Catalogi bibliothecarum antiqui* (Bonn 1885)

Bieler, *Irish Penitentials* = L. Bieler (ed.), *The Irish Penitentials* (Scriptores Latini Hiberniae 5; Dublin 1963)

Bischoff, 'Panorama der Handschriftenüberlieferung' = B. Bischoff, 'Panorama der Handschriftenüberlieferung aus der Zeit Karls des Großen', *Karl der Große, Lebenswerk und Nachleben* 2 (Düsseldorf 1965) 233–254

Bischoff, *Schreibschulen* = B. Bischoff, *Die südostdeutschen Schreibschulen und Bibliotheken in der Karolingerzeit* 1: *Die bayerischen Diözesen*^{2} (Wiesbaden 1960); 2: *Die vorwiegend österreichischen Diözesen* (Wiesbaden 1980)

Bischoff-Hofmann, *Libri Sancti Kyliani* = B. Bischoff and J. Hofmann, *Libri Sancti Kyliani, Die Würzburger Schreibschule und die Dombibliothek im VIII. und IX. Jahrhundert* (Quellen und Forschungen zur Geschichte des Bistums und Hochstifts Würzburg 6; Würzburg 1952)

Blumenthal, *Early Councils* = U.-R. Blumenthal, *The Early Councils of Pope Paschal II. 1100–1110* (Toronto 1978)

Blumenthal, 'Fälschungen' = U.-R. Blumenthal, 'Fälschungen bei Kanonisten der Kirchenreform', *Fälschungen im Mittelalter* 2.241–262

Boese, *Sammlung Hamilton* = H. Boese, *Die lateinischen Handschriften der Sammlung Hamilton zu Berlin* (Wiesbaden 1966)

Brett, 'Collectio Lanfranci' = M. Brett, 'The Collectio Lanfranci and its Competitors', *Intellectual Life in the Middle Ages: Essays presented to Margaret Gibson*, ed. L. Smith and B. Ward (London 1992) 157–174

Brett, 'Collections attributed to Ivo' = M. Brett, 'Urban II and the collections attributed to Ivo', *Proceedings San Diego* 27–46

Brommer, 'Bischöfliche Gesetzgebung' = P. Brommer, 'Die bischöfliche Gesetzgebung Theodulfs von Orléans', ZRG Kan. Abt. 60 (1974) 1–120

Brommer 'Fragmente' = P. Brommer, 'Unbekannte Fragmente von Kanonessammlungen im Staatsarchiv Marburg', *Hessisches Jahrbuch für Landesgeschichte* 24 (1974) 228–233

Brommer, 'Kirchenrechtliche Sammlungen' = P. Brommer, 'Kirchenrechtliche Sammlungen der vorgratianischen Zeit in Koblenz', *Landeskundliche Vierteljahresblätter* 21 (1975) 86–89

Brommer, 'Kurzformen' = P. Brommer, 'Kurzformen des Dekrets Bischof Burchards von Worms', *Jahrbuch für westdeutsche Landesgeschichte* 1 (1975) 19–45

Brommer, 'Rezeption' = P. Brommer, 'Die Rezeption der bischöflichen Kapitularien Theodulfs von Orléans', ZRG Kan. Abt. 61 (1975) 113–160

Brooke, *English Church* = Z. N. Brooke, *The English Church and the Papacy from the Conquest to the Reign of John* (Cambridge 1931, repr. Cambridge 1968 and 1989)

Bruckner, *Scriptoria medii aevi Helvetica* = A. Bruckner, *Scriptoria medii aevi Helvetica; Denkmäler schweizerischer Schreibkunst des Mittelalters* 1–5 (Geneva 1935–1943)

Bruns, *Canones apostolorum* = H. T. Bruns, *Canones Apostolorum et Conciliorum Veterum Saeculorum IV–VII* 1–2 (Berlin 1889; repr. Torino 1959)

Busch, *Placidus von Nonantola* = J. W. Busch, *Der Liber de Honore Ecclesiae des Placidus von Nonantola, eine kanonistische Problemerörterung aus dem Jahre 1111: Die Arbeitsweise ihres Autors und seine Vorlagen* (Quellen und Forschungen zum Recht im Mittelalter 5; Sigmaringen 1990)

Chiesa, diritto e ordinamento = *Chiesa, diritto e ordinamento della 'Societas Christiana' nei secoli XI e XII:. Atti della nona Settimana internazionale di studio, Mendola, 28 agosto–2 settembre 1983* (Miscellanea del Centro di Studi Medioevali XI; Milan 1986)

Chiesa e riforma = *Chiesa e riforma nella spiritualità del sec. XI* (Convegno di studi sulla spiritualità medievale; Todi 1968)

Christ, 'Überlieferung' = K. Christ, 'Die Schloßbibliothek von Nikolsburg und die Überlieferung der Kapitulariensammlung des Ansegis', DA 1 (1937) 281–322

CLA = *Codices latini antiquiores*, ed. E. A. Lowe (=Loew), *A paleographical guide to latin manuscripts prior to the ninth century* 1–2 (Oxford 1934–1972) 1: *Vatican City* (Oxford 1934)

Clavis = E. Dekkers and E. Gaar, *Clavis Patrum Latinorum*^{2} (SE 3; Steenbrugge 1961)

Concilio III de Toledo = *Concilio III de Toledo: XIV Centenario, 589–1989* (Toledo 1991)

Contreni, 'Description' = J. J. Contreni, 'A New Description of the Lost Laon Manuscript of the *Collectio Hispana Gallica*,' BMCL 7 (1977) 85–89 (repr. *Carolingian Learning, Masters and Manuscripts* [1992] no. xiv)

Conrat, *Geschichte* = M. Conrat (Cohn), *Geschichte der Quellen und Literatur des römischen Rechts im früheren Mittelalter* 1 (Leipzig 1891; repr. Aalen 1963)

Coquin, 'Sort' = M. Coquin, 'Le sort des *Statuta Ecclesiae antiqua* dans les collections canoniques jusqu'à la *Concordia* de Gratien', *Recherches de Théologie ancienne et médiévale* 28 (1961) 193–224

De Clercq, *Législation* = C. De Clercq, *La législation religieuse franque: Etude sur les actes de conciles et les capitulaires, les statuts diocésains et les règles monastiques* 1: *de Clovis à Charlemagne (507–814)* (Louvain-Paris 1936); 2: *De Louis le Pieux à la fin du IXe siècle (814–900)* (Anvers 1958)

Delisle, *Cabinet des manuscrits* = L. Delisle, *Cabinet des manuscrits* 1 (Paris 1868); 2 (Paris 1874); 3 (Paris 1881)

Devisse, *Hincmar et la loi* = J. Devisse, *Hincmar et la loi* (Université de Dakar: Faculté des lettres et sciences humaines, Publications de la section d'histoire 5; Dakar 1962)

Die Salier = *Die Salier und das Reich*, ed. S. Weinfurter 1–3 (Sigmaringen 1992)

Dobschütz, *Decretum Gelasianum* = E. von Dobschütz, *Das Decretum Gelasianum de libris recipiendis et non recipiendis, in kritischem Text hg. und untersucht* (Texte und Untersuchungen zur Geschichte der altchristlichen Literatur, 3. Reihe, 8. Bd, Heft 4; Leipzig 1912)

Duchesne, 'Collection romaine' = L. Duchesne, 'La première collection romaine des décrétales', *Atti del II° congresso internazionale di archeologia cristiana* (Rome 1902) 159–162

Duchesne, *Fastes épiscopaux* = L. Duchesne, *Fastes épiscopaux de l'ancienne Gaule* 1–3, 2e édition revue et corrigée (Paris 1907–1915)

Duchesne, *Liber pontificalis* = L. Duchesne, *Le Liber pontificalis* 1–2 (Paris 1886–1892)

Essays in Honor of Stephan Kuttner (1977) = *Law, Church, and Society: Essays in Honor of Stephan Kuttner*, ed. K. Pennington and R. Somerville (Philadelphia 1977)

Etudes . . . Le Bras = *Etudes d'histoire du droit canonique dédiées à Gabriel Le Bras* 1 (Paris 1965)

Etudes Metman = *Etudes d'histoire du droit médiéval en souvenir de Josette Metman* (Mémoires de la Société pour l'Histoire du Droit et des Institutions des anciens pays bourguignons, comtois et romands 45; Dijon 1988)

Fälschungen im Mittelalter = *Fälschungen im Mittelalter: Internationaler Kongreß der Monumenta Germaniae Historica München, 16.–19. September 1986*, 1–6 (MGH Schriften 33.1–6; Hannover 1988)

Festschrift Becker (1987) = *Deus qui mutat tempora. Menschen und Institutionen im Wandel des Mittelalters: Festschrift für Alfons Becker zu seinem fünfundsechzigsten Geburtstag*, edd. E. D. Hehl et al. (Sigmaringen 1987)

Festschrift Elze (1992) = *Rom im hohen Mittelalter. Studien zu den Romvorstellungen und zur Rompolitik vom 10. bis zum 12. Jahrhundert: Reinhard Elze zur Vollendung seines siebzigsten Lebensjahres gewidmet*, edd. B. Schimmelpfennig and L. Schmugge (Sigmaringen 1992)

Festschrift Fuhrmann (1991) = *Papsttum, Kirche und Recht im Mittelalter: Festschrift für Horst Fuhrmann zum 65. Geburtstag*, ed. H. Mordek (Tübingen 1991)

Festschrift Kempf (1983) = *Aus Kirche und Reich. Studien zu Theologie, Politik und Recht im Mittelalter: Festschrift für Friedrich Kempf zu seinem fünfundsiebzigsten Geburtstag und fünfzigjährigen Doktorjubiläum*, ed. H. Mordek (Sigmaringen 1983)

Festschrift Kottje (1992) = *Aus Archiven und Bibliotheken: Festschrift für Raymund Kottje zum 65. Geburtstag*, ed. H. Mordek (Frankfurt 1992)

Festschrift Reindel (1995) = *Regensburg, Bayern und Europa: Festschrift für Kurt Reindel*, ed. L. Kolmer (Regensburg 1995)

Festschrift Tellenbach (1985) = *Reich und Kirche vor dem Investiturstreit: Vorträge beim wissenschaftlichen Kolloquium aus Anlass des achtzigsten Geburtstags von Gerd Tellenbach*, ed. K. Schmidt (Sigmaringen 1985)

Festschrift Zimmermann (1991) = *Ex ipsis rerum documentis. Beiträge zur Mediävistik: Festschrift für Harald Zimmermann zum 65. Geburtstag*, ed. K. Herbers, H. H. Kortüm and C. Servatius (Sigmaringen 1991)

Finsterwalder, *Canones Theodori* = P. W. Finsterwalder, *Die Canones Theodori Cantuariensis und ihre Überlieferungsformen* (Untersuchungen zu den Bußbüchern des 7., 8. und 9. Jahrhunderts 1; Weimar 1929)

Fliche, *Réforme grégorienne* = A. Fliche, *La Réforme grégorienne et la Reconquête chrétienne 1057–1123* (Histoire de l'église depuis les origines à nos jours 8; Paris 1950)

Fournier, 'Angleterre' = P. Fournier, 'Note sur les anciennes collections canoniques conservées en Angleterre', RHD, 4e série, 12 (1933) 129–134

Fournier, 'Anselmo dedicata' = P. Fournier, 'L'origine de la collection Anselmo dedicata', *Mélanges P. F. Girard* 1 (Paris 1912) 475–498 (repr. *Mélanges de droit canonique* 2.189–212)

Fournier, 'Caesaraugustana' = P. Fournier, 'La collection canonique dite Caesaraugustana', *Nouvelle* RHD 45 (1921) 53–79 (repr. *Mélanges de droit canonique* 2.815–841)

Fournier, 'Collection canonique italienne' = P. Fournier, 'Une collection canonique italienne du commencement du XIIe siècle', *Annales de l'enseignement supérieur de l'Université de Grenoble* 6 (1894) 209–233, 343–438

Fournier, 'Collections canoniques attribuées à Yves de Chartres' = P. Fournier, 'Les collections canoniques attribuées à Yves de Chartres', BEC 57 (1896) 645–698; BEC 58 (1897) 26–77, 293–326, 410–444, 624–676 (repr. *Mélanges de droit canonique* 1.451–678)

Fournier, 'Collections canoniques issues du Décret de Burchard' = P. Fournier, 'De quelques collections canoniques issues du Décret de Burchard', *Mélanges Paul Fabre, Etudes d'histoire du moyen âge* (Paris 1902) 189–214 (repr. *Mélanges de droit canonique* 1.205–230)

Fournier, 'Collections canoniques romaines' = P. Fournier, 'Les collections canoniques romaines de l'époque de Grégoire VII', *Mémoires de l'Institut National de France, Académie des Inscriptions et Belles-Lettres* 41 (1920) 271–397 (repr. *Mélanges de droit canonique* 2.425–550)

Fournier, 'Décret' = P. Fournier, 'Le Décret de Burchard de Worms: Ses caractères, son influence', RHE 12 (1911) 451–473, 670–701 (repr. *Mélanges de droit canonique* 1.393–448)

Fournier, 'Etudes critiques' = P. Fournier, 'Etudes critiques sur le Décret de Burchard de Worms', *Nouvelle* RHD 34 (1910) 41–112, 213–221, 289–331, 564–584 (repr. *Mélanges de droit canonique* 1.247–391)

Fournier, 'Fausses Décrétales' = P. Fournier, 'Etude sur les Fausses Décrétales', RHE 7 (1906) 33–51, 301–316, 543–564, 761–784; RHE 8 (1907) 19–56 (repr. *Mélanges de droit canonique* 1.83–201)

Fournier, 'Groupe de recueils' = P. Fournier, 'Un groupe de recueils canoniques inédits du Xe siècle (Troyes, 1406; Bibliothèque Nationale, Latin 2449; Ambrosienne, A.46.inf.)', *Annales de l'Université de Grenoble* 11 (1899) 345–402

Fournier, 'Influence' = P. Fournier, 'De l'influence de la collection irlandaise sur la formation des collections canoniques', *Nouvelle* RHD 23 (1899) 27–78 (repr. *Mélanges de droit canonique* 2.93–144)

Fournier, 'Manuel' = P. Fournier, 'Le premier manuel canonique de la réforme du XIe siècle', *Mélanges d'archéologie et d'histoire de l'Ecole française de Rome* 14 (1894) 147–223, 285–290 (repr. *Mélanges de droit canonique* 2.551–633)

Fournier, 'Manuscrit de Montpellier' = P. Fournier, 'Notice sur le Manuscrit H. 137 de l'Ecole de Médecine de Montpellier', *Annales de l'Université de Grenoble* 9 (1897) 357–389

Fournier, 'Notices' = P. Fournier, 'Notices sur trois collections canoniques inédites de l'époque carolingienne: I. L'Institutio canonum. II. La collection de Laon. III. La collection en deux livres', *Revue des sciences religieuses* 6 (1926) 78–92, 217–230, 513–526 (repr. *Mélanges de droit canonique* 2.145–187)

Fournier, 'Observations' = P. Fournier, 'Observations sur diverses recensions de la collection canonique d'Anselme de Lucques', *Annales de l'Université de Grenoble* 13 (1901) 427–458 (repr. *Mélanges de droit canonique* 2.635–666)

Fournier, 'Polycarpus' = P. Fournier, 'Les deux recensions de la collection canonique romaine dite le *Polycarpus*', *Mélanges d'archéologie et d'histoire de l'école française de Rome* 37 (1918/1919) 55–101 (repr. *Mélanges de droit canonique* 2.703–750)

Fournier, 'Question des Fausses Décrétales' = P. Fournier, 'La question des Fausses Décrétales', *Nouvelle* RHD 11 (1887) 70–104 (repr. *Mélanges de droit canonique* 2.23–64)

Fournier, 'Recueil canonique allemand' = P. Fournier, 'La collection canonique dite collectio XII partium: Etude sur un recueil canonique allemand du XIe siècle', RHE 17 (1921) 31–62, 229–259 (repr. *Mélanges de droit canonique* 2.751–813)

Fournier, 'Recueils canoniques italiens' = P. Fournier, 'Un groupe de recueils canoniques italiens des Xe et XIe siècles', *Mémoires de l'Institut national de France, Académie des inscriptions et belles-lettres* 40 (1916) 95–213 (repr. *Mélanges de droit canonique* 2.213–331)

Fournier, 'Réginon' = P. Fournier, 'L'oeuvre canonique de Réginon de Prüm', BEC 81 (1920) 5–44 (repr. *Mélanges de droit canonique* 2.333–372)

Fournier, 'Tournant' = P. Fournier, 'Un tournant de l'histoire du droit', RHD 41 (1917) 129–180 (repr. *Mélanges de droit canonique* 2.373–424)

Fournier, 'Yves de Chartres et le droit canonique' = P. Fournier, 'Yves de Chartres et le droit canonique', *Revue des questions historiques* 63 (1898) 51–98, 384–405 (repr. *Mélanges de droit canonique* 1.679–748)

Fournier-Le Bras = P. Fournier and G. Le Bras, *Histoire des collections canoniques en Occident depuis les Fausses Décrétales jusqu'au Décret de Gratien* 1–2 (Bibliothèque de l'histoire du Droit 4–5; Paris 1931–1932, repr. Aalen 1972)

Fowler-Magerl, 'Vorgratianische Kanonessammlungen' = L. Fowler-Magerl, 'Vier französische und spanische vorgratianische Kanonessammlungen', *Aspekte europäischer Rechtsgeschichte: Festschrift für Helmut Coing zum 70. Geburtstag* (Ius Commune, Sonderheft 17; Frankfurt 1982) 123–146

Fransen, 'Abrégés' = G. Fransen, 'Les abrégés de collections canoniques: Essai de typologie', RDC 28 (1978) 157–166

Fransen, 'Essai de classement' = G. Fransen, 'Le Décret de Burchard de Worms: Valeur du texte de l'édition, Essai de classement des manuscrits', ZRG Kan. Abt. 63 (1977) 1–19

Fransen, 'Manuscrit de Montpellier' = G. Fransen, 'Le manuscrit de Burchard de Worms conservé à la Bibliothèque municipale de Montpellier, *Mélanges Aubenas* 301–311

Fransen, 'Manuscrits' = G. Fransen, 'Manuscrits des collections canoniques', BMCL 6 (1976) 67–72

Fransen, 'Réflexions' = G. Fransen, 'Réflexions sur l'étude des collections canoniques à l'occasion de l'édition d'une lettre de Bruno de Segni', SGreg 9 (1972) 316–533

Fransen, 'Trois notes' = G. Fransen, 'Trois Notes: Note sur le Ms. Saint-Omer 107, Collections canoniques oubliés, Burchard de Worms: Quête de manuscrits' *Traditio* 26 (1970) 444–447

Fuhrmann, *Einfluß und Verbreitung* = H. Fuhrmann, *Einfluß und Verbreitung der pseudoisidorischen Fälschungen, von ihrem Auftauchen bis in die neuere Zeit* 1–3 (MGH Schriften 24.1–3; Stuttgart 1972–1974)

Fuhrmann, 'Fragmente' = H. Fuhrmann, 'Fragmente der Collectio Anselmo dedicata', DA 44 (1988) 539–543

Fuhrmann, 'Papstbriefe' = H. Fuhrmann, 'Zu kirchenrechtlichen Vorlagen einiger Papstbriefe aus der Zeit Karls des Großen', DA 35 (1979) 357–367

Fuhrmann, 'Pseudoisidor in Rom' = H. Fuhrmann, 'Pseudoisidor in Rom vom Ende der Karolingerzeit bis zum Reformpapsttum', ZKG 78 (1967) 15–66

García y García, *Historia* = A. García y García, *Historia del Derecho Canónico* 1: *El Primer Milenio* (Instituto de Historia de la Teologia Española, Subsidia 1; Salamanca 1967)

Gassò-Batlle, *Pelagii I papae epistulae* = P. M. Gassò and C. M. Batlle, *Pelagii I papae epistulae quae supersunt* (Scripta et Documenta 8; Montserrat 1956)

Gaudemet, 'Capitula Martini' = J. Gaudemet, '*Traduttore, traditore*—Les Capitula Martini', *Fälschungen im Mittelalter* 2.51–65

Gaudemet, 'Primauté' = J. Gaudemet, 'La Primauté pontificale dans le Décret de Gratien', *Studia in Honorem A. M. Stickler* 137–156

Gaudemet, *Sources* = J. Gaudemet, *Les sources du droit de l'église en occident du IIe au VIIe siècle* (Paris 1985)

Gaudemet, 'Survivances romaines' = J. Gaudemet, 'Survivances romaines dans le droit de la monarchie franque du Ve au Xe siècle', TRG 23 (1955) 149–206

Gilchrist, *Diuersorum patrum sententie* = J. Gilchrist, *Diuersorum patrum sententie siue*

Collectio in LXXIV titulos digesta (MIC, Series B: Corpus Collectionum 1; Vatican City 1973)

Gilchrist, 'Economic Policy' = J. Gilchrist, 'Eleventh and Early Twelfth Century Canonical Collections and the Economic Policy of Gregory VII', SGreg 9 (1972) 377–417

Gilchrist, 'Epistola Widonis' = J. Gilchrist, 'Die Epistola Widonis oder Pseudo-Paschalis: Der erweiterte Text', DA 37 (1981) 576–604

Gilchrist, 'Manuscripts' = J. Gilchrist, 'The Manuscripts of the Canonical Collection in Four Books', ZRG Kan. Abt. 69 (1983) 64–120

Gilchrist, 'Monastic Forgeries' = J. Gilchrist, 'The Influence of the Monastic Forgeries attributed to Pope Gregory I (JE †1951) and Boniface IV (JE †1996)', *Fälschungen im Mittelalter* 2.263–287

Gilchrist, 'Reception 1' = J. Gilchrist, 'The Reception of Pope Gregory VII into the Canon Law (1073–1141) 1', ZRG Kan. Abt. 59 (1973) 35–82

Gilchrist, 'Reception 2' = J. Gilchrist, 'The Reception of Pope Gregory VII into the Canon Law (1073–1141) 2', ZRG Kan. Abt. 66 (1980) 192–229

Gossman, *Urban II* = F. J. Gossman, *Pope Urban II and Canon Law* (Washington 1960)

Hartmann, 'Autoritäten' = W. Hartmann, 'Autoritäten im Kirchenrecht und Autorität des Kirchenrechts in der Salierzeit', *Die Salier* 3.425–446

Hartmann, 'Kanonessammlung' = W. Hartmann, 'Die Kanonessammlung der Handschrift Rom, Biblioteca Vallicelliana, B.89', BMCL 17 (1987) 45–64

Hartmann, *Worms* = W. Hartmann, *Das Konzil von Worms 868: Überlieferung und Bedeutung* (Abh. Göttingen; phil.-hist. Kl. 3. Folge, Nr. 105; Göttingen 1977)

Hispana Christiana = *Hispana Christiana: Estudios en honor del Prof. Dr. José Orlandis Rovira en su septuagésimo aniversario,* ed. J. I. Saranyana and E. Tejero (Pamplona 1988)

Hoffmann, *Buchkunst* = H. Hoffmann, *Buchkunst und Königtum im ottonischen und frühsalischen Reich* 1 (MGH Schriften 30.1; Stuttgart 1986)

Hoffmann, *Bamberger Handschriften* = H. Hoffmann, *Bamberger Handschriften des 10. und 11. Jahrhunderts* (MGH Schriften 39, Stuttgart 1995)

Hoffmann-Pokorny = H. Hoffmann and R. Pokorny, *Das Dekret des Bischofs Burchard von Worms* (MGH Hilfsmittel 12; Munich 1991)

Horst, *Polycarpus* = U. Horst, *Die Kanonessammlung Polycarpus des Gregor von S. Grisogono* (MGH Hilfsmittel 5; Munich 1980)

Il secolo di ferro = *Il secolo di ferro: Mito e realtà del secolo X: 19–25 aprile 1990, Spoleto, Centro Italiano di Studi sull'Alto Medioevo 1991* (Settimane di studio del Centro Italiano di Studi sull'Alto Medioevo 38; Spoleto 1991)

Jasper, *Papstwahldekret* = D. Jasper, *Das Papstwahldekret von 1059: Überlieferung und Textgestalt* (Beiträge zur Geschichte und Quellenkunde des Mittelalters 12; Berlin-New York 1986)

John, *Collectio canonum Remedio . . . ascripta* = H. John (ed.), *Collectio canonum Remedio Curiensi episcopo perperam ascripta* (MIC, Series B: Corpus Collectionum 2; Vatican City 1976)

Ker, *Medieval Libraries of Great Britain*[2] = N. R. Ker, *Medieval Libraries of Great Britain. A List of Surviving Books*[2] (London 1964)

Ker, *Medieval Manuscripts* = N. R. Ker, *Medieval Manuscripts in British Libraries* 1 (London 1969) 2–3 (Oxford 1977–1983)

Kerff, *Quadripartitus* = F. Kerff, *Der Quadripartitus: Ein Handbuch der karolingischen Kirchenreform: Überlieferung, Quellen und Rezeption* (Quellen und Forschungen zum Recht im Mittelalter 1; Sigmaringen 1982)

Kerner et al., 'Textidentifikation' = M. Kerner, F. Kerff, R. Pokorny, K. G. Schon and H. Tills, 'Textidentifikation und Provenienzanalyse im Decretum Burchardi', SG 20 (=*Miscellanea Gérard Fransen* 2; 1976) 17–63

Kottje, *Bußbücher Halitgars* = R. Kottje, *Die Bußbücher Halitgars von Cambrai und des Hrabanus Maurus: ihre Überlieferung und ihre Quellen* (Beiträge zur Geschichte und Quellenkunde des Mittelalters 8; Berlin-New York 1980)

Kottje, 'Einheit und Vielfalt' = R. Kottje, 'Einheit und Vielfalt des kirchlichen Lebens in der Karolingerzeit', ZKG 76 (1965) 323–342

Kottje, 'Salzburger Handschrift' = R. Kottje, 'Eine Salzburger Handschrift aus Köln', RhV 28 (1963) 286–290

Kölzer, *Collectio canonum* = T. Kölzer (ed.), *Collectio canonum Regesto Farfensi inserta* (MIC, Series B: Corpus Collectionum 5; Vatican City 1982)

Kölzer, 'Farfenser Kanonessammlung' = T. Kölzer, 'Die Farfenser Kanonessammlung des Cod. Vat. lat. 8487 (Collectio Farfensis)', BMCL 7 (1977) 94–100

Kölzer, 'Mönchtum und Kirchenrecht' = T. Kölzer, 'Mönchtum und Kirchenrecht: Bemerkungen zu monastischen Kanonessammlungen der vorgratianischen Zeit', ZRG Kan. Abt. 69 (1983) 121–142

Krause, 'Acten' = V. Krause, 'Die Acten der Triburer Synode 895', NA 17 (1892) 49–82, 281–326

Kretzschmar, *Alger von Lüttich* = R. Kretzschmar (ed.), *Alger von Lüttichs Traktat 'De misericordia et iustitia': Ein kanonistischer Konkordanzversuch aus der Zeit des Investiturstreits: Untersuchungen und Edition* (Quellen und Forschungen zum Recht im Mittelalter 2; Sigmaringen 1985)

Kurtscheid-Wilches = B. Kurtscheid and F. A. Wilches, *Historia iuris canonici* 1: *Historia fontium et scientiae iuris canonici ad usum scholarium* (Rome 1943)

Kuttner, 'Autorité des collections canoniques' = S. Kuttner, 'Quelques observations sur l'autorité des collections canoniques dans le droit classique de l'Eglise', *Actes du Congrès de droit canonique, Paris 22–26 avril 1947* (Paris 1950) 305–312 (repr. *Medieval Councils, Decretals and Collections of Canon Law* [1980] no. I)

Kuttner, 'Roman Manuscripts' = S. Kuttner, 'Some Roman Manuscripts of Canonical Collections', BMCL 1 (1971) 7–29 (repr. Kuttner, *Medieval Councils, Decretals and Collections of Canon Law* [1980] no. II with supplements)

Kuttner, 'Turning point' = S. Kuttner, 'Urban II and the doctrine of interpretation: A turning point ?', *Post scripta: Essays on Medieval Law and the Emergence of the European State in Honor of Gaines Post*, SG 15 (1972) 53–85 (repr. Kuttner, *The History of Ideas and Doctrines of Canon Law in the Middle Ages* [1980] no. IV)

Kuttner-Elze, *Catalogue* = S. Kuttner and R. Elze, *A Catalogue of Canon and Roman Law Manuscripts in the Vatican Library* 1 (Studi e testi 322; Vatican City 1986); 2 (Studi e Testi 328; Vatican City 1987)

Kuttner-Somerville = S. Kuttner and R. Somerville, 'The so-called Canons of Nîmes (1096)', TRG 38 (1970) 175–189

Landau, 'Dekret' = P. Landau, 'Das Dekret des Ivo von Chartres: Die handschriftliche Überlieferung im Vergleich zum Text in den Editionen des 16. und 17. Jahrhunderts', ZRG Kan. Abt. 70 (1984) 1–44

Landau, 'Eheschließung' = P. Landau, 'Die Eheschließung von Freien mit Unfreien bei Burchard von Worms und Gratian: Ein Beitrag zur Textkritik der Quellen des kanonischen Rechts und zur Geschichte christlicher Umformung des Eherechts', *Studi in onore di Luigi Prosdocimi* 1.2, 453–461

Landau, 'Erweiterte Fassungen' = P. Landau, 'Erweiterte Fassungen der Kanonessammlung des Anselm von Lucca aus dem 12. Jahrhundert', *Sant'Anselmo, Mantova* 323–338

Landau, 'Gefälschtes Recht' = P. Landau, 'Gefälschtes Recht in den Rechtssammlungen bis Gratian', *Fälschungen im Mittelalter* 2.11–49

Landau, 'Kanonessammlungen in Bayern' = P. Landau, 'Kanonessammlungen in Bayern in der Zeit Tassilos III. und Karls des Großen', *Festschrift Reindel* (1995) 137–160

Landau, 'Kanonessammlungen in der Lombardei' = P. Landau, 'Kanonessammlungen in der Lombardei im frühen und hohen Mittelalter', *Atti dell'11° congresso internazionale di studi sull'alto medioevo, Milano, 26–30 ottobre 1987*, 1 (Spoleto 1989) 425–457

Landau, 'Kirchweihe' = P. Landau, 'Das Verbot der Wiederholung einer Kirchweihe in der Geschichte des kanonischen Rechts: Ein Beitrag zur Entwicklung der Sakramentenlehre', *Studia in Honorem A. M. Stickler* 225–240

Landau, 'Regensburg' = P. Landau, 'Kanonistische Aktivität in Regensburg im frühen Mittelalter', *Zwei Jahrtausende Regensburg: Vortragsreihe der Universität Regensburg*, hg. von D. Albrecht (= U. R. Schriftenreihe der Universität Regensburg 1; Regensburg 1979) 55–74

Landau, *Officium* = P. Landau, *Officium und Libertas christiana* (SB Munich 1991, 3; Munich 1991)

Landau, 'Vorgratianische Kanonessammlungen bei den Dekretisten' = P. Landau, 'Vorgratianische Kanonessammlungen bei den Dekretisten und in frühen Dekretalensammlungen', *Proceedings San Diego* 93–116

Landau, 'Wandel und Kontinuität' = P. Landau, 'Wandel und Kontinuität im kanonischen Recht bei Gratian', *Sozialer Wandel im Mittelalter: Wahrnehmungsformen, Erklärungsmuster, Regelungsmechanismen*, edd. J. Miethke and K. Schreiner (Sigmaringen 1994) 215–233

Le Bras, 'Isidore de Seville' = G. Le Bras, 'Sur la part d'Isidore de Séville et des Espagnols dans l'histoire des collections canoniques, à propos d'un livre récent (P. Séjourné)', *Revue des sciences religieuses* 10 (1930) 218–257

Le Bras, 'Notes I' = G. Le Bras, 'Notes pour servir à l'histoire des collections canoniques I: Richesses méconnues de la Bibliothèque publique d'Albi', RHD, 4e sér., 8 (1929) 767–775

Le Bras, 'Notes II' = G. Le Bras, 'Notes pour servir à l'histoire des collections canoniques, 2: Sur la date et la patrie de la collection dite d'Angers', RHD, 4e sér. 8 (1929) 775–780

Le Bras, 'Notes III' = G. Le Bras, 'Notes pour servir à l'histoire des collections canoniques III: Un moment décisif dans l'histoire de l'Eglise et du droit canon: la renaissance gélasienne, RHD, 4e sér., 9 (1930) 506–518

Le Bras 'Notes IV' = G. Le Bras, 'Notes pour servir à l'histoire des collections canoniques IV: A propos de la *Dacheriana*', RHD, 4e sér., 9 (1930) 518–524

Le travail = Le travail au Moyen Age: Une approche interdisciplinaire: Actes du Colloque international de Louvain-la-Neuve, 21–23 mai 1987, ed. J. Hamesse and C. Muraille-Samaran (Louvain-la-Neuve 1990)

Loew-Brown, *Beneventan Script* = E. A. Loew (Lowe), *The Beneventan Script: A History of the South Italian Minuscule,* ed. V. Brown ([2]1 Rome 1980), 2: *Hand List of Beneventan MSS.* (Sussidi eruditi 34; Rome 1980)

Maassen, 'Bibliotheca' = F. Maassen, 'Bibliotheca Latina iuris canonici manuscripta 1: Die Canonessammlungen vor Pseudoisidor', *SB Vienna* 53, 1866 (1867) 373–427 (part 1.1); 54, 1866 (1867) 157–288 (part 1.2); 56, 1867 (1867) 157–212 (part 1.3–6)

Maassen, *Geschichte* = F. Maassen, *Geschichte der Quellen und der Literatur des canonischen Rechts im Abendlande,* 1: *Die Rechtssammlungen bis zur Mitte des 9. Jahrhunderts* (Graz 1870; repr. Graz 1956)

Manitius, *Literatur* = M. Manitius, *Geschichte der lateinischen Literatur des Mittelalters,* 1: *Von Justinian bis zur Mitte des 10. Jahrhunderts* (Munich 1911; repr. 1959); 2: *Von der Mitte des zehnten Jahrhunderts bis zum Ausbruch des Kampfes zwischen Kirche und Staat* (Munich 1923); 3: *Vom Ausbruch des Kirchenstreites bis zum Ende des 12. Jahrhunderts* (Munich 1931)

Mansi = J. D. Mansi, *Sacrorum conciliorum nova et amplissima collectio* 1–53 (Paris [2]1901–1927; repr. Graz 1960–1961)

Martínez Díez, *Colección Hispana* = G. Martínez Díez, *La colección canónica Hispana,* 1: Estudio (Monumenta Hispaniae sacra, Ser. can. 1, 1966); G. Martínez Díez (ed.), *La colección canónica Hispana,* 2: *Colecciónes derivadas* 1–2, (Monumenta Hispaniae Sacra, Ser. can. 1; Madrid 1976); G. Martínez Díez and F. Rodríguez (edd.), *La colección canónica Hispana,* 3: *Concilios griegos y africanos,* (Monumenta Hispaniae Sacra, Ser. can. 3; Madrid 1982); G. Martínez Díez and F. Rodríguez, *La colección canónica Hispana,* 4: *Concilios galos, Concilios hispanos, primera parte* (Monumenta Hispaniae sacra, Ser. can. 4; Madrid 1984); G. Martínez Díez and F. Rodriguez, *La colección canónica Hispana,* 5: *Concilios Hispanos: segunda parte* (Monumenta Hispaniae sacra, Ser. can. 5; Madrid 1992)

Martínez Díez, 'El Epítome Hispánico' = G. Martínez Díez, 'El Epítome Hispánico. Una colección canónica española del siglo VII: Estudio y texto critico', *Miscelánea Comillas* 36 (Comillas-Santander 1961) 6–90 and 37 (1962) 321–466

Martínez Díez, 'Novara' = G. Martínez Díez, 'La colección del ms. de Novara', *Anuario de Historia del Derecho Español* 33 (1963) 391–538

Masson, *Manuscrits des Bibliothèques sinistrées* = A. Masson, *Manuscrits des Bibliothèques sinistrées de 1940 à 1944* (Catalogue général des manuscrits des bibliothèques publiques de France 53; Paris 1962)

Mélanges Aubenas = *Mélanges Roger Aubenas* (Recueil de mémoires et travaux publiés par la société d'Histoire du Droit et des Institutions des anciens Pays de droit écrit 9; Montpellier 1974)

Mélanges de droit canonique = P. Fournier, *Mélanges de droit canonique,* ed. T. Kölzer avec avant-propos par J. Gaudemet 1–2 (Aalen 1983)

Mélanges Fransen = *Mélanges Gérard Fransen* 1–2 (= SG 19–20), ed. S. Kuttner, A. M. Stickler, E. Van Balberghe and D. Van den Auweele (Rome 1976)

Meyer, 'Überlieferung' = O. Meyer, 'Überlieferung und Verbreitung des Dekrets des Bischofs Burchard von Worms', ZRG Kan. Abt. 24 (1935) 141–183

MGH AA = MGH Auctores antiquissimi

MGH Capit. = MGH Capitularia

MGH Capit. n.s. = MGH Capitularia, nova series

G. Schmitz (ed.) *Die Kapitulariensammlung des Ansegis*, MGH Capitularia regum Francorum, nova series 1 (Hannover 1996)

MGH Capit. episc. = MGH Capitula episcoporum

P. Brommer (ed.), MGH Capitula episcoporum 1 (Hannover 1984)

R. Pokorny and M. Stratmann (edd.) MGH Capitula episcoporum 2 (Hannover 1995)

R. Pokorny (ed.), MGH Capitula episcoporum 3 (Hannover 1995)

MGH Conc. = MGH Concilia

A. Werminghoff (ed.), *Concilia Aevi Carolini* 1 (MGH Concilia 2; Hannover and Leipzig 1906)

W. Hartmann (ed.), *Die Konzilien der karolingischen Teilreiche 843–859 (Concilia aevi Karolini DCCCXLIII–DCCCLIX)* (MGH Concilia 3; Hannover 1984)

W. Hartmann (ed.), *Die Konzilien der karolingischen Teilreiche 860–874 (Concilia aevi Karolini DCLX–DCLXXIV)* (MGH Concilia 4; Hannover 1998)

R. Schieffer (ed.), *Die Streitschriften Hinkmars von Reims und Hinkmars von Laon 869–871* (MGH Concilia 4, Suppl. 2; Hannover 1998)

E.-D. Hehl and H. Fuhrmann (edd.), *Die Konzilien Deutschlands und Reichsitaliens 916–1001 (Concilia aevi Saxonici et Salici DCCCCXVI–MI)* (MGH Concilia 6.1: [916–961]; Hannover 1987)

MGH Const. = MGH Constitutiones et acta publica

L. Weiland (ed.), MGH *Constitutiones et acta publica imperatorum et regum inde ab a. DCCCCXI usque ad a. MCXCVII (911–1197)* (MGH Constitutiones 1; 1893; repr. Hannover 1963)

MGH Epp. = MGH Epistolae

E. Dümmler (ed.), MGH *Epistolae Karolini Aevi* 2 (MGH Epistolae 4; Berlin 1895)

MGH Ldl =Libelli de lite

F. Thaner (ed.), MGH Ldl 2 (Hannover 1892, repr. 1956)

MGH LL = MGH Leges

MGH Ordines = H. Schneider (ed.), MGH *Ordines de celebrando concilio: Die Konzilsordines des Früh- und Hochmittelalters* (Hannover 1996)

MGH SS = MGH Scriptores

Mor, 'Digesto' = C. G. Mor, 'Il Digesto nell'età preirneriana e la formazione della Vulgata', *Per il XIV centenario delle Pandette e del Codice di Giustiniano* (Pavia 1934) 631–647, 679–692

Mor, 'Diritto romano e diritto canonico' = C. G. Mor, 'Diritto romano e diritto canonico nell'età pregrazianea', *L'Europa e il diritto romano: Studi in memoria di Paolo Koschaker* 2 (Milan 1954) 13–32 (repr. *Scritti di storia giuridica altomedievale* [Pisa 1977] 345–363)

Mor, 'Droit romain' = C. G. Mor, 'Le droit romain dans les collections canoniques des Xème et XIème siècles', RHD 4e sér., 6 (1927) 512–524

Mor, 'La Bibbia e il diritto canonico' = C. G. Mor, 'La Bibbia e il diritto canonico', *La Bibbia nell'alto medioevo* (Settimane de studio del centro italiano di studi sull' alto medioevo 10; Spoleto 1963) 163–179

Mor, 'Manoscritto canonistico francese' = C. G. Mor, 'Un manoscritto canonistico francese del secolo IX', *Rendiconti del Reale Istituto Lombardo di Scienze e Lettere 76, Classe di Lettere e Scienze Morali e Storiche* (Milan 1942–1943) 188–202

Mor, 'Reazione al *Decretum Burchardi*' = C. G. Mor, 'La reazione al *Decretum Burchardi* in Italia avanti la riforma gregoriana' SGreg 1 (1947) 197–206

Mor, 'Recezione' = C. G. Mor, 'La recezione del diritto romano nelle collezioni canoniche dei secoli IX–XI in Italia e oltr'Alpe', *Acta congressus iuridici internationalis, VII saeculo a decretalibus Gregorii IX et XIX e Codice Iustiniano promulgatis: Romae 12–17 Novembris 1934*, 2 (Rome 1935) 281–302 (repr. *Scritti di storia giuridica altomedievale* [Pisa 1977] 289–309)

Mordek, 'Addenda' = H. Mordek, 'Codices Pseudo-Isidoriani: Addenda zu dem gleichnamigen Buch von Schafer Williams', AKKR 147 (1978) 471–478

Mordek, 'Aera', = H. Mordek, 'Aera', DA 25 (1969) 216–222

Mordek, 'Analecta canonistica' = H. Mordek, 'Analecta canonistica I', BMCL 16 (1986) 1–16

Mordek, *Bibliotheca capitularium* = H. Mordek, *Bibliotheca capitularium regum Francorum manuscripta: Überlieferung und Textzusammenhang der fränkischen Herrschererlasse* (MGH Hilfsmittel 15; Munich 1995)

Mordek, 'Bischofsabsetzungen' = H. Mordek, 'Bischofsabsetzungen in spätmerowingischer Zeit: Justelliana, Bernensis und das Konzil von Malay (677)', *Festschrift Fuhrmann* (1991) 31–53

Mordek, 'Bonneval' = H. Mordek, 'Die Rechtssammlungen der Handschrift von Bonneval—ein Werk der karolingischen Reform', DA 24 (1968) 339–434

Mordek, 'Dacheriana' = H. Mordek, 'Zur handschriftlichen Überlieferung der Dacheriana', QF 47 (1967) 574–595

Mordek, 'Dionysio-Hadriana' = H. Mordek, 'Dionysio-Hadriana und Vetus Gallica—historisch geordnetes und systematisches Kirchenrecht am Hofe Karls des Großen', ZRG Kan. Abt. 55 (1969) 39–63

Mordek, 'Handschriftenforschungen' = H. Mordek, 'Handschriftenforschungen in Italien', QF 51 (1971) 626–651

Mordek, 'Herovalliana' = H. Mordek, 'Die historische Wirkung der Collectio Herovalliana', ZKG 81 (1970) 220–243

Mordek, 'Isaak der Gute' = H. Mordek, 'Isaak der Gute in Freiburg im Breisgau: Ein neuer Textfund und die Capitula des Bischofs von Langres überhaupt', *Freiburger Diözesan-Archiv* 100 (1980) 203–210

Mordek, 'Kanonistik und gregorianische Reform' = H. Mordek, 'Kanonistik und gregorianische Reform: Marginalien zu einem nicht-marginalen Thema', *Festschrift Tellenbach* (1985) 65–82

Mordek, 'Kanonistische Aktivität' = H. Mordek, 'Kanonistische Aktivität in Gallien in der ersten Hälfte des 8. Jahrhunderts', *Francia* 2 (1974) 19–25

Mordek, 'Karolingische Kapitularien' = H. Mordek, 'Karolingische Kapitularien', ed. H. Mordek, *Überlieferung und Geltung normativer Texte des frühen und hohen Mittelalters* (Sigmaringen 1986) 25–50

Mordek, 'Kirchenrecht in Rätien' = H. Mordek, 'Spätantikes Kirchenrecht in Rätien: Zur Verwandtschaft von Tuberiensis und Weingartensis als Tradenten des ältesten lateinischen Corpus canonum', ZRG Kan. Abt. 79 (1993) 16–33

Mordek, *Kirchenrecht und Reform* = H. Mordek, *Kirchenrecht und Reform im Frankenreich: Die Collectio Vetus Gallica, die älteste systematische Kanonessammlung des fränkischen Gallien: Studien und Edition* (Beiträge zur Geschichte und Quellenkunde des Mittelalters 1; Berlin-New York 1975)

Mordek, 'Kirchenrechtliche Autoritäten' = H. Mordek, 'Kirchenrechtliche Autoritäten im Frühmittelalter', *Recht und Schrift im Mittelalter*, ed. P. Classen (Vorträge und Forschungen 23; Sigmaringen 1977) 237–255

Mordek, 'Primat' = H. Mordek, 'Der römische Primat in den Kirchenrechtssammlungen des Westens vom IV. bis VIII. Jahrhundert', *Il primato del vescovo di Roma nel primo millenio: Ricerche e testimonianze: Atti del Symposium Storico-Teologico (Roma, 9–13 Ottobre 1989)*, ed. M. Maccarrone (Vatican City 1991) 523–566

Mordek, 'Riforma gregoriana' = H. Mordek, 'Dalla riforma gregoriana alla *Concordia discordantium canonum* di Graziano: Osservazioni marginali di un canonista su un tema non marginale', *Chiesa, diritto e ordinamento* 89–112

Mordek, 'Suche' = H. Mordek, 'Auf der Suche nach einem verschollenen Manuskript . . . Friedrich Maassen und der Traktat *De immunitate et sacrilegio et singulorum clericalium ordinum compositione*', *Festschrift Kempf* (1983) 187–200

Mordek, 'Systematische Kanonessammlungen' = H. Mordek, 'Systematische Kanonessammlungen vor Gratian: Forschungsstand und neue Aufgaben', *Proceedings Berkeley* 185–201

Motta, 'Liber canonum' = G. Motta, 'Il *Liber canonum diversorum sanctorum patrum* e la disciplina canonica', *Chiesa, diritto e ordinamento* 331–339

Motta, 'Regula Benedicti' = G. Motta, 'La Regula Benedicti in alcune collezioni canoniche dei secoli VIII–XII', *Benedictina* 28 (1981) 261–279

Müller, *Collectio Duodecim Partium* = J. Müller, *Untersuchungen zur Collectio Duodecim Partium* (Abhandlungen zur rechtswissenschaftlichen Grundlagenforschung 73; Ebelsbach 1989)

Munier, *Sources patristiques* = Ch. Munier, *Les sources patristiques du droit de l'Eglise du VIIIe au XIIIe siècle.* (Dissertation University of Strasbourg; Mulhouse 1957)

Mynors-Thomson, *Catalogue of Hereford* = R. A. B. Mynors and R. M. Thomson, *Catalogue of the manuscripts of Hereford Cathedral Library* (Cambridge 1993)

Ommanney, *Early History of the Athanasian Creed* = G. W. D. Ommanney, *Early History of the Athanasian Creed* (London-Oxford-Cambridge 1880)

Ommanney, *A Critical Dissertation on the Athanasian Creed* = G. W. D. Ommanney, *A Critical Dissertation on the Athanasian Creed* (Oxford 1897)

Ourliac, 'Manuscrit toulousain' = P. Ourliac, 'Le manuscrit toulousain de la collection d'Albi', RDC 28 (1978) *(= Mélanges Jean Gaudemet)* 223–338 (repr. *Etudes de droit et d'histoire* [Paris n.d. 1980 ?] 49–62)

Peitz, *Originalregister Gregors VII.* = W. M. Peitz, *Das Originalregister Gregors VII. im Vatikanischen Archiv (Reg. Vat. 2) nebst Beiträgen zur Kenntnis der Originalregister Innocenz' III. und Honorius' III. (Reg. Vat. 4–11)* (SB Vienna, Phil.-Hist. Klasse, 165. Band, 5. Abh.; Vienna 1911)

Peitz, *Dionysius Exiguus* = W. M. Peitz, *Dionysius Exiguus als Kanonist* (1945) (Spanish translation by P. Galindo Romeo, REDC 2 [1947] 9–32)

Pelster, 'Dekret' = F. Pelster, 'Das Dekret Bischof Burkhards von Worms (1000–1025) in vatikanischen Handschriften', *Miscellanea Giovanni Mercati* 2 (Studi e testi 122; Vatican City 1946) 114–157

Petersmann, 'Kanonistische Überlieferung' = J. Petersmann, 'Die kanonistische

Überlieferung des Constitutum Constantini bis zum Dekret Gratians: Untersuchung und Edition', DA 30 (1974) 356–449

Picasso, *Collezioni canoniche Milanesi* = G. Picasso, *Collezioni canoniche Milanesi del secolo XII* (Pubblicazioni dell'Università Cattolica del S. Cuore, Saggi e richerche, ser. terza, scienze stor. 2; Milan 1969)

Picasso, 'Identificazioni' = G. Picasso, 'Nuove identificazioni nelle Collezioni canoniche Milanesi del sec. XII', BMCL 3 (1973) 139–141

Picasso, 'Reformatio ecclesiae' = G. Picasso, '*Reformatio Ecclesiae* e disciplina canonica', *Chiesa, diritto e ordinamento* 70–88

Plöchl, *Geschichte des Kirchenrechts* = W. M. Plöchl, *Geschichte des Kirchenrechts* ²1–2 (Vienna-Munich 1960–1962)

Pokorny, 'Triburer Synodalakten' = R. Pokorny, 'Die drei Versionen der Triburer Synodalakten von 895', DA 48 (1992) 429–511

Proceedings Boston = *Proceedings of the Second International Congress of Medieval Canon Law, Boston College*, ed. S. Kuttner and J. J. Ryan (MIC, Series C: Subsidia 1; Vatican City 1965)

Proceedings Strasbourg = *Proceedings of the Third International Congress of Medieval Canon Law, Strasbourg, 3–6 September 1968*, ed. Stephan Kuttner (MIC, Series C: Subsidia 4; Vatican City 1971)

Proceedings Salamanca = *Proceedings of the Fifth International Congress of Medieval Canon Law, Salamanca, 21–25 September 1976*, edd. S. Kuttner and K. Pennington (MIC, Series C: Subsidia 6; Vatican City 1980)

Proceedings Berkeley = *Proceedings of the Sixth International Congress of Medieval Canon Law, Berkeley, California, 28 July–2 August 1980*, edd. S. Kuttner and K. Pennington (MIC, Series C: Subsidia 7; Vatican City 1985)

Proceedings Cambridge = *Proceedings of the Seventh International Congress of Medieval Canon Law, Cambridge, 23–27 July 1984*, ed. P. Linehan (MIC, Series C: Subsidia 8; Vatican City 1988)

Proceedings San Diego = *Proceedings of the Eighth International Congress of Medieval Canon Law, San Diego, University of California at La Jolla, 21–27 August 1988*, ed. S. Chodorow (MIC, Series C: Subsidia 9; Vatican City 1992)

Rambaud-Buhot, 'Baluze, bibliothécaire et canoniste' = J. Rambaud-Buhot, 'Baluze, bibliothécaire et canoniste', *Etudes . . . Le Bras* 1.325–342

Rambaud-Buhot, 'Critique' = J. Rambaud-Buhot, 'La critique des faux dans l'ancien droit canonique', BEC 126 (1968) 5–62

Rambaud-Buhot, 'Corpus inédit' = J. Rambaud-Buhot, 'Un Corpus inédit de droit canonique de la réforme Carolingienne à la réforme Grégorienne', *Humanisme actif: Mélanges d'art et de littérature offerts à Julien Cain* 2 (Paris 1968) 271–281

Reynolds, 'Excerpta' = R. E. Reynolds, 'Excerpta from the *Collectio Hibernensis* in three Vatican Manuscripts', BMCL 5 (1975) 1–9

Reynolds, 'Salzburg' = R. E. Reynolds, 'Canon Law Collections in Early Ninth-Century Salzburg', *Proceedings Salamanca* 15–31

Reynolds, 'South Italian Collection' = R. E. Reynolds, 'The South-Italian Collection in Five Books and its Derivatives: New Evidence on its Origins, Diffusion and Use', MS 52 (1990) 278–295

Reynolds, 'Turin Collection' = R. Reynolds, 'The Turin Collection in Seven Books: A Poitevin Canonical Collection', *Traditio* 25 (1969) 508–514

Reynolds, 'Unity and Diversity' = R. E. Reynolds, 'Unity and Diversity in Carolingian Canon Law Collections: The Case of the *Collectio Hibernensis* and Its Derivatives', *Carolingian Essays: Andrew W. Mellon Lectures in Early Christian Studies*, ed. U.-R. Blumenthal (Washington D.C. 1983) 99–135

Richter, 'Stufen' = J. Richter, 'Stufen pseudoisidorischer Verfälschung: Untersuchungen zum Konzilsteil der pseudoisidorischen Dekretalen', ZRG Kan. Abt. 64 (1978) 1–72

Rose, *Handschriften-Verzeichnisse* = V. Rose, *Die Handschriften-Verzeichnisse der Königlichen Bibliothek zu Berlin*, 13: *Verzeichnis der lateinischen Handschriften* 2.1 (Berlin 1901)

Ryan, 'Observations' = J. J. Ryan, 'Observations on the Pre-Gratian Canonical Collections: Some Recent Work and Present Problems', *Congrès de Droit Canonique Médiéval, Louvain et Bruxelles 22–26 juillet 1958* (Bibliothèque de la RHE 33; Louvain 1959) 88–103

Ryan, *Saint Peter Damiani* = J. J. Ryan, *Saint Peter Damiani and his Canonical Sources: A Preliminary Study in the Antecedents of the Gregorian Reform* (Pontifical Institute of Mediaeval Studies; Studies and Texts 2, Toronto 1956)

Sackur, *Cluniacenser* = E. Sackur, *Die Cluniacenser in ihrer kirchlichen und allgemeingeschichtlichen Wirksamkeit bis zur Mitte des 11. Jahrhunderts* 1–2 (Halle 1894, repr. Darmstadt 1965)

Sant'Anselmo, Mantova = *Sant'Anselmo, Mantova e la lotta per le investiture: Atti del convegno Internazionale di studi (Mantova, 23–25 maggio 1986)*, ed. P. Golinelli (Bologna 1987)

Savigny, *Geschichte* = F. C. von Savigny, *Geschichte des römischen Rechts im Mittelalter* (Heidelberg [2]1834, repr. Darmstadt 1956)

Sant'Anselmo vescovo = *Sant'Anselmo vescovo di Lucca (1073–1086) nel quadro delle trasformazioni sociali e della riforma ecclesiastica, Atti del Convegno internazionale di studio, Lucca, 25–28 settembre 1986*, ed. C. Violante (Rome 1992)

Scherer, *Handbuch* = R. von Scherer, *Handbuch des Kirchenrechtes* 1 (Graz 1886)

Schieffer, *Investiturverbot* = R. Schieffer, *Die Entstehung des päpstlichen Investiturverbots für den deutschen König* (MGH, Schriften 28; Stuttgart 1981)

Schieffer, 'Rätische Sammlung' = R. Schieffer, 'Spätantikes Kirchenrecht in einer rätischen Sammlung des 8. Jahrhunderts', ZRG Kan. Abt. 66 (1980) 164–191

Schmitz, 'Abbreviatio Ansegisi' = G. Schmitz, 'Die Überlieferung der sog. *Abbreviatio Ansegisi et Benedicti Levitae*; mit einem Anhang: Die Abbreviatio- und Dacheriana-Rezeption in der 17-Bücher-Sammlung', DA 40 (1984) 176–199

Schmitz, 'Ansegis und Regino' = G. Schmitz, 'Ansegis und Regino: Die Rezeption der Kapitularien in den *Libri duo de synodalibus causis*', ZRG Kan. Abt. 74 (1988) 95–132

Schmitz, 'Überlieferung' = G. Schmitz, 'Zur Überlieferung von Thegans *Vita Hludowici* und der Kapitulariensammlung des Ansegis', RhV 44 (1980) 1–15

Schmitz, 'Vier Bücher Sammlung' = G. Schmitz, 'Die Vier-Bücher-Sammlung des Cod. Köln 124: Zur kirchenrechtlichen Kenntnis im 10. Jahrhundert', *Festschrift Zimmermann* (1991) 233–255

Schulte, 'Iter Gallicum' = J. F. von Schulte, 'Iter Gallicum', SB Vienna 59 (1868) 355–496

Schwartz, 'Kanonessammlungen' = E. Schwartz, 'Die Kanonessammlungen der alten Reichskirche', ZRG Kan. Abt. 25 (1936) 1–114 (repr. Schwartz, *Gesammelte Schriften*, 4: *Zur Geschichte der alten Kirche und ihres Rechts* [Berlin 1960] 159–275)

Schwartz, *Publizistische Sammlungen* = E. Schwartz, *Publizistische Sammlungen zum acacianischen Schisma* (Abh. Munich, philos.-hist. Kl., N.F. 10; Munich 1934)

Schwartz, 'Zweisprachigkeit' = E. Schwartz, 'Zweisprachigkeit in den Konzilsakten', *Philologus: Zeitschrift für das Klassische Altertum* 88, N.F. 46 (1933) 245–253

Sdralek, *Wolfenbüttler Fragmente* = M. Sdralek, *Wolfenbüttler Fragmente: Analekten zur Kirchengeschichte des Mittelalters aus Wolfenbüttler Handschriften* (Kirchengeschichtliche Studien, 1.2; Münster 1891)

Seckel, 'Benedictus Levita' = E. Seckel, 'Benedictus Levita decurtatus et excerptus: Eine Studie zu den Handschriften der falschen Kapitularien', *Festschrift für Heinrich Brunner zum fünfzigjährigen Doktorjubiläum am 8. April 1914 überreicht von der Juristenfakultät der Universität Berlin* (Munich-Leipzig 1914) 377–464

Seckel-Fuhrmann, *Die erste Zeile Pseudoisidors* = E. Seckel, *Die erste Zeile Pseudoisidors, die Hadriana-Rezension 'In nomine domini incipit praefatio libri huius' und die Geschichte der Invokationen in den Rechtsquellen: Aus dem Nachlaß mit Ergänzungen* ed. H. Fuhrmann (SB Berlin, Heft 4; Berlin 1959)

Seibert, 'Unbekannte Überlieferung' = H. Seibert, 'Eine unbekannte Überlieferung der 74-Titel-Sammlung aus Rheinau', *Festschrift Becker* (1987) 87–100

Séjourné, *Saint Isidore* = P. Séjourné, *Le dernier Père de l'Eglise, Saint Isidore de Séville: Son rôle dans l'histoire du droit canonique* (Paris 1929)

Semmler, 'Monastische Gesetzgebung' = J. Semmler, 'Zur Überlieferung der monastischen Gesetzgebung Ludwigs des Frommen', DA 16 (1960) 309–388

Siems, *Handel und Wucher* = H. Siems, *Handel und Wucher im Spiegel frühmittelalterlicher Rechtsquellen* (MGH Schriften 35; Hannover 1992)

Silva-Tarouca, 'Beiträge' = C. Silva-Tarouca, 'Beiträge zur Überlieferungsgeschichte der Papstbriefe des IV., V. u. VI. Jahrhunderts', ZKTh 43 (1919) 467–481 and 657–692

Silva-Tarouca, 'Nuovi studi' = C. Silva-Tarouca, 'Nuovi studi sulle antiche lettere dei papi', *Gregorianum* 12 (Rome 1931) 3–56, 349–425, 547–598

Somerville, 'Berengar' = R. Somerville, 'The Case against Berengar of Tours—A New Text', SGreg 9 (1972) 53–75

Somerville, *Decreta Claromontensia* = R. Somerville, *The Councils of Urban II*, 1: *Decreta Claromontensia* (AHC Supplementum 1; Amsterdam 1972)

Sprandel, *Ivo von Chartres* = R. Sprandel, *Ivo von Chartres und seine Stellung in der Kirchengeschichte* (Pariser Historische Studien 1; Stuttgart 1962)

Staerk, *Manuscrits Latins* = A. Staerk, *Manuscrits Latins du Ve au XIIIe siècle conservés à la Bibliothèque Impériale de Saint-Pétersbourg* 1–2 (Saint Petersburg 1910; repr. Hildesheim-New York 1976)

Steinacker, 'Deusdedithandschrift' = H. Steinacker, 'Die Deusdedithandschrift (cod. Vat. lat. 3833) und die ältesten gallischen libri canonum' (MIÖG, Ergänzungsband 6; Innsbruck 1901) 113–144

Stickler, *Historia* = A. M. Stickler, *Historia iuris canonici Latini*, 1: *Historia fontium* (Torino 1950)

Stickler, 'Potere coattivo' = A. Stickler, 'Il potere coattivo materiale della chiesa nella riforma gregoriana secondo Anselmo di Lucca', SGreg 2 (1947) 235–285

Studi in onore Luigi Prosdocimi (1994) = *Cristianità ed Europa: Miscellanea di studi in onore di Luigi Prosdocimi*, ed. C. Alzati, 1–2 (Rome-Freiburg-Vienna 1994)

Studia in Honorem A. M. Stickler (1992) = *Studia in Honorem eminentissimi cardinalis Alphonsi M. Stickler*, ed. Rosalio Iosepho Card. Castillo Lara (Studia et Textus historiae iuris canonici 7; Rome 1992)

Stürner, 'Die Quellen der Fides Konstantins' = W. Stürner, 'Die Quellen der Fides Konstantins im Constitutum Constantini (3–5)', ZRG Kan. Abt. 55 (1969) 64–206

Tardif, *Sources* = J. Tardif, *Histoire des sources du droit canonique* (Paris 1887)

Tarré, 'Sources' = J. Tarré, 'Les sources de la législation ecclésiastique dans la province Tarraconaise depuis les origines jusqu'à Gratien', *Positions des thèses de l'Ecole des chartes* (Paris 1927) 125–134

Tarré, 'Etudes' = J. Tarré, 'Etudes des collections de droit ecclésiastique avant Charlemagne', RHD, 4e sér., 12 (1933) 208–210

Theiner, *Über Ivo's vermeintliches Decret* = A. Theiner, *Über Ivo's vermeintliches Decret: Ein Beitrag zur Geschichte des Kirchenrechts und ins Besondere zur Critik der Quellen des Gratian* (Mainz 1832)

Theiner, *Disquisitiones criticae* = A. Theiner, *Disquisitiones criticae in praecipuas canonum et decretalium collectiones seu sylloges Gallandianae dissertationum de vetustis canonum collectionibus continuatio* (Rome 1836)

Thomson, *Catalogue of Lincoln* = R. M. Thomson, *Catalogue of the Manuscripts of Lincoln Cathedral Chapter Library* (Cambridge 1989)

Turner, EOMIA = C. H. Turner (ed.), *Ecclesiae occidentalis monumenta iuris antiquissima, canonum et conciliorum Graecorum interpretationes Latinae* 1–2, ed. E. Schwartz (Oxford 1899–1939)

Van Hove, *Prolegomena* = A. Van Hove, *Prolegomena* (Commentarium Lovaniense in codicem iuris canonici, 1.1; Mechelen-Rome ^{2}1945)

Verfasserlexikon = *Die deutsche Literatur des Mittelalters: Verfasserlexikon*, ed. Kurt Ruh 1–7 (Berlin-New York^{2} 1978–1989)

Waelkens-Van den Auweele, 'Codex Gandavensis' = L. Waelkens and D. Van den Auweele, 'La collection de Thérouanne en IX livres à l'abbaye de Saint-Pierre-au-Mont-Blandin: le codex Gandavensis 235', SE 24 (1980) 115–153

Wasserschleben, *Beiträge* = F. G. A. Wasserschleben, *Beiträge zur Geschichte der vorgratianischen Kirchenrechtsquellen* (Leipzig 1839)

Williams, *Codices Pseudo-Isidoriani* = Sch. Williams, *Codices Pseudo-Isidoriani: A Paleographico-Historical Study* (MIC, Series C: Subsidia 3; New York 1971)

Wretschko, *Theodosiani libri XVI* = A. von Wretschko, 'De usu Breviarii Alariciani forensi et scholastico per Hispaniam, Galliam, Italiam regionesque vicinas', *Theodosiani libri XVI cum constitutionibus Sirmondianis*, ed. Theodor Mommsen 1.1–2 (Berlin 1905)

Wurm, *Studien und Texte* = H. Wurm, *Studien und Texte zur Dekretalensammlung des Dionysius Exiguus* (Kanonistische Studien und Texte 16; Bonn 1939; repr. Amsterdam 1964)

Zechiel-Eckes, *Cresconius* = K. Zechiel-Eckes, *Die Concordia canonum des Cresconius: Studien und Edition* 1–2 (Freiburger Beiträge zur Mittelalterlichen Geschichte 5; Frankfurt 1992)

Canonical Collections of the Early Middle Ages (ca. 400–1140)

I

Late Antique and Early Medieval Collections to the End of the Eighth Century

Corpus canonum Africanum(-Romanum)

1. Author: Unknown. *2. Date:* About 420. *3. Place:* Unknown. *4. Type:* Oldest important canonical collection. The origins of this collection are connected to the *Causa Apiarii,* in which the claims of the African bishops for autonomy from Rome were presented.

5. Editions

Only in Latin (the so-called *Versio Isidori antiqua*); the Greek text is lost.

Turner, EOMIA 1.1.2 (1904) 175 and 177, each col. 2 (Creed of Nicaea)
Turner, EOMIA 1.1.2 (1904) 179–239, each col. 2 (Canones of Nicaea)
Turner, EOMIA 2.1 (1907) 54–140, each col. 1 (Ancyra and Neocaesarea)
Turner, EOMIA 2.2 (1913) 170, 174–214, each col. 1 (Gangra); 228–230, 232, 234etc.–312, each col. 2 (Antioch)
Turner, EOMIA 2.3 (ed. Schwartz 1939) 340, 342, 344–388, 390, 392 (Laodicaea), 406, 408, 410–420, each col. 2 (Constantinople)

6. Manuscripts

Only indirectly transmitted; cf. manuscripts of the *Collectiones Frisingensis prima* and *Wirceburgensis;* cf. also *Collectio Quesnelliana* (only Wien lat. 2141, Prov. Lorsch?) and *Collectio Weingartensis* (partial transmissions); cf. Mordek, 'Karthago oder Rom' (as below) 362 including n. 18 and 19

7. Bibliography

Van Hove, *Prolegomena* 146–147; Stickler, *Historia* 1.35, 45

C. H. Turner, 'Chapters in the History of Latin MSS of Canons. V. The Version called Prisca: (a) The Justel manuscript (J) now Bodl. e Mus. 100–102, and the *editio princeps* (Paris 1661)', JTS 30 (1929) 338–340
Turner, EOMIA 1.2.3 (Oxford 1930) p. x–xi and 623–624
Schwartz, 'Zweisprachigkeit' 249–250
Schwartz, *Publizistische Sammlungen* 274–275
Schwartz, 'Kanonessammlungen' 58–95
E. Schwartz, *Über die Bischofslisten der Synoden von Chalkedon, Nicaea und Konstantinopel* (Abh. Munich, N.F. Part 13, Munich 1937) 64–65
Wurm, *Studien und Texte* 30 n. 70
F. L. Cross, 'History and Fiction in the African Canons', JTS, n.s. 12 (1961) 227–247
G. L. Dossetti, *Il Simbolo di Nicea e di Constantinopoli. Edizione critica* (Testi e ricerche di scienze religiose 2; Rome 1967) 144
Ch. Munier, 'Vers une édition nouvelle des conciles africains (345–525)', *Revue des études augustiniennes* 18 (1972) 249–259
Ch. Munier, *Concilia Africae a. 345–a. 525* (CCL 149, Turnhout 1974) 79–149; cf. review by Mordek, ZRG Kan. Abt. 72 (1986) 368–376
Ch. Munier, 'La tradition littéraire des canons africains (345–525)', *Recherches augustiniennes* 10 (1975) 3–22
Mordek, *Kirchenrecht und Reform* 9, 149 n. 243
Ch. Pietri, *Roma Christiana: Recherches sur l'Eglise de Rome, son organisation, sa politique, son idéologie de Miltiade à Sixte III (311–440)* (Bibliothèque des Ecoles Françaises d'Athènes et de Rome 224; Rome 1976) 2.1259–1264
Ch. Munier, 'La tradition littéraire des dossiers africains', RDC 29 (1979) 41–52
H. Mordek, 'Karthago oder Rom? Zu den Anfängen der kirchlichen Rechtsquellen im Abendland', *Studia in Honorem A. M. Stickler* (1992) 359–374
Landau, 'Kanonessammlungen in Bayern' 149 with n. 64

Cf. *Collectiones Frisingensis prima, Wirceburgensis, Quesnelliana, Weingartensis*

Collectio Frisingensis prima

1. Author: Unknown. *2. Date:* Soon after 495 (Wurm 81); according to Turner and Schwartz ('Kanonessammlungen') the original core of the *Frisingensis prima* dates to the second decade of the fifth century. Cf. 'Corpus canonum Africanum(-Romanum)'. *3. Place:* Italy, probably Rome. *4. Type:* Chronologically arranged collection of conciliar canons and decretals that was partly the basis of the *Collectio Diessensis* (München Clm 5508). *5. Edition:* None.

6. Manuscripts

München, Bayerische Staatsbibliothek, Clm 5508, saec. IX, Reichenau?, fol. 135ff (probably copied from Clm 6243, cf. Bischoff, *Schreibschulen* 2.88, Mordek, *Bibliotheca capitularium* 367 and Landau, 'Kanonessammlungen in Bayern' 152–154)

München, Bayerische Staatsbibliothek, Clm 6243, saec. VIII^{ex}, fol. 11ra–189ra; (fol. 200^{r}–216^{v}, 233–238: Freising; fol. 1–199, 217–232: in the Lake Constance region; cf. Bischoff, *Schreibschulen* 1.86; CLA 9 no. 1255, p. 8, p. 62; Suppl. p. 63; Mordek, *Bibliotheca capitularium* 321–324, esp. 322)

Würzburg, Universitätsbibliothek, M.p.th.f. 146, saec. IX1/3, Main river region (cf. Bischoff-Hofmann, *Libri Sancti Kyliani* 50, 111–112 and Schieffer, 'Rätische Sammlung' 175)

According to Bischoff-Hofmann, *Libri Sancti Kyliani* 31 and 135, the fragments of the conciliar canons from Würzburg (Würzburg, Universitätsbibliothek, M.p.th.f. 47 and 64a, saec. IX2/4, Würzburg; late Hunbert-script) show a remarkable affinity with the *Collectio Frisingensis prima*

7. *Bibliography*

Maassen, *Geschichte* 476–486 esp. 477, 833 (cf. Mordek, *Kirchenrecht und Reform* 149 n. 243); Fournier-Le Bras 1.25; Van Hove, *Prolegomena* 157; Kurtscheid-Wilches, 1.90–91; Stickler, *Historia* 1.51

Turner, EOMIA 1.1, p. x
Turner, EOMIA 1.2, 623–624
C. H. Turner, 'Documents: Latin Lists of the Canonical Books. 1. The Roman Council under Damasus, A.D. 382', JTS 1 (1900) 554–560
C. H. Turner, 'Documents: Latin Lists of the Canonical Books. 2. An unpublished stichometrical list from the Freisingen MS of canons', JTS 2 (1901) 236–253
Dobschütz, *Decretum Gelasianum* 147
ACO 1.2, p. viii–xii
Silva-Tarouca, 'Beiträge' 467–481, 657–692
A. Scharnagl, 'Die kanonistische Sammlung der Hs. von Freising', *Wissenschaftliche Festgabe zum zwölfhundertjährigen Jubiläum des heiligen Korbinian*, ed. J. Schlecht (Munich 1924) 126–146
Le Bras, 'Notes III' 506–518
Schwartz, ZRG Kan. Abt. 20 (1931) 599 (review of Turner, EOMIA)
Silva-Tarouca, 'Nuovi studi' 381
Schwartz, *Publizistische Sammlungen* 262
Schwartz, 'Kanonessammlungen' 60–83; cf. *Collectio Sanblasiana*
Wurm, *Studien und Texte* 81–82, 206–209, 236–240
Bischoff, *Schreibschulen* 1.86–88 and 2.87–88
Bischoff, 'Panorama der Handschriftenüberlieferung' 244 n. 80
Mordek, *Kirchenrecht und Reform* 9 n. 32 and 149 n. 243
Ch. Munier, 'La tradition littéraire des dossiers africains', *Etudes offertes à Jean Gaudemet* = RDC 29 (1979) 41–52
Schieffer, 'Rätische Sammlung' 175–177
Zechiel-Eckes, *Cresconius* 1.80, 101 n. 131, 136, 143, 2.413 n. 11
Mordek, 'Kirchenrecht in Rätien' 18
Landau, 'Kanonessammlungen in Bayern' 139, 142, 148–154

Cf. below, *Collectio Frisingensis secunda*

Collectio Diessensis

1. Author: Unknown. *2. Date:* Seventh century. *3. Place:* Gaul. *4. Type:* Chronologically arranged collection of conciliar canons and decretals; the second part of the collection (Clm 5508, fol. 131–213) is taken from the *Collectio Frisingensis prima*

5. *Edition*

E. Amort, *Elementa iuris canonici veteris et moderni* 2 (Augsburg 1757) 273–594 (Only second part [from Siricius to Himerius] including the appendix at the end of München, Clm 5508, which derives from the *Collectio Frisingensis prima,* cf. Mordek, *Kirchenrecht und Reform* 149 n. 243)

6. *Manuscripts*

München, Bayerische Staatsbibliothek, Clm 5508, saec. VIII^{ex}, written at Salzburg, Prov. Diessen, fol. 1–130, cf. Bischoff, *Schreibschulen* 2.56–57 and 2.87–88; CLA 9, no. 1247, p. 6 and 61, CLA Suppl. (1971) p. 63

7. *Bibliography*

Maassen, *Geschichte* 624–636; Fournier-Le Bras 1.98 n. 2; Kurtscheid-Wilches 1.98; Van Hove, *Prolegomena* 276; Stickler, *Historia* 1.99

Turner, EOMIA 1.2.1, p. vi–vii and 1.2.3, p. x
Dobschütz, *Decretum Gelasianum* 185
ACO 1.2, p. ix–x
Silva-Tarouca, 'Beiträge' 675
A. Scharnagl, 'Die kanonistische Sammlung der Hs. von Freising', *Wissenschaftliche Festgabe zum zwölfhundertjährigen Jubiläum des hl. Korbinian*, ed. J. Schlecht (Munich 1924) 126–146, esp. 136
Wurm, *Studien und Texte* 99–101, 165
Katalog der Ausstellung 'Karl der Große: Werk und Wirkung' (Aachen 1965) 220 (description of manuscripts)
Mordek, 'Bonneval' 345 and n. 35
Stürner, 'Die Quellen der Fides Konstantins' 84–85
Mordek, *Kirchenrecht und Reform* 9 n. 32
Reynolds, 'Salzburg' 21
R. McKitterick, 'Knowledge of Canon Law in the Frankish Kingdoms before 789: The Manuscript Evidence', JTS n.s. 36 (1985) 97–117, esp. 102
Landau, 'Gefälschtes Recht' 19
Landau, 'Kanonessammlungen in Bayern' 152–154

Collectio Wirceburgensis (Würzburg, M.p.th.f. 146)

1. Author: Unknown. *2. Date:* Sixth or seventh century? *3. Place:* Not of Gallican origin (Maassen, *Geschichte* 555). *4. Type:* A chronologically arranged collection of conciliar canons. *5. Edition:* None.

6. *Manuscripts*

Würzburg, Universitätsbibliothek, M.p.th.f. 146, saec. IX1/3, river Main region, Franconia, probably not at Würzburg; cf. Bischoff-Hofmann, *Libri Sancti Kyliani* 50, 111–112 and J. Hofmann, 'Altenglische und althochdeutsche Glossen aus Würzburg und dem weiteren angelsächsischen Missionsgebiet', *Beiträge zur Geschichte der deutschen Sprache und Literatur* 85 (1963) 27–131, esp. 83

7. *Bibliography*

Maassen, *Geschichte* 551–555 (close affinity to the *Collectio Frisingensis prima*; both works are considered to be part of the collections of the *Collectio Maassen*, cf. Mordek, *Kirchenrecht und Reform* 240); Van Hove, *Prolegomena* 269

C. H. Turner, 'The manuscript of the Jesuit College of Clermont in Paris', JTS 1 (1900) 435–441
Le Bras, 'Notes III' 506–518
Schwartz, 'Kanonessammlungen' 60–83
Bischoff-Hofmann, *Libri Sancti Kyliani* 50, 111–112
Mordek, *Kirchenrecht und Reform* 81 n. 88, 173 n. 358
Schieffer, 'Rätische Sammlung' 164–191
Zechiel-Eckes, *Cresconius* 1.15–17 and 146–147 (cf. also index)

Constitutiones Sirmondianae

1. Author: Unknown. *2. Date:* Between 425 and 438. *3. Place:* Probably Southern Gaul (cf. Landau). *4. Type:* Small collection of 16 constitutions of Roman emperors (between 333 and 425) without any system, but all concerning ecclesiastical matters.

5. *Editions*

J. Sirmond, *Appendix Codicis Theodosiani novis constitutionibus cumulatior* (Paris 1631)
Th. Mommsen and P. Meyer (edd.), *Theodosiani libri XVI cum constitutionibus Sirmondianis et leges novellae ad Theodosianum pertinentes* (Berlin 1905, repr. 1970) 1.2 907–921; English translation: C. Pharr, *The Theodosian Code and Novels and the Sirmondian Constitutions* (Princeton 1952) 477–486

6. *Manuscripts*

Paris, Bibliothèque nationale, lat. 1452, saec. IX^{ex} or IX–X, Burgundy, Rhône region
St. Petersburg, Rossiyskaya Natsional'naya Biblioteka, F.v.II.3 and Berlin, Staatsbibliothek Preußischer Kulturbesitz, Phill. 1745, saec. VII, Burgundy

7. *Bibliography*

Maassen, *Geschichte* 792–796; Conrat, *Geschichte* 93–94, 146–147; J. Gaudemet, DDC 7 (1965) 1229–1230; H. Mordek, 'Constitutiones Sirmondianae', LMA 3 (1986) 179–180

F. Maassen, 'Ein Commentar des Florus von Lyon zu einigen der sog. Sirmond'schen Constitutionen', SB Vienna 92 (1878) 301–325
P. Krüger, *Geschichte der Quellen und der Litteratur des Römischen Rechts* (Munich-Leipzig ^{2}1912) 333–334

M. Conrat, 'Römisches Recht im frühesten Mittelalter', ZRG Rom. Abt. 24 (1913) 13–45
Mor, 'Recezione' 281–302
L. Wenger, *Die Quellen des römischen Rechts* (Vienna 1953) 542
Gaudemet, 'Survivances romaines' 176–177
J. Devisse, *Hincmar et la loi* (Dakar 1962) 14, 21, 48–49
J. Gaudemet, *La formation du droit séculier et du droit de l'Eglise aux IVe et Ve siècles* (Paris [2]1979) 73–74
P. Landau, 'Findelkinder und Kaiserkonstitutionen: Zur Entstehung der Constitutiones Sirmondianae', *Rivista internazionale di diritto comune* 3 (1992) 37–45
M. Vessey, 'The Origins of the Collectio Sirmondiana: a new look at the evidence', *The Theodosian Code. Studies in the Imperial Law of Late Antiquity*, ed. J. Harris and I. Wood (London 1993) 178–199
D. Liebs, 'Die im spätantiken Gallien verfügbaren römischen Rechtstexte', *Recht im frühmittelalterlichen Gallien: Spätantike Tradition und germanische Wertvorstellung*, ed. H. Siems, K. Nehlsen-v. Stryk and D. Strauch (Cologne 1995) 1–28

Collectio 'concilii secundi Arelatensis'

1. Author: Unknown. *2. Date:* Fifth century, between 442 and 506. *3. Place:* Arles. *4. Type:* Private collection, 56 canons of a putative council of Arles; in fact these canons are from Nicea and various Gallican councils; not identical with the so-called 'Collection of the church of Arles' (cf. Maassen, *Geschichte* 766, mss. Paris lat. 2777 and Paris lat. 3849).

5. Edition

Ch. Munier (ed.), *Concilia Galliae a. 314–a. 506* (CCL 148; Turnhout 1963) 111–130

6. Manuscripts

Only indirect transmissions Cf. *Collectio Albigensis, Collectio Remensis (Phill. 1743), Collectio Lugdunensis, Collectio Coloniensis (Köln 212), Collectio Sancti Mauri, Collectio Pithouensis, Collectio Sancti-Amandi, Collectio Corbeiensis (Paris lat. 12097), Collectio Laureshamensis*

7. Bibliography

Maassen, *Geschichte* 578–579 ('Can. Arelatensis episcoporum XVII'); Fournier-Le Bras 1.20 n. 1; Van Hove, *Prolegomena* 152; Stickler; *Historia* 1.40–41; Plöchl, *Geschichte des Kirchenrechts* 1.283; *Clavis* 395, no. 1777

Ballerini, *De antiquis . . . collectionibus et collectoribus* P. II, cap. X, § 2, c. 19 (PL 56.153–154)
G. Morin, 'Les Statuta ecclesiae antiqua sont-ils de S. Césaire d'Arles?' RB 30 (1913) 334–342, esp. 340 ('forgery')
Turner, EOMIA 1: Suppl.; ed. E. Schwartz (1939) 426
Gaudemet, 'Survivances romaines' 166

J. Gaudemet, *La formation du droit séculier et du droit de l'Eglise aux IVe et Ve siècles* (Paris 1957)
K. Schäferdiek, *Die Kirche in den Reichen der Westgoten und Suewen bis zur Errichtung der westgotischen katholischen Staatskirche* (Arbeiten zur Kirchengeschichte 39; Berlin 1967) 28 n. 82
K. Schäferdiek, 'Das sogenannte zweite Konzil von Arles und die älteste Kanonessammlung der arelatenser Kirche', ZRG Kan. Abt. 71 (1985) 1–19
Landau, 'Gefälschtes Recht' 15–16
Siems, *Handel und Wucher* 524–525

Statuta ecclesiae antiqua

1. Author: Unknown; perhaps Gennadius of Marseille (ca. 500?); cf. Munier. *2. Date:* Probably during the second half of the fifth century. *3. Place:* Probably Southern Gaul (Arles?). *4. Type:* Systematic collection. Circulated as the Fourth Council of Carthage (*Hispana*) or alternatively as 'Concilium Valentinum' (*Collectio Novariensis*).

5. Editions

C. Munier (ed.), *Les Statuta ecclesiae antiqua* (Université de Strasbourg, Bibliothèque de l'Institut de droit canonique 5; Paris 1960)
C. Munier (ed.), *Concilia Galliae a. 314–a. 506* (CCL 148; Turnhout 1963) 162–188
C. Munier (ed.), *Concilia Africae a. 345–a. 525* (CCL 149; Turnhout 1974) 342–354

6. Manuscripts

Only indirect transmissions; cf. *Collectio Albigensis, Collectio Bigotiana, Collectio Bonnaevallensis prima, Collectio Bonnaevallensis secunda, Collectio Burgundiana, Collectio Colonienis* (Köln 212), *Collectio Corbeiensis* (Paris lat. 12097), *Collectio Diessensis, Collectio Dionysiana adaucta, Collectio Herovalliana, Collectio Hibernensis, Collectio Hispana Gallica Augustodunensis, Collectio Laureshamensis, Collectio Novarienis, Collectio Quesnelliana, Collectio Sancti Amandi, Collectio Sancti Mauri, Collectio Sangermanensis, Collectio Vaticana* (Vat. lat. 1342 etc.), *Collectio Vetus Gallica, Epitome Hispana, Pseudo-Isidorus Mercator*

7. Bibliography

Maassen, *Geschichte* 383–390; Stickler, *Historia* 1.40

C. Munier, 'Une forme abrégée du rituel des ordinations des Statuta ecclesiae antiqua', *Revue des sciences religieuses* 32 (1958) 79–84
C. Munier, 'Nouvelles recherches sur les Statuta ecclesiae antiqua', RDC 9 (1959) 170–180
C. Munier (ed.), *Les Statuta ecclesiae antiqua* (Paris 1960) 56–58 and 69
Coquin, 'Sort' 193–224
Mordek, *Kirchenrecht und Reform* 51–52
Landau, 'Gefälschtes Recht' 11–12

Martinus of Braga, Capitula

1. Author: Martin, Bishop of Dumium (about 556) and later Archbishop of Braga, capital of the Suebian kingdom (569, †about 580). *2. Date:* Shortly after the Second Council of Braga (572). *3. Place:* Northern Spain, Galicia. *4. Type:* A systematic collection, the second of its kind after the *Breviatio canonum* of Fulgentius Ferrandus (546); there are no indications of any direct connection between them (Le Bras and Séjourné disagree, cf. García y García); became part of the *Hispana.*

5. Editions

Mansi 9.845–860

Antonio Caetano do Amaral, *Colleçao de canones ordenada por S. Martinho Bracarense com a versao en portuguez* (Lisboa 1803)

PL 84.575–587 and PL 130.574–586

Bruns, *Canones apostolorum* 2.43–59

C. P. Gaspari, *Martin von Bracaras Schrift De correctione rusticorum mit Anmerkungen begleitet und mit einer Abhandlung . . . über Martins Leben und übrige Schriften* (Christiania 1883)

C. W. Barlow, *Martini episcopi Bracarensis opera omnia* (Papers and Monographs of the American Academy in Rome 12; New Haven 1950) 80–144 (no improvement on Gonzalez's edition [PL 84], because several manuscripts of the *chronological Hispana* had not been consulted)

6. Manuscripts

Only indirectly transmitted; cf. manuscripts of the *Collectio Hispana* and the *Collectio Sancti Amandi*

7. Bibliography

Maassen, *Geschichte* 802–806; E. Amann, 'Martin de Braga', DThC 10 (1928) 203–207; Fournier-Le Bras 1.65–66; Kurtscheid-Wilches 1.103; Van Hove, *Prolegomena* 279; M. McGuire, 'Martin of Braga', NCE 9 (1967) 303; U. Domínguez del Val, 'Martin de Braga', DHEE 3 (Madrid 1973) 1429–1430

Bardenhewer, *Literatur* 5.379–388

A. de Jesus da Costa, S. Martinho de Dume (Braga 1950)

J. Madoz, 'Martin de Braga', *Estudios Eclesiásticos* 25 (1951) 219–242

G. Martínez Díez, 'La Colección canónica de la iglesia sueva: los capitula Martini', *Bracara Augusta* 21–22 (1967) *(=Actas do Congreso de Estudos da comemoraçao do XIII Centenário da morte de S. Frutuoso 19–23 Oct. 1966)* 224–243

J. L. Moralejo, 'Notas criticas a Martín de Braga (Capitula Martini 9–10)', *Emerita* 34 (1966) 85–86

Rambaud-Buhot, 'Critique' 16–19

G. Martínez Díez, 'Los concilios suevos de Braga en las colecciones canónicas de los siglos VI–XII', *El Concilio de Braga y la funcion de la legislación particular en la Iglesia* (Salamanca 1975) 93–105

Mordek, *Kirchenrecht und Reform* 34, 62, 191

S. Kuttner, 'A forgotten definition of justice', SG 20 (1976) 73–109 (repr. *The History of Ideas and Doctrines of Canon Law in the Middle Ages* [London ^{2}1992])
A. Fontán, 'Martin de Braga, un testigo de la tradición clásica y cristiana', *Anuario de estudios medievales* 9 (1974–1979) 329–341
Gaudemet, *Sources* 152–153
Gaudemet, 'Capitula Martini' 51–65
Zechiel-Eckes 1.31–32
A. Torres, 'António Caetano do Amaral, como autor das Memórias e tradutor das obras latinas de S. Martinho et S. Frutuoso', *Euphrosyne* 21 (1993) 319–328

Collectio Dionysiana

1. Author: Dionysius Exiguus (†537–555). *2. Date:* About 500. *3. Place:* Rome. *4. Type:* A chronologically arranged collection of councils and decretals.

5. Editions

First Recension

A. Strewe (ed.), *Die Canonessammlung des Dionysius Exiguus in der ersten Redaktion* (Leipzig 1931) (based on Cod. Vat. Pal. lat. 577, saec. VIII–IX, river Main region); cf. K. Christ, 'Eine unbekannte Hs. der ersten Fassung der Dionysiana und der Capitula e canonibus excerpta a. 813', *Festschrift für Georg Leidinger,* ed. A. Hartmann (Munich 1930) 25–36

Second Recension

Christophe Justel, *Codex canonum ecclesiasticorum Dionysii Exigui* (Paris 1628 and 1643) from Cod. Oxford Bodl. Libr., e Mus. 103 (olim 3689, saec. IX ca. 3/4, probably Eastern France) repr. G. Voellius et H. Justellus, *Bibliotheca iuris canonici veteris* 1 (Paris 1661) 101–174 (councils) und 183–248 (decretals), PL 67.137–316 (Councils: 137–230; Decretals: 230–316)

A third recension can be deduced from the existence of a Praefatio in Cod. Novara, Biblioteca Capitolare, XXX (66):
Maassen, *Geschichte* 964–965

Editions of *'Praefationes'*

Maassen, *Geschichte* 960–965

F. Glorie (ed.), 'Dionisii Exigui Praefationes Latinae Genuinae in variis suis translationibus ex Graeco', *Scriptores 'Illyrici' Minores* (CCL 85; Turnhout 1972) 27–81, esp. 35–42, 43–47 and 49–51

6. Manuscripts

A. Councils

First Recension

Gotha, Forschungs- und Landesbibliothek, Mbr. I.75, saec. VIII^{in}, probably from Chelles, by the fifteenth century at Murbach (fragment)
Kassel, Gesamthochschul-Bibliothek: Landesbibliothek und Murhardsche Biblio-

thek, 4° theol. 1, fol. 2r–94v, saec. IXin, Main river region, Prov. Fulda. Cf. Bischoff, 'Panorama der Handschriftenüberlieferung' 248 n. 117, cf. Mordek, *Bibliotheca capitularium* 190–191

Vaticano, Città del, Biblioteca Apostolica Vaticana, Pal. lat. 577, saec. VIII–IX, Main river region (used by Turner in EOMIA 1, cf. p. 562), cf. CLA 1.29 no. 97 (with facsimile); German-Insular scriptorium (Hersfeld or Mainz) according to Mordek, Prov. Mainz, fol. 11v–69v, cf. Mordek, *Bibliotheca capitularium* 777

Second Recension

Erfurt, Wissenschaftliche Allgemeinbibliothek (olim Stadtbücherei), Ampl. 2° 74, saec. VI², very early fragment, probably Italy (CLA 8 no. 1190, p. 47 and 67)

Oxford, Bodleian Library, e Mus. 103 (olim 3689), saec. IX ca. 3/4, probably Eastern France

Paris, Bibliothèque nationale, lat. 1536, saec. X

Paris, Bibliothèque nationale, lat. 3837, saec IX, also decretals

Paris, Bibliothèque nationale, lat. 3845, saec. IX, also decretals

Paris, Bibliothèque nationale, lat. 3848, saec. XIII

St. Petersburg, Rossiyskaya Natsional'naya Biblioteka, F.v.II.3, saec. VII, Burgundy (oldest manuscript discovered by Turner: CLA 11 no. 1061, p. 8 and 31), Staerk, *Manuscrits Latins* 1.13–15

Vaticano, Città del, Biblioteca Apostolica Vaticana, lat. 5845, saec. X1/2, between 915 and 934, Capua, also decretals; all texts of the Symmachian forgeries, cf. Landau, 'Gefälschtes Recht' 19

Third Recension

Novara, Biblioteca Capitolare, XXX (66), saec. IXex, probably written in Northern Italy according to Reynolds, cf. also Mordek, *Kirchenrecht und Reform* 242; Mordek, *Bibliotheca capitularium* 396

Praefationes* of the *Dionysiana* without *Concilia

El Escorial, Real Biblioteca de San Lorenzo, F.II.13 (16), saec. XVI

Paris, Bibliothèque nationale, lat. 4280A, saec. IX2/2 and X1/2

Roma, Biblioteca Casanatense, 2407 (olim XX.I.21), saec. XVI–XVII

Roma, Biblioteca Vallicelliana, C.20, saec. XVI–XVII

***Praefatio* to the First Recension of the Councils**

Köln, Erzbischöfliche Diözesan- und Dombibliothek, 212 (Darmst. 2326), saec. VII–VIII

Paris, Bibliothèque nationale, lat. 1451 (Saint-Maur-des Fossés), saec. IX

Paris, Bibliothèque nationale, lat. 3846, saec. IXin, (Saint-Amand), fol. 2v, cf. Mordek, *Bibliotheca capitularium* 440

Vaticano, Città del, Biblioteca Apostolica Vaticana, Pal. lat. 577, saec. VIII–IX, Main river region

***Praefatio* to the Second Recension of the Councils**

Brescia, Biblioteca Civica Queriniana, B.II.13, saec. IX–X, Italian

München, Bayerische Staatsbibliothek, Clm 6288 (olim Freising 88), saec. XI–XII

München, Bayerische Staatsbibliothek, Clm 14008, saec. IX2/2, Sankt Emmeram, Regensburg

Novara, Biblioteca Capitolare, XXX (66), saec. IXex, probably Northern Italy, cf. Mordek, *Bibliotheca capitularium* 396

Paris, Bibliothèque nationale, lat. 1536, saec. X, Prov. Bobbio
Paris, Bibliothèque nationale, lat. 3838, saec. IX3/4, France, fol. 21vb–22rb, cf. Mordek, *Bibliotheca capitularium* 435–438, esp. 436
Paris, Bibliothèque nationale, lat. 3848, saec. XIII
Paris, Bibliothèque nationale, lat. 4280A, saec. IX^{ex}, Reims, Prov. Saint-Remi, fol. 14^{v}–15^{r}; cf. Mordek, *Bibliotheca capitularium* 453
Vercelli, Biblioteca Capitolare, CXI, saec. X, Prov. Bobbio

Excerpts

Warszawa, Biblioteka Uniwersytecka, 1, saec. IX$^{1\text{-}2}$, Tours, fol. 254^{v}–268^{r}, excerpt from the conciliar part of the *Collectio Dionysiana* (versio II); cf. Mordek, *Bibliotheca capitularium* 900–901

B. Decretals (Second Recension)

Paris, Bibliothèque nationale, lat. 3837, saec. IX, Angers, cf. Silva-Tarouca, 'Beiträge' 660 (including *praefatio* to the decretals)
Vaticano, Città del, Biblioteca Apostolica Vaticana, lat. 5845, saec. X1/2 (between 915 and 934), Capua (including *praefatio* to the decretals)

Small Collections of Excerpts

Paris, Bibliothèque nationale, lat. 10399, fol. 20–25 (cf. Fransen, 'Manuscrits' 67)
Paris, Bibliothèque nationale, lat. 3847, saec. XII, mutilated (cf. Wurm, *Studien und Texte* 32 n. 6 according to Maassen, 'Bibliotheca' 1.2, *SB Vienna* 54 [1867] 240)

7. *Bibliography*

Maassen, *Geschichte* 422–440; Fournier-Le Bras 1.24–26, 36–37, 94–98; Kurtscheid-Wilches 1.87–89; Van Hove, *Prolegomena* 157–161; Rambaud-Buhot, 'Denys le Petit', DDC 4 (1949) 1131–1152; Stickler, *Historia* 1.46–50; Plöchl, *Geschichte des Kirchenrechts* 1.279–280; Rambaud-Buhot, 'Dionysiana collectio', NCE 4 (1967) 876; M. Richter, 'Dionysius Exiguus', TRE 9 (1981) 1–4; Mordek, 'D(ionysius) Exiguus', LMA 3 (1985) 1088–1092

Maassen, 'Bibliotheca', SB Vienna 53 (1866) 373–427; 54 (1867) 157–288; 56 (1867) 157–212
A. Amelli, S. Guerrino, *Leone Magno e l'Oriente* (Rome 1882)
A. Amelli, *Prolegomena* c.III: *De codicis Novariensis XXX collectione Dionysio-Hadriana* p. lxxi–lxxx; Pars 2: 'Collectionis Dionysio-Hadrianae excerpta', *Spicilegium Casinense complectens analecta sacra et profana* 1 (Monte Cassino 1888), p. lxxi–lxxx and 197–252
Turner, EOMIA 1 p. x,
Turner, 'The MSS of Councils in the Library of the College of Clermont', JTS 1 (1899–1900) 438–441
Turner, 'The Lyon-Petersburg MS of Councils', JTS 4 (1902–1903) 426–434
P. Versaime, *Denis le Petit et le droit canonique au VIe siècle* (Diss. Fac. Cath. Lyon; Paris 1913)
ACO 4.2 p. xvi–xx and 1.5.2 p. iiii–v
Silva-Tarouca, 'Beiträge' 659–660
L. Duchesne, *L'Eglise au sixième siècle* (Paris 1925) 134–137
M. Cappuyns, 'L'origine des Capitula pseudo-célestiniens contre le sémipélagianisme', RB 41 (1929) 156–170

K. Christ, 'Eine unbekannte Handschrift der ersten Fassung der Dionysiana und der Capitula e canonibus excerpta a. 813', *Festschrift für Georg Leidinger*, ed. A. Hartmann (Munich 1930) 25–36

E. Schwartz, Review of Turner, EOMIA in ZRG Kan. Abt. 20 (1931) 590–607

A. Strewe, *Die Kanonessammlung des Dionysius Exiguus in der ersten Redaktion* (Arbeiten zur Kirchengeschichte 16; Berlin 1931)

A. Van de Vyver, 'Cassiodore et son oeuvre', *Speculum* 6 (1931) 244–292

Caspar, *Geschichte des Papsttums* 2.79–80, 307–311

Schwartz, 'Zweisprachigkeit' 245–253

Schwartz, *Publizistische Sammlungen* 274 n. 1, 278, 285–286

Schwartz, 'Kanonessammlungen' 108–114

Wurm, *Studien und Texte* passim

H. Wurm, 'Decretales selectae ex antiquissimis Romanorum Pontificum epistulis decretalibus', *Apollinaris* 12 (1939) 40–93

A. Van de Vyver, 'Les Institutiones de Cassiodore et sa fondation à Vivarium', RB 53 (1941) 59–88

W. M. Peitz, 'Gratian und Dionysius Exiguus', SG 1 (1953) 51–81

H. Steinacker, 'Die römische Kirche und die griechischen Sprachkenntnisse des Frühmittelalters', MIÖG 62 (1954) 28–66, especially 51–55

W. M. Peitz, *Dionysius Exiguus Studien: Neue Wege der philologischen und historischen Text- und Quellenkritik*, revised and ed. H. Foerster (Arbeiten zur Kirchengeschichte 33; Berlin 1960), [Spanish translation by P. Galindo Romeo, REDC 2, 1947, 9–32] cf. the reviews by Martínez Díez, 'A proposito de la obra de Wilhelm Peitz 'Dionysius Exiguus Studien', *Miscelanea Comillas* 39 (1963) 297–308, C. Munier, 'L'oeuvre canonique de Denis le Petit, d'après les travaux du R. P. Wilhelm Peitz, S.I.', SE 14 (1963) 236–250, K. Schäferdiek, review of 'Wilhelm Peitz, Dionysius Exiguus Studien', ZKG 3–4 (1963) 353–367 and the critical reviews mentioned in AHP 1 (1963) 518 and 2 (1964) 413

H. Müllejans, *Publicus und Privatus im römischen Recht und im älteren kanonischen Recht* (Münchner theologische Studien 3, Kan. Abt. 14; Munich 1961) 67–69

A. Chavasse, 'Les lettres de saint Léon le Grand dans le supplément de la Dionysiana et de l'Hadriana et dans la collection du manuscrit du Vatican', *Revue des sciences religieuses* 38 (1964) 154–176

Rambaud-Buhot, 'Critique' 10–14

Brommer, 'Fragmente' 228–230

Mordek, *Kirchenrecht und Reform* 46 n. 35, 241–243

Fuhrmann, 'Papstbriefe' 364–367

W. Berschin, *Griechisch-lateinisches Mittelalter. Von Hieronymus zu Nikolaus von Kues* (Bern-Munich 1980) (Italian translation: Naples 1989)

F. De Marini Avonzo, 'Secular and clerical culture in Dionysius Exiguus' Rome', *Proceedings Berkeley* 83–92

G. Limouris, 'L'oeuvre canonique de Denys le Petit (VIe s.)', RDC 37 (1987) 127–142

M. Cardinale, 'La 'Concordia canonum' di Cresconio e la sua diffusione nella cultura giuridica dell'Europa medievale, 1: Problemi generali e criteri metodologici', *Apollinaris* 62 (1989) 283–331

Busch, *Placidus von Nonantola* 126–134

F. S. Paxton, '*Bonus liber*: A Late Carolingian Clerical Manual from Lorsch (Biblioteca Vaticana MS. Pal. lat. 485)', *The Two Laws: Studies in Medieval Legal History Dedicated to Stephan Kuttner*, ed. L. Mayali and S. A. J. Tibbetts (Washington D.C. 1990) 1–30

Landau, 'Kanonessammlungen in der Lombardei' 427–430

Schmitz, 'Vier-Bücher-Sammlung' 237–238

G. May, 'Die Kanonistik um das Jahr 1000', *1000 Jahre St. Stephan in Mainz: Festschrift*, ed. Helmut Hinkel (Quellen und Abhandlungen zur mittelrheinischen Kirchengeschichte 63; Mainz 1990) 113–157

Th. F. X. Noble, 'Literacy and the Papal Government in Late Antiquity and the Early Middle Ages', *The Uses of Literacy in Early Mediaeval Europe*, ed. R. McKitterick (Cambridge 1990) 82–108

Zechiel-Eckes, *Cresconius* (cf. index)

N. Dura, 'Denys Exiguus (465–550). Précisions et correctifs concernant sa vie et son oeuvre', REDC 50 (1993) 279–290

Landau, 'Kanonessammlungen in Bayern' 142

Collectio Dionysiana Bobiensis

1. Author: Unknown. *2. Date:* Seventh century, with later additions during the pontificate of Pope Zacharias (743) and Eugene II (826). *3. Place:* Possibly in Bobbio (cf. Landau, 'Kanonessammlungen in der Lombardei' 427–428). *4. Type:* A collection of conciliar canons and decretals arranged in chronological order. *5. Edition:* None.

6. *Manuscripts*

Milano, Biblioteca Ambrosiana, S.33.sup., saec. IX; on the first folio a hand of the tenth or eleventh century had written: 'Liber sci Columbani de Bobio'

Vercelli, Biblioteca Capitolare, CXI, saec. X (on the relationship of the manuscripts cf. Wurm, *Studien und Texte* 32 n. 8)

7. *Bibliography*

Maassen, *Geschichte* 471–476; Van Hove, *Prolegomena* 268

Wurm, *Studien und Texte* 32–33, 53–58

Landau, 'Kanonessammlungen in der Lombardei' 427–428

Zechiel-Eckes, *Cresconius* (cf. index)

Cf. also *Collectio Mutinensis*

Collectio Dionysio-Hadriana

1. Author: Unknown. *2. Date:* Before 774, on the command of Pope Hadrian I. *3. Place:* Rome. *4. Type:* A collection of conciliar canons and decretals arranged chronologically.

5. Editions

A. A partial edition of the *Canones apostolorum* and the Greek councils of this collection can be found in:

Turner, EOMIA

ACO 2.2.2, p. 49–60

B. The African councils are edited by Ch. Munier, *Concilia Africae* (CCL 149; Turnhout 1974)

C. Printed editions of the sixteenth to eighteenth centuries

J. Cochlaeus (Wendelstein), *Canones apostolorum, veterum conciliorum constitutiones. Decreta Pontificum antiquiora* (Moguntiae [Mainz] 1525)

F. Pithou, *Codex canonum vetus Ecclesiae Romanae restitutus* (Paris 1609 and ²1687)

D. Editions that contain only the conciliar canons

E. Amort, *Elementa iuris canonici* 2 (1757) 75–235

J. F. Schannat and J. Hartzheim, *Concilia Germaniae* 1 (Cologne 1759) 131–235

PL 67.135–137 and 315–346 (Dedicatory acrostic and decretals)

A. Amelli, *Spicilegium Casinense* I, 2, 197*–252: Excerpts from the *Dionysio-Hadriana* from Cod. Novara XXX (66)

6. Manuscripts

Aosta, Biblioteca Capitolare, C.103, saec. VIII–IX, Aosta; 72 fol., fragment, cf. A. P. Frutaz, *Le fonti per la storia della Valle d'Aosta* (Thesaurus ecclesiarum Italiae I, 1, 1966) 17

Bamberg, Staatsbibliothek, Can. 3 (P.I.2), saec. IX2/4 or IX$^{med.}$, Eastern France or Western Germany

Barcelona, Archivo de la Corona de Aragón, Ripoll 105, saec. XIII; according to Rius, 'El Concili de Nicea', *Analecta sacra Tarraconensia* 2 (1926) 585–591; cf. Mordek, *Kirchenrecht und Reform* 245

Barcelona, Biblioteca Central de la Diputación Provincial, 945, saec. XII (cf. Martínez Díez, *Colección Hispana* 1.14)

Berlin, Staatsbibliothek Preußischer Kulturbesitz, Hamilton 132, fol. 1ra–128va; saec. IX$^{in\text{-}med}$, Corbie (fol. 1–251); saec. IX2/2, probably Northern France (fol. 152–261, 263); revised in the middle of the ninth century into the *Collectio Hispana Gallica Augustodunensis*; cf. Mordek, *Kirchenrecht und Reform* 273–274; Mordek, *Bibliotheca capitularium* 29–34 and below

Berlin, Staatsbibliothek Preußischer Kulturbesitz, Phill. 1741, saec. IX$^{med\text{-}3/4}$, Reims

Berlin, Staatsbibliothek Preußischer Kulturbesitz, Phill. 1744, saec. X

Berlin, Staatsbibliothek Preußischer Kulturbesitz, Phill. 1749, saec. VIII–IX, Southern Burgundy; CLA 8 no. 1063, 13 and 62; CLA Suppl. 61; the councils of the *Dionyisana* reworked into a *Dionysio-Hadriana*

Bern, Burgerbibliothek, 89 and A.26, fol. 17ra–169vb, saec. IX^{in}, perhaps Alsace (Councils), cf. Mordek, *Bibliotheca capitularium* 72–77, esp. 76

Bruxelles, Bibliothèque Royale Albert Ier, 495–505 (Cat. no. 2494), saec. IX$^{med\text{-}3/4}$, Northeastern France (Aurivalle)

Cambrai, Bibliothèque municipale, 600–601 (559–558), saec. X

Cambrai, Bibliothèque municipale, 625 (576) saec. IX3/4, Northern France, cf. Kottje, 'Einheit und Vielfalt' 338; cf. Mordek, *Bibliotheca capitularium* 93–94 (fragment), cf. Paris lat. 3182

Düsseldorf, Universitätsbibliothek, E.1, saec. IX^{2}, Italy (probably Rome); Prov. Essen; according to Zechiel-Eckes, *Cresconius* 1.219, this codex is not a transmission of the *Collectio Dionysio-Hadriana* but of the *Collectio Vaticana* (Vat. lat. 1342 etc.), below

Düsseldorf, Universitätsbibliothek, E.2, saec. IX^{1}, Werden

Einsiedeln, Stiftsbibliothek, 199, p. 258–430, saec. IX (fragment) Rhaetia

Frankfurt am Main, Stadt- und Universitätsbibliothek, Barth. 64, saec. IX^{med}, Mainz (Councils)

Freiburg (Breisgau), Universitätsbibliothek, 8, saec. IX^{2}, Lake Constance region

Ivrea, Biblioteca Capitolare, LXXIV, saec. IX$^{med\text{-}2}$, France

Ivrea, Biblioteca Capitolare, LXXV, saec. IX ca. med., Northern Italy

Karlsruhe, Badische Landesbibliothek, Aug. CIII, Sankt Paul im Lavanttal, Carinthia

København, Kongelike Bibliotek, Gl. Kgl. Saml. 192 fol., saec. IX^{1}, Saint-Germain-des-Prés

Köln, Erzbischöfliche Diözesan- und Dombibliothek, 115 (olim Darmst. 2114), saec. IX^{in}, Cologne, cf. L. W. Jones, 'The Script of Cologne from Hildebald to Hermann' (Mediaeval Academy Books 10; Cambridge, Mass. 1932) 46–47

Köln, Erzbischöfliche Diözesan- und Dombibliothek, 116 (olim Darmst. 2115), saec. IX^{in}, Western Germany or Eastern France (Councils)

Köln, Erzbischöfliche Diözesan- und Dombibliothek, 117 (olim Darmst. 2116), fol. 1–60, saec. IX^{1}, Eastern France? (Councils)

Laon, Bibliothèque municipale, 200, saec. IX3/4, France, south of Laon

Leipzig, Universitätsbibliothek, II.6 (olim Stadtbibliothek, Cat. no. ccxxxix), saec. IX^{1}, Hildesheim

London, British Library, Arundel 393, fol. 1–93, saec. IX1/4, Southern Germany

Lucca, Biblioteca Capitolare Feliniana, 125, saec. IX ca. 3/4, Italy

Mantova, Biblioteca Comunale, C.II.23, saec. XII^{2} (*Hadriano-Hispanica*, cf. Mordek, *Kirchenrecht und Reform* 12 n. 43)

Monte Cassino, Archivio e Biblioteca dell'Abbazia, 522 (olim 472), saec. XII, Southern Italy: pp. 228–231, 236–372, cf. Gilchrist, *Diversorum patrum sententie* xxxii–xxxiv ('A collection of texts from the Dionysiana') (Councils)

Monza, Biblioteca Capitolare, h-3/151, saec. IX^{2}, Northern Italy (Councils)

München, Bayerische Staatsbibliothek, Clm 3860, saec. X

München, Bayerische Staatsbibliothek, Clm 3860a, saec. IX^{2}, Northern Italy

München, Bayerische Staatsbibliothek, Clm 5258, saec. X (Councils)

München, Bayerische Staatsbibliothek, Clm 5525, saec. XII

München, Bayerische Staatsbibliothek, Clm 6242, saec. IX1/3 (after 811), Freising

München, Bayerische Staatsbibliothek, Clm 6244 (Freising 44), saec. IX^{in}, before 805, Southeastern Germany (Councils)

München, Bayerische Staatsbibliothek, Clm 6355 (Freising 155), saec. IX2/4

München, Bayerische Staatsbibliothek, Clm 14407, saec. X (Councils)

München, Bayerische Staatsbibliothek, Clm 14422, fol. 5–138, saec. IX (ca. a. 800), Southern Germany (Councils)

München, Bayerische Staatsbibliothek, Clm 14517, saec. VIII–IX, Southwestern Germany, Switzerland, or Northern Italy and München, Clm lat. 14567, saec. X^{med}, Regensburg
München, Bayerische Staatsbibliothek, Clm 18217, saec. XI (Councils)
München, Universitätsbibliothek, 2° 254, saec. XV or XVI^{in}; from the library of Johannes Eck [d. 1543] with his annotations (fol. 192^{v} and 193^{r})
München, Universitätsbibliothek, 2° 292, saec. XI, Central Italy, fol. 116ra bis 132vb; fragment (Councils up to c. 15 of Serdica)
Novara, Biblioteca Capitolare, XV (30), saec. XII, Novara (cf. Landau, 'Kanonessammlungen in der Lombardei' 430 n. 20: literature); copy of Novara XXX; fol. 1ra–46ra (cf. Mordek, *Bibliotheca capitularium* 393)
Novara, Biblioteca Capitolare, XXX (66), saec. IX^{ex}, probably Northern Italy, fol. 118^{r}–232^{v} (cf. Mordek, *Bibliotheca capitularium* 395–399, esp. 396)
Oxford, Bodleian Library, Laud. misc. 421 (olim Nr. 893), saec. IX^{ex}, Western Germany
Palermo, Archivio della Cattedrale, 14, saec. XII; Councils to Chalcedon and Council of Gregory II (721) (cf. Mordek, *Kirchenrecht und Reform* 194–195 n. 495)
Paris, Bibliothèque nationale, lat. 1452, saec. IX 4/4 or IX–X, region of the Rhône
Paris, Bibliothèque nationale, lat. 1453, saec. IX 1/4, probably Orléans
Paris, Bibliothèque nationale, lat. 3182, saec. X^{2}, Bretagne, written by a *Discipulus Maeloc*, Prov. Fécamp (cf. Mordek, *Bibliotheca capitularium* 433–435)
Paris, Bibliothèque nationale, lat. 3838, saec. IX3/4, France, fol. 12ra–19rb, 23ra–128vb, 151ra–158vb, 129ra–150rb, 159ra–161va (cf. Mordek, *Bibliotheca capitularium* 436)
Paris, Bibliothèque nationale, lat. 3839, saec. XI^{2}, France
Paris, Bibliothèque nationale, lat. 3839A, saec. XI^{2}, Angers (cf. Mordek, *Kirchenrecht und Reform* 181 n. 394)
Paris, Bibliothèque nationale, lat. 3840, saec. IX
Paris, Bibliothèque nationale, lat. 3841, saec. X
Paris, Bibliothèque nationale, lat. 3842, ca. saec. X–XI, probably region of Angers (Councils)
Paris, Bibliothèque nationale, lat. 3843, saec. IX
Paris, Bibliothèque nationale, lat. 3844, saec. IX ca. $2/4^{-med}$, Loire region
Paris, Bibliothèque nationale, lat. 3846, saec. IX^{in}, Northeastern France? Prov. Saint-Amand, fol. 3ra–123ra (cf. Mordek, *Bibliotheca capitularium* 439–442)
Paris, Bibliothèque nationale, lat. 4278, saec.IX^{2}
Paris, Bibliothèque nationale, lat. 8921, cf. below Reims, Bibliothèque municipale, 2102
Paris, Bibliothèque nationale, lat. 11710 (olim Sangerm. 367), a. 805, Burgundy
Paris, Bibliothèque nationale, lat. 11711 (olim Sangerm. 365), saec. VIII–IX, Corbie
Paris, Bibliothèque nationale, lat. 12445, (olim Sangerm. 366), saec. IX3/4, Reims, cf. L. Böhringer (ed.), 'Der eherechtliche Traktat im Paris. lat. 12445, einer Arbeitshandschrift Hinkmars von Reims', DA 46 (1990) 18–47
Paris, Bibliothèque nationale, lat. 12446 (olim Sangerm. Harl. 391), saec. IX1–2/4, probably Central France
Paris, Bibliothèque nationale, lat. 12447 (olim Sangerm. Harl. 503), saec. IX ca. 4/4, Southern France

Paris, Bibliothèque nationale, lat. 12448 (olim Sangerm. Harl. 386), saec. IX–X or X^{in}, probably Eastern France

Paris, Bibliothèque nationale, lat. 17526, saec. XII, France; cf. Mordek, *Kirchenrecht und Reform* 181 n. 394

Praha, Národní Muzeum, XII.C.12 (olim I.G.13), saec. XI or XII

Princeton, University Library, John Hinsdale Scheide Collection 139 (olim Dublin, A. Chester Beatty Collection, W.14), saec. IX^{ex} probably Lyon, Prov. Mettlach, near Trier; Phillipps Collection manuscript 390; sold in 1969 by Sotheby's to B. Rosenthal, New York)

Reims, Bibliothèque municipale, 671 (olim 513–510), saec. IX^{in}, Reims, fol. 13–196

Reims, Bibliothèque municipale, 2102 (fol. 1–8) and Paris, Bibliothèque nationale, lat. 8921 (fol. 1–140), saec. VIII^{ex}, written probably at Corbie, Prov. Beauvais, cf. CLA 5 (1950) no. 574, 17 and 57

Roma, Biblioteca Nazionale Centrale, Sessor. LXIII, saec. IX ca. 2/4, Nonantola recension of the *Hadriana*, cf. Wurm, *Studien und Texte* 31 and 44

St. Gallen, Stiftsbibliothek, 671, saec. IX^{in}, Swabia (cf. Autenrieth, *Domschule* 81), p. 2–82

St. Paul im Lavanttal, Stiftsbibliothek, 6/1 [olim 25.4.12; XXV. a.6] together with Karlsruhe, Badische Landesbibliothek, Aug. CIII, saec. IX1/3, Reichenau

Vaticano, Città del, Biblioteca Apostolica Vaticana, lat. 631, fol. 339–406, saec. XIII4/4, probably Flanders

Vaticano, Città del, Biblioteca Apostolica Vaticana, lat. 1337, saec. IX^{in}, Upper Rhine

Vaticano, Città del, Biblioteca Apostolica Vaticana, lat. 4979, saec. IX1/4, Verona during the time of archdeacon Pacificus, fragment (from Serdica to Symmachus, PL 67.175–325)

Vaticano, Città del, Biblioteca Apostolica Vaticana, lat. 7222, saec. IX1/4 or 2/3, Salzburg

Vaticano, Città del, Biblioteca Apostolica Vaticana, Borghes. 28, saec. XIII^{2} or XIV^{1}, Northern France or Flanders, Prov. Avignon

Vaticano, Città del, Biblioteca Apostolica Vaticana, Ottobon. lat. 312, saec. XI–XII

Vaticano, Città del, Biblioteca Apostolica Vaticana, Pal. lat. 578, saec. IX^{1}, Mainz (Decretals)

Vaticano, Città del, Biblioteca Apostolica Vaticana, Reg. lat. 1021, saec. IX1/4, Saint-Amand

Vaticano, Città del, Biblioteca Apostolica Vaticana, Reg. lat. 1043, saec. IX^{1}, probably Burgundy, Rhône region

Vercelli, Biblioteca Capitolare, CLXV, saec. IX2/4, Northern Italy (cf. Bischoff, quoted by Kottje, 'Einheit und Vielfalt' 339 n. 69) (only councils); cf. also Zechiel-Eckes, *Cresconius* 1.172–175

Verdun, Bibliothèque municipale, 46 (olim 21), saec. XI, Prov. Saint-Vannes

Wien, Österreichische Nationalbibliothek, lat. 361 (olim iur. can. 40), saec. XII

Wolfenbüttel, Herzog August Bibliothek, Weißenburg 3, saec. IX^{1}, Wissembourg (Alsace)

Würzburg, Universitätsbibliothek, M.p.th.f. 70, saec. IX ca 3/4, probably Italian

Würzburg, Universitätsbibliothek, M.p.th.f. 72, probably saec. IX2/4 or IX3/4 Fulda (Fragment: Councils up to c. 9 of Serdica)

Fragments from the *Dionysiana* or the *Hadriana* (according to Mordek)

Karlsruhe, Badische Landesbibliothek, fragment Aug. 146 and 198 and 200 and Stuttgart, Württembergische Landesbibliothek, Theol. et phil. fol. 95, saec. IX, according to A. Holder, *Die Reichenauer Handschriften, 2: Die Papierhandschriften: Fragmenta, Nachträge* (Die Handschriften der Badischen Landesbibliothek in Karlsruhe 6 [Heidelberg 1914; repr. Wiesbaden 1971 with bibliographical additions]) 594–601 and 738 etc.

Maria Laach, Stiftsbibliothek, sine num. and Dülken, Katholisches Pfarramt, sine num., saec. VIII–IX, Central Italy CLA 9, no. 1230, 2; CLA Suppl., 5 and 63 (cf. Mordek, *Kirchenrecht und Reform* 247)

München, Bayerische Staatsbibliothek, Clm 29952/1 (olim 29083m), bifolium; saec. IX^{in}, region of Salzburg (the text is printed in: PL 67.152–153)

München, Bayerische Staatsbibliothek, Clm 29952/2 (olim Clm 14922) and Washington, The Library of Congress, Rare Book Division, 18, saec. IX^{in}, Southern Germany; cf. S. de Ricci-W. J. Wilson, *Census of Medieval and Renaissance Manuscripts in the United States and Canada* 1 (New York 1935) 233 no. 118 (cf. Mordek, *Kirchenrecht und Reform* 247)

München, Universitätsbibliothek, sine num.—2 fragments mentioned by P. Lehmann and O. Glauning, *Mittelalterliche Handschriftenbruchstücke der Universitätsbibliothek und des Georgianum zu München* (Zentralblatt für Bibliothekswesen, Beiheft 72 [1940]) 44, no. LVIII and LIX, saec. IX^{1}, Eastern France or region of the Rhine and saec. IX$^{in.}$, Western Germany or Eastern France (fragments destroyed in 1944)

Philadelphia, Free Library, John F. Lewis Collection 202, saec. IX^{1}, Germany; cf. B. Löfstedt, *Studien über die Sprache der langobardischen Gesetze: Beiträge zur frühmittelalterlichen Latinität* (Acta Universitatis Upsaliensis: Studia Latina Upsaliensia 1, Stockholm 1961) 5 n. 1

Regensburg, Staatliche Bibliothek, sine num.

Schaffhausen, Staatsarchiv, sine num., fragments of a manuscript of the *Collectio Dionysio-Hadriana* written in Western Germany or Eastern France, saec. IX^{ex}

Würzburg, Universitätsbibliothek, M.p.th.f. 38 and 5 and 13 and 37 and 60 and M.p.th.q. 2 and M.p.misc.f. 3 and 5a, saec. VIII–IX, in Anglo-Saxon minuscule, probably written on the Continent; CLA 9, no. 1401, 46 and 68

7. *Bibliography*

Maassen, *Geschichte* 441–471, 965–967; Conrat, *Geschichte* 1.254–255; Fournier-Le Bras 1.94–97 (cf. ZRG Kan. Abt. 55, 42–43 n. 10); Kurtscheid-Wilches 1.89–90; Van Hove, *Prolegomena* 268, 291–293 and 416; Stickler, *Historia* 1.107–109; R. Naz, 'Hadriana', DDC 5 (1953) 1083–1084; Plöchl, *Geschichte des Kirchenrechts* 1.444; Rambaud-Buhot, 'Hadriana Collectio', NCE 6 (1967) 887; Mordek, 'Dionysio-Hadriana', LMA 3 (1985) 1074–1075; G. Fransen, 'Hadriana ou Dionysio-Hadriana', DHGE 22 (1988) 1430–1432

Bernold von Konstanz, *De excommunicatis vitandis* c. 29 and 43, ed. F. Thaner, MGH Ldl 2.125, 131

L. Chr. Rudolph, *De codice canonum quem Hadrianus Carolo Magno dono dedit* (Erlangen 1754)

L. Chr. Rudolph, *Nova commentatio de codice canonum quem Hadrianus I Carolo Magno dono dedit* (Erlangen 1777)

J. Hartzheim, 'Collectio Dionysio-Hadriana', *Concilia Germaniae* 1 (Cologne 1759) 131–235

F. Maassen, 'Glossen des canonischen Rechts aus dem karolingischen Zeitalter', SB Vienna 84 (1877) 235–298

P. Ewald, 'Studien zur Ausgabe des Registers Gregors I.', NA 3 (1878) 433–628

P. Ewald, in: W. Wattenbach, 'Die Handschriften der Hamiltonschen Sammlung', NA 8 (1883) 332–335

P. Hinschius, 'Die kanonistischen Handschriften der Hamilton'schen Sammlung im Kupferstich-Kabinett des königlichen Museums zu Berlin', ZKG 6 (1884) 193–246

W. Gundlach, *Epistolae Merowingici et Karolini aevi* (MGH Epistolae 3; Berlin 1892) 479–487

M. Conrat (Cohn), 'Hinkmariana im Cod. Paris Sangerm. 12445', NA 35 (1910) 769–775

R. Massigli, 'Sur l'origine de la collection canonique dite Hadriana augmentée', *Mélanges d'Archéologie et d'Histoire* 32 (1912) 363–383

A. M. Koeniger, *Grundriss einer Geschichte des katholischen Kirchenrechts* (Cologne 1919) 35, 75 n. 152

De Clercq, *Législation* 1.125–128

Séjourné, *Saint Isidore* 395

Wurm, *Studien und Texte* 33–35

Seckel-Fuhrmann, *Die erste Zeile Pseudoisidors* 24–32

A. Chavasse, 'Les lettres de saint Léon le Grand dans le supplément de la Dionysiana et de l'Hadriana et dans la collection du manuscrit du Vatican', *Revue des sciences religieuses* 38 (1964) 154–176

Kottje, 'Einheit und Vielfalt' 336–338 esp. nn. 54–58, 60–62 (manuscripts)

Mordek, 'Bonneval' 340 n. 5

Mordek, 'Dionysio-Hadriana' 39–63

Fuhrmann, *Einfluß und Verbreitung*, index 1084–1085

Mordek, *Kirchenrecht und Reform* 151–162, 241–249

H. Mordek, 'Bemerkungen zum mittelalterlichen Schatzverzeichnis von Porto/Rom', *Mélanges Fransen* 2.233–240 (fragment of the *Dionysio-Hadriana* Clm 2° 292)

R. McKitterick, *The Frankish Church and the Carolingian Reforms 789–895* (London 1977) 1–44 passim

Mordek, 'Kirchenrechtliche Autoritäten' 237–255

Fuhrmann, 'Papstbriefe' 365–367

Kottje, *Bußbücher Halitgars* 192–194

H. Mordek, 'Il diritto canonico fra Tardo Antico e Alto Medioevo: La *svolta dionisiana* nella canonistica', *La cultura in Italia fra tardo antico e alto medioevo* (Atti del Convegno tenuto a Roma, Consiglio nationale delle Ricerche, 12–16 nov. 1979; Rome 1981) 149–164

Kretzschmar, *Alger von Lüttich* 72–78 (use of the *Collectio Dionysio-Hadriana* by Alger of Liège)

C. Leonardi, 'Von Pacificus zu Rather: Zur Veroneser Kulturgeschichte im 9. und 10. Jahrhundert', DA 41 (1985) 390–417 (cf. on Vat. lat. 4979)

Mordek, 'Kanonistik und gregorianische Reform' 74–75 (Bernold of Constance's evaluation of the *Collectio Dionysio-Hadriana*)

J. F. Hanselmann, 'Der Codex Vat. Pal. 289: Ein Beitrag zum Mainzer Skriptorium im 9. Jahrhundert', *Scriptorium* 41 (1987) 78–87. (List of manuscripts from Mainz saec. IX contains three copies of the *Collectio Dionysio-Hadriana*)

H. Mordek, 'Rom, Byzanz und die Franken im 8. Jahrhundert', *Person und Gemeinschaft im Mittelalter: Karl Schmid zum 65. Geburtstag*, ed. H. Mordek (Sigmaringen 1988) 123–156

Landau, 'Kanonessammlungen in der Lombardei' 429–430

R. Newhauser, 'Towards 'modus in habendo': Transformation in the Idea of Avarice: The Early Penitentials through the Carolingian Reforms', ZRG Kan. Abt. 75 (1989) 1–22

L. Böhringer (ed.), 'Der eherechtliche Traktat im Paris. lat. 12445, einer Arbeitshandschrift Hinkmars von Reims', DA 46 (1990) 18–47

K. Bierbrauer, 'Die vorkarolingischen und karolingischen Handschriften der Bayerischen Staatsbibliothek', *Katalog der illuminierten Handschriften der Bayerischen Staatsbibliothek in München* 1 (Wiesbaden 1990)

Th. F. X. Noble, 'Literacy and the Papal Government in Late Antiquity and the Early Middle Ages', *The Uses of Literacy in Early Mediaeval Europe*, ed. R. McKitterick (Cambridge 1990) 82–108

F. S. Paxton, '*Bonus liber*: A Late Carolingian Clerical Manual from Lorsch (Biblioteca Vaticana MS Pal. lat. 485)', *The Two Laws: Studies in Medieval Legal History Dedicated to Stephan Kuttner*, ed. Laurent Mayali and Stephanie A. J. Tibbetts (Washington 1990) 1–30

Landau, 'Vorgratianische Kanonessammlungen bei den Dekretisten' 93–116

Siems, *Handel und Wucher* 516–517, 727–728

Zechiel-Eckes, *Cresconius* (cf. index)

H. Mordek, 'Zur Kirchenrechtsreform am Beispiel des Frankfurter Kapitulars', *794 - Karl der Große in Frankfurt am Main: Ein König bei der Arbeit: Ausstellung zum 1200-Jahre-Jubiläum der Stadt Frankfurt am Main*, ed. J. Fried, R. Koch, L. E. Saurma-Jeltsch, and A. Thiel (Sigmaringen 1994) 134–136

K. Rebro, 'La Grande Moravia: Gli inizi del cristianesimo e dell'ordine giuridico', *Studi in onore Luigi Prosdocimi* (1994) 1.2, 357–368

Landau, 'Kanonessammlungen in Bayern' 151, 154–160

Collectio Dionysiana adaucta

1. Author: Unknown. *2. Date:* Between 850 and 872. *3. Place:* Ravenna (Wurm 35); perhaps Rome (cf. Landau, 'Kanonessammlungen in der Lombardei' 429–430 n. 19). *4. Type:* A chronologically arranged collection of conciliar canons and decretals. *5. Edition:* None.

6. Manuscripts

München, Bayerische Staatsbibliothek, Clm 14008, saec. IX^{2}, Rome, Prov. St. Emmeram, Regensburg

Roma, Biblioteca Vallicelliana, A.5, saec. IX ca. 3/4, Central Italy (probably Rome; according to Turner and Massigli: Ravenna)

Vaticano, Città del, Biblioteca Apostolica Vaticana, lat. 1343, saec. X–XI, Italy, Pavia (only parts of the *Collectio Dionysiana adaucta*, together with Pseudo-Isidore)
Vaticano, Città del, Biblioteca Apostolica Vaticana, lat. 1353 (a. 1461, copy of an old manuscript from Bergamo)
Vaticano, Città del, Biblioteca Apostolica Vaticana, lat. 5845, saec. X1/2, between 915 and 934, Capua (including *praefatio* to the decretals)
Vercelli, Biblioteca Capitolare, LXXVI, saec. X, Vercelli

7. *Bibliography*

Maassen, *Geschichte* 454–465; corr. by: A. L. Feder, *Hilarii Pictaviensis opera* (CSEL LXV) p. xlvii; Kurtscheid-Wilches 1.90; Van Hove, *Prolegomena* 268; Mordek, 'Dionysius Exiguus', LMA 3 (1985) 1090

Ballerini, *De antiquis . . . collectionibus et collectoribus* P. III cap. 3, c. 2–3 (PL 56.211–212)
Turner, EOMIA 1.2.1, p. IX and 1.2.3, p. IX and 535
R. Massigli, 'Sur l'origine de la collection canonique dite Hadriana augmentée', *Mélanges d'Archéologie et d'Histoire* 32 (1912) 363–383
ACO 1.5.2, p. xi and 2.2, p. v–vi
Schwartz, *Publizistische Sammlungen* 278
Wurm, *Studien und Texte* 35
W. Lettenbauer, 'Eine lateinische Kanonessammlung in Mähren im 9. Jahrhundert', *Orientalia Christiana Periodica* 18 (1952) 246–269
Mordek, *Kirchenrecht und Reform* 59 n. 94, 243
Landau, 'Gefälschtes Recht' 19
Landau, 'Kanonessammlungen in der Lombardei' 429–430 n. 19
Zechiel-Eckes, *Cresconius* (cf. index)

Breviarium ad inquaerendum sententias infra

1. *Author:* Unknown. 2. *Date:* Certainly datable to the reign of Emperor Charles the Great. 3. *Place:* Unknown. 4. *Type:* A summary of the *Collectio Dionysio-Hadriana*. 5. *Edition:* None.

6. *Manuscripts*

Barcelona, Archivo de la Corona de Aragón, Ripoll 105, saec. XIII
Berlin, Staatsbibliothek Preußischer Kulturbesitz, Phill. 1744, saec. X
Hamburg, Staats- und Universitätsbibliothek, cod. 26 in scrinio, saec. IX^{in}, Southern Burgundy; 24 foll., (cf. T. Brandis, *Die Codices in scrinio der Staats- und Universitätsbibliothek Hamburg 1–110* [Katalog der Handschriften der Staats- und Universitätsbibliothek Hamburg 7, Hamburg 1972] 72–73) (fragment)
Paris, Bibliothèque nationale, lat. 1452, saec. IX4/4, Rhône region
Paris, Bibliothèque nationale, lat. 3844 (cf. Mordek, *Kirchenrecht und Reform* 244)
Paris, Bibliothèque nationale, lat. 11710, saec. IX^{in}, a. 805, Burgundy
Paris, Bibliothèque nationale, lat. 12446, saec. IX1–2/4, probably Central France
Vaticano, Città del, Biblioteca Apostolica Vaticana, Reg. lat. 1021, saec. IX1–2/4, St.

Amand) perhaps a separate collection (similar to the *Concordia canonum* of Cresconius, but arranged chronologically)
Wien, Österreichische Nationalbibliothek, lat. 524, saec. IX, Salzburg
Wien, Österreichische Nationalbibliothek, lat. 737, saec. IX, Salzburg

7. *Bibliography*

Maassen, *Geschichte* 465–466; Van Hove, *Prolegomena* 293

Mordek, *Kirchenrecht und Reform* 248–249

Collectio Mutinensis

1. Author: Unknown. *2. Date:* Probably at the beginning of the seventh century. *3. Place:* Italy, Bobbio. *4. Type:* A chronologically arranged collection of decretals, copied out of the *Dionysiana* (as well as the *Liber Pontificalis* and the Symmachian forgeries); closely related with the *Dionysiana Bobiensis* (cf. Wurm, *Studien und Texte* 32).

5. *Edition*

M. Fornasari, 'Collectio Canonum Mutinensis', SG 9 (1966) 245–356

6. *Manuscript*

Modena, Biblioteca Capitolare, O.I.12, saec. VII^{ex} or saec. VIII^{in} according to Hinschius, *Zeitschrift für Rechtsgeschichte* 2 (1863) 463–464; saec. VII/IX according to Wurm, *Studien und Texte* 32; Northern Italy; CLA 3 no. 369 p. 30

7. *Bibliography*

Maassen, *Geschichte* 796–797; H. Leclercq, 'Liber pontificalis', DACL 9/1 (1930) 354–460; Van Hove, *Prolegomena* 267

P. Hinschius, 'Nachrichten über juristische (insbesondere kanonische) Handschriften in italienischen Bibliotheken. II und III.', *Zeitschrift für Rechtsgeschichte* 2 (1863) 455–473, esp. 463–473 (Modena)
Maassen, 'Bibliotheca' SB Vienna 53 (1866) 382
Turner, EOMIA 1.1.1, p. 1
Duchesne, *Liber pontificalis* 1.cxcvii–cxcix
Th. Mommsen, *Gestorum pontificum Romanorum* 1: *Libri pontificalis pars prior* (Berlin 1898)
J. M. March, *Liber pontificalis prout exstat in codice Dertusiensi* (Barcelona 1925)
M. Buchner, 'Zur Überlieferungsgeschichte des Liber pontificalis und zu seiner Verbreitung im Frankenreich im 9. Jahrhundert', RQ 34 (1926) 141–166
E. Caspar, *Geschichte des Papsttums* 2 (Tübingen 1933) 314–320, 774–775
Wurm, *Studien und Texte* 32
M. Fornasari, 'Collectio canonum Mutinensis', SG 9 (1966) 245–356
Landau, 'Kanonessammlungen in der Lombardei' 428–429 n. 15

Fulgentius Ferrandus, Breviatio canonum

1. Author: Fulgentius Ferrandus, Deacon at Carthage (†546–547). *2. Date:* About 535 (cf. Zechiel-Eckes, *Cresconius* 1.68). *3. Place:* Carthage. *4. Type:* Systematic collection of conciliar canons, arranges the old Greek and African canons in a systematic order without citing their text; frequently circulated together with Cresconius' *Concordia canonum*.

5. Editions

G. Voellius and H. Justellus, *Bibliotheca iuris canonici* 1 (Paris 1661) 448–455 (PL 67.949–962 and PL 88.817–830)

C. Munier, *Concilia Africae a. 345–a. 525* (CCL 149; 1974) 287–306

6. Manuscripts

Montpellier, Bibliothèque Interuniversitaire, H.233 saec. IX1/3, Rhaetia, Prov. Troyes, then Pithou and the Oratorium of Troyes, cf. below, 'Cresconius' and cf. Zechiel-Eckes, *Cresconius* 1.72 and 2.325–327

Paris, Bibliothèque nationale, lat. 12097, fol. 144^{v}–158^{r} (olim Sangerm. 936, cf. *Collectio Corbeiensis*), Southern France, Arles or Lyon, cf. CLA 5 no. 619, p. 30; fol. 1^{r}–139^{v}: shortly after 524; fol. 139^{v}–224^{v}: saec. VI/VII cf. Mordek, *Kirchenrecht und Reform* 90 n. 126

Vercelli, Biblioteca Capitolare, CLXV, saec. IX2/4, Northern Italy (cf. below, 'Cresconius'); cf. Zechiel-Eckes, *Cresconius* 1.172–175 (detailed description of the manuscript)

Cf. Zechiel-Eckes, *Cresconius* 1.72, 172–184 and 179 n. 24 about two other presumable manuscripts of the *Breviatio canonum* in the time from saec. VIII^{2} to IX^{in}

Partial Tradition

Paris, Bibliothèque nationale, lat. 2796, about a. 813, France, fol. 142^{v}–145^{r}, cf. Mordek, *Kirchenrecht und Reform* 148 n. 242 (dependent on Paris lat. 12097)

7. Bibliography

Maassen, *Geschichte* 799–802; P. Godet, 'Ferrand Fulgence', DThC 5 (1924) 2174–2175; Fournier-Le Bras 1.34–35; G. Bardy, 'Afrique', DDC 1 (1935) 289–290; A. Vetulani, 'Breviatio canonum Ferrandi', DDC 2 (1937) 1111–1113; Kurtscheid-Wilches 1.93; Van Hove, *Prolegomena* 265–266; Stickler, *Historia* 1.74; Mordek, 'Ferrandus', LMA 4 (1989) 385 (bibliography)

Ballerini, *De antiquis . . . collectionibus et collectoribus* P. IV, cap. I (PL 56.273–279)

Tardif, *Sources* 114

Fessler-Jungmann, *Institutiones patrologiae* (Innsbruck 1896) 2b.423

W. Schanz, C. Hosius, G. Krüger, 'Geschichte der römischen Literatur. Die Literatur des 5. und 6. Jahrhunderts', in: I. Müller, *Geschichte der klassischen Altertums-Wissenschaft* 8.4.2 (Munich 1920) 572–575

G. G. Lapeyre, *Saint Fulgence de Ruspe* (Paris 1929) lxxii–lxxiii, 72–73

G. G. Lapeyre, *Ferrand diacre de Carthage. Vita S. Fulgentii* (Paris 1929)

Bardenhewer, *Literatur* 5.316–319

W. Pewesin, *Imperium, Ecclesia universalis, Rom: Der Kampf der afrikanischen Kirche um die Mitte des 6. Jahrhunderts* (Forschungen zur Kirchen- und Geistesgeschichte 11; Stuttgart 1937)
Wurm, *Studien und Texte* 37–39
Gaudemet, *Sources* 137–138
Landau, 'Vorgratianische Kanonessammlungen bei den Dekretisten' 93–116
Zechiel-Eckes, *Cresconius* 1.68, 72–74 and 115–116

Collectio Teatina (Ingilramni)

1. Author: Unknown. *2. Date:* About 525; after the death of Hormisda (523); sixth century. *3. Place:* Italy. *4. Type:* Unstructured collection of conciliar canons and decretals. *5. Edition:* None.

6. *Manuscript*

Vaticano, Città del, Biblioteca Apostolica Vaticana, Reg. lat. 1997, saec. VIII–IX or IX^{med}, Chieti, CLA 1 no. 113, p. 34, 44, CLA Suppl. p. 45, cf. Loew-Brown, *Beneventan script* 1.208

7. *Bibliography*

Maassen, *Geschichte* 526–533; Fournier-Le Bras 1.25–26; Kurtscheid-Wilches 1.91; Van Hove, *Prolegomena* 162; Stickler, *Historia* 1.52

A. Reifferscheid, *Bibliotheca patrum latinorum Italica* 1 (Vienna 1865) 333–336
Duchesne, *Liber pontificalis* 1.XV
E. Carusi, 'Notizie su codici delle Biblioteca Capitolare de Chieti e sulla collezione canonica Teatina del cod. Vat. Reg. 1997', *Bulletino della R. Deputazione Abruzzese di Storia Patria* Series 3, vol. 4 (1913) 7–75, esp. 22ff.
ACO 2.2.2, p. xv
Silva-Tarouca, 'Beiträge' 664–665
C. H. Turner, 'Chapters in the History of Latin MSS of Canons VI: The Version called Prisca (b) The Chieti MS (=I), now Vatic. Regin. 1997', JTS 31 (1929–1930) 9–20
Le Bras, 'Notes III' 506–518
E. Schwartz, ZRG Kan. Abt. 20 (1931) 599 (review of Turner, EOMIA)
Schwartz 'Kanonessammlungen' 1–114 (cf. *Collectio Sanblasiana*) esp. 53–57, 103–104
Wurm, *Studien und Texte* 88 and 257–260
Mordek, *Kirchenrecht und Reform* 11 n. 41 (circulation of the collection outside of Italy)
P. Supino Martini, 'Per lo studio delle scritture altomedievali italiane: La collezione canonica chietina (Vat. Reg. lat. 1997)', *Scrittura e civiltà* 1 (1977) 133–154
Landau, 'Gefälschtes Recht' 19–20
R. Reynolds, 'The Ritual of Clerical Ordination of the Sacramentarium Gelasianum saec. VIII: Early Evidence from Southern Italy', *Rituels: Mélanges offerts au Père Gy O.P.*, ed. P. De Clerck and E. Palazzo (Paris 1990) 437–445
Zechiel-Eckes, *Cresconius* (cf. index)

Collectio Vaticana (Vat. lat. 1342 etc.)

1. Author: Unknown. *2. Date:* First quarter of the sixth century. *3. Place:* Rome. *4. Type:* Partly a chronologically arranged collection of conciliar canons and decretals (cf. Maassen, *Geschichte* 522); used the *Collectio Dionysiana*, contains all the texts of the Symmachian forgeries (cf. Landau). *5. Edition:* None.

6. *Manuscripts*

Düsseldorf, Universitätsbibliothek, E.1, Italy (probably Rome), saec. IX^2, fol. 3ra–44ra; cf. Zechiel-Eckes, *Cresconius* 1.218–223. A previously unknown partial version of the text, combined with the *Dionysio-Hadriana* tradition; it is more similar to Firenze, Biblioteca Medicea Laurenziana, Aedil. 82 and Vat. Barb. lat. 679 than to Vat. lat. 1342

Firenze, Biblioteca Medicea Laurenziana, Aedil. 82, saec. IX3/4, probably Northern Italy (cf. Mordek, *Kirchenrecht und Reform* 278–279), contains a variant version of the text. Cf. Maassen, *Geschichte* 513 u. 524–526; cf. also Kölzer, 'Farfenser Auszüge aus der *Sammlung der Vatikanischen Handschrift*', BMCL 12 (1982) 6 n. 37

Vaticano, Città del, Biblioteca Apostolica Vaticana, lat. 1342, saec. VIII or older, Central Italy, cf. CLA 1, no. 9, p. 4 and p. 38; CLA Suppl., p. 43; Stürner, 'Die Quellen der Fides Konstantins' 150; Mordek, *Kirchenrecht und Reform* 667

Vaticano, Città del, Biblioteca Apostolica Vaticana, Barb. lat. 679 (olim XIV. 52; 2888), saec. VIII–IX, Northern Italy, perhaps Aquileia; fol. 1–295^r; it can be traced in Tuscany in the eleventh century (San Salvatore di Montamiata); cf. CLA 1 no. 65 p. 20 and p. 41; CLA Suppl., p. 44; in the CLA erroneously identified as a *Concordia canonum* of Cresconius, an error which the Ballerini, *De antiquis . . . collectionibus*, P. II, cap. VII (PL 56.135–141) sought to correct during their dispute with some Anonymi and L. Holste, who is mentioned on the flyleaf of Cod. Vat. Barb. lat. 679. Martínez Díez, *Colección Hispana* 1.13 erroneously attributed it to the Pseudo-Isidorian tradition. Addition copied on fol. 298^r (saec. XI) is edited by R. E. Reynolds, RB 80 [1970] 246–247); cf. also Mordek, *Bibliotheca capitularium* 751–754

Only *Capitulatio*

Novara, Biblioteca Capitolare, XXX (66), saec. IX^2, probably Northern Italy

Oxford, Bodleian Library, Laud. misc. 421 (olim no. 893), saec. IX^{ex}, Prov. Würzburg, cf. Bischoff-Hofmann, *Libri Sancti Kyliani* 58, 139; contains only fragments of the *Vaticana*-Capitulatio (fol. 1ra–1rb), whereas the *Corpus canonum* was taken over from the *Dionysio-Hadriana*, cf. Maassen, *Geschichte* 513

Excerpt

Lucca, Biblioteca Capitolare Feliniana, 125, saec. IX ca. 3/4, Italy, cf. Mordek, *Kirchenrecht und Reform* 244, fol. 190ra–209va, for a detailed description of the contents, cf. Zechiel-Eckes 1.220 n. 51

Roma, Biblioteca Nazionale Centrale, Sessor. CCV (2100), saec. XV (cf. Mordek, *Kirchenrecht und Reform* 10 n. 40

7. *Bibliography*

Maassen, Geschichte 500–504, 512–526; Fournier-Le Bras 1.25–26; Van Hove, *Prolegomena* 162; Stickler, *Historia* 1.52

ACO 2.2.2, p. xvii; 2.4, p. iv

Silva-Tarouca, 'Beiträge', 664–665

Le Bras, 'Notes III' 506–518

C. H. Turner, 'The version called prisca: The Chieti MS. now Vatican Regina 1997', JTS 31 (1930) 10

C. H. Turner, 'The collection named after the MS of St. Maur, Paris lat. 1451', JTS 32 (1931) 9–11

G. Le Bras, 'Quantam partem habuerint Romani in libris canonum ante decretum Gratiani confectis', *Ius Pontificium* 13 (1933) 237–240

Schwartz, 'Kanonessammlungen' 84–86

Wurm, *Studien und Texte* 89–92, 265–271

A. Chavasse, 'Les lettres de Saint Léon le Grand dans le Supplément de la Dionysiana et de l'Hadriana et dans la Collection du ms. du Vatican', *Revue des sciences religieuses* 38 (1964) 154–176

Stürner, 'Die Quellen der Fides Konstantins' 150–152

Mordek, *Kirchenrecht und Reform* 10, n. 40, 278–279 and 667

R. Riedinger, 'Papst Martin I. und Papst Leo I. in den Akten der Lateran-Synode von 649', JBOeB 33 (1983) 87–88

G. Billanovich, 'Treviso e Ceneda', IMU 27 (1984) 17–29

Gaudemet, *Sources* 139–140

Landau, 'Gefälschtes Recht' 19

Zechiel-Eckes, *Cresconius* 1.101–102 n. 131, 219–222 (cf. also index)

Collectio of Vat. lat. 6808

1. Author: Unknown. *2. Date:* Unknown (between eighth and eleventh century) *3. Place:* Copy of an older source from Farfa (Kölzer). *4. Type:* Unstructured collection of conciliar canons and decretals. Excerpts from the *Collectio Vaticana* (Vat. lat. 1342 etc.). *5. Edition:* None.

6. *Manuscript*

Vaticano, Città del, Biblioteca Apostolica Vaticana, lat. 6808, saec. XI1/2, fol. 113^{v}–138^{v}; cf. Kölzer

7. *Bibliography*

B. Albers, *Consuetudines monasticae* 1 (Stuttgart-Vienna 1900) p. x

E. Monaci, *Archivio paleografico italiano* 2 (Rome 1884–1907) p. ix

T. Kölzer, 'Farfenser Auszüge aus der *Sammlung der Vatikanischen Handschrift*', BMCL 12 (1982) 1–12

Zechiel-Eckes, *Cresconius* 1.221–222

Collectio Quesnelliana

1. Author: Unknown. *2. Date:* About the turn of the fifth to the sixth century; according to J. Van der Speeten, 'Le dossier de Nicée dans la Quesnelliana', SE 28 (1985) 383–450, esp. 384, the *Collectio Quesnelliana* was used by Dionysius Exiguus at Rome. *3. Place:* Gaul (Maassen), Arles (Duchesne), Rome (Silva-Tarouca, 'Beiträge', 661–662; Silva-Tarouca, 'Nuovi studi' 552–559; Le Bras, 'Notes III', 511–513; Fournier-Le Bras 1.27; Wurm, *Studien und Texte* 82–87, 221–223, 240–257; Stickler, *Historia* 1.41 and 50–51; Lefebvre, DDC 7 [1965] 434–440; see also Mordek, *Kirchenrecht und Reform* 239). *4. Type:* Chronologically arranged collection of conciliar canons and decretals; served as a source for later collections; was used especially for the letters of Leo I.

5. Editions

Pasquier Quesnel, *Ad S. Leonis Magni Opera Appendix* 2 (Paris 1675) 13–242

Ballerini, 'Codex canonum ecclesiasticorum et constitutorum sanctae sedis apostolicae', *Appendix ad S. Leonis Magni opera* 3 (Venice 1757) 1–472 (=PL 56.359–746); the Greek councils of the *Quesnelliana* are available in a critical edition by Turner, EOMIA und Schwartz, ACO

Wurm, *Studien und Texte* 240–257 (contains only a critical inventory of the decretals)

6. Manuscripts

Arras, Bibliothèque municipale, 644 (572), saec. VIII–IX, probably Northeastern France or Northwestern Austrasia; probably from the same scriptorium as Einsiedeln 191; Prov. Saint-Vaast at Arras; cf. A. Goldbacher, CSEL 58 (1923) LXI; CLA 6, no. 713, p. 4 and p. 42; CLA Suppl. p. 56

Einsiedeln, Stiftsbibliothek, 191 (277), saec. VIII–IX, probably Northeastern France or Northwestern Austrasia like Arras 644 "ein des Königs würdiges Buch" [Bischoff, 'Die Hofbibliothek Karls des Großen', *Karl der Große, Lebenswerk und Nachleben* 2 (Düsseldorf 1965) 42–62, esp. 55] Prov. Constance; saec. XI–XII with many comments by Bernold of Constance and an anonymous reader; cf. CLA 7, no. 874, p. 12 and p. 55; CLA Suppl. p. 58

Oxford, Oriel College, 42, saec. XII (Silva-Tarouca, 'Beiträge' 661: saec. XIII, Prov. Malmesbury [Wiltshire]; cf. Ker, *Medieval Libraries of Great Britain*^{2} 128); Quesnel's edition is based on a copy of this latest and most reliable manuscript of the collection which is now kept at the Bodleian Library, Oxford (cf. R. M. Thompson, 'The Reading of William of Malmesbury', RB 85 [1975] 362–402)

Paris, Bibliothèque nationale, lat. 1454, saec. IX3/4, probably from the region around Paris, Saint-Denis? Prov. cathedral chapter of Beauvais; cf. Mordek, *Bibliotheca capitularium* 409–410

Paris, Bibliothèque nationale, lat. 3842A, saec. IX^{med} or 3/4, perhaps from Paris (one of the manuscripts used for the preparation of the *Editio princeps* of the *Quesnelliana*; it also contains the *Constitutum Silvestri* belonging to the Symmachian forgeries); cf. Mordek, *Bibliotheca capitularium* 438–439

Paris, Bibliothèque nationale, lat. 3848A, saec. IX1/4, from the region around Metz; Prov. Troyes

Wien, Österreichische Nationalbibliothek, lat. 2141, about 780, from the region around Lorsch; cf. CLA 10, no. 1505, p. 20 and p. 49; CLA Suppl. p. 66; cf. Mordek, *Kirchenrecht und Reform* 10 including n. 38

Wien, Österreichische Nationalbibliothek, lat. 2147, about 780, from the region around Lorsch; cf. CLA 10, no. 1506, p. 20 and p. 49; CLA Suppl. p. 66

Further manuscripts of the *Quesnelliana* that are now lost are mentioned in Turner, EOMIA 1.2.1, p. xi; Silva-Tarouca, 'Beiträge' 660 and Stürner, 'Die Quellen der Fides Konstantins' 77

Fragment

Düsseldorf, Universitätsbibliothek, E.32, fragment consisting of four leaves, about 800, possibly from the monastery of Werden (Ruhr); cf. Levison, 'Analecta pontificia, 1: Neue Bruchstücke der Quesnelschen Sammlung', *Papsttum und Kaisertum: P. Kehr zum 65. Geburtstag dargebracht* (Munich 1926) 138–140; CLA 8, no. 1188, p. 46 and p. 67; CLA Suppl. p. 62

Excerpts

Vaticano, Città del, Biblioteca Apostolica Vaticana, lat. 4982, saec. XVI (after 1572), fol. 185^r–196^v; cf. Mordek, *Bibliotheca capitularium* 878

Cf. *Collectio Colbertina* (especially its second part, which took over most of its material from the *Quesnelliana*, cf. Mordek, *Kirchenrecht und Reform* 240)

7. *Bibliography*

Maassen, *Geschichte* 413; 486–500; Conrat, *Geschichte* 145; Fournier-Le Bras 1.26–29; Kurtscheid-Wilches 1.95–96; Van Hove, *Prolegomena* 156–157; Stickler, *Historia* 1.50–51; *Clavis* 393–394, no. 1770; Ch. Lefebvre, 'Quesnelliana Collectio', DDC 7 (1965) 434–440: very instructive; but erroneously identifies the Pseudo-Isidorian manuscripts, Paris lat. 9629 [olim Suppl. lat. 840, not nouv. acq. lat. 840], Rouen E.27 (702) [olim 15/9 E], Vat. lat. 3791 and Vat. Ottobon. lat. 93 as *Quesnelliana*-Codices (criticized by Stürner, 'Die Quellen der Fides Konstantins' 77 n. 44); *García y García,* Historia 1.174–175; J. M. Buckley, 'Quesnelliana Collectio', NCE 12 (1967) 22; *Rep. font.* 3 (1970) 507; Mordek, LMA 7 (1995) 365

Pierre Coustant (ed.), *Epistolae Romanorum Pontificum* 1 (Paris 1721, reprint Farnborough 1967) Praefatio lxvii–lxxix

Ballerini, *De antiquis . . . collectionibus et collectoribus* P. II, cap. VIII (PL 56.141–143)

Maassen, 'Bibliotheca' SB Vienna 54 (1867) 192, 232

P. Schneider, *Die Lehre von den Kirchenrechtsquellen: Eine Einleitung in das Studium des Kirchenrechts*[2] (Regensburg-New York-Cincinnati 1892) 58–59

Duchesne, 'Collection romaine' 159–162

Steinacker, 'Deusdedithandschrift' 131

E. Friedberg, *Lehrbuch des katholischen und evangelischen Kirchenrechts*[6] (Leipzig 1909, repr. Frankfurt 1965) 131–132

Turner, EOMIA 1.2.1, p. xi–xii

R. Massigli, 'La plus ancienne collection des décrétales', *Revue d'histoire et de littérature religieuse*, N.S. 5 (1914) 402–424

C. H. Turner, 'Arles and Rome', JTS 17 (1916) 237

Silva-Tarouca, 'Beiträge' 447–478 u. 660–662

Silva-Tarouca, 'Edizioni delle antiche lettere dei papi', *Civiltà cattolica* 72.1 (1921) 3–22, 323–336
ACO 1.5.2, p. xiv–xvii and ACO 2.4, p. i–iv
Tarré, 'Sources' 125–134
J. Tarré, 'Sur les origines arlésiennes de la collection canonique, dite Hispana', *Mélanges Paul Fournier* (Paris 1929) 705–724
Le Bras, 'Notes III' 506–518; on the origins of the collection, cf. 512–513 including 512 n. 4 (on Silva-Tarouca).
Schwartz, *Publizistische Sammlungen*
Silva-Tarouca, 'Nuovi studi' 3–56, 349–425, 547–598
G. Le Bras, 'Quantam partem habuerint Romani in libris canonum ante decretum Gratiani confectis', *Ius Pontificium* 13 (1933) 237–240
Tarré, 'Etudes' 208–209
De Clercq, *Législation* 1, passim
Schwartz, 'Kanonessammlungen' 85 and 88–90
Wurm, *Studien und Texte* 82–87, 143–149, 209–223, 240–257
N. M. Haring, 'The Character and Range of the Influence of St. Cyril of Alexandria on Latin Theology (430–1260)', MS 12 (1950) 4–5
R. Buchner, *Die Rechtsquellen*, in: W. Wattenbach and W. Levison, *Deutschlands Geschichtsquellen im Mittelalter: Vorzeit und Karolinger* (Weimar 1953) 64–65
R. Losada Cosme, 'Las colecciones canonicas en foncion de autenticidad, universalidad y unificacion de Derecho', REDC 10 (1955) 61–111
R. Losada Cosme, 'La unificacion interna del derecho y las colecciones anteriores a Graciano', REDC 10 (1955) 353–384
De Clercq, *Législation* 2, passim
J. Autenrieth, 'The Canon Law Books of the Curia episcopalis Constantiensis from the Ninth to the Fifteenth Century', *Proceedings Boston* 3–15, 4–5
Mordek, 'Bonneval' 340 with n. 3
Stürner, 'Die Quellen der Fides Konstantins' 74–79
Ch. Munier, 'La tradition manuscrite de *l'Abrégé d'Hippone* et le canon des Ecritures des églises africaines', SE 21 (1972) 43–55
Mordek, 'Kanonistische Aktivität' 22–23
Mordek, *Kirchenrecht und Reform* 238–240
Fuhrmann, 'Papstbriefe' 365–367
Gaudemet, *Sources* 133 (cf. on latest developments in research)
J. Van der Speeten, 'Le dossier de Nicée dans la Quesnelliana', SE 28 (1985) 383–450
Landau, 'Gefälschtes Recht' 19
E. Vodola, 'Sovereignty and Tabu: Evolution of the Sanction against Communication with Excommunicates, 2: Canonical Collections, *Studia in honorem A. M. Stickler* (1992) 581–598
Zechiel-Eckes, *Cresconius* (cf. index)

Collectio Sanblasiana

1. Author: Unknown. *2. Date:* At the beginning of the sixth century. *3. Place:* Italy, possibly Rome. *4. Type:* Chronologically arranged collection of conciliar canons and decretals; the author used the *Dionysiana*. Maassen, *Geschichte* 504–512 gives a minute description of the collection.

5. Edition

There is only an edition of the Greek councils by Turner, EOMIA and Schwartz, ACO

6. Manuscripts

Detailed information about the manuscripts and further reading in Stürner, 'Die Quellen der Fides Konstantins' 79–82

Köln, Erzbischöfliche Diözesan- und Dombibliothek, 213 (olim Darmstadt 2336), saec. VIII^{in}, Northumbria or region on the continent where missionaries from Northumbria worked; by the eighth century it was already at Cologne; cf. CLA 8, no. 1163, p. 40 and p. 66; CLA Suppl. p. 62; J. Hofmann, 'Altenglische und althochdeutsche Glossen aus Würzburg und dem weiteren angelsächsischen Missionsgebiet', *Beiträge zur Geschichte der deutschen Sprache und Literatur* 85 (1963) 36, 42

Lucca, Biblioteca Capitolare Feliniana, 490, saec. VIII–IX, Lucca; fol. 236^{r}–271^{v}, cf. L. Schiaparelli, *Il codice 490 della Biblioteca Capitolare di Lucca e la Scuola Scrittoria Lucchese (sec. VIII–IX): Contributi allo studio della minuscola precarolina in Italia* (Rome 1924); CLA 3 no. 303b, p. 9 and p. 43; CLA Suppl., p. 49

Paris, Bibliothèque nationale, lat. 1455, saec. IX^{2}, probably near Reims; cf. Mordek, *Kirchenrecht und Reform* 127 n. 118. The *Collectio Sanblasiana* is combined with excerpts from the *Quesnelliana* in this manuscript. Maassen, *Geschichte* 536–542 identified the combination as the collection of the Colbert manuscript

Paris, Bibliothèque nationale, lat. 3836, saec. VIII^{2}, Northern France (Corbie or surrounding region) cf. CLA 5, no. 554, pp. 11 and 55; CLA Suppl. p. 54.

Paris, Bibliothèque nationale, lat. 4279, saec. IX^{med}, probably Western France (B. Bischoff); on the transmission of parts of the collection cf. Maassen, *Geschichte* 509 (only beginning of the *Sanblasiana*)

Sankt Paul im Lavanttal, Stiftsbibliothek, 7/1 (olim XXIX Kassette 1; XXV a. 7), saec. VIII, Italy; by the eighth century it was already on the island of Reichenau; Prov. St. Blasien, cf. CLA 10 no. 1457, pp. 7 and 46; Stürner, 'Die Quellen der Fides Konstantins' 79 n. 53)

A large fragment of the collection was kept at Cheltenham, Phillipps Collection, 17849, saec. VIII^{ex} Italy; cf. CLA 2^{2}, no. 143, pp. 8, 49, 57. After World War II it was acquired by Dr. M. Bodmer (Cologny near Geneva); cf. A. N. L. Munby, 'The Dispersal of the Phillipps Library', *Phillipps Studies* 5 (1960) 104, 108.

Parts of the *Sanblasiana* were taken over into the collection of the manuscript of Diessen, cf. Mordek, *Kirchenrecht und Reform* 9 n. 32

Cf. *Collectio Colbertina,* which incorporated entirely the *Collectio Sanblasiana*

7. *Bibliography*

Maassen, *Geschichte* 504–512; Fournier-Le Bras 1.25–26; Van Hove, *Prolegomena* 161–162; Stickler, *Historia* 1.51–52; Lefebvre, 'Quesnelliana', DDC 7 (1965) 439

Turner, EOMIA 1.2.1, p. VIII and 1.2.3, p. 444
A. L. Feder, 'Studien zu Hilarius von Poitiers 1', SB Vienna 162.4 (1910) 24–25
Dobschütz, *Decretum Gelasianum* 163
ACO 2.2.2, p. v–ix
Silva-Tarouca, 'Beiträge' 664–665
Josep Rius, 'El Concili de Nicea en la provincia eclesiástica Tarraconense', *Analecta Tarraconensia* 2 (1926) 553–592
Le Bras, 'Notes III' 508–518
C. H. Turner, 'The Chieti manuscript now Vat. Reg. 1997', JTS 31 (1930) 9–13
E. Schwartz, ZRG Kan. Abt. 20 (1931) 602 (review of Turner, EOMIA)
Schwartz, 'Kanonessammlungen' 86
Wurm, *Studien und Texte* 88–89, 261–264
Stürner, 'Die Quellen der Fides Konstantins' 79–82
Mordek, *Kirchenrecht und Reform* 240–241
Landau, 'Gefälschtes Recht' 18–19
Zechiel-Eckes, *Cresconius* 1.176–177 (cf. also index)

Collectio Colbertina

1. Author: Unknown. *2. Date:* By the middle of the sixth century at the earliest, possibly during the seventh or eighth centuries. *3. Place:* Gaul (Maassen); Northern France or Rhine region (Van Hove) (Stickler: more likely in Italy); Le Bras, 'Notes III' 514 n. 3: perhaps Rome? *4. Type:* Collection of unstructured materials; decretals and conciliar canons (esp. from the *Collectiones Sanblasiana* and *Quesnelliana*). *5. Edition:* None.

6. *Manuscript*

Paris, Bibliothèque nationale, lat. 1455, fol. 3^{r}–77ra, saec. IX3–4/4, perhaps near Reims (cf. Bischoff, quoted in Stürner, 'Die Quellen der Fides Konstantins' 85 n. 83); detailed description of the contents: Maassen, *Geschichte* 536–541 and Maassen, 'Bibliotheca' SB Vienna 54, 1866 (1867) 195–198; see also Mordek, 'Herovalliana' 229–230 (*Herovalliana*-excerpts in Paris lat. 1455) and *Collectio Sancti Amandi* below; Mordek, *Bibliotheca capitularium* 410–411

7. *Bibliography*

Maassen, *Geschichte* 536–542; Fournier-Le Bras 1.26 n. 4; Van Hove, *Prolegomena* 267–268; Stickler, *Historia* 1.65

Tarré, 'Sources' 130
Wurm, *Studien und Texte* 90
H. Fuhrmann, 'Konstantinische Schenkung und abendländisches Kaisertum; Ein Beitrag zur Überlieferungsgeschichte des Constitutum Constantini', DA 22 (1966) 63–178, 69–71, esp. 69 n. 12

Stürner, 'Die Quellen der Fides Konstantins' 85–86
Mordek, *Kirchenrecht und Reform* 127–128
Gaudemet, *Sources* 141

Collectio Novariensis

1. Author: Unknown. *2. Date:* After the Sixth Council of Toledo (638), perhaps as early as 550, because it contains the first recension of the Synod of Lérida (546); later councils up to Toledo IV (633) and Toledo VI (638) were added (Van Hove 280; also Martínez Díez 406: about 550, after the Synod of Lérida and before the Third Council of Toledo [589]). *3. Place:* Spain, Province of Tarragona. *4. Type:* Chronologically arranged collection of conciliar canons (particularly Spanish councils).

5. Editions

A. Amelli, *Spicilegium Casinense* 1.255–326 (according to manuscript XXX from Novara)
Martínez Díez, 'Novara' 391–538

6. Manuscripts

Brescia, Biblioteca Civica Queriniana, B.II.13, saec. X, fol. 177^{v}–214^{r} (Williams, *Codices Pseudo-Isidoriani* 12–14: saec. IX–X), Northern Italy
Lucca, Biblioteca Capitolare Feliniana, 124, saec. XI4/4, Central Italy, fol. 173^{r}–191^{r}, cf. Gilchrist, 'Reception 2' 197 and Landau, 'Kanonessammlungen in der Lombardei' 435 including n. 40
Monza, Biblioteca Capitolare, h-3/151, saec. X, without manuscript foliation (Williams, *Codices Pseudo-Isidoriani* 37–38: saec. IX^{2}, Northern Italy)
Novara, Biblioteca Capitolare, XV (olim 30), saec. XII or XII^{1} (Northern?) Italy, fol. 46ra–56vb, 61ra–62vb, 57ra–58ra, cf. Mordek, *Bibliotheca capitularium* 393 (copy of Novara XXX)
Novara, Biblioteca Capitolare, XXX (olim 66), saec. IX^{ex}, Northern Italy; cf. Mordek, *Bibliotheca capitularium* 395–399, esp. 396, fol. 233^{r}–265^{v} (copy of Novara LXXXIV)
Novara, Biblioteca Capitolare, LXXXIV (olim 54), saec. VIII–IX, Northern Italy, fol. 2^{r}–78^{r}, cf. Mordek, *Kirchenrecht und Reform* 11 n. 41 (*Constitutum Silvestri* traceable for the first time in this manuscript of the Spanish collection)

Excerpts

Firenze, Biblioteca Medicea Laurenziana, Calci 9, saec. XII1/4, Central Italy; cf. Mordek, 'Handschriftenforschungen' 637 (affiliated with Lucca 124)
Oxford, Bodleian Library, Laud. Misc. 421 (olim 893), saec. X; but cf. Mordek, *Kirchenrecht und Reform* 11 n. 41 and 10 n. 40. saec. IX^{ex}, Western Germany, Prov. Würzburg (copy of Paris lat. 12448); fol. 123^{v}–139^{v},
Paris, Bibliothèque nationale, lat. 12448 (olim Saint-Germain, Harlay 386), saec. X (IX–X, in the opinion of B. Bischoff, probably Eastern France, cf. Mordek, *Kirchenrecht und Reform* 11 n. 41), fol. 124^{v}–131^{v}

Two codices contain four councils from the *Novariensis* as an appendix to the *Collectio Dionysio-Hadriana* (Martínez Díez 396)

7. *Bibliography*

Maassen, *Geschichte* 717–721; Fournier-Le Bras 1.70 and 237; Van Hove, *Prolegomena* 280

Antonius Franciscus Zacharias, *Iter litterarium per Italiam ab a. 1753 ad a. 1757* (Venetiis 1762) 14
Maassen, 'Bibliotheca' SB Vienna 53 (1866) 385–387
Amelli, *Spicilegium Casinense* (cf. above 'Edition') p. lxxxi–lxxxiv
Martínez Díez, 'Novara' 391–410
G. Picasso, 'I codici canonistici della biblioteca capitolare di Novara nella recente storiografia', *Novarien.* 5 (1973) 3–11 [on the manuscripts of the *Collectio Novariensis* and other collections before Gratian (codd. LXXIV, XXX, XV, LXXI)]
Novara e la sua terra nei secoli XI e XII: Storia, documenti, architettura, cur. M. L. Gavazzoli Tomea (Novara 1980)
Gaudemet, *Sources* 151–152
Landau, 'Kanonessammlungen in der Lombardei' 434–435 and 438–439
Landau, 'Gefälschtes Recht' 20 including n. 36
B. Carboni, 'Il Codice XXX della Capitolare di S. Maria portato a Milano, Montecassino e Roma è tornato a Novara, Studio del quaterno *alieno* XXXVI', *Novarien* 19 (1989) 199–215

Cresconius, Concordia canonum

1. Author: 'Cresconius'; cf. Zechiel-Eckes, *Cresconius* 1.82–85. *2. Date:* About the middle of the sixth century. *3. Place:* Italy (cf. Zechiel-Eckes). *4. Type:* Systematic collection (cf. Zechiel-Eckes, *Cresconius* 1.62).

5. *Editions*

G. Voellius and H. Justellus (eds.), *Bibliotheca iuris canonici veteris,* 1 (Paris 1661) *Appendix,* p. xxxiii–cxii (PL 88.829–942)
Turner, EOMIA, passim
Zechiel-Eckes, *Cresconius* 2.419–798

6. *Manuscripts*

Berlin, Staatsbibliothek Preußischer Kulturbesitz, lat. fol. 626, saec. XII^1, probably diocese of Liège, Prov. Louvain, then Ashburnham collection, fol. 59rb–79va (including cap. 226,1) cf. Zechiel-Eckes, *Cresconius* 2.314–317
Berlin, Staatsbibliothek Preußischer Kulturbesitz, Phill. 1748, about 800, Southern Burgundy, fol. 1^v–101^r, cf. Zechiel-Eckes, *Cresconius* 2.313–314
Einsiedeln, Stiftsbibliothek, 197 (530), saec. X^{med-2}, written at Einsiedeln during the second half of the tenth century; fol. 1^v–233; on the contents, cf. G. Meier, *Catalogus codicum manuscriptorum, qui in bibliotheca monasterii Einsidlensis O.S.B. servantur* 1 (Einsiedeln 1899) 153–154; Maassen, 'Bibliotheca' SB Vienna 56 (1867) 200–205 and Maassen, *Geschichte* 807, 811–812 (erroneous signature 196 instead of 197, 196 is Ivos *Panormia*); G. Folliet, '*Expositio de secreto gloriosae Incarnationis D.N.I.C.*: Histoire d'un texte attribué à saint Augustin', *Corona Gratiarum: Miscellanea patristica, historica et liturgica Eligio Dekkers O.S.B. XII lustra*

complenti oblata 1 (Bruges-'s-Gravenhage 1975) 375; A. Bruckner, *Scriptoria medii aevi Helvetica: Denkmäler schweizerischer Schreibkunst des Mittelalters* 5 (Geneva 1943) 25, 27–28, 180; Mordek, *Kirchenrecht und Reform* 254; Zechiel-Eckes, *Cresconius* 2.318–319

Köln, Erzbischöfliche Diözesan- und Dombibliothek, 120 (Darmstadt 2119), saec. X^{in}, Eastern France or Belgium, fol. 1va–122^{r}, cf. Zechiel-Eckes, *Cresconius* 2.319–321

Kraków, Biblioteka Jagiellonska, 1894 (olim Berlin, lat. qu. 104), saec. IX2/3, fol. 4^{r}–88^{r}, cf. Zechiel-Eckes, *Cresconius* 2.321–322

Monte Cassino, Archivio e Biblioteca dell'Abbazia, 541 (123), saec. XI1/4, Monte Cassino, Southern Italy, fol. 9^{a}–123^{b}; according to Zechiel-Eckes probably the manuscript of the *Concordia canonum*, which was written by order of abbot Theobald of Monte Cassino (1022–1035) in the beginning of his term of office. According to Mordek and Kerff (*Quadripartitus* 18–20) a direct copy taken from Vat. lat. 1347. Cf. Zechiel-Eckes, *Cresconius* 2.323

Montpellier, Bibliothèque Interuniversitaire, H.233, saec. IX1/3, Rhaetia, Italian glosses [Bischoff], fol. 1^{v}–110^{v}; Prov. St. Peter at Troyes; cf. Zechiel-Eckes, *Cresconius* 2.325–327

München, Bayerische Staatsbibliothek, Clm 6288 (olim Freising 88) and lat. 29390/1, saec. X3/3, script from Freising and Northern Italy, probably written during the exile of Bishop Abraham of Freising in Northern Italy; fol. 46^{v}–191^{r}, cf. N. Daniel, *Handschriften des zehnten Jahrhunderts aus der Freisinger Dombibliothek* (Munich 1973) 111–113; cf. Zechiel-Eckes, *Cresconius* 2.327–330

Novara, Biblioteca Capitolare, LXXI (134), fol. IX$^{med\text{-}3/4}$, fol. 49^{v}–169^{r}, cf. G. Picasso, 'I codici canonistici della biblioteca capitolare di Novara nella recente storiografia', *Novarien.* 5 (1973) 3–11; Kottje, *Bußbücher Halitgars* 47, probably written at Novara; Zechiel-Eckes, *Cresconius* 2.331–332

Oxford, Bodleian Library, Laud. misc. 436 (SC 882), saec. IX1/3, Würzburg, fol. 1^{r}–161^{v} (Bischoff-Hofmann 24 and 113); Zechiel-Eckes, *Cresconius* 2.332–334

Roma, Biblioteca Vallicelliana, T.XVIII, saec. X^{ex}–XI^{in}, Central Italy, near Rome; fol. 1ra–49rb, cf. Zechiel-Eckes, *Cresconius* 2.336–337

Salzburg, Bibliothek der Erzabtei St. Peter, a.IX.32, cf. G. Phillips, 'Der Codex Salisburgensis S. Petri IX.32: Ein Beitrag zur Geschichte der vorgratianischen Rechtsquellen', SB Vienna 44 (1863) 443–444, saec. XI1/2, Cologne (cf. Kottje, 'Salzburger Handschrift' 286–290; Zechiel-Eckes, *Cresconius* 2.337–338; Mordek, *Bibliotheca capitularium* 644–652) or Salzburg; cf. E.-D. Hehl, '*Iuxta canones et instituta sanctorum patrum*: Zum Mainzer Einfluß auf Synoden des 10. Jahrhunderts', *Festschrift Fuhrmann* (1991) 125 n. 24, fol. 2^{r}–90^{v}

Vaticano, Città del, Biblioteca Apostolica Vaticana, lat. 1347, saec. IX$^{med\text{-}2}$, Reims, fol. 1^{r}–63^{v}, cf. Kerff, *Quadripartitus* 27, according to Bernhard Bischoff; Zechiel-Eckes, *Cresconius* 2.344–346

Vaticano, Città del, Biblioteca Apostolica Vaticana, lat. 5748, saec. IX–X, Northern Italy, Prov. Bobbio, fol. 17^{v}–121^{v}, cf. Zechiel-Eckes, *Cresconius* 2.346–347

Vaticano, Città del, Biblioteca Apostolica Vaticana, Pal. lat. 579, saec. IX2/4, Western Germany (Mainz?) (based on insular master copy), fol. 1ra–94ra, cf. Zechiel-Eckes, *Cresconius* 2.338–339

Vaticano, Città del, Biblioteca Apostolica Vaticana, Reg. lat. 423, saec. IX^{2}, Weißenburg, fol. 26^{r}–61^{v} contains the collection which was named by Martínez Díez,

Colección Hispana 1.347–350 'Collection of the Weissenburg-Manuscript' and after fol. 61^{v} texts which can also be traced, for example, in the Cresconius, Oxford Bodl. Laud. misc. 436 and Einsiedeln 197 (not 196: it contains Ivo's *Panormia*), cf. Maassen, 'Bibliotheca' SB Vienna 56 (1867) I.4.4, 181–190 (Oxford, Bodleiana) and I.6.2.200–201 (Einsiedeln 196); Zechiel-Eckes, *Cresconius* 2.339–341

Vaticano, Città del, Biblioteca Apostolica Vaticana, Reg. lat. 849, saec. X^{in}, France, Eastern?; fol. 118^{r}–216^{r}, Zechiel-Eckes, *Cresconius* 2.341–344

Verona, Biblioteca Capitolare, LXII (60), saec. VIII–IX, Northern Italy, probably Verona, cf. CLA 4, no. 512, p. 31; fol. 4^{r}–103^{r}, greatest part of the manuscript (now fol. 4–81) palimpsest of the *Codex Iustinianus* (saec. VI), cf. Zechiel-Eckes, *Cresconius* 2.349–351

Wolfenbüttel, Herzog August Bibliothek, Helmst. 219 (Cat. no. 251); saec. XVI, fol. 1^{r}–126^{v}; copy of a Carolingian model (Wolfenbüttel Helmst. 842). It once belonged to Matthias Flacius Illyricus, the leading personality of the 'Magdeburger Centuriatoren' (†1575); Zechiel-Eckes, *Cresconius* 2.351–352

Wolfenbüttel, Herzog August Bibliothek, Helmst. 842 , saec. IX2/4, written by Ercanbertus in Fulda about 840, belonged also to M. Flacius Illyricus, fol. 2^{r}–79^{r}, cf. Zechiel-Eckes, *Cresconius* 2.352–354

Excerpts and Fragments

Berlin, Deutsches Historisches Museum, fragment sine num., fol. 1^{r-v}, text from cap. 30,2 to cap. 33,3. Cf. Zechiel-Eckes, *Cresconius* 2.317–318

Köln, Erzbischöfliche Diözesan- und Dombibliothek, 124, fol. 224^{v}–235^{r} (cf. G. Schmitz, 'Vier-Bücher-Sammlung' 252: excerpt of about twenty pages)

Münster, Nordrhein-Westfälisches Staatsarchiv, VII.5201, saec. X^{med}, Corvey, additions from Cresconius' *Concordia canonum* to the Paenitentiale of Halitgar of Cambrai; cf. Zechiel-Eckes, *Cresconius* 1.259–261; Mordek, *Bibliotheca capitularium* 385

Paris, Bibliothèque nationale, lat. 1455, saec. IX3/4, Reims region, cf. Zechiel-Eckes, *Cresconius* 1.240–241; Mordek, *Bibliotheca capitularium* 410

Paris, Bibliothèque nationale, lat. 3182, saec. X, Brittany, pp. 182–183 (cf. Mordek, *Kirchenrecht und Reform* 153)

Paris, Bibliothèque nationale, lat. 3851, saec. IX^{1}, Lorsch, fol. 1^{v}–23^{v}, cf. Mordek-Schmitz, 'Neue Kapitularien und Kapitulariensammlungen', DA 43 (1987) 361–439, esp. 379–380; Zechiel-Eckes, *Cresconius* 2.334–335; cf. Mordek, *Bibliotheca capitularium* 443

Paris, Bibliothèque nationale, lat. 3851A, saec. X/XI (?), Southwestern France (Diocese of Limoges?), fol. 1^{r}–8^{v}, Zechiel-Eckes, *Cresconius* 2.335–336

Vaticano, Città del, Biblioteca Apostolica Vaticana, lat. 15204, saec. X, fol. 3^{r-v}: text from cap. 147 to cap. 152; fol. 4^{r-v}: text from the addition before cap. 190,1 to cap. 195,1; cf. Zechiel-Eckes, *Cresconius* 2.347–348

Verona, Biblioteca Capitolare, LXI (59), saec. VII–VIII, probably Verona, fol. 69^{r}–76^{v}: text of title 1 and 2 (by far the most ancient existing piece of evidence of the collection); Zechiel-Eckes, *Cresconius* 2.348–349

Wien, Österreichische Nationalbibliothek, lat. 501, saec. IX–X, probably Northern Italy, fol. 61^{v}–62^{r}, fol. 115^{v}–116^{r}, excerpts; cf. Zechiel-Eckes, *Cresconius* 1.255–259; 671–672, 624 and 666, 767–768; Mordek, *Bibliotheca capitularium* 905

Wolfenbüttel, Herzog August Bibliothek, Novi 404.7 (25a), saec. X$^{1?}$, fol. 1^{r-v}, fragment (one single leaf with the ending of cap. 159 to cap. 164; PL 88.894–895); Zechiel-Eckes, *Cresconius* 2.354

Modern Copies

Cf. Mordek, *Kirchenrecht und Reform* 254 and Zechiel-Eckes, *Cresconius* 1.293

Roma, Biblioteca Casanatense, 2407 (olim XX.I.21); written after a. 1567, fol. 3^{r}–25^{r}

Roma, Biblioteca Nazionale Centrale, Gesuit. 793 (2922) [Brommer] (copy on paper)

Roma, Biblioteca Vallicelliana, C.20, saec. XVI or XVII, fol. 1^{r}–15^{v}

Revised Version Dating from the Carolingian Period: *'Cresconius Gallicus'*

Paris, Bibliothèque nationale, lat. 4280A, saec. IX^{2} (fol. 1–100) and X^{1} (fol. 102–107), Reims, Prov. Saint-Remi; fol. 17^{v}–79^{r}; cf. Maassen, *Geschichte* 846–847; Kurtscheid-Wilches, 1.94–95; saec. X (Mordek, 'Aera' 221 including n. 33), see also Mordek, *Kirchenrecht und Reform* 255; Zechiel-Eckes, *Cresconius* 1.226–240; Mordek, *Bibliotheca capitularium* 451–456

7. *Bibliography*

Maassen, *Geschichte* 806–813 and 846–847 (Gallican Cresconius); von Scherer, *Handbuch* 1.207; H. Leclercq, 'Liber canonum Africae', DACL 9/1 (1930) 159–178; Fournier-Le Bras 1.35; Kurtscheid-Wilches 1.93–95; Van Hove, *Prolegomena* 266; J.-P. Lévy, 'Cresconius ou Crisconius', DDC 4 (1949) 762–763; Stickler, *Historia* 1.75; *Clavis* 393, no. 1769; Mordek, 'Cresconius', LMA 3 (1986) 345–346

Ballerini, *De antiquis . . . collectionibus et collectoribus* P. IV, cap. III (PL 56.282–286)

H. P. C. Henke, *De Cresconii concordia canonum eiusque codice manuscripto* (Helmstedt 1788, Leipzig 1802)

H. von Schubert, *Geschichte der christlichen Kirche im Frühmittelalter* (Tübingen 1921, repr. Darmstadt 1962) 532

Bardenhewer, *Literatur* 5.319–320

Wurm, *Studien und Texte* 37–39

P. Lehmann, 'Mittelalterliche Büchertitel 1', SB Munich 1948, 4 (Munich 1948) 13 (expresses doubts about the originality of the collection's name)

G. Le Bras, 'Miettes pour une nouvelle édition de l'Histoire', RHD, 4e sér., 38 (1960) 309–312

P. Pinedo, 'Fragmentacion, titulación y sistema', *Homenaje a Don Ramón Carande* 1 (Madrid 1963) 285–297

P. Pinedo, 'Concordia canonum Cresconii', *Ius canonicum* 4 (1964) 35–64

Kottje, 'Einheit und Vielfalt' 339 including n. 69

Fuhrmann, 'Pseudoisidor in Rom' 47

Mordek, *Kirchenrecht und Reform* 122–124, 253–255

Gaudemet, *Sources* 138–139

Mordek, 'Analecta canonistica' 1–4

M. Cardinale, 'La 'Concordia canonum' di Cresconio e la sua diffusione nella cultura giuridica dell'Europa medievale, 1: Problemi generali e criteri metodologici', *Apollinaris* 62 (1989) 283–331 (Manuscripts)

Landau, 'Kanonessammlungen in der Lombardei' 430–432
Zechiel-Eckes, *Cresconius* passim
Landau, 'Vorgratianische Kanonessammlungen bei den Dekretisten' 93–116

Collectio Avellana

1. Author: Unknown. *2. Date:* About 555. *3. Place:* Rome. *4. Type:* Chronologically arranged collection of decretals, esp. letters of popes and emperors which are not preserved in other collections. One of the author's main goals seems to have been to supplement other collections (the author must have made extensive use of ecclesiastical and private archives).

5. Edition

O. Günther, *Epistulae Imperatorum, Pontificum, aliorum inde ab anno 367 ad annum 553 datae Avellana quae dicitur collectio* (CSEL 35/1–2; Vienna 1895–1898)

6. Manuscripts

Vaticano, Città del, Biblioteca Apostolica Vaticana, lat. 3787, saec. XII
Vaticano, Città del, Biblioteca Apostolica Vaticana, lat. 4961, saec. X^{ex}–XI^{in}, Prov. Santa Croce, Avellana

Early Modern Copies

El Escorial, Real Biblioteca de San Lorenzo, C.II.21, saec. XVII, cf. P. Ewald, NA 6 (1881) 235; copy of Vat. lat. 4961
Roma, Biblioteca Angelica, 292, saec. XVI/XVII, cf. Ballerini, *De antiquis . . . collectionibus et collectoribus* P. II. cap. XII c. 3 (PL 56.180)
Roma, Biblioteca dell'Accademia Nazionale dei Lincei, Corsin. 817, saec. XVI–XVII
Vaticano, Città del, Biblioteca Apostolica Vaticana, lat. 3786, saec. XVI, according to Thiel a copy of Cod. Vat. 4961, cf. Thiel, *Epistolae Romanorum pontificum* (as below) xxv–xxvi
Vaticano, Città del, Biblioteca Apostolica Vaticana, lat. 4903, saec. XVI, according to Thiel also a copy of Cod. Vat. 4961, cf. Thiel, *Epistolae Romanorum pontificum* (as below) xxv–xxvi
Vaticano, Città del, Biblioteca Apostolica Vaticana, lat. 5617, saec. XVI
Vaticano, Città del, Biblioteca Apostolica Vaticana, Ottobon. lat. 1105, saec. XVI
Venezia, Biblioteca Nazionale Marciana, Iur. can. 13 (171) saec. XV (according to a note on the last page, it was commissioned by the Cardinal Bessarion and completed on Febr. 28, 1469)
Venezia, Biblioteca Nazionale Marciana, Iur. can. 14 (172), saec. XVI

7. Bibliography

Maassen, *Geschichte* 787–792; Fournier-Le Bras 1.39; Naz, 'Avellana collectio', DDC 1 (1935) 1491; Kurtscheid-Wilches, 1.91; Van Hove, *Prolegomena* 267; Stickler, *Historia* 1.65; García y García, *Historia* 1.186–187; *Rep. font.* 3 (1979) 504

A. Thiel (ed.), *Epistolae Romanorum pontificum genuinae et quae ad eos scriptae sunt a S. Hilaro usque ad Pelagium II* (Braunsberg 1867; repr. Hildesheim-New York 1974) xxv–xxvi

Duchesne, *Liber pontificalis* 1, errata ad p. ccxxxi and 2.563

O. Günther, 'Avellana Studien', SB Vienna 134,V (1895,III) 1–134

Dobschütz, *Decretum Gelasianum* 184

Silva-Tarouca, 'Beiträge' 471

Wurm, *Studien und Texte* 98

Gaudemet, 'Survivances romaines' 172

M. Green, 'The Supporters of the Anti-Pope Ursinus', JTS 22 (1971) 531–538

S. Cristo, 'Some notes on the Bonifacian-Eulalian schism', *Aevum* 51 (1977) 163–177

M. Palma, 'Da Nonantola a Fonte Avellana: a proposito di dodici manoscritti e di un domnus Damianus', *Scrittura e civiltà* 2 (1978) 221–230

Fuhrmann, 'Papstbriefe' 363–367

Gaudemet, *Sources* 100, 140

Mordek, 'Kanonistik und gregorianische Reform' 74 n. 50

Collectio Theodosii diaconi (Verona LX)

1. Author: Deacon Theodosius. *2. Date:* Before the seventh century (cf. dating of the manuscript). *3. Place:* Probably Italy. *4. Type:* A chronologically arranged collection of conciliar canons. *5. Edition:* None.

6. Manuscript

Roma, Biblioteca Casanatense, 378 (olim A.III.24) and Verona, Biblioteca Capitolare, LX (58), saec. VII/VIII, Italy, fol. 37–126^{v}, CLA 4, no. 416, 510, pp. 4, 31, 34, 40, Suppl. pp. 51, 53

7. Bibliography

Maassen, *Geschichte* 546–551; Van Hove, *Prolegomena* 269

C. H. Turner, 'The Verona MSS of Canons: The Theodosian MS and Its Connection with S. Cyril', *The Guardian*, 11 Dec. 1895, 1921–22

E. Schwartz, 'Zur Geschichte des Athanasius', *Nachrichten von der königlichen Gesellschaft der Wissenschaften zu Göttingen, philol.-hist. Kl.*, 1904, 357–391

Hefele-Leclercq, *Histoire des conciles* 2 (Paris 1908) 1367–1372

E. Schwartz, 'Über die Sammlung des Cod. Veronensis LX', *Zeitschrift für die Neutestamentliche Wissenschaft und die Kunde der älteren Kirche* 35 (1936) 1–23

Schwartz, 'Kanonessammlungen' 73–75

W. Telfer, 'The Codex Verona LX 58', *Harvard Theological Review* 36 (1943) 169–246

G. Muzzioli, 'Il codice Veronese LX (58) (and Casan. 378) e il vescovo Raterio', *Atti del Congresso Internazionale di Diritto Romano e di Storia del Diritto, Verona 1948* (Milan 1953) 1.217–231

Ch. Munier, 'Cinq canons inédits du concile d'Hippone du 8 octobre 393', RDC 18 (1968) 16–29

Collectio Novariensis concilii Chalcedonensis
(Vat. lat. 1322 etc.)

1. Author: Unknown. *2. Date:* About the beginning of the sixth century. *3. Place:* Italy. *4. Type:* Collection of conciliar acts.

5. Edition

ACO 2.1

6. Manuscripts

Novara, Biblioteca Capitolare, XXX (66), saec. IX^{ex}; perhaps Northern Italy, but France is also possible, fol. 28^{r}–34^{r}, probably the same archetype as Vat. lat. 1322; cf. Maassen, SB Vienna 53 (1866) 387–391; A. Reifferscheid, SB Vienna 68 (1871) 613–627; ACO 4.2, p. xiii–xvi; C. Silva-Tarouca, 'Originale o Registro? La tradizione manoscritta del Tomus Leonis', *Pubblicazioni della Università Cattolica del Sacro Cuore*, Ser. 5 (Scienze Storiche), 16 (1937) 151–170, esp. 154; Martínez Díez, 'Novara' 395–396; Mordek, *Bibliotheca capitularium* 395–399

Vaticano, Città del, Biblioteca Apostolica Vaticana, lat. 1322, main part of the manuscript: saec. VI^{ex}, collection of the acts of the Council of Chalcedon fol. 1–24, saec. IX, both parts written at Verona; cf. Lowe, CLA 1 no. 8; cf. Mordek, *Kirchenrecht und Reform* 43 n. 32

7. Bibliography

Maassen, *Geschichte* 737–738

Turner, EOMIA 1.2.1, p. 7

E. Schwartz, 'Verhandlungen des chalkedonischen Konzils', SB Munich 32 (1925) 9

E. Schwartz, 'Das Nicaenum und das Constantinopolitanum auf der Synode von Chalkedon', *Zeitschrift für Neutestamentliche Wissenschaft* 25 (1926) 38–88

ACO 2.2.2, p. v

G. L. Dossetti, *Il Simbolo di Nicea e di Constantinopoli. Edizione critica* (Rome-Freiburg-Basel 1967) 82–85

Stürner, 'Die Quellen der Fides Konstantins' 82–83

Mordek, *Kirchenrecht und Reform* 43 n. 32

Collectio Bigotiana (Paris lat. 2796)

1. Author: Unknown. *2. Date:* Probably shortly after 600. *3. Place:* Unknown. *4. Type:* A chronologically arranged collection of conciliar canons (containing Oriental, African, and Gallican councils). A source of this collection is the *Collectio Corbeiensis*. *5. Edition:* None.

6. Manuscript

Paris, Bibliothèque nationale, lat. 2796, saec. IX (a. 813–815), France; fol. 108^{r}–152^{r}, cf. Mordek, *Bibliotheca capitularium* 430–431

7. *Bibliography*

Maassen, *Geschichte* 611–613; Fournier-Le Bras 1.44 n. 3; Van Hove, *Prolegomena* 276

C. H. Turner, 'The *Liber ecclesiasticorum dogmatum* attributed to Gennadius', JTS 7 (1905–1906) 78–99, 8 (1906–1907) 103–114

J. Rambaud-Buhot, 'Note sur la collection canonique de Bigot. ms. lat. de la Bibliothèque nationale 2796', *Revue du moyen âge latin* 2 (1946) 176–179

Gaudemet, *Sources* 148

Mordek, *Kirchenrecht und Reform* 148 n. 242

Landau, 'Gefälschtes Recht' 19

Collectio Parisiensis (Paris lat. 3858C)

1. Author: Unknown. *2. Date:* Maassen, Van Hove: 'Gelasian Renaissance' (End of the fifth, beginning of the sixth century), about 523 (Gaudemet). *3. Place:* Italy (Rome?). *4. Type:* A chronologically arranged collection of conciliar canons (especially African councils).

6. *Manuscript*

Paris, Bibliothèque nationale, lat. 3858C, saec. XII^{in}, Italy, fol. 56–88

7. *Bibliography*

Maassen, *Geschichte* 542–546; Fournier-Le Bras 1.26; Van Hove, *Prolegomena* 269

Le Bras, 'Notes III' 514 n. 3

Schwartz, 'Kanonessammlungen' 71 n. 1

C. Munier, *Concilia Africae a. 345–a. 525* (CCL 149; Turnhout 1974) 177–181

C. Munier, 'La tradition littéraire des canons africains (345–525)', *Recherches augustiniennes* 10 (1975) 3–22

C. Munier, 'La tradition littéraire des dossiers africains', RDC 29.2–4 (1979) 41–52

Gaudemet, *Sources* 78, 140

Gaudemet, 'Capitula Martini' 55

Collectio (ecclesiae) Thessalonicensis

1. Author: Unknown. *2. Date:* Unknown. *3. Place:* Unknown. *4. Type:* Collection of 27 papal and imperial letters; circulated only fragmentarily. There is, however, a remark of Pope Nicholas I (858–867) dating from 860 referring to the letters of popes which used to follow in an intact form of the collection (MGH Epistola 6.438.31–439.2 and *Traditio* 14 [1958] 376).

5. *Editions*

L. Holstenius, *Collectio Romana bipartita veterum aliquot historiae ecclesiasticae monumentorum,* Pars 1 (Rome 1662) 1–163

C. Silva-Tarouca, *Epistularum Romanorum pontificum ad vicarios per Illyricum aliosque episcopos collectio Thessalonicensis* (Textus et Documenta 22; Rome 1937)

6. *Manuscripts*

Vaticano, Città del, Biblioteca Apostolica Vaticana, lat. 5751, saec. IX–X, Northern Italy (Bobbio or Verona?), fol. 55^r–75^r

Vaticano, Città del, Biblioteca Apostolica Vaticana, lat. 6339, saec. XVI

Vaticano, Città del, Biblioteca Apostolica Vaticana, Barb. lat. 3386a (copy of Vat. lat. 5751)

7. *Bibliography*

Maassen, *Geschichte* 766–767

K. Friedrich, 'Über die Sammlung der Kirche von Thessalonich und das päpstliche Vicariat für Illyricum', *SB Munich* (1891) 771–887

F. Streichhan, 'Die Anfänge des Vikariats von Thessalonich', ZRG Kan. Abt. 12 (1922) 330–384

W. Völker, 'Studien zur päpstlichen Vikariatspolitik im 5. Jahrhundert', ZKG 9 (1928) 355–380, esp. 370–380

E. Schwartz, 'Die sog. Sammlung der Kirche von Thessalonich', *Festschrift Richard Reitzenstein dargebracht* (Berlin-Leipzig 1931) 137–159

C. Silva-Tarouca, *Collectio Thessalonicensis ad fidem Cod. Vat. lat. 5751* (Textus et documenta 23; Rome 1937)

Wurm, *Studien und Texte* 5, 103, 199

H. Fuhrmann, 'Ein Bruchstück der Collectio ecclesiae Thessalonicensis', *Traditio* 14 (1958) 371–377

E. Chrysos, 'Zur Echtheit des *Rescriptum Theodosii ad Honorium* in der *Collectio Thessalonicensis*', *Kleronomia* 4 (1972) 240–247

Fuhrmann, 'Papstbriefe' 363 and 365–367

Gaudemet, *Sources* 140

Collectio Iustelliana

1. Author: Unknown. *2. Date:* End of sixth century? *3. Place:* Italy. *4. Type:* A chronologically arranged collection of conciliar canons (taken from the *versio prisca*)

5. *Editions*

G. Voellius and H. Justellus, *Bibliotheca iuris canonici veteris* 1 (Paris 1661) 277–320 (PL 56.747–816)

Mordek, 'Bischofsabsetzungen' 45–53

6. *Manuscript*

Oxford, Bodleian Library, e Mus. 100 and 101 and 102 (3686–3688), saec. VI–VII; Italy; CLA 2^2 no. 255, p. 38 further reading pp. 54, 60

7. *Bibliography*

Maassen, *Geschichte* 533–536; Van Hove, *Prolegomena* 148

C. H. Turner, 'Chapters in the History of Latin MSS of Canons V: The Version called Prisca (a) The Justel MS (J), now Bodl. e. Mus. 100–102, and the editio princeps (Paris 1661)', JTS 30 (1928–29) 337–346
Le Bras, 'Notes III' 506–518
Schwartz, 'Kanonessammlungen' 96–98
Mordek, 'Kanonistische Aktivität' 22
Ch. Munier, 'La tradition littéraire des canons africains (345–525)', REAug 10 (1975) 3–22
Ch. Munier, 'La tradition littéraire des dossiers africains', RDC 29 (1979) 41–52
Mordek, 'Bischofsabsetzungen' 31–53

Collectio Tuberiensis ('Rhaetian Collection', Collection of Müstair)

1. Author: Unknown. *2. Date:* About 580. *3. Place:* Diocese of Trent. *4. Type:* A chronologically arranged collection of conciliar canons and decretals. Taken from an earlier version of the *Collectio Frisingensis*; very close relationship to *Collectio Weingartensis*. *5. Edition:* None.

6. Manuscript

München, Bayerische Staatsbibliothek, Clm 29550/1 (olim 29168a), saec. VIII3/3, Prov. probably monastery of Müstair, Taufers? (cf. Schieffer, 'Rätische Sammlung' 166)

7. Bibliography

Bischoff, *Schreibschulen* 1.51–52
Mordek, *Kirchenrecht und Reform* 251
I. Müller, 'Karl der Große und Müstair', *Schweizerische Zeitschrift für Geschichte* 26 (1976) 273–287
I. Müller, *Geschichte des Klosters Müstair* (1978)
Schieffer, 'Rätische Sammlung' 164–191
Mordek, 'Kirchenrecht in Rätien' 16–33

Collectio Weingartensis

1. Author: Unknown. *2. Date:* End of the sixth century. *3. Place:* Rome. *4. Type:* A chronologically arranged collection of conciliar canons and decretals (only very few decretals); influenced by or even directly relying on the *Collectio Quesnelliana*. *5. Edition:* None.

6. Manuscripts

Stuttgart, Württembergische Landesbibliothek, HB.VI.113, saec. VIII^{ex}, Rhaetia [probably Chur]; fol. 1^{v}–66^{v}, 68–89^{v}, 97–98^{v}, 90–91^{v} [cf. Van der Speeten] *Collectio Weingartensis* (together with the *Vetus Gallica*), Prov. Weingarten

7. *Bibliography*

Van Hove, *Prolegomena* 269; Stickler, *Historia* 1.64

J. F. Schulte, 'Vier Weingartner jetzt Stuttgarter Handschriften' *SB Vienna* 117, 11 (1888,II) 1–30
ACO 2.2.2, p. xviii
Turner, EOMIA 1.2.3, p. x–xi
Wurm, *Studien und Texte* 99, 294
Mordek, *Kirchenrecht und Reform* 9 n. 31 and 294
J. Van der Speeten, 'Quelques remarques sur la collection canonique de Weingarten', SE 29 (1986) 25–118
Mordek, 'Kirchenrecht in Rätien' 16–33

Collectio Lugdunensis

1. Author: Unknown. *2. Date:* In the middle or shortly after the middle of the sixth century (cf. Mordek, *Kirchenrecht und Reform* 45 n. 34). *3. Place:* Rhône valley (or Arles). *4. Type:* Chronologically arranged collection of conciliar canons (only one decretal); a combination of the second recension of the *Dionysiana* with the canons of the Gallican councils. *5. Edition:* None.

6. *Manuscripts*

Paris, Bibliothèque nationale, lat. 1452, fol. 153–196, saec. IX4/4 or IX–X, cf. B. Bischoff quoted in Kottje, 'Einheit und Vielfalt' 338 n. 62, Rhône region; from the tenth to the seventeenth century at Le Puy, cf. E. Lesne, *Histoire de la propriété ecclésiastique en France* 4: *Les 'Scriptoria' et Bibliothèques du commencement du VIIIe à la fin du XIe siècle* (Mémoires et travaux publiés par des professeurs des Facultés catholiques de Lille 46 [Lille 1938, repr. New York 1964]) 518; cf. Mordek, *Bibliotheca capitularium* 58

St. Petersburg, Rossiyskaya Natsional'naya Biblioteka, F.v.II.3 and Berlin, Staatsbibliothek Preußischer Kulturbesitz, Phill. 1745, saec. VII, Burgundy; by the ninth century at the latest, it is traceable at Lyon; cf. CLA 8 no. 1061, pp. 12 and 62; CLA Suppl. p. 60–61. The first part of the codex containing the councils of the *Dionysiana* in the *Interpretatio secunda* and several canons of the First Council of Arles (a. 314), is kept today in St. Petersburg, Rossiyskaya Natsional'naya Biblioteka, F.v.II.3, cf. Turner's argument in: 'The MSS of Councils in the Library of the College of Clermont', JTS 1 (1899) 438–441; for detailed information about the Saint Petersburg Codex, cf. Turner, 'The Lyon-Petersburg MS of Councils', JTS 4 (1902–03), 426–434; A. Staerk, *Manuscrits Latins* 1.13–15; CLA 11, no. 1061, p. 8 and 31; Mordek, *Bibliotheca capitularium* 58 and above *Collectio Dionysiana*

7. *Bibliography*

Maassen, *Geschichte* 775–777; Fournier-Le Bras 1.44 n. 1; Kurtscheid-Wilches 1.98; Van Hove, *Prolegomena* 275; Stickler, *Historia* 1.98

Turner, EOMIA 2.1, p. 33, 48–51, 54–142

C. H. Turner, 'The manuscripts of the Jesuit Collège de Clermont in Paris', JTS 1 (1899–1900) 435–441

C. H. Turner, 'Chapters in the History of Latin Manuscripts III, The Lyon-Petersburg MS of Councils', JTS 4 (1902–1903) 426–434

Duchesne, *Fastes episcopaux* 1.144 n. 8

Silva-Tarouca, 'Beiträge' 659

Tarré, 'Sources' 130–131

Séjourné, *Saint Isidore* 364–365

Schwartz, 'Zweisprachigkeit' 251

Wurm, *Studien und Texte* 43, 101

Mordek, *Kirchenrecht und Reform* 45–49, esp. 45 n. 34 and 46 n. 35

Gaudemet, *Sources* 143

Zechiel-Eckes, *Cresconius* 1.8–9, 12 with n. 21, 14–17, 22–23, 25–28 (cf. also index)

Collectio Coloniensis (Köln 212)

1. Author: Unknown. *2. Date:* Compiled by the middle or during the second half of the sixth century. *3. Place:* Probably ecclesiastical province of Arles (Fournier-Le Bras 1.44 n. 1); Southern Gaul (Mordek, *Kirchenrecht und Reform* 15, n. 63). *4. Type:* Chronologically arranged collection of conciliar canons and decretals. *5. Edition:* None.

6. *Manuscripts*

Köln, Erzbischöfliche Diözesan- und Dombibliothek, 212 (olim Darmstadt 2326), saec. VII (originated about 600, since the eighth or ninth century traceable at Cologne) E. A. Lowe, 'A Hand-List of Half Uncial Manuscripts', *Miscellanea Francesco Ehrle* 4 (Studi e testi 42; Rome 1924) 34–61, esp. 51, no. 2 (including a bibliography); CLA 8, no. 1162, pp. 40, 66; CLA Suppl. p. 62

7. *Bibliography*

Maassen, *Geschichte* 574–585 and 958–960 (catalogue of popes); Fournier-Le Bras 1.44, n. 1; J.-L.-J. Van de Kamp, 'Cologne, Collection de', DDC 3 (1942) 1004–1005; Kurtscheid-Wilches, 1.98; Van Hove, *Prolegomena* 273–274

Ph. Jaffé and W. Wattenbach, *Ecclesiae Metropolitanae Coloniensis codd. mss.* (Berlin 1874) 93–95

Duchesne, *Liber pontificalis* 1.xv and 24–25

Turner, EOMIA 1.2.1, p. ii and vii

Steinacker, 'Deusdedithandschrift' 113–144

Duchesne, 'Collection romaine' 161

Duchesne, *Fastes épiscopaux* 1.144

R. Massigli, 'La plus ancienne collection des décrétales', *Revue d'histoire et de littérature religieuse* NS 5 (1914) 402–424, esp. 412

G. Morin, 'Les Statuta ecclesiae antiqua sont-ils de S. Césaire d'Arles', RB 30 (1913) 339

C. H. Turner, 'Arles and Rome', JTS 17 (1916) 237
Silva-Tarouca, 'Beiträge' 669–670
Schwartz, 'Kanonessammlungen' 85
Wurm, *Studien und Texte* 94, 276–278
Gaudemet, 'Survivances romaines' 169
Mordek, 'Bonneval' 345 including n. 36
Mordek, *Kirchenrecht und Reform* 3 n. 7, 37 n. 2, 38, 47 n. 38 and 41, 48–49, 67 n. 18, 71, 80–81 n. 82
Gaudemet, *Sources* 88–91

Collectio Sancti Mauri

1. Author: Unknown. *2. Date:* In the second half, probably near the end, of the sixth century. *3. Place:* Southern Gaul (cf. Mordek, *Kirchenrecht und Reform* 15 n. 63). The various theses concerning its place of origin (Narbonne, Arles) that do not permit any final conclusion are discussed in: Van Hove, *Prolegomena* 276 n. 1; see also Stürner, 'Die Quellen der Fides Konstantins' 84 including n. 76. *4. Type:* Chronologically arranged collection of conciliar canons and a relatively small number of decretals; some texts closely resemble those of the *Quesnelliana*, which is likely to have been used as a source; others bear a resemblance to texts in the *Sanblasiana*. *5. Edition:* None.

6. Manuscripts

'S Gravenhage (Den Haag), Museum Meermanno-Westreenianum, 10.B.4 (olim 9; Par. Clarom. 562, Meerm. 583); saec. VIII^{2}; according to Lowe [CLA 10 no. 1572a, p. 39] it originated in Northern France, according to Bischoff ['Panorama der Handschriftenüberlieferung' 241 n. 57] in Central France [Bourges?]); cf. W. Levison, 'Hss. des Museum Meermanno-Westreenianum im Haag', NA 38 (1913) 513–518; ACO 2.2.2, p. ix–x; M. Huglo, 'Christe fave votis', *Scriptorium* 8 (1954) 110

Paris, Bibliothèque nationale, lat. 1451, saec. IX^{in} (between 800 and 816), region around Tours; Prov. Saint-Maur-des-Fossés near Paris; Lowe, CLA 5, no. 528; Stürner, 'Die Quellen der Fides Konstantins' 83 nn. 73 and 74

Vaticano, Città del, Biblioteca Apostolica Vaticana, Reg. lat. 1127, saec. IX2/4, France; Prov. Angoulême; cf. Stürner, 'Die Quellen der Fides Konstantins' 84 n. 75

Missing manuscript

Laon; cf. Paris, Bibliothèque nationale, Collection Baluze 2, saec. XVII^{ex}, fol. 180^{r}–181^{v}, 183^{r} and 184^{r}, for a survey of the manuscript's contents; cf. Tarré, 'Etudes' 209; according to Baluze the *Codex Laudunensis* which was probably written in 793 cannot be identified with any of the three known manuscript traditions. Like Cod. Vat. Reg. lat. 1127 it must have contained some more material following the Third Council of Toledo such as: *Capitula de diversis canonibus. Excerptum ex Gregorio Turon. lib. VIII. cap. XXX. Synodus Autisiodorensis. Concilium Cabilonense I. Canon XXIV. Concilii Turonensis II. Statuta Ecclesiae antiqua.* Cf. Contreni (cf. below, *Bibliography*)

7. *Bibliography*

Maassen, *Geschichte* 613–624 (on Paris lat. 1451); Fournier-Le Bras 44 n. 3; Kurtscheid-Wilches 1.98; Van Hove, *Prolegomena* 276; Stickler, *Historia* 1.98; Naz, 'Saint-Maur (Collection de)', DDC 7 (1965) 836–837

Bernard de Montfaucon, *Antiquissima canonum collectio* (Paris 1739)

Bernard de Montfaucon, 'Catalogus mss ecclesiae cathed. Laudunensis', *Bibliotheca bibliothecarum manuscriptorum nova* 1–2 (Paris 1739) 2.1292–1299

E. Ch. Babut, 'La plus ancienne décrétale' (1904) 69ff. (edited the letter of Pope Damasus I to the bishops of Gaul in the version given by the Parisian and the Vatican manuscripts, cf. Schieffer, 'Rätische Sammlung' 180 n. 85 and 86)

Duchesne, *Fastes épiscopaux* 1.144 n. 6

ACO 2.2.2, p. ix–x

Silva-Tarouca, 'Beiträge' 673

Turner, EOMIA 1.2.3, p. ix and 1.2.1, p. viii–ix

Turner, EOMIA 1.2, appendix viii

C. H. Turner, 'The Collection Named after the MS of St. Maur' JTS 32 (1930–1931) 1–11

Tarré, 'Etudes' 208–210

Schwartz, 'Kanonessammlungen' 85–86

Wurm, *Studien und Texte* 97–98, 292–293

Martínez Díez, *Colección Hispana* 1.339–340

Stürner, 'Die Quellen der Fides Konstantins' 83–84

Mordek, *Kirchenrecht und Reform* 55–56 n. 81

J. J. Contreni, 'Two Descriptions of the Lost Laon Copy of the *Collection of Saint-Maur*', BMCL 10 (1980) 45–51

Schieffer, 'Rätische Sammlung' 179–182, 186–187

Zechiel-Eckes, *Cresconius* (cf. index)

Mordek, 'Kirchenrecht in Rätien' 19–20

Collectio Albigensis

1. Author: Perpetuus presbyter, on the order of the Bishop Dido of Albi (Ourliac, 'Manuscrit toulousain' 55). *2. Date:* Date of origin is contested (cf. Mordek, *Kirchenrecht und Reform* 39 n. 13 and 14). Wurm, *Studien und Texte* 95, concluded that the collection was compiled after the death of Gregory I; Mordek argues that the collection was compiled in the middle or during the second half of the sixth century (shortly after 549?) (Mordek, *Kirchenrecht und Reform* 39–40 n. 14). About 600 (Ourliac, 'Manuscrit toulousain' 49–62); *3. Place:* With great certainty in Southern Gaul (Mordek, *Kirchenrecht und Reform* 15 n. 63); because of its contents, it is supposed to be from Arles (Mordek, *Kirchenrecht und Reform* 39 n. 13; cf. Duchesne, 'Collection romaine' 161; Silva-Tarouca, 'Beiträge' 670–671; Fournier-Le Bras 1.44 n. 1; Wurm, *Studien und Texte* 95). Albi according to Ourliac. *4. Type:* Unstructured collection of materials; used the same source as the *Collectio Vetus Gallica*. *5. Edition:* None.

6. *Manuscripts*

Albi, Bibliothèque municipale, 2 (147), saec. IX^2, Southern France (probably Albi), a copy of the manuscript from Toulouse; cf. Turner, *A Group of MSS of Canons at Toulouse, Albi and Paris*, JTS 2 (1900–1901) 266–267; Wurm, *Studien und Texte* 94–95 n. 15; additional material deriving from Merovingian councils

Toulouse, Bibliothèque municipale, 364 (I. 63) and Paris, Bibliothèque nationale, lat. 8901, before a. 666–667, written by Perpetuus at Bishop Dido of Albi's behest; cf. CLA 6, no. 836, pp. 39 and 48; CLA Suppl. p. 58, cf. Ourliac, 'Manuscrit toulousain' 54: ca. 600

Important Excerpt of the Collection

Albi, Bibliothèque municipale, 38, saec. X, fol. 35^r–114^r, cf. Mordek, *Kirchenrecht und Reform* 268–69 (description of the manuscript)

7. *Bibliography*

Maassen, *Geschichte* 592–603; Fournier-Le Bras 1.44 n. 1; Kurtscheid-Wilches 1.98; Van Hove, *Prolegomena* 274; Stickler, *Historia* 1.98

Schulte, 'Iter Gallicum' 422

Duchesne, *Liber pontificalis* 1.xv and 26–27 and 3.26 and 48

Turner, 'Chapters in the History of Latin MSS 2: A Group of Canons at Toulouse, Albi and Paris, JTS 2 (1900–1901) 266–273

Duchesne, 'Collection romaine' 159–162

Duchesne, *Fastes episcopaux* 1.144

Silva-Tarouca, 'Beiträge' 670–671

Le Bras, 'Notes I' 767–775, esp. 768

F. Galabert, 'Notice sur deux manuscrits des bibliothèques de Toulouse et d'Albi', *Annales du Midi* 45 (1933) 353–372

Wurm, *Studien und Texte* 94–95, 279–283

G. Morin, *S. Caesarii episcopi Arelatensis opera omnia, 2: Opera varia* (Maredsous 1942)

Ch. Munier, *Les Statuta ecclesiae antiqua* (Paris 1960) 53

Ch. Munier, *Concilia Galliae A. 314–A. 506* (CCL 148; Turnhout 1963) X

C. De Clercq, *Concilia Galliae A. 511–A. 695* (CCL 148A; Turnhout 1963) IX

Mordek, 'Bonneval' 345 including n. 34

Mordek, *Kirchenrecht und Reform* 39–43

Ourliac, 'Manuscrit toulousain' 223–238

Gaudemet, *Sources* 143–144

Zechiel-Eckes, *Cresconius* (cf. index)

Collectio Corbeiensis (Paris lat. 12097)

1. Author: Unknown. *2. Date:* Written during the pontificate of Pope Vigilius (537–555) cf. Ourliac, 'Manuscrit toulousain' 59. *3. Place:* Ecclesiastical province of Vienne (Silva-Tarouca, 'Beiträge' 669), with great certainty in Southern Gaul (Mordek, *Kirchenrecht und Reform* 15 n. 63), presumably at Arles. *4. Type:* Chronologically arranged collection of conciliar canons and decretals; close connection with the *Collectio Pithouensis*; Merovingian councils as additions. *5. Edition*: None.

6. *Manuscripts*

Paris, Bibliothèque nationale, lat. 12097, fol. 1ʳ–232ᵛ; the main part (fol. 1ʳ–139ᵛ) of Paris lat. 12097 was written saec. VI2/4 (shortly after a. 524) in Southern France, the other part (fol. 139ᵛ–224ᵛ): saec. VI–VII in Southern France; cf. CLA 5 no. 619, pp. 29–30 and 59, CLA Suppl. p. 55; see also E. A. Lowe, 'A Hand-list of Half Uncial Manuscripts' *Miscellanea Francesco Ehrle* 4 (Studi e Testi 42; Rome 1924) 34–61, esp. 49 (including a bibliography); saec. VIII^1, France: fol. 225–232; cf. also Mordek, *Bibliotheca capitularium* 607–609

On the *Collectio Corbeiensis systematica* (Paris lat. 12097, fol. 177ᵛ–178ᵛ) cf. Mordek, *Kirchenrecht und Reform* 17 n. 72

7. *Bibliography*

Maassen, *Geschichte* 556–574; Fournier-Le Bras 1.44 n. 1; Kurtscheid-Wilches 1.97–98; Van Hove, *Prolegomena* 273 (earlier publications); J.-L.-J. Van de Kamp, DDC 4 (1949) 605–606; Stickler, *Historia* 1.98

Duchesne, *Liber pontificalis* 1.xvi and 16–17

Duchesne, *Fastes épiscopaux* 1.144 n. 1 (cited as Paris lat. '12079')

G. Morin, 'Les Statuta ecclesiae antiqua sont-ils de S. Césaire d'Arles?' RB 30 (1913) 339

ACO 2.4, p. xiii and 155–156

Silva-Tarouca, 'Beiträge' 667–669

C.H. Turner, 'The Corbie MS', JTS 30 (1929) 225–237

Silva-Tarouca, 'Nuovi studi' 350–352

Schwartz, 'Kanonessammlungen' 85

G. Morin, 'Castor et Polychronicus: Un épisode peu connu de l'histoire ecclésiastique des Gaules', RB 51 (1939) 31–36 (edited some pieces from this collection)

Wurm, *Studien und Texte* 93–94, 119–120, 272–276

J. M. Moynihan, *Papal Immunity and Liability in the Writings of Medieval Canonists* (Analecta Gregoriana 120; Rome 1961), but cf. Landau, 'Gefälschtes Recht' 20 n. 38

Martínez Díez, *Colección Hispana* 1.290–291

K. Schäferdiek, *Die Kirche in den Reichen der Westgoten und Suewen bis zur Errichtung der westgotischen katholischen Staatskirche* (Arbeiten zur Kirchengeschichte 39; Berlin 1967)

Mordek, 'Bonneval' 345 including n. 33

Mordek, *Kirchenrecht und Reform* 90 n. 126 (distribution), 91 n. 127 (research), 15 n. 63 (place of origin, see above; further information cf. Index)

Collectio Pithouensis (Paris lat. 1564)

1. Author: Unknown. *2. Date:* End of sixth or beginning of the seventh century. *3. Place:* Central Gaul, perhaps Sens or Auxerre. *4. Type:* A chronologically arranged collection of conciliar canons and decretals; close relationship with the *Collectio Corbeiensis* (Paris lat. 12097). *5. Edition:* None.

6. *Manuscript*

Paris, Bibliothèque nationale, lat. 1564, saec. VIII–IX (785–810), Northern France (probably Chelles); only a fragment of the collection is preserved, the first 8 quaterneries are missing, cf. CLA 5, no. 529 pp. 5, 54; Suppl. p. 53

7. *Bibliography*

Maassen, *Geschichte* 604–611; Fournier-Le Bras 1.44 n. 3; Van Hove, *Prolegomena* 275

Duchesne, *Fastes épiscopaux* 1.141–142
Silva-Tarouca, 'Beiträge' 672
Wurm, *Studien und Texte* 96, 119–120, 283–287
Stürner, 'Die Quellen der Fides Konstantins' 153–154
Mordek, *Kirchenrecht und Reform* 56 n. 82
Zechiel-Eckes, *Cresconius* 1.233–236 (source of the Gallican Cresconius)

Collectio Laureshamensis

1. Author: Unknown. *2. Date:* By the middle (second half) of the sixth century. *3. Place:* Southern Gaul. *4. Type:* A chronologically arranged collection of conciliar canons and decretals. *5. Edition:* None.

6. *Manuscripts*

Gotha, Forschungsbibliothek, Mbr. I.85, saec. VIII–IX, Alsace, Wissembourg? by the fifteenth century at Murbach (Cod. Murbacensis)
Vaticano, Città del, Biblioteca Apostolica Vaticana, Pal. lat. 574, saec. VIII–IX, Upper Rhine region, Prov. Lorsch, cf. Mordek, *Bibliotheca capitularium* 771–773

7. *Bibliography*

Maassen, *Geschichte* 585–591; Fournier-Le Bras 1.144 n. 1; Van Hove, *Prolegomena* 274–275; Stickler, *Historia* 1.98

Turner, EOMIA 1.1.2, p. 153
Duchesne, 'Collection romaine' 159–163
Duchesne, *Fastes épiscopaux* 1.141–142, 144
Dobschütz, *Decretum Gelasianum* 141
G. Morin, 'Les Statuta ecclesiae antiqua sont-ils de S. Césaire d'Arles', RB 30 (1913) 339
R. Massigli, 'La plus ancienne collection de décrétales', *Revue d'histoire et de littérature religieuses* 5 (1914) 402–424
Silva-Tarouca, 'Beiträge' 671–672
CLA 1 pp. 28 and 42 (including facsimile and bibliography), Suppl. 62
Wurm, *Studien und Texte* 96

Ch. Munier (ed.), *Concilia Galliae A. 314–A.506* (CCL 148; Turnhout 1963)
Mordek, *Kirchenrecht und Reform* 9 n. 33
Gaudemet, *Sources* 143
Zechiel-Eckes, *Cresconius* 1.31–32, 232–233 (cf. also index)

Collectio Remensis (Berlin, Phill. 1743)

1. Author: Unknown. *2. Date:* Second half of the sixth century. *3. Place:* Gaul. *4. Type:* A chronologically arranged collection of conciliar canons and decretals (especially of Pope Leo I). *5. Edition:* None.

6. Manuscript

Berlin, Staatsbibliothek Preußischer Kulturbesitz, Phill. lat. 1743, saec. VIII^2, Prov. Bourges; cf. V. Rose, *Die Lateinischen Meerman-Handschriften des Sir Thomas Phillipps in der königlichen Bibliothek zu Berlin* (Berlin 1892) 171–179 no. 84: Saint-Remi at Reims, but according to Bischoff it is not from Reims; more closely related to a group of manuscripts whose place of origin seems to have been Bourges (Bischoff, 'Panorama der Handschriftenüberlieferung' 241 including n. 57; Mordek, *Kirchenrecht und Reform* 10 n. 38), cf. also Mordek, *Bibliotheca capitularium* 56–57

7. Bibliography

Maassen, *Geschichte* 638–640; Fournier-Le Bras 1.44 n. 3; Van Hove, *Prolegomena* 275; Stickler, *Historia* 1.98

Turner, EOMIA 1.2.3, p. 444 and 535
Dobschütz, *Decretum Gelasianum* 137
R. Massigli, 'La plus ancienne collection des décrétales', *Revue d'histoire et de littérature religieuse*, n. s. 5 (1914) 402–424, esp. 414
ACO 2.2.2, p. xviii (on the canons of Chalcedon)
Duchesne, *Liber pontificalis* 1.xv and 20
Tarré, 'Sources' 131
Silva-Tarouca, 'Beiträge' 673–674
Wurm, *Studien und Texte* 97, 116, 287–292
Mordek, *Kirchenrecht und Reform* 10 n. 38

Collectio Vetus Gallica (Collectio [codicis] Andegavensis)

1. Author: In all probability, it was Bishop Etherius of Lyon (about 586–602) author or initiator (Mordek, *Kirchenrecht und Reform* 79–82). *2. Date:* Between 585 and 626–627. *3. Place:* Lyon. *4. Type:* Systematic collection.

5. Edition

Mordek, *Kirchenrecht und Reform* 343–617

6. *Manuscripts*

Cf. Mordek, *Kirchenrecht und Reform* 267–301; for the classification of the manuscripts, cf. Mordek, *Kirchenrecht und Reform* 301–334

French Class: Northern French Subclass

Complete manuscripts

Bruxelles, Bibliothèque Royale Albert Ier, 10127–44, saec. VIII–IX, Northeastern France or Belgium, fol. 1^{v}–39^{v}, including the additions and appendices ending at fol. 79^{v} (cf. Mordek, *Kirchenrecht und Reform* 276–277)

Köln, Erzbischöfliche Diözesan- und Dombibliothek, 91 (Darmstadt 2179), saec. VIII–IX, Burgundy or Corbie? (cf. Mordek, *Kirchenrecht und Reform* 279–280); fol. 2^{r}–48^{r} including the additions and appendices ending at fol. 112^{v},

Paris, Bibliothèque nationale, lat. 1603, saec. VIII–IX, Northeastern France, Prov. Saint-Amand, fol. 7^{r}–66^{v}, including the additions and appendices ending at fol. 163^{r}, cf. Mordek, *Kirchenrecht und Reform* 281–283 and Mordek, *Bibliotheca capitularium* 420–421

Stuttgart, Württembergische Landesbibliothek, HB.VI.109, saec. IX1/4, presumably Southwestern Germany, Prov. Constance, library of the cathedral chapter, from there it was transferred to Weingarten, fol. 2^{r}–83^{v}, including the additions and appendices ending at fol. 132^{v} (cf. Mordek, *Kirchenrecht und Reform* 292–293)

Fragments

Paris, Bibliothèque nationale, Collection Baluze 270, fol. 72 (71), saec. IX1/4, possibly from the region around Paris (cf. Mordek, *Kirchenrecht und Reform* 288–289)

Trier, Stadtbibliothek, fragment sine numero, written about 770 in Northeastern France (presumably at Corbie or in its region), cf. Mordek, *Kirchenrecht und Reform* 295–297

Excerpts

Oxford, Bodleian Library, 572, saec. IX^{1}, Northern France, fol. 73^{v}–80^{r}; cf. Mordek, *Kirchenrecht und Reform* 98 n. 3; Reynolds, 'Unity and Diversity' 108

Salzburg, Bibliothek der Erzabtei St. Peter, a.IX.32, saec. XI^{1}, Cologne (Kottje), fol. 157^{v}–166^{r} (cf. Mordek, *Kirchenrecht und Reform* 289–290; Kottje, 'Salzburger Handschrift' 287–290); cf. also Mordek, *Bibliotheca capitularium* 644–652, esp. 647

Würzburg, Universitätsbibliothek, M.p.th.q. 31, fol. 42^{r}–51^{v}, saec. VIII–IX, probably written in (Western-)Germany in a scriptorium with Insular influence (cf. Mordek, *Kirchenrecht und Reform* 300–301)

French Class: Southern French Subclass

Complete manuscripts

Albi, Bibliothèque municipale, 38bis, saec. $IX^{ca.\ med.}$, probably Southern France (perhaps Bourges?), from the same scriptorium as Phill. 1763 (cf. Mordek, *Kirchenrecht und Reform* 269–271)

Berlin, Staatsbibliothek Preußischer Kulturbesitz, Phill. 1763, saec. IX^{in}, Southern France, later at Dijon, fol. 1^{r}–48^{r}, including the appendix ending at fol. 50^{v} and a Latin glossary ending at fol. 55^{v} (cf. Mordek, *Kirchenrecht und Reform* 271–273)

Excerpts

Albi, Bibliothèque municipale, 38, saec. X^{1}, Southern France, fol. 120^{v}–123^{v} (the writer used manuscript Albi, Bibliothèque municipale, 38bis as a source), Prov. library of the cathedral chapter of Albi (cf. Mordek, *Kirchenrecht und Reform* 268–269)

Southern German Class

Complete Manuscripts

Einsiedeln, Stiftsbibliothek, 205, saec. IX2/4, Switzerland, p. 41–166, including the additions and appendices ending at p. 230 (cf. Mordek, *Kirchenrecht und Reform* 277–278)

Monte Cassino, Archivio e Biblioteca dell'Abbazia, 372, saec. XI^{in}, Beneventan script, Prov. monastery S. Nicola della Cicogna (cf. Mordek, *Kirchenrecht und Reform* 280–281), p. 169–221, additions ending at p. 224,

Paris, Bibliothèque nationale, lat. 10588 (olim Suppl. lat. 302), saec. IX^{1}, possibly originated in Burgundy or in another region of Southern France, Prov. Saint-Martial at Limoges, fol. 1^{r}–41^{r}, including the additions and appendices ending at fol. 74^{r} (cf. Mordek, *Kirchenrecht und Reform* 286–288)

St. Gallen, Stiftsbibliothek, 675, saec. IX^{1}, Southern Germany, probably Bavaria, p. 3–137, including the additions and appendices ending at p. 267, largely corresponds with the once unmutilated codices Einsiedeln 205 and Wien, lat. 2171 cf. Mordek, *Kirchenrecht und Reform* 291; Mordek, *Bibliotheca capitularium* 655–658

Stuttgart, Württembergische Landesbibliothek, HB.VI.112, saec. X, region around Lake Constance, probably Constance, Prov. Weingarten, fol. 2^{r}–39^{r}, additions and supplements on fol. 39^{r}–40^{v}, 65^{v}–80^{v}, cf. Mordek, *Kirchenrecht und Reform* 293–294 and Mordek, *Bibliotheca capitularium* 720–723, esp. 721

Stuttgart, Württembergische Landesbibliothek, HB.VI.113; saec. VIII^{ex}, Churrhaetia (presumably Chur), later in possession of the monastery in Weingarten, fol. 92^{v}–155^{v}, including the additions and appendices ending at fol. 195^{v} or 223^{r} (cf. Mordek, *Kirchenrecht und Reform* 294–295) cf. below, *Collectio Weingartensis*

Wien, Österreichische Nationalbibliothek, lat. 2171, saec. IX3/4, Southwestern Germany, fol. 2^{r}–24^{v}, including the additions and appendices ending at fol. 47^{r} (cf. Mordek, *Kirchenrecht und Reform* 299–300)

Excerpts

Bruxelles, Bibliothèque Royale Albert Ier, 8654–72, saec. VIII–IX or IX^{in}, Prov. Saint-Bertin, fol. 130^{r}–133^{r}, cf. Mordek, *Kirchenrecht und Reform* 274–276; Mordek, *Bibliotheca capitularium* 88

Firenze, Biblioteca Medicea Laurenziana, Aedil. 82, saec. IX3/4, Italy (probably Northern Italy), *Vetus-Gallica* addition on fol. 169rb, saec. XI^{1}, Italian (cf. Mordek, *Kirchenrecht und Reform* 278–279)

Roma, Biblioteca Nazionale Centrale, Sessor. XXX

Vaticano, Città del, Biblioteca Apostolica Vaticana, Reg. lat. 982, saec. IX2/4, France, fol. 12^{v}–14^{r} and fol. 14^{v}–15^{v} (it is partly a copy of the excerpt contained in the manuscript Bruxelles, Bibliothèque Royale 8654–72, cf. Mordek, *Kirchenrecht und Reform* 297–299)

7. *Bibliography*

Maassen, *Geschichte* 821–828; H. Leclercq, 'Léger d'Autun', DACL 8/2 (1929) 2460–2493; Fournier-Le Bras 1.49–51; Kurtscheid-Wilches, 1.99–100; Van Hove, *Prolegomena* 276–277; Stickler, *Historia* 1.103; G. Fransen, 'Gallica, Vetus', DHGE 19 (1980) 838–839

G. Phillips, 'Der Codex Salisburgensis S. Petri IX.32: Ein Beitrag zur Geschichte der vorgratianischen Rechtsquellen', SB Vienna 44 (1863) 437–510

Le Bras, 'Notes II' 775–780

G. Le Bras, 'Un manuscrit et un fragment de la collection d'Angers', RHD, 4e sér., 8 (1929) 769–771

G. Le Bras, 'Autun dans l'histoire du droit canon', *Mémoires de la Société Eduenne,* n.s. 48 (1937) 161–174

Mordek, 'Bonneval' 339 including n. 2

Mordek, 'Aera' 220–221

H. Mordek, 'Der Codex Andegavensis Jacques Sirmonds', *Traditio* 25 (1969) 485–498

Mordek, 'Dionysio-Hadriana' 39–63

H. Mordek, 'Sur la tendance, la date, la patrie et l'influence de la *Collectio Vetus Gallica*: Contribution à l'histoire des sources canoniques dans la Gaule du haut moyen âge', RHD, 4e sér., 47 (1969) 441–453

H. Mordek, 'Die Collectio Vetus Gallica: Die älteste systematische Canonessammlung des fränkischen Gallien', *Francia* 1 (1973) 45–61 (first published in: *Proceedings Strasbourg* 15–30)

Mordek, 'Kanonistische Aktivität' 23–25

Mordek, *Kirchenrecht und Reform*

Motta, 'Regula Benedicti' 261–279

O. Capitani, 'Monachesimo occidentale e collezioni canoniche: secc. V–VII', *Atti del VII congresso internazionale di studi sull'alto medioevo. Norcia, Subiaco, Cassino, Montecassino: 28 settembre–5 ottobre 1980* (Centro italiano di studi sull'alto medioevo 1–2; Spoleto 1982) 231–253

Reynolds, 'Unity and Diversity' 108–109

Landau, 'Gefälschtes Recht' 20 including n. 37

Mordek, 'Primat' 523–566

H. Mordek and R. Reynolds, 'Bischof Leodegar und das Konzil von Autun', *Festschrift Kottje* (1991) 71–92

R. E. Reynolds (ed.), 'A Beneventan Monastic Excerptum from the Collectio Vetus Gallica', RB 102 (1992) 298–308

Zechiel-Eckes, *Cresconius* 1.140–141 and 297–298 (cf. also index)

Collectio Bernensis (Bern 611)

1. Author: Unknown. *2. Date:* About 727. *3. Place:* Corbie? (Mordek, *Kirchenrecht und Reform* 109). *4. Type:* Systematic collection; used the *Collectio Vetus Gallica* in a form prior to the Corbie-recension (Mordek, *Kirchenrecht und Reform* 109).

5. Edition

Mordek, 'Bischofsabsetzungen' 45–53

6. Manuscript

Bern, Burgerbibliothek, 611, fol. 138^{v}–140^{r} and Paris, Bibliothèque nationale, lat. 10756, fol. 62–69, saec. VIII^{1} (about 727), cf. CLA 7, no. 604a–e, pp. 9–10 and 55; CLA Suppl. p. 54; CLA 5, no. 604, p. 25 and 58

7. Bibliography

G. Le Bras, 'Autun dans l'histoire du droit canon', *Mémoires de la Société Eduenne*, nouv. sér. 48 (1937) 161–174
Mordek, 'Kanonistische Aktivität' 23
Mordek, *Kirchenrecht und Reform* 107–109
Mordek, 'Bischofsabsetzungen' 31–53

Collectio Herovalliana

1. Author: Unknown. *2. Date:* Second half of the eighth century. *3. Place:* Gaul. *4. Type:* Systematic collection; its main source is the *Collectio Vetus Gallica.*

5. Editions

Theodori sanctissimi et doctissimi archiepiscopi Cantuariensis Poenitentiale, Omnibus quae potuerunt ejusdem Capitulis adauctum, per Canones selectos ex antiquissima Canonum Collectione MS. nec non per plura ex variis Poenitentialibus hactenus inéditis excerpta expositum . . . Jacobus Petit primus in lucem edidit 1 (Paris 1677) 97–280 (= PL 99.989–1086)
Ballerini, *De antiquis . . . collectionibus et collectoribus* P. IV cap. 7 § 2 c. 8 (Capitulatio taken over from Petit's edition) (PL 56.306–308, no. 8)
Maassen, *Geschichte* 969–971: printed the collection's index based on the evidence of three different manuscripts.
Incipit-Explicit-Edition in which the canons of each title will be listed separately is announced by Mordek, *Kirchenrecht und Reform* 111 n. 57

6. Manuscripts

Original Form A Represented by the Older Manuscripts

Ivrea, Biblioteca Capitolare, XLII, saec. IX1/4, Northern France) fol. 57^{r}–111^{v}; the ending is missing; cf. W. M. Lindsay, *Notae Latinae: An Account of Abbreviation in Latin MSS. of the Early Minuscule Period (c.700–850) with a Supplement (Abbreviations in Latin MSS. of 850 to 1050) by D. Bains* (Cambridge 1915 and 1936; repr. Hildesheim 1963) 458; A. Professione and I.Vignono, *Inventario dei Manoscritti della Biblioteca Capitolare di Ivrea* (1967) 21
Paris, Bibliothèque nationale, lat. 2123, about 814–816, Flavigny, fol. 65^{v}–104^{v}, cf. *Bibliothèque nationale: Catalogue général des manuscrits latins* 2 (1940) 329–330;

also Migne-Hamann PL Suppl. 3.56 and esp. Ommanney, *Early History of the Athanasian Creed* 96ff., 393ff. on the dating, cf. Mordek, 'Herovalliana' 222 n. 10. Maassen, *Geschichte* 828–833 (829 n. 2) described the *Herovalliana* based on Cod. Paris lat. 2123. As Mordek has shown, Maassen made a rather unfortunate choice among the manuscripts known to him because a great number of the collection's chapters are missing in Paris lat. 2123. This manuscript should be regarded as an extensive excerpt of the *Collectio*. Consequently Maassen's description of the *Herovalliana* is far from being correct (cf. Mordek, *Kirchenrecht und Reform* 111 n. 61). A copy of the *Herovalliana*-Chapter LXIX 31 (PL 99.1073 [ibid. Kap. LXVIII 30]) of Cod. Paris lat. 2123 is contained in the manuscript Paris, Collection Baluze 4 (saec. XVII) fol. 129^{r} together with the following information about the provenance of the manuscript: *In codice 116 bibliothecae Tuanae fol. 103 antiquissimo.*

Paris, Bibliothèque nationale, lat. 2400, saec. XI1/3, Angoulême, fol. 103^{r}–130^{r}; cf. Mordek, *Kirchenrecht und Reform* 112 n. 65

Paris, Bibliothèque nationale, lat. 3848B, saec. VIII–IX, Flavigny, fol. 70^{r}–178^{v} (according to Maassen: fol. 70–180), cf. CLA 5 no. 555, pp. 11 and 55; CLA Suppl. 54 with further bibliographical references; see also Ommanney, *Early History of the Athanasian Creed* 92ff., 393ff. and by the same author, *A Critical Dissertation on the Athanasian Creed* 117–118

Paris, Bibliothèque nationale, lat. 4281, saec. IX1/4, Burgundy or Eastern France, Prov. Saint-Martial at Limoges; fol. 1^{r}–63^{v} (according to Maassen: fol. 1^{v}–55); an exact dating and localisation of the manuscript is given by B. Bischoff. On the contents, cf. *Catalogus codicum manuscriptorum Bibliothecae Regiae* Part 3, Vol. 3 (Paris 1744) 574; Ommanney, *Early History of the Athanasian Creed* 104; in Mordek's opinion (*Kirchenrecht und Reform* 114) it is the version which perhaps comes closest to the original form of the *Herovalliana*.

Revised Form B

After the middle of the ninth century; is augmented and numerous texts are appended to the end (cf. Mordek, *Kirchenrecht und Reform* 113 including n. 71)

Paris, Bibliothèque nationale, lat. 13657, saec. XI^{2}, France, fol. 5^{r}–111^{r} (manuscript of Antoine Vyon d'Hérouval [d. 1689], model for Petit's edition [cf. above]) see also Mordek, *Kirchenrecht und Reform* 110 n. 56 and 112 n. 66

Poitiers, Bibliothèque municipale, 6 (121), saec. XI^{2}, France, fol. 2^{r}–33^{r}; Prov. Saint-Hilaire le Grand at Poitiers, cf. Mordek, 'Herovalliana' 223 n. 16 and Mordek, *Kirchenrecht und Reform* 112 n. 67

Vaticano, Città del, Biblioteca Apostolica Vaticana, Reg. lat. 263, saec. XII, probably France, fol. 221^{r}–226^{v}, 205^{r}–212^{r}, cf. Mordek, *Kirchenrecht und Reform* 113 n. 68: 'Fragment eines früher sicher auch kompletten Codex'

Excerpts

Bamberg, Staatsbibliothek, Patr. 101 (olim B.V.19), saec. IX2/2

Ivrea, Biblioteca Capitolare, LXXV, saec. IX ca. med., Northern Italy

Padova, Biblioteca Antoniana, VI.103, saec. X^{ex}–XI^{in}, Northern Italy, perhaps from Verona, fol. 105^{r}–107^{v}, cf. Mordek, 'Analecta canonistica' 4 n. 11 and 5

Paris, Bibliothèque nationale, lat. 1455, saec. IX3/4, Reims region, fol. 1^{r}–2^{v}; cf. Mordek, *Bibliotheca capitularium* 410

Roma, Biblioteca Vallicelliana, T.XVIII, cf. Mordek, *Kirchenrecht und Reform* 135; Zechiel-Eckes, *Cresconius* 2.336–337

Sankt Paul im Lavanttal, Stiftsbibliothek 4/1, saec. IX1/3, Northern Italy (written in the same scriptorium as Vat. Barb. lat. 679), fol. 168vb–169rb: *Capitula excerpta canonica*; cf. Mordek, *Bibliotheca capitularium* 691

Special Form of the Herovalliana

Vercelli, Biblioteca Capitolare, CLXXV, saec. IX1/4, France or Northern Italy), fol. 1^{r}–86^{r}, cf. A. Reifferscheid, *Bibliotheca Patrum Latinorum Italica* 2.2 (1871) 176–178; MGH Capit. 2.xxxii; R. Pastè, in: G. Mazzatinti and A. Sorbelli, *Inventari dei Manoscritti delle Biblioteche d'Italia* 31 (1925) 120; S. F. Wemple, 'The Canonical Resources of Atto of Vercelli (926–960)', *Traditio* 26 (1970) 340. Cod. Vercelli CLXXV which omits some canons of the *Herovalliana*, can be traced with great certainty in ninth-century Italy, cf. ZKG 81 (1970) 222 including n. 12; Atto of Vercelli did not use it when he wrote his *Capitulare* (ca. saec. X^{med}) (neither did he use it as a source for 'De pressuris ecclesiasticis'). Cf. Mordek, *Kirchenrecht und Reform* 112 n. 64; Mordek, *Bibliotheca capitularium* 893–894 (Mordek classified it as belonging to Form A [113]; he characterized it, however, as an 'Italian version', because the editor had considerably revised the text of the collection; [cf. Mordek, 'Herovalliana' 222 n. 12 and idem, *Kirchenrecht und Reform* 114]. Mordek discovered that the collection had a considerable influence throughout Italy until the time of the Gregorian Reform movement.)

7. *Bibliography*

Maassen, *Geschichte* 828–833, 969–971; Scherer, *Handbuch* 1.207 n. 51; Fournier-Le Bras 1.84; Kurtscheid-Wilches 1.100; Van Hove, *Prolegomena* 277 (according to Mordek it contains several errors); Stickler, *Historia* 1.103; R. Naz, 'Herovalliana (Collectio)', DDC 5 (1953) 1112–1113 (according to Mordek it contains several errors); García y García, *Historia* 1.292; Mordek, 'Herovalliana, Collectio', LMA 4 (1989) 2176

Ballerini, *De antiquis . . . collectionibus et collectoribus*, P. IV, cap. VII, § 2 (PL 56.304–308)

Ommanney, *Early History of the Athanasian Creed* 92–105 (with excellent analyses of the manuscripts which go beyond Maassen's work)

Ommanney, *A Critical Dissertation on the Athanasian Creed* 53ff.

Tardif, *Sources* 120

G. Le Bras, review of G. Lardé, 'Le Tribunal du clerc dans l'Empire romain et la Gaule franque', *Le moyen âge* 24 (1922) 126–132, 129–130

Roque Losada Cosme, 'Las colecciones canónicas en función de autenticidad, universalidad y unificación del Derecho', REDC 10 (1955) 61–111, 73ff.

Coquin, 'Sort' 202–203

B. De Gaiffier, 'La lecture des passions des martyrs à Rome avant le IXe siècle', *Analecta Bollandiana* 87 (1969) 64–65

H. Mordek, 'Der Codex Andegavensis Jacques Sirmonds', *Traditio* 25 (1969) 485–498

G. Le Bras, 'Les apocryphes dans les collections canoniques', *La critica del testo* 1 (Atti del secondo Congresso internazionale della Società Italiana di Storia del Diritto 1; Florence 1971) 371–391, esp. 374–375
Mordek, 'Herovalliana' 220–243
Mordek, *Kirchenrecht und Reform* 109–143
H. Mordek, 'Ehescheidung und Wiederheirat in der Frühkirche. Zu Kanon 11 (10) des Konzils von Arles (a. 314)', *Etudes offertes à Jean Gaudemet* = RDC 28 (1978) 218–222
Mordek, 'Systematische Kanonessammlungen' 187
Mordek, 'Analecta canonistica' 4–6 (on the impact of the *Herovalliana* in Italy)
Landau, 'Kanonessammlungen in der Lombardei' 443–444
Zechiel-Eckes, *Cresconius* 2.375–376, 401–402 (cf. also index)

Collectio Frisingensis secunda

1. Author: Unknown. *2. Date:* Second half of the eighth century. *3. Place:* Gallican origin? probably Lake Constance region, according to Landau, 'Kanonessammlungen in Bayern' 151. *4. Type:* A systematically arranged collection of conciliar canons and decretals, the only source used, was the *Collectio Vetus Gallica*; traceable only in the manuscript München Clm 6243.

5. Edition

Mordek, *Kirchenrecht und Reform* 618–633

6. Manuscript

München, Bayerische Staatsbibliothek, Clm 6243, saec. VIII^{ex}, fol. 192^{r}–196^{v}; cf. Th. Mommsen, *Die Chronica minora* 1, MGH AA 9 (Berlin 1892, repr. 1961) 1.564, no. 18 (MGH SS 3.2 54): fol. 200–216, 233–238: Freising; fol. 1–199, 217–232: Constance region); cf. Mordek, *Bibliotheca capitularium* 322

7. Bibliography

Maassen, *Geschichte* 833

Mordek, *Kirchenrecht und Reform* 147–151
Landau, 'Kanonessammlungen in Bayern' 150–151

Epitome Hispana

1. Author: Unknown. *2. Date:* Between 598 (Council of Huesca) and 619 (Council of Sevilla), cf. Martínez Díez (see below) 71, or, more likely, before the Council of Toledo (610), cf. García y García. *3. Place:* Spain, probably Tarragona. *4. Type:* A chronologically arranged collection, primitive excerpt of decrees of Greek, Gallican, and Spanish councils and decretals.

5. Editions

Mansi, *Ad Concilia Veneto Labbaeana Supplementum* 1–6 (Lucca 1748–1752) and in the first few volumes of his edition of councils (only a few fragments)

Turner, EOMIA 1.113–114, 2.4–25, 55–115, 119–141, 185–211, 233–309 (single councils)

A. Ariño Alafont, *Colección Canónica Hispana* (Avila 1941) 124–144 (based exclusively on the manuscript Vat. lat. 5751)

Martínez Díez, 'El Epítome Hispánico' 322–466

6. Manuscripts

København, Kongelike Bibliothek, Ny Kgl. Saml. 58 8°, saec. VIII1/2: written shortly after 731 in Gaul, in a hand whose writing clearly betrays Spanish influence (indication that the *Epitome* was known in Southern France), Prov. Regensburg, fol. 52ʳ–69ᵛ, cf. CLA 10, no. 1568, p. 37 and 52; Mordek, 'Kanonistische Aktivität' 21–22; Landau, 'Regensburg' 57–58 and F. B. Asbach, *Das Poenitentiale Remense und der sogen. Excarpsus Cummeani* (Regensburg 1975) 43–44

Lucca, Biblioteca Capitolare Feliniana, 490 (olim 89), saec. VIII^{ex}–IX^{in}; written probably at Lucca, fol. 288ʳ–309, cf. L. Schiaparelli, *Il codice 490 della Biblioteca Capitolare di Lucca e la scuola scrittoria Lucchese (sec. VIII–IX),* (Studi e testi 36; 1924); E. A. Lowe, CLA 3 (1938) 9–10 and 43; Mordek, 'Aera' 219

Merseburg, Archiv des Domkapitels, 104, saec. X, according to Pertz, *Archiv* 8 (1831) 668; fol. 10ʳ–36ᵛ

München, Bayerische Staatsbibliothek, Clm 14468, written a. 821 under abbot-bishop Baturich in Regensburg (cf. Landau, 'Regensburg' 58–59); Mordek, *Bibliotheca capitularium* 336 (excerpt) and 912

Paris, Bibliothèque nationale, Collection Baluze 270, saec. IX, fol. 177ʳ–178ᵛ, and Lyon, Bibliothèque de la ville, 788, fol. 100ʳ–101ᵛ, saec. IX (fragments)

Vaticano, Città del, Biblioteca Apostolica Vaticana, lat. 5751, saec. X, Northern Italy (ownership note by the monastery of Bobbio), fol. 31ʳ–41ᵛ, excerpt of the *Epitome*; cf. Martínez Díez; Kottje, *Bußbücher Halitgars* 73–74 (manuscript possibly written at Verona; it may have been among the manuscripts acquired under Abbot Agilulf [about 887–896]); cf. also Mordek, *Bibliotheca capitularium* 885–886 (saec. IX–X)

Verona, Biblioteca Capitolare, LXI (59), saec. VII–VIII, Verona (first instance of manuscript evidence, cf. Martínez Díez, 'El Epítome Hispanico' 23, basic text for the edition of Martínez Díez); fol. 1ᵛ–68ᵛ, cf. also Zechiel-Eckes 1.166 and 2.348–349; Landau, 'Kanonessammlungen in Bayern' 143 n. 33

Excerpts

Heiligenkreuz, Stiftsbibliothek, 217, saec. X^{ex}, Southern Germany, cf. Landau, 'Kanonessammlungen in Bayern' 145 n. 40

London, British Library, Add. 16413, saec. XI^{in}, fol. 107ʳ–110ʳ; cf. L. Mahadevan, 'Überlieferung und Verbreitung des Bußbuchs *Capitula Iudiciorum*', ZRG Kan. Abt. 72 (1986) 24–28; Hoffmann-Pokorny 78 n. 44

München, Bayerische Staatsbibliothek, Clm 3852, saec. XI, probably Freising, fol. 65^{r}–65^{v} (the same special version of excerpts as in München Clm 6241, cf. Hoffmann-Pokorny 77–80)
München, Bayerische Staatsbibliothek, Clm 3853, saec. X, fol. 129^{v}–153^{r}, cf. R. Haggenmüller, *Die Überlieferung der Beda und Egbert zugeschriebenen Bußbücher* (Europäische Hochschulschriften, Reihe 3, Band 461; Frankfurt 1991) 76–78
München, Bayerische Staatsbibliothek, Clm 6241, saec. X3/3, Freising (cf. Hoffmann-Pokorny 76–81); fol. 31^{v}–33^{v}; comprehensive description of this manuscript by John, *Collectio canonum Remedio . . . ascripta* 33–36; complete edition of the text by Martínez Díez, *Epitome* 229–232 (cf. above München Clm 3852; Hoffmann-Pokorny 78)
St. Gallen, Stiftsbibliothek, 676, p. 55, 83–98 (Hoffmann-Pokorny 78 n. 44)
Stuttgart, Württembergische Landesbibliothek, HB.VI.107, fol. 63^{v}–64^{r}, 81^{v}–82^{r}, 85^{v}–96^{v} (Kottje, *Bußbücher Halitgars* 60–62; Hoffmann-Pokorny 78 n. 44)
Vaticano, Città del, Biblioteca Apostolica Vaticana, Ottobon. lat. 3295, saec. IX^{2}, Prov. Mainz, fol. 76^{r}–v, cf. Mordek, *Kirchenrecht und Reform* 11 (parallel text of Clm 6241)
Wien, Österreichische Nationalbibliothek, lat. 2232, saec. IX^{in}, Southeastern Germany; excerpt, fol. 63^{r}–74^{v}; cf. Mordek, *Bibliotheca capitularium* 911–915

Reception

Collectio 4 librorum (Köln 124)

7. *Bibliography*

Maassen, *Geschichte* 646–666; Fournier-Le Bras 1.66–67; Kurtscheid-Wilches 1.103–104; Van Hove, *Prolegomena* 279; García y García, *Historia* 1.180–181; Martínez Díez, DHEE 1 (Madrid 1972) 445; Rep. font. 4 (1976) 365–366

Ballerini, *De antiquis . . . collectionibus et collectoribus* P. IV, cap. IV (PL 56.286–291)
Pertz, *Archiv* 8 (1831) 668–669
Tarré, 'Sources' 131
Séjourné, *Saint Isidore* 270–281
Le Bras, 'Isidore de Séville' 238–244
García Villada, *Historia Eclesiástica de España* 2.2 (Madrid 1933) 132–134
García Villada, 'Las colecciones canónicas en la época visigoda', *Razón y Fé* 102 (1933) 471–480
Tarré, 'Etudes' 208–210
A. García Gallo, *Historia del Derecho Español,* 1: *Exposición Histórica* (Madrid ^{2}1941) 325
Martínez Díez, cf. 'El Epitome Hispánico' 6–90
M. Torres López, 'La Iglesia en la España Visigoda', *Historia de España,* 3: *España Visigoda* (Madrid ^{2}1963) 310
Martínez Díez, *Colección Hispana* 1.290–300 and passim
A. García Gallo, *Manual de Historia del Derecho Español* 1 (Madrid ^{3}1967) no. 652
M. Díaz y Díaz, 'La circulation des manuscrits dans la Péninsule Ibérique du VIIIe au XIe siècle', CCM 12 (1969) 219–241, 383–392
Mordek, 'Aera' 219

Mordek, 'Kanonistische Aktivität' 19–25
Gaudemet, *Sources* 153–155
Landau, 'Kanonessammlungen in der Lombardei' 433–434
Landau, 'Kanonessammlungen in Bayern' 143–148

Excerpta Hispana

1. Author: Isidor of Seville, corrections by Bishop Julian of Toledo (680–690) (Séjourné 321–331, cf. Appendix IV, 502–504), but cf. Le Bras: written after the middle of the seventh century, later than the 'Tabula'; García y García: between the X. (656) and XI. Councils of Toledo (675). *2. Date:* Cf. 'Author' *3. Place:* Spain. *4. Type:* A systematic Repertorium of the *Collectio Hispana* that is arranged according to titles, with references to conciliar canons and decretals; included in manuscripts of the *Hispana.*

5. Editions

C. Cenni, *De antiquitate ecclesiae Hispanae dissertationes . . .* 1 (Rome 1741) xxxiii–cxxvii (Mansi 8.1179–1260)
F. A. Gonzalez, *Collectio Canonum Ecclesiae Hispanae* III–LX (PL 84.23–92)
C. García Goldáraz (on the basis of manuscript Vat. lat. 4887, a late copy [saec. XV] of the *Hispana*, cf. below *Collectio Hispana* 'Editions')
Martínez Díez, *Colección Hispana* 2.1.43–214

6. Manuscripts

El Escorial, Real Biblioteca de San Lorenzo, D.I.1 (a. 992–94), fol. 19v–52v: *Juliana*-recension of the *Hispana*, with numerous additions, *Liber iudiciorum* etc. (known as *Codex Emilianensis*); cf. Martínez Díez 1.117–120 (E)
El Escorial, Real Biblioteca de San Lorenzo, D.I.2 (26 May 974), fol. 20v–56r: *Juliana*-recension with a few additions (known as *Codex Albeldensis* or *Vigilianus*); cf. Martínez Díez 1.114–117 (A)
El Escorial, Real Biblioteca de San Lorenzo, E.I.12, saec. IX, fol. 1r–10v: *Juliana*-recension of the chronological *Hispana* (known as Codex *Oxomensis*); cf. Martínez Díez 1.109–114 (O)
Madrid, Biblioteca Nacional, 1872 (olim P. 21: Vitr. 14.4), fol. 2r–35v: chronological *Hispana, Vulgata*-recension, 'forma Común'. (known as *Codex of the Biblioteca Regia*); cf. Martínez Díez 1.128–130 (R)
Madrid, Biblioteca Nacional, 10041 (olim Toledo, Biblioteca Capitular 15–16), (a. 1034, based on a source dating from 948), fol. 1v–37v: chronological *Hispana, Vulgata*-recension, 'forma Común' (known as *Codex Toledanus*); cf. Martínez Díez 1.124 128 (T)
Toledo, Archivo y Biblioteca Capitular, 15–17 (a. 1095), fol. 1v–33r: chronological *Hispana, Vulgata*-recension (known as *Codex Complutensis*); cf. Martínez Díez 1.137–139; A. García y García and R. Gonzálvez Ruiz, *Catálogo de los manuscritos juridicos medievales de la Catedral de Toledo* (Rome-Madrid 1970) 47–48 (C)

Fragment

Orense, Biblioteca Capitular, 43 (T 664), saec. X: chronological *Hispana, Vulgata*-recension (Fragment of lib. 9, tit. 6 up to lib. 10, tit. 4 of the *Excerpta*). Cf. Martínez Díez 1.144 (Q)

Copies of Juan Bautista Pérez from the Codex Luccense (Vat. lat. 4887)

For late copies (saec. XV–XVI) of the *Excerpta,* cf. Martínez Díez, *Colección Hispána* 1.12 no. V ('Copias y Cotejas de la Hispana')

7. *Bibliography*

Maassen, *Geschichte* 819–820; J. Forget, 'Julien de Tolède', DThC 8 (1925) 1940–1942; Fournier-Le Bras 1.70, 103–106, 109; Van Hove, *Prolegomena* 282

Séjourné, *Saint Isidore* 321–331

Le Bras, 'Isidore de Séville' 350

E. Tejero Tejero, 'Los "excerpta" de la Hispana: Originalidad de su sistemática', *La norma en el derecho canónico: Actas del III Congresso internacional de derecho canonico, Pamplona 10–15 octubre 1976,* 1 (Pamplona 1979) 143–161

Gaudemet, *Sources* 158–159

Collectio Hispana

1. Author: Isidor of, Seville according to Martínez Díez; other scholars have rejected his authorship: Ch. Munier, 'Saint Isidore de Séville est-il l'auteur de l'Hispana chronologique', SE 17 (1966) 230–241; Ch. Munier, 'Nouvelles recherches sur l'*Hispana* chronologique', *Revue des sciences religieuses* 40 (1966) 400–410, 405–406; J. Gaudemet, RHD, 4e sér., 45 (1967) 122–124; K. Schäferdiek, ZKG 78 (1967) 144–148; P. Landau ZRG Kan. Abt. 54 (1968) 406–414; Mordek, 'Aera' 219–220. *2. Date:* Oldest recension (*Form A*) is from the time of the Fourth Council of Toledo (633); the definitive version (*Form B*—most of the manuscripts) contains the Seventeenth Council of Toledo (694) (Fournier-Le Bras 1.68). *3. Place:* Spain. *4. Type:* A chronologically arranged collection of conciliar canons and decretals (also known in a systematic form, cf. below, *Collectio Hispana systematica*).

5. *Editions*

G. Loaysa, *Collectio conciliorum Hispaniae* (Madrid 1593) (partly)

Franciscus Antonius González, *Collectio Canonum Ecclesiae Hispanae ex probatissimis ac pervetustis codicibus nunc primum in lucem edita publica Matritensi Bibliotheca* 1–2 (Madrid 1808–1821) (PL 84.93–848)

Epistolae Decretales ac Rescripta Romanorum Pontificum (Madrid 1821); Colección de canónes de la Iglesia española, publicada . . . por F. Gonzalez, Traducida por J Tejada 1 (1849), 2 (1850)

C. García Goldáraz, *El Codice Lucense de la Colección canónica Hispana* (Biblioteca de la Escuela Española de Historia y Arquelogía en Roma 10, 11, 12; Rome 1954) [with facsimile of the codices Vat. lat. 4887 and 4888]

G. Martínez Díez, *La colección canónica Hispana* 1: *Estudio* (Monumenta Hispaniae sacra, Series canonica 1; Madrid 1966)

G. Martínez Díez (ed.), *La colección canónica Hispana* 2: *Colecciónes derivadas* 1–2 (Monumenta Hispaniae Sacra, Ser. can. 1; Madrid 1976)

G. Martínez Díez, and F. Rodríguez (edd.), *La colección canónica Hispana* 3: *Concilios griegos y africanos* (Monumenta Hispaniae Sacra, Ser. can. 3; Madrid 1982)

G. Martínez Díez and F. Rodríguez, *La colección canónica Hispana* 4: *Concilios galos, Concilios hispanos: primera parte* (Monumenta Hispaniae sacra, Ser. can. 4; Madrid 1984)

G. Martínez Díez and F. Rodriguez, *La colección canónica Hispana 5: Concilios Hispanos: segunda parte* (Monumenta Hispaniae sacra, Ser. can. 5; Madrid 1992)

For further editions, cf. Martínez Díez, *Colección Hispana* 1: *Estudio* (Madrid 1966) 25–102

6. *Manuscripts*

Several recensions (according to Martínez Díez 1.11–15, 103–205, 384–386)

1. Primitive *Hispana* (*Isidoriana*, lost today; its existence can be deduced from the evidence given by two codices: the now-lost *Codex Rachionis* and the manuscript W of the Galician version of the *Vulgata*-recension, written 633–636)

2. *Juliana*-recension (after 681), supplements one codex of the *Isidoriana*-recension by adding the eight Toledean councils from Toledo V (636) up to Toledo XII (681), written shortly after 681. Two subcategories:

   a. Gallican—as far as the councils of Agde, Orléans and Toledo III–XI are concerned, the signatures of the bishops are omitted. The arrangement of the decretals is also changed (manuscripts DVW) for the first time in a manuscript from the beginning of the eighth century.

   b. Toletanian—varying additions of Toledo XII, written before 775

3. *Vulgata*-recension (694–702); adds fourteen new councils up to Toledo XVII (694); most widely circulated version of the *Hispana;* see below, *Collectio Hispana Gallica.* Two subcategories:

   a. 'Común'—almost all the manuscripts: CPRSTVZ and those now lost from Lugo, Carrión de los Condes and San Juan de la Peña

   b. Catalan—Two manuscripts (GU)

El Escorial, Real Biblioteca de San Lorenzo, D.I.1, written between 992 and 994, Prov. San Millán de la Cogolla, fol. 19^{v}–316^{v}, *Juliana*-recension with numerous additions (known as *Codex Emilianus*); cf. Martínez Díez, *Colección Hispana* 1.117–20 (E)

El Escorial, Real Biblioteca de San Lorenzo, D.I.2, written between 974 and 976, Prov. San Martin de Alvelda (Logroño), fol. 20^{r}–238^{v} and 248–341^{r}, *Juliana*-recension with some additions (known as *Codex Albeldensis* or *Vigilianus*); cf. Martínez Díez, *Colección Hispana* 1.114–17 (A)

El Escorial, Real Biblioteca de San Lorenzo, E.I.12, saec. IX, Prov. Andalusia, Córdoba? fol. 1^{r}–323^{v}, *Juliana*-recension (known as *Codex Oxomensis*); cf. Martínez Díez, *Colección Hispana* 1.109–114(O)

El Escorial, Real Biblioteca de San Lorenzo, E.I.13, saec. X–XI, Prov. Córdoba (?), fol. 1^{r}–103^{v} (very fragmentary), *Vulgata*-recension, 'forma Común' (known as *Codex Soriensis*); cf. Martínez Díez, *Colección Hispana* 1.130–132 (S)

El Escorial, Real Biblioteca de San Lorenzo, O.I.13, saec. XV, Prov. unknown, fol.

1^{r}–136^{v}, probably copied from a Visigothic codex; collection of decretals from the *Hispana*, Martínez Díez, *Colección Hispana* 1.143 (K)

Firenze, Biblioteca Medicea Laurenziana, Ashburnham 1554, saec. XII^{1}, fol. 99^{v}–119^{v} (in the second part of the collection which Fournier-Le Bras 2.135–39 called collection of Lord Ashburnham's manuscript); cf. Mordek, *Kirchenrecht und Reform* 251

Firenze, Biblioteca Riccardiana, 258, saec. XII; the Greek and Spanish councils of the *Hispana*; the second part of the manuscript contains *Polycarpus*; Mordek, *Kirchenrecht und Reform* 251

Gerona, Archivo de la Santa Iglesia Catedral Basílica, Códice Conciliar, saec. IX^{in}, Prov. probably Gerona, fol. I^{r}–XXIII^{v} and 1^{r}–365^{v}, *Vulgata*-recension, Catalan form (known as *Codex Gerundensis*); cf. Martínez Díez, *Colección Hispana* 1.141–142 (G)

Madrid, Biblioteca Nacional, 1872 (olim P.21, Vitrina 14.4), Prov. mozarabian-andalusian, fol. 2^{r}–345^{v}, *Vulgata*-recension, 'forma Común', (known as *Codex of the Biblioteca Regia*); Martínez Díez, *Colección Hispana* 1.128–130 (R)

Madrid, Biblioteca Nacional, 10041 (olim Toledo XV,16), 1034–1072 (?), Prov. Córdoba? since 1455 at Toledo (known as *Codex Toledanus*); fol. 1^{v}–237^{v}, *Vulgata*-recension, 'forma Común', cf. Martínez Díez, *Colección Hispana* 1.124–128 (T)

Oxford, Bodleian Library, Holkham misc. 19, saec. XII^{in}, Tuscany (probably Pistoia), cf. Brooke, *English Church* 230; Fournier, 'Angleterre' 132–133; Mordek, *Kirchenrecht und Reform* 251

Oxford, Bodleian Library, lat.th.c.5 (SC. 32.564) (olim Sir Thomas Philipps Library 6.735, El Escorial, Real Biblioteca de San Lorenzo, D.II.20) fol. 2^{r}–81^{v}, saec. XII, Spanish, Prov. Toledo? fragments of the chronological *Hispana*, councils of Toledo in the *Vulgata*-recension (known as *Codex Zuritanus*); Martínez Díez, *Colección Hispana* 1.132–135 (Z)

Paris, Bibliothèque nationale, lat. 4280, saec. XII; cf. Rambaud-Buhot, 'Baluze, bibliothécaire et canoniste' 329 n. 25; Mordek, *Kirchenrecht und Reform* 251

Roma, Biblioteca Angelica, 1.091 (olim s.1.15), saec. IX–X, Prov. Carolingian empire, p. 1–184; Gallican and Spanish councils of the Hispana, *Vulgata*-recension (known as *Codex Passionei*, named after the cardinals who owned it); cf. Martínez Díez, *Colección Hispana* 1.136–137 (P)

Roma, Biblioteca Vallicelliana, D.18, cf. Martínez Díez, *Colección Hispana* 1.142–143 (D) and for further details see below *Collectio Hispana Gallica*

Seo de Urgel, Biblioteca Capitular, 2005, saec. XI^{ex}, Prov. probably Seo de Urgel, fol. 1^{r}–290vb, *Vulgata*-recension, Catalan form (known as *Codex Urgelensis*); Martínez Díez, *Colección Hispana* 1.139–141 (U)

Toledo, Archivo y Biblioteca Capitular, 15–17 (olim Tol. 31,5), saec. XI^{ex}, ('Iulianus indignus presbiter scripsit; a. 1095, IIII feria, XVII K. Iunius, era ICXXXIII'); Prov. Alcatá de Henares; fol. 1va–348rb, *Vulgata*-recension, purest form of the *Vulgata* recension (complete), (known as *Codex Complutensis*); cf. A. García y García and R. Gonzálvez Ruiz, *Catálogo de los manuscrito juridicos medievales de la Catedral de Toledo* (Rome-Madrid 1970) 47–48) (C)

Vaticano, Città del, Biblioteca Apostolica Vaticana, Pal. lat. 575, saec. IX–X, unknown Prov. (notation concerning a former owner fol. 3^{r}: 'Iste liber pertinet ad librarium Sancti Martini ecclesiae Maguntinae. M. Sindicus est 1479'), fol.

1–158, contains characteristics of both, the *Gallica* and the *Vulgata* (known as Codex Vaticanus); cf. Martínez Díez, *Colección Hispana* 1.120–124 (V) and below *Collectio Hispana Gallica*

Wien, Österreichische Nationalbibliothek, lat. 411 (iur. can. 41), cf. Martínez Díez, *Colección Hispana* 1.104–109 (W) and below *Collectio Hispana Gallica*

Moreover, there existed another fourteen codices (according to García y García), which are now lost (some from Sevilla, Lugo, Oviedo, Carrión de los Condes, San Pedro de Montes, Celanova, Oña, S. Juan de la Peña, S. Pedro de Cardeña, S. Pedro de Arlanza, Strasbourg [the Codex of Rachio destroyed in 1870] and Soissons). Fifteen other codices are erroneously cited as manuscripts of the *Collectio Hispana,* but contain different works. On the eight late copies cf. Martínez Díez, *Colección Hispana* 1.146–200

Fragments

Burgos, Archivo y Biblioteca de la Catedral, Codex n° 2, saec. X, Prov. probably Castille, Cardeña?; fol. 71^{rv}, fragment of the decretals, *Vulgata*-recension, cf. Martínez Díez, *Colección Hispana* 1.145–146 (J)

Orense, Biblioteca Capitular, 43 (T 664), saec. X^2; fragments of the *Vulgata*-recension, cf. Martínez Díez, *Colección Hispana* 1.144 (Q)

Solothurn, Staatsarchiv, sine num. and Zürich, Staatsarchiv, A.G.19, no. VI (fol. 18=pp. 49–50) and C VI 1, no. IV 2 (fol. 5), saec. VIII–IX, Rhaetia (probably Chur); cf. CLA 7, no. 1006, pp. 47 and 61; CLA Suppl. p. 27, the supplementary volume of the CLA identifies them as texts belonging to the *Hispana* (cf. Mordek, *Kirchenrecht und Reform* 251)

For late copies (saec. XV–XVI) of the *Hispana,* cf. Martínez Díez, *Colección Hispána* 1.12 no. V ('Copias y Cotejas de la Hispana')

7. *Bibliography*

Maassen, *Geschichte* 667–716; 802–806; Fournier-Le Bras 1.68–71, 100–106; Kurtscheid-Wilches 1.85–86 and 104–108; Van Hove, *Prolegomena* 280–282

Cf. above 'Author'

Petrus De Marca, 'Dissertatio de veteribus collectionibus canonum', *Opuscula Petri de Marca,* ed. Baluze (Paris 1681) 201–358, see also Paris, Bibliothèque nationale, Collection Baluze 372, fol. 1^r–41^v

Ballerini, *De antiquis . . . collectionibus et collectoribus* P. III, c. IV (PL 56.218–238)

A. De Morales, *Viage de Ambrosio de Morales per Orden del Rey D. Felipe II . . .* (Madrid 1765) 32–33, 38–39, 93, 103–104, 155, 174, 199, 204, 214, 216

P. Coustant, *Dissertatio de antiquis Canonum Collectionibus* (Venice 1778) 50–51, 55

L. Blanco, *Noticia de las antiguas y genuinas Colecciones canónicas inéditas de la Iglesia española que de orden del Rey nuestro Señor se publicaron por su Real Biblioteca de Madrid* (Madrid 1798)

C. De la Serna Santander, *Praefatio historico-critica in veram et genuinam collectionem veterum canonum Ecclesiae Hispaniae* (Brussels 1800), text printed in PL 84.849–914

J. M. Eguren, *Memoria descriptiva de los códices notables conservados en los archivos eclesiésticos de España* (Madrid 1859) 63–80

P. Gams, 'Das altspanische Kirchenrecht', *Theologische Quartalschrift* 49 (1867) 3–23

Silva-Tarouca, 'Beiträge' 675
ACO 2.4, p. vi–x
Tarré, 'Sources' 125–134
Séjourné, *Saint Isidore*
J. Tarré, 'Sur les origines arlésiennes de la collection canonique dite *Hispana*', *Mélanges Paul Fournier* (Paris 1929) 705–724
Le Bras, 'Isidore de Séville' 218–257
A. Wilmart, 'Fragments Carolingiens du Fonds Baluze', RB 43 (1931) 106–115 (Fragments of the chronological *Hispana*)
Z. García Villada, 'Las colecciónes canónicas en la época Visigoda', *Razón y Fe* 102 (1933) 471–480
Tarré, 'Etudes' 208–210
J. A. De Aldama, 'El símbolo Toledano I. Su texto, su origen, su posicion en la historia de los símbolos', *Analecta Gregoriana* 7 (1934) 26–43
J. Ruiz Goyo, 'San Isidoro de Sevilla y la antigua Colección canónica Hispana', *Estudios Eclesiasticos* 15 (1936) 119–136
Wurm, *Studien und Texte* 143–150
A. Ariño Alafont, *Colección canónica Hispana: Estudio de su formación y contenido* (Avila 1941)
A. García Gallo, *Historia del Derecho Español,* 1: *Exposición historica* (Madrid [2]1941) 326–328
A. Ariño Alafont, 'Edición crítica de la Colección canónica Hispana' *Revista Española de derecho canónico* 1 (1946) 195–201, 257–259, 268, 562; 2 (1947) 11, 718 and 723
A. Ariño Alafont, 'La Colección canónica Hispana en el códice 15–17 de Toledo', *Anales de la Universidad de Murcia* (1948–1949) 381–413
L. Rodriguez Sotillo, 'Las fuentes ibéricas del Decreto Graciano', *Miscelánea Comillas* 20 (1953) 299–329 (also in: SG 2 [Bologna 1954] 13–48)
C. García Goldáraz, *El códice Lucense de la Colección canónica Hispana* 1–3 (Biblioteca de la Escuela Española de Historia y Arqueología en Roma 10–12; Rome 1954) (reconstruction of the Codex of Lugo destroyed by a fire in the library of the Escorial in 1671 by using notes taken during the 16th century) cf. above 'Edition'
B. Franck, 'Recherches sur le ms. de l'Hispana de l'évêque Rachio' *Archives de l'Eglise d'Alsace* 23 (1956) 67–82 (cf. Le Bras, RHD, 4e sér., 36 [1958] 133)
P. Pinedo, 'A propósito de la reconstrucción del mejor manuscrito de la Hispana', AHDE 26 (1956) 767–770
M. Díaz y Díaz, *Index scriptorum latinorum medii aevi Hispanorum* 1–2 (1958–1959)
C. García Goldáraz, *Los concilios de Cartago de un códice Soriense* (Biblioteca de la Escuela Española de Historia y Arqueología en Roma 13; Rome 1960)
J. Madoz, 'La Colección Canónica Hispana', *Archivos Leoneses* 14 (1960) 89–117
Clavis 397–399 nr. 1790 and 1790a
Martínez Díez, 'El Epitome Hispánico' 14
M. Díaz y Díaz, 'Pequeñas aportaciones para el estudio de la Hispana', *Revista Española de Derecho Canónico* 17 (1962) 373–390
G. Martínez Díez, 'Una colección canónica pirenaica del siglo XI', *Miscelánea Comillas* 38 (1962) 211–270
G. Martínez Díez, 'Fragmentos canónicos del siglo VI', HS 15 (1962) 389–399

Martínez Díez, 'Novara' passim

M. Torres López, 'La Iglesia en la España Visigoda', in: *Historia de España, 3: España Visigoda* (Madrid [2] 1963) 310–311

G. Martínez Díez, 'Hacia la edición crítica de la Hispana', *Miscelánea Comillas* 41 (1964) 257–269 (with a preliminary edition of the Second Council of Toledo)

G. Martínez Díez, 'Prolegómenos a la edición crítica de la Hispana', *Etudes . . . Le Bras* 1.263–272

G. Martínez Díez, 'Algunas normas críticas para la edición de textos jurídicos', AHDE 35 (1965) 527–551

Martínez Díez, *Colección Hispana* 1

Ch. Munier, 'Saint Isidore de Séville est-il l'auteur de l'Hispana chronologique?' SE 17 (1966) 230–241

C. Munier, 'Nouvelles recherches sur l'Hispana Chronologique', *Revue des Sciences Religieuses* 40 (1966) 400–410

J. Gaudemet, Review of: G. Martínez Díez, *La colección canónica Hispana* 1', RHD, 4e sér., 45 (1967) 122–124

K. Schäferdiek, Review of 'Martínez Díez, *La colección canónica Hispana* 1', ZKG 78 (1967) 144–148

V. Castell Maiques, 'Un elenco de Códices de la Hispana del año 1239', *Anthologica annua* 16 (1968) 329–343

P. Landau, Review of 'Gonzalo Martínez Díez, *La Colección Canónica Hispana* (Monumenta Hispaniae Sacra, Series Canonica 1; Madrid 1966)' ZRG Kan. Abt. 54 (1968) 406–414

M. Díaz y Díaz, 'La circulation des manuscrits dans la Péninsule Ibérique du VIIIe au XIe siècle', CCM 12 (1969) 219–241, esp. 227, 383–392, esp. 386–390

Mordek, 'Aera' 216–222

G. Martínez Díez, 'La edición crítica de las varias recensiones y formas de un texto', *La critica del testo* (Atti del secondo Congresso internazionale della Società Italiana di Storia del Diritto 1; Firenze 1971) 401–413

R. Kottje, 'Isidor von Sevilla und der Chorepiskopat', DA 28 (1972) 533–537

F. Rodríguez, 'El crecimiento de la Colección Canónica Hispana a través de sus 'Capitula',' *Miscelánea Comillas* 30 (1972) 5–24

Brommer, 'Fragmente' 228–230

F. Rodríguez, 'Las listas episcopales de Nicea en la Colección Canónica Hispana', *Burgense* 15 (1974) 341–358

M. Breydy, 'La labor de dos maronitas acerca de la Arábico-Hispana Escurialense', *El Concilio de Braga y la función de la legislación particular en la Iglesia* (Salamanca 1975) 169–183

A. Chavasse, 'Les lettres du Pape Léon le Grand (440–461) dans l'Hispana et la collection dite des Fausses Décrétales', RDC 25 (1975) 28–39

Mordek, 'Kanonistische Aktivität' 21

Mordek, *Kirchenrecht und Reform* 250–252

F. Rodríguez, 'Observaciones y sugerencias sobre algunos manoscritos de la Colección canónica Hispana', *Burgense* 16 (1975) 119–143 (on the manuscripts Barcelona Biblioteca Central 945 and Vat. Pal. lat. 575)

F. Rodríguez, 'Los antiguos concilios españoles y la edición critica de la Colección Canónica Hispana', *Proceedings Salamanca* 3–13

Contreni, 'Description' 85–89
Richter, 'Stufen' 3–5
Fuhrmann, 'Papstbriefe' 359 and 365–367
J. Orlandis and D. Ramos-Lissón, *Die Synoden der Iberischen Halbinsel bis zum Einbruch des Islam (711)* (Konziliengeschichte Reihe A, Paderborn-Munich-Zurich 1981)
A. Mundo, 'El fragmento de Celanova de la *Hispana* reaparecido', HS 36 (1983) 591–600
H. J. Sieben, *Die Konzilsidee des lateinischen Mittelalters* (Paderborn-Munich-Zurich 1984)
Gaudemet, *Sources* 155–161
E. J. Kilmartin, 'Early African Legislation Concerning Liturgical Prayer', EL 99 (1985) 105–127
S. De Silva y Verástegui, 'Imágenes de los concilios Africanos en los codices altomedievales hispánicos: los concilios de Cartago y el concilio Milevitano', REAug 32 (1986) 108–123
Gaudemet, 'Capitula Martini' 51–65
S. De Silva y Verástegui, 'L'illustration des manuscrits de la Collection Canonique Hispana', CCM 32 (1989) 247–261
A. García y García, 'Proyección del Concilio III de Toledo en las colecciones canónicas medievales', *Concilio III de Toledo* 511–522
Mordek, 'Primat' 523–566
F. Rodriguez, 'La tradición manuscrita del Concilio III de Toledo', *Concilio III de Toledo* 729–744
F. Salvador Ventura, 'El Concilio III de Toledo y los concilios béticos', *Concilio III de Toledo* 627–640
P. Sjoerd van Koningsveld, 'La literatura cristiano-árabe de la España medieval y el significado de la transmisión textual en árabe de la Collectio Conciliorum', *Concilio III de Toledo* 695–710
A. García y García, 'Vocabulario de las escuelas en la Península Ibérica', *Vocabulaire des écoles et des méthodes d'enseignement au moyen âge: Actes du colloque, Rome 21–22 octobre 1989*, ed. O. Weijers (Turnhout 1992) 157–176
Siems, *Handel und Wucher* 522, 531, 559, 672
Zechiel-Eckes, *Cresconius* 19–20 (cf. also index)
Mordek, *Bibliotheca capitularium* 452

Collectio Hispana Gallica

1. Author: Unknown. *2. Date:* End of the seventh century at the earliest, contains Toledo XIII (683) and Braga III (675) *3. Place:* Circulated in the Frankish part of Gaul. *4. Type:* A chronologically arranged collection of conciliar canons and decretals. *5. Edition:* None.

6. Manuscripts

Roma, Biblioteca Vallicelliana, D.18, fol. '1–168' (only 165 folios, fol. 10 is also counted as no. 11 and 12; 133 is also counted as 134), saec. X, Prov. unknown, cf. Richter, 'Stufen' 12–13, (known as *Codex Vallicellianus*); cf. Martínez Díez, *Colección Hispana* 1.142–143 (D)

Vaticano, Città del, Biblioteca Apostolica Vaticana, Pal. lat. 575, saec. IX–X, unknown Prov. (notice concerning a former owner fol. 3^{r}: 'Iste liber pertinet ad librarium Sancti Martini ecclesiae Maguntinae. M. Sindicus est 1479'), fol. 1–158 contains characteristics of both, the *Gallica* and the *Vulgata* (known as *Codex Vaticanus*); cf. Martínez Díez, *Colección Hispana* 1.120–124 (V); cf. Richter, 'Stufen' 8–10

Wien, Österreichische Nationalbibliothek, lat. 411, saec. VIII–IX, Prov. Eastern France adjoining the Rhineland (probably from Gaul), fol. 1^{v}–310^{r}, cf. complete facsimile edition in the original format of the Codex Vindobonensis 411. Introduction by O. Mazal (Codices selecti phototypice impressi 41; Graz 1974) and CLA 10, no. 1477 pp. 12 and 47; cf. Martínez Díez, *Colección Hispana* 1.104–109 (W); Richter, 'Stufen' 14–15.

A Strasbourg manuscript connected to Bishop Rachio of Strasbourg [a. 787–788] was burnt in 1870 and is described by Dom Pitra in Séjourné, *Saint Isidore* 514–523; cf. also Fuhrmann, *Einfluß und Verbreitung* 1.153 n. 27 with full bibliography on this manuscript

7. *Bibliography*

Maassen, *Geschichte* 710–716; Fournier-Le Bras 1.100–103, 138–139; Kurtscheid-Wilches, 1.109; Van Hove, *Prolegomena* 293

F. H. Knust, *De fontibus et consilio Pseudo-Isidorianae collectionis commentatio* (Göttingen 1832) (cf. the review in: *Freimüthige Blätter über Theologie und Kirchenthum* 5 [1833] 246–250)

F. Maassen, 'Pseudoisidor-Studien', *SB Vienna* 108 (1884) 1061–1104; 109 (1885) 801–860

Séjourné, *Saint Isidore* 427–433

B. Franck, 'Recherches sur le manuscrit de l'Hispana de l'évêque Rachio', *Archives de l'église d'Alsace*, nouv. sér. 7 (1956) 67–82

Contreni, 'Description' 85–89

Williams, *Codices Pseudo-Isidoriani* 107

Fuhrmann, *Einfluß und Verbreitung* 1.151–161

Richter, 'Stufen' 5–16

Collectio Weissenburgensis (Vat. Reg. lat. 423)

1. Author: Unknown. *2. Date:* Eighth century. *3. Place:* Gaul. *4. Type:* Chronologically arranged collection of conciliar councils and decretals; taken from the *Collectio Hispana Gallica*. *5. Edition:* None.

6. *Manuscript*

Vaticano, Città del, Biblioteca Apostolica Vaticana, Reg. lat. 423, saec. IX^{2}, Wissembourg: 'Codex sanctorum Petri et Pauli in Wissenburg ordinis beati Benedicti', fol. 1^{v}–25^{v} cf. Martínez Díez, *Colección Hispana* 1.347–350; Zechiel-Eckes 2.340–341

7. *Bibliography*

Séjourné, *Saint Isidore de Séville* 273–274
A. Wilmart, *Codices Reginenses Latini* 2 (Vatican City 1945) 518–522
C. W. Barlow, *Martini episcopi Bracarensis opera omnia* (Papers and Monographs of the American Academy in Rome 12; New Haven 1950) 94
Martínez Díez, *Colección Hispana* 1.347–350
Mordek, *Kirchenrecht und Reform* 254
Zechiel-Eckes, *Cresconius* 1.192 and 2.340–341

Collectio Hadriano-Hispanica

1. Author: Unknown. *2. Date:* First half of the ninth century. *3. Place:* Unknown. 4. *Type.* Collection of conciliar canons and decretals (cf. Fournier-Le Bras 1.103 n. 2). Synoptic version of the material contained in the *Dionysio-Hadriana* and the *Hispana* in its *Hispana-Gallica* form. *5. Edition:* None.

6. *Manuscripts*

Mantova, Biblioteca Comunale, C.II.23, saec. XII2/2
St. Gallen, Stiftsbibliothek, 671, saec. IX^{in}, Swabia (cf. Autenrieth, *Domschule* 81), pp. 2–82
Vaticano, Città del, Biblioteca Apostolica Vaticana, lat. 1338, saec. XI, France
Venezia, Biblioteca Nazionale Marciana, lat. IV.48 (2301), saec. XV1/2, Italy

7. *Bibliography*

Maassen, *Geschichte* 454; Fournier-Le Bras 1.103

Ballerini, *De antiquis . . . collectionibus et collectoribus* P. III. C. V (PL 56.238–239)
H. Mordek, '*Dictatus papae* e *Proprie auctoritates Apostolice Sedis.* Intorno all'idea del primato pontificio di Gregorio VII', RSCI 28 (1974) 1–22

Collectio Hispana Gallica Augustodunensis

1. Author: Unknown. *2. Date:* Probably after the mid-forties of the ninth century; was consulted by the compilers of the *False Decretals* as well as by Benedictus Levita in the *False Capitularies*; it was probably available for the forgers (if only in parts) by the beginning of the fifties at the latest. *3. Place:* Gaul (manuscript circulation). *4. Type:* Preliminary text for the major part of the Pseudo-Isidorian Decretals. *5. Edition:* None.

6. *Manuscripts*

Berlin, Staatsbibliothek Preussischer Kulturbesitz, Hamilton 132, saec. IX^{in-med}, Prov. Corbie; fol. 1ra–128va, it originally contained a combination of the *Collectio Dionysio-Hadriana* and the *Collectio Sancti Amandi*, but was reworked by the middle of the ninth century into a *Hispana Gallica Augustodunensis*, cf. Boese, *Sammlung Hamilton* 72–75; Mordek, *Bibliotheca capitularium* 29–34

Vaticano, Città del, Biblioteca Apostolica Vaticana, lat. 1341, saec. IX (Wurm 37: saec. X^{ex}), Prov. Autun (the only complete manuscript of this collection), but according to B. Bischoff it was written in Corbie (cf. Mordek, *Kirchenrecht und Reform* 252; Richter, 'Stufen' 22)

Councils based on or derived from the *Collectio Hispana Gallica Augustodunensis* (decretals from Pseudo-Isidore) in the following manuscripts, cf. Richter, 'Stufen' 25–31:

Eton, College Library, B.1.I.6 (James 97), saec. XII

London, British Library, Royal 11.D.IV, saec. XV, copy of Eton, College Library, B.1.I.6

Paris, Bibliothèque nationale, lat. 3855, saec. XV

According to P. Coustant (1721) manuscripts which are now lost were in his day still to be found at Beauvais, Noyon and Laon, cf. Richter, 'Stufen' 30–31

7. *Bibliography*

E. Seckel, 'Pseudoisidor', RE ^{3}16 (1905) 293–295; Fournier-Le Bras 1.138–141, 185–187, 201–202; Van Hove, *Prolegomena* 281–282, 293, 303

Ballerini, *De antiquis . . . collectionibus et collectoribus* pars III, cap. IV § 5 c. 13–17 (PL 56.231–234)

F. H. Knust, *De fontibus et consilio Pseudo-Isidorianae collectionis commentatio* (Göttingen 1832) esp. 7 (cf. *Freimüthige Blätter über Theologie und Kirchentum* 5 [1833] 246–250)

P. Hinschius, 'Die kanonistischen Handschriften der Hamilton'schen Sammlung', ZKG 6 (1884) 193–246

F. Maassen, 'Pseudoisidor-Studien, 2: Die Hispana der Handschrift von Autun und ihre Beziehungen zum Pseudoisidor', *SB Vienna* 108 (1885) 1061–1104 and 109 (1885) 801–860, here 109 (1885) 824–825 and 860

Finsterwalder, *Canones Theodori* 122ff.

Séjourné, *Saint Isidore* 434–443

G. Le Bras, 'Autun dans l'histoire du droit canon', *Mémoires de la Société Eduenne* 48 (1939) 161–174, esp. 165

J. Tarré, 'L'influence des Ecoles dans la transmission des canons médiévaux', *Etudes . . . Le Bras* 1.354

Martínez Díez, *Colección Hispana* 1.355–357 (Emendations based on the *Dionysio-Hadriana* were not taken into account) and 3–5 (1982–1992)

S. Williams, 'Appollinaris Sidonii Epistola ad Dominicum IV, 25', *Manuscripta* 11 (1967) 48–51

Fuhrmann, *Einfluß und Verbreitung* 1.151–161

Richter, 'Stufen' 16–31

Contreni, 'Description' 85–89

R. E. Reynolds, 'Pseudonymous Liturgica in early mediaeval canonical collections', *Fälschungen im Mittelalter* 2.67–77

Tabulae Hispanae

1. Author: Unknown. *2. Date:* About 590 (Séjourné, Tarré) but second half of the seventh century according to Le Bras ('Isidore de Séville' 239–240). Perhaps tenth century (García y García), cf. G. Martínez Díez, 'Una colección canónica Pirenaica del s. XI', *Miscelánea Comillas* 28 (1959) 213–270; *3. Place:* Perhaps Catalonia. *4. Type:* Index of the *Collectio Hispana.*

5. Edition

Martínez Díez, *Colección Hispana* 2.501–583

6. Manuscripts

Gerona, Archivo de la Santa Iglesia Catedral Basílica, Códice Conciliar, saec. IX^{in}, Prov. probably Gerona, fol. I^{v}–XXII^{r}, chronological *Hispana, Vulgata*-recension, Catalan-Form (known as *Codex Gerundensis*); cf. Martínez Díez 1.141–142 (G)

Paris, Bibliothèque nationale, lat. 1568 (*Tabulae* and *Collectio Sancti Amandi*); saec. IX–XV, miscellaneous codex, Prov. probably France (the manuscript came from the Biblioteca Colbertina, cf. Martínez Díez 489); fol. 67^{r}–74^{r}, saec. XII: *Tabulae Hispanae* ('las mismas que encabezan los dos manuscritos de la Familia Catalan') cf. Martínez Díez, *Coleccion Hispana* 1.365–366

Paris, Bibliothèque nationale, lat. 3850, saec. XVI (copy of the manuscript Seo de Urgel 2005)

Seo de Urgel, Biblioteca Capitular, 2005, saec. XI^{ex}, fol. 5^{r}–13^{r} (incomplete), chronological *Hispana, Vulgata*-recension, Catalan-Form (known as Codex Urgelensis); cf. Martínez Díez 1.139–141 (U)

7. Bibliography

Fournier-Le Bras 1.69–70; Van Hove, *Prolegomena* 282

Tarré, 'Sources' 132–133
Séjourné, *Saint Isidore* 321–336, esp. 324–327
Le Bras, 'Isidore de Séville' 239–242
Martínez Díez, *Colección Hispana* 2.487–498

Collectio Hispana systematica

1. Author. Bishop Julian of Toledo (680–690)? (cf. Maassen, Séjourné). *2. Date:* cf. 'Author', but according to Le Bras written in Gaul, the middle of the ninth century. *3. Place:* cf. 'Author', 'Date'. *4. Type:* Systematic collection.

5. Editions

Martínez Díez, *Colección Hispana* 2.1.277–426 (Books, titles and rubrics of the 1630 chapters of the collection)

Description of the Mozarabic version with concordance to *Collectio Hispana systematica:* ibid., 2.619–715

6. *Manuscripts*

Lyon, Bibliothèque de la ville, 336 (olim 383), saec. IX, Lyon (Waitz, *Archiv* 7, 211 and Schulte, 'Iter Gallicum' 389; saec. VIII^{med}–IX according to Delandine, *Manuscrits de la bibliothèque de Lyon* [Paris 1812])

Paris, Bibliothèque nationale, lat. 1565, saec. X–XI, Southern France; perhaps Lyon according to A. Wilmart, 'Fragments carolingiens du fonds Baluze', RB 43 (1931) 106–115, esp. 108,

Paris, Bibliothèque nationale, lat. 11709 (olim St. Germain 364), saec. IX^{in}, Lyon

Arabic Translation

El Escorial, Real Biblioteca de San Lorenzo, ms. arab. 1623, saec. XI, fol. 1^{r}–435^{v}, in Arabic. This codex was kept at the Biblioteca Nacional in Madrid for several years under the shelf-mark manuscript 4879. Cf. G. de Andrés, 'Un valioso códice árabe de concilios españoles recuperado para El Escorial', *La Ciudad de Dios* 179 (1966) 681–695; P. Sjoerd van Koningsveld, 'La literatura cristiano-árabe de la España medieval y significado de la transmisión textual en árabe de la Collectio Conciliorum', *Concilio III de Toledo* 695–710

Lisboa, Arquivo Nacional da Torre do Tombo, Sé de Coimbra, 2^{a}. incorporaçao 45, Doc. 1806 (saec. XI, according to A. Keller this manuscript contains a fragment of the Arab version of the *Hispana*)

7. *Bibliography*

Maassen, *Geschichte* 813–821; Fournier-Le Bras 1.102; Kurtscheid-Wilches 1.108; Van Hove, *Prolegomena* 282

Séjourné, *Saint Isidore* 331–333

Le Bras, 'Isidore de Séville' 250–252

G. de Andrés, 'Un valioso códice árabe de concilios españoles recuperado para el Escorial', *La Ciudad de Dios* 179 (1966) 681–695

G. Martínez Díez, 'Un tratado visigótico sobre la penitencia', HS 19 (1966) 89–98

G. Haenni, 'Notes sur les sources de la Dacheriana', SG 11 (1967) 3–22

M. Díaz y Díaz, 'La circulation des manuscrits dans la Péninsule Ibérique du VIIIe au XIe siècle', CCM 12 (1969) 219–241, 383–392

F. Rodríguez, 'El crecimiento de la Colección Canónica Hispana a través de sus "Capitula",' *Miscelánea Comillas* 30 (1972) 5–24

Mordek, *Kirchenrecht und Reform* 12, 22 n. 7, 181, 259–260

Martínez Díez, *Colección Hispana* 2.587–615 ('IV. La Colección sistematica mozarabe')

R. E. Reynolds, 'The "Isidorian" *Epistula ad Leudefredum*: An Early Medieval Epitome of the Clerical Duties', MS 41 (1979) 252–330

E. Tejero Tejero, 'Los "excerpta" de la Hispana: Originalidad de su sistemática', *La norma en el derecho canónico: Actas del III Congresso internacional de derecho canonico, Pamplona 10–15 octubre 1976*, 1 (Pamplona 1979) 143–161

Mordek, 'Systematische Kanonessammlungen' 186

R. E. Reynolds, 'Rites and signs of conciliar decisions', *Segni e Riti nella Chiesa altomedievale occidentale (11–17 aprile 1985)* (Settimane di Studio del Centro Italiano di Studi sull'alto Medioevo 33; Spoleto 1987) 1.207–249

M.-T. Urvoy, 'Note de Philologie Mozarabe', *Arabica* 36 (1989) 236–237

Collectio Hibernensis

1. Author: Unknown. *2. Date:* First half of the eighth century at the latest, cf. O'Corráin. *3. Place:* Ireland. *4. Type:* Systematic collection.

5. Edition

H. Wasserschleben (ed.), *Die irische Kanonensammlung* (Leipzig ^{2}1885; repr. Aalen 1966)

6. Manuscripts

Form A (Shorter Version)

London, British Library, Cotton Otho E. XIII, saec. X^{in} according to L. Bieler, *Irish Penitentials* 14 and R. Kottje, *Studien zum Einfluß des Alten Testamentes auf Recht und Liturgie des frühen Mittelalters (6.–8. Jahrhundert)* (Bonner Historische Forschungen 23; Bonn 1964) 65, n.44; saec. X–XI according to Ker, *Medieval Libraries of Great Britain*^{2} 43; Prov. Canterbury (Part 1 is, according to Sheehy, a corrected version of the alpha-form; Part 2 has not been classified)

Orléans, Bibliothèque municipale, 221 (193), saec. IX^{in}, Brittany: Bischoff, 'Panorama der Handschriftenüberlieferung' 239; saec. VIII–IX, Prov. Fleury: Bieler, *Irish Penitentials* 12; written by Junobrus

Paris, Bibliothèque nationale, lat. 3182, saec. X^{2}: Bischoff, saec. X^{1}: Bieler, *Irish Penitentials* 12; written by a Breton named Maeloc; Prov. Fécamp; on the manuscript cf. Mordek, *Kirchenrecht und Reform* 153 and Mordek, *Bibliotheca capitularium* 433–435

Paris, Bibliothèque nationale, lat. 12021 (olim Sangerman. 121), saec. X^{in}, written in Brittany by Arbedoc; Prov. Corbie; fol. 33–139, cf. Bieler, *Irish Penitentials* 14. The whole content analyzed by Maassen, *Geschichte* 786–787 under the heading of 'Sammlung des Codex Sangermanensis 121'; cf. below, *Collectio Sangermanensis (Paris lat. 12021)*

St. Gallen, Stiftsbibliothek, 243, saec. IX^{1}, Saint Gall; cf. Bruckner, *Scriptoria medii aevi Helvetica* 2 (1936) 74, 3 (1938) 23

Form B (Longer Version)

Karlsruhe, Badische Landesbibliothek, Aug. XVIII, saec. IX^{in}, Reichenau, fol. 75^{r}–90^{v}, fragment; cf. A. Holder, 'Die Reichenauer Handschriften 1: Die Pergamenthandschriften', *Die Handschriften der Badischen Landesbibliothek in Karlsruhe* 5 (Heidelberg 1906, repr. Wiesbaden 1970 with supplementary bibliographical references) 58–69 (esp. 68) and 645–646; supplement also in Vol. 2 (6, ^{2}1971) 659 (According to Sheehy: 'Alpha-Form')

Livorno, Biblioteca Comunale, Fondo Labronica, sine num. (olim no. 10), saec. XI–XII, probably Northern Italy, cf. A. Gaudenzi, 'Un nuovo ms. delle collezioni irlandese e pseudoisidoriana e degli estratti bobbiesi', QF 10 (1907) 370–379; C. G. Mor, 'Una piccola collezione di testi gregoriani del secolo VIII', *Etudes . . . Le Bras* 1.283–291; Williams, *Codices Pseudo-Isidoriani* 28–29, 136–137, 143–144 and Landau, 'Kanonessammlungen in der Lombardei' 446 including n. 84; according to Sheehy 'Alpha-Form'

Oxford, Bodleian Library, Hatton 42, saec. IX^{1} and med. according to Bischoff, saec. IX^{2} according to Bieler, *Irish Penitentials* 13; saec. IX–X according to Ker, *Medieval Libraries of Great Britain*^{2} 209, Bretagne; Prov. Worcester, like Cod. Cambridge CCC. 279 (cf. 'Derivations of the *Hibernensis* according to Reynolds')

Roma, Biblioteca Vallicelliana, T.XVIII, about saec. X^{ex}, Italy; Mordek, *Kirchenrecht und Reform* 134, n. 172; saec. XI^{1}, Southern Italy (Reynolds); cf. below, *Collectio Bibliotecae Vallicellianae T.XVIII*

Fragments

München, Bayerische Staatsbibliothek, Clm 29051(b), saec. VIII–IX, written on the continent in a scriptorium under Irish influence; according to CLA 2^{2} no. 144, pp. 8 and 49

München, Bayerische Staatsbibliothek, Clm 29410/2, written on the continent in an Irish hand, cf. Reynolds, 'Unity and Diversity' 104

Trier, Stadtbibliothek, 137/50, saec. VIII^{2}, written in Ireland or on the continent in a scriptorium under Irish influence, fol. 48^{r}–61^{v}, palimpsest, younger script (saec. XI): Augustine, *De civitate Dei*; according to CLA 9 no. 1368, pp. 37 and 66; CLA Suppl. p. 64

Excerpt

Dates from the eighth century transmitting the first half of the collection up to title XXXVIII, Chapter 18

Cambrai, Bibliothèque municipale, 679 (619), saec. VIII^{2}, between 763 and 790, Northeastern France (Péronne?); cf. Bischoff, 'Panorama der Handschriftenüberlieferung' 237; CLA 6 no. 741, pp. 12–13 and 43; CLA Suppl. p. 57

Chartres, Bibliothèque municipale, 124 (127), saec. XI^{in} from Notre-Dame at Chartres, according to A. Wilmart, 'Lettres de l'époque carolingienne', RB 34 (1922) 238. The manuscript was destroyed during World War II, cf. *Speculum* 29 (1954) 336 and Masson, *Manuscrits des Bibliothèques sinistrées* 11

Köln, Erzbischöfliche Diözesan- und Dombibliothek, 210 (olim Darmstadt 2178), saec. VIII^{2}, Northeastern France; cf. CLA 8 no. 1161, pp. 39 and 65–66; CLA Suppl. p. 62

Tours, Bibliothèque municipale, 556, saec. IX4/4, from Marmoutier near Tours; cf. A. Wilmart, 'Lettres de l'époque carolingienne', RB 34 (1922) 239; E. K. Rand, *Studies in the Script of Tours, 1: A Survey of the Manuscripts of Tours* (The Mediaeval Academy of America 3, Cambridge, Mass. 1929) no. 174, 72 and 187 and Table CLXXVII, 2 (reproduction of fol. 48^{r}). Like Chartres 124 this codex was also destroyed during World War II, cf. *Speculum* 29 (1954) 337 and Masson, *Manuscrits des Bibliothèques sinistrées* 12

Excerpts

For the separate circulation of title XLVI [*'De ratione matrimonii'*] or excerpts from title XLVI cf. Maassen, *Geschichte* 885 n. 7, Fournier, 'Influence' 33–34, Fournier-Le Bras 1.276 n. 1 and n. 2; Mordek, *Kirchenrecht und Reform* 259 and Reynolds, 'Unity and Diversity' 115–116)

Albi, Bibliothèque municipale, 38bis, saec. IX$^{ca.\ med}$, Southern France

Arras, Bibliothèque municipale, 425

Avranches, Bibliothèque municipale, 146

Bamberg, Staatsbibliothek, Can. 9 (olim P.I.9)

Bamberg, Staatsbibliothek, 127 (B V 24), saec. XII, together with the *Collectaneum* of Sedulius Scottus; cf. Reynolds, 'Unity and Diversity' 117

Barcelona, Archivo de la Corona de Aragón, Ripoll 105, saec. XIII, Ripoll

Berlin, Staatsbibliothek Preußischer Kulturbesitz, Phill. 1763, saec. IX^{in}, Southern part of France

Bern, Burgerbibliothek, 89, saec. IX^{in}, probably Alsace, fol. 2ra and fol. 3^{rb-va}: *Collectio Hibernensis* XXI, 29; fol. 3vb and fol. 169vb–171va other short texts and excerpts from the *Collectio Hibernensis*, cf. Mordek, *Bibliotheca capitularium* 73–74 and 76

Bernkastel-Kues, Bibliothek des St.-Nikolaus-Hospitals, 52 (37; C 14), saec. XII; together with the *Collectaneum* of Sedulius Scottus (cf. Reynolds, 'Unity and Diversity' 117)

Bruxelles, Bibliothèque Royale Albert Ier, 8654–72, saec. VIII–IX, Prov. Saint-Bertin

Cambridge, Library of Corpus Christi College, 279, saec. IX^{2}, region around Tours: B. Bischoff (quoted in Bieler, *Irish Penitentials* 15), later at Worcester; cf. Ker, *Medieval Libraries of Great Britain*^{2} 206

Einsiedeln, Stiftsbibliothek, 205, saec. IX2/4, Switzerland

Firenze, Biblioteca Medicea Laurenziana, VII sin. 1 (excerpts from Burchard), fol. 152va–155ra (S. Croce, cf. Fransen, 'Manuscrits' 67)

Firenze, Biblioteca Medicea Laurenziana, XX 48

Firenze, Biblioteca Medicea Laurenziana, Ashburnham 82 (32), saec. IX3/4 Western France

Firenze, Biblioteca Medicea Laurenziana, Calci 11, fol. 181rb–183rb, cf. Mordek, 'Handschriftenforschungen' 637, 646; Fransen, 'Manuscrits' 67

Freiburg (Breisgau), Universitätsbibliothek, 8, saec. IX^{2}, Lake Constance region, cf. Autenrieth, *Domschule* 68

Laon, Bibliothèque municipale, 201, saec. IX$^{ca\,.\,.med}$, Cambrai?

London, British Library, Cotton Cleopatra C. VIII, saec. XII

London, British Library, Royal 5.E.XIII, saec. IX, Prov. Worcester, fol. 52^{r}–68^{v}: used excerpts from the *Hibernensis*

Madrid, Biblioteca Nacional, 373 (olim A. 151), saec. XII, Southern Italy

Metz, Bibliothèque municipale, 236, saec. VIII–IX, probably Rhine region, destroyed

Monte Cassino, Archivio e Biblioteca dell'Abbazia, 1, saec. XI, Southern Italy

Monte Cassino, Archivio e Biblioteca dell'Abbazia, 297, saec. XI^{in}, Southern Italy (Reynolds), p. 204–248, Beneventan script; cf. E. A. Loew (=Lowe), *The Beneventan Script: A History of the South Italian Minuscule* (Oxford 1914) 220, 348; M. Inguañez, *Codicum Casinensium manuscriptorum catalogus* 2.1 (Monte Cassino 1928) 118–119

Monte Cassino, Archivio e Biblioteca dell'Abbazia, 439, saec. X, Southern Italy, chap. 128–129 (ed. *Spicilegium Casinense* 1.397–398, including the chapters XXXIX, 4c, a, b also in the *Vetus Gallica* [XLVI, 22–24])

Montpellier, Bibliothèque Interuniversitaire, H.137, cf. Fournier, 'Manuscrit de Montpellier' 357–389

München, Bayerische Staatsbibliothek, Clm 4592, saec. IX2/4, from Benediktbeuern, cf. Mordek, *Kirchenrecht und Reform* 258

München, Bayerische Staatsbibliothek, Clm 6241, saec. X3/3, Freising; cf. Mordek, *Bibliotheca capitularium* 319–321
München, Bayerische Staatsbibliothek, Clm 6242, saec. IX1/3, Freising
München, Bayerische Staatsbibliothek, Clm 6245, saec. X^2, Freising, fol. 59^v, cf. Mordek, *Bibliotheca capitularium* 325
München, Bayerische Staatsbibliothek, Clm 6433, saec. VIII, Freising
München, Bayerische Staatsbibliothek, Clm 6434, saec. VIII^{ex}, Freising
München, Bayerische Staatsbibliothek, Clm 14468 (a. 821) St. Emmeram, Regensburg, fol. 16^r–20^r: *Collectio Hibernensis* 38.1; 40.5; 27.8–9; 29.2; 28.11; 17.6; 64.4; cf. Mordek, *Bibliotheca capitularium* 336
Münster, Nordrhein-Westfälisches Staatsarchiv, VII.5201, saec. X2/4 (probably 945 or later), Corvey; p. 94–103, cf. Mordek, *Bibliotheca capitularium* 381
Oxford, Bodleian Library, 572, saec. IX1/2, Northern France
Padova, Biblioteca Antoniana, 27, saec. IX^{ex} (after 880) Verona
Palermo, Archivio della Cattedrale, 14, saec. XII, Palermo
Paris, Bibliothèque nationale, lat. 1557, saec. IX3/4, Northern France, Laon?
Paris, Bibliothèque nationale, lat. 2316, saec. IX2/4, Southern France
Paris, Bibliothèque nationale, lat. 3839, saec. XI2/2, France
Paris, Bibliothèque nationale, lat. 3839A, saec. XI2/2, Saint-Aubin, Angers
Paris, Bibliothèque nationale, lat. 3852
Paris, Bibliothèque nationale, lat. 3859, saec. $IX^{med\text{-}3/4}$, Gaul
Paris, Bibliothèque nationale, lat. 4281A, saec. XII, Prov. a monastery of Beaupré
Paris, Bibliothèque nationale, lat. 10588, saec. IX1/2, Southern France, Burgundy
Paris, Bibliothèque nationale, lat. 12444 (olim Sangerman. 938), saec. VIII–IX, probably from Fleury; Prov. Corbie; cf. Bischoff, 'Panorama der Handschriftenüberlieferung' 241 n. 53; Böhringer, DA 46 (1990) 23; cf. also Mordek, *Kirchenrecht und Reform* 145. According to Maassen, *Geschichte* 885 and Wasserschleben, *Irische Kanonensammlung*[2] (cf. above 'Edition'), p. xxvii, the shorter excerpts contained in the codices München, Bayerische Staatsbibliothek, Clm 4592, saec. IX1/2, Prov. Benediktbeuern; cf. Bischoff, *Schreibschulen* 1.46, and Wien, Österreichische Nationalbibliothek, lat. 522, saec. IX2/3, Salzburg [B. Bischoff] are closely related to this excerpt. The *Hibernensis*-canons in Clm 6434, fol. 41^r–75^r, saec. VIII^{ex}, Freising; CLA 9 no. 1285, p. 16 and 63 are part of the same tradition
Rouen, Bibliothèque municipale, 702 (E.27)
Salzburg, Bibliothek der Erzabtei St. Peter a.IX.32, saec. XI, Cologne, cf. Kottje, 'Salzburger Handschrift' 286–290 or Salzburg
St. Gallen, Stiftsbibliothek, 675, saec. IX1/2, probably Bavaria
St. Petersburg, Rossiyskaya Natsional'naya Biblioteka, Q.v.II.5, saec. IX4/4, Cambrai?
Torino, Biblioteca Nazionale Universitaria, E.IV.44, saec. XIII
Vaticano, Città del, Archivio di San Pietro, H.58, ca. 1000, Rome; cf. Kottje, *Bußbücher Halitgars* 65–69; Date: F. De Marco, 'Censimento dei codici dei secoli X–XII', SM 11 (1970) 1132–1133; cf. also the date assigned by B. Bischoff, cf. D. Sicard, *La Liturgie de la mort dans l'église latine des origines à la réforme carolingienne* (Liturgiewissenschaftliche Quellen und Forschungen 63; Münster 1978) xiv and 115 n. 33; Reynolds, 'Excerpta' 4–9; cf. G. Schmitz, 'Vier-Bücher-Samm-

lung' 234: the following fol. 117^{r}–118^{r} contain 16 canons [3.96–99 and 4.38–49] of the *Collectio 4 librorum* (Cod. Köln 124); cf. also Hoffmann-Pokorny 75 n. 38

Vaticano, Città del, Biblioteca Apostolica Vaticana, lat. 1349, saec. XI1/2, Southern Italy

Vaticano, Città del, Biblioteca Apostolica Vaticana, lat. 3791

Vaticano, Città del, Biblioteca Apostolica Vaticana, lat. 4162, saec. XII, fol. 35^{r}–37^{v} (from books I–IV; cf. Reynolds, 'Excerpta' 3–4)

Vaticano, Città del, Biblioteca Apostolica Vaticana, lat. 5748, saec. X^{in}, fol. 7^{r-v}, Prov. Bobbio, saec. IX–X, cf. Kottje, 'Einheit und Vielfalt' 339 n. 69 and Landau, 'Kanonessammlungen in der Lombardei' 446 with n. 84

Vaticano, Città del, Biblioteca Apostolica Vaticana, Ottobon. lat. 6, saec. X, Nonantola, cf. Reynolds, 'Excerpta' 2–3

Vaticano, Città del, Biblioteca Apostolica Vaticana, Pal. lat. 577, saec. VIII–IX, German-Insular scriptorium (Hersfeld or Mainz), fol. 2^{r}: *Collectio Hibernensis* XI.1a and XXI, 16, 17g and 13a, cf. Mordek, *Bibliotheca capitularium* 775

Vaticano, Città del, Biblioteca Apostolica Vaticana, Reg. lat. 407, saec. IX^{med}, region around St. Gallen

Vaticano, Città del, Biblioteca Apostolica Vaticana, Reg. lat. 421, saec. IX2–3/3, Saint Gall

Verona, Biblioteca Capitolare, LXIII (61), saec. X$^{med-2/2}$, Northern Italy, Verona?

Vesoul, Bibliothèque municipale, 79 (73), saec. X^{ex}

Wien, Österreichische Nationalbibliothek, lat. 424, saec. IX2/4, Salzburg

Wien, Österreichische Nationalbibliothek, lat. 522, saec. IX2/3, Salzburg, cf. Mordek, *Kirchenrecht und Reform* 258

Wien, Österreichische Nationalbibliothek, lat. 1370, saec. IX1/4, Mondsee

Wien, Österreichische Nationalbibliothek, lat. 2171, saec. IX3/4, Southwestern Germany

Wien, Österreichische Nationalbibliothek, lat. 2198

Wien, Österreichische Nationalbibliothek, lat. 2232, saec. IX^{in}; Southeastern Germany, fol. 78^{v}–84^{r}, cf. Mordek, *Bibliotheca capitularium* 911–915

Wolfenbüttel, Herzog August Bibliothek, Helmst. 532 (579), saec. IX2/4, Salzburg; fol. 137^{v}; cf. Reynolds, 'Unity and Diversity' 116 ('Salzburg Fragments'); Mordek, *Bibliotheca capitularium* 955

Würzburg, Universitätsbibliothek, M.p.th.q. 31, saec. VIII–IX, probably Germany (Anglo-Saxon scriptorium); fol. 1^{r}–41^{r}, and 52^{r}–59^{r}, cf. CLA 9 no. 1439, p. 56 and 70; CLA Suppl. p. 65; analyzed by Nürnberger, 'Über die Würzburger Handschrift der irischen Canonensammlung', AKKR 60 (1888) 3–84, cf. Würzburg, Universitätsbibliothek M.p.th.q. 31, fol. 52–59 defined by Reynolds as a separate collection dependent on the *Hibernensis* (Reynolds, 'Unity and Diversity' 110) cf. Mordek, *Bibliotheca capitularium* 960–964

Now-lost manuscript written in early Carolingian Salzburg: cf. B. Bischoff, 'Salzburger Formelbücher und Briefe aus Tassilonischer und Karolingischer Zeit', SB Munich 1972, 5 (Munich 1973) 51–52; Reynolds, 'Unity and Diversity' 116–117

Additionally there are the following collections and penitentials containing excerpts of the Hibernensis: *Capitula Theodori; Excerpta Egberti;* Council of Tribur, *Collectio duodecim partium, Decretum Burchardi, Collectio 4 librorum;* cf. esp. Fournier, 'Influence', and Reynolds, 'Unity and Diversity'

Derivations of the Hibernensis

According to Reynolds, 'Unity and Diversity' 105–108

Cambridge, Library of Corpus Christi College, 279, saec. IX^2, near Tours, copy of a Breton manuscript according to A. J. Frantzen, 'The Significance of the Frankish Penitentials', JEH 30 (1979) 419 n. 73

Würzburg, Universitätsbibliothek M.p.th.q. 31

Collectio 250 capitulorum—cf. below

Paris, Bibliothèque nationale, lat. 12444, fol. 75^v–96^v and 105^r–136^v (the *Sangermanensis*-derivation, Prov. Fleury?), cf. Reynolds 'Unity and Diversity' 107

London, British Library, Royal 5.E.XIII, saec. IX, Prov. Worcester, fol. 52^r–68^v

7. *Bibliography*

Maassen, *Geschichte* 877–885; Fournier-Le Bras 1.62–64; Kurtscheid-Wilches 1.110–112; Van Hove, *Prolegomena* 290–291; Zeiger, *Historia iur. can.* 1.43–44; Stickler, *Historia* 1.93–94; R. Naz, 'Hibernensis (collectio)', DDC 5 (1953) 1124–1125; Ludwig Bieler, 'Hibernensis Collectio', NCE 6 (1967) 1095; D. O'Corráin, 'Hibernensis. Collectio canonum', LMA 4 (1989) 2207

Ballerini, *De antiquis . . . collectionibus et collectoribus*, P. IV, c. VII, § 1 (PL 56.302–304)

A. J. Nürnberger, 'Über die Würzburger Handschrift der irischen Canonensammlung', AKKR 60 (1888) 3–84

A. J. Nürnberger, 'Über eine ungedruckte Kanonessammlung aus dem 8. Jahrhundert', *25. Bericht der wissenschaftlichen Gesellschaft Philomathie in Neisse vom Oktober 1888 bis zum Oktober 1890* (Neisse 1890) 125–197

H. Bradshaw, *The Early Collection of Canons Known as the Hibernensis: Two Unfinished Papers* (Cambridge 1893)

Fournier, 'Influence' 27–78

E. W. B. Nicholson, 'The Origin of the 'Hibernian' Collection of Canons', *Zeitschrift für Celtische Philologie* 3 (1901) 99–103

T. S. Hellmann, *Sedulius Scottus* (Quellen und Untersuchungen zur lateinischen Philologie des Mittelalters I, 1; 1906) 136–144

A. Gaudenzi, 'Un nuovo Ms delle collezioni Irlandese e Pseudoisidoriana e degli estratti Bobbiesi', QF 10 (1907) 370–379

R. Thurneysen 'Zur irischen Kanonensammlung', *Zeitschrift für Celtische Philologie* 6 (1907) 1–5

P. Fournier, 'Le *Liber ex lege Moysi* et les tendances bibliques du droit canonique irlandais', *Revue celtique* 30 (1909) 221–234

W. Levison, 'Die Iren und die fränkische Kirche', HZ 109 (1912) 1–22, esp. 9–12 (repr.: *Aus rheinischer und fränkischer Frühzeit* [Düsseldorf 1948] 247–263)

Fournier, 'Recueils canoniques italiens' 95–213

H. von Schubert, *Geschichte der christlichen Kirche im Frühmittelalter* (Tübingen 1921, repr. Darmstadt 1962) 533

A. Wilmart, 'Lettres de l'époque carolingienne', RB 34 (1922) 234–242 (edition of the *praefatio* to the *Hibernensis*)

Fournier, 'Notices' 219

J. F. Kenney, *The Sources for the Early History of Ireland,* 1: *Ecclesiastical* (Records of Civilization: Sources and Studies; New York 1929, repr. New York 1966) 247–250

K. Christ, *Die Bibliothek des Klosters Fulda im 16. Jahrhundert. Die Handschriftenverzeichnisse* (64. Beiheft zum Zentralblatt für Bibliothekswesen Leipzig 1933; repr. Wiesbaden 1968) (on the still unidentified codex of the *Collectio Hibernensis* which used to be kept at the library of the monastery of Fulda p. 138, 265 and passim)

Munier, *Sources patristiques* 30–32

Ryan, 'Observations' 91

Clavis 399, no. 1794 (giving a mistaken account of the results of Wilmarts' research: W. examined only the special introduction contained in Chartres 124 [127], which he interpreted as a letter of Hrabanus Maurus to the empress Judith, not as a prologue characteristic of the form A)

Bieler, *Irish Penitentials* passim

Mor, 'La Bibbia e il diritto canonico', 163–179

R. Kottje, *Studien zum Einfluß des Alten Testamentes auf Recht und Liturgie des frühen Mittelalters (6.–8. Jahrhundert)* (Bonner Historische Forschungen 23; Bonn 1964) 11–12

M. Sheehy, 'Influences of Ancient Irish Law on the Collectio Canonum Hibernensis', *Proceedings Strasbourg* 31–41.

J. Morales, 'La doctrina teologica y los doctos en la Colección Hibernense', *Ius canonicum* 12 [24] (1972) 280–286

Mordek, *Kirchenrecht und Reform* 13, 255–259

Reynolds, 'Excerpta' 1–9

M. J. Faris (ed.), *The Bishop's Synod ('The First Synod of St. Patrick'): A Symposium with Text Translation and Commentary* (ARCA Classical and Mediaeval Texts, Papers and Monographs 1; Liverpool 1976)

K. Hughes, '*Synodus II S. Patricii* in Latin Script and Letters A.D. 400–900', *Festschrift presented to Ludwig Bieler on the occasion of his 70th birthday,* ed. J. J. O'Meara and B. Naumann (Leiden 1976) 141–147

P. Salmon, 'Un 'Libellus officialis' du XIe siècle', RB 87 (1977) 257–288

J. J. Contreni, *The Cathedral School of Laon from 850 to 930: Its Manuscripts and Masters* (Münchener Beiträge zur Mediävistik und Renaissance-Forschung 29; Munich 1978) 82 (copies of the *Hibernensis* at Cambrai during the late eighth century)

M. P. Sheehy, 'The *Collectio canonum Hibernensis*—A Celtic phenomenon', *Die Iren und Europa im früheren Mittelalter,* ed. H. Löwe (Veröffentlichungen des Europa Zentrums Tübingen, Kulturwissenschaftliche Reihe; Stuttgart 1982) 1.525–535

L. Breatnach, 'Canon Law and Secular Law in Early Ireland: The Significance of Bretha Nemed', *Peritia* 3 (1983) 439–458

A. Breen, 'Some Seventh-Century Hiberno-Latin Texts and their Relationships', *Peritia* 3 (1983) 204–214

C. Doherty, 'The Basilica in Early Ireland', *Peritia* 3 (1983) 303–315

Reynolds, 'Unity and Diversity' 99–135 (Manuscripts and derivations of the *Hibernensis)*

D. N. Dumville, 'On the Dating of Early Breton Lawcodes' ECelt 21 (1984) 207–221

T. O'Raifeartaigh, 'A Rationale for the Censuring of Saint Patrick by the Seniores', *Celtica* 16 (1984) 13–32

J. Gaudemet, 'La Bible dans les collections canoniques', *Le Moyen Age et la Bible*, ed. P. Riché and G. Lobrichon (Bible de tous les temps 4; Paris 1984) 327–367

D. O'Corráin, 'Irish law and canon law', *Irland und Europa/Ireland and Europe: Die Kirche im Frühmittelalter/The Early Church*, ed. P. N. Chatháin and M. Richter (Veröffentlichungen des Europa Zentrums Tübingen, Kulturwissenschaftliche Reihe; Stuttgart 1984) 157–166

D. O'Corrain, L. Breatnach, A. Breen, 'The laws of the Irish', *Peritia* 3 (1984) 382–438 (review, cf. DA 42 [1986] 295 by R. Schieffer)

R. Sharpe, 'Gildas as a Father of the Church', *Gildas: New Approaches*, ed. M. Lapidge and D. N. Dumville (Woodbridge 1984) 193–205

M. Enright, *Iona, Tara and Soissons: The Origin of the Royal Anointing Ritual* (Arbeiten zur Frühmittelalterforschung 17; Berlin-New York 1985)

L. M. Bitel, 'Women's Monastic Enclosures in Early Ireland: A Study of Female Spirituality and Male Monastic Mentalities', JMH 12 (1986) 15–36

M. Pryce, 'Early Irish Canons and Medieval Welsh Law', *Peritia* 5 (1986) 107–127

M. Gerriets, 'Kingship and Exchange in Pre-Viking Ireland' *Cambridge Medieval Celtic Studies* 13 (1987) 39–72

C. Piacitelli, 'L'Europa nei secoli XI e XII fra novità e tradizione: Sviluppi di una cultura' (Passo della Mendola 25–29 agosto 1986), RSCI 47 (1987) 239–247

M. P. Sheehy, 'The Bible and the Collectio canonum Hibernensis', *Irland und die Christenheit, Ireland and Christendom: Bibelstudium und Mission: The Bible and the Missions*, ed. P. N. Chatháin and M. Richter (Veröffentlichungen des Europa Zentrums Tübingen, Kulturwissenschaftliche Reihe; Stuttgart 1987) 277–283

J. Higgitt, 'The Iconography of St. Peter in Anglo-Saxon England and St. Cuthbert's Coffin', *St. Cuthbert, His Cult and His Community to AD 1200*, ed. G. Bonner, D. Rollason, and C. Stancliffe, (Woodbridge 1989) 267–285

Landau, 'Kanonessammlungen in der Lombardei', 446

M. Walsh and D. O. Crónin (ed. trad.), *Cummian's Letter 'De controversia paschali', Together with a Related Irish Computistical Tract 'De ratione computandi'* (Toronto 1989)

Marilyn Gerriets, 'Theft, Penitentials and the Compilation of the Early Irish Laws', *Celtica* 22 (1991) 18–32

J. Gaudemet, 'Sagesse biblique et droit canonique', *Letture cristiane dei Libri Sapienziali: XX Incontro di studiosi dell'antichità cristiana, Roma, 9–11 maggio 1991* (Studia Ephemeridis 'Augustinianum' 37; Rome 1992) 127–144

Siems, *Handel und Wucher* 580–583

Zechiel-Eckes, *Cresconius* (cf. index)

P. Petitmengin, 'La compilation 'De vindictis magnis magnorum peccatorum'. Exemples d'anthropophagie tirés des sièges de Jérusalem et de Samarie', *Philologia Sacra: Biblische und patristische Studien für Hermann J. Frede und Walter Thiele zu ihrem siebzigsten Geburtstag*, ed. R. Gryson (Freiburg 1993) 2.622–638

R. Meens, 'A Background to Augustine's Mission in Anglo-Saxon England', *Anglo-Saxon England* 23 (1994) 5–17

Collectio 30 capitulorum (De ratione matrimonii)

1. *Author:* Unknown. 2. *Date:* Ninth century. 3. *Place:* Germany. 4. *Type:* Excerpt of Book 46 of the *Collectio Hibernensis.*

5. Edition

F. Kunstmann, 'Das Eherecht des Bischofes Bernhard von Pavia, mit geschichtlicher Einleitung', AKKR 6 (1861) 3–14 (according to München, Clm 6242)

6. Manuscripts

Avranches, Bibliothèque municipale, 146, saec. XII, Reims region
Bamberg, Staatsbibliothek, Can. 9 (P.I.9), fol. 1–127: saec. XI1–2/3, Freising; fol. 128–232: saec. XI^{in}, Southern Germany
Firenze, Biblioteca Medicea Laurenziana, XX 48
London, British Library, Cotton Cleopatra C.VIII, saec. XII
Monte Cassino, Archivio e Biblioteca dell'Abbazia, 1, saec. XI; Southern Italy
Montpellier, Bibliothèque Interuniversitaire, H.137, saec. XI, France
München, Bayerische Staatsbibliothek, Clm 6241, saec. X3/3, Freising
München, Bayerische Staatsbibliothek, Clm 6242, saec. IX1/3, Freising
München, Bayerische Staatsbibliothek, Clm 6245, saec. X2/2, Carinthia, Prov. Freising
Palermo, Archivio della Cattedrale, 14, saec. XII, France
Paris, Bibliothèque nationale, lat. 1557, part of Paris, lat. 9629, saec. IX3/4, Prov. Laon? (cf. Contreni)
Paris, Bibliothèque nationale, lat. 3839, saec. XI2/2, France
Paris, Bibliothèque nationale, lat. 3839A, saec. XI2/2, St-Aubin, Angers
Paris, Bibliothèque nationale, lat. 3852, saec. XI–XII, probably Angers
Rouen, Bibliothèque municipale, 702 (E.27), saec. XI^{ex}
Vaticano, Città del, Biblioteca Apostolica Vaticana, lat. 3791, saec. XI^{ex}, Northern France
Vaticano, Città del, Biblioteca Apostolica Vaticana, Pal. lat. 973, saec. IX2/2, Northeastern France
Vaticano, Città del, Biblioteca Apostolica Vaticana, Reg. lat. 407, saec. ca. IX^{med}; near St. Gall
Vaticano, Città del, Biblioteca Apostolica Vaticana, Reg. lat. 421, saec. IX2–3/3, St. Gall
Wien, Österreichische Nationalbibliothek, 424, saec. IX2/4, Salzburg
Wien, Österreichische Nationalbibliothek, 1370, saec. IX1/4, Mondsee
Wien, Österreichische Nationalbibliothek, 2198, saec. X$^{1/2\text{-}med}$; Southern Germany

Excerpt
Freiburg (Breisgau), Universitätsbibliothek, 8, saec. IX^2; Lake Constance

7. Bibliography

Maassen, *Geschichte* 885; Fournier-Le Bras 1.276–277; Van Hove, *Prolegomena* 319

F. Kunstmann (cf. above, 'edition') 10–11

M. Sdralek, 'Handschriftlich-kritische Untersuchungen über eine Gruppe von Briefen Papst Nikolaus I.', AKKR 47 (1882) 177–215, esp. 192–193
V. Krause, 'Die Acten der Triburer Synode 895', NA 17 (1892) 319–323
Fournier, 'Manuscrit de Montpellier' 357–389
Fournier, 'Influence' 27–78
Rambaud-Buhot, 'Corpus inédit' 271–281
Mordek, *Kirchenrecht und Reform* 259
J. J. Contreni, 'Codices Pseudo-Isidoriani: The Provenance and Date of Paris, B.N. MS lat. 9629', *Viator* 13 (1982) 1–14
Reynolds, 'Unity and Diversity' 99–135

Collectio Sangermanensis (Paris lat. 12444)

1. Author: Unknown. *2. Date:* Eighth century. *3. Place:* Gaul. *4. Type:* A systematic collection deriving from the *Collectio Hibernensis*.

5. Edition

Cf. A. J. Nürnberger, 'Über eine ungedruckte Canonensammlung aus dem 8. Jahrhundert', *25. Bericht der wissenschaftlichen Gesellschaft Philomathie in Neisse vom Oktober 1888 bis zum Oktober 1890* (Mainz 1890) 118–197

6. Manuscripts

München, Bayerische Staatsbibliothek, Clm 14508, saec. IX3/4, Northeastern France, already at St. Emmeram (Regensburg) at an early date, fol. 75^r–105^v, large fragment, cf. Maassen, *Geschichte* 840–841; Nürnberger (see above) 123 with description of the contents; Landau, 'Regensburg' 63–64, 74; Mordek, *Kirchenrecht und Reform* 172 n. 356; Reynolds, 'Unity and Diversity' 121; Mordek, *Bibliotheca capitularium* 340

Paris, Bibliothèque nationale, lat. 12444 (olim Sangerm. 938), saec. VIII^{ex}–IX^{in}, written probably at Fleury, the only complete manuscript of this collection

***Excerpt or source of the Collectio Sangermanensis* (cf. Mordek, *Kirchenrecht und Reform* 145)**

Albi, Bibliothèque municipale 38, saec. X, Southern France, fol. 126^v–127^r, 127^v (cf. Mordek, *Kirchenrecht und Reform* 268–269), excerpt of Albi 38bis

Albi, Bibliothèque municipale, 38bis, saec. IX ca. med., Southern France; fol. 38^v–42^r, Mordek, *Kirchenrecht und Reform* 269–271; cf. also Reynolds, 'Unity and Diversity' 121 and 123 (contains a supplement-text to the *Collectio Sangermanensis* which can also be found in the manuscripts St. Gallen, Stiftsbibliothek, 40, p. 304 [saec. IX] and Albi, Bibliothèque municipale, 43 [15])

Köln, Erzbischöfliche Diözesan- und Dombibliothek, 117 (olim Darmstadt 2116), saec. IX ca. med., France; fol. 69^r–89^r, the first part of the manuscript (fol. 1–60) also containing the *Dionysio-Hadriana* is older; cf. Mordek, *Kirchenrecht und Reform* 145 n. 223; Reynolds, 'Unity and Diversity' 121

London, British Library, Harley 3034, saec. X, fol. 1^r–10^r (cf. Reynolds, 'Unity and Diversity' 122)

Orléans, Bibliothèque municipale, 116 (94), saec. IX^{in}, Salzburg, later Fleury, cf. Reynolds, 'Unity and Diversity' 113 and 122

Vaticano, Città del, Biblioteca Apostolica Vaticana, Pal. lat. 485, saec. IX^{med}, Lorsch; the isolated excerpts from the *Sangermanensis* are transmitted under the name of Isidore; contains also parts of the *Dionysio-Hadriana* as well as the *Capitula* by Theodulf of Orléans; cf. Mordek, *Kirchenrecht und Reform* 247; Reynolds, 'Unity and Diversity' 122

Vesoul, Bibliothèque municipale, 79 (73), fol. 81^{r}–83^{v}

7. *Bibliography*

Maassen, *Geschichte* 836–841; Fournier-Le Bras 1.85; Kurtscheid-Wilches 1.100; R. Naz, 'Saint-Germain (Collection de) ou Sangermanensis', DDC 7 (1965) 835; Van Hove, *Prolegomena* 278; Stickler, *Historia* 1.106

Jean Mabillon, *De re diplomatica libri VI* (Paris 1681) 5.360

A. J. Nürnberger, 'Über eine ungedruckte Kanonessammlung aus dem 8. Jahrhundert', *25. Bericht der wissenschaftlichen Gesellschaft Philomathie in Neisse vom Oktober 1888 bis zum Oktober 1890* (Neisse 1890) 125–197

E. Seckel, 'Nachtrag zur Benedictus-Studie VI', NA 31 (1906) 238

Finsterwalder, *Canones Theodori* 76

Coquin, 'Sort' 203

Mordek, 'Bonneval' 342 n. 8

R. E. Reynolds, 'A Florilegium on the Ecclesiastical Grades in Clm 19414: Testimony to Ninth-Century Clerical Instruction', *Harvard Theological Review* 63 (1970) 248 n. 71

Mordek, *Kirchenrecht und Reform* 144–147

R. McKitterick, *The Frankish Church and the Carolingian Reforms, 789–895* (London 1977) 148

Reynolds, 'Unity and Diversity' 106–107, 119–124

Collectio 250 capitulorum

1. Author: Unknown. *2. Date:* Second half of the eighth century? *3. Place:* Northern France? *4. Type:* Derivative of the *Collectio Hibernensis*. *5. Edition:* None.

6. *Manuscripts*

München, Bayerische Staatsbibliothek, Clm 4592, saec. IX2/4, Prov. Benediktbeuern

München, Bayerische Staatsbibliothek, Clm 6434, saec. VIII^{ex}, Freising, fol. 41^{r}–75^{r}

Wien, Österreichische Nationalbibliothek, lat. 522, saec. IX2/3, Salzburg, cf. Bischof, *Schreibschulen* 2.159–160

7. *Bibliography*

Fournier, 'Influence' 27–78

Mordek, *Kirchenrecht und Reform* 258

Reynolds, 'Salzburg' 32
Reynolds, 'Unity and Diversity' 106

Collectio Sancti Amandi

1. Author: Unknown. *2. Date:* End of the seventh century at the earliest or second half of the eighth century (cf. Mordek, *Kirchenrecht und Reform* 250 and 72 n. 38). On opinions favoring an earlier dating, see: Van Hove, *Prolegomena* 277; Stickler, *Historia* 1.99; Martínez Díez, *Colección Hispana* 1.342–344 (saec. VIII^1). *3. Place:* Gaul. *4. Type:* A chronologically arranged collection of conciliar canons. *5. Edition:* None.

6. *Manuscripts*

In all extant manuscripts the *Collectio Sancti Amandi* is transmitted together with the *'Dionysio-Hadriana'*

Complete Manuscripts

Berlin, Staatsbibliothek Preussischer Kulturbesitz, Hamilton 132, saec. $IX^{in\text{-}med}$, Corbie, fol. 131ra–238vb, cf. Mordek, *Kirchenrecht und Reform* 273–274; Mordek, *Bibliotheca capitularium* 29–34

Paris, Bibliothèque nationale, lat. 1455, saec. IX3–4/4, Northern France, fol. 80ra–188vb, cf. Mordek, *Kirchenrecht und Reform* 127 with n. 118; cf. also Mordek, 'Herovalliana' 229–230 (*Herovalliana*-excerpts in this manuscript) and Mordek, *Bibliotheca capitularium* 410–411: augmented and corrected version of the *Collectio Sancti Amandi*, copy of Paris lat. 3846

Paris, Bibliothèque nationale, lat. 3846, saec. IX^{in}, Northeastern France?, Prov. Saint Amand, fol. 128ra–253rb, cf. Mordek, *Bibliotheca capitularium* 439–442

Partial Transmissions of the Collection

Paris, Bibliothèque nationale, lat. 1568, saec. X, fol. 122^r–124^v (according to Martínez Díez, *Colección Hispana* 1.366 a fragment of the *Collectio Sancti Amandi* deriving directly from Paris lat. 3846)

Paris, Bibliothèque nationale, lat. 4280, saec. XII, fol. 81^v–115^v, excerpt following a chronologically arranged collection (cf. Mordek, *Kirchenrecht und Reform* 251)

Paris, Bibliothèque nationale, lat. 12445, saec. IX3/4, Reims, a manuscript of the *Dionysio-Hadriana*, which, according to Mor, 'Manoscritto canonistico francese' 191–192 and 201 contains canons of the *Collectio Sancti Amandi* in its final part. Finsterwalder, *Canones Theodori* 136 had already assigned the version on fol. 153–156 of the so-called *Penitentiale Theodori* to the tradition of the *Collectio Sancti Amandi*. He also found that it did not derive from any of the known manuscripts of the collection. Cf. also Böhringer, DA 46 (1990) 23

Vaticano, Città del, Biblioteca Apostolica Vaticana, Ottobon. lat. 312, saec. XI–XII, cf. Boese, *Sammlung Hamilton* 73–74; on the second liturgical part of the collection from the fifteenth century [beginning fol. 137], cf. Andrieu, *Ordines Romani* 1.316–317) fol. 136^v, fragment containing the *tituli* of the councils of Arles I (a. 314), Arles IV (a. 524) and Arles II (a. 442–506) following the *Dionysio-Hadriana*.

7. *Bibliography*

Maassen, *Geschichte* 780–784; Fournier-Le Bras 1.102; Van Hove, *Prolegomena* 277; Stickler, *Historia* 1.99

P. Ewald, in: W. Wattenbach, 'Die Handschriften der Hamiltonschen Sammlung', NA 8 (1883) 332–335

P. Hinschius, 'Die kanonistischen Handschriften der Hamilton'schen Sammlung im Kupferstich-Kabinett des königlichen Museums zu Berlin', ZKG 6 (1884) 193–246

Finsterwalder, *Canones Theodori* 136

Séjourné, *Saint Isidore* 273–275, 362, 430

Le Bras, 'Isidore de Séville' 230, 240 n. 3 and 243 n. 2

Mor, 'Manoscritto canonistico francese' 191–192 and 201

Mordek, 'Aera' 221 including n. 31

Martínez Díez, *Colección Hispana* 1.342–347 and 366

Mordek, 'Bonneval' 345 with n. 32

Mordek, *Kirchenrecht und Reform* 249–250

Gaudemet, *Sources* 149

L. Böhringer (ed.), 'Der eherechtliche Traktat im Paris. lat. 12445, einer Arbeitshandschrift Hinkmars von Reims', DA 46 (1990) 18–47

Zechiel-Eckes, *Cresconius* 1.233–234

Mordek, *Bibliotheca capitularium* 439

Collectio Bellovacensis

1. Author: Unknown. *2. Date:* Second half of the ninth century. *3. Place:* France? *4. Type:* Chronologically arranged collection of councils and decretals. Same source as the *Collectio Sancti Amandi* (for the councils). *5. Edition:* None.

6. *Manuscripts*

Vaticano, Città del, Biblioteca Apostolica Vaticana, lat. 3827, saec. IX3/3, Northern France, Prov. Beauvais, fol. 1r–125r; (the same Merovingian councils contained in Paris lat. 1458 [from Beauvais], a codex of fragments dating from the ninth to the fourteenth century, and Paris lat. 1454 [in the appendix of the *Collectio Quesnelliana*]); cf. Mordek, *Bibliotheca capitularium* 858–863

Partial Copies of Vat. lat. 3827

Roma, Biblioteca Vallicelliana, C.23, cf. Mordek, *Bibliotheca capitularium* 858 (early-modern paper manuscript)

Roma, Biblioteca Vallicelliana, C.24; cf. Mordek, *Bibliotheca capitularium*, 858–859 (early-modern paper manuscript)

Vaticano, Città del, Biblioteca Apostolica Vaticana, Chigi C. VIII. 239, saec. XVI2, cf. Mordek, *Bibliotheca capitularium* 754

Vaticano, Città del, Biblioteca Apostolica Vaticana, Reg. lat. 1041; cf. Mordek, *Bibliotheca capitularium* 858 (early-modern paper manuscript)

7. *Bibliography*

Maassen, *Geschichte* 778–780, 782; Fournier-Le Bras 1.93; Van Hove, *Prolegomena* 277

Ballerini, *De antiquis . . . collectionibus et collectoribus* P. II cap. X § 4 (PL 56.157–158)
Mordek, *Kirchenrecht und Reform* 71 and 72 n. 38

Collectio Burgundiana (Bruxelles 8789–8793)

1. Author: Unknown. *2. Date:* Beginning of the eighth century. *3. Place:* Northern France. *4. Type:* Unstructured collection of material (penitential books and mostly Gallican councils). *5. Edition:* None.

6. *Manuscript*

Bruxelles, Bibliothèque Royale Albert Ier, 8780–8793, saec. VIII–IX, probably Northern France; CLA 10 n. 1543 pp. 30, 50; Suppl. p. 66

7. *Bibliography*

Maassen, *Geschichte* 636–638; Fournier-Le Bras 1.90; Van Hove, *Prolegomena* 277

H. J. Schmitz, *Die Bußbücher und die Bußdisciplin der Kirche* 2 (Düsseldorf 1898) 319–322
C. Munier (ed.), *Concilia Galliae, a. 314–a. 506* (CCL 148; Turnhout 1963)
C. De Clercq (ed.), *Concilia Galliae, a. 511–a. 695* (CCL 148A; Turnhout 1963)
C. Munier, 'La tradition manuscrite de l'abrégé d'Hippone et le canon des Ecritures des églises africaines', SE 21 (1972) 43–55
Mordek, *Kirchenrecht und Reform* 10, 55, 72

Collectio 'Pro causa iniustae excommunicationis'

1. Author: Unknown. *2. Date:* Seventh to eighth century. *3. Place:* Probably Northern Italy. *4. Type:* Fourteen Patristic and biblical excerpts. *5. Edition:* None (Transcription taken from the manuscripts of Montpellier and Verona: Folliet [see below] 296–300)

6. *Manuscripts*

Montpellier, Bibliothèque Interuniversitaire, H.233, saec. IX, fol. 123r–125r
Vercelli, Biblioteca Capitolare, CLXV, saec. IX2/4, Northern Italy, fol. 220r–224v, cf. Zechiel-Eckes, *Cresconius* 1.172–175
Verona, Biblioteca Capitolare, LXII (60), saec. VIII–IX, fol. 103v–107r

7. *Bibliography*

G. Folliet, 'Une collection anonyme "Pro causa iniustae excommunicationis" des VIIe–VIIIe siècles', *Miscellanea di studi agostiniani: Studi in onore A. Trapé = Augustinianum* 25 (1985) 295–308
Zechiel-Eckes, *Cresconius* (cf. index)

Carolingian and Post-Carolingian Collections to the Eve of the Gregorian Reform

(From the End of the Eighth to the Middle of the Eleventh Century)

Collectio Dacheriana

1. Author: Intellectual personality who could well have been a member of the leading circles of the Carolingian reform clergy; perhaps Agobard of Lyon (Mordek, *Kirchenrecht und Reform* 12–13). *2. Date:* About 800. At the center of the collections of the Carolingian reform; most important source for all the collections dating from the first half of the ninth century. *3. Place:* Southern France, possibly Lyon. *4. Type:* Systematic collection.

5. Editions

Luc D'Achery, *Veterum aliquot scriptorum qui in Galliae Bibliothecis, maxime Benedictorum latuerant, Spicilegium* 2 (Paris 1672) 1–200; cf. new edition of the *Spicilegium* by L.-F.-J. De la Barre, *Spicilegium sive collectio veterum aliquot scriptorum qui in Galliae Bibliothecis delituerant* 1 (Paris 1723) 509–564 (based on Paris lat. 4287, cf. Le Bras and Haenni)

M. Murjanoff, 'Leningrader Fragmente der Dacheriana', SG 9 (1966) 6–10; based on St. Petersburg, Rossiyskaya Natsional'naya Biblioteka, Q.v.II.24 (fragment of Book 2)

6. Manuscripts

Albi, Bibliothèque municipale, 43 (15), saec. IX4/4, probably Southern France (without *praefatio*), cf. Mordek, 'Dacheriana' 594 n. 45: (Form A according to Le Bras); cf. Reynolds, 'Unity and Diversity' 123

Arras, Bibliothèque municipale, 224 (897), saec. X–XI (Form A changed into B)

Barcelona, Archivo de la Corona de Aragón, Ripoll 77, a. 1776, Ripoll; fol. 5vb–39va, copy probably based on a Carolingian source, cf. F. Valls-Taberner, 'Les collecions canóniques a Catalunya durant l'època comtal (872–1162)', *Estudis d'Història juridica Catalana* (Barcelona 1929) 70–83, repr. 'Obras selectas', 2: *Estudios histórico-juridicos* (Madrid-Barcelona 1954) 96–106; (excerpt of Form B)

Berlin, Staatsbibliothek Preußischer Kulturbesitz, Phill. 1765, saec. X, from Reims (Form B)

Berlin, Staatsbibliothek Preußischer Kulturbesitz, Phill. 1777, saec. X^1, Southern France, closely related to the Valère-manuscript

Bern, Burgerbibliothek, 425, saec. IX^2, Reims (Bischoff, cf. O. Homburger, *Die illustrierten Handschriften der Burgerbibliothek Bern* [Bern 1962] 124) (Form A according to Haenni 386)

Bologna, Biblioteca Universitaria, 376 (Cat. 242), saec. IX^{med-2}, not saec. XII, as in the catalogue of L. Frati, *Studi italiani di filologia classica* 16 (1908) 201; Southern France? Colophon on fol. 132^v: 'Rogo vos ergo fratres karissimi qui legitis in codicem istum ut oretis pro aldefredo peccatore sive minimum omnium presbiterorum ut deum habeatis auxiliatorem . . .' ; fol. 44^r–132^v (after fol. 120 there are losses of leaves and parts of the text) (Form A, *Versio adaucta* with additions after the third book)

Bruxelles, Bibliothèque Royale Albert Ier, 1312 (Cat. 2497), saec. IX ca. 3/4, near Reims

Canterbury, Cathedral and Chapter Library, Lit. B.7, saec. XII, fol. 74^r–88^v, only Book I (Form B) following the collection in four books; cf. Brooke, *English Church* 240–241 [on the dating of this manuscript];

Ivrea, Biblioteca Capitolare, XXXVII bis, saec. IX ca. med., probably Rhône valley (Form A, according to Le Bras)

Ivrea, Biblioteca Capitolare, XXXVIII, saec. IX ca 3/4, probably Northern Italy (Form A, according to Le Bras)

Köln, Erzbischöfliche Diözesan- und Dombibliothek, 121 (Darmstadt 2120), saec. X (damage at beginning and end)

Köln, Erzbischöfliche Diözesan- und Dombibliothek, 122 (Darmstadt 2121), about 805, probably Northeastern France (without *Praefatio*)

Köln, Erzbischöfliche Diözesan- und Dombibliothek, 123 (Darmstadt 2122), saec. IX^1, perhaps Northwestern Germany

Leiden, Bibliotheek der Rijksuniversiteit, BPL 127 AB, saec. IX3/4, Northern France (Form A)

London, British Library, Harley 3845, saec. IX^2, Northeastern France, notation of its provenance fol. 1^r below: 'Liber sancti Petri Gandensis aecclesiae. Servanti benedictio, tollenti maledictio. Qui folium tulerit vel cortaverit, anathena (!) sit', [saec. XII] and fol. 1^r above *Liber Humfredi Wanley, . . A.D. 1714* [Wanley died in 1726 as librarian to the Earl of Oxford], fol. 1^r–122^r (Form A), cf. Mordek, *Kirchenrecht und Reform* 262

Lyon, Bibliothèque de la ville, 571 (486), saec. IX2/4, Southern France, damaged at the beginning, *Dacheriana augmentée*, cf. Mordek, 'Dacheriana' 594 n. 45 (Form A)

Mainz, Stadtbibliothek, II 4, saec. XI (Books I and II: Form B; Book III: Form A); cf. Mordek, 'Dacheriana' 574 n. 45

Marburg, Hessisches Staatsarchiv, Hr. 5 fasc. 3, saec. IX^{ex}, probably Northern France (fragment); cf. Mordek, *Kirchenrecht und Reform* 667

Merseburg, Archiv des Domkapitels, 100, saec. IX3/4, Reims. According to the librarian it was destroyed during World War II. Photos in possession of Prof. B. Bischoff, Munich

Metz, Bibliothèque municipale, 236 (olim E.29), saec. X–XI according to Waitz, *Archiv* 8 (1843) 454 and Seckel, 'Benedictus Levita' 411; saec. XI according to Werminghoff, NA 26 (1901) 17; fol. 3^{r}–121^{v}. Marthe Dulon in her paleographical study of the codex on 5 January 1935 (Bischoff) distinguished two different parts: fol. 1–142, saec. IX^{ex} 'very much the Tours style, or perhaps rather St. Denis, anyhow very French'; fol. 143–206 [with a fragment of the collection in 400 chapters], saec. IX^{in}, perhaps VIII^{ex}, Rhineland. Prov. St. Arnulph at Metz (Form B); destroyed in 1944

Monte Cassino, Archivio e Biblioteca dell'Abbazia, 541, saec. XI^{in}, Southern Italy, (Form B; probably copy of Vat. lat. 1347); p. 147^{b}–235^{b}; cf. Mordek, 'Dacheriana' 577 and *Kirchenrecht und Reform* 101 n. 15; Kerff, *Quadripartitus* 18–20

Monte Cassino, Archivio e Biblioteca dell'Abbazia, 554, saec. X, Italy, damaged at the beginning, p. 1–203 (Form A); cf. M. Inguañez, *Codicum Casinensium manuscriptorum catalogus* 3.2 (Monte Cassino 1940–1941) 218–219 and Mordek, 'Dacheriana' 580–581

Montpellier, Bibliothèque Interuniversitaire, H.137, saec. XI, France, beginning at fol. 230^{v} (Form A, according to Le Bras)

Montpellier, Bibliothèque Interuniversitaire, H.301, saec. IX$^{med\text{-}2}$, probably Lyon; without *Praefatio* (Form A, according to Le Bras)

Palermo, Archivio della Cattedrale, 14, saec. XII (cf. E. Besta, 'Di una collezione canonistica palermitana', *Il Circolo Giuridico* 40 [1909] 10–11 and Mordek, 'Bonneval' 341 n. 7)

Paris, Bibliothèque de l'Arsenal, 1199 (577 T.L.), saec. IX^{2}, probably France, from the Carmelite convent of St. Joseph at Paris (the *Catalogue des manuscrits de la Bibliothèque de l'Arsenal* 2 [1886] 344 erroneously lists it as the Penitential of Egbert of York), fol. 1^{r}–107^{v} (Form A)

Paris, Bibliothèque nationale, lat. 1927, saec. IX ca. med., Southern France, Prov. Saint-Martial at Limoges (cf. Delisle, *Cabinet des manuscrits* 1.397 and Mordek, 'Dacheriana' 594 n. 45), fol. 27^{v}–124^{r}: (Form A; *Dacheriana augmentée*)

Paris, Bibliothèque nationale, lat. 2341, saec. IX2/4, Orléans (without *Praefatio*)

Paris, Bibliothèque nationale, lat. 3839, saec. XI^{2}, France, fragment (only beginning of *Praefatio*)

Paris, Bibliothèque nationale, lat. 3839A, saec. XI^{2}, Angers, cf. Mordek, *Kirchenrecht und Reform* 181 n. 194

Paris, Bibliothèque nationale, lat. 3879, saec. IX^{med}, probably Southern France (without *Praefatio, Dacheriana augmentée*), cf. Mordek, 'Dacheriana' 594 n. 45 (Form A)

Paris, Bibliothèque nationale, lat. 3880, saec. XII

Paris, Bibliothèque nationale, lat. 4287, saec. X (*Praefatio* and *Capitulatio* of Book I are missing according to Haenni 378–380: losses of texts); cf. Mordek, 'Dacheriana' 577 (cf. above 'edition')

Paris, Bibliothèque nationale, lat. 7561, p. 33–46 and lat. 4287, saec. IX3/4, region around Reims (first leaf is missing; Form B, the third book was later changed from A to B), cf. Mordek, 'Dacheriana' 594 n. 45

Paris, Bibliothèque nationale, lat. 10741 (olim Suppl. lat. 205), saec. IX^2, Lyon (damaged at the beginning; *Dacheriana augmentée*), cf. Mordek, 'Dacheriana' 594 n. 45 (Form A)

Paris, Bibliothèque nationale, lat. 13655 (olim Sangerm. 939), saec. IX–X

St. Petersburg, Rossiyskaya Natsional'naya Biblioteka, Q.v.II.24, saec. IX3/4, Reims, fragment (2 fol.) from Book 2, ed. Murjanoff, SG 9 (1966) 6–10

Valère near Sion (Sitten), Archives du Chapitre, 120, saec. IX3/4, region around Lyon, cf. O. Perler, 'Eine *Dacheriana* aus der ersten Hälfte des IX. Jahrhunderts in Sitten', ZSKG 31 (1937) 145–150 (Form A), closely related to Berlin 1777 (cf. Mordek, 'Dacheriana' 590 n. 39); for this manuscript cf. also J. Leisibach, *Scriptoria Medii Aevi Helvetica: Denkmäler Schweizerischer Schreibkunst des Mittelalters, XIII: Schreibstätten der Diözese Sitten,* ed. A. Bruckner (Geneva 1973) 14–15 (and plates) (Information provided by A. Firey)

Vaticano, Città del, Biblioteca Apostolica Vaticana, lat. 1347, saec. IX^2, Reims (Form B), fol. 80^r–143^v, cf. Kerff, *Quadripartitus* 27–30; (by the eleventh century at the latest it was in Italy, cf. above, Cod. Monte Cassino 541)

Vaticano, Città del, Biblioteca Apostolica Vaticana, Ottobon. lat. 261, saec. IX^{ex}, Northern France, fol. 1^r–123^r (revised version of Form A, AB-Recension, cf. extensive discussion in Mordek, 'Dacheriana' 583–593)

Vaticano, Città del, Biblioteca Apostolica Vaticana, Reg. lat. 425, saec. X, France, fol. 1^r–103^v (Form B) cf. Mordek, 'Dacheriana' 576–578 and 580 n. 21

Vaticano, Città del, Biblioteca Apostolica Vaticana, Reg. lat. 446, saec. IX2/4, Lyon (damaged at the beginning)

Vaticano, Città del, Biblioteca Apostolica Vaticana, Reg. lat. 845, saec. IX3/4, Reims (Form A); cf. Mordek, 'Dacheriana' 578: saec. X^1, fol. 1^r–94^r

Vaticano, Città del, Biblioteca Apostolica Vaticana, Reg. lat. 847, saec. X–XI, Northern France, Prov. Saint-Magloire, Paris (Form A); cf. Mordek, 'Dacheriana' 578, (the mss. Vat. Reg. lat. 845 and 847 seem to be closely related to each other)

Vaticano, Città del, Biblioteca Apostolica Vaticana, Reg. lat. 848, saec. IX3/4 (probably shortly after 858), France, fol. 2^r–106^v (Form A) cf. Mordek, 'Dacheriana' 578–580

Vaticano, Città del, Biblioteca Apostolica Vaticana, Reg. lat. 849, saec. X^{in} France (originally Form A, later changed into Form B) cf. Mordek, 'Dacheriana' 582–583

Vaticano, Città del, Biblioteca Apostolica Vaticana, Reg. lat. 1000A, saec. IX^2, Reims, fol. 4^r–113^v (Form A) cf. Mordek, 'Dacheriana' 580

Wien, Österreichische Nationalbibliothek, lat. 2231, saec. IX$^{med\text{-}2}$ or IX–X, Italy or Southern France

Wolfenbüttel, Herzog August Bibliothek, Helmst. 1062 [Cat. 1164], saec. X (Form A changed into B)

Würzburg, Universitätsbibliothek, M.p.th.f. 22, saec. IX ca. med., probably Rhine region (Form A, according to Le Bras); cf. F. Gillmann, 'Eine Würzburger Dacheriana', AKKR 87 (1907) 587–598

Excerpts Resp. Special Recension

Berlin, Staatsbibliothek Preußischer Kulturbesitz, lat. fol. 626, saec. XII^1; Prov. presumably Liège area; cf. Mordek, 'Dacheriana' 594–595 n. 45; G. Schmitz,

'Wucher in Laon: Eine neue Quelle zu Karl dem Kahlen und Hinkmar von Reims', DA 37 (1981) 529–558, especially 529–541; Zechiel-Eckes, *Cresconius* 2.315–316; Mordek, *Bibliotheca capitularium* 42 (combination with Cresconius, above)

Separate Tradition of the 'Praefatio'

Angers, Bibliothèque municipale, 891 (803), saec. XVII, fol. 71^{r}–76^{v}

Paris, Bibliothèque nationale, lat. 14497, saec. XIII, fol. 134ra–135rb

Rodez, Bibliothèque municipale, 23, saec. XIII, p. 94–99 (a parallel codex to Paris lat. 14497)

Vaticano, Città del, Biblioteca Apostolica Vaticana, lat. 5751, saec. IX–X, Northern Italy, Prov. Bobbio (according to the ownership note on fol. 2^{r}), fol. 9^{r}–11^{v}, cf. Maassen, 'Bibliotheca', *SB Vienna* 53 (1866) 369–370; Mordek, 'Dacheriana' 574; Mordek, *Bibliotheca capitularium* 884

7. *Bibliography*

Maassen, *Geschichte* 848–852; Fournier-Le Bras 1.104–109 and passim; Kurtscheid-Wilches, 1.100; Van Hove, *Prolegomena* 293–294; R. Naz, 'Dacheriana (Collectio)', DDC 4 (1949) 1013; Stickler, *Historia* 1.110–111; Haenni, 'Dacheriana Collectio', NCE 4 (1967) 610; Mordek, 'Dacheriana', LMA 3 (1986) 426

Ballerini, *De antiquis . . . collectionibus et collectoribus* P. IV, cap. VIII, § 1–2, (PL 56.309–310)

Waitz, *Archiv* 8 (1843) 454

G. Phillips, 'Der Codex Salisburgensis S. Petri IX 32: Ein Beitrag zur Geschichte der vorgratianischen Rechtsquellen', SB Vienna 44 (1863) 437–510

H. J. Schmitz, *Die Bußbücher und die Bußdisciplin der Kirche* 1 (Mainz 1883) 716

F. Maassen, 'Pseudo-Isidor Studien', SB Vienna 108 (1884) 1061–1104; 109 (1885) 801–860

A. Decker, 'Die Hildebold'sche Manuskriptensammlung des Kölner Domes', *Festschrift der 43. Versammlung deutscher Philologen und Schulmänner dargeboten von den Höheren Lehranstalten Kölns* (Bonn 1895) 227 [Nr. 79] (Decker gives references to *Dacheriana* codices from medieval library catalogues; for example, from the ninth-century [833] catalogue from Cologne)

E. Ehrmann, 'Der kanonische Prozess nach der Collectio Dacheriana', AKKR 77 (1897) 260–266

Fournier, 'Manuscrit de Montpellier' 357–389

A. Werminghoff, 'Reise nach Frankreich und Belgien im Frühjahr 1899', NA 26 (1901) 9–35

A. Werminghoff, 'Reise nach Italien im Jahre 1901', NA 27 (1902) 587 n. 15

G. Morin, 'Le catalogue des manuscrits de l'abbaye de Gorze au XIe siècle', RB 22 (1905) 6 (refers to *Dacheriana-Codices*)

G. Le Bras, 'Les deux formes de la *Dacheriana*', Mélanges Paul Fournier (Paris 1929) 395–414

G. Le Bras, 'Notes pour servir à l'histoire des collections canoniques, 4: A propos de la Dacheriana', RHD 8 (1929) 777 ['Dacheriana augmentée'] and 9 (1930) 518–524

G. Le Bras, 'Sur la part d'Isidore de Séville et des Espagnols dans l'histoire des collections canoniques', *Revue des sciences religieuses* 10 (1930) 218–257

G. Haenni, 'La Dacheriana mérite-t-elle une réedition?' RHD 34 (1956) 376–390 (announces the publication of a critical edition)
G. Haenni, 'Note sur la Dacheriana', ZSKG 50 (1956) 277–281
Ryan, 'Observations' 91
Kuttner, *Traditio* 16 (1960) 533 ('Annual report')
J. Fohlen, 'Dom Luc d'Achery (1609–1685) et les débuts de l'érudition Mauriste', *Revue Mabillon* 55 (1965) 149–175
G. Martinez Diez, *Colección Hispana* 1.371–373 (on the source for the *Dacheriana*)
G. Haenni, 'Note sur les sources de la Dacheriana', SG 11 (1967) 1–22
Rambaud-Buhot, 'Corpus inédit' 271–281 (The manuscript Palermo, Bibl. Comunale, 2.Qq.E.17 is actually Palermo, Archivio della Cattedrale, 14)
Mordek, 'Dacheriana' 574–595 with additional information in: DA 24 (1968) 341 n. 7 and ZRG Kan. Abt. 55 (1969) 40–41 n. 6 and 7
Mordek, 'Bonneval' 339–434
Mordek, 'Dionysio-Hadriana' 40–41 with n. 6 and 7
Mordek, *Kirchenrecht und Reform* 259–263
Mordek, 'Kirchenrechtliche Autoritäten' 237–253
Mordek, 'Systematische Kanonessammlungen' 188
Schmitz, 'Abbreviatio Ansegisi' 191–199
Landau, 'Kanonessammlungen in der Lombardei' 444–445
Müller, *Collectio Duodecim Partium* 326–335
R. Newhauser, 'Towards "modus in habendo": Transformation in the Idea of Avarice: The Early Penitentials through the Carolingian Reforms', ZRG Kan. Abt. 75 (1989) 1–22
Schmitz, 'Vier-Bücher-Sammlung' 237–238
Hartmann, 'Autoritäten' 428
Siems, *Handel und Wucher* 443, 523, 530, 721
Zechiel-Eckes, *Cresconius* 1.297–298; 2.315–316

Ansegis, Collectio capitularium

1. Author: Ansegis (†20 July, 833) was Abbot of Fontenelle (St. Wandrille) in Northern France. *2. Date:* Completed before 28 January 827. *3. Place:* Unknown (probably Fontanelle); cf. MGH Capit. n.s. 1.12. *4. Type:* Combination of chronologically arranged and systematic collection.

5. Editions

Alfred Boretius (ed.) *Ansegisi abbatis capitularium collectio,* MGH Capit. 1 (Hannover 1883; repr. 1984) 394–450, no. 183
Gerhard Schmitz (ed.) *Die Kapitulariensammlung des Ansegis,* MGH Capit. n.s. 1 (Hannover 1996)

6. Manuscripts

Avranches, Bibliothèque municipale, 145 (olim 121), saec. XII^{2}, written on the order of Abbot Robert de Torigni (1154–June 1186) at Mont-Saint-Michel, fol.

1^{v}–46^{v}; Mordek, *Bibliotheca capitularium* 3–6; MGH Capit. n.s. 1.71–73, 279–281 (D with strong elements of Class C)

Bamberg, Staatsbibliothek, Can. 12 (P.I.1), saec. X1/4, Prov. unknown, fol. 2^{v}–66^{v}, cf. Hoffmann, *Bamberger Handschriften* 92, 124 and plates no. 244 and 245; Mordek, *Bibliotheca capitularium* 12–15; MGH Capit. n.s. 1.73–75 and 277–278 (Group D)

Barcelona, Archivo della Corona de Aragón, Ripoll 40, saec. XI^{1}, Prov. Santa María de Ripoll (in the library catalogue of 1046), fol. 9ra–27vb, cf. Mordek, *Bibliotheca capitularium* 19–27; MGH Capit. n.s. 1.75–77, 245–249 (Group B, with an overlying text from C almost in Books 2 and 4, and appendices from group C)

Berlin, Staatsbibliothek Preußischer Kulturbesitz, Hamilton 132, saec. $IX^{in\text{-}2/2}$, Western France, fol. 255^{r}–263^{v}, only Books 3 and 4, cf. Mordek, *Bibliotheca capitularium* 29–34, especially 32; MGH Capit. n.s. 1.77–78 and 255–257 (Group C1)

Berlin, Staatsbibliothek Preußischer Kulturbesitz, lat. fol. 626; saec. XII^{1}, diocese of Liège, Prov. Jesuit college Louvain (Ashburnham-Barrois 43), fol. 1ra–23vb: *Praefatio* and Books 1–4; fol. 32va–33ra: Book 2, cc. 21, 34–38; cf. Mordek, *Bibliotheca capitularium* 34–43; MGH Capit. n.s. 1.78–79 and 276–278 (Group D)

Berlin, Staatsbibliothek Preußischer Kulturbesitz, lat. qu. 931 (Bibliotheca Jagiellonska, Krakau), saec. $IX^{ex,}$ St. Gall?, Prov. Mondsee, *praefatio*, Books 1–4, Appendices 1–3, (once again Book 2.1–13 on fol. 84^{v}–89^{r}), cf. Mordek, *Bibliotheca capitularium* 43–47, especially 44; MGH Capit. n.s. 1.79–81 and 197–205 (Group A)

Berlin, Staatsbibliothek Preußischer Kulturbesitz, Phill. 1737, saec. X^{2}, Eastern France (Metz?); Prov. perhaps Mainz, fol. 7^{r}–27^{v}, (1.105–4.13), addition at the end of Book 1; fol. 37^{r-v} (4.71–74), cf. Mordek, *Bibliotheca capitularium* 51–55, especially 52 and 53–54; MGH Capit. n.s. 1.81–83 and 197–205 (Group A)

Berlin, Staatsbibliothek Preußischer Kulturbesitz, Phill. 1762, before 860, Reims, Prov. Saint-Remi at Reims, fol. 1^{r}–68^{v}, Books 1–4; cf. Mordek, *Bibliotheca capitularium* 58–69, especially 61–62; MGH Capit. n.s. 1.83–85 and 269–276 (Group D); cf. also Landau, 'Gefälschtes Recht' 27 (forged canons: fol. 137^{v}–138^{v})

Bonn, Universitätsbibliothek, S. 402 (olim 96a), saec. XII, Germany (Rhineland?); p. 47–131, cf. Schmitz, 'Überlieferung' 1–15, especially 5–8, Mordek, *Bibliotheca capitularium* 81–85, especially 82; MGH Capit. n.s. 1.85–87 and 234–238 (Group B2), see below Schaffhausen, Stadtbibliothek, Min. 75

Gotha, Forschungs- und Landesbibliothek, Mbr. I.84 (olim 54), saec. X–XI (cf. Hoffmann, *Buchkunst* 239, Prov. Cathedral Library at Mainz (1479), fol. 1ra–29rb: *Praefatio*, Books 1–4 and Appendices 1–3 (Group C2); fol. 376rb–396rb: combination of Ansegis (Group B1, without Book 4.71–74) and capitularies of Louis the Pious, cf. Mordek, *Bibliotheca capitularium* 131–149, especially 132 and 141–144; MGH Capit. n.s. 1.87–91, 221–224; 260–261

Hamburg, Staats- und Universitätsbibliothek, 141a in scrinio (olim ms. 83), saec. IX3/4, Script. Fulda (cf. Hoffmann, *Buchkunst* 151), Prov. Corvey (saec. XIV), p. 1–145, *Praefatio,* Books 1–4 and Appendices 1–3, cf. Mordek, *Bibliotheca capitularium* 153–157, especially 154–155; MGH Capit. n.s. 1.92 and 197–205

Heiligenkreuz, Stiftsbibliothek, 217, saec. X^{ex}, Southeastern Germany (cf. Mordek and MGH Capit. n.s. 1.93), fol. 205^{r}–265^{r}, *Praefatio,* Books 1–4; cf. Mordek, *Bib-*

liotheca capitularium 158–172, especially 163–164; MGH Capit. n.s. 1.93–96 and 212–215 (Group A)

Leiden, Bibliotheek der Rijksuniversiteit, BPL 22, saec. X, France, Prov. Saint-Nicaise (Reims?), fol. 1^{r}–42^{v}, Books 1–4 and Appendices 1–3; cf. Mordek, *Bibliotheca capitularium* 205; MGH Capit. n.s. 1.96–98 and 258–259 (Group C)

London, British Library, Add. 22398, saec. IX^{ex}–X, France; Prov. St. Pierre de Vierzon (region of Bourges)?, fol. 3ra–55ra, *Praefatio,* Books 1–4; Mordek, *Bibliotheca capitularium* 220–223, especially 221; MGH Capit. n.s. 1.98–99 and 253–255 (Group C)

Milano, Biblioteca Ambrosiana, C.51 sup., saec. XI3/3 (cf. L. Jordan and S. Wool, *Inventory of Western Manuscripts in the Bibliotheca Ambrosiana, 2: C - D Superior* [Publications in Medieval Studies 22.2; 1986] 78), probably France (additions saec. XII1/4), fol. 129^{r}–153^{v}: *Praefatio,* Books 1–2, Excerpts from Book 3 and 4; cf. Mordek, *Bibliotheca capitularium* 241–242; MGH Capit. n.s. 1.99–102 (Group C, Copy of London, Add. 22398); cf. also *Collectio 4 librorum*

München, Bayerische Staatsbibliothek, Clm 3853, saec. X^{2}, Southern Germany, Prov. Augsburg?; fol. 183^{r}–245^{r}, *Praefatio,* Book 1–4; fol. 247^{v}: Ansegis 3.57; fol. 262^{r-v}: Excerpts from Appendix 1 and 2; cf. Mordek, *Bibliotheca capitularium* 294–296, 299; MGH Capit. n.s. 1.102–104 and 212–215 (Group A)

München, Bayerische Staatsbibliothek, Clm 4460 (aquired about 1863), saec. XI^{2}, Southern Germany(?), Prov. Dominican friars at Bamberg, cf. Hoffmann, *Bamberger Handschriften* 100 and 182; fol. 33^{v}–40^{v}, 25^{r}–32^{v}, 41^{r}–92^{r}, *Praefatio,* Book 1–4, Appendices 1–3; cf. Mordek, *Bibliotheca capitularium* 308–312, especially 310–311; MGH Capit. n.s. 1.104–106 and 210–211 (Group A)

München, Bayerische Staatsbibliothek, Clm 6360, saec. X3/3 written in Freising or in Southern Carinthia during the exile of Bishop Abraham of Freising (974–983); cf. Daniel, *Freisinger Dombibliothek* 111; Prov. Freising, Cathedral (Boretius no. 15, cites it wrongly as Fris. 234); fol. 1^{v}–40^{r}, 57^{r}–72^{v}, 41^{r}–56^{v}, 73^{r}–85^{r}: *Praefatio,* Books 1–4, Appendices 1–3; fol. 85^{r}–89^{r}: Ansegis 2.1–13, *Capitulatio* and text; fol. 89^{r}: Ansegis 3.57; cf. Mordek, *Bibliotheca capitularium* 329–333, especially 330–331 and 332; MGH Capit. n.s. 1.106–108 (Group A)

New Haven, Yale University, Beinecke Library, 413, about 875, Reims, fol. 2^{v}–66^{v}: Books 1–4 including the *Capitulationes,* cf. Mordek, *Bibliotheca capitularium* 386–391, especially 388; MGH Capit. n.s. 1.109–110 and 262–265 (Group C2)

Oxford, Bodleian Library, Hatton 42, saec. IX^{med}, Brittany, Prov. Glastonbury, later Worcester (cf. Ker, *Medieval Libraries of Great Britain*[2] 209), fol. 188^{v}–204^{v}: only Book 1 and additions from Book 2; cf. Mordek, *Bibliotheca capitularium* 404–406; MGH Capit. n.s. 1.110–113 and 229–230 (Group B1)

Paris, Bibliothèque nationale, lat. 3878, saec. X–XI, Southern Germany, Bressanone (according to H. Hoffmann), fol. 98^{r}–156^{v}, *Praefatio* (fragments in the beginning), Books 1–4; cf. Mordek, *Bibliotheca capitularium* 447–448; MGH Capit. n.s. 1.114–115 and 212–215 (Group A)

Paris, Bibliothèque nationale, lat. 4417, saec. IX^{ex}, Burgundy (?), Prov. Canonry Le Puy-en-Velay, fol. 185^{v}–252^{v}, *Praefatio,* Books 1–4 and Appendix 2 (extracts); cf. Mordek, *Bibliotheca capitularium* 467–468; MGH Capit. n.s. 1.115–117 and 234–238 (Group B2)

Paris, Bibliothèque nationale, lat. 4628A, saec. X–XI (fol. 93–100: saec. XV), Northern France, Prov. Saint-Denis, fol. 80^r–144^r: *Praefatio,* Books 1–4 and Appendices 1 and 2; with additions; cf. Mordek, *Bibliotheca capitularium* 496–497, 500; MGH Capit. n.s. 1.117–120 and 269–279 (Group D, Copy of Paris lat. 10758)

Paris, Bibliothèque nationale, lat. 4631, saec. XV, Northern France, fol. 46^r–88^v, without *Praefatio,* rest of Book 1, Books 2, 3, and 4 (each with preceding *Capitulatio*), Appendices 1 and 2 (copy of Paris lat. 4628A) Mordek, *Biblioteca capitularium* 510–511, 513; MGH Capit. n.s. 1.120–121 (Group D)

Paris, Bibliothèque nationale, lat. 4634, saec. X; France, Prov. Cathedral of Sens, fol. 1^v–34^v: *Praefatio,* Books 1–4 and Appendices 1–3; cf. Mordek, *Bibliotheca capitularium* 519–521; MGH Capit. n.s. 1.121–123 and 262 (Group C2)

Paris, Bibliothèque nationale, lat. 4635, saec. X, probably Italy (according to Mordek, *Bibliotheca capitularium* 521), in the property of Jean du Tillet (Bishop of Meaux, †1570) who used it for his edition (Paris 1548, cf. MGH Capit. n.s. 1.377–381) and the Cardinal Jules Mazarin (1602–1661); p. 3–48, 33–69: Ansegis, Books 1–4 (without 4.71–74) and Appendices 1–3; cf. Mordek, *Bibliotheca capitularium* 521–522 and MGH Capit. n.s. 1.123–125 and 171–172 (Group B1)

Paris, Bibliothèque nationale, lat. 4636, saec. IX^{med}, written at Tours, fol. 3^r–24^v: Books 1–4 and Appendices 1–3, cf. Mordek, *Bibliotheca capitularium* 522–524; MGH Capit. n.s. 1.126–127 and 262 (Group C2)

Paris, Bibliothèque nationale, lat. 4637, saec. IX^2; France, perhaps Le Mans, fol. 1^r–65^r: *Praefatio,* Books 1–4 and Appendices 1–3; cf. Mordek, *Bibliotheca capitularium* 524–526; MGH Capit. n.s. 1.127–129 and 259 (Group C2)

Paris, Bibliothèque nationale, lat. 4638, saec. XI, France (Reims according to Semmler, 'Monastische Gesetzgebung' 370, but see also Devisse, *Hincmar et la loi* 67 n. 3) fol. 1^r–70^r: *Praefatio,* Books 1–4 and Appendices 1 and 2; Appendix 3 from a modern hand; cf. Mordek, *Bibliotheca capitularium* 526–533; MGH Capit. n.s. 1.129–130 and 275–276 (Group D, probably a copy of Berlin, Phill. 1762); cf also Landau, 'Gefälschtes Recht' 27 (five forged canons: fol. 137^v–139);

Paris, Bibliothèque nationale, lat. 4761, saec. X^1, France, perhaps Besançon (thirteenth century), fol. 1^v–90^r: *Praefatio,* Books 1–4.70 (without 4.71–74) and Appendices 1–3 (as Book 5, without App. 2.31); with additions, cf. Mordek, *Bibliotheca capitularium* 540–545; MGH Capit. n.s. 1.130–132 and 224–227 (Group B1)

Paris, Bibliothèque nationale, lat. 4762, saec. IX^2, Northeastern France? The manuscript has been in the property of Jacques-Auguste de Thou (1553–1617) and Colbert (1619–1683); 1732 acquired by the Bibliotheca Regia; fol. 1^r–133^v: *Praefatio,* Books 1–4 and Appendices 1–3, cf. Mordek, *Bibliotheca capitularium* 545–546; MGH Capit. n.s. 1.132–133 and 255–257 (Group C1)

Paris, Bibliothèque nationale, lat. 9654, saec. X^{ex}–XI^{in}, Prov. Saint-Vincent, Metz, fol. 29^v–66^r: *Praefatio,* Books 1–4, Appendices 1 and 2; cf. Schmitz, 'Ansegis und Regino' 110 with n. 45 and Mordek, *Bibliotheca capitularium* 562–578, esp. 571–572; MGH Capit. n.s. 1.133–135 and 231–234 (Group B2)

Paris, Bibliothèque nationale, lat. 10758, saec. IX3/4, Prov. Saint-Remi, Reims, p. 141–255: *Praefatio,* Books 1–4, Appendices 1 and 2; additions; cf. Mordek, *Bibliotheca capitularium* 595–596; MGH Capit. n.s. 1.135–139 and 276–277 (Group D); cf. also above Paris lat. 4628A

Paris, Bibliothèque nationale, lat. 18237, saec. IX2/4; France (near Tours?); in the possession of Antoine Loisel (1536–1617); three parts: part I (fol. 1–64): part II (fol. 65–120): part III (fol. 121–144), fol. 1^r–64^v: Ansegis, fragmentary from Book 1.59 to 3.82; cf. Mordek, *Bibliotheca capitularium* 612–616, especially 614 and MGH Capit. n.s. 1.139–140 and 262–263 (Group C)

Paris, Bibliothèque nationale, lat. 18238, with the exception of Ansegis (saec. IX–X) the manuscript dates from saec. IX1/2, Northern France, (Saint-Amand? according to Mordek); fol. 21^r–40^v: only Book 3 and *Praefatio* (fragmentary); cf. Mordek, *Bibliotheca capitularium* 617–619, especially 618 and MGH Capit. n.s. 1.140–141 and 255–257 (Group C1)

Paris, Bibliothèque nationale, lat. 18239, saec. XI, Prov. Sainte-Marie at Cambron (Hainaut, dioc. of Cambrai) and was later owned by the Jacobine convent at Paris (1671–1790); cf. Schmitz, 'Ansegis und Regino' 109 with n. 44 (further bibliographical references to this manuscript); p. 2–fol. 73^v: *Praefatio,* Books 1–4; with the preface of Book 4 (fol. 59^v) begins another recension; Appendices 1–2 with Addenda like in mss. Vat. Pal. lat. 582 and Paris lat. 9654; cf. Mordek, *Bibliotheca capitularium* 619–621, especially 620 and MGH Capit. n.s. 1.141–144, 231–234 and 260 (Books 1–3: Group B2, Book 4: Group C2)

Paris, Bibliothèque nationale, nouv. acq. lat. 1632, saec. X^{in}, France (probably Orléans), Prov. Orléans (cf. Christ, 'Überlieferung' 317 n. 1), fol. 119^v–147^v: *Praefatio,* Books 1–4, Appendices 1 and 2, but without Book 4.19–21 and 70–74; cf. Mordek, *Bibliotheca capitularium* 624–625; MGH Capit. n.s. 1.144–146 and 241–242 (Group B2)

St. Gallen, Stiftsbibliothek, 727 (Sang. 1), saec. IX3/4; Reims, during the episcopate of Hincmar? (cf. Devisse, *Hincmar et la loi* 64–65) p. 1–106: *Praefatio,* Books 1–4 and Appendices 1–3; cf. Mordek, *Bibliotheca capitularium* 664–665; MGH Capit. n.s. 1.146–147 and 261 (Group C2)

St. Gallen, Stiftsbibliothek, 728 (Sang. 2), saec. IX2/2, (Eastern) France, Prov. St. Gall (close relationship to Cod. Berlin Hamilton 132), p. 24–95: Books 3 and 4, Appendices 1–3, cf. Mordek, *Bibliotheca capitularium* 665–668, especially 666; MGH Capit. n.s. 1.147–148 and 255–256 (Group C1)

Schaffhausen, Stadtbibliothek, Min. 75, saec. XI–XII, Prov. Allerheiligen; fol. 32^r–86^v: *Praefatio,* Books 1–4 and excerpts from Appendix 2, addition (excerpt from Gelasius I., JK 637) like Cod. Bonn S. 402 and Paris lat. 4417; cf. Mordek, *Bibliotheca capitularium* 705–707; MGH Capit. n.s. 1.148–150 and 234–238 (Group B2)

Sélestat (Schlettstadt), Bibliothèque Humaniste, 14 (104), saec. $IX^{2-3/3}$; Western France (Wissembourg), cf. H. Mordek, 'Weltliches Recht im Kloster Weißenburg i. Elsaß - Hinkmar von Reims und die Kapitulariensammlung des Cod. Sélestat, Bibliothèque Humaniste, 14 (104)', *Litterae Medii Aevi: Festschrift für Johanne Autenrieth zu ihrem 60. Geburtstag,* ed. M. Borgolte and H. Spilling (Sigmaringen 1988) 69–85; cf. also H. Mordek, 'Von Patrick zu Bonifatius . . . Alkuin, Ferrières und die irischen Heiligen in einem westfränkischen Reliquienverzeichnis', *Festschrift Zimmermann* (1991) 61; fol. 70^r–93^v, 99^r–127^r: including Appendices 1 and 2, without *Praefatio* and without Book 4.71–74; fol. 128^{r-v}: 4.71–74; Mordek, *Bibliotheca capitularium* 708–714; MGH Capit. n.s. 1.150–152 and 277–278 (Group D)

Stuttgart, Württembergische Landesbibliothek, HB.VI.112, saec. X^{2}, region around the Lake Constance, Prov. Weingarten (cf. J.- F. von Schulte, 'Vier Weingartner jetzt Stuttgarter Handschriften', *SB Vienna* 117, 1888); fol. 87^{r}–124^{r}: *Praefatio,* Books 1–4, (Appendices 1–3 are missing); cf. Christ, 'Überlieferung' 322; Mordek, *Bibliotheca capitularium* 720–723; MGH Capit. n.s. 1.152–153 and 210–211 (Group A)

Stuttgart, Württembergische Landesbibliothek, iur. 4° 134, saec. X–XI, written at St. Gall (according to H. Hoffmann), Prov. Weißenau, fol. 34^{r}–136^{v}: Books 1–4; fol. 177^{r}–183^{r}: Ansegis 4.15–33; fol. 183^{r}–199^{v}: Excerpts from Ansegis; cf. Mordek, *Bibliotheca capitularium* 724–728; MGH Capit. n.s. 1.153–155, 210–211 (Group A) and 340–357 (partial edition)

Vaticano, Città del, Biblioteca Apostolica Vaticana, lat. 4159, saec. IX^{2}, probably France, fol. 1^{r}–112^{v}, Book 4.71–74 missing; cf. Mordek, *Bibliotheca capitularium* 864–865; MGH Capit. n.s. 1.170–171 and 224–227 (Group B1)

Vaticano, Città del, Biblioteca Apostolica Vaticana, Ottobon. lat. 258 (olim Vat. Reg. 1233), saec. IX^{2}–X^{1}, Compiègne? (B. Bischoff), fol. 1^{r}–84^{r}: *Praefatio,* Books 1–4.70 (Book 4.71–74 and Appendices missing); cf. Mordek, *Bibliotheca capitularium* 768–769, MGH Capit. n.s. 1.155–156 (Group B1)

Vaticano, Città del, Biblioteca Apostolica Vaticana, Pal. lat. 582, saec. XI/2, Northeastern France (Schmitz), Prov. St. Martin at Mainz (1479), related to Cod. Paris lat. 9654; fol. 33^{r}–75^{r}: *Praefatio,* Books 1–4, Appendices 1 and 2, cf. Mordek, 'Karolingische Kapitularien' 38 n. 72; Schmitz, 'Ansegis und Regino' 111 including n. 49–52 and 115–132; Mordek, *Bibliotheca capitularium* 780–797, especially 790; MGH Capit. n.s. 1.156–158 and 231–234 (Group B2)

Vaticano, Città del, Biblioteca Apostolica Vaticana, Pal. lat. 583, saec. X^{med} (cf. Hoffmann, *Buchkunst* 259–260) Fulda-Mainz, Prov. Cathedral library, Mainz (1479), fol. 1^{r}–43^{r}: after the fragmentary Book 1.48, complete transmission of all the books and appendices; cf. Mordek, *Bibliotheca capitularium* 797–799; MGH Capit. n.s. 1.158–159 and 260–261 (Group C2)

Vaticano, Città del, Biblioteca Apostolica Vaticana, Pal. lat. 973, saec. IX^{2}, Northeastern France, region of Reims (cf. B. Bischoff, 'Lorsch im Spiegel seiner Handschriften', *Die Reichsabtei Lorsch: Festschrift zum Gedenken an ihre Stiftung 764* [Darmstadt 1977] 2.7–128, especially 116–117); fol. 43^{r}–123^{v}: *Praefatio,* Books 1–4, Appendices 1–2; cf. Mordek, *Bibliotheca capitularium* 801–805, especially 803; MGH Capit. n.s. 1.159–160 and 201–202 (Group A)

Vaticano, Città del, Biblioteca Apostolica Vaticana, Reg. lat. 417, saec. X^{1}, 900–950 according to F. M. Carey, 'The scriptorium of Reims during the Archbishopric of Hincmar (845–882 A.D.)', *Classical and Mediaeval Studies in Honor of Edward Kennard Rand,* ed. L. W. Jones (New York 1938) 41–60, especially 59; Reims, Prov. Saint-Remi at Reims; fol. 1^{r}–67^{v}: *Praefatio,* Books 1–4 and Appendices 1 and 2 with additions from the 'Reims group' (Group D); cf. Mordek, *Bibliotheca capitularium* 823–825; MGH Capit. n.s. 1.160–162 and 239–240 (Group B)

Vaticano, Città del, Biblioteca Apostolica Vaticana, Reg. lat. 447, saec. IX–X, (for the several differing dates cf. MGH Capit. n.s. 1.162), Northern France; fol. 1^{r}–8^{v}, 25^{r}–32^{v}, 9^{r}–16^{v}, 33^{r}–50^{r}: *Praefatio,* Books 1–4, Appendices 1–3; cf. Mordek, *Bibliotheca capitularium* 825–827; MGH Capit. n.s. 1.162–164 and 255–257 (Group C1)

Vaticano, Città del, Biblioteca Apostolica Vaticana, Reg. lat. 974, saec. X, France (the manuscript was owned by Alexandre Petau), not a copy of Vat. Pal. lat. 583, as Seckel; 'Benedictus Levita' 383, indicated (cf. MGH Capit. n.s. 1.166); fol. 1^r–38^v: complete transmission of Ansegis; cf. Mordek, *Bibliotheca capitularium* 833–834; MGH Capit. n.s. 1.165–167 and 260–261 (Group C2)

Vaticano, Città del, Biblioteca Apostolica Vaticana, Reg. lat. 1000B, saec. IX³, Western Germany with additions from Corbie (fol. 11^r, 42^v - according to B. Bischoff); fol. 1^r–87^v: *Praefatio,* Books 1–4, Appendices 1–3; cf. G. Schmitz, 'Vier-Bücher-Sammlung' 241 including n. 38; and 238–239 (Ansegis-version used in the compilation of the *Collectio 4 librorum* of Köln 124); cf. Mordek, *Bibliotheca capitularium* 841–842; MGH Capit. n.s. 1.167–169 and 206–208 (Group A with numerous characteristics of Group C, illustrates the transition from A to C)

Vaticano, Città del, Biblioteca Apostolica Vaticana, Reg. lat. 1036, saec. XV, the manuscript was owned by Alexandre Petau; du Tillet used it for his edition (cf. MGH Capit. n.s. 1.378); fol. 53^v–147^r: Books 1–4 (the Appendices are missing); cf. Mordek, *Bibliotheca capitularium* 844–847; MGH Capit. n.s. 1.169–170 and 265–266 (Group C2)

Vercelli, Biblioteca Capitolare, CLXXIV, saec. IX², Northern Italy; fol. 1^r–76^v *Praefatio,* Book 1–4 (Book 4.71–74 missing) and Appendices 1–3, fragmentary in the beginning; same addition as Paris lat. 4635; cf. Mordek, *Bibliotheca capitularium* 891–893; MGH Capit. n.s. 1.171–172 and 227–229 (Group B1)

Fragments

Blois, Archives départementales de Loir-et-Cher, saec. X–XI (according to J. Soyer, 'Un fragment des capitulaires de l'Empereur Louis le Pieux, 814–840, aux Archives départementales de Loir-et-Cher', *Bulletin du Comité des travaux historiques et scientifiques, Sect. 4, Bulletin historique et philologique* [1903] 466–468), cf. Mordek, *Bibliotheca capitularium* 80–81; MGH Capit. n.s. 1.172–173 (lost fragment)

Frankfurt am Main, Stadt- und Universitätsbibliothek, lat. oct. 139, fol. 11, 14, 17–69; saec. IX (palimpsest: saec. XII: *Gesta Treverorum*), Prov. St. Eucharius, Trier; Books 1–4, cf. Mordek, *Bibliotheca capitularium* 124–125; MGH Capit. n.s. 1.173

München, Bayerische Staatsbibliothek, Clm 29555/1 (olim 29084); Prov. Benediktbeuern, saec. IX–X; remains of a manuscript containing capitularies, related to Gotha, Mbr. I 84 (cf. MGH Capit. n.s. 1.89); cf. G. Seeliger, 'Mittheilungen aus einer Münchener Handschrift der Capitularien', NA 19 (1894) 670–679; P. Lehmann and O. Glauning, 'Mittelalterliche Handschriftenbruchstücke der Universitätsbibliothek und des Georgianum zu München', *72. Beiheft zum Zentralblatt für Bibliothekswesen* (1940) 45 n. LXI; Mordek, *Bibliotheca capitularium* 369–376; MGH Capit. n.s. 1.173–174; (part B I, single leaf; saec. IX–X, Northern Italy; Ansegis, Book 1, c. 100 from *pape gelasii* to c. 104; single leaf sine num., saec. IX–X, Northern Italy: Ansegis, Book 2, c. 28 (from *comes uicarios*) to c. 29 (*pueri pascuntur*); part B II, two double leaves, saec. IX–X, Northern Italy: fol. 1^r–2^r: Ansegis, Book 4, cc. 57–70, cf. Mordek, *Bibliotheca capitularium* 372)

München, Bayerische Staatsbibliothek, Clm 29555/3 (olim 29085), saec. IX–X, Southern Germany, three strips of paper from three leaves (two from Clm

3717 and one from Clm 3852) Mordek, *Biblioteca capitularium* 377–378; MGH Capit. n.s. 1.153 and 175 (Group A, related to Stuttgart, Württembergische Landesbibliothek, HB.VI.112)

München, Universitätsbibliothek, double leaf, p. 2, saec. IX–X, Northern Italy: Book 1, from c. 104 to c. 115 and p. 3: Book 1.138–157, cf. Mordek, *Bibliotheca capitularium* 372 and MGH Capit. n.s. 1.173 (burnt in World War II)

Wien, Österreichische Nationalbibliothek, Ser. n. 3761, saec. IX^{2}, probably Lorraine (Wissembourg?) according to H. Hoffmann; fol. 1^{r-v}; cf. Mordek, *Bibliotheca capitularium* 915–916; Southern Germany according to MGH Capit. n.s. 1.175

Excerpts

Leiden, Bibliotheek der Rijksuniversiteit, Voss. lat. qu. 13, written in France, saec. X2/2; fol. 18^{r}–26^{v}; Prov. Avignon; cf. Mordek, *Bibliotheca capitularium* 208–209; MGH Capit. n.s. 1.175–177

Milano, Biblioteca Ambrosiana, A.46 inf., saec. IX^{ex}, Reims, fol. 131^{r}–151^{r}, 90 excerpts from Ansegis; the text indicates that it is part of a collection of 142 chapters; cf. Mordek, *Bibliotheca capitularium* 235–236; MGH Capit. n.s. 1.177–182 (probably a collection of excerpts compiled after 857 and copied together with other materials for a 'Collectio 142 capitulorum', the Ansegis' excerpts must be copied from a manuscript of Group B2)

Lost Manuscripts

Beauvais, Prov. Cathedral of Beauvais, used by Pithou, Sirmond and Baluze; according to Baluze the best and most complete manuscript known to him, cf. Pertz 268. Seckel 381, 461, proves that the Vat. lat. 4982 and Vat. Reg. 291 contain excerpts from this manuscript dating from the sixteenth and seventeenth centuries; collations from this manuscript are found in the Paris B.N. Coll. Baluze 2 (cf. Auvray-Poupardin, *Catalogue des mss. de la Collection Baluze* [Paris 1921] 4); collations from Ansegis' texts can be found only in Vaticano, Città del, Biblioteca Apostolica Vaticana, Reg. lat. 291, saec. XVI^{2} (ca. 1573?), Northern France, fol. 123bis^{v}–127^{v}: excerpts from all the books and appendices of Ansegis' *Collectio capitularium* with additions; cf. Mordek, *Bibliotheca capitularium* 819; MGH Capit. n.s. 1.182–184 (lost Beauvais codex transmitted a complete Ansegis-text of the B2-Group)

Strasbourg, Bibliothèque municipale, C.V.6, saec. IX3/3, probably Southern Germany or Switzerland, Prov. Sélestat (Schlettstadt), burnt in 1870, cf. Pertz, MGH LL 1.267–268 and Mordek, *Bibliotheca capitularium* 714–716; MGH Capit. n.s. 1.184–188 (Group A)

7. *Bibliography*

HLF 4 (Paris 1738) 509–511; P. Hinschius, 'Ansegis', RE 1 (^{3}1896) 560; P. Fournier, 'Anségise', DHGE 3 (1924) 447–448; A. Amanieu, 'Anségise', DDC 1 (1935) 564–567; Van Hove, *Prolegomena* 256–257; R. Buchner, 'Ansegis', NDB 1 (1953) 309; A. Zimmermann 'Ansegis', LThK 1 (1957) 591–592; Ch. Lefebvre, 'Ansegiso', *Bibliotheca Sanctorum* 1 (1961) 1339–1340; W. A. Eckhardt, 'Ansegis', HRG 1 (1971) 178–179; J. Laporte, 'Fontenelle', DHGE 17 (1971) 915–953; J. Wollasch, 'Ansegis', LMA 1 (1979) 677–678

Schmitz, 'Ansegis und Regino' 95–132

G. Schmitz, 'The Capitulary Legislation of Louis the Pious', *Charlemagne's Heir: New Perspectives on the Reign of Louis the Pious (814–840)*, ed. P. Godman and R. Collins (Oxford 1990) 425–436

Schmitz, 'Vier-Bücher-Sammlung' 237–239

G. Schmitz, 'Intelligente Schreiber: Beobachtungen aus Ansegis- und Kapitularien-handschriften', *Festschrift Fuhrmann* (1991) 79–93

Siems, *Handel und Wucher* 323–324, 442–444, 535

Mordek, *Bibliotheca capitularium* (cf. index, p. 1100 no. 183)

MGH Capit. n.s. 1.(cf. 'Edition') 1–416 ('Einleitung')

Pseudo-Isidorus Mercator, Decretales

1. Author: Unknown. *2. Date:* About the middle of the ninth century. *3. Place:* Probably western part of the Frankish empire. *4. Type:* Chronologically arranged collection of decretals and conciliar canons.

5. Editions

Jacques Merlin, *Tomus primus quatuor conciliorum generalium, Quadraginta septem conciliorum provincialium authenticorum, Decretorum sexaginta novem Pontificum ab Apostolis et eorum canonibus, Usque ad Zachariam primum, Isidoro authore* (Paris 1524) (according to Cod. Paris, Bibliothèque de l'Assemblée nationale, 27; saec. XII) (PL 130 (1853)

P. Hinschius, *Decretales Pseudo-Isidorianae et Capitula Angilramni* (Leipzig 1863; repr. Aalen 1963) (cf. Fuhrmann, HRG 4 [1990] 83)

6. Manuscripts

Cf. S. Williams, *Codices Pseudo-Isidoriani*; Fuhrmann, *Einfluß und Verbreitung* 1.168–170 n. 61 and Mordek, 'Addenda' 471–478; see also the important corrections and additional information to Williams in the following reviews: R. E. Reynolds, *Speculum* 47 (1972) 818–823; A. García y García, REDC 28 (1972) 434–435; J. Gilchrist, TRG 42 (1974) 130–134; P. Landau, ZRG Kan. Abt. 60 (1974) 402–405

Albi, Bibliothèque municipale, 30; Pseudo-Isidorian part comprises 33 unnumbered folios, difficult to date, saec. XI?, cf. Reynolds, *Speculum* 47 (1972) 821: probably earlier than saec. XI. Script. Liège, Prov. Albi

Albi, Bibliothèque municipale, 108 (olim 115) (saec. IX–X)

Angers, Bibliothèque municipale, 367, saec. X (Hinschius: Class A-1), Script. Angers, Prov. Angers

Aosta, Biblioteca Capitolare, C.102, saec. IX^2, Northern Italy, fol. 1^r–93^v (Class A-2, cf. Mordek, 'Addenda' 473)

Avesnes, Société archéologique et historique de l'arrondissement d'Avesnes (Nord), sine num., saec. XII2/2, Script. Flanders, Prov. Avesnes

Avranches, Bibliothèque municipale, 146, saec. XII (Hinschius: Class A-1); Script. Northern France (Thérouanne?), Prov. Avranches

Bamberg, Staatsbibliothek, Can. 4 (P.I.8, olim Dombibliothek C.47), saec. X; Script. Northern Italy, Prov. Bamberg (Class A-2)

Bern, Burgerbibliothek, 451, fol. 1–8, saec. IX^2 (excerpt from the Pseudo-Isidorian Decretals from Clemens to Zephyrinus)

Bernkastel-Kues, Bibliothek des St.-Nikolaus Hospitals, 52 (olim 37; C.14), saec. XI; Script. Liège, Prov. Bernkastel-Kues (Class A-1?), according to K. Manitius (*Forschungen und Fortschritte* 29, 1955, 317–319) from the monastery of S. Eucharius-Matthias at Trier

Boulogne, Bibliothèque municipale, 115, saec. XII (Hinschius: Class B); Script. Flanders, Prov. Boulogne

Boulogne, Bibliothèque municipale, 116, saec. XII; Script. Flanders, Prov. Boulogne (Class B)

Brescia, Biblioteca Civica Queriniana, B.II.13, saec. IX–X (according to Maassen, abridged version, Hinschius: Class A-2); Script. Northern Italy, Prov. Brescia

Bruxelles, Bibliothèque Royale Albert Ier, 5219–31, saec. XI; Script. Flanders, Prov. Belgium

Bruxelles, Bibliothèque Royale Albert Ier, II.2532, saec. XII; Script. Flanders, Prov. Binche (Belgium)

Cambrai, Bibliothèque municipale, 624 (575), saec. XII

Cambridge, University Library, Dd.I.10–11, saec. XIV (Hinschius: Class A-1), copy of London, British Library, Cotton Claudius E.V (no. 27), Script. England, Prov. Cambridge

Chartres, Bibliothèque municipale, 26 (olim 67bis), saec. X (completely destroyed on 26 May 1944) (Hinschius. Class A-1), Prov. library of the cathedral chapter of Notre-Dame at Chartres; Script. Chartres

Chartres, Bibliothèque municipale, 376 (olim 140), saec. XI; Script. Chartres, Prov. Chartres

Córdoba, Archivo Catedralicio y Biblioteca del Cabildo, 38 (saec. XVI; cf. Fuhrmann, *Einfluß und Verbreitung* 2.403 including n. 120)

Douai, Bibliothèque municipale, 582, saec. XII; Script. Saint-Bertin, Prov. Marchiennes

Douai, Bibliothèque municipale, 583, saec. XII (ca. 1138–1143); Script. Saint-Bertin, Prov. Anchin

Edinburgh, National Library of Scotland, 10.1.5, fol. 267^r–382^r (saec. XV) (only councils)

Eton, College Library, B.1.I.6 (97), saec. XII, Script. Normandy? Prov. cathedral chapter of Exeter, connections with Saint-Omer 189 and London, Royal 11.D.IV; cf. Somerville, 'Lanfranc's Canonical Collection and Exeter', BIHR 45 (1972) 303–306; Ker, *Medieval Manuscripts* 2.708–711

Firenze, Biblioteca Medicea Laurenziana, Plut. XVI 18, saec. XV (Hinschius: Class A-1) (incomplete copy of Firenze, Conv. soppr. J.III.18), Script. Florence, Prov. Florence

Firenze, Biblioteca Nazionale Centrale, Conv. soppr. J.III.18, saec. X–XI; Script. Northern Italy, Prov. Florence (Class A-1)

Firenze, Biblioteca Nazionale Centrale, Panciatichi 135, saec. XV (Class A-1, particular form without the part containing the councils, cf. Mordek, 'Addenda' 474)

Grenoble, Bibliothèque municipale, 473 (olim 16), saec. XII; Script. France?, Prov. Grenoble

Ivrea, Biblioteca Capitolare, LXXXVIII, saec. IX^{ex} (Hinschius: Class A-2) closely related to the codices Köln 114, Stuttgart HB.VI.105, St. Gallen 670 and Vercelli LXXX; Script. Ivrea, Prov. Ivrea

Köln, Erzbischöfliche Diözesan- und Dombibliothek, 113 (olim Darmstadt 2112), saec. X, Script. Cologne?, Prov. Cologne

Köln, Erzbischöfliche Diözesan- und Dombibliothek, 114 (olim Darmstadt 2113), saec. X (Hinschius: Class A-2), Script. Cologne?, Prov. Cologne

Köln, Historisches Archiv, W 50, saec. XI–XII

Köln, Historisches Archiv, W 101, saec. XII (both Mss. from Cologne seem to contain the decretals of Class A-1 in an abridged version, cf. Fuhrmann, *Einfluß und Verbreitung* 1.170 n. 61); cf. above

Leipzig, Universitätsbibliothek, II.7 (olim Stadtbibliothek, Naumann CCXLI), saec. IX (Hinschius: Class A/B), Script. Corbie? Prov. Leipzig

Leipzig, Universitätsbibliothek, II.8 (olim Stadtbibliothek, Naumann CCXL), saec. XII (Hinschius: Class A/B); Script. and Prov. unknown

Livorno, Biblioteca Comunale, Fondo Labronica sine num., saec. XII, (Hinschius: Class A-2) Script. Northern Italy, Prov. Brescia

London, British Library, Cotton Claudius E.V., saec. XII (Hinschius: Class A-1), Script. Normandy, Prov. England

London, British Library, Royal 11.D.IV, saec. XV (Hinschius: Class A-1); according to Brooke either direct or indirect copy of Eton, College Library, B.1.I.6 (97), Script. England, Prov. England

Lucca, Biblioteca Capitolare Feliniana, Plut. II 123, saec. IX (Hinschius: Class A-2), striking resemblance to Pistoia, Archivio Capitolare del Duomo, 102; Script. Lucca, Prov. Lucca

Madrid, Biblioteca Nacional, 12187, saec. XVII (copy of the now-lost Cod. Madrid Ff.8), Script. Spain, Prov. Spain

Mantova, Biblioteca Comunale, B.III.1 (205), saec. XI–XII, Class A-2; cf. Fuhrmann, MIÖG 78 (1970) 54 n. 12; Reynolds, *Speculum* 47 (1972) 822 including n. 2; Fuhrmann, *Einfluß und Verbreitung* 1.169 n. 61; Mordek, 'Addenda' 476

Mantova, Biblioteca Comunale, B.III.5 (209), saec. XII (Fuhrmann, *Einfluß und Verbreitung* 1.169 n. 61); Mordek, 'Addenda' 476 (Class A-2)

Melk, Stiftsbibliothek, 410 (I 22, 506), saec. XV

Milano, Biblioteca Ambrosiana, A.87 inf., saec. XI; Script. Angers, Prov. Milan (Class A-1)

Modena, Biblioteca Capitolare, O.I.4, saec. IX; Script. Italy, Prov. Modena

Monte Cassino, Archivio e Biblioteca dell'Abbazia, 1, saec. XI (Hinschius: Class A/B); Script. Monte Cassino, Prov. Monte Cassino

Montpellier, Bibliothèque Interuniversitaire, H.3, saec. XII (1144–1145) (Hinschius Class C); Script. Northern France, Prov. Clairvaux

Montpellier, Bibliothèque Interuniversitaire, H.13, saec. XIII (cf. Reynolds, *Speculum* 47 [1972] 821: saec. XII^{ex}), Script. Northern France, Prov. Pontigny

Monza, Biblioteca Capitolare, h-3/151, saec. IX; Script. Northern Italy, Prov. Monza (Class A-2)

München, Bayerische Staatsbibliothek, Clm 2940, saec. IX3/4, Northern Italy (fragmentary strips of a Pseudo-Isidorian codex in binding)

New Haven, Yale University, Beinecke Library, 442, saec. IX3/4; Script. probably Diocese of Reims; not written during the decade after 850 (Williams) but rather during the pontificate of Pope John VIII (872–882) (see list of popes; cf. Kerner et al., 'Textidentifikation' 37 n. 86); on the provenance of this manuscript, cf. C. McCurry, 'On the Provenance of the Yale-Pseudo-Isidore', BMCL 2 (1972) 61–67; but cf. the criticism of D. Jasper, DA 29 (1973) 251–252 (Class A-1)

Oxford, Bodleian Library, Canon. Patr. lat. 194, saec. XI^{2}, Northern (?) Italy (Class A-2, cf. Mordek, 'Addenda' 474)

Oxford, Bodleian Library, Hatton 6 (=Misc. 4129), saec. XIII^{in}; Script. Northern France, Prov. Oxford

Paris, Bibliothèque de l'Arsenal, 679 (6 J.1), saec. XIV^{in}; Script. France? Prov. Paris

Paris, Bibliothèque de l'Assemblée nationale 27 (B.19, olim 681), saec. XII (striking correspondance to Reims, Bibliothèque municipale, 672 and Venezia, Zanetti lat. 168 and 169), saec. XII^{ex} (April or May 1191), Script. Northern France, Prov. Paris (Class C)

Paris, Bibliothèque nationale, Collection Baluze 271, fol. 9, 10–11, saec. IX–X (see also Mordek, 'Addenda' 477) fragment

Paris, Bibliothèque nationale, lat. 3852, saec. XI; Script. Angers, Prov. Paris

Paris, Bibliothèque nationale, lat. 3853, saec. XII (1154–59) (Hinschius: Class B); Script. Saint-Amand, Prov. Saint-Amand

Paris, Bibliothèque nationale, lat. 3854, saec. XII (Hinschius: Class A-2), Script. Normandy (Jumièges?), Prov. Normandy

Paris, Bibliothèque nationale, lat. 3855, saec. XV (Hinschius: Class A-1), Script. uncertain, Prov. Paris

Paris, Bibliothèque nationale, lat. 3857, saec. XIV

Paris, Bibliothèque nationale, lat. 4280AA, saec. X–XI (Hinschius: Class A-2); Prov. Moissac

Paris, Bibliothèque nationale, lat. 5141, saec. XIV, probably a copy of Paris lat. 16897 (Hinschius: Class A-2); Script. France, Prov. Troyes

Paris, Bibliothèque nationale, lat. 9629 (Reg. 3887.8.A), saec. IX–XI (cf. Reynolds, *Speculum* 47 [1972] 821: the dating is to be thoroughly reexamined; not one manuscript, but parts of two different ones) (Hinschius: Class A-1), Script. France, Prov. France

Paris, Bibliothèque nationale, lat. 14314 (olim Saint-Victor 184), saec. XII (1138–1143) (Hinschius: Class B), Script. Flanders, Prov. Paris

Paris, Bibliothèque nationale, lat. 15391 (olim Sorbonne 729), saec. XV (Hinschius: Class A-1); Script. France, Prov. Paris

Paris, Bibliothèque nationale, lat. 16897 (olim Navarre 7), saec. XIII (Hinschius: Class A-2), Script. uncertain, Prov. Paris

Paris, Bibliothèque nationale, nouv. acq. lat. 2253, saec. XI (resembles Cod. Lucca, Bibl. Capit. Plut. II 123 which Hinschius subsumed under Class A-2); Script. France (or Italy?), Prov. Cluny (Fuhrmann, *Einfluß und Verbreitung* 1.169 n. 61: saec. X–XI)

Pistoia, Archivio Capitolare del Duomo, C. 130 (olim 102), saec. IX–X (Hinschius: Class A-2); Script. Pistoia, Prov. Pistoia

Praha, Knihovna Metropolitní Kapituli, K.XXX./1 (1224), saec. XV, fragment (Fuhrmann, *Einfluß und Verbreitung* 1.169 n. 61; Mordek, 'Addenda' 476)

Praha, Národní Muzeum, XII.D.2, saec. XIV (Schulte: Hinschius-Class C, cf.

Williams, *Codices Pseudo-Isidoriani* 50: older tradition), Script. uncertain, Prov. Prague (identical with Praha, Národní Museum, I.G.15 [old shelf-mark], saec. XV), (Class B) (Fuhrmann, *Einfluß und Verbreitung* 1.169 n. 61, corrected by Mordek, 'Addenda' 475 n. 19)

Praha, Národní Knihovna Ceské Republiky, IV. B.12, saec. XV (late twelfth-century source from the diocese of Reims), Script. uncertain, Prov. Prague (Class C)

Praha, Národní Knihovna Ceské Republiky, VI. D.9, saec. XV^{in} (source saec. XII, Hinschius: Class A-2, cf. Fuhrmann, *Einfluß und Verbreitung* 1.169 n. 61: Class A1 [?]), Script. uncertain, Prov. Chomutov (CSFR)

Reims, Bibliothèque municipale, 672 (G. 166), fol. 7–191^{v}, saec. XII (1154–1159) (greatest correspondance to Hinschius' Class C); Script. Reims?, Prov. Reims, cf. Mordek, *Bibliotheca capitularium* 625–628

Rennes, Bibliothèque municipale, 134 (112), saec. IX–X (see also Fuhrmann, *Einfluß und Verbreitung* 1.169 n. 61: saec. XI) Script. probably diocese of Reims or Rouen; part 2 in Rennes, Bibliothèque municipale, 135, saec. XVII presumably a copy of the original part 2 (Williams, *Codices Pseudo-Isidoriani* 149–150)

Roma, Biblioteca Casanatense, 221 (D.III.16; olim A.II.14), saec. XV (Hinschius: Class A-1) (source probably saec. XII), Script. uncertain, Prov. Italy

Roma, Biblioteca Casanatense, 496 (olim A. V. 40), saec. XII (Class A-1)

Roma, Biblioteca Vallicelliana, D.38, saec. IX (Hinschius: Class A-2), Script. Italy, Prov. Italy

Rouen, Bibliothèque municipale, 702 (E.27), saec. XI (Hinschius Cl. A-1; cited under its old shelf-mark 15/9); Script. Angers, Prov. Rouen

Saint-Omer, Bibliothèque municipale, 189, saec. XI, prov. chapter library of Notre-Dame at Saint-Omer (Hinschius: Class A/B); Script. Northern France, Prov. Saint-Omer

St. Gallen, Stiftsbibliothek, 670, saec. IX (Hinschius: Class A-2), Script. St. Gall, Prov. St. Gall

Stuttgart, Württembergische Landesbibliothek, HB.VI.105, saec. X, Prov. Weingarten (1630), written probably at St. Gall or in a scriptorium influenced by St. Gall (Class A 2)

Torino, Biblioteca Nazionale Universitaria, E.II.26, saec. XV (may be a copy of the Milano, Biblioteca Ambrosiana, A.87 inf., saec. XI), Script. Italy, Prov. Italy (Class A-1)

Toulouse, Bibliothèque municipale, 365 (I.9), saec. XIII^{ex}, Script. France, Prov. Dominican friars of Toulouse (Class A-2?)

Vaticano, Città del, Biblioteca Apostolica Vaticana, lat. 629, saec. XII (Hinschius: Class A-2), Script. Montalcino, Prov. Italy

Vaticano, Città del, Biblioteca Apostolica Vaticana, lat. 630, saec. IX^{med} (Hinschius: Class A/B), Script. Corbie, Prov. Northern France (Arras), cf. Richter, 'Stufen' 35–42 and 46–58

Vaticano, Città del, Biblioteca Apostolica Vaticana, lat. 631, saec. XIII (Hinschius: Class B), Script. Flanders, Prov. France

Vaticano, Città del, Biblioteca Apostolica Vaticana, lat. 1340, saec. XIII (Hinschius: Class C); Script. France, Prov. France?

Vaticano, Città del, Biblioteca Apostolica Vaticana, lat. 1344, saec. XII (Hinschius: Class A-1), Script. France, Prov. France?

Vaticano, Città del, Biblioteca Apostolica Vaticana, lat. 3788, saec. XI–XII (Hinschius: Class A2), Script. Italy, Prov. Italy

Vaticano, Città del, Biblioteca Apostolica Vaticana, lat. 3791, saec. XI (Hinschius: Class A1), Script. Northern France, Prov. Northern France?

Vaticano, Città del, Biblioteca Apostolica Vaticana, lat. 4873, saec. XVI (written in 1566 by Vincentius Navarra, scribe of the Vatican Library) (Hinschius: Class A2); Script. Vatican; Prov. Vatican

Vaticano, Città del, Biblioteca Apostolica Vaticana, lat. 4978, saec. XV (fragmentary transmission of a Pseudo-Isidorian augmented version, cf. Mordek, 'Addenda' 474–475)

Vaticano, Città del, Biblioteca Apostolica Vaticana, Ottobon. lat. 93, saec. IX^{med}, (Hinschius: Class A-1), Script. Northern France?, Prov. Northern France, cf. also Richter, 'Stufen' 42–53

Vaticano, Città del, Biblioteca Apostolica Vaticana, Reg. lat. 976, saec. XIII (Hinschius: Class B), Prov. probably a Northern French or Flemish convent, cf. Erickson, 'New Pseudo-Isidore manuscripts' 115; Mordek, 'Addenda' 476

Vaticano, Città del, Biblioteca Apostolica Vaticana, Reg. lat. 978, saec. XII (Class A1, cf. Fuhrmann, *Einfluß und Verbreitung* 3.757–768) see also Erickson, 'New Pseudo-Isidore manuscripts' 115–117, Mordek, 'Addenda' 476)

Vaticano, Città del, Biblioteca Apostolica Vaticana, Reg. lat. 1038, fragment (the part containing the councils is missing), saec. X, fol. 1^r–80^v, cf. Reynolds, *Speculum* 47 (1972) 822 including n. 1; Fuhrmann, *Einfluß und Verbreitung* 1.169 n. 61; saec. IX–X, Mordek, 'Addenda' 476

Vaticano, Città del, Biblioteca Apostolica Vaticana, Reg. lat. 1054, saec. XI, (Hinschius: Class A-1), Script. France, Prov. France

Vaticano, Città del, Biblioteca Apostolica Vaticana, Urb. lat. 46

Vaticano, Città del, Biblioteca Apostolica Vaticana, Urb. lat. 179 (a. 1483)

Vendôme, Bibliothèque municipale, 91, saec. XI (Hinschius: Class A-1), Script. Angers, Prov. Vendôme

Venezia, Biblioteca Nazionale Marciana, lat. IV.47 (Num. Progr. 2126), saec. XV (Hinschius: Class A-1), Script. uncertain, Prov. Northern Italy

Venezia, Biblioteca Nazionale Marciana, lat. IV.48 (Num. Progr. 2301), saec. XV (Hinschius: Class A-2) (source saec. XI–XII), Script. uncertain, Prov. Northern Italy

Venezia, Biblioteca Nazionale Marciana, Zanetti lat. 168 and 169 (Num. progr. 1615, 1616), saec. XV (source from Northern France, saec. XII2/2) (Hinschius: Class C), Script. uncertain, Prov. Venice

Vercelli, Biblioteca Capitolare, LXXX, saec. IX–X (Hinschius: Class A2), written at Vercelli? Prov. Vercelli (saec. X, cf. Fuhrmann, *Einfluß und Verbreitung* 1.170 n. 61)

Wien, Österreichische Nationalbibliothek, lat. 2133, saec. XII (Hinschius: Class A1), Script. uncertain, Prov. uncertain

Wien, Österreichische Nationalbibliothek, lat. 2161, saec. XI (abridged version similar to Hinschius' Class A-2), Script. uncertain, Prov. Salzburg?

York, Minister Library, Add. 8; dating from 1469; cf. N. R. Ker and A. J. Piper, *Medieval Manuscripts in British Libraries* 4 (Oxford 1992) 795–797 (Class B)

Zürich, Zentralbibliothek, Z XIV 10, saec. IX^2 (One leaf with Pseudo-Isidorian texts of Anterus and Fabianus)

Excerpts

For other excerpts see below, Hincmar of Laon, Pittaciolus, Pseudo-Remedius of Chur, *Collectio canonum* and *Collectio Lanfranci*

Berlin, Staatsbibliothek Preußischer Kulturbesitz, Phill. 1664, saec. XI (eleventh-century collection containing extensive excerpts from Pseudo-Isidore), Prov. Limoges

Berlin, Staatsbibliothek Preußischer Kulturbesitz, Phill. 1764, saec. X, Script. probably Soissons (this collection of excerpts can be traced back to Hincmar of Laon, cf. Fuhrmann, *Einfluß und Verbreitung* 3.633–650; G. Schmitz, 'Vier-Bücher-Sammlung' 250–251)

Berlin, Staatsbibliothek Preußischer Kulturbesitz, Theol. lat. qu. 313, Prov. France or Southern Italy (cf. Hoesch, *Traditio* 25 [1969] 499–507)

Brugge (Bruges), Stedelijke Bibliotheek (Bibliothèque de la ville), 99, saec. XI–XII, Prov. Cistercian abbey of Ter Duinen (Dunes), tripartite excerpt from Pseudo-Isidore (fol. 63^r–82^r)

Budapest, Országos Széchényi Könyvtár (Széchényi Library of the National Museum), 203, saec. XV^2

Chartres, Bibliothèque municipale, 193 (olim 172), saec. XI, destroyed in 1944

Chartres, Bibliothèque municipale, 409 (olim 424), saec. XIV, destroyed in 1944; large group of excerpts from Pseudo-Isidore, cf. Mordek, *Bibliotheca capitularium* 111–112

Dijon, Bibliothèque municipale, 2975; fragment of a Pseudo-Isidorian manuscript dating from the second half of the twelfth century; probably from the Cistercian Abbey of Pontigny, cf. Y. Zaluska, *Manuscrits enluminés de Dijon* (1991) 170–171

Durham, Cathedral Library, B.IV.18, saec. XII, Script. Christ Church, Canterbury, according to Brooke excerpt from the *Collectio Lanfranci* (see below, *Collectio Lanfranci*)

Firenze, Biblioteca Medicea Laurenziana, Ashburnham 53, saec. XII

Freiburg (Breisgau), Universitätsbibliothek, 8, saec. IX (about 850–888)

Fribourg, Bibliothèque Cantonale et Universitaire, L 32, saec. XII^2

Leipzig, Universitätsbibliothek, 836, saec. XII, Prov. convent of St. Thomas at Leipzig (Hinschius: Class C)

Leiden, Bibliotheek der Rijksuniversiteit, Voss. lat. oct. 29, saec. IX^{ex} (cf. *Additional Collections to the Capitula of Isaac of Langres* below)

Leiden, Bibliotheek der Rijksuniversiteit, lat. qu. 108, fol. 68^r–81^r, saec. IX^2

London, British Library, Cotton Cleopatra C.VIII, saec. XII, Prov. Germany?

London, British Library, Cotton Vespasian A.XV, saec. XII, during the twelfth century in the possession of Cirencester Abbey; it shows a great similarity to the so-called 'Canterbury abbreviation' of the *Collectio Lanfranci*; cf. Göttweig, Stiftsbibliothek, 53 (56), saec. XII, probably from Passau, fol. 8–107, cf. J. F. Schulte, 'Die Rechtshandschriften der Stiftsbibliotheken von Göttweig, Heiligenkreuz, Klosterneuburg, Melk, Schotten', SB Vienna 57 (1868) 560–569; M. Sdralek, *Die Streitschriften Altmanns von Passau und Wezilos von Mainz* (Paderborn 1890) 64–65 and Brett, 'Collectio Lanfranci' 161 n. 14

London, British Library, Harley 633, saec. XII

London, Lambeth Palace Library 351, saec. XII

Madrid, Biblioteca Nacional, 428 (olim C.40), saec. XII–XIII, Collection in three books based on excerpts from Pseudo-Isidore and Burchard of Worms (cf. below)

Madrid, Biblioteca de la Faculdad de Ciencias Politicas y Economicas, no. 53, saec. XII (olim: signatura moderna 117-2-51; signatura antigua E-26-no. 69; Bibliotheca Complutense Ildefonsiana, Mss. latinos E-2-C2-no. 10; Libreria del Colegio Mayor 25D [Alcalá])

Merseburg, Archiv des Domkapitels, 104, saec. X, small collection of letters from Pseudo-Isidore, cf. below

Milano, Biblioteca Ambrosiana, A.46 inf., saec. IX^{ex}, Reims, collection influenced by Pseudo-Remedius (cf. below); additions saec. XI from the Pseudo-Isidorian Decretals: fol. 150^{r-v}, fol. 156^{r}, 157^{v}–158^{r}; cf. Mordek, *Bibliotheca capitularium* 238

Montserrat, Archivo y Biblioteca de la Abadía, 605, saec. XVIII, excerpts from Pseudo-Isidore; cf. A. Olivar, *Catálog dels manuscrits de la Biblioteca del Monestir de Montserrat* (Scripta et documenta 25; Montserrat 1977) 129–131

München, Bayerische Staatsbibliothek, Clm 14581, saec. XI–XII, St. Emmeram (Regensburg) fol. 162^{v}–163^{v}: two excerpts

Münster, Nordrhein-Westfälisches Staatsarchiv, VII.5201, saec. X, pp. 88–91 (short excerpts of decretals) see above, *Cresconius,* and below *Capitula Angilramni;* Mordek, *Bibliotheca capitularium* 381

Oxford, Bodleian Library, Holkham misc. 19, saec. XII^{in} (*Hispana*-manuscript with a Pseudo-Isidorian appendix including the *Capitula Angilramni*)

Oxford, Bodleian Library, Rawlinson A.433, saec. XII, Prov. Waltham Abbey

Palermo, Archivio della Cattedrale, 14, saec. XII; sister manuscript of Paris lat. 17526 (=Williams, Excerpta no. 26); closely related to Paris lat. 3839A and Paris lat. 17526, cf. MGH Ordines 162

Paris, Bibliothèque nationale lat. 1569, saec. XV

Paris, Bibliothèque nationale, 2449, saec. IX^{ex}, distinct collection which makes extensive use of Pseudo-Isidorian material (cf. *Additional Collections to the Capitula of Isaac of Langres,* below)

Paris, Bibliothèque nationale, lat. 2830, saec. X

Paris, Bibliothèque nationale, lat. 3839A (olim Baluze 90), saec. XI (Hinschius: Class A-1, not a Pseudo-Isidorian codex, but a derivative collection, closely related to Palermo 14, Paris lat. 17526, cf. MGH Ordines 163)

Paris, Bibliothèque nationale, lat. 12445 (olim Saint-Germain-des-Prés 366), saec. IX (845–882), Script. Diocese of Reims, perhaps Cathedral of Laon

Paris, Bibliothèque nationale, lat. 14992, saec. XII, Prov. convent of Saint-Victor, excerpts from the decretals and the councils as well as canons from the *Capitula Angilramni* and the *Canones Apostolorum*

Paris, Bibliothèque nationale, lat. 17526 (olim Notre Dame 105); closely related to Palermo 14 and Paris lat. 3839A, cf. MGH Ordines 165

Paris, Bibliothèque nationale, lat. 18219, saec. XII–XIII, Prov. Library of Notre Dame, contains letters by Ivo of Chartres and a great number of excerpts from Pseudo-Isidore

Roma, Biblioteca Nazionale Centrale, Fondo Varia 1, fol. 199^{r}–297^{v}, saec. XV, Prov. probably Farfa (cf. Mordek, 'Handschriftenforschungen' 630 n. 8)

Salzburg, Bibliothek der Erzabtei St. Peter, a.IX.32 (olim X.28), saec. X–XI, Prov. Cologne (cf. Kottje, 'Salzburger Handschrift' 286–290; fol. 172–194: *Pittaciolus*, fol. 208–212: *Capitula Angilramni*); saec. XI1/4, Salzburg (according to H. Hoffmann, cf. Pokorny, 'Triburer Synodalakten' 435 n. 20); cf. below *Pittaciolus* and *Collectio* of Salzburg, *St. Peter a.IX.32*

Troyes, Bibliothèque municipale, 1064, saec. X, Prov. probably Burgundy

Troyes, Bibliothèque municipale, 1406, saec. X, Prov. probably Burgundy

Vaticano, Città del, Biblioteca Apostolica Vaticana, lat. 1343, distinct collection saec. X, Prov. Italy (transferred from the Diocese of Pavia to the Diocese of Milan, cf. Ballerini); cf. Kuttner-Elze, *Catalogue* 1.86–94, especially 90

Vaticano, Città del, Biblioteca Apostolica Vaticana, lat. 3829, beginning of the twelfth century, independent collection: *Collectio Vaticana* (see below), Northern Italy

Verona, Biblioteca Capitolare, LXIV (62), saec. XI, according to Fournier is this incomplete manuscript evidence of a tenth-century collection from Northern Italy; Prov. library of the chapter of Verona; substantial and systematic excerpts from the abridged version of Pseudo-Isidore (cf. Fournier-Le Bras 1.218–220); cf. also below *Collectio of Verona LXIV*

Würzburg, Universitätsbibliothek, M.p.th.f. 70, saec. IX3/4 (excerpt, based on the *Dionysio-Hadriana*)

7. *Bibliography*

Ph. Schneider, 'Pseudoisidor', *Wetzer und Welte's Kirchenlexikon* ²10 (1897) 600–624; E. Seckel, 'Pseudoisidor', RE ³16 (1905) 265–307; Fournier-Le Bras 1.127–233, especially 171–187, 192–201, 209–212; Kurtscheid-Wilches 1.138–146; H. Fuhrmann, 'False Decretals' NCE 5 (1967) 820–824; H. Fuhrmann, 'Pseudoisidorische Fälschungen', HRG 4 (1990) 80–85; H. Fuhrmann, 'Pseudoisidorische Dekretalen', LMA 7 (1994) 307–309

M. Flacius Illyricus, *Ecclesiastica historia . . . congesta per aliquot et pios viros in urbe Magdeburgica* 2 (Basel 1560) c. VII, 147.59–149.12

D. Blondel, *Pseudo-Isidorus et Turrianus vapulantes* (Geneva 1628)

B. Malvasia, *Apologiae pro Epistolis veterum Romanorum pontificum a B. Clemente usque ad Syricium et a Syricio usque ad D. Gregorium, S. Isidoro Hispalense collectore et P. Francisco Turriano defensore: Liber I in Davidem Blondellum Catalaunum* (Rome 1658)

Ballerini, *De antiquis . . . collectionibus et collectoribus* P. III cap. VI (PL 56.240–264)

C. Blasco, *De collectione canonum Isidori Mercatoris commentarius: Adnectitur in calce operis appendix de Pseudo-Cyriaco Papa, comite S. Ursulae, etc. itemque diatriba de capitulis Hadriano I papae tributis* (Naples 1760)

A. Theiner, *De Pseudo-Isidoriana canonum collectione dissertatio historico-canonica* (Breslau 1827)

J. A. Möhler, 'Fragmente aus und über Pseudo-Isidor', *Theologische Quartalschrift* 1829, 477–520 and 1832, 3–52 (also in: *Gesammelte Schriften und Aufsätze*, ed. J. J. I. von Döllinger [Regensburg 1839–1840] 1.283–347)

F. H. Knust, *De fontibus et consilio Ps.-Isidorianae collectionis commentatio* (Göttingen 1832)

F. G. A. Wasserschleben, *De patria decretalium pseudo-isidorianarum* (Diss. Breslau 1843)

F. G. A. Wasserschleben, *Beiträge zur Geschichte der falschen Dekretalen* (Breslau 1844)

F. Kunstmann, 'Fragmente über Pseudo-Isidor', *Neue Sion* 1 (1845) 241–243, 245–247, 249–251 and 253–255

K. J. Hefele, 'Ueber den gegenwärtigen Stand der pseudoisidorischen Frage', *Theologische Quartalschrift* 29 (1847) 583–665

J. C. E. F. Rosshirt, *Zu den kirchenrechtlichen Quellen des ersten Jahrtausends und zu den pseudoisidorischen Decretalen: Mit besonderer Rücksicht auf noch nicht bekannte Manuscripte* (Heidelberg 1849)

J. Weizsäcker, 'Hinkmar und Pseudo-Isidor', *Zeitschrift für historische Theologie* 28 (1858) 327–430

J. Weizsäcker, *Der Kampf gegen den Chorepiskopat des fränkischen Reichs im 9. Jahrhundert* (Tübingen 1859)

J. Weizsäcker, 'Die pseudo-isidorische Frage in ihrem gegenwärtigen Stande', HZ 3 (1860) 42–96

C. von Noorden, 'Ebo, Hinkmar und Pseudo-Isidor', HZ 7 (1862) 311–350

P. Hinschius, *Decretales Pseudo-Isidorianae et Capitula Angilramni* (Leipzig 1863, repr. Aalen 1963)

P. Hinschius, 'Nachrichten über juristische (insbesondere kanonistische) Handschriften in italienischen Bibliotheken', *Zeitschrift für Rechtsgeschichte* 2 (1863) 455–473

P. Hinschius, 'Über Pseudo-Isidor-Handschriften und Kanonensammlungen in Spanischen Bibliotheken (II)', ZKR 3 (1863) 122–146

R. W. Dove, 'Die erste kritische Ausgabe des Pseudo-Isidor', ZKR 4 (1864) 260–265

H. Wasserschleben, 'Die pseudo-isidorische Frage', ZKR 4 (1864) 273–303

E. Herrmann, 'Decretales Pseudo-Isidorianae et Capitula Angilramni: Ad fidem librorum manuscriptorum rec. . . . Paulus Hinschius (review)', *Göttinger Gelehrte Anzeigen* 1865, 1521–1536

P. Hinschius, 'Der Beiname 'Mercator' in der Vorrede Pseudo-Isidor's', ZKR 6 (1866) 148–152

P. Roth, 'Pseudo-Isidor', *Zeitschrift für Rechtsgeschichte* 5 (1866) 1–27

F. X. Kraus, *Theologische Quartalschrift* 48 (1866) 479–514 (review of Hinschius' edition)

E. Dumont, 'Les fausses décrétales', *Revue des questions historiques* 1 (1866) 392–426 and 2 (1867) 97–154

A. De Margerie, *Les Fausses Décrétales et les Pères de l'église, seconde lettre au R. P. Gratry* (Paris 1870)

F. Maassen, 'Eine Rede des Papstes Hadrian II. vom Jahre 869. Die erste umfassende Benutzung der Falschen Decretalen zur Begründung der Machtfülle des römischen Stuhles', *SB Vienna* 72 (1872) 521–554

R. von Scherer, *Ueber das Eherecht bei Benedict Levita und Pseudo Isidor* (Graz 1879)

C. J. M. Bottemanne, 'Over den invloed der valsche Dekretalen op de Pauselijke magt', *De Katholiek* 77 (1880) 1–64, 65–107, 281–309 and 78 (1880) 65–95 and 225–242

H. Denzinger, 'Ecloge et epicrisis eorum quae a recentioribus criticis de Pseudoisidorianis Decretalibus statuta sunt', PL 130 v–xvi

A. Lapôtre, 'Hadrien II et les Fausses décrétales', *Revue des questions historiques* 27 (1880) 377–431

C. H. Föste, *Die Reception Pseudo-Isidors unter Nicolaus I. und Hadrian II.* (Diss. Leipzig 1881)

J. Langen, 'Nochmals: wer ist Pseudo-Isidor?' HZ 48 (1882) 473–493

F. Maassen, 'Zur pseudoisidorischen Frage', *Anzeiger der Kaiserlichen Akademie der Wissenschaften (in Wien)* 24 (1882) 73–76

H. Schroers, *Hinkmar, Erzbischof von Reims* (Freiburg 1884)

F. Maassen, 'Pseudoisidor-Studien I: Die Textrecension der ächten Bestandtheile der Sammlung', *SB Vienna* 108 (1884) 1061–1104; 'Pseudoisidor-Studien II: Die Hispana der Handschrift von Autun und ihre Beziehungen zum Pseudoisidor', *SB Vienna* 109 (1885) 801–860

B. von Simson, 'Pseudoisidor und die Geschichte der Bischöfe von Le Mans', ZKR 21 (1886) 151–169

B. von Simson, *Die Entstehung der Pseudo-isidorischen Fälschungen in Le Mans* (Leipzig 1886)

Fournier, 'Question des fausses décrétales' 70–104

P. Fournier, 'De l'origine des *Fausses Décrétales*', *Compte rendu du Congrès scientifique international des Catholiques tenu à Paris en 1888: Section des sciences historiques* (1889) 403–419

F. Patetta, 'Sopra due manoscritti della collezione Pseudo-Isidoriana', *Rivista italiana per le scienze giuridiche* 10 (1890) 3–11 (repr. *Studi sulle fonti giuridiche medievali*, ed. G. Astuti, Torino 1967, 709–717)

H. Wasserschleben, 'Über das Vaterland der falschen Dekretalen', HZ 64 (1890) 234–250

G. Lurz, *Über die Heimat Pseudoisidors* (Hist. Abh. 12; Munich 1898)

H. M. Gietl, 'Die Heimat der Pseudo-Isidorischen Dekretalen', HJb 20 (1899) 441–455

A. V. Müller, 'Zum Verhältnisse Nicolaus' I. und Pseudo-Isidors', NA 25 (1900) 625–663

F. Liebermann, 'De accusatoribus aus Pseudo-Isidor', *Deutsche Zeitschrift für Kirchenrecht* 11 (1902) 1–5

W. Sommer, *Inhalt, Tendenz und kirchenrechtlicher Erfolg der Pseudo-Isidorischen Dekretalen-Sammlung* (Theol. Diss Jena 1902)

H. Schrörs, 'Papst Nikolaus I. und Pseudo-Isidor', HJB 25 (1904) 1–33

J. F. von Schulte, 'Marius Mercator und Pseudo-Isidor', SB Vienna 147 (1904) 167–172

E. Perels, 'Zur Frage nach dem Verhältnis zwischen Nikolaus I. und Pseudo-Isidor', NA 30 (1905) 473–476

H. Schrörs, 'Die pseudo-isidorische Exceptio spolii bei Papst Nikolaus I.', HJB 26 (1905) 275–298

P. Fournier, 'Fausses Décrétales', RHE 7 (1906) 33–51, 301–316, 543–564, 761–784; RHE 8 (1907) 19–56

F. Lot, 'La question des Fausses Décrétales', RH 94 (1907) 290–299 (repr. *Recueil des travaux historiques de Ferdinand Lot* 1 [Geneva-Paris 1968] 524–533)

H. Jäger, *Das Kirchenrechtssystem Pseudoisidors* (Jur. Diss. Würzburg 1908)

E. Seckel, 'Pseudo-Isidorian Decretals and other Forgeries', *The New Schaff-Herzog*

Encyclopedia of Religious Knowledge, ed. S. Macauley Jackson 9 (New York 1911) 343–344

M. W. Speyer, 'Ueber Hincmar's von Laon Auslese aus Pseudo-Isidor, Ingilramn und aus Schreiben des Pabstes Nicolaus I.', *Nachrichten der Gesellschaft der Wissenschaften Göttingen, Philol.-hist. Klasse* (1912) 219–227

B. von Simson, 'Pseudoisidor und die Le Mans-Hypothese', ZRG Kan. Abt. 4 (1914) 1–74

E. H. Davenport, *The False Decretals* (Oxford 1916)

G. Hartmann, *Der Primat des römischen Bischofs bei Pseudoisidor* (Stuttgart 1930)

A. Dold, 'Ein altes Konstanzer Handschriftenblatt des 9. Jahrhunderts mit Auszügen aus Pseudoisidor über das Verhalten der Bischöfe in Anklagefällen', AKKR 111 (1931) 17–30

P. Funk, 'Pseudo-Isidor gegen Heinrichs III. Kirchenhoheit', HJB 56 (1936) 305–330

J. Haller, *Nikolaus I. und Pseudoisidor* (Stuttgart 1936)

C. Silva-Tarouca, 'Un codice di Pseudo-Isidoro coevo del falso?' *Miscellanea Isidoriana: Homenaje a S. Isidoro de Sevilla en el XIII centenario de su muerte 636–634 de abril 1936* (Rome 1936) 357–363

M. Buchner, 'Pseudoisidor und die Hofkapelle Karls des Kahlen', HJb 57 (1937) 180–208

G. Oesterle, 'De Pseudo-Isidoro et capella aulica Caroli Calvi', *Jus Pontificium* 18 (1938) 142–150, 219–221

F. Lot, 'Textes manceaux et fausses décrétales 1–2', BEC 101 (1940) 5–48 and 102 (1941) 5–34 (repr. *Recueil de travaux historiques de F. Lot* 1 [Geneva-Paris 1968] 534–577 and 578–607)

J. Haller, 'Pseudoisidors erstes Auftreten im deutschen Investiturstreit', SGreg 2 (1947) 91–101

A. Michel, 'Pseudo-Isidor, die Sentenzen Humberts und Burkard von Worms im Investiturstreit', SGreg 3 (1948) 149–161; also in: ZRG Kan. Abt. 35 (1948) 329–339

S. Williams, *Visio Aetatis Ecclesiae Pseudo-Isidoriana,* (Ph.D. dissertation, University of California; Berkeley 1951)

Sch. Williams, 'The Pseudo-Isidorian Problem Today', *Speculum* 29 (1954) 702–707

R. Grand, 'Nouvelles remarques sur l'origine du Pseudo-Isidore: Source du Décret de Gratien', SG 3 (1955) 1–16

H. Fuhrmann, 'Studien zur Geschichte mittelalterlicher Patriarchate', ZRG Kan. Abt. 39 (1953) 112–176; 40 (1954) 1–84; 41 (1955) 95–183

H. Fuhrmann, 'Die pseudoisidorischen Fälschungen und die Synode von Hohenaltheim (916)', *Zeitschrift für bayerische Landesgeschichte* 20 (1957) 136–151

B. Leeming, 'The False Decretals, Faustus of Riez and the Pseudo-Eusebius', *Studia patristica, 2: Papers presented to the . . . International Conference held at Christ Church, Oxford, 1955,* ed. K. Aland and F. L. Cross (Texte und Untersuchungen zur Geschichte der altchristlichen Literatur 64; Berlin 1957) 122–140

H. Fuhrmann, 'Pseudoisidor und die Abbreviatio Ansegisi et Benedicti Levitae', ZKG 69 (1958) 308–311

Ryan, 'Observations' 92–94

Seckel-Fuhrmann, *Die erste Zeile Pseudoisidors* passim (bibliography until 1958)

G. May, 'Die Bedeutung der pseudoisidorischen Sammlung für die Infamie im kanonischen Recht', ÖAKR 12 (1961) 87–113 and 191–207

H. Fuhrmann, 'Die sogenannte Kanonessammlung des Remedius von Chur', DA 18 (1963) 231–235

S. Williams, 'The Oldest Text of the *Constitutum Constantini', Traditio* 20 (1964) 448–461

H. Fuhrmann, 'Die Fälschungen im MA', HZ 197 (1963) 529–554

H. Fuhrmann, 'Pseudoisidor im Kloster Cluny', *Proceedings Boston* 17–22

K.-U. Betz, 'Hinkmar von Reims, Nikolaus I., Pseudo-Isidor. Fränkisches Landeskirchentum und römischer Machtanspruch im 9. Jahrhundert (Ev. Theol. Diss. Bonn 1965)

Fuhrmann, 'Pseudoisidor in Rom' 15–66

S. Williams, 'Pseudo-Isidore from the Manuscripts', *Catholic Historical Review* 53 (1967) 58–66

S. Williams, *Codices Pseudo-Isidoriani* passim

Rambaud-Buhot, 'Critique' 25–31

H. Fuhrmann, 'Päpstlicher Primat und pseudoisidorische Dekretalen', QF 49 (1969) 313–339

H. Hoesch, 'Ein Auszug aus Pseudoisidor im MS Berlin Theol. Lat. 313', *Traditio* 25 (1969) 499–507

A. Marchetto, *Episcopato e primato pontificio nelle decretali pseudo isidoriane* (Rome 1971)

Mordek, 'Handschriftenforschungen' 630 including n. 8

C. McCurry, 'On the Provenance of the Yale Pseudo-Isidore', BMCL 2 (1972) 61–67 (cf. D. Jasper, DA 29 [1973] 251–252)

C. Munier, 'La tradition du IIe concile de Carthage (390)', *Revue des sciences religieuses* 46 (1972) 193–211

Fuhrmann, *Einfluß und Verbreitung* 1–3 (cf. reviews listed in HRG 4, 1990, 83)

A. Chavasse, 'Les lettres de pape Léon le Grand (440–461) dans l'Hispana et la collection dite des Fauses Décrétales', RDC 25 (1975) 28–39

J. H. Erickson, 'New Pseudo-Isidore Manuscripts', BMCL 5 (1975) 115–117 (Vat. Reg. lat. 976 and 978)

H. Fuhrmann, 'Justinians *Edictum de recta fide* bei Pseudoisidor: Nach Notizen von Emil Seckel', SG 19 (1976) 217–223

K.-G. Schon, 'Exzerpte aus den Akten von Chalkedon bei Pseudoisidor und in der 74-Titel-Sammlung', DA 32 (1976) 546–557

Mordek, 'Addenda' 471–478

Richter, 'Stufen' 1–72

K.-G. Schon, 'Eine Redaktion der pseudoisidorischen Dekretalen aus der Zeit der Fälschung', DA 34 (1978) 500–511

H. Fuhrmann, 'Reflections on the Principles of Editing Texts. The Pseudo-Isidorian Decretals as an Example', BMCL 11 (1981) 1–7

J. J. Contreni, 'Codices Pseudo-Isidoriani: The Provenance and Date of Paris, B.N. MS lat. 9629', *Viator* 13 (1982) 1–14

H. Fuhrmann, 'Kritischer Sinn und unkritische Haltung: Vorgratianische Einwände zu Pseudo-Clemens-Briefen', *Festschrift Kempf* (1983) 81–95

H. Fuhrmann, 'Eine Fälschung im Stile der Pseudo-Clemensbriefe', *Variorum munera florum: Latinität als prägende Kraft mittelalterlicher Kultur: Festschrift H. F. Haefele zu seinem 60. Geburtstag*, ed. A. Reinle, L. Schmugge and P. Stotz (Sigmaringen 1985) 157–167

Kretzschmar, *Alger von Lüttich* 99–105

K. Christensen, 'The Schafer Williams Papers at the Institute of Medieval Canon Law', BMCL 16 (1986) 101–104

G. Motta, 'I codici canonistici di Polirone', *Sant'Anselmo, Mantova* 349–374

F. Yarza, *El obispo en la organización eclesiástica de las Decretales Pseudoisidorianas* (Pamplona 1985) (a few errors resulting from the wrong wording in Hinschius' edition, cf. review by Fuhrmann, DA 44, 1988, 660–661; Weigand, AKKR 155, 1986, 301–302)

J. Ruysschaert, 'Les 'Decretales' du Ps-Isidore du Vat. lat. 630: Péripéties Vaticanes d'un manuscrit de Jean Jouffroy, consulté par Bernardino Carvajal', *Miscellanea Bibliothecae Apostolicae Vaticanae* (Vatican City 1987) (Studi e testi 329) 111–115

A. Marchetto, 'La 'fortuna' di una falsificazione: Lo spirito dello Pseudo-Isidoro aleggia nel nuovo Codice di diritto canonico per la Chiesa latina?' *Apollinaris* 61 (1988) 311–326 (also in *Fälschungen im Mittelalter* 2.397–411)

L. Mezey, A. Fodor, E. Madas, G. Sarbak, T. Wehli, I. Lauf-Nobilis, K. Fülep, L. Veszpremy, Z. Falvy, W. Pass, P. Erdö and C. Boross (adiuv.), *Fragmenta latina codicum in Bibliotheca Seminarii Clari Hungariae Centralis* 1.2 (Wiesbaden 1988)

R. E. Reynolds (ed. praef.), 'A South Italian Liturgico-Canonical Mass Commentary', MS 50 (1988) 626–670

H. Schneider, 'Ademar von Chabannes und Pseudoisidor—der 'Mythomane' und der Erzfälscher', *Fälschungen im Mittelalter* 2.129–250

M. M. Sheehan, 'Theory and Practice: Marriage of the Unfree and the Poor in Medieval Society', MS 50 (1988) 457–487

The Cambridge History of Medieval Political Thought c. 350–c. 1450, ed. J. H. Burns (Cambridge 1988)

P. Cramer, 'Ernulf of Rochester and Early Anglo-Norman Canon Law', JEH 40 (1989) 483–510

Fälschungen im Mittelalter 2, passim (see index 6.180 s.v. 'Pseudoisidor')

Landau, 'Gefälschtes Recht' 20–22

R. H. Rouse and M. A. Rouse, 'Ennodius in the Middle Ages: Adonics, Pseudo-Isidore, Cisterciens, and the Schools', *Popes, Teachers, and Canon Law in the Middle Ages: Essays in Honor of Brian Tierney,* ed. J. R. Sweeney and S. Chodorow (Ithaca, N.Y. and London 1989) 91–113

G. Arnaldi, *Natale 875, Politica, ecclesiologia, cultura del papato altomedievale* I (Istituto Storico Italiano per il Medio Evo; Rome 1990)

Busch, *Placidus von Nonantola* 134–151

H. J. Sieben, *Die Partikularsynode: Studien zur Geschichte der Konzilsidee* (Frankfurt 1990)

H. Fuhrmann, 'Pseudoisidor und das Constitutum Constantini', *In iure veritas: Studies in Canon Law in Memory of Schafer Williams,* ed. S. B. Bowman and B. E. Cody (Cincinnati 1991) 80–84

J. Gilchrist, 'Changing the Structure of a Canonical Collection', *In iure veritas: Studies in Canon Law in Memory of Schafer Williams,* ed. S. B. Bowman and B. E. Cody (Cincinnati 1991) 93–117

Il primato del vescovo di Roma nel primo millenio: Ricerche e testimonianze, Atti del Symposium Storico-Teologico (Roma, 9–13 Ottobre 1989), ed. M. Maccarrone (Vatican City 1991)

R. Knox, 'Accusing Higher Up', ZRG Kan. Abt. 77 (1991) 1–31

Mordek, 'Primat' 523–566

Schmitz, 'Vier-Bücher-Sammlung' 250–251

H. J. Sieben, 'Pseudoisidor auf dem Konzil von Florenz (1438/9)', ThPh 66 (1991) 226–238

Brett, 'Collectio Lanfranci' 157–174

R. Schieffer, 'Kreta, Rom und Laon, Vier Briefe des Papstes Vitalian vom Jahre 668', *Festschrift Fuhrmann* (1991) 14–30

E. Frauenknecht (ed.), *Der Traktat 'De ordinando pontifice'* (MGH, Studien und Texte 5; Hannover 1992)

G. Giordanengo, '*Scientia canonum:* Droit et réforme dans l'oeuvre de Geoffrey, abbé de Vendôme (1093–1132)', CCM 35 (1992) 27–47

A. Marchetto, 'In partem sollicitudinis . . . non in plenitudinem potestatis: Evoluzione di una formula di rapporto Primato-Episcopato', *Studia in Honorem A. M. Stickler* (Rome 1992) 269–298

Landau, 'Kirchweihe' 225–240

S. Scholz, *Transmigration und Translation: Studien zum Bistumswechsel der Bischöfe von der Spätantike bis zum Hohen Mittelalter* (Cologne-Weimar-Vienna 1992)

M. Stark, 'Die liturgiegeschichtlichen Angaben im *Lucidarius*', *Zeitschrift für deutsche Philologie* 111 (1992) 51–64

Zechiel-Eckes, *Cresconius* (cf. index)

J. Gaudemet, 'La primauté pontificale dans les collections canoniques grégoriennes', *Studi in onore Luigi Prosdocimi* (1994) 1.1, 59–90

Pseudo-Isidorus, Capitula Angilramni

1. Author: Unknown. *2. Date:* About the middle of the ninth century. *3. Place:* See above, *Pseudo-Isidorus Mercator, Decretales*. *4. Type:* Small tract of criminal procedure outlining proceedings for cases brought against bishops.

5. Editions

P. Hinschius, *Decretales Pseudo-Isidorianae et Capitula Angilramni* (Leipzig 1863) 757–769

P. Ciprotti, *I capitula Angilramni con appendice di documenti connessi* (Università degli studi di Camerino, Istituto giuridico, testi per esercitazioni sez. 7.1; 1966) (revised reprint of Hinschius' edition, not citing variants)

6. Manuscripts

Circulated almost always together with the longer version of the Pseudo-Isidorian Decretals (A1 resp. A/B and their derivatives)

Avranches, Bibliothèque municipale, 146, saec. XII; Reims, fol. 156ra–159rb

Boulogne, Bibliothèque municipale, 115, saec. XII, St-Bertin, fol. 288vb–192rb

Boulogne, Bibliothèque municipale, 116, saec. XII, fol. 142ra–144va

Chartres, Bibliothèque municipale, 409 (424), *Capitula Angilramni* up to c. 43; saec. XIV, destroyed in World War II, cf. *Speculum* 29 (1954) 337; Masson, *Manuscrits des Bibliothèques sinistrées* 11; Mordek, *Bibliotheca capitularium* 111–112

Douai, Bibliothèque municipale, 582, saec. XII, fol. 152va–155rb

Douai, Bibliothèque municipale, 583, saec. XII, fol. 153^{v}–155^{v}

Eton, College Library, B.1.I.6 (James 97), saec. XII, Script. Normandy? Prov. cathedral chapter of Exeter, fol. 232va–235rb

Firenze, Biblioteca Nazionale Centrale, Panciatichi 135, saec. XV, cf. Mordek, 'Addenda' 474

Grenoble, Bibliothèque municipale, 473 (olim 16), saec. XII, fol. 120vb–122vb

Köln, Erzbischöfliche Diözesan- und Dombibliothek, 113 (olim Darmstadt 2112), saec. X, fol. 144va–147ra

London, British Library, Cotton Claudius E.V., saec. XII, Northern France, fol. 131vb–133rb

London, British Library, Royal 11.D.IV, saec. XV, fol. 131vb–133rb

Monte Cassino, Archivio e Biblioteca dell'Abbazia, 1, saec. XI^{ex}, Southern Italy,

Montpellier, Bibliothèque Interuniversitaire, H.3, saec. XII^{med}, Flanders, or Northern France, fol. 191rb–193vb

Montpellier, Bibliothèque Interuniversitaire, H.13, saec. XII–XIII, fol. 181ra–183va

New Haven, Yale University, Beinecke Library, 442, saec. IX3/4, Aquitaine, fol. 238ra–239vb

Oxford, Bodleian Library, Hatton 6 (=Misc. 4129), saec. XIII, northwestern France, fol. 184rb–186va

Paris, Bibliothèque de l'Arsenal, 679 (6.J.1), saec. XIV^{in}, fol. 289rb–292ra

Paris, Bibliothèque de l'Assemblée nationale, 27 (B.19, olim 681), saec. XII; Northern France

Paris, Bibliothèque nationale, lat. 3853, saec. XII (1154–1159), Flanders or Northern France, fol. 269ra–271ra

Paris, Bibliothèque nationale, lat. 5141, saec. XIV, France, fol. 195va–197va

Paris, Bibliothèque nationale, lat. 9629 (olim suppl. lat. 840), saec. IX3/4, Laon?), fol. 214

Paris, Bibliothèque nationale, lat. 14314 (olim St-Victor 184), saec. XII, Northern France

Paris, Bibliothèque nationale, lat. 14992 (saec. XII, St-Victor)

Paris, Bibliothèque nationale, lat. 15391 (olim Sorbonne 729), saec. XV

Paris, Bibliothèque nationale, lat. 16897 (olim Navarre 7), saec. XIII

Paris, Bibliothèque nationale, nouv. acq. lat. 2253, saec. XI, Cluny, fol. 140ra–141vb

Reims, Bibliothèque municipale, 672, saec. XII, fol. 222va–224ra

Rouen, Bibliothèque municipale, 702 (E.27), saec. XI, Angers, fol. 186rb–188va

Saint-Omer, Bibliothèque municipale, 189, saec. XI

Toulouse, Bibliothèque municipale, 365 (I.9), saec. XIII, fol. 346rb–349rb

Vaticano, Città del, Biblioteca Apostolica Vaticana, lat. 630, saec. IX$^{med.}$, Corbie, Prov. Arras, fol. 310ra–312rb (cf. Richter, 'Stufen' 35–42)

Vaticano, Città del, Biblioteca Apostolica Vaticana, lat. 631, saec. XIII3/4, probably Flanders, fol. 326vb–328va

Vaticano, Città del, Biblioteca Apostolica Vaticana, lat. 1340, saec. XIII, France, fol. 357va–359vb

Vaticano, Città del, Biblioteca Apostolica Vaticana, lat. 1344, saec. XII, France, fol. 90va–93ra

Vaticano, Città del, Biblioteca Apostolica Vaticana, lat. 3791, saec. XI, Northern France, fol. 278^{v}–282^{v}

Vaticano, Città del, Biblioteca Apostolica Vaticana, Reg. lat. 978, saec. XII

Venezia, Biblioteca Nazionale Marciana, lat. IV.47 (Num. Progr. 2126), saec. XV, Northern Italy

Venezia, Biblioteca Nazionale Marciana, Zanctti lat. 169, saec. XV, fol. 237va–240rb

Special Recension

Berlin, Staatsbibliothek Preußischer Kulturbesitz, Phill. 1764 (second part of the manuscript = fol. 27–47), fol. 138^{r}–141^{v}

As Part of the *Collectio Lanfranci*

Cambridge, Corpus Christi College, 130, saec. XI–XII, fol. 117^{v}–120^{v}

Cambridge, Library of Peterhouse College, 74, saec. XI^{ex}, fol. 113^{r}–115^{v}

Cambridge, Library of Trinity College, B.16.44, saec. XI, pag. 203–208

Hereford, Cathedral Library, O.IV.5, saec. XII^{1}, written by an English hand at and for Hereford Cathedral, fol. 182rb–187ra, cf. Mynors-Thomson, *Catalogue of Hereford* 27

Hereford, Cathedral Library, O.VIII.8, saec. XI^{ex}, written in French hand, Prov. Hereford Cathedral, fol. 131^{r}–134^{v}, cf. Mynors-Thomson, *Catalogue of Hereford* 57

Lincoln, Cathedral Chapter Library, 161, saec. XII^{in}, written in an English hand at and for Lincoln Cathedral, fol. 4^{r}–250^{v}, cf. Thomson, *Catalogue of Lincoln* 130 (see also Plate 37)

London, British Library, Cotton Claudius D.IX, saec. XI–XII, fol. 122^{v}–125^{v}

London, British Library, Royal 9.B.XII, saec. XII, Worcester, fol. 149^{r}–151^{v}

London, British Library, Royal 11.D.VIII, saec. XII, fol. 125ra–128vb

Paris, Bibliothèque nationale, lat. 1458, (fourth part of the manuscript); saec. IX^{1}, Northern France, fol. 97va–101va

Paris, Bibliothèque nationale, lat. 1563, saec. XV, fol. 271ra–274va

Paris, Bibliothèque nationale, lat. 3856, saec. XII, fol. 174^{v}–177^{r}

Rouen, Bibliothèque municipale, 701, saec. XII, fol. 130va–133va

Rouen, Bibliothèque municipale, 1408, saec. XII

Salisbury, Library of the Cathedral Church, 78, saec. XI–XII, Salisbury, fol. 94^{v}–96^{v}

In a Group of Manuscripts from Lotharingia

Luxembourg, Bibliothèque nationale, 29 (102), saec. XII, Prov. Orval. fol. 1^{r}–6^{r} (fragmentary at the beginning)

Münster, Nordrhein-Westfälisches Staatsarchiv VII.5201, p. 64–87, from Corvey, saec. X^{med}, about 945, p. 64–87; cf. Fuhrmann, *Einfluß und Verbreitung* 2.278 n. 105; Mordek, *Bibliotheca capitularium* 378–386, especially 381; cf. also *Cresconius*, above

Salzburg, Bibliothek der Erzabtei St. Peter, a.IX.32, saec. XI^{1}, Cologne, fol. 202^{r}–207^{r}, cf. Mordek, *Bibliotheca capitularium* 649; Salzburg (according to H. Hoffmann, cf. Pokorny, 'Triburer Synodalakten' 435 n. 20)

Trier, Stadtbibliothek, 927 (1882), saec. X^{2}, St. Maximin, Trier, Prov. Maria Laach, p. 382–400, cf. G. Fransen, *Traditio* 26 (1970) 446

Other Separate Traditions

Oldenburg, Niedersächsisches Staatsarchiv, Best. 291 Nr. 1, Fragment 35, saec. X (according to H. Hoffmann), fragment: chapters 16bis–20bis (information by R. Pokorny)

Oxford, Bodleian Library, Holkham misc. 19, saec. XII^{in}, Tuscany, perhaps Pistoia, cf. Mordek, 'Addenda' 476 n. 20

Paris, Bibliothèque nationale, lat. 2449, saec. IX^{ex}–X^{in}, fol. 76^{r}–81^{v}

Paris, Bibliothèque nationale, lat. 12445 (olim Sangerm. 366), saec. IX3/4, Reims; fol. 163ra–166vb; cf. Böhringer (as below) 17–32

Pistoia, Archivio Capitolare del Duomo, C. 101, saec. XII^{in}, fol. 2^{r}–6^{r} (cf. Mordek, 'Addenda' 476 n. 20)

Vaticano, Città del, Biblioteca Apostolica Vaticana, Vat. Pal. lat. 587, saec. XII

7. *Bibliography*

Conrat, *Geschichte* 304–308; A. Humbert, DHGE 3 (1924) 125–127; Fournier-Le Bras 1.142–145, 188–190, 192–202, 223–224; A. Amanieu, 'Angilramne', DDC 1 (1935) 522–526; Kurtscheid-Wilches 1.136; Van Hove, *Prolegomena* 303–304; H. Fuhrmann, NCE 5 (1967) 820–824; Mordek, 'Capitula Angilramni (Hadriani)', LMA 2 (1983) 1479

F. Lot, *'Etudes sur le règne de Hugues Capet'* (Paris 1903) 370–371

E. Seckel, 'Pseudoisidor', RE ^{3}16 (1905) 295–296

E. Seckel, 'Studien zu Benedictus Levita VII', NA 35 (1910) 491–505

E. Seckel, 'Studien zu Benedictus Levita VIII' NA 40 (1915) 15–130

F. Lot, 'Textes manceaux et Fausses Décrétales 2', BEC 102 (1941) 33–34; also in: *Recueil des travaux historiques de F. Lot* 1, (Geneva-Paris 1968) 606–607 (Metz as place of origin of the *Capitula Angilramni*)

A. Hauck, Kirchengeschichte Deutschlands 2 (Berlin-Leipzig ^{6}1952) 539–542

S. Williams, 'The Pseudo-Isidorian Problem', *Speculum* 29 (1954) 702–707

W. Ullmann, *The Growth of Papal Government in the Middle Ages* (London 1955, ^{2}1962) 179–180

Seckel-Fuhrmann, *Die erste Zeile Pseudoisidors* 8

G. May, 'Zu den Anklagebeschränkungen, insbesondere wegen Infamie, in den Capitula Angilramni', ZKG 72 (1961) 106–112

O.G. Oexle, 'Die Karolinger und die Stadt des heiligen Arnulf', FMSt 1 (1967) 296

Williams, *Codices Pseudo-Isidoriani* passim

Fuhrmann, *Einfluß und Verbreitung* 1.161–63 and see also index 1080

Schmitz, 'Vier-Bücher-Sammlung' 237 n. 24.

L. Böhringer (ed.), 'Der eherechtliche Traktat im Paris. lat. 12445, einer Arbeitshandschrift Hinkmars von Reims', DA 46 (1990) 18–47

Zechiel-Eckes, *Cresconius* 1.250; 2.329, 343, 353

Cf. also *Pseudo-Isidorus Mercator, Decretales*

Benedictus Levita, Collectio capitularium

1. Author: 'Benedictus Levita'. *2. Date:* Middle of the ninth century (847–852). *3. Place:* Western Francia, diocese Reims. *4. Type:* Intended to be a supplement to Ansegis' collection of capitulary texts (cf. above) with which they always circulated in the manuscripts; Benedictus began numbering the books of his collection by continuing the numbering of Ansegis' books; see also *Abbreviatio Ansegisi et Benedicti Levitae* (below).

5. Editions

E. Baluze, *Capitularia regum Francorum* 1 (Paris 1677) 801–910, according to Seckel 'grundlegend und die Textgestalt im wesentlichen abschließend' cf. Fuhrmann, *Einfluß und Verbreitung* 1.164 n. 52; new edition ed. by P. de Chiniac [Paris 1780] 801–910;

G. H. Pertz, MGH LL 2.2 (Hannover 1837) 17–158, critical introduction to the sources by F. H. Knust (19–39) (repr. PL 97.698–912)

Critical Edition of the Add. I (Without Rubrics)

J. Semmler (ed.) 'Collectio capitularis Benedicti Levitae monastica', *Corpus Consuetudinem Monasticarum,* ed. by K. Hallinger 1 (1963) 537–554

6. Manuscripts

Class 1

Paris, Bibliothèque nationale, lat. 4634, saec. X, France, Prov. Cathedral of Sens: 'Liber sanctae Mariae sanctique Stephani Senonum', (cf. Semmler, 'Monastische Gesetzgebung' 369); fol. 34^{v}–179^{v}:Books 1–3 and Additiones 1–4, cf. Seckel, 'Benedictus Levita' 379; cf. Mordek, *Bibliotheca capitularium* 519–521 and especially MGH Capit. n.s. 1.121–122

Paris, Bibliothèque nationale, lat. 4636, saec. IX^{med}, written at Tours; fol. 24^{v}–142^{v}: Books 1–3 and Additiones 1–4, cf. Semmler, 'Monastische Gesetzgebung' 369; Mordek, *Bibliotheca capitularium* 522–524 (manuscript used by Ivo of Chartres); MGH Capit. n.s. 1.126

Codex Bellovacensis (now lost); Baluze called it the best and most complete of all the manuscripts known to him (Class 1)

Modern copies of the lost Beauvais manuscript:

Vaticano, Città del, Biblioteca Apostolica Vaticana, lat. 4982, saec. XVI (after 1572), fol. 1^{r}–66^{v}; cf. Mordek, *Bibliotheca capitularium* 865–881, especially 868

Vaticano, Città del, Biblioteca Apostolica Vaticana, Reg. lat. 291, saec. XVI^{2}, Northern France, excerpt only: fol. 128^{r}–140^{r}, cf. Mordek, *Bibliotheca capitularium* 819

Class 2

Avranches, Bibliothèque municipale, 145 (old nos.: 121 and 40.56), saec. XII^{2} written on the instructions of abbot Robert de Torigni (1154–June 1186) at Mont-Saint-Michel (cf. fol. 110^{v}), fol. 46^{v}–110^{v}; abbreviated form (Benedictus Levita 1–2, 362), cf. Seckel, 'Benedictus Levita' 389–392; Mordek, *Bibliotheca capitularium* 6; MGH Capit. n.s. 1.71

Barcelona, Archivo de la Corona de Aragón, Ripoll 40, saec. XI^{1}, Prov. monastery of Santa María de Ripoll, fol. 27vb–48vb; Seckel, 'Benedictus Levita' 384–387; MGH Capit. n.s. 1.75–76; Mordek, *Bibliotheca capitularium* 19–27

Gotha, Forschungs- und Landesbibliothek, Mbr. I.84, saec. X–XI (cf. Hoffmann, *Buchkunst* 239), fol. 29rb–145vb, Books 1–3 and Additiones 2–4; Prov. Fulda according to Fuhrmann, *Einfluß und Verbreitung* 1.164 n. 52; belonged to St. Martin at Mainz, cf. the catalogue of the exposition: *Karl der Grosse: Werk und Wirkung* (Aachen 1965) 505 no. 688; cf. Seckel, 'Benedictus Levita' 384; Mordek, *Bibliotheca capitularium* 131–149, especially 132–133; MGH Capit. n.s. 1.87–88

Paris, Bibliothèque nationale, lat. 4635, saec. X; perhaps Italy (according to Mordek); fol. 69–240^{v}: Books 1–3 and Additiones 2–4; cf. Seckel, 'Benedictus Levita' 397–399; Mordek, *Bibliotheca capitularium* 521–522; MGH Capit. n.s. 1.123–124

Paris, Bibliothèque nationale, lat. 4637, saec. IX^{2}, Prov. France, perhaps Le Mans; fol. 65^{r}–152^{v}, 153^{r}–160^{v}, fol. 161^{r}–175^{v}: fragments, cf. Seckel, 'Benedictus Levita' 386–387; Mordek, *Bibliotheca capitularium* 524–526; MGH Capit. n.s. 1.127–128

Paris, Bibliothèque nationale, lat. 18239, saec. XI; Prov. monastery of Ste-Marie at Cambron (Hainaut, dioc. of Cambrai); fol. 73^{v}–118^{v}: abbreviated form of Book 1, cf. Seckel, 'Benedictus Levita' 392–394; Mordek, *Bibliotheca capitularium* 619–621; MGH Capit. n.s. 1.141–142

St. Gallen, Stiftsbibliothek, 727, saec. IX3/4, Reims, p. 106–256, fragmentary transmission up to 2.101; Seckel, 'Benedictus Levita' 385; cf. Mordek, *Bibliotheca capitularium* 664–665; MGH Capit. n.s. 1.146

Vaticano, Città del, Biblioteca Apostolica Vaticana, Pal. lat. 583, saec. X^{med}, Fulda/Mainz, Prov. Cathedral Library, fol. 43^{r}–244^{r}: Books 1–3 and Additiones 2–4; cf. Seckel, 'Benedictus Levita' 383; Mordek, *Bibliotheca capitularium* 797–799; MGH Capit. n.s. 1.158

Vaticano, Città del, Biblioteca Apostolica Vaticana, Reg. lat. 447, saec. IX–X, Northern France, fol. 50^{v}–72^{v}, Seckel, 'Benedictus Levita' 386; cf. Mordek, *Bibliotheca capitularium* 826; MGH Capit. n.s. 1.162–163

Vaticano, Città del, Biblioteca Apostolica Vaticana, Reg. lat. 974, saec. X, France, fol. 38^{v}–187^{v}: Books 1–3 and Additiones 2–4; cf. Seckel, 'Benedictus Levita' 383–384; Mordek, *Bibliotheca capitularium* 833–834; MGH Capit. n.s. 1.165–166

Special Manuscripts of the Abridged Four *'Additiones'*

Berlin, Staatsbibliothek Preußischer Kulturbesitz, Phill. 1762, before 860, Reims; fol. 78^{r}–137^{r}; the four Additiones of Benedictus Levita, partly abridged (striking similarity to Paris lat. 4638); cf. Seckel, 'Benedictus Levita' 399–400; Semmler, 'Monastische Gesetzgebung' 369–370; Mordek, *Bibliotheca capitularium* 58–69, especially 63–64; MGH Capit. n.s. 1.83–84

Paris, Bibliothèque nationale, lat. 4638, saec. XI; France, perhaps Reims (cf. Semmler, 'Monastische Gesetzgebung' 370); cf. Berlin, Phill. 1762 and Seckel, 'Benedictus Levita' 400–404; fol. 80^{r}–137^{r}; cf. Mordek, *Bibliotheca capitularium* 525–533; MGH Capit. n.s. 1.129

Reception/Excerpts

Isaac of Langres, *Capitula* (ed. R. Pokorny, MGH Capit. episc. 2.161–241, especially 163: Isaac's *Capitula* are excerpted from the *Capitularia* by Benedictus Levita), cf. below

Abbreviatio Ansegisi et Benedicti Levitae, cf. below

'Capitulare incerti anni datum in synodo, cui interfuit Bonifacius apostolicae sedis legatus, circa annum Christi 744', cf. Seckel, 'Benedictus Levita' 419; Mordek, *Biblioteca capitularium* 1033

Metz, Bibliothèque municipale, 236 (olim E. 29), Prov. S. Arnulph at Metz, saec. X–XI (containing the *Dacheriana* and incomplete *Collectio 400 capitulorum,* cf. analysis in Seckel, 'Benedictus Levita' 410–413) 'Appendix Dacherianae Mettensis'

Milano, Biblioteca Ambrosiana, A.46 inf., saec. IX^{ex}, *Collectio Ambrosiana* (cf. *Collectio duorum librorum I* of Cod. Milano Ambrosiana A.46 inf.)

Chartres, Bibliothèque municipale, 193 (olim 172), saec. XI; cf. Seckel, 'Benedictus Levita' 409–410

Vaticano, Città del, Biblioteca Apostolica Vaticana, Reg. lat. 612, cf. Seckel, 'Benedictus Levita' 418; MGH Capit. 2, 124

A larger excerpt from Benedictus used by Ivo of Chartres? Cf. Seckel, 'Benedictus Levita' 453–454

Cf. also Mordek, *Bibliotheca capitularium* (index)

Other Transmissions

Two separate transmissions of the *Collectio Benedicti Levitae monastica* Semmler, 'Monastische Gesetzgebung' 370

Milano, Biblioteca Ambrosiana, S.17 sup., fol. 67^{v}–71^{v}, saec. X^{ex}–XI^{in}, Italy, Prov. San Giusto di Susa in Piemont (cf. fol. 98^{v}); cf. Mordek, *Bibliotheca capitularium* 251

Montserrat, Archivo y Biblioteca de la Abadía, 995, fol. 136^{r}–137^{r} (fragmentary), saec. XV, Spain (copy of Cod. Milano, Biblioteca Ambrosiana, S.17 sup.?), Prov. Sant Pere de Galligants (Gerona); cf. Mordek, *Bibliotheca capitularium* 280–281

7. *Bibliography*

Conrat, *Geschichte* 299–302, 306–311; Seckel, 'Pseudoisidor', RE ^{3}16 (1905) 296–304; Fournier-Le Bras 1.145–171, 183–184, 187–192, 202–209; F. Baix, 'Benoît le Lévite', DHGE 8 (1935) 213–218; F. Baix, 'Benedictus Levita', DDC 2 (1937) 400–406; Kurtscheid-Wilches 1.136–138; Van Hove, *Prolegomena* 237, 257, 262, 304–305; Stickler, *Historia* 1.128–131; Stickler, 'Benedikt Levita', LThK 2^{2} (1958) 181; W. A. Eckhardt, 'Benedictus Levita', HRG 1 (1971) 362–364; *Rep. font.* 2 (1967) 481–482 U. Mattejiet, 'Benedikt Levita', LMA 1 (1980) 1857

P. Hinschius, *Decretales Pseudo-Isidorianae et Capitula Angilramni* (Leipzig 1863) cxliii–clxiii, clxxxiii–clxxxvi

R. von Scherer, *Ueber das Eherecht bei Benedict Levita und Pseudo-Isidor* (Graz 1879)

B. Simson, *Die Entstehung der pseudo-isidorischen Fälschungen in Le Mans* (Leipzig 1886)

Fournier, 'Question des Fausses Décrétales' 70–104

F. Maassen, 'Zwei Excurse zu den falschen Capitularien des Benedictus Levita', NA 18 (1893) 294–302

P. Schneider, *Die Lehre von den Kirchenrechtsquellen* (Regensburg ^{2}1892) 75–78

M. Conrat, 'Der Novellenauszug De ordine ecclesiastico, eine Quelle des Benedikt Levita', NA 24 (1899) 341–348

E. Seckel, 'Studien zu Benedictus Levita', NA 26 (1901) 37–72, NA 29 (1904) 275–331, NA 31 (1906) 59–139 and 238–239, NA 34 (1909) 319–381, NA 35 (1910) 105–191 and 433–539, NA 39 (1914) 327–431, NA 40 (1915) 15–130, NA 41 (1917) 157–263

Wretschko, *Theodosiani libri XVI*, p. cccxiii–cccxiv

F. Lot, *Etudes sur le règne de Hugues Capet* (Paris 1903) 367–370 and 370–375

H. Brunner, *Deutsche Rechtsgeschichte* 1² (Leipzig 1906) 553–558
Fournier, 'Fausses Décrétales', RHE 7 (1906) 33–51, 301–316, 543–564, 761–784; RHE 8 (1907) 19–56
E. Seckel, 'Die ältesten Canones von Rouen', *Historische Aufsätze: Karl Zeumer zum sechzigsten Geburtstag als Festgabe dargebracht von Freunden und Schülern* (Weimar 1910) 608–635
Seckel, 'Benedictus Levita' 377–464
B. Simson, 'Pseudo-Isidor und die Le Mans-Hypothese', ZRG Kan. Abt. 35 (1914) 1–74
M. Tangl, 'Studien zur Neuausgabe der Bonifatius-Briefe', NA 41 (1919) 76–100
B. Lijdsman, *Introductio in jus canonicum* 1 (Hilversum 1924) 146–150
Fournier, 'Notices' 78–92
B. Krusch, *Neue Forschungen über die drei oberdeutschen Leges: Bajuvariorum, Alamannorum, Ribuariorum* (Berlin 1927) 51–58
Seckel, 'Studien zu Benedictus Levita VIII' expanded and edited posthumously by J. Juncker, ZRG Kan. Abt. 23 (1934) 269–377, 24 (1935) 1–112 (sources of texts in III, 447–478)
M. Buchner, 'Pseudoisidor und die Hofkapelle Karls des Kahlen', HJB 57 (1937) 180–208
Christ, 'Überlieferung' 281–322
F. Lot, 'Textes manceaux et fausses décrétales', BEC 101 (1940) 5–48, 102 (1941) 5–34
W. Schwer, 'Die Schenkung an die Kirche in den Pseudokapitularien des Benedictus Levita', *Aus Theologie und Philosophie: Festschrift für Fritz Tillmann* (Düsseldorf 1950) 477–485
R. Buchner, 'Die Rechtsquellen', in: W. Wattenbach and W. Levison, *Deutschlands Geschichtsquellen im Mittelalter, Vorzeit und Karolinger* (Weimar 1953) 72
A. Gerlich, 'Die Reichspolitik des Erzbischofs Otgar von Mainz (826–847)', RhV 19 (1954) 315
Sch. Williams, 'The Pseudo-Isidorian Problem Today', *Speculum* 29 (1954) 702–707
Gaudemet, 'Survivances romaines' 172, 175, 176
W. Ullmann, *The Growth of Papal Government in the Middle Ages* (London 1955) 184–189
H. Fuhrmann, 'Pseudoisidor und die Abbreviatio Ansegisi et Benedicti Levitae', ZKG 69 (1958) 309–311
W. A. Eckhardt, 'Die von Baluze benutzten Handschriften der Kapitularien-Sammlungen' *Mélanges offerts par ses confrères étrangers à Charles Braibant* (Brussels 1959) 113–140
G. May, 'Die Infamie bei Benedikt Levita', ÖAKR 11 (1960) 16–36
J. Semmler, 'Zur Überlieferung der monastischen Gesetzgebung Ludwigs des Frommen', DA 16 (1960) 309–388, especially 369–378 (on the Add. I of Book III by Benedictus Levita)
F.-L: Ganshof, *Was waren die Kapitularien?* (Weimar 1961) 111
F.-L. Ganshof, *Le droit romain dans les capitulaires, 2: Le droit romain dans la collection de Benoît le Lévite* (IRMA Pars I 2 b cc a–ß, Milan 1969) 23–24 (Benedictus Levita as mediator of Roman law)
P. Landau, 'Ursprünge und Entwicklung des Verbotes doppelter Strafverfolgung

wegen desselben Verbrechens in der Geschichte des kanonischen Rechts', ZRG Kan. Abt. 56 (1970) 124–156, especially 135–144

H. Mordek, 'Une nouvelle source de Benoît le Lévite', RDC 20 (1970) 241–251

Fuhrmann, *Einfluß und Verbreitung* 1.163–167

P. Brommer, 'Benedictus Levita und die *Capitula Episcoporum*', *Mainzer Zeitschrift* 70 (1975) 145–147

Mordek, *Kirchenrecht und Reform* 190–196, 268–269

R. McKitterick, *The Frankish Church and the Carolingian Reform (789–895)* (London 1977)

G. Schmitz, 'Das Konzil von Trosly (909): Überlieferung und Quellen', DA 33 (1977) 341–434, especially 373–386

Richter, 'Stufen' 1–72

J. Hannig, 'Zentrale Kontrolle und regionale Machtbalance: Beobachtungen zum System der karolingischen Königsboten am Beispiel des Mittelrheingebiets', *Archiv für Kulturgeschichte* 66 (1984) 15

Schmitz, 'Abbreviato Ansegisi' 176–199

Mordek, 'Karolingische Kapitularien' 25–50, especially 36

H. Mordek and G. Schmitz, 'Neue Kapitularien und Kapitulariensammlungen', DA 43 (1987) 361–439

G. Schmitz, 'Die Waffe der Fälschung zum Schutz der Bedrängten? Bemerkungen zu gefälschten Konzils- und Kapitularientexten', *Fälschungen im Mittelalter* 2.79–110

Schmitz, 'Vier-Bücher-Sammlung' 251

MGH Capit. n.s. 1.315–320

Abbreviatio Ansegisi et Benedicti Levitae

1. *Author:* Unknown. 2. *Date:* Eleventh century (after 1028)? 3. *Place:* France, probably in the north. 4. *Type:* Shortened form of the *Capitularia* of Ansegis, combined with texts from the *Capitularia* of Benedictus Levita. 5. *Edition:* None.

6. *Manuscripts*

Cf. Schmitz, 'Abbreviatio Ansegisi' 176–191

First Recension

Montpellier, Bibliothèque Interuniversitaire, H.137, saec. XI, France, fol. 127v–229v, see also Fournier, 'Manuscrit de Montpellier' 357–389; Prov.: belonged to F. Pithou, then to the Biblioteca Oratorii Trecensis (Troyes), (Boretius p. 392 [fragments], cf. Seckel, 'Benedictus Levita' no. 22)

Vaticano, Città del, Biblioteca Apostolica Vaticana, Ottobon. lat. 93, fol. 101v (Excerpt, cf. Fuhrmann, ZKG 69 [1958] 309–311)

Cf. *Collectio 17 librorum*

Second Recension

Palermo, Archivio della Cattedrale, 14, saec. XII, France, fol. 71r–112v, cf. Besta, 'Di una collezione canonistica Palermitana', *Il Circolo Giuridico* 40 [1909] 3–16;

Mordek, *Kirchenrecht und Reform* 181 n. 394 and 194 n. 495; Rambaud-Buhot, 'Baluze, bibliothécaire et canoniste' 334 including n. 117, erroneously assigns the shelf-mark 2 Qq E 17 (like Fournier-Le Bras 2.380) to the originally numberless codex; same mistake in 'Corpus inédit' 280–281 (French origin of the manuscript); see also Eckhardt, 'Die von Baluze benutzten Handschriften der Kapitularien-Sammlungen', *Mélanges offerts par ses confrères étrangers à Charles Braibant* (Brussels 1959) 113–140

Paris, Bibliothèque nationale, lat. 3839 (olim 533.3887), saec. XI^{ex}, France, fol. 86^{v}–121^{v} (Boretius p. 392, fragment; cf. Seckel, 'Benedictus Levita' no. 23)

Paris, Bibliothèque nationale, lat. 3839A, saec. XI^{2}, France, Prov. St. Aubin at Angers, fol. 34^{r}–76^{r}; (Boretius p. 392, fragment; cf. Seckel, 'Benedictus Levita' no. 24); on Codd. Paris lat. 3839 and 3839A, see also W. A. Eckhardt, 'Die von Baluze benutzten Handschriften der Kapitularien-Sammlungen', *Mélanges offerts par ses confrères étrangers à Charles Braibant* (Brussels 1959) 123 and 124; on Paris, B.N. lat. 3839A cf. J. Vezin, *Les 'scriptoria' d'Angers au IXe siècle* (Bibliothèque de l'Ecole des Hautes Etudes, IVe Section, Sciences historiques et philologiques 322, 1974) 57, 99 and especially 263–265; Mordek, *Kirchenrecht und Reform* 181 n. 394

Paris, Bibliothèque nationale, lat. 17526, saec. XII, France, fol. 24^{r}–58^{r}, fragment, cf. Seckel, 'Benedictus Levita' no. 25

Epitome Ansegisi et Benedicti Levitae

Paris, Bibliothèque nationale, lat. 3851, fol. 24^{r}–44^{v}, saec. X, France, Prov. Northwestern France (Angers, Le Mans), cf. Mordek-Schmitz, 'Neue Kapitularien und Kapitulariensammlungen', DA 43 (1987) 361–439, especially 378–390 and 424–439 (partial edition of the *Epitome Ansegisi et Benedicti Levitae*); cf. also Mordek, *Bibliotheca capitularium* 443–444; MGH Capit. n.s. 1.338–340

Cf. also *Collectio 342 capitulorum*

7. *Bibliography*

Fournier-Le Bras 1.206–207 and 2.150

Fournier, 'Manuscrit de Montpellier' 357–389

E. Besta, 'Di una collezione canonistica palermitana', *Il Circolo giuridico* 40 (1909) 3–16

Seckel, 'Benedictus Levita' 420–453

H. Fuhrmann, 'Pseudoisidor und die Abbreviatio Ansegisi et Benedicti Levitae', ZKG 69 (1958) 309–311

W. A. Eckhardt, 'Die von Baluze benutzten Handschriften der Kapitularien-Sammlungen', *Mélanges offerts par ses confrères étrangers à Charles Braibant* (Brussels 1959) 113–140

Rambaud-Buhot, 'Baluze, bibliothécaire et canoniste' 334 including n. 117

Rambaud-Buhot, 'Corpus inédit' 271–281

J. Vezin, *Les 'scriptoria' d'Angers au XIe siècle* (Bibliothèque de l'école des Hautes Etudes, IVe section, Sciences historiques et philologiques 322; Paris 1974) 57, 99, 263

Mordek, *Kirchenrecht und Reform* 181 n. 394 and 194 n. 495

Schmitz, 'Abbreviatio Ansegisi' 176–199
H. Mordek and G. Schmitz, 'Neue Kapitularien und Kapitulariensammlungen', DA 43 (1987) 361–439, especially 379–380, 391–395 and 424–439
Mordek, *Bibliotheca capitularium* 524–525
MGH Capit. n.s. 1.335–340

On the *Collectio Hispana Gallica Augustodunensis* cf. above

Collectio Anselmo dedicata

1. *Author:* Unknown. 2. *Date:* Last quarter of the ninth century. 3. *Place:* Northern Italy, perhaps Vercelli; cf. Ph. Levine, 'Historical Evidence for Calligraphic Activity in Vercelli from St. Eusebius to Atto', *Speculum* 30 (1955) 575–581. 4. *Type:* Systematic collection (introduces large parts of the Pseudo-Isidorian forgeries into the sources of canon law; taken from manuscripts of the A-2 class).

5. *Editions*

Ballerini, *De antiquis . . . collectionibus et collectoribus* P. IV cap. X, p. cclxxxv–cclxxxvi (praefatio and index including the titles of the respective parts) (PL 56.315–316)
A. Mai, *Novae patrum Bibliothecae tomus primus* VII/3 (Rome 1854) v–vii (Praefatio, index of the twelve parts and some particular titles from the fifth part concerning the formation of clerics)
J.-C. Besse, *Histoire des textes du droit de l'église au moyen-âge de Denys à Gratien: Collectio Anselmo dedicata: Etude et textes (extraits),* (Paris 1957): Incipit-explicit index of chapters based on Paris lat. 15392; cf. the devastating criticism of G. Le Bras, *Bibliothèque de la Revue d'histoire ecclésiastique* 33 (1959) 103
J.-C. Besse, *Collectionis 'Anselmo dedicata' liber primus,* RDC 9 (1959) 207–296 (only first book, according to Paris lat. 15392)
G. Russo, *Tradizione manoscritta di Leges Romanae* (as below) 75–239 (only Roman law texts according to Modena, O.II.2)

6. *Manuscripts*

The dating of the groups have to be analyzed again, since B. Bischoff (quoted in O. Bertolini, 'La Collezione canonica beneventana del Vat. Lat. 4939', *Collectanea Vaticana in honorem A. M. Card. Albareda* 1 [Studi e Testi 219; Rome 1962] 119–137, especially 123 n. 3 compare also *Scritti scelti* 2 [1968] 777 n. 10) established that the codices Vat. lat. 580 and 581 were actually written in the ninth century in Northern Italy; cf. Fuhrmann, *Einfluß und Verbreitung* 2.426–427 n. 8

First Italian Group

Modena, Biblioteca Capitolare, O.II.2, saec. X^1, Northern or Central Italy (Ravenna?), cf. Mordek, *Bibliotheca capitularium* 268–269
Roma, Biblioteca dell'Accademia Nazionale dei Lincei, Corsin. 41. A 24 (14), cf. Mordek, *Bibliotheca capitularium* 269 (partial copy saec. XVI of Modena O.II.2)
Roma, Biblioteca Vallicelliana, C.18 (partial copy saec. XVI of Modena O.II.2)

Roma, Biblioteca Vallicelliana, C.23 (partial copy saec. XVI of Modena O.II.2)
Roma, Biblioteca Vallicelliana, C.24 (partial copy saec. XVI of Modena O.II.2)
Vaticano, Città del, Biblioteca Apostolica Vaticana, lat. 4899 (a. 1578) (complete copy of Modena O.II.2)
Vercelli, Biblioteca Capitolare, XV (53), saec. X^{1}; some additions saec. X^{1-2}; Northern Italy, vicinity of Vercelli; cf. F. Patetta, 'Nota sull'età del codice Vercellese della collezione di canoni Anselmo dedicata', *Antologia giuridica di Catania* 4.3 (1890) (repr. *Studi sulle fonti giuridiche medievali,* ed. G. Astuti [Torino 1967] 701–707); F. Patetta, 'Nuove osservazioni sui manoscritti della collezione di canoni *Anselmo dedicata* et del capitolo di Lamberto', *Rivista italiana per le scienze giuridiche* 11 (1891) 374–383 (repr. *Studi sulle fonti giuridiche medievali,* ed. G. Astuti [Torino 1967] 743–752); Fournier, 'Groupe de recueils' 345–402; A. Werminghoff, 'Capitula episcoporum', NA 27 (1902) 603 (on the additions in this manuscript); cf. Mordek, *Bibliotheca capitularium* 888–890

Second Italian Group

Vaticano, Città del, Biblioteca Apostolica Vaticana, Pal. lat. 580 (Fournier: saec. XI, St. Martin at Mainz, corrected by Bischoff: saec. IX^{ex}, Milan)
Vaticano, Città del, Biblioteca Apostolica Vaticana, Pal. lat. 581 (Fournier: saec. XI; corr. Bischoff saec. IX^{ex}, Northern Italy)

Cisalpine Group

Bamberg, Staatsbibliothek, Can. 5 (P.I.12), saec. X or XI^{in}; Italy, cf. Hoffmann, *Bamberger Handschriften* 122 (a gift of Emperor Henry II to the cathedral of Bamberg)
Darmstadt, Hessische Landes- und Hochschulbibliothek, 2318, saec. XIX. cf. Mordek, 'Analecta canonistica' 6–7 (modern copy of Bamberg Can. 5)
Leipzig, Universitätsbibliothek, Haenel 32 (3529), made by Dr. Meier from Esslingen in 1833; cf. R. Helssig, *Katalog der lateinischen und deutschen Handschriften der Universitäts-Bibliothek zu Leipzig* 3 (Leipzig 1905) 307–308 (modern copy of Bamberg Can. 5)
Metz, Bibliothèque municipale, 100, saec. XI–XII, from the cathedral library (burnt in 1944, cf. Brommer, BMCL 9 [1979] 82)
Paris, Bibliothèque nationale, lat. 15392 (olim Sorbonne 752, from the library of the Cathedral of Verdun, where it has resided since 1009)

Partial Manuscript

Karlsruhe, Badische Landesbibliothek, Aug. CXLII, saec. X^{in}; Reichenau (contains parts 5–10)

Fragments

Koblenz, Landeshauptarchiv, 701 no. 759,37, fly leaf, saec. XI1/3, Mainz, cf. Hoffmann, *Schreibschulen* 1.241 (1 double leaf: Texts added to the end of Book III; Book IV chapters 1–19); cf. P. Brommer, 'Ein Koblenzer Fragment der *Collectio Anselmo dedicata*', BMCL 9 (1979) 82–83
Pavia, Archivio di Stato, Archivio notarile di Pavia, Frammenti, saec. IX^{ex}–X^{in}; region around Pavia; 3 leaves: two of them edited by Fiorina, 'Due Frammenti' 250–253 (chapters VII 62 and VII 95–100), the third added by Fiorina, *Il libro: Mille anni di storia documentati dalle testimonianze conservate a Pavia, Catalogo della Mostra* (1982) 35 no. 10 (without edition: chapters VII 39–40)

Strasbourg, Archives du Bas-Rhin, J. suppl. 1985–25, fol. 1^{rv} and 2^{rv}, J suppl. 1985–43, J suppl. 1985–44 and 45, about 900, Western Francia; cf. Reynolds: with Italian characteristics; cf. Fuhrmann, 'Fragmente' 541–543

Vercelli, Biblioteca Capitolare, fly leaf, saec. X, cf. Fuhrmann, *Einfluß und Verbreitung* 427 no. 8

Excerpt

Vaticano, Città del, Biblioteca Apostolica Vaticana, lat. 624, fols. I–II, saec. X; Kuttner-Elze, *Catalogue* 2.327 (1 double leaf: chapters X 108–108); this manuscript is not a fragment of a lost manuscript; cf. Fuhrmann, 'Fragmente' 543 n. 18

7. *Bibliography*

Maassen, *Geschichte* 717–721 (on the *Collectio Novariensis*); Conrat, *Geschichte* 212–215; Fournier-Le Bras 1.234–243; A. Amanieu, 'Anselmo dedicata (collection)', DDC 1 (1935) 578–583; Kurtscheid-Wilches 1.150–151; Van Hove, *Prolegomena* 232; 314; Stickler, *Historia* 1.150; M. G. Bertolini, 'Anselmo', DBI 3 (1961) 382–384; C. G. Mor, 'Anselmo dedicata, collectio', NCE 1 (1967) 585; R. E. Reynolds, 'Law, Canon: to Gratian', *Dictionary of the Middle Ages* 7 (1986) 406

Ballerini, *De antiquis . . . collectionibus et collectoribus* P. IV, cap. X. (PL 56.318)

Theiner, *Über Ivo's vermeintliches Decret* 13–14

E. L. Richter, *Beiträge zur Kenntnis der Quellen des canonischen Rechts* (Leipzig 1834) 36–63

F. Maassen, 'Über eine Lex romana canonice compta. Ein Beitrag zur Geschichte der Beziehung beider Rechte im Mittelalter', SB Vienna 35 (1861) 73–108

F. Maassen, 'Zur Geschichte der Quellen des Kirchenrechts und römischen Rechts im Mittelalter', *Kritische Vierteljahrschrift* 5 (Munich 1863)

J. F. Schulte, 'Über drei in Prager Handschriften enthaltene Canonen-Sammlungen. I. Eine aus der Collectio Anselmo dedicata excerpirte Sammlung', *SB Vienna* 57, 1867 (1868) 171–174

J.-B. Pitra, *Analecta novissima Spicilegii Solesmensis altera continuatio* 1 (1885) 140–141

F. Patetta, 'Il capitolare di Lamberto imperatore e gli atti del concilio di Ravenna dell'898', *Antologia giuridica di Catania* (1890) 335–348 (repr. *Studi sulle fonti giuridiche medievali,* ed. G. Astuti [Torino 1967] 729–742)

F. Patetta, 'Nota sull'età del codice Vercellese della collezione di canoni Anselmo dedicata e sopra una classe di manoscritti che da esso ebbe origine' *Antologia Giuridica* 4 (1890) 209–215 (repr. *Studi sulle fonti giuridiche medievali,* ed. G. Astuti [Torino 1967] 701–707)

F. Patetta, 'Nuove osservazione sui mss. della collezione di canoni Anselmo dedicata e del capitolare di Lamberto', *Rivista Italiana per le Scienze Giuridiche* 11 (1891) 375–384 (repr. *Studi sulle fonti giuridiche medievali,* ed. G. Astuti [Torino 1967] 743–752)

F. Patetta, 'Il Breviario Alariciano in Italia', *Archivio Giuridico* 47 (1891) 22–27 (repr. *Studi sulle fonti giuridiche medievali,* ed. G. Astuti [Torino 1967] 601–644)

Fournier, 'Groupe de recueils' 345–402

A. Gaudenzi, 'Lo svolgimento parallelo del diritto longobardo e del diritto romano a Ravenna,' *Memorie della R. Accademia delle scienze dell'Istituto di Bologna, Classe di scienze morali* 1 (1906–1907) 46–48 (origin in Ravenna)

A. Bachofen, Review of Fournier, 'Etudes sur le Décret de Burchard de Worms', AKKR 91 (1911) 772

Dobschütz, *Decretum Gelasianum* 37 (Milan as the place of origin of the *Collectio Anselmo dedicata*)

Fournier, 'Anselmo dedicata' 475–498

C. G. Mor, 'Lex Romana canonice compta', *Testo di leggi romano-canoniche del sec. IX pubblicato sul ms. parigino Bibl. Naz. 12448* (Pubblicazioni della R. Università di Pavia, Facultà di Giurisprudenza 31; Pavia 1927) 25–35 (edition of the collection's source in Roman law)

C. G. Mor, 'Recezione del diritto romano', *Testo di leggi romano-canoniche del sec. IX pubblicato sul ms. parigino Bibl. Naz. 12448* (Pubblicazioni della R. Università di Pavia, Facultà di Giurisprudenza 31; Pavia 1927) 297 and 299

Mor, 'Recezione' 298–300

Mor, 'Reazione al *Decretum Burchardi*' 197–206

J. De Ghellinck, *Le mouvement théologique du XIIe siècle* (Bruges ²1948) 424–425

A. G. Bergamaschi, 'La partecipazione del monastero di Bobbio alla attività di compilazione delle collezioni canoniche anteriori a Graziano', *San Columbano e la sua opera in Italia: Convegno storico Columbaniano, Bobbio 1–2 sett. 1951* (1953) 113–127 (Bobbio as the place of origin of the *Collectio Anselmo dedicata*)

E. Besta, *Storia di Milano* 2 (Milan 1954) 419–424

G. P. Bognetti, *Storia di Milano* 2 (Milan 1954) 787–803

Mor, 'Diritto romano e diritto canonico' 28–30

P. Levine, 'Historical Evidence for Calligraphic Activity in Vercelli from St. Eusebius to Atto', *Speculum* 30 (1955) 561–581, especially 573–577

Ryan, *Saint Peter Damiani* 13, 161, 166

C. G. Mor, (contribution to the discussion), 'Il monachesimo nell'alto medioevo e la formazione della civiltà occidentale', *Settimane di studio del centro Italiano di Studi sull'Alto Medioevo* 4, 1956 (Spoleto 1957) 514

J.-C. Besse, *Histoire des textes du droit de l'église au moyen âge de Denys à Gratien. Collectio Anselmo dedicata. Etude et texte* (Extraits) (Paris 1957) cf. Le Bras' criticism (see above, 'Edition')

Ryan, 'Observations' 94–95

J.-C. Besse, 'Collectionis Anselmo dedicata liber primus', RDC 9 (1959) 207–211 and 295–296

G. Le Bras, 'Miettes pour une nouvelle édition de l'Histoire des collections canoniques III: A propos de l'Anselmo dedicata', RHD 4e sér. 38 (1960) 309–312

J.-C. Besse, 'La suprématie romaine dans la collection 'Anselmo dedicata' à travers quelques textes conciliaires', *L'année canonique* 8 (1961–1962) 67–70

Martínez Díez, 'Novara' 408–409

C. G. Mor, 'Una piccola collezione di testi gregoriani del secolo VIII', *Etudes . . . Le Bras* 1.283–291 (cf. also Fuhrmann, *Einfluß und Verbreitung* 2.425 n. 7)

S. F. Wemple, 'The Canonical Resources of Atto of Vercelli', *Traditio* 26 (1970) 335–350

Fuhrmann, *Einfluß und Verbreitung* 2.425–435 and 3.774

Petersmann, 'Kanonistische Überlieferung' 364–365, 367

Mordek, *Kirchenrecht und Reform* 4–5 n. 12, 180, 184

Kerner et al., 'Textidentifikation' 23–24, 33

U. Fiorina, 'Frammenti di codici giuridici (saec. IX–XV) recentemente recuperati nell'Archivio di Stato di Pavia', RSDI 52 (1979) 7–8

G. Russo, *Tradizione manoscritta di Leges Romanae nei codici dei secoli IX e X della Biblioteca Capitolare di Modena* (Deputaz. di storia patria per le antiche Provincie Modenesi, Biblioteca n.s. 56; Modena 1980)

U. Fiorina, 'Due frammenti della 'Collectio Anselmo dedicata' rinventi nell'Archivio di Stato di Pavia', *Athenaeum, Studi periodici di Letteratura e Storia dell'Antichità. N.S.* 60 (Pavia 1982) 248–253

U. Fiorina, 'Pavia e la cultura del Medioevo', *Le Scienze* (edizione italiana di *Scientific American*) 30 (June 1983) 60–75, especially 74 with a reproduction on p. 66

U. Fiorina, 'Rendiconto sul recupero di frammenti di codici dal sec. IX in poi compiuto recentemente dall'Archivio di Stato di Pavia', *Istituto Lombardo: Academia di Scienze e Lettere, Classe di Lettere e Scienze Morali e Storiche: Rendiconti 115* (1981, published in 1984) 56–57

Mordek, 'Systematische Kanonessammlungen' 185–201

C. Märtl (ed.), *Die falschen Investiturprivilegien* (MGH *Fontes iuris Germanici antiqui* 13; Hannover 1986) 49 including n. 150

Fuhrmann, 'Fragmente' 539–543

Landau, 'Kanonessammlungen in der Lombardei' 439–443

Müller, *Collectio Duodecim Partium* 316–325

Gaudemet, 'Primauté' 155–156

Landau, 'Vorgratianische Kanonessammlungen bei den Dekretisten' 93–116

Siems, *Handel und Wucher* 179, 295, 320, 538, 618–619, 789

Zechiel-Eckes, *Cresconius* 1.245–247

Landau, 'Eheschließung' 456

Regino of Prüm, *Libri duo de synodalibus causis*

1. Author: Regino of Prüm (†906–915). *2. Date:* About 906. *3. Place:* Convent of St. Martin at Trier. 4. *Type:* Systematic collection ('Sendhandbuch').

5. Editions

J. Hildebrand (ed.), *Reginonis Prumiensis de disciplina ecclesiastica veterum presertim Germanorum Libri duo* (Helmstedt 1659): based on Wolfenbüttel Helmst. 32, including its Appendices: Appendix I, followed by Appendix III based on the copy in Wien 694, finally Appendix II based on Wolfenbüttel 83.21

Etienne Baluze (ed.), *Reginonis abbatis Prumiensis de ecclesiasticis disciplinis et religione christiana libri duo* (Paris 1671): based on Paris lat. 17527 including its Appendices: Appendix I 1–28 and Appendix II; followed by Appendix I 29–58 of Wolfenbüttel Helmst. 32; according to Hildebrand, Appendix III was not taken over; the missing quire in the text of the Parisian codex was filled in with the text of Hildebrand's edition, cf. the manuscripts Paris, Collection Baluze 264 and 274 with materials for this edition

A. Graf Christiani (ed.), *Reginonis abbatis Prumiensis libri duo de ecclesiasticis disciplinis* (Vienna 1765): based on Baluze, but changed the order of his Nota

J. F. Schannat and J. Hartzheim (ed.), *Concilia Germaniae* 2 (Cologne 1760) 438–582: based on Baluze, omitting the appendices

PL 132.183–400: based on Baluze

F. G. A. Wasserschleben, *Reginonis abbatis Prumiensis Libri duo de synodalibus causis et disciplinis ecclesiasticis,* (Leipzig 1840; repr. Graz 1964)

Editions of Selected Groups of Chapters before the Oldest Complete Edition

M. Flacius Illyricus, *Ecclesiastica historia . . . secundum singulas centurias . . . digesta* 9 (Basel 1565), 406–412 (Canons of Meaux-Paris, 845–846, based on Wolfenbüttel Helmst. 32); cf. MGH Conc. 3.69

L. Surius, *Conciliorum omnium, tum generalium, tum provincialium atque particularium . . .* 3 (Cologne 1567) 569–572 (*Canones Namnetenses* based on a codex of the interpolated version); cf. E. Seckel, 'Studien zu Benedictus Levita I. Benedictus Levita und das Konzil von Nantes', NA 26 (1901) 39–72

J. Morinus, *Commentarius historicus de disciplina in administratione sacramenti poenitentiae* (Paris 1651) 40–42 (Excerpts based on Paris lat. 17527)

6. *Manuscripts*

Information provided by R. Pokorny

I. Genuine Form

Arras, Bibliothèque municipale, 723 (olim 675, not 673, as Naz, DDC 7, 535 noted), saec. XI, Prov. Saint-Vaast at Arras (notation of ownership of 1628); this manuscript is not mentioned in the old library catalogue of Saint-Vaast, saec. XII, cf. P. Grierson, 'La Bibliothèque de St-Vaast d'Arras au XIIe siècle', RB 52 (1940) 117–140 especially 138: 'Omissions'

Gotha, Forschungs- und Landesbibliothek, Mbr. II.131, saec. X, Metz, Prov. St-Symphorien, Metz (eleventh- and seventeenth-century notations of ownership)

Luxembourg, Bibliothèque nationale, 29 (olim 102), saec. XII^{1}, Prov. Orval in Luxembourg (eighteenth-century notations of ownership), fol. 25^{v}ff., quire one lost (with beginning of the *Capitula Angilramni*)

Trier, Stadtbibliothek, 927 (olim 1882), saec. X^{2}, Trier (St. Maximin), Prov. Maria Laach (notation of ownership p. xii); cf. Hoffmann, *Buchkunst* 1.446, 491

II. Interpolated Version

Düsseldorf, Universitätsbibliothek, E.3, saec. X, Werden, Prov. Werden (twelfth- and fourteenth-century notations of ownership)

Paris, Bibliothèque nationale, lat. 17527 (olim Fonds de l'Oratoire no. 20), saec. XI^{1}, Eastern France; Prov. ecclesiastical province of Reims (?); one quire lost after fol. 149 with II 201–247, cf. C. Erdmann, *Die Entstehung des Kreuzzugsgedankens* (Stuttgart 1935) 337–338; MGH Conc. 6.1.181 and MGH Capit. episc. 3.150

Stuttgart, Württembergische Landesbibliothek, HB.VI.108, saec. XI^{2}, Southwestern Germany, Prov. Constance(?), later at Weingarten (notation of ownership); cf. MGH Conc. 6.1.146 and 188;

Stuttgart, Württembergische Landesbibliothek, HB.VI.114, saec. X^{ex}, Hersfeld; Prov. Constance; later at Weingarten (notation of ownership dated 1630); Hoffmann, *Buchkunst* 1.200–201; MGH Conc. 6.1.146 and 188

Wien, Österreichische Nationalbibliothek, lat. 694, about 1000, Mainz; by 1576 it was already in possession of the Hofbibliothek at Vienna; cf. Hoffmann, *Buchkunst* 1.262–263; MGH Conc. 6.1.181; MGH Ordines 329–330

Wolfenbüttel, Herzog August Bibliothek, August. 83.21, about 1000, Prov. St. Jakob, Mainz (twelfth century); probably between 1653 and 1656 the Duke August the Younger of Wolfenbüttel acquired it; cf. Hoffmann, *Buchkunst* 1.266; MGH Conc. 6.1.181; MGH Ordines 330

Wolfenbüttel, Herzog August Bibliothek, Helmst. 32, about 1000 (it was not written at Reims as was supposed previously but in the region around Hildesheim) it was part of Matthias Flacius' library (beginning of the seventeenth century); cf. Hoffmann-Pokorny 115–129; MGH Ordines 222–223

III. Fragments (Single Leaves)

Göttingen, Niedersächsische Staats- und Universitätsbibliothek, Fragmentenkasten III, Fasz. 2, a single leaf (II 216–228), saec. X, Cologne (Information from H. Hoffmann)

Konstanz, Stadtarchiv, M.1 U.11 no. 1, remains of two double leaves (II 76–77, 80–82, 90–94, 98–99, 100–101, 104–106, 108–110, 112–113, 115–118; 122–123) (Information from H. Hoffmann)

Trier, Bibliothek der Abtei St. Eucharius und St. Matthias, belonged to the Carthusian monastery of St. Alban at Trier; three lengthwise strips, II, 387–401; saec. X^1, written in the region around Trier, cf. Petrus Becker, 'Neu gefundene Fragmente zu Reginos Werk *De synodalibus causis*', RB 93 (1983) 126–127, saec. X2/3 (Northwestern Germany, fragment of a codex of the interpolated version); cf. Hoffmann, *Buchkunst* 1.503

Kept at an unknown place: two inner double leaves of the same quire immediately following each other: I 7–I 10; I 18–23 and I 10–14/I 15–17; saec. X^1, Werden? (H. Hoffmann; copies were in the possession of †B. Bischoff)

IV. Manuscripts of Regino in Medieval and Early Modern Library Catalogues

Gorze, cf. G. Morin, 'Le catalogue des manuscrits de l'abbaye de Gorze au XIe siècle', RB 22 (1905) 1–14

Mainz (Cathedral?); cf. Worms

Mönchengladbach; inventory of precious manuscripts from about 1790 to 1795; A. Wendehorst, 'Zur Geschichte der Gladbacher Abteibibliothek', *Lebendiges Münster* 2 (1954) 90 (no. 17)

Nienburg/Saale; Catalogue from 1473; cf. F. P. Schmidt, 'Der Katalog der Klosterbibliothek Nienburg a. S.', *Thüringische Studien: Festschrift zur Feier des 250jährigen Bestehens der Thüringischen Landesbibliothek Altenburg*, ed. F. P. Schmidt (Altenburg 1936), 59 (Signatur: H.X.)

Trier, Cathedral; reference dating from 1626: C. Brower, *Antiquitates et Annales Trevirenses* (Cologne ^{1}1626) 535, unfinished and only one copy remains in Göttingen; Liège ^{2}1670 in two volumes, reference (in vol. 2, p. 437) to a codex of the *Libri duo* in the cathedral library of Trier ('Treviris aedis primariae bibliotheca); the supposition expressed by P. Lehmann, 'Nachrichten von der alten Trierer Dombibliothek', *Erforschung des Mittelalters* 1 (Stuttgart 1941; repr. Stuttgart 1959) 251, that this codex could be identified with the Wien 694, cannot be correct, because it was already in the possession of the Hofbibliothek at Vienna by 1597

Worms (Cathedral); reference on p. xvi; in the Praefatio of his edition of Regino's Chronicle, Sebastianus de Rotenthan mentions two manuscripts of the *Libri duo*, one from Mainz and another from Worms, the former might be identical with the Codex Wolfenbüttel 83.21 and the latter is possibly identical with Wien 694, because Burchard used a codex of the same type

7. *Bibliography*

Conrat, *Geschichte* 258–259; Fournier-Le Bras 1.244–268; E. Amann, 'Reginon de Prum', DThC 13 (1937) 2117–2120; Kurtscheid-Wilches 1.151–153; Van Hove, *Prolegomena* 238, 263, 317–318; P. Hofmeister, 'Regino von Prüm', LThK 8^2 (1963) 1099–1100; R. Naz, 'Réginon de Prüm', DDC 7 (1965) 533–536; G. May, 'Regino of Prüm, Collection of', NCE 12 (1967) 204–205; B. Schneidmüller, 'Regino von Prüm', HRG 4 (1990) 492–495; G. Schmitz, 'Regino von Prüm', *Verfasserlexikon* 7 (1988) 1115–1122, especially 1117–1118

Ballerini, *De antiquis . . . collectionibus et collectoribus* P. IV, cap. XI (PL 56.319–320)

A. J. Binterim, *Pragmatische Geschichte der deutschen National-, Provinzial- und vorzüglichsten Diöcesanconcilien* 1 (Mainz 1835) 256

H. Wasserschleben, 'Über Regino's Libri II de synodalibus causis et disciplinis ecclesiasticis, ihre Quellen und ihr Verhältnis zu spätern Sammlungen', *Beiträge* 1 (Leipzig 1839) 1–33

G. Phillips, 'Die große Synode von Tribur', *SB Vienna* 49 (1865) 713–784

G. Phillips, 'Der Codex Salisburgensis S. Petri IX 32: Ein Beitrag zur Geschichte der vorgratianischen Rechtsquellen', *SB Vienna* 44 (1863) 437–510

L. Weiland, 'Über eine Handschrift von Regino's Liber de Synodalibus causis', ZKR 20, N.F. 5 (1885) 455–460

K. Zeumer, *Formulae Merovingici et Karolini aevi*, MGH LL Formulae (Hannover 1886) 544

L. Weiland, 'Handschriften der vormaligen königlichen Handbibliothek zu Stuttgart, Nachlese zu N.A. X, 600', NA 15 (1890) 386

Krause, 'Acten' 49–82, 281–326

E. Seckel, 'Zu den Acten der Triburer Synode 895', NA 18 (1893) 365–409

V. Krause, 'Die Münchner Handschriften 3851.3853 mit einer Compilation von 181 Wormser Beschlüssen', NA 19 (1894) 85–139 (cf. correction by G. Schmitz, 'Vier-Bücher-Sammlung' 240 n. 35)

M. Manitius, 'Regino und Justin', NA 25 (1900) 192–201

Seckel, 'Studien zu Benedictus Levita I', NA 26 (1901) 37–72, especially 45, 47, 57; 'Studien zu Benedictus Levita VIII', NA 41 (1919) 157–263, especially 172, 173 and 179

Wretschko, *Theodosiani libri XVI*, p. cccxlii–cccxliii

A. M. Koeniger, *Die Sendgerichte in Deutschland* 1 (Veröffentlichungen aus dem Kirchenhistorischen Seminar München, Reihe 3, No. 2, Munich 1907)

E. Seckel, 'Die ältesten Canones von Rouen', *Historische Aufsätze: Karl Zeumer zum 60. Geburtstag als Festgabe dargebracht* (Weimar 1910) 624

Fournier, 'Réginon' 5–44

G. Flade, 'Germanisches Heidentum und christliches Erziehungsbemühen in Karolingischer Zeit nach Regino von Prüm', *Theologische Studien und Kritiken* 106 (1934–35) 213–240

G. Flade, *Vom Einfluß des Christentums auf die Germanen (secundum librum de synodalibus causis Reginonis Prumiensis)* (Stuttgart 1936)

P. W. Finsterwalder, 'Die sogenannte Homilia Leonis IV, ihre Bedeutung für Hinkmars Capitula und Reginos Inquisitio', ZRG Kan. Abt. 27 (1938) 639–664

N. Kyll, 'Das Visitationshandbuch Reginos von Prüm als Quelle heimischer Volkskunde', *Einhundert Jahre Reginoschule (Festschrift Prüm 1952)* 26–44, 112–117

H. Löwe, 'Regino von Prüm und das historische Weltbild der Karolingerzeit', RhV 17 (1952) 152–173 (repr. Löwe, *Von Cassiodor zu Dante: Ausgewählte Aufsätze zur Geschichtsschreibung und politischen Ideenwelt des Mittelalters* [Berlin-New York 1973] 149–179)

K. F. Werner, 'Zur Arbeitsweise des Regino von Prüm', *Die Welt als Geschichte* 19 (1959) 96–116 (concentrating especially on the Chronicle)

H. Hüschen, 'Regino von Prüm, Historiker, Kirchenrechtler und Musiktheoretiker', *Festschrift für K. G. Fellerer* (1962) 205–223

J. Autenrieth, 'Die Handschriften der ehemaligen Hofbibliothek Stuttgart 3, Codices iuridici et politici HB VI, 1–139, Patres HB VII 1–71', *Die Handschriften der Württembergischen Landesbibliothek Stuttgart* 2.3 (Wiesbaden 1963)

W. Hellinger, 'Die Pfarrvisitation nach Regino von Prüm' ZRG Kan. Abt. 48 (1962) 1–116 and 49 (1963) 76–137

C. Vogel, 'Les rites de la pénitence publique aux Xe et XIe siècles', *Mélanges offerts à René Crozet*, ed. by P. Gallais and Y.-J. Riou (Poitiers 1966) 1.137–144

J. Rambaud-Buhot, 'La critique des faux dans l'ancien droit canonique', BEC 126 (1968) 5–62, especially 31

M. Kerner, *Studien zum Dekret des Bischofs Burchard von Worms* 1–2 (Aachen, phil. Diss. 1969; 1971) 1.22–25 and 107–119

N. Kyll, 'Zum Zeugniswert des Visitationshandbuches Reginos von Prüm für die Trierer Volkskunde um 900', *Kurtrierisches Jahrbuch* 11 (1971) 5–23

N. Kyll, *Tod, Grab, Begräbnisplatz, Totenfeier: Zur Geschichte ihres Brauchtums im Trierer Lande und in Luxemburg unter besonderer Berücksichtigung des Visitationshandbuchs des Regino von Prüm (†915)* (Rheinisches Archiv 81; Bonn 1972)

Fuhrmann, *Einfluß und Verbreitung* 2.435–441

Brommer, 'Rezeption' 113–160

D. A. Bullough, 'The Continental Background of the Tenth-Century English Reform', *Tenth-Century Studies: Essays in Commemoration of the Millennium of the Council of Winchester and 'Regularis Concordia'*, ed. D. Parsons (London-Chichester 1975; repr. *Carolingian Renewal, Sources and Heritage* [Manchester-New York 1991])

Mordek, *Kirchenrecht und Reform* 4–5 n. 12

J. Gaudemet, 'Le pseudo-concile de Nantes', RDC 25 (1975) 40–60 (repr. J. Gaudemet, *La formation du droit canonique médiéval* [1980] no. V)

E. Hlawitschka, 'Regino von Prüm', *Rheinische Lebensbilder* 6, ed. B. Poll (1975) 7–27

John, *Collectio canonum Remedio . . . ascripta* 106–108

D. Aupest-Conduché, 'De l'existence du concile de Nantes', *Bulletin philologique et historique, Année 1973* (1976) 29–59 (not very convincing, cf. review by W. Hartmann, DA 35, 1979, 250)

Kerner et al. 'Textidentifikation' 44–62

F. Lotter, 'Ein kanonistisches Handbuch über die Amtspflichten des Pfarrklerus als gemeinsame Vorlage für den Sermo synodalis 'Fratres presbyteri' und Reginos Werk *De synodalibus causis*', ZRG Kan. Abt. 62 (1976) 1–57
Hartmann, *Worms* 109–111
Mordek, 'Kirchenrechtliche Autoritäten' 254
Motta, 'Regula Benedicti' 261–279
Kerff, *Quadripartitus* 71–72
Landau, 'Dekret' 29–30 (Regino is not a direct source of Ivo's Decree)
P. J. Payer, *Sex and the Penitentials: The Development of a Sexual Code 550–1150* (Toronto 1984)
J. Bishop, 'Bishops as Marital Advisors in the Ninth Century', *Women of the Medieval World, Essays in Honor of John H. Mundy,* ed. J. Kirshner and S. F. Wemple (Oxford 1985) 53–84
R. Pokorny, 'Nochmals zur Admonitio synodalis', ZRG Kan. Abt. 71 (1985) 20–51, especially 42–48
Landau, 'Gefälschtes Recht' 22–26
Schmitz, 'Ansegis und Regino' 95–132
M. M. Sheehan, 'Theory and Practice: Marriage of the Unfree and the Poor in Medieval Society', MS 50 (1988) 457–487
Müller, *Collectio Duodecim Partium* 301–315
G. Fransen, 'La notion d'oeuvre servile dans le droit canonique', *Le travail* 177–184
J. Gaudemet, 'Le serment dans le droit canonique médiéval', *Le serment,* ed. R. Verdier (Paris 1991) 2.63–75
E.-D. Hehl, 'Iuxta canones et instituta sanctorum patrum: Zum Mainzer Einfluß auf Synoden des 10. Jahrhunderts', *Festschrift Fuhrmann* (1991) 117–133
Hoffmann-Pokorny, passim
J. Longère, 'L'enseignement du 'Credo': Conciles, synodes et canonistes médiévaux jusqu'au XIIIe siècle', SE 32 (1991) 309–341
Schmitz, 'Vier-Bücher-Sammlung' passim, especially 239
Brett, 'Collectio Lanfranci' 168–169
Hartmann, 'Autoritäten' 428–429
R. McKitterick, 'Continuity and Innovation in Tenth-Century Ottonian Culture', *Intellectual Life in the Middle Ages: Essays presented to Margaret Gibson,* ed. L. Smith and B. Ward (London 1992) 15–24
Pokorny, 'Triburer Synodalakten' 429–511, especially 440–441
H.-H. Kortüm, '*Necessitas temporis:* Zur historischen Bedingtheit des Rechtes im früheren Mittelalter', ZRG Kan. Abt. 79 (1993) 34–55
MGH Capit. n.s. 1.330–335

Burchard of Worms, Decretum

1. Author: Bishop Burchard I. of Worms (†1025); cf. *Vita Burchardi,* MGH SS 4.829–846 (PL 140.505–536); H. Boos, *Quellen zur Geschichte der Stadt Worms* 3.99–126; on the *Vita,* cf. Manitius, NA 13 (1886) 197–202. *2. Date:* Between 1008 and 1012 (Fournier-Le Bras 1.366 n. 2); before 1023 (R. Pokorny). *3. Place:* Worms. *4. Type:* Systematic collection.

5. Editions

Bartoldus de Questenburgh, Cologne, Melchior Neuss (Novesianus) 1548, copied from a manuscript which must have closely resembled Vat. Pal. 585–586. This edition was essentially taken from and reprinted by Jean Foucher (Paris 1549) (the edition of Foucher from 1550 was published with a different date on the title page)

Jean Birckmann Jr. edited the second edition of Cologne in 1560

PL 140.537–1065 reprinted the text of Jean Foucher (Paris 1549) (the editions dating before the fire of 1868 contain fewer errors than the newly drafted text by Garnier, cf. E. van Balberghe, 'Les éditions du Décret de Burchard de Worms', *Recherches de Théologie ancienne et médiévale* 37 (1970) 5–22 and Fransen, 'Essai de classement' 3 (progressive deterioration of the printed text)

G. Fransen and T. Kölzer (edd.), *Burchard von Worms: Decretorum libri XX* (Köln 1548, repr. Aalen 1992)

6. Manuscripts

Mss. of the *Decretum Burchardi* according to R. Pokorny. In the following list, 'additions' means additional texts written by one and the same hand; 'supplements' means texts added later. Cf. Meyer, 'Überlieferung' 141–183 and Mordek, QF 51 (1971) 626–651, especially 633; reprinted with additional information in SG 20 (1976) 240 n. 33 and especially Hoffmann-Pokorny

I. Complete Codices

1. 'Order of Worms, Type A'

Vaticano, Città del, Biblioteca Apostolica Vaticana, Pal. lat. 585–586; saec. XI1/4, Worms; cf. Hoffmann-Pokorny 29–37 and passim; MGH Ordines 471; Additions: *Ordo synodalis* 17; Council of Seligenstadt (1023) following Book XX

Würzburg, Universitätsbibliothek, M.p.th.f. 86, saec. XII, Eastern Franconia, Prov. Würzburg, St. Stephan; Additions: *Ordo synodalis* 17, with the *Admonitio synodalis* inserted at the beginning; Seligenstadt (1023) following Book XX

Würzburg, Universitätsbibliothek, M.p.th.f. 167, saec. XI3/4, Amorbach, Prov. Amorbach; (fragmentary beginning at rubric 226 of the *Capitulatio* on Book III; also ending at XX 61; one leaf is almost totally missing between fol. 3 and 5: III 41–50, another is missing between fol. 72 and 73: X 15–44), cf. Hoffmann-Pokorny 59–61, 143–147

2. 'Order of Worms, Type B': German Group of Manuscripts

Bamberg, Staatsbibliothek, Can. 6, saec. XI1/4, Worms; Prov. Bamberg, Cathedral; (missing leaves between fol. 76 and 77: II 215–230 as well as between 77 and 78: II 236 - *Capitulatio* III); cf. Hoffmann-Pokorny 16–18 and passim. Additions: *Admonitio synodalis* and (in a different hand) Seligenstadt (1023) at the beginning, inserted on fol. 3^r–5^v on a separate quire between the *Praefatio* of the *Decretum* and the *Capitulatio* of Book I (probably misbound, originally followed Book XX)

Bruxelles, Bibliothèque Royale Albert Ier, 3819–20 (Cat. 2499), saec. XI; Prov. Kues, Hospital St. Nikolaus (notation of ownership) Trier, St. Mattias

Chartres, Bibliothèque municipale, 161 (154), saec. XII, largely destroyed in 1944, vgl. *Catalogue général, Départements* 53 (1962) 4; it was fragmentary at the end even before its destruction; cf. *Catalogue général, Départements* 11 (1889) 84

Durham, Cathedral Library, B.IV.17, saec. XI. Additions: *Admonitio synodalis* and Seligenstadt (1023) following Book XX (closely related to the mss. St-Omer 194 and Vat. Reg. lat. 979)

Eichstätt, Universitätsbibliothek, st. 772 (olim manuscript 6 or 48); saec. XI^{med}, Bavaria/Franconia; Prov. Eichstätt, Cathedral; cf. Hoffmann-Pokorny 136–137, 143. Additions: *ius synodale* for the Slavs in the Main region following Book I (ed. W. Dove, ZKR 4 [1864], 160–162), *Admonitio synodalis* following Book XX. Supplement: Synod of Dingolfing (932), MGH Conc. 6.1 (Hannover 1987) 115–124 (closely related to Freiburg Universitätsbibliothek 7)

Frankfurt am Main, Stadt- und Universitätsbibliothek, Barth. 50, saec. XI1/4, Worms; Prov. Frankfurt, St. Bartholomäus, cf. Hoffmann-Pokorny 37–39 and passim

Freiburg (Breisgau), Universitätsbibliothek, 7, saec. XI2/4, Constance? script of St. Gall and Lorsch, Prov. Constance, Cathedral (notation of donation by Bishop Eberhard of Constance [1034–1046], cf. Meyer, 'Überlieferung' 153–154 including 153 n. 1 [Bibliography] and 161–162, 180–181 [parenthetical remarks]); Hoffmann, *Buchkunst* 1.208–209. Additions: *ius synodale* for the Slavs in the Main region following Book I (Edition cf. Eichstätt 772), *Admonitio synodalis* following Book XX. Supplements saec. XII: Innocent II (JL 7740) to the clergy and people of Constance, Paschal II (JL-; *Germania Pontificia* 2.135 no. 46) to the canons of Constance (closely related to Eichstätt 772 and St. Gallen 674)

Köln, Erzbischöfliche Diözesan- und Dombibliothek, 119, saec. XI1/4, Worms, Prov. Cologne, Cathedral; cf. Hoffmann-Pokorny 20–21 (fragmentary, missing the quires I–IX, XXIV, quires at the end: *Praefatio*–II 196, XIX 102–159, XX 57–110)

Lambach, Bibliothek des Benediktinerstifts, XVI, saec. XI^2, Southern Germany, Prov. Lambach *praefatio,* fragmentary: about a fifth of the codex is lost due to various missing leaves); cf. R. Weigand, 'Die Lambacher Handschrift XVI des Dekrets Burchards von Worms und Bischof Adalbero von Würzburg', *Würzburger Diözesan-Geschichtsblätter* 52 (1990) 25–36. Additions: *Admonitio synodalis* following Book XX (closely related to, although an earlier version than, München Clm 4570 and Vat. lat. 3809)

München, Bayerische Staatsbibliothek, Clm 4570, the manuscript was finished on March 20, 1108 (entry on fol. 239^v); Prov. Benediktbeuern; cf. A. M. Koeniger, 'Beiträge zu den fränkischen Kapitularien und Synoden', AKKR 87 (1907) 393–406; without the *Praefatio,* but with a reformulated table of contents, ed. F. Pelster, 'Das Dekret Burkhards von Worms in einer Redaktion aus dem Beginn der Gregorianischen Reform (Cod. Vat. lat. 3809 und Cod. Monacen. lat. 4570)', SGreg 1 (1947) 321–331, 342–343. Additions: *Fraterne mortis* (JL †6613a) following Book I; Lucius III JL 14688 to the cathedral chapter of Chur on a separate quire. Supplements: *Admonitio synodalis* following Book XX (closely related to Vat. lat. 3809 and Lambach)

München, Bayerische Staatsbibliothek, Clm 5801c, saec. XI^2, Prov. Ebersberg; (missing leaves after fol. 33, 52, 57, 60, 64a, 115, 127, 143 and 146: II 16–39, III

45–53, III 104–124, III 153–160, III 221–224, Capitulatio XI, rubric 28–XI 3, XIII 23–XV 44, XVII 56–middle of the *ordo* before XVIII, XVIII 15–24) (closely related to Clm 18094)

München, Bayerische Staatsbibliothek, Clm 18094, saec. XI–XII, Prov. Tegernsee. (closely related to Clm 5801c)

Orléans, Bibliothèque municipale, 229 (200), saec. XI, France, Prov. Fleury; missing quires between p. 80–81 and p. 174–175: III 5–IV 98 and XVI 29–Capitulatio-rubric XIX 27; fragmentary ending at XIX 5 (PL 140.971D); also leaf lost between p. 72 and 73: II 184–197 and large parts of p. 93–94: VI 5–22. Supplements: verses in honor of Abbot Veranus of Fleury (1080–1096) at the fly leaf

Paris, Bibliothèque nationale, lat. 3860, saec. XI^2, Prov . Angers, St. Aubin; cf. Kuttner-Somerville 175–189. Additions: Seligenstadt (1023) inserted between the Books XIX and XX. Supplement: the so-called acts of Nîmes (1096), edited on the basis of this codex; books 17 and 18 are switched in the manuscript with the exception that the *ordo infirmorum* of book 18 is placed at the end (closely related to Reims 673 and 674 and the short version Paris lat. 8922, see below)

Paris, Bibliothèque nationale, lat. 12449, saec. XII^1, Prov.: 1732 as a legacy by Henri du Cambout, Duc de Coislin, Bishop of Metz, to St-Germain-des-Prés. Additions: Seligenstadt (1023) following Book XX (fol. 216 has to be inserted between 225 and 226)

Parma, Biblioteca Palatina, 3777, saec. XI^1, Prov. Parma, cathedral; cf. G. Catalano and C. Pecorella, 'Inventario ragionato de manoscritti giuridici della Biblioteca Palatina di Parma', *Studi Parmensi* 5 (1955) 386–394, MGH Ordines 470–471. Additions: *Ordo synodalis* 17, with the *Admonitio synodalis* inserted at the beginning, Seligenstadt (1023) following Book XX. Supplements: Lateran (1059), epitaphs of some bishops of Parma dating from 980–1072, letter concerning the Peace of God in the ecclesiastical province of Arles 1037–1041 (MGH Const. 1.596–597), Pavia (1046) or Lombardy (1077) and *Pax Italica* (1077) (MGH Const. 1.116–117) on some leaves bound together with the manuscript

Pommersfelden, Gräflich Schönbornsche Schloßbibliothek, 198 (2816), saec. XI–XII, German? (only XIX *Capitulatio*–XX 110 [=End]; Fragment or rather partial transmission?). fol. 65^v a certain 'Otto persbiter (!)' is mentioned as the person who commissioned the codex

Reims, Bibliothèque municipale 673; saec. XI, Prov. Reims, cathedral, a modern notation describes it as a donation by Archbishop Manasses I (1069–1080) or Manasses II (1096–1106); core of the codex is fol. 4–240. Supplement: fol. 1–3 and 241–243: fragment of an additional manuscript of the *Decretum Burchardi,* see below

Reims, Bibliothèque municipale, 674; saec. XII, Prov. Reims, St-Remi; (according to the colophon on fol. 154ra written by Garnerus) Additions: Seligenstadt (1023) following Book XIX. Supplement: Third Lateran Council (1179) following Book XX (perhaps a direct copy of Reims 673, cf. also Paris 3860)

Saint-Omer, Bibliothèque municipale, 194, saec. XI^2, Prov. Saint-Omer. Additions: *Admonitio synodalis,* Seligenstadt (1023), Tribur (1036) and the genealogy of Otto and Irmingard of Hammerstein (MGH Const. 1.639) following Book XX. Supplements: Gregory VII JL 5157 to Hubert of Thérouanne; list of the 'censuales' of Saint-Omer saec. XII^{ex}; negotiations between Henry V and Paschal II in Rome 1111 (MGH Const. 1.142–145, no. 94, 95, 91, 92, 93, 96) (closely related to Durham B.IV.17 and Vat. Reg. lat. 979)

St. Gallen, Stiftsbibliothek, 674, saec. XI², missing leaves between p. 54–67: I 182–rubric of the *Capitulatio* II 120 (closely related to Freiburg 7)

Vaticano, Città del, Biblioteca Apostolica Vaticana, Reg. lat. 979, saec. XI², Prov. Bruges, then Haluin (French part of Flanders); cf. Pelster, 'Dekret' 133–135. Additions: *Admonitio synodalis,* Seligenstadt (1023), Tribur (1036) and genealogy of Otto and Irmingard of Hammerstein (MGH Const. 1.639) following Book XX. Supplements: Quedlinburg (1085) MGH Const. 1.651; inventory of relics saec. XIII of the church of Haluin (closely related to Durham B.IV.17 and Saint-Omer 194)

Vaticano, Città del, Biblioteca Apostolica Vaticana, lat. 3809, saec. XI², cf. F. Pelster, 'Das Dekret Burkharts von Worms in einer Redaktion aus dem Beginn der Gregorianischen Reform', SGreg 1 (1947) 321–351; Pelster, 'Dekret' 135–138. Additions: *Admonitio synodalis* following Book XX (closely related to Clm 4570 and Lambach) without the *Praefatio,* but with a reformulated table of contents, ed. Pelster, SGreg 1, 1947, 342–343

3. 'Order of Worms, Type B': Early Lombard-Burgundian Codices

London, British Library, Cotton Claudius C.VI (Part I: fol. 1–165); saec. XI² Prov. Canterbury (?); presumably a copy of a codex traceable in the ecclesiastical province of Besançon about 1049 during the episcopate of Archbishop Hugues de Salins (1031–1066). Additions: *Notitia Galliarum* as well as Leo I JK 407 and Zosimus JK 335 at the beginning (both for the ecclesiastical province of Vienne; same order as in Codex Troyes 246 of the *Collectio XII partium* on fol. 12bis^{vb}–14ra), Mainz (1049) = Leo IX JL 4188 in favor of Hugues de Salins following XX 57, the closing chapter of the *Decretum* (MGH Const. 1.97)

Milano, Biblioteca Ambrosiana, E.144 sup., saec. XI², Prov. Milan, cathedral; cf. A. Ambrosioni, 'Il più antico elenco di chierici della diocesi Ambrosiana ed altre aggiunte al Decretum di Burcardo in un codice della biblioteca Ambrosiana (E. 144 sup.)', *Aevum* 50 (1976) 274–320; (missing leaves between fol. 24 and 25: I 104 Inq. 87 - I 170). Supplements: following XX 57 as the last chapter of the *Decretum:* list of the priests of the Diocese of Milan, saec. XI–XII; excommunication of (the leader of the Pataria?) Ariald according to the formula XI 6, XI 7 and XI 4 of the *Decretum*

Mantova, Biblioteca Comunale, D.IV.15 (461), saec. XI–XII; Prov. San Benedetto di Polirone, Benedictine Congregation of Montecassino and Santa Giustina-Padova

Vercelli, Biblioteca Capitolare, XCIV (94), saec. XI. Additions: Seligenstadt (1023) (without the *Praefatio* and with an additional chapter after c. 4), *Admonitio synodalis* following Book XX; *Fraterne mortis* (JL †6613a) following Book I

4. 'Order of Worms, Type B': Italian Main Group of Manuscripts

Angers, Bibliothèque municipale, 368 (355), saec. XI, Prov. Angers, St-Aubin; before that apparently at Tours. Additions: *Ordo synodalis* 5 following Book III; Supplements: Gregory VII JL 5232 to the canons of Saint-Martin at Tours, JL 5225 to Archbishop R. of Tours, a letter of Archbishop Radulf of Tours to Bishop Hoellus of Le Mans; entries about due taxes to the archbishop and the canons of Saint-Martin at Tours

Bologna, Biblioteca Universitaria, 2239 (1107), saec. XII, Italy, cf. MGH Ordines 231–232. Additions: *Ordo synodalis* 5 following Book III; *Admonitio synodalis* (including the end of *Ordo* 17), Seligenstadt (1023) and *Nicaeno-Constantinopolitanum* following Book XX; *Fraterne mortis* (JL †6613a) following Book I and between XIX 108 and XIX 109 (closely related to Monza h-5, also to Burgo de Osma)

Burgo de Osma, Biblioteca de la Santa Iglesia Catedral, 157, saec. XII^2, cf. MGH Ordines 232. Additions: *Ordo synodalis* 5 following Book III, *Fraterne mortis* (JL †6613a) between XIX 108 and XIX 109; Seligenstadt (1023) (without *Praefatio* and with an additional chapter following c. 4) and *Admonitio synodalis* following XX 108 as last chapter of the Decretum (closely related to Bologna 2239 and Vercelli XCIV)

Calci, Archivio delle Certosa Monumentale, 9, saec. XII1/4, Tuscany, Prov. Carthusian monastery of SS. Maria and Gorgonius on the island of Gorgona near Pisa; cf. Mordek, 'Handschriftenforschungen' 636–637. Additions: Seligenstadt (1023), and the *Collectio Novariensis* (excerpt) following Book XX (closely related to Lucca 124)

Cortona, Biblioteca Comunale e dell'Accademia Etrusca, 75 saec. XII1/2, central Italy; cf. Mordek, 'Handschriftenforschungen' 637–638 and MGH Ordines 264–272 and 39–40. Additions: *Admonitio synodalis* (including the end of *Ordo* 17) following Book XIX; *Ordo synodalis* 5b following Book XX (the leaves 1–3 and 160–172 were added in another contemporary hand)

El Escorial, Real Biblioteca de San Lorenzo, T.I.14, saec. XI^{ex}–XII^{in}, cf. MGH Ordines 233 (missing parts of the text: VI 44–VII 3, VII 28; XI 71–XII 1; XVII 48–XIX, XIX *Capitulatio*-rubric 20, XIX 152–XX 28; Capitulatio XVII bound before *Capitulatio* XI). Additions: *Ordo synodalis* 5 following Book III

Firenze, Biblioteca Medicea Laurenziana, Plut. XVI 21, saec. XI–XII, central Italy; Prov. Camaldulensian abbey of Fontebuona (now: Tavagnaco) Friaul, cf. MGH Ordines 233. Additions: *Ordo synodalis* 5 following Book III. Supplement: *Capitulare Ticinense de praediis ecclesiarum* (MGH Const. 1.49–51) and *Admonitio synodalis* (including the end of *Ordo* 17) at the end of the codex

Firenze, Biblioteca Nazionale Centrale, Conv. soppr. F.IV.255, saec. XI–XII, Italy, Prov. Vallombrosa; cf. Fransen, 'Réflexions', 315–533, MGH Ordines 233. Additions: *Ordo synodalis* 5 following Book III; Urban II (JL 5451) to Rusticus of Vallombrosa and to Martin of Camaldoli

Firenze, Biblioteca Riccardiana, 240, saec. XI4/4, Italy, cf. MGH Ordines 233 (missing leaves between fol. 88 and 89: *Arbor consanguinitatis* and *Capitulatio*-rubric VIII 38). Additions: *Ordo synodalis* 5 following Book III

Ivrea, Biblioteca Capitolare, XCIV (50), saec. XI4/4, Prov. Ivrea, cathedral; cf. Mordek, 'Handschriftenforschungen' 638–639; MGH Ordines 233. Additions: *Ordo synodalis* 5 following Book III; *Admonitio synodalis* (including the end of *Ordo* 17) following Book XX. Supplements: three letters by the Archipresbyter S. of Ivrea, one is addressed to the Antipope Clement III (1080–1100) (cf. Fransen, 'Manuscrit de Montpellier' 303 n. 6), Hymn on Henry IV, Clement III and Bishop Ogerius of Ivrea (1075–1090)

Lisboa, Biblioteca Nacional, Alcobaça CCCIII/365, saec. XII4/4, Prov. Alcobaça (fragmentary, beginning at XI3 to XX110)

Lucca, Biblioteca Capitolare Feliniana, 124, saec. XI4/4, Central Italy; Prov. Lucca, cathedral; cf. MGH Ordines 233–234. Additions: *Ordo synodalis* 5 following Book III; Seligenstadt (1023) following Book XX. Supplements: *Notitiae donationis* for the Cathedral of Lucca and *Fraterne mortis* (JL †6613a) as part of the preceding materials; *Collectio Novariensis,* materials from the *ordines officiorum,* cf. Landau, *Officium* 21; *Admonitio synodalis* (including the end of *Ordo* 17) as well as the Council of Piacenza (1095) following Book XX (closely related to Calci 9)

Madrid, Biblioteca Nacional, 386 (C 6), saec. XI; cf. MGH Ordines 234 (fragmentary, breaks off at XX 54b; after that, fol. 269–272 the end of Book XIX). Additions: *Ordo synodalis* 5 following Book III

Madrid, Biblioteca Nacional, 391 (C 7), saec. XII; Italy, cf. MGH Ordines 298 (fragmentary, beginning at the Prologue). Additions: *Ordo synodalis* 7 following Book XX written by a later hand

Manchester, John Rylands University Library, 42, saec. XI, Italy (fragmentary, 42 leaves; ca. one third of the existing 1800 canons of the *Decretum* are preserved)

Manchester, John Rylands University Library, 96 saec. XII1/4, Central Italy (Tuscany), (fragmentary, ends at XX 98). Additions: *Ordo synodalis* 5 following Book III. Supplement: Urban II (JL 5367) to King Alfons VI of Castile-Leon

Milano, Archivio Storico Civico e Biblioteca Trivulziana, 601, saec. XI, Italy, Prov. S. Croce at Novara; cf. MGH Ordines 234 (fragmentary beginning at I 94 Inq. 38; finally breaking off in the middle of c. 10 of the Synod of Seligenstadt; missing leaves between fol. 75 and 76: V 35–VI *Capitulatio*-rubric 46). Additions: *Ordo synodalis* 5 following Book III; Seligenstadt (1023) without the Prologue and fragmentary following Book XX

Modena, Biblioteca Capitolare, O.II.15, saec. XI^2; Italy; cf. MGH Ordines 234–235. Supplements: *Ordo synodalis* 5 as a fragmentary supplement on three integrated additional leaves (fol. 127–129), interrupting now the *Ordo infirmorum* preceding Book XVIII; *Constitutio Langobardica de beneficiis* (1052) (MGH Const. 1.100) Concordat of Worms (1122), papal version (MGH Const. 1.160–161); the same order of offices as in Parma 3777

Monte Cassino, Archivio e Biblioteca dell'Abbazia, 44, saec. XI^2 (in Romanesca); cf. MGH Ordines 235; (various missing leaves). Additions: *Ordo synodalis* 5 following Book III

Monte Cassino, Archivio e Biblioteca dell'Abbazia, 45, saec. XI^2, Italy (p. 398–404 written in Beneventan script); Prov. Montecassino; cf. MGH Ordines 235 (fragmentary, ends at XX 65, various missing leaves). Additions: *Ordo synodalis* 5 following Book III (related to Vat. lat. 11731?)

Montpellier, Bibliothèque municipale, 7, saec. XII; Prov.: St. Bernard de Romans?; cf. Fransen, 'Manuscrit de Montpellier', passim; MGH Ordines 235. Additions: *Ordo synodalis* 5 following Book III, *Fraterne mortis* (JL †6613a) following Book XVI. Supplements: Urban II (JL 5374) in favor of St. Bernard de Romans (closely related to Paris 3861 and Troyes 1386/Paris 4283)

Monza, Biblioteca Capitolare, d-10/152 (T.II.212), saec. XI^2, Italy (fragmentary, beginning at I 32, ending at XX 96). Addition: *Fraterne mortis* (JL †6613a) following Book I

Monza, Biblioteca Capitolare, h-5/154 (T.IV.214), saec. XI, Northern Italy; Prov.

Plebe Seveso; cf. MGH Ordines 235–236 (loss of quire XXV; after XIX 108 and *Fraterne mortis*–XX 8). Additions: *Ordo synodalis* 5 following Book III; *Fraterne mortis* (JL †6613a) following XIX 108; *Admonitio synodalis* (including the end of *Ordo* 17), Seligenstadt (1023) and *Nicaeno-Constantinopolitanum* following Book XX. Supplement: seating plan of the Provincial Synod of Milan written on fly leaf (closely related to Bologna 2239)

Napoli, Biblioteca Nazionale Vittorio Emanuele II, Vind. lat. 23, saec. XII1/4, central Italy; Prov. S. Giustina at Padova, SS. Severino e Sossio, Napoli, cf. Mordek, 'Handschriftenforschungen' 649–650; R. Somerville, 'Pope Clement in a Roman Synod and Pastoral Work by Monks', *Fälschungen im Mittelalter* 2.151–156; MGH Ordines 236 (missing leaves between fol. 8/9, 56/57, 59/60, 62/63, 68/69: I 90–192, IX 53–XI 4, XI 67–XII 20, XV 1–6, XVII 8–34). Addition: *Ordo synodalis* 5 following Book III. Supplements: *Admonitio synodalis* among additional materials following XX 67, here the closing chapter of the *Decretum*

Novara, Biblioteca Capitolare, XV (16) (part II: fol. 69–140), saec. XII^{1}, cf. Mordek, 'Handschriftenforschungen' 643; MGH Ordines 236 (fragmentary ending at III 196; missing leaves also between fol. 84/85: I 85–127)

Novara, Biblioteca Capitolare, XXVIII (17), saec. XI, Italy; cf. MGH Ordines 236. Addition: *Ordo synodalis* 5 following Book III

Padova, Biblioteca del Seminario Vescovile, 529, saec. XI, Italy; Prov.: Polirone, 1814; it was brought to Padova by Mauro Mari, Abbot of Polirone, cf. Mordek, 'Handschriftenforschungen' 649; MGH Ordines 236. Additions: *Ordo synodalis* 5 following Book III; Seligenstadt (1023) and excommunication formulas following Book XX (in the second the Martyrs Stephanus, Vitalis and Appolinaris as well as the Confessors Silvester, Probus, Severus and Martinus are invoked: copy of a codex from Ravenna?); inserted between IV 99 and 100 is the letter of Nicholas I about the sentences passed at Rome (861) against Johannes of Ravenna (MGH Epistolae 6.613–617 and Mansi 15.602–606)

Paris, Bibliothèque de l'Arsenal, 678 saec. XI (in Roman minuscule [Romanesca]); Prov. Angers, Saint-Aubin; cf. MGH Ordines 236 and 299 (fragmentary, breaks off at XX 110). Additions: *Ordo synodalis* following Book III, *Ordo synodalis* 7 following Book 1

Paris, Bibliothèque nationale, lat. 3861, saec. XII; Prov. Le Puy, cathedral, cf. Fransen, 'Manuscrit de Montpellier', passim. Additions: *Ordo synodalis* 5 following Book III, *Fraterne mortis* (JL †6613a) following Book XVI (closely related to Montpellier 7 and Troyes 1386)

Paris, Bibliothèque nationale, lat. 3862, saec. XII2/4, Central Italy (Tuscany); cf. MGH Ordines 237 (fol. 25–26 including II 63–100 has to be placed between fol. 32 and 33). Additions: *Ordo synodalis* 5 following Book III

Paris, Bibliothèque nationale, lat. 3863 saec. XII; Prov. Moissac, cf. MGH Ordines 237; (fragmentary, ending at XX 100). Additions: *Ordo synodalis* 5 following Book III

Paris, Bibliothèque nationale, lat. 4283; a Quaternio (fol. 1–8): Prologue–I 28. It is the missing first quire of the Troyes codex; cf. Fransen, 'Manuscrits de Montpellier' 68

Paris, Bibliothèque nationale, lat. 9630, saec. XII1/4, Central Italy, Prov. Fréjus, Cathedral; cf. MGH Ordines 237–238. Additions: *Admonitio synodalis* (including the end of *Ordo* 17) following Book XX

Paris, Bibliothèque nationale, lat. 11578, (part II of the codex: fol. 131–209), saec. XII, Italy? Prov. St-Germain-des-Prés, St-Maur-des Fossés, cf. G. Fransen, 'La tradition manuscrite du Décret de Burchard de Worms: Une première orientation', *Ius sacrum: Festschrift Klaus Mörsdorf zum 60. Geburtstag,* ed. A. Scheuermann and G. May (Munich-Paderborn-Vienna 1969) 115 (the manuscript, ending at the end of Book III apparently has never been completed; from fol. 157^{r-v} rubrics and numbering are missing, from fol. 188^{r} also the Initia)

Pistoia, Archivio Capitolare del Duomo, C. 125 (C. XII), saec. XII1/4, Pistoia; Prov. Pistoia, Cathedral; cf. G. Fransen, 'Les textes ajoutés au Décret de Burchard de Worms dans deux manuscrits Toscans', *Studi Senesi* 100, Supplement 2 (1988) 536–552; MGH Ordines 238. Additions: *Ordo synodalis* 5 following Book III; *Fraterne mortis* (JL †6613a) between XIX 108 and XIX 109; materials from the *ordines officiorum,* and Seligenstadt (1023) together with other texts following XX 57 (here the closing chapter of the *Decretum*) (closely related to Prato)

Pistoia, Archivio Capitolare del Duomo, C. 140 (C.XIII), saec. XII1/4, Central Italy; cf. MGH Ordines 238. Additions: *Ordo synodalis* 5 following Book III; Material from the *ordines officiorum,* cf. Landau, *Officium* 17, following XX 57 (here the closing chapter of the *Decretum*). Supplements: Nicolaus II (JL 4406) to the bishops of the ecclesiastical province of Amalfi; Eugene III (JL 8963) to Bishop Azo of Florence

Prato, Biblioteca Roncioniana, Q.VIII.4 (3), saec. XII1/4, Pistoia; Prov. Prato, cathedral; cf. Mordek, 'Handschriftenforschungen' 639–640. Fransen, 'Textes ajoutés' passim; MGH Ordines 238. Additions: *Ordo synodalis* following Book III; Seligenstadt (1023) and *Fraterne mortis* (JL †6613a) following XIX 108 (closely related to Pistoia 125)

Roma, Biblioteca Vallicelliana, A.20, saec. XII^{1}, Central Italy (Umbria/Rome), cf. Mordek, 'Handschriftenforschungen' 640–641. Additions: *Ordo synodalis* 5 following Book III; *Admonitio synodalis* (including the end of *Ordo* 17) following XIX 108 (here the closing chapter of the *Decretum*) (closely related to Vat. lat. 7790)

Troyes, Bibliothèque municipale, 1386; Part III: Fol. 137–301; beginning at I 28, today the first quire is fol. 1–8 of Paris lat. 4283; saec. XII; cf. Fransen, 'Manuscrit de Montpellier', passim; R. Somerville, 'Cardinal Stephan of St. Grisogono: Some Remarks on Legates and Legatine Councils in the Eleventh Century', *Essays in Honor of Stephan Kuttner* (1977) 162–163; MGH Ordines 239. Additions: *Ordo synodalis* following Book III; *Fraterne mortis* (JL †6613a) following Book XVI (closely related to Paris 3861 and Montpellier 7)

Vaticano, Città del, Biblioteca Apostolica Vaticana, lat. 1355, saec. XI, Central Italy; cf. Pelster, 'Dekret' 140–141; Kuttner-Elze, *Catalogue* 1.119–120; MGH Ordines 239. Additions: *Ordo synodalis* 5 following Book III; *Admonitio synodalis* following XX 103 (here the closing chapter of the *Decretum*)

Vaticano, Città del, Biblioteca Apostolica Vaticana, lat. 4880, saec. XI–XII, Central Italy; cf. Pelster, 'Dekret' 144; MGH Ordines 239 (fragmentary, beginning at I *Capitulatio*–rubric 157, ending at XX 92). Additions: *Ordo synodalis* 5 following Book III; *Admonitio synodalis* (including the end of *Ordo* 17) following Book XIX

Vaticano, Città del, Biblioteca Apostolica Vaticana, lat. 4981, saec. XII (Beneventan script), cf. Pelster, 'Dekret' 143; MGH Ordines 240 (fragmentary, only I 89–XI 1 is preserved). Addition: *Ordo synodalis* 5 following Book III

Vaticano, Città del, Biblioteca Apostolica Vaticana, lat. 7790, saec. XII^1, Central Italy, cf. Pelster, 'Dekret' 144; Mordek, 'Handschriftenforschungen' 641; MGH Ordines 240 (fragmentary, beginning at I *Capitulatio*-rubric 61, various missing leaves). Additions: *Ordo synodalis* following Book III; *Admonitio synodalis* (including the end of *Ordo* 17) following XIX 108 (here the closing chapter of the *Decretum*) (closely related to Roma, Bibl. Vallicell. A 20)

Vaticano, Città del, Biblioteca Apostolica Vaticana, lat. 14731 (olim Caiazzo, sine num.), saec. XI^2 (in Beneventan script), cf. Pelster, 'Dekret' 143; MGH Ordines 240. Additions: *Ordo synodalis* 5 following Book III; *Admonitio synodalis* (including the end of *Ordo* 17) following Book XX

Vaticano, Città del, Biblioteca Apostolica Vaticana, Barb. lat. 1450, saec. XI, central Italy, Prov. San Salvatore di Montamiata; cf. Pelster, 'Dekret', 145–146; Mordek, 'Handschriftenforschungen' 645 n. 55; MGH Ordines 239 (fragmentary, breaks off at XX 43). Additions: *Ordo synodalis* 5 following Book III. Supplement: Rome 1079 *Confessio Berengarii*

Vaticano, Città del, Biblioteca Apostolica Vaticana, Urb. lat. 180, saec. XI, Northern Italy; cf. Pelster, 'Dekret' 146; the leaves 1–7: Prologue and *Capitulatio* about Book I, as well as 243–256: XVI 13–XVIII 24 were added in a fifteenth-century script; Book XX is missing.

Vercelli, Biblioteca Capitolare, XLI (11), saec. XI, Italy (fragmentary; only the quires VII–XXI and XXVI–XXXI are still extant: II 30–XI 68 and XVIII 5–XX 54)

5. Manuscript That Cannot be Traced at Present

Cheltenham, Sir Thomas Phillipps Collection, 'saec. XI^{ex} Burchardi Wormatiensis Collectio Canonum (in 12 [20?] Books)' mentioned in H. Schenkl, *Bibliotheca patrum latinorum Britannica* 1.2 (Vienna 1892) 153 = *SB Vienna* 123 no. 5 (Vienna 1892) (Or might this be a manuscript of the *Collectio duodecim partium* containing the *Praefatio* of the *Decretum Burchardi* similar to the manuscripts Troyes, Bibl. mun. 246 and Saint-Claude, Bibl. mun. 17, cf. Müller, *Collectio Duodecim Partium* 34–35 and 37?)

6. Changes of Shelf-Mark

Caiazzo, Archivio Capitolare (Meyer no. 5) now: Vat. lat. 14731

Firenze, Biblioteca Nazionale Centrale, Conv. soppr. A.IV.254 (Meyer no. 9): erroneous identification; it is not Burchard's text (cf. Fransen, 'Trois notes' 446)

Olomouc (Olmütz), Kapitulni knihovna (now: Státni vedecké knihovna, Universitni knihovna), 202 (not 203) (Meyer no. 36); this is a manuscript with parts of Burchard's *Decretum,* and parts of the *Collectio duodecim partium,* see below

Paris, Bibliothèque nationale, lat. 297/298 (Meyer no. 41): identical with Paris lat. 11578

Paris, Bibliothèque nationale, lat. 375 (Meyer no. 42): identical with Paris lat. 12449

Paris, Bibliothèque nationale, lat. 393 (Meyer no. 43): identical with Paris lat. 9630

Saint-Claude, Bibliothèque municipale, 17 (3) (Meyer no. 66): a manuscript of the *Collectio duodecim partium* not of Burchard's *Decretum* (cf. below)

Torino, Biblioteca Comunale, 150 (Meyer no. 67): wrong reference instead of Ivrea, Biblioteca Capitolare, XCIV

Vaticano, Città del, Biblioteca Apostolica Vaticana, lat. 1450 (Meyer no. 59): miscited in Meyer; the correct signature is Vat. Barb. lat. 1450; cf. Mordek, 'Handschriftenforschungen' 645 n. 55

Vaticano, Città del, Biblioteca Apostolica Vaticana, lat. 9201: wrong reference; it is not Burchard's text; cf. Mordek, 'Handschriftenforschungen' 649

Vaticano, Città del, Biblioteca Apostolica Vaticana, lat. 9522: wrong reference; it is not Burchard's text; cf. Mordek, 'Handschriftenforschungen' 649

Vercelli, Biblioteca Capitolare, T. IV (214): wrong reference (of Pelster) instead of Monza, Biblioteca Capitolare, h-5/154 (olim T.IV.214)

Wien, Österreichische Nationalbibliothek, 354 (Meyer no. 70): a manuscript with parts of Burchard's *Decretum* and parts of the *Collectio duodecim partium*

Wien, Österreichische Nationalbibliothek, 2044 (Meyer no. 71): now Napoli, Biblioteca Nazionale Vittorio Emanuele II, Vind. lat. 23; cf. Mordek, 'Handschriftenforschungen' 649–650

II. Fragments (Single Leaves)

Augsburg, Universitätsbibliothek, Cod. I.2.2° 42, saec. XI^{ex}, Main river region. One single leaf, removed from the cover of Augsburg, Universitätsbibliothek, 02/XIII.8.4° 609 (prints from the beginning of the seventeenth century), Book 2, chapters 28–37, written in long lines (information by H. Hoffmann)

Bologna, Collegio di Spagna, 37, saec. XII^{1}; cf. Mordek, 'Handschriftenforschungen' 641–642. Four leaves, bound up in a fourteenth-century codex (in two columns): *Praefatio - Capitulatio* I (rubric 57), 1.21–35

Frankfurt am Main, Stadt- und Universitätsbibliothek, Fragm. lat. I 34, saec. XII; cf. Mordek, *Kirchenrecht und Reform* 183 n. 402; Hoffmann-Pokorny 11 n. 2; G. Powitz, *Mittelalterliche Handschriftenfragmente der Stadt- und Universitätsbibliothek Frankfurt am Main* (Frankfurt 1994) 7–8

Fulda, Hessische Landesbibliothek, Cod. Fragm. 4 (no. 73), saec. XII4/4; Prov. presumably Fulda (cf. lost mss.). Three double leaves (two columns), only one of them is completely transmitted: 5.13–24 and 6.23–24, 9.69–71 and 9.74–77, 10.1–3 and 10.34; cf. H. Köllner, *Die illuminierten Handschriften der Hessischen Landesbibliothek Fulda* 1 (Stuttgart 1976) p. xxvii and reproduction no. 777

Hannover, Niedersächsisches Hauptstaatsarchiv, Dep. 76, Heine-Halberstadt, Ms. 44, Mappe 2 No. 14, saec. XI^{2}; Prov.: Halberstadt; cf. Hoffmann-Pokorny 152–154. Double leaf (two columns): 2.30–59

Los Angeles, University of California, University Research Library, Department of Special Collections, Collection of Loose Leaves, 1/XI/ITA/15, saec. XI (Northern) Italy; cf. M. Ferrari; *Medieval and Renaissance Manuscripts at the University of California, Los Angeles,* ed. R. H. Rouse (Berkeley-Los Angeles 1991) 103. Single leaf (two columns): 15.16–19

Lucca, Biblioteca Capitolare Feliniana, 597, saec. XI^{2}, Central Italy; cf. Mordek, *Kirchenrecht und Reform* 183 n. 402. Two fly leaves in an eleventh-century codex: 1.94 Interrogatio 53–1.96, 1.131–135

Marburg, Hessisches Staatsarchiv, Hr. 8 fasc. 14, saec. XII^{2}; cf. Brommer, 'Fragmente' 231. A double leaf (two columns): 6.40–46, *Arbor consanguinitatis*, 7.29–30, 8th *Capitulatio* (up to rubric 20)

Monza, Biblioteca Capitolare, c-1/61. Single leaf, considerably trimmed: Seligenstadt (1023) cc. 1–10 (probably from a manuscript of the *Decretum Burchardi*)

Paris, Bibliothèque nationale, lat. 3454, only the *Capitulationes* of Books 1–3; cf. MGH Ordines 231 n. 2

Paris, Bibliothèque nationale, lat. 8922, saec. XI. Single leaf, bound as a fly leaf (two columns) to Tarragona 35, a codex of the *Decretum Burchardi* (beginning of the *Praefatio* of Burchard's *Decretum*)

Pavia, Archivio di Stato, Archivio notarile di Pavia, Frammenti III 3, saec. XI^{ex}. Six fragments; cf. Ugo Fiorina, 'Frammenti di codici giuridici (secc. IX–XV) recentemente recuperati nell'Archivio di stato di Pavia', RSDI 52 (1979) 8

Reims, Bibliothèque municipale, 673; an incomplete quire of a Burchard manuscript with two columns, saec. XI, bound with a complete Burchard manuscript; two flyleaves at the beginning and end of the manuscript came from an unfinished manuscript (the initials and numbers of the chapter rubrics are missing). The leaves were once part of a beginning quire containing an index of the chapters of Book 1.

San Miniato, Biblioteca Comunale (sin. num.); saec. XI. One leaf with texts taken from Book 3; cover of an inquistion register, saec. XVI; cf. Mordek, 'Bemerkungen zum mittelalterlichen Schatzverzeichnis von Porto/Rom', SG 20 (1976) 240 n. 33

St. Gallen, Stiftsbibliothek, 1398a, saec. XII^{1}. Two slightly trimmed leaves (two columns) in a composite codex including fragments (pag. 15–18): 19.127–133, 20.27–36,

Siena, Archivio di Stato, A-191 (82) (fol. 1–16), saec. XI; 16 only fragmentarily preserved leaves (two columns): Parts of Books 3, 4, 6, 14, 15, 17, 19, 20; cf. Mordek, 'Handschriftenforschungen' 650

[Torino, Biblioteca Nazionale Universitaria, K.V.9]. One half of a single fly leaf containing chapters from the series 19.61–71; apparently burnt in 1944; cf. Mordek, 'Handschriftenforschungen' 639 n. 40]

Vaticano, Città del, Archivio di San Pietro B.41 (fol. 121), saec. XII^{1}, cf. 'Censimento dei codici dei secoli X–XII', *Studi medievali,* ser. 3, 11 (1970) 1106–1107; Mordek, 'Handschriftenforschungen' 643–644. Single leaf (two columns) at the end of a codex dating from the second half of the eleventh century: beginning-middle of the *Praefatio*

Vaticano, Città del, Biblioteca Apostolica Vaticana, lat. 4980 (fol. 76), about 1100, Mordek, 'Handschriftenforschungen' 645. Single leaf (two columns): 6.34–40; (on the partial transmission of a manuscript of the *Decretum* contained on fol. 1–75 in the same codex, cf. below)

Vich, Archivo Capitular, Fragmenta XV, saec. XII; cf. Mordek, 'Analecta canonistica' 8. Two halves of two different leaves (two columns); 19.46–52

Vich, Archivo Capitular, Fragmenta (without signature), saec. XII; cf. Mordek, 'Analecta canonistica' 8–9. Two leaves (long lines); 10.23–37

Wolfenbüttel, Herzog August Bibliothek, Novi 404.5 (8), saec. XI1/4, Wissembourg, Prov. Wissembourg; cf. Hoffmann-Pokorny 108–110. Three double leaves (long lines): *Capitulatio* 1.1–140 (as far as the text is concerned this is the most ancient instance of the Burchard tradition)

Wolfenbüttel, Niedersächsisches Staatsarchiv, Mappe 12 Slg 5, saec. XI3/4, Hildesheim (?), Prov. St. Blasius, Braunschweig, cf. Hoffmann-Pokorny 155–156. Single leaf (two columns): 1.6–17

Würzburg, Universitätsbibliothek, M.p.j.f. 15, saec. XI2/4, Bamberg, Michelsberg?; cf. R. Weigand, ZRG Kan. Abt. 58 (1972) 393; Hoffmann-Pokorny 132–136. Single leaf (long lines): 11.75–78 and *Capitulatio* 12 (apparently copied from Bamberg, Staatsbibliothek, Can. 6)

III. Manuscripts of the Decretum Mentioned in Old Library Catalogues

Angers, St. Aubin (catalogue dating from saec. XII; Delisle, *Cabinet des manuscrits* 2.486 no. 62); one of today's three codices Angers, Bibliothèque municipale, 386, Paris, Arsenal 678 or Paris lat. 3860, on the latter, cf. Kuttner-Somerville 187–188

Arras, St-Vaast (catalogue dating from saec. XII; Becker, *Catalogi* 125, p. 250 no. 104); P. Grierson, 'La Bibliothèque de St-Vaast d'Arras au XIIe siècle', RB 52 (1940) 131 n. 141

Bamberg, Michelsberg ('Summa Richardi Bormacensis [*sic*] episcopi' among the codices of canon law; catalogue dating from 1483, P. Ruf, *Mittelalterliche Bibliothekskataloge Deutschlands und der Schweiz* 3.3 [Munich 1939] 378, lines 16–17); it is presumably the codex of which Würzburg M.p.j.f. 15 used to be a part, cf. Hoffmann-Pokorny 132–136

Bayeux, Cathedral (two copies) (catalogue dating from 1436; *Catalogue général, Départements* 10 [1889] 282–283, no. 130 and 132)

Bec (two copies); legate of Bishop Philipp of Bayeux [1142–1164]); (catalogues dating from 1142–1164 and saec. XII; Becker, *Catalogi* 86, p. 200, no. 47 and 127, p. 265, no. 125)

Besançon, Cathedral (P. Pithou, *Synopsis . . . eorum qui canones et decreta collegerunt,* quoted in J. H. Boehmer, *Corpus iuris canonici* 1 [Halle 1747] 1239)

Bordeaux, Cathedral (P. Pithou, *Synopsis . . . eorum qui canones et decreta collegerunt,* quoted in J. H. Boehmer, *Corpus iuris canonici* 1 [Halle 1747] 1239)

Chartres, Cathedral

Cluny (catalogue dating from saec. XII; Delisle, *Cabinet des manuscrits* 2.475 no. 434)

[Cremona, cathedral] (catalogue dating from 1201; mentioned in Meyer, 'Überlieferung' 149–150 n. 1; this manuscript was probably not a Burchard text, cf. Mordek, 'Handschriftenforschungen' 646–648

Durham, Cathedral (two copies) (catalogue dating from saec. XII; Becker, *Catalogi* 117, p. 240 no. 80 and 81); probably one of them is identical with the manuscript from Durham

Ebersberg, Catalogue dating from saec. XII[ex]; cf. *Mittelalterliche Bibliothekskataloge Deutschlands und der Schweiz* 4.2 (Munich 1979) 616, line 11 (= today's codex Clm 5801c; this catalogue is entered on the front flyleaf of this manuscript and refers to this codex as 'Iste liber Burchardi')

Fleury, Catalogue dating from 1552: *Notices et extraits des manuscrits de la Bibliothèque nationale et autres bibliothèques* 31.1, p. 432, no. 129), *Catalogue général, Départements* 12 (1889) p. xii no. 129; probably today the Orléans manuscript

Fulda (catalogues dating from saec. XV and XVI; cf. K. Christ, *Die Bibliothek des Klosters Fulda* [Leipzig 1933] 109–110, 256, 299); cf. the fragment at Fulda

Genève, Cathedral (legate of Bishop Frederic of Geneva 1031–1070) (entry in an eleventh-century Bible; J. Senebier, *Catalogue raisonné des manuscrits conservés dans la bibliothèque de la ville et république de Genève* [Geneva 1779] 57)

Konstanz, Cathedral (catalogue dating from 1343; P. Lehmann, *Mittelalterliche Bibliothekskataloge Deutschlands und der Schweiz* 1 [Munich 1918] 196, 19–22), is the Freiburg manuscript (see above)

Limoges, St-Martial (catalogue dating from saec. XII–XIII; Delisle, *Cabinet des manuscrits* 2.494 no. 80)

Liège, Saint-Laurent (catalogue dating from saec. XII–XIII; J. Gessler, *La bibliothèque de l'abbaye de Saint-Laurent à Liège* [Bulletin de la société des bibliophiles liégeois 12; Tongres 1927] 91–135); R. C. van Caenegem, SG 12 [1967] 270 n. 10)

Lyon, Cathedral (donation of Archbishop Hugo of Lyon) catalogue dating from 1085–1106; *Obituarium Lugdunensis ecclesiae,* ed. M.-C. Guigue (Lyon 1867) 130

Maillezais (catalogue dating from saec. XII^{ex}; Delisle, *Cabinet des manuscrits* 2.507 no. 69)

Mainz, Cathedral (catalogue saec. XVIII, cf. Hoffmann-Pokorny 160, n. 131)

Moissac, two catalogues dating from saec. XI^{ex}–XII^{in} and one saec. XVII: J. Dufour, 'La composition de la Bibliothèque de Moissac à la lumière d'un inventaire du XVIIe siècle nouvellement découvert', *Scriptorium* 35 (1981) 184 and 196 no. 67; Paris lat. 3836

Napoli, San Severino (catalogue dating from saec. XVIII, B. de Montfaucon, *Bibliotheca bibliothecarum manuscriptorum nova* [Paris 1739] 1.233D); probably the codex which is kept today at Naples

Nonantola (three copies) (one codex is already mentioned in the inventory of the books acquired during the abbacy of Abbot Rudolf [1002–1035], ed. G. Gullotta, *Gli antichi cataloghi e i codici della Abbazia di Nonantola* [Studi e testi 155; Rome 1955] 5 no. 11 and 11; the library catalogue dating from 1331 lists three copies, cf. Gullotta 86–87, 208–209 and 213, no. 40, 142 and 151, see also J. Ruysschaert, *Les manuscrits de l'Abbaye de Nonantola* [Studi e testi 182bis; Vatican City 1955] 38–39)

Padova, Santa Giustina (an eighteenth-century notation is cited by Ballerini, *De antiquis . . . collectionibus et collectoribus,* P. IV cap. XII [Venice 1757]; PL 56.321 and PL 140.498); may not be identical with Padova 529 or Naples Vind. Lat. 23, cf. Mordek, 'Handschriftenforschungen' 649

[Paderborn, Cathedral] (mentioned in Meyer, 'Überlieferung' 149–150, n. 1 with a reference to the *Vita Meinwerci* [saec. XII]; actually the text only characterizes some bishops of Meinwerc's time; among them he mentioned 'Burchardus Wormatiensis studio suo in collectione canonum in ecclesia laudabilis': c. 192, MGH SS rer. Germ. [59] 110, 16–18)

Pistoia, Cathedral (*Duo Brocardi*), catalogue dating from saec. XII^{1}: S. Ferrali, *Vita di S. Atto, monaco vallombrosano e vescovo di Pistoia* (Pistoia 1953) 62 (the two manuscripts from Pistoia)

Polirone (San Benedetto Po) (an eighteenth-century notation is cited in Ballerini, *De antiquis . . . collectionibus et collectoribus* P. IV cap. XII [Venice 1757] PL 56.321 and PL 140.498) (the manuscripts from Mantova D.IV.15 and Padova 529 contain marks of ownership from Polirone)

Porto, Cathedral (donation from Bishop Johannes [III.] of Porto [1085–1087 to 1095]; edited by G. Swarzenski in RQ 14 [1900] 130 no. 13), cf. Mordek, 'Bemerkungen zum mittelalterlichen Schatzverzeichnis von Porto/Rom', SG 20 (1976) 238–239; Munich, Universitätsbibliothek, 2° 292, in which the inventory of treasures is also recorded

Ravenna, Archivescovado (inventory of the archives dating from 1480; cf. Bethmann, *Archiv* 12 [1872–74] 583; in Bethmann's lifetime this and other codices mentioned in the inventory had disappeared); perhaps identical with Padova 529

Roma, a Burchard manuscript of Cardinal Sirleto from which a notation of the Synod of Pavia (1046) was taken in 1583, which granted to the bishop of Verona the first seat to the right of the Patriarch during a provincial synod in the Province of Aquileia, see MGH Const. 1, no. 48, p. 94–95. This manuscript, which may have come from Verona, is now lost

St. Pons de Thomières (two copies) (catalogue dating from 1276; Delisle, *Cabinet des manuscrits* 2.541 no. 55)

Speyer, Cathedral (P. Lehmann, *Erforschung des Mittelalters* [Munich 1959] 2.221)

Tegernsee, Catalogue dating from 1483: cf. *Mittelalterliche Bibliothekskataloge Deutschlands und der Schweiz* 4.2 (Munich 1979) 774, 709; München Clm 18094

Troyes, Cathedral; Troyes 1386

Verona, San Zeno; Catalogue dating from about 1400, cf. G. Moschetti, 'I frammenti Veronesi del secolo IX delle istituzioni di Giustiniano', *Atti del Congresso internazionale di diritto Romano e di storia del diritto, Verona 27–28–29 IX 1948* (Milan 1953) 1.491 (no. 129; a codex beginning with the *Praefatio* and ending with 20.109)

Villeneuve-lez-Avignon, St. André (catalogue dating from 1307; Delisle, *Cabinet des manuscrits* 3.7 no. 7)

IV. Abridged Forms of the *Decretum*

Bologna, Biblioteca Universitaria, 2599 (1358), saec. XII, cf. Mordek, 'Handschriftenforschungen' 646 (Italian group of mss.). Excerpts from Books 1–15

Firenze, Biblioteca Medicea Laurenziana, Plut. VII sin. 1, saec. XI XII, Prov. S. Croce, Firenze, cf. MGH Ordines 232. Excerpts from Books 1–20 and *Ordo synodalis* 5 following Book 3; for a survey, cf. Fransen, 'La tradition manuscrite du Décret de Burchard de Worms: Une première orientation', *Ius sacrum: Festschrift Klaus Mörsdorf zum 60. Geburtstag*, ed. A. Scheuermann and G. May (Munich-Paderborn-Vienna 1969) 113 n. 6 (Italian group of manuscripts; closely related to the the complete codices Lucca 124 and Calci 9)

Firenze, Biblioteca Nazionale Centrale, Conv. soppr. C.I.2777; saec. XI–XII; Prov. Badia Fiorentina; cf. Mordek, 'Handschriftenforschungen' 642; fol. 9^{v}–57^{r}. Excerpts from Books 1–20; (incomplete) survey: Brommer, 'Kurzformen' 39 (Italian group of mss.)

København, Kongelike Bibliotek, Gl. Kgl. Saml. 1617 4°, saec. XII^{in}; Prov. Minden, St. Martin. Excerpts from Books 1–20 (including the *Admonitio synodalis* as a supplement, fol. 1^{v}–2^{v}); for a survey, cf. Brommer, 'Kurzformen' 39–40 (German group of manuscripts)

München, Universitätsbibliothek, 2° 292 (Part I: fol. 1–115; 1.179–2.28 and 3.129–5.40 are lost due to missing quires); saec. XI^{2}, in Roman minuscule (Romanesca); Prov. Porto (cf. III. above). Excerpts from Books 1–20 (Italian group, originally about three-fourths of all the chapters of the *Decretum*)

Paris, Bibliothèque nationale, lat. 4283, fol. 11^{r}–47, saec. XII. Excerpts from Books 1–16; for a survey, cf. Brommer, 'Kurzformen' 31–32 (German group). See also Fransen, 'Manuscrits' 68 and Fransen, 'Collections canoniques dans le manuscrit 4283 de la Bibliothèque nationale de Paris', *Liber amicorum Monseigneur Onclin* (Biblioteca Ephemeridum Theologicarum Lovaniensium 42; Gembloux 1976) 169–197 and Fransen, 'Abrégés' 158 n. 4

Paris, Bibliothèque nationale, lat. 8922; originated between 1051 and 1081 during the abbacy of Abbot Reginbert (cf. fol. 2^{v}), Prov. Echternach, cf. Hoffmann-Pokorny 129 n. 92. Excerpts from Books 1–20, only very slightly shortened version; Additions: Seligenstadt (1023) inserted between Book 19 and 20. Supplements: Concordat of Worms (papal and imperial version), charter for Echternach (1090) fol. 94^{v}, Alexander II (JL 4258) to Udo of Trier, Paschal II (JL 6099) to Bruno of Trier. (German group; related to Paris 3860, Reims 673 and 674); (for the fly leaf of another Burchard-codex in this codex cf. above

Tarragona, Biblioteca Provincial, 35 (18), saec. XII^{1}, Prov. Santes Creus (OCist.); First quire lost; fragmentary beginning at 1.43). Excerpts from the Books 1–20 (fol. 1^{r}–132^{v}), about one third of all the chapters of the *Decretum* and Seligenstadt (1023) c. 3 and 16–17 following Book 20; cf. G. Fransen, 'Textes grégoriens dans un manuscrit espagnol', ZRG Kan. Abt. 75 (1989) 58–69 (Italian group of mss.)

Vaticano, Città del, Biblioteca Apostolica Vaticana, lat. 1356, saec. XI–XII; Italy; cf. Pelster, 'Dekret' 147–148; Kuttner-Elze, *Catalogue* 1.121–122. Partial transmission of Books 10–19 with some omissions now and then, ending fragmentarily at 19.48 (Italian group of mss.)

Vaticano, Città del, Biblioteca Apostolica Vaticana, lat. 4980 (Part I: fol. 1–75); saec. XII^{1}, Italy; cf. Pelster, 'Dekret' 148; Mordek, 'Handschriftenforschungen' 644–645. Fragmentary transmission of the *Decretum* with occasional omissions: 7.10 - 17.60 and 19.1–53 (on another single leaf of a manuscript of the *Decretum* contained in the same codex, cf. above, 'Fragments')

V. Manuscripts Containing Individual Books of the *Decretum Burchardi*

Books 7 and 8

Oxford, St. John's College, 125, saec. XII, beginning at fol. 79^{v} Book 7 and 8 (up to c. 33) of the *Decretum Burchardi;* Book 7 of the *Decretum* directly follows Book 7 of Ivo of Chartres' *Panormia*, however, Book 8 of the *Decretum* is represented as Book 8 of the *Panormia*; thus, it seems as if the manuscript contained a complete version of Ivo's *Panormia* (cf. Brooke, *English Church* 237–239)

Books 17–19

Assisi, Biblioteca Comunale, CL 227, saec. XII, fol. 51va–80vb: a separate transmission of the Books 17–19 (without *Capitulationes* at the beginning, up to 19.148) before the beginning of the *Collectio 8 partium,* cf. below

Books 19 and 20

London, British Library, Add. 18371, saec. XII–XIII, Prov. St. Georgenberg-Fiecht (cf. fol. 1^{r}), fol. 130^{v}–176^{v} (also *Admonitio synodalis*) following Ivo of Chartres, *Panormia*

Pommersfelden, Gräflich-Schönborn'sche Schloßbibliothek 198 (2816)

Book 20

Madrid, Biblioteca Nacional, 6367 (Vitr. 5.5); separate transmission of Book 20, fol. 1^{v}–95^{r}, saec. XIII (Visigothic script, according to Reynolds); Prov. Juan Bautista Cardona, bishop of Vich (1584–1587); cf. A. García y García, 'Canonistica Hispanica IV', BMCL 1 (1971) 71

7. *Bibliography*

Conrat, *Geschichte* 261–262; Fournier-Le Bras 1.364–421; A. Pétrau-Gay, 'Burchard de Worms', DDC 2 (1937) 1141–1157; G. Allemang, 'Burchard' DHGE 10 (1938) 1245–1247; Kurtscheid-Wilches 1.153–156; Van Hove, *Prolegomena* 239, 263, 298, 320; Stickler, *Historia* 1.154–159; K. Weinzierl, 'Burchard, Bischof v. Worms', LThK 2 (1958) 783–784; García y García, *Historia* 1.311; *Rep. font.* 2 (1967) 610–611; Merzbacher, HRG 1 (1971) 541–543; M. Kerner, 'Burchard von Worms', *Verfasser-lexikon* 1 (1978) 1121–1127; R. Kaiser and M. Kerner, 'Burchard I., Bf. v. Worms', LMA 2 (1983) 946–951

D. Blondel, *Pseudo-Isidorus et Turrianus vapulantes* (Geneva 1628)

C. Oudin, *Commentarius de scriptoribus ecclesiasticis antiquis* 2 (Leipzig 1722) 525–530 (excerpt repr. PL 140.491–496)

Ballerini, *De antiquis . . . collectionibus et collectoribus,* P. IV, cap. XII (PL 56.320–326 and 140.491–536)

Theiner, *Über Ivo's vermeintliches Decret* 13–14

E. L. Richter, *Beiträge zur Kenntnis der Quellen des kanonischen Rechts* (Leipzig 1834)

Theiner, *Disquisitiones criticae* 151–152, 311–317; Appendix 2.39–166

Wasserschleben, *Beiträge* 624–682

F. G. A. Wasserschleben (ed.), *Reginonis Abbatis Prumiensis Libri Duo de Synodalibus Causis et Disciplinis Ecclesiasticis* (Leipzig 1840; repr. Graz 1964)

H. Wasserschleben, *Die Bussordnungen der abendländischen Kirche* (Halle 1851) 624–692

H. Hüffer, *Beiträge zur Geschichte der Quellen des Kirchenrechts und des römischen Rechts im Mittelalter* (Münster 1862) 42–44

F. Maassen, 'Zur Geschichte der Quellen des Kirchenrechts und des römischen Rechts im Mittelalter', *Kritische Vierteljahrsschrift für Gesetzgebung und Rechtswissenschaft* 5 (1863) 186–214

L. Bethmann, 'Reise durch Deutschland und Italien in den Jahren 1844, 1845, 1846', *Archiv* 9 (1871) 513–568 and 12 (1874) 201–426

J. von Pflugk-Harttung, 'Die Synode von Seligenstadt und Burchards Decretum', *Forschungen zur deutschen Geschichte* 16 (1876) 587–593

H. J. Schmitz, *Die Bußbücher und die Bußdisciplin der Kirche* 1 (Mainz 1883) 765; 2 (Düsseldorf 1898) 385–386, 403–467 (on Book 19)

H. Grosch, *Bischof Burchard I. zu Worms* (Diss. Leipzig, Jena 1890)

F. Patetta, 'Il Breviario Alariciano in Italia', *Archivio giuridico* 47 (1891) 35 n. 3 (mss.) (repr. *Studi sulle fonti giuridiche medievali,* ed. G. Astuti, Torino 1967, 633 n. 3)

K. Müller, *Der Umschwung in der Lehre von der Busse während des 12. Jahrhunderts* (Theologische Abhandlungen C. v. Weizsäcker; Freiburg 1892) 287–320

H. Boos, *Quellen zur Geschichte der Stadt Worms* 3 (Berlin 1893) 99–126 and xxvi–xxvii

P. Fournier, 'La collezione canonica del regestro di Farfa', *Archivio della R. Società Romana di Storia Patria* 17 (1894) 285–301, especially 293 n. 2

A. Hauck, 'Über den Liber decretorum Burchard's von Worms', *Berichte über die Verhandlungen der Königlich Sächsischen Gesellschaft der Wissenschaften zu Leipzig, philol.-hist. Classe* 1 (1894) 65–86 (cf. review by M. Gietl, HJB 16 (1895) 116–119

Sackur, *Cluniacenser* 2.308, 310

H. Boos, *Geschichte der rheinischen Städtekultur* 1 (Berlin ^{2}1897) 235–309
Fournier, 'Collections canoniques issues du décret de Burchard' 189–214
G. Meier, *Zentralblatt für Bibliothekswesen* 20 (1903) 16–32
A. M. Koeniger, *Burchard I. von Worms und die deutsche Kirche seiner Zeit (1000–1025): Ein kirchen- und sittengeschichtliches Zeitbild* (Veröffentlichungen aus dem kirchenhistorischen Seminar München, 2nd Series, No. 6; Munich 1905)
A. Hauck, *Kirchengeschichte Deutschlands* 3 (Leipzig $^{3/4}$1906) 437–442
M. Manitius, 'Geschichtliches aus mittelalterlichen Bibliothekskatalogen', NA 32 (1907) 647–709, especially 685
A. M. Koeniger, 'Beiträge zu den fränkischen Kapitularien und Synoden', AKKR 87 (1907) 393–406
E. Diederich, *Das Dekret des Bischofs Burchard von Worms: Beiträge zur Geschichte seiner Quellen* 1 (Kath.-Theol. Diss. Breslau 1908)
A. M. Koeniger, 'Ein deutscher Beichtspiegel von der Wende des 13. Jahrhunderts', *Katholik* 37 (1908) 286–300
Fournier, 'Etudes critiques' 41–112, 213–221, 289–331, 564–584 (also as a separate publication with consecutive numbering from 1 to 144)
P. Fournier, 'Les Capitula Pseudo-Theodori et le décret de Burchard de Worms', *Florilegium Melchior de Vogüé* (Paris 1910) 241–255
A. Lagarde, 'Le manuel du confesseur au XIe siècle', *Revue d'histoire et de littérature religieuses* n.s. 1 (1910) 542–555
Fournier, 'Décret' 451–473, 670–701
Manitius, *Literatur* 2.56–61
H. Schmitt, 'Bischof Burchard im Urteil der Zeitgenossen', *Wormatia sacra: Beiträge zur Geschichte des ehemaligen Bistums Worms aus Anlaß der Feier der 900. Wiederkehr des Todestages des Bischofs Burchard* (Worms 1925) 43–44
H. Schmitt, 'Aus der Geschichte der Wormser Domschule', *Wormatia sacra* (same as above) 52–60
G. Le Bras, 'La part de la Belgique dans l'histoire des collections canoniques', RHD, 4e séries 9 (1930) 588–589
Brooke, *English Church* 237–239 (English manuscripts of Burchards *Decretum*)
E. N. Johnson, *The Secular Activities of the German Episcopate 919–1024* (Lincoln 1932)
S. Inglot, 'Les serfs dans les Decreta de Burchard de Worms', *Przewodnik histoyczno prawny (Revue d'histoire du droit)* 4 (1933) 72–80
J. C. Naber, 'De Gregorio Papa et Constantina regina (Burchardi Decretum L. XI, c.26)', RHD 4e séries 13 (1934) 727–731
Meyer, 'Überlieferung' 141–183
A. Boutemy, 'En lisant Sigebert de Gembloux, 1: Le canoniste Burchard de Worms étudia-t-il en Lotharingie?', *Revue belge de philologie et d'histoire* 15 (1936) 987–996
W. Wattenbach and R. Holtzmann, *Deutschlands Geschichtsquellen im Mittelalter, Deutsche Kaiserzeit* 1.2 (Berlin ^{2}1943) 210–212
A. Van Hove, 'En inleiding tot bronnen van het Kerkelijk Recht op het einde den XI de eeuw', *Miscellanea A. de Meyer* (Louvain 1946) 358–372
Pelster, 'Dekret' 114–157 (Supplement to Meyer, 'Überlieferung')
Mor, 'Reazione al *Decretum Burchardi*' 197–206
F. Pelster, 'Das Dekret Burkhards von Worms in einer Redaktion aus dem Beginn

der Gregorianischen Reform (Cod. Vat. lat. 3809 und Clm 4570)', SGreg 1 (1947) 321–351 (Humbert of Moyenmoutier as the author of the Gregorian recension of the *Decretum*)

A. Michel, 'Pseudoisidor, die Sentenzen Humberts und Burkhard von Worms im Investiturstreit', SGreg 3 (1948) 149–161

J. Ruysschaert, *Les Mss de l'Abbaye de Nonantola* (Studi e Testi 182bis; Vatican City 1955) (Burchard's *Decretum* mentioned in Catalogue A of the Abbey of Nonantola in 1035 - cf. Ryan, 'Observations' 97)

Ryan, *Saint Peter Damiani* 160–162 (on his use of Burchard's *Decretum*)

H. Büttner, 'Das Bistum Worms und der Neckarraum während des Früh- und Hochmittelalters', *Archiv für mittelrheinische Kirchengeschichte* 10 (1958) 9–38

Ryan, 'Observations' 95–97

E. Seckel, 'Bisher nicht identifizierte Texte im Dekret des Burchard von Worms: Aus dem Nachlaß hg. und ergänzt von H. Fuhrmann', DA 15 (1959) 16–22

H. Büttner, 'Zur Stadtgeschichte von Worms in Früh- und Hochmittelalter', *Aus Geschichte und Landeskunde: Festschrift für Franz Steinbach* (Bonn 1960) 389–401

Sprandel, *Ivo von Chartres* 53–54, 57–58, 65–71

G. Theuerkauf, 'Burchard von Worms und die Rechtskunde seiner Zeit', FMSt 2 (1968) 144–161

G. Fransen, 'La tradition manuscrite du Décret de Burchard de Worms. Une première orientation', *Ius sacrum: Festschrift Klaus Mörsdorf zum 60. Geburtstag*, ed. A. Scheuermann and G. May (Munich-Paderborn-Vienna 1969) 111–118

G. Fransen, 'Une suite de recherches sur le Décret de Burchard de Worms', *Traditio* 25 (1969) 514–515

Fransen, 'Trois notes' 446–447

P. Landau, 'Bericht über das Seminar "Das Decretum Burchards von Worms"', *Traditio* 26 (1970) 469–470

E. Van Balberghe, 'Les éditions du Décret de Burchard de Worms: Avatars d'un texte', RTAM 37 (1970) 5–22 (Supplément: concordance entre l'ordre 'de Constance' et l'ordre de la PL)

M. Kerner, *Studien zum Dekret des Bischofs Burchard von Worms* 1–2 (phil. Diss. Aachen 1969, 1971) [cf. review by G. Fransen, RHE 67 [1972] 479–482]

Mordek, 'Handschriftenforschungen' 626–651

A. García y García, 'Canonistica Hispanica (IV)' BMCL 1 (1971) 70–73, 71 (on the manuscript Madrid, Biblioteca Nacional, 6367, which contains Book 20 of the *Decretum Burchardi* [fol. 1^{v}–95^{r}], saec. XIII)

U. Bubenheimer, 'Der Aufenthalt Burchards von Worms im Kloster Lobbes als Erfindung des Johannes Trithemius: Zur literarischen Arbeitsweise und Quellenkenntnis des Sponheimer Abts', ZRG Kan. Abt. 58 (1972) 320–337

G. Fransen, 'Réflexions sur l'étude des collections canoniques à l'occasion de l'édition d'une lettre de Bruno de Segni', SGreg 9 (1972) 3–15 (on Firenze, Biblioteca Nazionale Centrale, Conv. soppr. F.IV.255)

Gilchrist, 'Economic Policy' 397–399

R. Knox, 'Finding the Law: Developments in Canon Law during the Gregorian Reform', SGreg 9 (Rom 1972) 448 ('a hardly tenable hypothesis', cf. Mordek, 'Kanonistik und gregorianische Reform' 73 n. 43, that the *Collection in 74 Titles* was a direct response to the *Decretum* of Burchard)

K. Kroeschell, *Deutsche Rechtsgeschichte* 1 (Hamburg 1972) 123–136

G. Fransen, 'Les sources de la Préface du Décret de Burchard de Worms', BMCL 3 (1973) 1–7 (including Appendice by Emile van Balberghe, 'La Préface du Décret et la *Collectio XII Partium*' 7–9)
Fuhrmann, *Einfluß und Verbreitung* 2.442–485
J. Morales, 'Las verdades catolicas en las colecciones canónicas anteriores a Graciano: Estudio del Decreto de Buchardo [sic] de Worms (s. XI)', *Ius canonicum* 13 (1973) 329–368
Brommer, 'Fragmente' 231
Fransen, 'Manuscrit de Montpellier' 301–311
Brommer, 'Kurzformen' 19–45 (on this, cf. Fransen, 'Abrégés' 157–166)
Mordek, *Kirchenrecht und Reform* 6 n. 12, 177–178, 183 n. 402
A. Ambrosini, 'Il più antico elenco di chierici della diocesi ambrosiana ed altre aggiunte al 'Decretum' di Burcardo in un codice della Biblioteca Ambrosiana (E 144 sup.): Una voce della polemica antipatarinica?' *Aevum* 50 (1976) 274–320
Fransen, 'Manuscrits de collections canoniques' 67–72
G. Fransen, 'Collections canoniques dans le manuscrit 4283 de la Bibliothèque nationale de Paris', *Liber Amicorum Monseigneur Onclin* (Biblioteca Ephemeridum Theologicarum Lovaniensium 42; Gembloux 1976) 169–197
John, *Collectio canonum Remedio . . . ascripta* 108–111
Kerner et al. 'Textidentifikation' 17–63
H. Mordek, 'Bemerkungen zum mittelalterlichen Schatzverzeichnis von Porto/Rom', SG 20 (1976) (=*Mélanges Fransen* 2) 231–240, especially 240 n. 33
G. Motta, '*In primo coniugio . . . :* Una falsa attribuzione milanese di Burcardo (9.8)', *Richerche storiche sulla Chiesa Ambrosiana* 6 (Milan 1976) 137–141
Fransen, 'Essai de classement' 1–19
Hartmann, *Worms* 111–113
Fransen, 'Abrégés' 157–166
Gilchrist, 'Reception 2' 196 and 196–197
Gilchrist, 'Epistola Widonis' 587–588 including n. 41
J. Gaudemet, 'Contribution à l'étude de la loi dans la doctrine canonique du XIIe siècle', *Etudes de droit contemporain, n.s., Contributions françaises au VIIe Congrès international de droit comparé Uppsala 1966, section I B—Droit canonique* (Paris 1966); (repr. *La formation du droit canonique médiéval* 3 [London 1980] 19–20)
Motta, 'Regula Benedicti' 261–279
G. M. Cantarella, 'Placido di Nonantola. Un progetto di ideologia', RSCI 37 (1983) 117–142, 406–436, especially 414 n. 25
B. Gloger and W. Zöllner, *Teufelsglaube und Hexenwahn* (Vienna-Cologne-Graz 1984)
P. J. Payer, *Sex and the Penitentials: The Development of a Sexual Code 550–1150* (Toronto 1984)
Mordek, 'Systematische Kanonessammlungen' 189 including n. 23 (reference to Cod. Lambach, XVI)
G. W. Olsen, 'Reference to the 'ecclesia primitiva' in the Decretum of Burchard of Worms', *Proceedings Berkeley* 289–307
J. H. Van Engen, 'Observations on *De consecratione*', *Proceedings Berkeley* 309–320
Mordek, 'Kanonistik und gregorianische Reform' 72–73
Picasso, 'Reformatio ecclesiae' 74–75

Mordek, 'Analecta canonistica' 8–9 ('4. Fragmente des Dekrets Bischof Burchards von Worms')

G. Picasso, G. Piana and G. Motta (trad.), *A pane e acqua: Peccati e penitenze nel Medioevo* (Novara 1986)

N. Wibiral, '*Admoneatur Imperator:* Altchristliche und frühmittelalterliche Texte zur Herrscherparänese', OOeHB 40 (1986) 208–233

J. Goering and F.A.C. Mantello (ed.), 'The Early Penitential Writings of Robert Grosseteste', RTAM 54 (1987) 52–112

Hartmann, 'Kanonessammlung' 45–64

E.-D. Hehl and H. Fuhrmann (ed.), *Die Konzilien Deutschlands und Reichsitaliens 916–100* (MGH Concilia 6.1: 916–960; Hannover 1987)

C. Lecouteux, 'Les fées au moyen âge: Quelques remarques', *Bulletin de la Société de mythologie française* 146 (1987) 26–31

F. Lotter, 'Zur Ausbildung eines kirchlichen Judenrechts bei Burchard von Worms und Ivo von Chartres', *Antisemitismus und jüdische Geschichte: Studien zu Ehren von Herbert A. Strauss,* ed. R. Erb and M. Schmidt (Berlin 1987) 69–96

E. Van Balberghe, *ABC Saint Claude, Bibliothèque municipale, Ms. 3 (17), Initiaalvariaties in een XIIe eeuws handschrift: Variétés des initiales d'un manuscrit du XIIe siècle: Variety of Initials in a Twelfth-Century Manuscript,* trans. D. Van den Auweele, M. Oppitz, and K. Jordá (Louvain 1987)

Landau, 'Gefälschtes Recht' 11–49

G. Motta (ed.), *Liber canonum diversorum sanctorum patrum sive Collectio in CLXXXIII titulos digesta* (MIC Series B. Corpus collectionum 7; Vatican City 1988)

C. Piacitelli, 'Milano e il suo territorio in età comunale (sec. XI–XIII) (Milano 26–30 ottobre 1987)', RSCI 42 (1988) 245–255

E. Cadoni and R. Turtas (ed.) *Umanisti sassaresi del '500: Le 'biblioteche' di Giovanni Francesco Fara et Alessio Fontana* (Pubblicazioni di 'Sandalion', Università degli Studi di Sassari 2; Sassari 1988)

R. E. Reynolds (ed. praef.), 'A South Italian Liturgico-Canonical Mass Commentary', MS 50 (1988) 626–670

M. M. Sheehan, 'Theory and Practice: Marriage of the Unfree and Poor in Medieval Society', MS 50 (1988) 457–487

P. Cramer, 'Ernulf of Rochester and Early Anglo-Norman Canon Law', JEH 40 (1989) 483–510

G. Fransen, 'Textes grégoriens dans un manuscrit espagnol', ZRG Kan. Abt. 75 (1989) 58–69

J. Gilchrist, 'The Canonistic Treatment of Jews in the Latin West in the Eleventh and Early Twelfth Centuries', ZRG Kan. Abt. 75 (1989) 70–106

W. Kozur, 'Index alphabeticus singulorum capitulorum Decreti Burchardi Wormatiensis', *Ius et historia: Festgabe für Rudolf Weigand zu seinem 60. Geburtstag,* ed. N. Höhl (Forschungen zur Kirchenrechtswissenschaft; Würzburg 1989) 64–101

Landau, 'Kanonessammlungen in der Lombardei' 446–447

L. Mauro, 'Dai peccati di pensiero alla volontarietà degli atti: un percorso attraverso i *libri paenitentiales', Seminari sassaresi* 4 (Sassari 1989) 65–81

G. May, 'Bemerkungen zu der Kirchenrechtswissenschaft um das Jahr 1000', AKKR 158 (1989) 29–68

G. Moretti, 'Arti e fate a banchetto, e i loro doni: Per la storia del reimpiego dottrinale di un motivo folklorico', *Testi e modelli antropologici: Seminario del Centro di ricerche in scienza della letteratura,* ed. M. Bonafin (Milan 1989) 137–165

Müller, *Collectio Duodecim Partium* passim (cf. index)

A. M. Piazzoni and P. Vian, *Manoscritti Vaticani latini 14666–15203, Catalogo sommario* (Studi e testi 332; Vatican City 1989)

R. Weigand, 'Burchardauszüge in Dekrethandschriften und ihre Verwendung bei Rufin als Paleae im Dekret Gratians', AKKR 158 (1989), 429–451

Busch, *Placidus von Nonantola* 76–101

R. Weigand, 'Die Lambacher Handschrift XVI des Dekrets Burchards von Worms und Bischof Adalbero von Würzburg', *Würzburger Diözesan-Geschichtsblätter* 52 (1990) 25–36

G. Fransen, 'La notion d'oeuvre servile dans le droit canonique', *Le travail* 177–184

Descriptive Inventories of Manuscripts Microfilmed for the Hill Monastic Manuscript Library. Portuguese Libraries 3: The 'Fundo Alcobaça' of the Biblioteca Nacional, Lisbon 3: Manuscripts 302–456, J. Black and Th. L. Amos, *Museu Nacional de Arte Antiga* by Jonathan Black, Collegeville Minnesota 1990, no. 365, p. 105–106 (a now-mutilated copy, twelfth-century Portugal, cf. DA 47 [1991], 589)

Hoffmann-Pokorny, passim

O. G. Oexle, 'Le travail au XIe siècle: réalités et mentalités', *Le travail* 49–60

C. Bologna, 'Le fate e il fato dei poeti', QuadS 77 (1991) 630–642

S. Coué, 'Acht Bischofsviten aus der Salierzeit', *Die Salier* 3.347–413, especially 350–359

Hartmann, 'Autoritäten' 425–427, 429–432, 434–437, 444

M. Ferrari, *Medieval and Renaissance Manuscripts at the University of California, Los Angeles* (Berkeley, Los Angeles, Oxford 1991)

D. Gatti, 'Curatrici e streghe nell'Europa dell'alto Medioevo', *Donne e lavoro nell' Italia medievale,* ed. Maria Giuseppina Muzzarelli, Paola Galetti, Bruno Andreolli (Torino 1991)

J. Gaudemet, 'Le serment dans le droit canonique médiéval', *Le serment,* ed. R. Verdier (Paris 1991) 2.63–75

G. Fransen, 'Textes ajoutés au Décret de Burchard de Worms dans deux manuscrits toscans', *Studi Senesi* 100, Supplement 2 (1988) 536–552

U.-R. Blumenthal, 'An Episcopal Handbook from Twelfth-Century Southern Italy: Codex Rome, Bibl. Vallicelliana F.54/III', *Studia in Honorem A. M. Stickler* (1992) 13–24

Brett, 'Collectio Lanfranci' 168

F. Cardini, 'Giacomo della Marca e le streghe', *Santi, monaci e contadini: La Marca tra agiografia e folklore: Atti del Convegno di studio svoltosi in occasione della quinta edizione del 'Premio internazionale Ascoli Piceno', Ascoli Piceno, 21–23 giugno 1991,* ed. E. Menestó (Ascoli Piceno 1992) 109–146

H. Fuhrmann, 'Kanonistische Konzilsüberlieferung und Archetyp: Zur Qualität von Burchardtexten', *Proceedings San Diego* 57–61

Gaudemet, 'Primauté' 155–156

Landau, 'Vorgratianische Kanonessammlungen bei den Dekretisten' 93–116

J. Müller, 'Collectio duodecim partium und Decretum Burchardi', *Proceedings San Diego* 63–76

Pokorny, 'Triburer Synodalakten' 429–511

J.-C. Schmitt, *Medioevo 'superstizioso'*, trans. M. Garin (Rome-Bari 1992)

E. Vodola, 'Sovereignty and Tabu: Evolution of the Sanction against Communication with Excommunicates, 2: Canonical Collections', *Studia in Honorem A. M. Stickler* (1992) 581–598, especially 590–592

J. B. Will, *Die Rechtsverhältnisse zwischen Bischof und Klerus im Dekret des Bischofs Burchard von Worms: Eine kanonistische Untersuchung* (Würzburg 1992)

Zechiel-Eckes, *Cresconius* 1.277–278, 281

J. Laudage, *Gregorianische Reform und Investiturstreit* (Darmstadt 1993)

P. Landau, 'Wandel und Kontinuität im kanonischen Recht bei Gratian', *Sozialer Wandel im Mittelalter. Wahrnehmungsformen, Erklärungsmuster, Regelungsmechanismen*, ed. J. Miethke and K. Schreiner (Sigmaringen 1994) 215–233, especially 217–221

Mordek, *Bibliotheca capitularium* 75, 112, 133–134, 293, 303, 333, 336, 350, 395, 696, 856, 913, 1029, 1035, 1039 (cf. also above, 'Manuscripts')

Landau, 'Eheschließung' 1.453–461

Collectio duodecim partium

1. Author: Unknown. *2. Date:* Between 1020 and 1050 (Fournier-Le Bras 1.440); 974–1039 (Müller, *Collectio Duodecim Partium* 356–364). *3. Place:* Southern Germany (Fournier-Le Bras 1.439–440); probably Freising (Müller 356). *4. Type:* Systematic collection.

5. Editions

Theiner, *Disquisitiones criticae* 320–331 (only excerpts)

Wasserschleben, *Beiträge* 42–45 (only excerpts)

6. Manuscripts

'1 CDP' (according to Müller)

Bamberg, Staatsbibliothek, Can. 7 (P I 13), saec. XI1/3; hands of Freising and Bamberg, Prov. Bamberg, Cathedral, 'late 1 CDP' (fully developed form); cf. Hoffmann, *Bamberger Handschriften* 122–123; cf. also Mordek, *Bibliotheca capitularium* 10–12

München, Bayerische Staatsbibliothek, Clm 19414, saec. XI^1, Prov. Tegernsee (no. 1414), fol. 1^r–68^r (only Books 7, 8 and 3); cf. Hoffmann, *Buchkunst* 123; cf. also Mordek, *Bibliotheca capitularium* 350

Wien, Österreichische Nationalbibliothek, lat. 2136; saec. XI^1, Freising, Prov. Salzburg, cathedral, 'late 1 CDP' (fully developed form); cf. also Mordek, *Bibliotheca capitularium* 910–911

Excerpts (of the Late 1 CDP)

Bamberg, Staatsbibliothek, Can. 8, saec. XII^2, Bamberg

Bamberg, Staatsbibliothek, Can. 9, saec. XI2/3, Freising, fol. 1–105 (cf. Hoffmann, *Bamberger Handschriften* 123)

Vaticano, Città del, Biblioteca Apostolica Vaticana, Pal. lat. 584, saec. XI, Mainz

Link between 1 CDP and 2 CDP

Berlin, Staatsbibliothek Preußischer Kulturbesitz, Savigny 2, saec. XI[1], Freising, (Prov. Cathedral of Freising) 'early 1 CDP'; cf. also Mordek, *Bibliotheca capitularium* 69

'2 CDP'

Saint-Claude, Bibliothèque municipale, 17, saec. XII, Prov. Abbey of Saint-Claude

Troyes, Bibliothèque municipale, 246, saec. XI[1], German, Prov. Cathedral of Troyes

Fragments

Schwäbisch-Gmünd, Stadtarchiv, Fragmentenmappe, saec. XII, Southern Germany, cf. P. Brommer, 'Ein Fund zur *Collectio duodecim partium*', BMCL 13 (1983) 57–58

Einsiedeln, Stiftsbibliothek, 370 (194); saec. XI[1], Freising, fol. 32 (cf. Hoffmann, *Buchkunst* 1.418 and Mordek, 'Analecta canonistica' 9–11 ('5. Ein weiterer Fund zur *Collectio XII partium*') (instance of another sub-category?)

Manuscripts containing individual books of the *Collectio duodecim partium* which are transmitted together with books of the *Decretum Burchardi*

Olomouc (Olmütz), Kapitulni Knihovna (now: Státni vedecké knihovna, Universitni knihovna) 202, saec. XII[med], Mainz? 'early 1 CDP'

Wien, Österreichische Nationalbibliothek, lat. 354, saec. XII[1], Salzburg, Cathedral

7. *Bibliography*

Conrat, *Geschichte* 262–263; Fournier-Le Bras 1.434–442, Van Hove, *Prolegomena* 263, 321; Stickler, *Historia* 1.159; R. Naz, 'Collectio duodecim partium' DDC 5 (1953) 71–74

Theiner, *Disquisitiones criticae* 308–333

H. Wasserschleben, 'Die Collectio duodecim partium und ihr Verhältnis zum Dekrete des Burchard von Worms', *Beiträge* 34–46

V. Krause, 'Die Münchener Handschriften 3851.3853 mit einer Compilation von 181 Wormser Beschlüssen', NA 19 (1894) 85–139 (corr. by G. Schmitz, 'Vier-Bücher-Sammlung' 240 n. 35)

Fournier, 'Recueil canonique allemand' 31–62; 229–259

E. Bohácek, 'Le opere delle scuole medievali di diritto nei manoscritti della Biblioteca del Capitolo di Olomouc', SG 8 (1962) 305–321

E. Van Balberghe, 'Un nouveau manuscrit du 'De ordinationibus' d'Auxilius', *Traditio* 26 (1970) 447–449

N. Daniel, *Handschriften des 10. Jahrhunderts aus der Freisinger Dombibliothek* (Münchener Beiträge zur Mediävistik und Renaissanceforschung 11; Munich 1973)

E. Van Balberghe, 'La Préface du Décret et la *Collectio XII Partium*', BMCL 3 (1973) 7–9

Petersmann, 'Kanonistische Überlieferung' 366–367

Mordek, *Kirchenrecht und Reform* 121 n. 91

John, *Collectio canonum Remedio . . . ascripta* 112–114
Hartmann, *Worms* 115–116
Hoffmann, *Buchkunst* 1.416–418
Mordek, 'Analecta canonistica' 9–11
H. Fuhrmann, 'Die Synode von Hohenaltheim quellenkundlich betrachtet', DA 43 (1987) 440–468
E.-D. Hehl and H. Fuhrmann (eds.), *Die Konzilien Deutschlands und Reichsitaliens 916–1001* (MGH Concilia 6.1: 916–960; Hannover 1987)
E. Van Balberghe, *ABC Saint Claude, Bibliothèque municipale, Ms. 3 (17): Initiaalvariaties in een XIIe eeuws handschrift: Variétés des initiales d'un manuscrit du XIIe siècle.—Variety of Initials in a Twelfth-Century Manuscript,* trans. D. Van den Auweele, M. Oppitz and K. Jordá (Leuven 1987)
Müller, *Collectio Duodecim Partium*
Hoffmann-Pokorny 87–107
Hartmann, 'Autoritäten' 426, 437
J. Müller, 'Collectio duodecim partium und Decretum Burchardi', *Proceedings San Diego* 63–76
Pokorny, 'Triburer Synodalakten' 429–511
Mordek, *Bibliotheca capitularium* 11, 69, 134, 348, 350, 448, 910, 1037
Landau, 'Eheschließung' 458 and 461

Collectio 5 librorum (Vat. lat. 1339 etc.)

1. Author: Advocate of reform in the early eleventh century; an Italian priest named Lupo is cited in one of the introductions as the initiator of the collection, cf. Fournier-Le Bras 1.429–430. *2. Date:* About 1020. *3. Place:* Central or Southern Italy. *4. Type:* A systematic collection deriving from the *Collectio Hibernensis.* Source of numerous collections including the *Collectio Farfensis.*

5. Edition

Edition of the First Three Books

M. Fornasari (ed.), *Collectio canonum in V libris, Libri I–III* (CCL, Continuatio mediaevalis 6, Turnhout 1970) cf. review by G. Fransen, RHE 66 (1971) 130–136 and Mordek, ZRG Kan. Abt. 60 (1974) 477–478; H. Fuhrmann, DA 27 (1971) 221–222; see also Mordek, 'Systematische Kanonessammlungen' 189 with n. 21

6. Manuscripts

Monte Cassino, Archivio e Biblioteca dell'Abbazia, 125, saec. XI2/4, 'post-Theobaldian, Montecassino', Reynolds; cf. M. Inguanez, *Codicum Casinensium manuscriptorum catalogus* 1 (Monte Cassino 1915) 206 (written during the first decades of the eleventh century, Mordek, *Kirchenrecht und Reform* 100 n. 15); probably identical with the *Liber canonum* of Abbot Theobald (1022–1035) of Montecassino (Fornasari, *Collectio canonum in V libris* p. ix; approving Mordek, *Kirchenrecht und Reform* 100 n. 15 and n. 12)

Roma, Biblioteca Vallicelliana, B.11, saec. XI1/2 (according to Fournier-Le Bras

1.421), Reynolds: written at S. Eutizio in Val Castoriana not far from Norcia by Ubertus (the later abbot), whose death is recorded by 1087

Vaticano, Città del, Biblioteca Apostolica Vaticana, lat. 1339, saec. XI^{med}, Narni? on the illuminations and the liturgical material both at the beginning and end of this manuscript, cf. C. Walter, 'Les dessins carolingiens dans un manuscrit de Verceil', *Cahiers archéologiques* 18 (1968) 107 n. 34; K. Gamber, *Codices liturgici latini antiquiores* 1.2. (Fribourg/Switzerland 1968) 573 no. 1599; Prov. from Farfa (Fornasari) is untenable, although the *Collectio 5 librorum* served as a source for the *Collectio Farfensis,* cf. Kölzer, *Collectio canonum* 49; Mordek, *Bibliotheca capitularium* 855–857

Fragment of the Collection?

Roma, Biblioteca Vallicelliana, R.32, saec. XI3/4, Central Italy, (fol. 50)

Excerpts of the *Collectio 5 librorum* (according to Reynolds)

El Escorial, Real Biblioteca de San Lorenzo, Z.III.19, saec. XI^{ex}, Southern Italy
Firenze, Biblioteca Medicea Laurenziana, V sin. 7
Firenze, Biblioteca Riccardiana, 300
Monte Cassino, Archivio e Biblioteca dell'Abbazia, 522, saec. XII, Southern Italy
Napoli, Biblioteca Nazionale Vittorio Emanuele II, XII.A.8
Rieti, Archivio Capitolare, 5
Roma, Biblioteca Angelica, 1447
Roma, Biblioteca Casanatense, 2010, saec. XII, Central Italy
Roma, Biblioteca Vallicelliana, B.63, saec. XI^{ex}, S. Eutizio in Val Castoriana near Norcia?
Vaticano, Città del, Biblioteca Apostolica Vaticana, lat. 7818, saec. XII, Chieti

Mixed with Canons from Other Collections

Roma, Biblioteca Vallicelliana, B.32
Roma, Biblioteca Vallicelliana, B.63
Roma, Biblioteca Vallicelliana, T.XXI

Combined with Material from Burchard's Decretum

Firenze, Biblioteca Medicea Laurenziana, Plut. 4, sin.4
Firenze, Biblioteca Riccardiana, 300
Monte Cassino, Archivio e Biblioteca dell'Abbazia, 216
Roma, Biblioteca Vallicelliana, F.2
Roma, Biblioteca Vallicelliana, F.8
Roma, Biblioteca Vallicelliana, F.92
Toledo, Archivo y Biblioteca Capitular, 22–32
Vaticano, Città del, Biblioteca Apostolica Vaticana, lat. 3830
Vaticano, Città del, Biblioteca Apostolica Vaticana, lat. 4977
Vaticano, Città del, Biblioteca Apostolica Vaticana, lat. 8487

Combined with Material from the *Collectio 74 titulorum*

El Escorial, Real Biblioteca de San Lorenzo, Z.III.19
Monte Cassino, Archivio e Biblioteca dell'Abbazia, 522
Roma, Biblioteca Angelica, 1447
Roma, Biblioteca Casanatense, 2010
Roma, Biblioteca Vallicelliana, F.54, fol. 67^{r}–169^{v}

7. *Bibliography*

Conrat, *Geschichte* 215–217; Fournier-Le Bras 1.421–431 and 445–450; Van Hove, *Prolegomena* 232, 263–264, 298, 316; Stickler, *Historia* 1.153; García y García, *Historia* 1.306.

Ballerini, *De antiquis . . . collectionibus et collectoribus,* P. IV, cap. XVIII, c. 4 (PL 56.349–350)

Theiner, *Disquisitiones criticae* 271–272

Fournier, 'Influence' 36–37

Fournier, 'Recueils canoniques italiens' 164–165

Mor, 'Reazione al *Decretum Burchardi*' 197–206

M. Fornasari, 'Un manoscritto e una collezione canonica del sec. XI proveniente da Farfa', *Benedictina* 10 (1956) 199–210 (further bibliographical references)

M. Fornasari, 'Enrico II e Benedetto VIII e i canoni del presunto concilio di Ravenna del 1014', RSCI 18 (1964) 46–55

Ryan, 'Observations' 97

F. Patetta, 'Contributi alla storia del diritto romano nel medio evo', BIDR 3 (1891) (repr. *Studi sulle fonti giuridiche medievali* [Torino 1967] 17–24)

G. Santini, *Ricerche sulle 'Exceptiones Legum Romanarum'* (Milan 1969) 191–192

Mordek, 'Herovalliana' 235 n. 82

Gilchrist, 'Economic Policy' 399–400

R. Reynolds, 'The *De officiis VII graduum:* Its Origins and Early Medieval Development', MS 34 (1972) 130 n. 71 (with bibliographical references)

Mordek, *Kirchenrecht und Reform* 6 n. 12; 100 n. 15; 138–139; 138 n. 187; 226 n. 56

Reynolds, 'Excerpta' 1–9

Y. Gélinas, 'Some Manuscripts from Farfa in the Vatican Library: Research on a Particular Type of Script', *Manuscripta* 21 (1977) 13 (Vat. lat. 1339)

Y. Gélinas, 'Researches in Analytical Paleography: The Utilization of Three Constitutive Elements of Writing for the Exact Isolation and Classification of a Proposed Handwriting (MSS Vat. lat. 1339, 3761, 3830, 6808)', *Manuscripta* 22 (1978) 7

P. Landau, 'Die Collectio Veronensis', ZRG Kan. Abt. 67 (1981) 85–86 (demonstrates that the *Collectio 5 librorum* was not used in the *Collectio Veronensis*)

Kölzer, *Collectio canonum* 48–55

Reynolds, 'Unity and Diversity' 134

J. Laudage, *Priesterbild und Reformpapsttum im 11. Jahrhundert* (Cologne-Vienna 1984) 78–83

L. Schmugge, 'The Canonistic Tradition of Leo IX's 'Relatum est' (JL 4269)' *Proceedings Cambridge* 91–101

R. E. Reynolds, 'A South Italian Ordination Allocution', MS 47 (1985) 438–444

Kuttner-Elze, *Catalogue* 1.71–74

R. E. Reynolds, 'Rites and Signs of Conciliar Decisions', *Segni e Riti nella Chiesa altomedievale occidentale (11–17 aprile 1985)* (Settimane di Studio del Centro Italiano di Studi sull'alto Medioevo 33; Spoleto 1987) 1.207–249

R. E. Reynolds, 'South Italian "liturgica" and "canonistica" in Catalonia (New York, Hispanic Society of America, ms. HC 380/819)', MS 49 (1987) 480–495, especially 483–489

P. Supino Martini, *Roma e l'area grafica romanesca (secoli X–XII)*, (Biblioteca di Scrittura e civiltà; Alessandria 1987) (Roma, Biblioteca Vallicelliana, B.11)
Landau, 'Gefälschtes Recht' 29, 37
Reynolds, 'South Italian Collection' 278–295
Schmitz, 'Vier-Bücher-Sammlung' 235
M. Wojtowytsch, 'Die Kanones Heinrici regis: Bemerkungen zur römischen Synode von Februar 1014', *Festschrift Fuhrmann* (1991) 155–168
R. E. Reynolds, 'The South-Italian Collection in Five Books and its Derivatives: The Collection of Vallicelliana Tome XXI', *Proceedings San Diego* 77–91
Siems, *Handel und Wucher* 180, 189, 668
Zechiel-Eckes, *Cresconius* 1.269–277
Mordek, *Bibliotheca capitularium* 474

Collections of Local Importance

Lex Romana canonice compta

1. Author: Unknown. *2. Date:* Probably middle of the ninth century. *3. Place:* Italy. *4. Type:* Systematically arranged collection ('Capitula Romanae legis ad canones pertinentia')

5. Edition

C. G. Mor (ed.), *Lex romana canonice compta: Testo di leggi romano-canoniche del sec. IX pubblicato sul ms. parigino Bibl. Nat. 12448* (Pubblicazioni della R. Università di Pavia, Facoltà di Giurisprudenza, A. Studi nell Scienze Giuridiche e Sociali 31; Pavia 1927)

6. Manuscript

Paris, Bibliothèque nationale, lat. 12448, saec. IX^{ex}–X^{in}, Eastern Francia (cf. Maassen, 'Über eine Lex Romana canonice compta', *SB Vienna 35*, 1860, 96ff.)

7. Bibliography

Maassen, *Geschichte* 888–896; Conrat, *Geschichte* 205–210, 631ff.; Fournier-Le Bras 1.116–119, 239; H.-J. Becker, HRG 2 (1978) 1934–1935; H. Mordek, LMA 5 (1991) 1930

F. Maassen, 'Über eine Lex Romana canonice compta', *SB Vienna* 35 (1860) 73–108

J. Flach, *Etudes critiques sur l'histoire du droit romain au moyen age avec textes inédits* (Paris 1890) 92–93, 167ff.

M. Conrat (Cohn), *Die Lex Romana canonice compta: Römisches Recht im frühmittelalterlichen Italien in systematischer Darstellung* (Verhandelingen der Koninglijke Akademie van de Wetenschappen te Amsterdam: Afdeeling Letterkunde: Nieuw Reeks VI, 1; Amsterdam 1904; repr. Wiesbaden 1967)

Fournier, 'Anselmo dedicata' 489–492

E. Besta, 'Fonti e legislazione', in: P. del Giudice, *Storia del diritto italiano* 1.1 (Milan 1923) 178ff., 262–271

C. G. Mor, 'Di una perduta compilazione di diritto romano ad uso del clero, fonte degli Excerpta Bobiensia e della *Lex romana canonice compta*', *Archivio giuridico* 11 (1926) 20–27 (also in: *Scritti di storia giuridica altomedievale,* Pisa 1977, 271–278)

Mor, 'Droit romain' 512–524

G. Moschetti, 'Tre documenti veronesi dei secoli XI e XII e la *Lex Romana canonice compta*', *Atti e Memorie della R. Accademia di Scienze, Lettere ed Arti in Padova* 48 (1932) 1–60

Mor, 'Recezione' 281–302
Mor, 'Diritto romano e diritto canonico' 13–32
G. Santini, *Ricerche sulle 'Exceptiones Legum Romanarum'* (Milan 1969) 183ff., 189
G. Russo, *Tradizione manoscritta di Leges Romanae* (Modena 1980) 33, 63ff.
Siems, *Handel und Wucher* especially 178–179, 300–302, 318–320, 618–619 (cf. also index)

Cf. *Collectio Anselmo dedicata* (extensive extracts)

Excerpta Bobiensia

1. Author: Unknown. *2. Date:* Carolingian period. *3. Place:* Northern Italy. *4. Type:* Systematically arranged collection of Roman Law (86 texts) concerning ecclesiastical matters (for the order of materials, cf. Maassen 897–898).

5. Edition

C. G. Mor, *Bobbio, Pavia e gli 'Excerpta Bobiensia'* (Contributi per la storia dell'Università di Pavia; Pavia 1925) 45–114

6. Manuscripts

Livorno, Biblioteca Comunale, Fondo Labronica, sine num., saec. XI–XII, Northern Italy
Milano, Biblioteca Ambrosiana, A.58 sup. saec. X–XI, Northern Italy

7. Bibliography

Maassen, *Geschichte* 896–900, Conrat, *Geschichte* 210–212; Fournier-Le Bras 1.117–118, 334; A. Stickler, 'Excerpta Bobiensia', DDC 5 (1953) 608–609

F. Maassen, 'Bobienser Excerpte des römischen Rechts', *SB Vienna* 46 (1864) 236–250
A. Gaudenzi, 'Un nuovo ms. delle collezioni irlandese e pseudoisidoriana e degli estratti bobbiesi', QF 10 (1907) 370–379
E. Besta, 'Fonti e legislazione', in: P. del Giudice, *Storia del diritto italiano* 1.1 (Milan 1923) 262–271
C. G. Mor, 'Di una perduta compilazione di diritto romano ad uso del clero, fonte degli *Excerpta Bobiensia* e della *Lex romana canonice compta'*, *Archivio giuridico* 11 (1926) 20–27 (repr. *Scritti di storia giuridica altomedievale,* Pisa 1977, 271–278)
Mor, 'Droit romain' 512–524
Mor, 'Recezione' 281–302
F. Calasso, *Medioevo del diritto* 1: *Le fonti* (Milan 1954) 327
G. Santini, *Ricerche sulle 'Exceptiones Legum Romanarum'* (Milan 1969) 183–189
Siems, *Handel und Wucher* 179, 187, 301, 320

Collectio of Vercelli CLXV

1. Author: Unknown. *2. Date:* First half of the ninth century. *3. Place:* Northern Italy. *4. Type:* Chronologically arranged collection of conciliar canons and decretals. *5. Edition:* None.

6. Manuscript

Vercelli, Biblioteca Capitolare, CLXV, saec. IX2/4, Northern Italy (cf. Zechiel-Eckes, *Cresconius* 1.172–175)

7. Bibliography

Zechiel-Eckes, *Cresconius* 1.172–184

Collectio 400 capitulorum (München Clm 4592 etc.)

1. Author: Unknown. *2. Date:* Eighth century at the earliest; at the latest during the first half of the ninth century. *3. Place:* Unknown, perhaps Gaul, cf. Gaudemet. *4. Type:* Unstructured collection of materials (taken from various penitentials, *Hibernensis* and *Vetus Gallica*). *5. Edition:* None.

6. Manuscripts

Metz, Bibliothèque municipale, 236 [olim E.29], saec. VIII^{ex}/IX, probably from the Rhineland, fol. 143–206; according to Fournier-Le Bras 1.90 n. 1, this manuscript, which contained only the preface of the collection, was destroyed during World War II, cf. *Speculum* 29 (1954) 337 and Masson, *Manuscrits des Bibliothèques sinistrées* 12; very detailed description by Seckel, 'Benedictus Levita' 410–413; on the dating cf. Mordek, *Kirchenrecht und Reform* 262

München, Bayerische Staatsbibliothek, Clm 4592, saec. IX ca. 2/4, Southeastern Germany, fol. 158^{r}–207^{v}, cf. Bischoff, *Schreibschulen* 1.46

Paris, Bibliothèque nationale, lat. 2316, saec. IX ca. 2/4, [Southern] France, fol. 84^{r}–118^{v}, cf. Mordek, *Kirchenrecht und Reform* 283–285

Wien, Österreichische Nationalbibliothek, lat. 522, saec. IX2/3, Salzburg [B. Bischoff]), fol. 113^{v}–192^{v}

García y García did not repeat his suggestion made in *Traditio* 21 (1965) 512 that Cod. 22–32 of the cathedral library of Toledo contained 'un Penitencial del mismo género que la *Collectio 400 capitulorum*' in an extensive study of the manuscript published in *Traditio* 23 (1967) 504–505.

7. Bibliography

Maassen, *Geschichte* 842–846, 971–972 (without knowledge of the collections' texts of Roman law); Scherer, *Handbuch* 1.208 n. 53; Conrat, *Geschichte* 46 n. 4 and 252–253; Fournier-Le Bras 1.90; Van Hove, *Prolegomena* 289; Stickler, *Historia* 1.106; R. Naz, 'Quatre cent chapitres (Collection en)', DDC 7 (1965) 425

R. von Scherer, *Über das Eherecht bei Benedict Levita und Pseudo-Isidor* (Graz 1879) 10 n. 1
Fournier, 'Influence' 40–41
Wretschko, *Theodosiani libri XVI* 1.1, p. cccxxxii
Gaudemet, 'Survivances romaines' 169–170
Coquin, 'Sort' 203
Mordek, 'Bonneval' 342 n. 9
Mordek, *Kirchenrecht und Reform* 162–164, 301
Reynolds, 'Unity and Diversity' 110–111

Collectio 2 librorum (Paris, nouv. acq. lat. 452 etc.)

1. Author: Unknown. *2. Date:* First half of the ninth century. *3. Place:* Salzburg, cf. Reynolds, 'Salzburg' 30. *4. Type:* First book: Handbook of theological instruction (patristic texts); second book: Gallican councils. *5. Edition:* None (Reynolds is preparing a critical edition, cf. Mordek, *Kirchenrecht und Reform* 120–121, n. 87).

6. *Manuscripts*

Paris, Bibliothèque nationale, nouv. acq. lat. 452; written at Salzburg during the last years of the episcopate of Bishop Adalramnus (†836), in the opinion of B. Bischoff

Vaticano, Città del, Biblioteca Apostolica Vaticana, Reg. lat. 407, saec. IX ca. 3/4, from the region around St. Gall, according to B. Bischoff, fol. 1–54; on this manuscript see also K. F. Werner, 'Die literarischen Vorbilder des Aimon von Fleury' (see below 'Bibliography') 80–81 n. 38

Fragment

Basel, Universitätsbibliothek, N.I.6, no. 9; saec. IX med., France; cf. A. Dold, 'Alte, teilweise unbekannte Väterfragmente auf dem Doppelblatt N I 6 Nr. 9 der Universitätsbibliothek Basel', RB 63 (1953) 239–245 including an edition of the text; cf. Reynolds, 'The Pseudo-Augustinian *Sermo de conscientia*' (see below 'Bibliography'), especially 310–311, who was able to trace the pseudo-Augustinian *Sermo De conscientia* also in München Clm 6314 (saec. IX2/4 from Freising)

Excerpt

Vaticano, Città del, Biblioteca Apostolica Vaticana, Pal. lat. 973, saec. IX^{2}, Northeastern France, fol. 123^{v}–126^{v}, also including the *Sermo De conscientia* like Basel N.I.6, no. 9

7. *Bibliography*

Van Hove, *Prolegomena* 295; Stickler, *Historia* 1.116

Fournier, 'Notices' 513–526 ('La collection en deux livres')
K. Werner, 'Die literarischen Vorbilder des Aimon von Fleury', *Medium aevum vivum: Festschrift für Walther Bulst* (Heidelberg 1960) 80–81 n. 38
Mordek, 'Herovalliana' 225–226 (not a derivative text of the *Herovalliana*)
R. E. Reynolds, 'A Florilegium on the Ecclesiastical Grades in Clm 19414: Testimo-

ny to Ninth-Century Clerical Instruction', *Harvard Theological Review* 63 (1970) 235–259, 244–251
R. E. Reynolds, 'The Pseudo-Augustinian *Sermo de conscientia* and the Related Canonical *Dicta sancti Gregorii papae*', RB 81 (1971) 310–317
Mordek, *Kirchenrecht und Reform* 120–121 including n. 87
Reynolds, 'Salzburg' 28–31
R. E. Reynolds, 'An Unexpected Manuscript Fragment of the Ninth-century Canonical Collection in Two Books', BMCL 8 (1978) 35–38
Mordek, 'Systematische Sammlungen' 190

Collectio 309 capitulorum (Paris lat. 4278)

1. *Author:* Unknown. 2. *Date:* Time of the Carolingian Reform. 3. *Place:* Unknown. 4. *Type:* Small systematic collection.

5. *Edition*

Incipit-Explicit edition: Rambaud-Buhot (as below) 60–73

6. *Manuscript*

Paris, Bibliothèque nationale, lat. 4278, saec. X^{ex}–XI^{in}, fol. 128–167

7. *Bibliography*

J. Rambaud-Buhot, 'Une collection canonique de la réforme carolingienne (ms. lat. de la Bibliothèque nationale no. 4278, fol. 128–167)', RHD 34 (1956) 50–73
Ryan, 'Observations' 91–92
Mordek, 'Bonneval' 342 n. 11
Mordek, 'Aera' 221 n. 32 (the *Collectio Herovalliana* has not been used as a source for Cod. Paris lat. 4278 despite the assertion of Rambaud-Buhot to the contrary)
Mordek, 'Herovalliana' 226–227

Collectio 91 capitulorum (Vesoul 79 [73])

1. *Author:* Unknown. 2. *Date:* About 800–820. 3. *Place:* Gaul? 4. *Type:* Unstructured collection of canonical materials.

5. *Edition*

R. Pokorny (ed.), MGH Capit. episc. 3.346–353 (Chapters 1–34)

6. *Manuscript*

Vesoul, Bibliothèque municipale, 79 (73), saec. XI, France, Prov. Abbey of Faverney, fol. 44^r–53^r; cf. Mordek, *Bibliotheca capitularium* 894–898, especially 896; Pokorny (ed.), MGH Capit. episc. 3.345

7. *Bibliography*

Fournier-Le Bras 1.113, 115, 154; Van Hove, *Prolegomena* 294 n. 5

Fournier, 'Notices' 78–92
De Clercq, *Législation* 1.131, 2.161
Mordek, 'Bonneval' 342 n. 11
Brommer, 'Bischöfliche Gesetzgebung' 16, 33, 115–116
F. B. Asbach, *Das Poenitentiale Remense und der sogen. Excarpsus Cummeani* (Regensburg 1975)
Mordek, *Kirchenrecht und Reform* 133 n. 169, 191
R. Pokorny (ed.), MGH Capit. episc. 3.339–345

Cf. *Collectio* of Laon 201 and St. Petersburg Q.v.II.5

Collectio of Laon 201 and St. Petersburg Q.v.II.5

1. Author: Perhaps Bishop Thierry of Cambrai (831–863) (cf. Seckel, Finsterwalder; Mordek expresses reservations about this attribution, cf. *Kirchenrecht und Reform* 165 n. 315). *2. Date:* Probably during the second quarter, at the latest by the middle of the ninth century (Fournier-Le Bras 1.115 n. 3; Mordek, *Kirchenrecht und Reform* 165). *3. Place:* Cambrai or region. *4. Type:* Excerpts from the works of the Fathers of the Church, conciliar canons, papal decrees, penitential books, other canon law collections, didactic writings about the sacraments and liturgical formularies.

5. *Editions*

Only partial editions

Seckel, 'Synode' (as below) 18–23 (eight canons from the Synod of Aachen, 819
R. Pokorny, MGH Capit. episc. 3.1–15 (the so-called *Capitula Corbeiensia*)
R. Pokorny, MGH Capit. episc. 3.333–338 (the so-called *Capitula Cameracensia*)
R. Pokorny, MGH Capit. episc. 3.354–366 (the so-called *Statuta Bonifatii*)

6. *Manuscripts*

Laon, Bibliothèque municipale, 201, saec. IX ca. med. 'written apparently at Cambrai, in the bishopric of Thierry, 831–863' (W. M. Lindsay, *Notae Latinae: An Account of Abbreviation in Latin MSS. of the Early Minuscule Period [c.700–859] with a Supplement [Abbreviations in Latin MSS. of 850 to 1050]* by D. Bains [Cambridge 1915–1936; repr. Hildesheim 1963] 459), fol. 38^r–94^v (*capitulatio* on fol. 33^r–35^v); cf. *Catalogue général Départments* 1 (Paris 1849) 141; Werminghoff, NA 26 (1901) 16; Bishop Thierry gave the manuscript to the Abbey of Saint-Pierre (later Saint-Aubert) at Cambrai (note of dedication at the beginning of the codex), cf. Mordek, *Kirchenrecht und Reform* 164 n. 312; Mordek, *Bibliotheca capitularium* 195–200, especially 197–198

St. Petersburg, Rossiyskaya Natsional'naya Biblioteka, Q.v.II.5, saec. IX4/4, Northeastern France (perhaps Cambrai, according to B. Bischoff), fol. 5^v–38^v (*Capitulatio* on fol. 2^v–4^v). Cf. Staerk, *Manuscrits Latins* 1.193–205 including a reproduction of fol. 53^v preceeding p. 203; see also A. Halban-Blumenstok, 'Die canonistischen Handschriften der kaiserlichen öffentlichen Bibliothek in St. Petersburg', *Deutsche Zeitschrift für Kirchenrecht* 5 (1895) 226; cf. also Mordek, *Bibliotheca capitularium* 698–702

7. *Bibliography*

Fournier-Le Bras 1.115 n. 3; Van Hove, *Prolegomena* 294; Stickler, *Historia* 1.116

Staerk, *Manuscrits Latins* 1.193–205
Lindsay, *Notae Latinae* 459
E. Seckel, 'Die Aachener Synode vom Januar 819', NA 44 (1922) 11–42, especially 13–17
Fournier, 'Notices' 217–230
P. W. Finsterwalder, 'Eine parteipolitische Kundgebung eines Anhängers Lothars I.', NA 47 (1928) 412
Andrieu, *Ordines Romani* 1.349–350
Mordek, 'Bonneval' 342 n. 10
Mordek, *Kirchenrecht und Reform* 164–166
Reynolds, 'Unity and Diversity' 112

Collectio 53 titulorum

1. Author: Unknown. *2. Date:* Ninth century? *3. Place:* France. *4. Type:* Collection of canons. *5. Edition:* None.

6. *Manuscripts*

München, Bayerische Staatsbibliothek, Clm 14508, saec. IX3/4, Northeastern France, fol. 128^{v}–146^{v}; cf. Mordek, *Bibliotheca capitularium* 341
St. Gallen, Stiftsbibliothek, 679, saec. IX^{2}, Prov. St. Gall, p. 152–217
Vendôme, Bibliothèque municipale, 55, saec. XI, Prov. Sainte-Trinité, Vendôme, fol. 42rb–51vb

7. *Bibliography*

G. Le Bras, 'Un manuscrit vendômois du Quadripartitus', *Revue des sciences religieuses* 11 (1931) 266–269
J. Autenrieth and R. Kottje, *Kirchenrechtliche Texte im Bodenseegebiet: Mittelalterliche Überlieferung in Konstanz, auf der Reichenau und in St. Gallen* (Vorträge und Forschungen, Sonderband 18; Sigmaringen 1975) 36
Mordek, *Kirchenrecht und Reform* 172–174
Kottje, *Bußbücher Halitgars* 61
Kerff, *Quadripartitus* 32–34

Quadripartitus

1. Author: Unknown (cf. Kerff, *Quadripartitus* 78–81). *2. Date:* Second or third quarter of the ninth century. *3. Place:* Ecclesiastical province of Reims, probably

Reims. 4. *Type:* Penitential or *Collectio canonum?* 'Handbook of the Carolingian Reform'.

5. Editions

E. L. Richter, *Antiqua canonum collectio qua in libris de synodalibus causis compilandis usus est Regino Prumiensis* (Marburg 1844) (only Book 4)

For other partial editions cf. Kerff, *Quadripartitus* 36–37

6. Manuscripts

Antwerpen, Museum Plantin-Moretus, M 82 (66), consisting of several parts, saec. XI–XII, saec. XII^{1} and saec. XII, Northeastern France, Prov. S'Coningsdale near Ghent, fol. 52^{r}–90^{v} (only Book 4); cf. R. Kottje, 'Eine Antwerpener Handschrift des Quadripartitus l.IV', BMCL 6 (1976) 65–67 and Kerff, *Quadripartitus* 15–18

Monte Cassino, Archivio e Biblioteca dell'Abbazia, 541, saec. XI^{in}, Southern Italy (1022–1035 at Monte Cassino?), p. 236^{a}–285^{b}, only prologue, *capitulatio* and text of Book 4; cf. Kerff, *Quadripartitus* 18–20

Oxford, Bodleian Library, Bodl. 718 (2632), saec. X–XI, Exeter? Prov. Exeter, fol. 22^{r}–178^{r}; special version of the *Quadripartitus* (First Capitulary of bishop Ghaerbald of Liège, an enlarged version of the *Paenitentiale Ps.-Egberti* and the last three books of the *Quadripartitus*), cf. Kerff, *Quadripartitus* 20–24

Stuttgart, Württembergische Landesbibliothek, HB.VII.62, saec. IX^{ex}, Lake Constance region (probably Reichenau), all four books of the *Quadripartitus,* most complete manuscript; probably a copy taken from a manuscript written in the west (France or Belgium); fol. 1^{v}–176^{r}; cf. Kerff, *Quadripartitus* 24–25

Trier, Stadtbibliothek, 1084/115, saec. XI, Prov. Trier, partly from St. Eucharius-St. Matthias and from St. Paulin; fol. 103^{vab}–128rb, Books 1–3, 10; cf. Kerff, *Quadripartitus* 25–27

Vaticano, Città del, Biblioteca Apostolica Vaticana, lat. 1347, saec. IX$^{med\text{-}3/4}$, Reims, Prov. Southern Italy, probably Monte Cassino (saec. XI^{in}); fol. 144^{r}–180^{v}; prologue, *capitulatio* and text of Book 4 (beginning at chapter 5) including the epilogue of the *Quadripartitus,* cf. Kerff, *Quadripartitus* 27–30

Vaticano, Città del, Biblioteca Apostolica Vaticana, lat. 1352, saec. XI^{2}, Italy, fol. 1^{r}–84^{r}, cf. Kerff, *Quadripartitus* 30–32

Vendôme, Bibliothèque municipale, 55, saec. XI, Prov. Sainte-Trinité at Vendôme, part 2 of the manuscript, fol. 1^{vab}–41vb; this manuscript transmits a special version of the *Quadripartitus* (Books 1, 2 and 4 together with the capitulary of Bishop Ghaerbald of Liége and the *Collectio 53 titulorum*); cf. Kerff, *Quadripartitus* 32–34

Wien, Österreichische Nationalbibliothek, lat. 1286 (Theol. 387), saec. XII^{1}, Austria, by 1576 it was already in the possession of the Hofbibliothek at Vienna; fol. 1^{r}–119^{v}; cf. Kerff, *Quadripartitus* 34–35

Excerpts

Collectio II of Milano A.46 inf.
Regino of Prüm, *Libri duo de synodalibus causis*
Paris, Bibliothèque nationale, nouv. acq. lat. 352
Excerptiones Egberti

Collectio Sinemuriensis
Ivo of Chartres, *Collectio Tripartia*
Collectio of Trier, Stadtbibliothek 1098/14
London, British Library, Cotton Cleopatra C.VIII, saec. XII^{2}, Northern France, miscellaneous canonical manuscript (fol. 35–178), exerpts of the *Quadripartitus* on fol. 146^{r}–160^{v} and 165^{r-v}, cf. R. Pokorny, 'Eine Kurzform der Konzilskanones von Trosly (909): Zur Reformgesetzgebung in der ausgehenden Karolingerzeit', DA 42 (1986) 118–144, especially 124–125 including n. 30

7. *Bibliography*

Maassen, *Geschichte* 852–863; Fournier-Le Bras 1.110; Van Hove, *Prolegomena* 296; Stickler, *Historia* 113; García y García, *Historia* 1.296

G. Le Bras, 'Un manuscrit vendômois du Quadripartitus', *Revue des sciences religieuses* 11 (1931) 266–269
C. Vogel, *Les 'Libri paenitentiales'* (Typologie des sources du moyen âge occidental 27; Turnhout 1978) 80–83
Kottje, *Bußbücher Halitgars* 183–184
Kerff, *Quadripartitus*

Collectio Bonaevallensis prima (Paris lat. 3859)

1. Author: Abbot Godo of Bonneval (according to Mordek, 'Bonneval' 355–360). *2. Date:* By 816 at the earliest, middle or third quarter of the ninth century at the latest (cf. dating of Paris lat. 3859). *3. Place:* Bonneval near Chartres? *4. Type:* Systematic collection.

5. *Edition*

Partial edition by Mordek, 'Bonneval' 361–429

6. *Manuscript*

Paris, Bibliothèque nationale, lat. 3859, saec. IX$^{med-3/4}$, Gaul, fol. 1^{r}–54^{r} (including the appendices up to fol. 55^{r}), immediately followed (fol. 55^{r}–142^{v}) by the second collection of the manuscript of Bonneval; in all probability the codex Paris Lat. 3859 transmits the original version of both collections of Bonneval (according to Mordek, *Kirchenrecht und Reform* 171); on Paris lat. 3859 see also Bieler, *Irish Penitentials* 16 (B. Bischoff's assessment of the manuscript); K. A. De Meyier, *Paul en Alexandre Petau en de geschiedenis van hun handschriften (voornamelijk op grond van de Petau-handschriften in de Universiteitsbibliotheek te Leiden)* (Leiden 1947) 85; Mordek, 'Bonneval' 355–360 and *Kirchenrecht und Reform* 170–171

7. *Bibliography*

Maassen, *Geschichte* 833–836; Scherer, *Handbuch* 1.207 n. 51; Fournier-Le Bras 1.84; Kurtscheid-Wilches 1.100; Van Hove, *Prolegomena* 277–278; Stickler, *Historia* 1.104

Theiner, *Über Ivo's vermeintliches Decret* 5–7
Theiner, *Disquisitiones criticae* 145–146
Maassen, 'Bibliotheca' *SB Vienna* 54 (1866/1867) 253
Tardif, *Sources* 120
C. Capelle, 'Le voeu d'obéissance des origines au XIIe siècle: Etude juridique', *Bibliothèque d'histoire du droit et droit romain* 2 (Paris 1959) 191–192
Coquin, 'Sort' 203
P. Andrieu-Guitrancourt, *Introduction sommaire à l'étude du droit en général et du droit canonique contemporain en particulier* (Paris 1963) 633
Mordek, 'Bonneval' 339–434
Mordek, *Kirchenrecht und Reform* 167–171
Mordek, 'Systematische Kanonessammlungen' 190
Reynolds, 'Unity and Diversity' 109

Collectio Bonaevallensis secunda (Paris lat. 3859)

1. Author: Abbot Godo of Bonneval near Chartres (cf. Mordek, 'Bonneval' 355–360). *2. Date:* After 816, by the middle or in the third quarter of the ninth century at the latest. *3. Place:* Bonneval near Chartres? *4. Type:* The collection maintains the order in which its immediate sources grouped their materials (mostly canonical collections arranged chronologically). *5. Edition:* None.

6. Manuscript

Paris, Bibliothèque nationale, lat. 3859, saec. IX$^{med.-3/4}$, Gaul, fol. 55^{r}–142^{v}

7. Bibliography

Maassen, *Geschichte* 841–842

Theiner, *Über Ivo's vermeintliches Decret* 10
Theiner, *Disquisitiones criticae* 148
Maassen, 'Bibliotheca' *SB Vienna* 54, (1866–1867) 253
Mordek, 'Bonneval' 347–351
Mordek, 'Systematische Kanonessammlungen' 190

Collectio of Paris lat. 12445 and Berlin, Phill. 1741

1. Author: Unknown. *2. Date:* Ninth century. *3. Place:* Francia. *4. Type:* A mixture of constitutions from the *Codex Theodosianus* and canon law texts; important because it contains a great number of constitutions from the *Codex Theodosianus* which are not found in the *Breviarium* of Alaric; this collection is more a systematic treatise than a canonical collection (cf. Gaudemet). *5. Edition:* None.

6. Manuscripts

Berlin, Staatsbibliothek Preußischer Kulturbesitz, Phill. 1741, saec. IX$^{med-3/4}$, Reims
Paris, Bibliothèque nationale, lat. 12445 (olim Sangerm. 366), saec. IX3/4, Reims

7. *Bibliography*

Conrat, *Geschichte* 255

T. Mommsen, *Prolegomena in Theodosianum LXXXVIII Berolinensis Philippsianus 1741* lxxxviii

Wretschko, *Theodosiani libri XVI*, p. cccxxxiii

Mor, 'Droit romain' 517–519 and 522

Gaudemet, 'Survivances romaines' 168–169, 171

Collectio of Paris lat. 12021

1. Author: Unknown. *2. Date:* Ninth century. *3. Place:* Ireland? Brittany? *4. Type:* Chronologically arranged collection. Completely analyzed by Maassen, *Geschichte* 786–787 under the heading of 'Sammlung des Codex Sangermanensis 121'; cf. above *Collectio Hibernensis. 5. Edition:* None.

6. *Manuscript*

Paris, Bibliothèque nationale, lat. 12021 (olim Sangerman. 121), saec. X^{in}, written in Brittany by Arbedoc, Prov. Corbie (cf. Bieler, *Irish Penitentials* 14), fol. 33–139

7. *Bibliography*

Maassen, *Geschichte* 786–787; Stickler, *Historia* 1.106

H. Bradshaw, *The Early Collection of Canons Known as the Hibernensis: Two Unfinished Papers* (Cambridge 1893)

Fournier, 'Influence' 27–78, especially 29 and 57

Finsterwalder, *Canones Theodori* 11–13

P. Fournier, 'Le liber ex lege Moysi et les tendances bibliques du droit canonique irlandais', *Revue celtique* 30 (1909) 221–234

Bieler, *Irish Penitentials*

R. Kottje, 'Überlieferung und Rezeption der irischen Bußbücher auf dem Kontinent', *Die Iren und Europa im früheren Mittelalter*, ed. H. Löwe (Veröffentlichungen des Europa Zentrums Tübingen, Kulturwissenschaftliche Reihe; Stuttgart 1982) 1.511–524

Mordek, *Kirchenrecht und Reform* 144 n. 216 and 257

Florus of Lyon, Collectio 'De coertione Iudeorum'

1. Author: Florus of Lyon (†860). *2. Date:* Mid-ninth century. *3. Place:* Lyon. *4. Type:* Systematic collection; apparently used manuscript Berlin, Phill. 1745 (cf. Blumenkranz).

5. *Editions*

Luc d'Achery and L.-F.-J. de la Barre, *Spicilegium sive collectio veterum aliquot scriptorum qui in Galliae Bibliothecis delituerant* (Paris 1723; repr. Farnborough 1967) 1.597–599 (PL 119.419–422)

E. Caillemer, 'Florus et Moduin: Episode de l'histoire de Lyon au IXe siècle', *Mémoires de l'Académie des sciences, belles lettres et arts de Lyon, Classe des Lettres* 21 (Paris-Lyon 1885)

6. *Manuscripts*

A thus-far-untraced manuscript from Auxerre (published in d'Achery)

Milano, Biblioteca Ambrosiana, A.46 inf., saec. IX^{ex}, Northern France

Troyes, Bibliothèque municipale, 1406, saec. IX^{ex} or saec. IX–X, Burgundy (according to B. Bischoff), fol. 14^{v}–16^{v}; cf. Mordek, *Kirchenrecht und Reform* 178 n. 387

7. *Bibliography*

Maassen, *Geschichte* 874–876; Fournier-Le Bras 1.313; R. Naz, 'Lyon (Collections de)', DDC 6 (1957) 686; C. Charlier, 'Florus de Lyon', *Dictionnaire de Spiritualité* 5 (1964) 516; Rep. font. 4 (1976) 476, J. Prelog, 'Florus v. Lyon', LMA 4 (1989) 577–578

F. Maassen, 'Ein Commentar des Florus von Lyon zu einigen der sogenannten Sirmond'schen Constitutionen', SB Vienna 92 (1878) 303

Fournier, 'Groupe de recueils' 351 and 381

Le Bras, 'Notes IV' 518–524

C. G. Mor, 'Di un trattato di Floro di Lione sui privilegi de'chierici', *Mélanges Paul Fournier* (Paris 1929) 565–572 (Bibliography)

B. Blumenkranz, 'Deux compilations canoniques de Florus de Lyon et l'action antijuive d'Agobard', RHD 4e séries 33 (1955) 227–254 and 560–582, here 227ff.

Gaudemet, 'Survivances romaines' 170–171

Mordek, *Kirchenrecht und Reform* 62, 175, 178–180

Isaac of Langres, Capitula

1. Author: Isaac, Bishop of Langres (857/59–880). *2. Date:* Third quarter of the ninth century. *3. Place:* Langres. *4. Type:* A collection of diocesan statutes taken from the False Capitularies of Benedictus Levita.

5. *Editions*

J. Sirmond, *Concilia antiqua Galliae* 3 (Paris 1629) 644–677 (according to Paris lat. 2449)

E. Baluze, *Capitularia regum Francorum* 1 (Paris 1677) (Mansi 17B. 1233–1284)

PL 124.1075–1110

MGH Capit. episc. 2.161–241

6. *Manuscripts*

Albi, Bibliothèque municipale, 38, saec. X^{1}, Southern France, Prov. Albi, Cathedral, fol. 143^{v}–148^{v} (only excerpts)

Freiburg (Breisgau), Universitätsbibliothek, 1122,5 (fragment, two bifolios)

Leiden, Bibliotheek der Rijksuniversiteit, Voss. lat. oct. 29, saec. IX3/3 or IX–X,

France; old ownership notation on fol. 1^r: *Liber sancti Stephani ex parte eiusdem*, fol. 1^r–43^v

New York, The Hispanic Society of America, MS HC 380/819, saec. XI, Southeastern France or Catalonia, Prov. S. Maria/Estany (near Vich), fol. 32^{r-v} (excerpts)

Oxford, Bodleian Library, Rawlinson C.290, saec. XII^1, France; fol. 76^r and 88^r–93^v, only excerpts

Paris, Bibliothèque nationale, lat. 2449, saec. IX^{ex} (after 894–895), Lyon; fol. 1^r–35^v; it is probably identical with the manuscript Sirmond used for his work (cf. 'Editions')

Paris, Bibliothèque nationale, lat. 3841, saec. X^2, France, fol. 117^r–130^r

Paris, Bibliothèque nationale, lat. 3877, saec. IX4/4 or IX/X, Saint-Germain at Auxerre, fol. 5^r–12^v , 15^v–58^v

Paris, Bibliothèque nationale, lat. 14993, saec. XII, France, Prov. St-Victor at Paris (cf. fol. 8^r); fol. 29^v–44^v

Vaticano, Città del, Biblioteca Apostolica Vaticana, Reg. lat. 994, saec. IX4/4, Saint-Amand, Prov. Saint Remi at Reims, fol. 1^r–42^r

Wolfenbüttel, Herzog-August-Bibliothek, 212 Gud., saec. XIII, Northern France, Prov. uncertain (Thérouanne?); saec. XVI at Saint-Germain-des-Prés; fol. 56^r (excerpt); cf. *Collectio 9 librorum*

According to a library catalogue in Cod. Reims, Bibliothèque municipale, 427 (E. 331) (saec. XI; Prov. Saint-Thierry, Reims) a manuscript of Isaac's work was kept at the Lorrainese monastery Gorze, cf. G. Morin (ed.), 'Le catalogue des manuscrits de l'abbaye de Gorze au XIe siècle', RB 22 (1905) 6, perhaps identical with Leiden Voss. lat. oct. 29; cf. Mordek, *Kirchenrecht und Reform* 176 n. 374

There is also evidence for the existence of an Isaac-codex in Spain (Brommer), San Juan de las Abadesas, Archivo 1, which cannot be found there (Mordek, *Kirchenrecht und Reform* 176 n. 374)

7. *Bibliography*

HLF 5 (1866) 528–530; Scherer, *Handbuch* 1.229 n. 6; Seckel, 'Pseudoisidor', RE ^{3}16 (1905) 303; Fournier-Le Bras 1.206; Van Hove, *Prolegomena* 185; P. Viard, 'Isaac, évêque de Langres', *Catholicisme* 6 (1967) 120–121; Stickler, 'Isaak der Gute', LThK 5 (1960) 774; N. Brieskorn, 'Isaak von Langres', LMA 5.3 (1990) 667

A. Werminghoff, 'Verzeichnis der Akten fränkischer Synoden von 843–918', NA 26 (1901) 607–678, especially 670

E. Seckel, 'Studien zu Benedictus Levita I IV', NA 29 (1904) 325–326, 328

Wretschko, *Theodosiani libri XVI*, p. cccxlii

Seckel, 'Benedictus Levita' 394, 419

B. Jacqueline, 'Une collection canonique inédite', *Ephemerides iuris canonici* 8 (1952) 207–212

Gaudemet, 'Survivances romaines' 172

De Clercq, *Législation* 2.372–375

H. Löwe, 'Die Karolinger vom Vertrag von Verdun bis zum Herrschaftsantritt der Herrscher aus dem sächsischen Hause: Das westfränkische Reich', in: W. Wattenbach and W. Levison, *Deutschlands Geschichtsquellen im Mittelalter, Vorzeit und Karolinger* 5 (Weimar 1973) 629 n. 566

Mordek, *Kirchenrecht und Reform* 126 n. 114; 175 n. 368, 176 n. 374
G. Schmitz, 'Das Konzil von Trosly (909): DA 33 (1977) 341–434, especially 366–367
H. Mordek and G. Schmitz, 'Papst Johannes VIII. und das Konzil von Troyes (878)', *Geschichtsschreibung und geistiges Leben im Mittelalter: Festschrift für Heinz Löwe zum 65. Geburtstag,* ed. K. Hauck and H. Mordek (Cologne-Vienna 1978) 179–225
Mordek, 'Isaak der Gute' 203–210

The 'Additiones' to the Capitula of Isaac of Langres

1. Author: Unknown. *2. Date:* During the last two decades of the ninth century (all codices contain the collection of Bishop Isaac of Langres, 859–880). *3. Place:* Gaul, presumably Langres. *4. Type:* Small systematic collection of excerpts: I. Twelve chapters from the Pseudo-Isidorian Decretals, 'De iniuria videlicet et honore episcoporum'. II. Six conciliar canons concerning monasteries. III. Thirteen chapters 'De Iudaeis'. IV. Four canons treating ecclesiastical property, 'De rebus ecclesiae'. V. 26 canons 'De modis accusatorum et accusationum'. VI. Thirteen more chapters taken from Pseudo-Isidore. *5. Edition:* None.

6. *Manuscripts*

Leiden, Bibliothek der Rijksuniversiteit, Voss. lat. oct. 29, saec. IX3/3, France; old ownership notation on fol. 1^{r}: 'Liber sancti Stephani ex parte eiusdem'
Paris, Bibliothèque nationale, lat. 2449, saec. IX^{ex} (after 894–895), Lyon; fol. 36^{v}–63^{r}. It is probably identical with the manuscript Sirmond used for his work (cf. 'Editions')
Paris, Bibliothèque nationale, lat. 3841, saec. X^{2}, France, fol. 130^{r}–135^{r}, fol. 136^{v}–137^{v}
Paris, Bibliothèque nationale, lat. 3877, saec. IX4/4 or IX/X, Saint-Germain at Auxerre, fol. 58^{v}–83^{v}
Vaticano, Città del, Biblioteca Apostolica Vaticana, Reg. lat. 994, saec. IX4/4, Saint-Amand, Prov. Saint Remi at Reims, fol. 42^{r}–63^{r}

Cf. MGH Capit. episc. 2.169–174

Reception
Berlin, Staatsbibliothek Preußischer Kulturbesitz, Phill. 1765 (cf. index)
Milano, Biblioteca Ambrosiana, A.46.inf.

7. *Bibliography*

Fournier-Le Bras 1.217; R. Naz, 'Lyon (collections de)', DDC 6 (1957) 685–686

Fournier, 'Groupe de recueils' 357–366
A. Werminghoff, 'Verzeichnis der Akten fränkischer Synoden von 843–918', NA 26 (1901) 670 (lists all the manuscripts but without giving any further information about their provenance and with inaccurate dates)
Wretschko, *Theodosiani libri XVI*, p. cccxlii

Gaudemet, 'Survivances romaines' 172–173

De Clercq, *Législation* 2.372

Mordek, 'Herovalliana' 220–243, especially 228–229. (In this article, Mordek discusses the collections in 19 and 22 chapters as one single collection; he calls it the *Collectio 29 capitulorum.)* In *Kirchenrecht und Reform* he uses the distinction between the *Collectio 19 capitulorum* and the *Collectio 22 capitulorum*

Mordek, *Kirchenrecht und Reform* 126–127 and 175–180 (as 'Collectio 19 capitulorum' and 'Collectio 22 capitulorum')

Mordek, 'Isaak der Gute' 203–210

Landau, 'Gefälschtes Recht' 27 including n. 64. (Five conciliar canons are forgeries. They can be traced for the first time in this collection.)

Hincmar of Laon, Pittaciolus

1. Author: Bishop Hincmar of Laon (858–871, d. 879), nephew of Archbishop Hincmar of Reims (845–882). *2. Date:* 869. *3. Place:* Laon. *4. Type:* Small collection of excerpts taken from the Pseudo-Isidorian Decretals, the *Capitula Angilramni* and authentic decretals. The collection was compiled for the defense of the Bishop of Laon against his uncle, the Archbishop Hincmar of Reims.

5. Editions

J. Sirmond, *Hincmari Opera 2* (Paris 1645) 355–376 (preferable to the edition of PL 124.993–1026, cf. Fuhrmann, DA 27 [1971], 517–524); following Paris B.N. lat. 5095 (cf. Fuhrmann 520–524)

R. Schieffer, ed., *Die Streitschriften Hinkmars von Reims und Hinkmars von Laon 869–871* (MGH Concilia 4 Suppl. 2; Hannover 1998) 57–97

6. Manuscripts

Metz, Bibliothèque municipale, 351, saec. IX^{ex} (before 882?), Prov. St. Arnulph at Metz, fol. 78^{v}–101^{r}

Paris, Bibliothèque nationale, lat. 5095, saec. IX^{ex} (written before 895), Prov. Laon, fol. 60^{v}–78^{r}

Salzburg, Bibliothek der Erzabtei St. Peter, a.IX.32, saec. XI^{1}, Salzburg, fol. 168^{v}–198^{v}

7. Bibliography

Fournier-Le Bras 1.215–216; R. Naz, DDC 6 (1957) 1508; R. Große, 'Hinkmar, Bischof von Laon', LMA 5 (1991) 29

H. Schrors, *Hinkmar, Erzbischof von Reims: Sein Leben und seine Schriften* (Freiburg 1884, repr. Hildesheim 1967) 315–353

E. Lesne, *La hiérarchie épiscopale: Provinces, métropolitaines, primats en Gaule et Germanie depuis la réforme de Saint Boniface jusqu'à la mort d'Hincmar, 742–882* (Lille - Paris 1902) especially 212ff.

Manitius, *Literatur* 1.347, 352, 354

M. W. Speyer, 'Über Hincmar's von Laon Auslese aus Pseudo-Isidor, Ingelramn und aus Schreiben des Pabstes Nicolaus I.', *Nachrichten der Wissenschaften zu Göttingen, Philol.-hist. Klasse* (1912) 219–227

H. Fuhrmann, 'Zur Überlieferung des Pittaciolus Bischof Hinkmars von Laon (869)', DA 27 (1971) 517–524

Fuhrmann, *Einfluß und Verbreitung* 1.219–224 and 3.625–756

J. Devisse, *Hincmar, archevêque de Reims 845–882,* 2 (Geneva 1976) 728–785

P. R. McKeon, *Hincmar of Laon and Carolingian Politics* (Chicago-London 1978)

H. Fuhrmann, 'Fälscher unter sich: Zum Streit zwischen Hinkmar von Reims und Hinkmar von Laon', *Charles the Bald: Court and Kingdom,* ed. M. Gibson and J. Nelson (Oxford 1981) 237–254

W. Hartmann, *Die Synoden der Karolingerzeit im Frankenreich und in Italien* (Paderborn 1989) 321–327

R. Schieffer, 'Der Pittaciolus Hinkmars von Laon in einer Salzburger Handschrift aus Köln, *Festschrift Kottje* (1992) 137–147

Collectio 72 capitulorum (Roma, Vallicelliana T.XVIII)

1. Author: Unknown. *2. Date:* Tenth century (Naz: ca. 930). *3. Place:* Rome? *4. Type:* Systematic collection. Mixture of texts; a first part contains excerpts from the *Collectio Herovalliana,* taken from the *Herovalliana excerpta* in Bamberg, Staatsbibliothek, Patr. 101 (saec. IX, Rome), cf. Mordek, *Kirchenrecht und Reform* 135.

5. Edition

Only printed version of the Capitulatio in Ballerini, *De antiquis . . . collectionibus et collectoribus* P. IV, cap. VII, § 3 (PL 56.308–309)

6. Manuscripts

Roma, Biblioteca Vallicelliana, T.XVIII, about saec. X^{ex} (on the dating, cf. Loew-Brown, *Beneventan Script* 131), fol. 49^{r}–58^{v}, for an extensive description of the manuscript cf. A. M. Giorgetti and S. Mottironi, *Catalogo dei manoscritti della Biblioteca Vallicelliana* 1 (Indice e cataloghi, New Series 7; Rome 1961) 243–252, reproduction of fol. 50^{r} in ZKG 81 (1970) after 236; cf. below *Collectio 44 capitulorum*

Excerpt

Roma, Biblioteca Casanatense, 2010, saec. XI, from Farfa or Rome perhaps

7. Bibliography

Maassen, *Geschichte* 869–870; Fournier-Le Bras 1.114–115; Van Hove, *Prolegomena* 294; R. Naz 'Soixante-douze chapitres (Collection en)', DDC 7 (1962) 1067; R. Naz, 'Vallicelliane (Manuscrits de la bibliothèque)', DDC 7 (1965) 1400–1401

Ballerini, *De antiquis . . . collectionibus et collectoribus* P. IV, cap. VII, § 3 (PL 56.308–309)

F. Patetta, 'Contributi alla storia del diritto romano nel Medio Evo', BIDR 3 (1890) 273–294
Fournier, 'Recueils canoniques italiens' 98
Mor, 'Diritto romano e diritto canonico' 28–29
H. Fuhrmann, 'Eine im Original erhaltene Propagandaschrift des Erzbischofs Gunthar von Köln (865)', AfD 4 (1958) 30–32
G. P. Pozzi, 'Le manuscrit tomus XVIIIus de la Vallicelliana e le libelle *De episcoporum transmigratione et quod non temere iudicentur regule quadraginta quattuor*', *Apollinaris* 31 (1958) 313–350, especially 315
J. Kunsemüller, *Die Chronik Benedikts von S. Andrea* (Phil. Diss. Erlangen 1961) 7 n. 23 and 72 n. 69
S. Lindemans, 'Auxilius et le manuscrit Vallicellian Tomus XVIII', RHE 57 (1962) 470–484
Mor, 'La Bibbia e il diritto canonico' 177–179
W. Wattenbach and W. Levison, *Deutschlands Geschichtsquellen im Mittelalter, Vorzeit und Karolinger*, Section 4, by H. Löwe (Weimar 1963) 447
Fuhrmann, 'Pseudoisidor in Rom' 17 n. 3, 32–33 n. 41
Mordek, 'Herovalliana' 235–236
Mordek, *Kirchenrecht und Reform* 135–136

Cf. below, *Collectio 44 capitulorum*

Collectio 44 capitulorum 'De Episcoporum transmigratione' (Roma, Vallicelliana T.XVIII)

1. *Author:* Perhaps Anastasius Bibliothecarius (†879) (cf. Pozzi, Lindemans), later used by Auxilius in the tenth century to defend ordinations made by Pope Formosus. 2. *Date:* About 870 (cf. Pozzi, Lindemans). 3. *Place:* Southern Italy (Naples, Benevento). 4. *Type:* A collection of canonical texts apparently related to the Formosan controversy of the early tenth century; series of excerpts from Pseudo-Isidore.

5. *Edition*

J. P. Pozzi, 'Le manuscrit Tomus XVIII de la Vallicelliana et le libelle *De episcoporum transmigratione et quod non temere judicentur regule quadraginta quattuor*', *Apollinaris* 31 (1958) 313–350

6. *Manuscripts*

Roma, Biblioteca Vallicelliana, T.XVIII, about saec. X^{ex} (on the dating of this codex, cf. Loew-Brown, *Beneventan Script* 131); fol. 143^{r}–149^{v}; for an extensive description of the manuscript cf. A. M. Giorgetti and S. Mottironi, *Catalogo dei manoscritti della Biblioteca Vallicelliana* 1 (Indice e cataloghi, new Ser. 7, Rome 1961) 243–252; cf. also Mordek, 'Herovalliana' 235 n. 82 and the *Collectio 72 capitulorum*
Roma, Biblioteca Casanatense, 2010, saec. XI, perhaps from Farfa or Rome (in an abridged form)

7. *Bibliography*

Fournier-Le Bras 1.270, 339–340; Van Hove, *Prolegomena* 315

Fournier, 'Influence' 59–60

F. Patetta, 'Contributi alla storia del diritto romano nel medio evo', BIDR 3 (1890) 273–294

Dobschütz, *Decretum Gelasianum* 164

Fournier, 'Recueils canoniques italiens' 96–123

Pozzi (cf. above 'Edition')

S. Lindemans, 'Auxilius et le manuscrit Vallicellian Tomus XVIII', RHE 57 (1962) 470–484

Mordek, 'Herovalliana' 235–236 n. 82

R. E. Reynolds, 'The *De officiis VII graduum:* Its Origins and Early Medieval Development', MS 34 (1972) 130 n. 71 (bibliographical references)

Reynolds, 'Excerpta' 1–9

Reynolds, 'Unity and Diversity' 134

Zechiel-Eckes, *Cresconius* 1.128–129, 248–249, 264 (cf. also index)

Cf. above *Collectio 72 capitulorum*

The Collections of Milano A.46 inf.

1. Author: Unknown. *2. Date:* Second half of the ninth century. *3. Place:* Northern France, region around Reims. *4. Type:* Four systematic collections of excerpt series: I. *Collectio duorum librorum I* (excerpts taken from *Cresconius, Collectiones Dacheriana* and *Herovalliana, Ansegis, Benedictus Levita,* the Pseudo-Isidorian Decretals etc.). II. *Collectio duorum librorum II,* (excerpts [penitential texts] taken from Augustine (*Enchiridion ad Laurentium*), the *Collectio Dacheriana* and the *Quadripartitus;* cf. Kerff 70. III: Excerpts taken from capitulary texts (*Ansegis* etc.) and councils; this is a collection in 142 chapters according to information in the text, cf. Mordek, *Bibliotheca capitularium* 235–240 and MGH Capit. n.s. 1.177–182. IV: Excerpts taken from the *Epitome Aegidii* (cf. Conrat, *Geschichte* 226–228). *5. Edition:* None.

6. *Manuscript*

Milano, Biblioteca Ambrosiana, A.46 inf., saec. IX^{ex}, Reims or the region, Prov. Benedictine Monastery of S. Dionigi at Milan (according to B. Bischoff, quoted in W. A. Eckhardt, 'Die Decretio Childeberti und ihre Überlieferung', ZRG Germ. Abt. 84 [1967] 15, part of this codex was written during the last quarter of the ninth century and part at the end of the ninth or the beginning of the tenth century, either at Reims or in the surrounding region); Catalogue reference: A. Amelli, 'Indice de codici manoscritti della Biblioteca Ambrosiana', *Rivista delle Biblioteche e degli Archivi* 20 (1909) 144; T. Mommsen, *Chronica minora*, MGH AA IX.566 no. 39; cf. Mordek, *Kirchenrecht und Reform* 130 n. 144; Mordek, *Bibliotheca capitularium* 233–240 (*Collectio I:* fol. 15^{v}–85^{v}; *Collectio II:* fol. 86^{r}–130^{v}; *Collectio III:* fol. 131^{r}–151^{r}; *Collectio IV:* fol. 152^{r}–156^{r})

7. *Bibliography*

Conrat, *Geschichte* 44, 226–228, 253–254, 256–257; Fournier-Le Bras 1.205, 217, 330–334; Van Hove, *Prolegomena* 315

F. Maassen, 'Ein Commentar des Florus von Lyon zu einigen der sogenannten Sirmond'schen Constitutionen', SB Vienna 92 (1878) 303

M. Conrat (Cohn), 'Kurze Notiz zur Hs. A.46 inf. der Ambrosiana', ZRG Germ. Abt. 9 (1888) 219

F. Patetta, 'Contributi alla storia del diritto romano nel medio evo', BIDR 3 (1890) 273–294

Fournier, 'Groupe de recueils' 373–402, especially 391

Wretschko, *Theodosiani libri XVI,* p. ccclvi

Seckel, 'Benedictus Levita' 414–417

B. Blumenkranz, 'Deux compilations canoniques de Florus de Lyon et l'action antijuive d'Agobard', RHD 4e sér. 33 (1955) 227–254 and 560–582

Mordek, 'Herovalliana' 241

Williams, *Codices Pseudo-Isidoriani* 89

Fuhrmann, *Einfluß und Verbreitung* 2.417–418, 3.693–696 (see also index of manuscripts)

Mordek, *Kirchenrecht und Reform* 130–131

John, *Collectio canonum Remedio . . . ascripta* 5, 7, 103–106, 117

R. E. Reynolds, 'An Unexpected Manuscript Fragment of the Ninth Century Canonical Collection in Two Books' BMCL 8 (1978) 35–38

Kerff, *Quadripartitus* 70–71, 103–114

MGH Conc. 3.261

Zechiel-Eckes, *Cresconius* 242–245

K. Zechiel-Eckes, 'Eine Mailänder Redaktion der Kirchenrechtssammlung Bischof Anselms II. von Lucca (1073–1086)', ZRG Kan. Abt. 81 (1995) 130–147 (fons formalis of Anselm Y)

MGH Capit. n.s. 1.177–182

Collectio of Troyes 1406

1. Author: Unknown. *2. Date:* Probably end of the ninth century. *3. Place:* Unknown. *4. Type:* Collection containing series of excerpts, mainly Pseudo-Isidorian excerpts; fragmentary at the end. *5. Edition:* None.

6. *Manuscript*

Troyes, Bibliothèque municipale, 1406, saec. IX[ex], perhaps Burgundy, Prov. Dijon, fol. 22[v]–55[v]

7. *Bibliography*

Fournier-Le Bras 1.312–316; Van Hove, *Prolegomena* 317

Fournier, 'Groupe de recueils' 345–356

Fuhrmann, *Einfluß und Verbreitung* 3.640–644, 681–685

Mordek, *Kirchenrecht und Reform* 178–180
John, *Collectio canonum* Remedio . . . *ascripta* 114
R. Pokorny, 'Ein unerkanntes Brieffragment Argrims von Lyon-Langres aus den Jahren 894/95 und zwei umstrittene Bischofsweihen in der Kirchenprovinz Lyon', *Francia* 13 (1985) 602–622, especially 602–603

The Argrim Dossier (Paris lat. 2449 etc.)

1. Author: Unknown. *2. Date:* Beginning of the tenth century. *3. Place:* Burgundy, probably Lyon. *4. Type:* Compilation of canonical texts concerning the installation of bishops. *5. Edition:* None.

6. Manuscripts

Cf. Pokorny, 'Brieffragment Argrims' (as below)

Albi, Bibliothèque municipale, 41, saec. X, Burgundy, fol. 1^r–16^v
Paris, Bibliothèque nationale, lat. 2449, saec. IX^{ex}, Burgundy, fol. 48^v–54^v
Troyes, Bibliothèque municipale, 1064, saec. IX^{ex}, Burgundy (dating according to B. Bischoff, cf. R. Pokorny, 'Eine bischöfliche Promissio aus Belley und die Datierung des Vereinigungs-Vertrages von Hoch- und Niederburgund (933?)', DA 43 (1987) 46–61, especially 55 n. 34); fol. 4ra–12rb
Troyes, Bibliothèque municipale, 1406, saec. X, Burgundy, fol. 1^r–11^r

7. Bibliography

Fournier-Le Bras 1.217 and 312–315; Van Hove, *Prolegomena* 317

Fournier, 'Groupe de recueils' 345–373
Seckel, 'Benedictus Levita' 400 n. 6
Gaudemet, 'Survivances romaines' 172–173
R. Reynolds, 'A Ninth-Century Treatise on the Origins, Office and Ordination of the Bishop', RB 85 (1975) 321–332
G. Schmitz, 'Das Konzil von Trosly (909): Überlieferung und Quellen', DA 33 (1977) 360–390, especially 362–367
R. Pokorny, 'Ein unerkanntes Brieffragment Argrims von Lyon-Langres aus den Jahren 894/95 und zwei umstrittene Bischofsweihen in der Kirchenprovinz Lyon', *Francia* 13 (1985) 602–622, especially 602–603 (for the mss.)

Cf. also Isaac of Langres, *Capitula,* and the *Additiones* to the *Capitula* of Isaac of Langres

Collectio 342 capitulorum (Montpellier H.137 etc.)

1. Author: Unknown. *2. Date:* Between the second half of the ninth century and the second half of the eleventh century. *3. Place:* Probably France (cf. Mordek, 'Kanonistik und gregorianische Reform' 75). *4. Type:* Series of excerpts of the *Collectio Hispana systematica. 5. Edition:* None.

6. *Manuscripts*

Montpellier, Bibliothèque Interuniversitaire, H.137, saec. XI^2, France, beginning fol. 272, MGH Capit. 2, p. xx; Seckel, 'Benedictus Levita' 420–421
Palermo, Archivio della Cattedrale, 14, saec. XII, France, beginning at fol. 118; cf. Besta, 'Di una collezione canonistica palermitana', *Il Circolo Giuridico* 40 (1909) 8–21; Fournier-Le Bras 2.150–151 (cited as manuscript Palermo, Biblioteca Comunale, 2.Qq.E.17)
Paris, Bibliothèque nationale, lat. 3839A, saec. XI^2, Prov. Saint-Aubin at Angers, fol. 110^r–134^r, cf. J. Vezin, 'Les "scriptoria" d'Angers au XIe siècle', *Positions des thèses de l'Ecole nationale des chartes* (Paris 1958) 134; Williams, *Codices Pseudo-Isidoriani* 85 (contains further bibliographical references on Paris 3839A)

Cf. the manuscripts of the *Abbreviatio Ansegisi et Benedicti Levitae,* above

Cf. the manuscripts of the *Collectio 114 capitulorum,* below

7. *Bibliography*

Fournier-Le Bras 1.311–312 and 2.150–51; Van Hove, *Prolegomena* 317

Schulte, 'Iter Gallicum' 407–413
Fournier, 'Manuscrit de Montpellier' 357–389
E. Besta, 'Di una collezione canonistica palermitana', *Il Circolo Giuridico* 40 (1909) 8–21
Seckel, 'Benedictus Levita' 420–421
J. Vezin, 'Les "scriptoria" d'Angers au XIe siècle', *Positions des thèses de l'Ecole nationale des chartes* (Paris 1958)
Rambaud-Buhot, 'Corpus inédit' 271–281
Mordek, *Kirchenrecht und Reform* 180–182
Mordek, 'Kanonistik und gregorianische Reform' 75

Collectio 114 capitulorum (Montpellier H.137 etc.)

1. Author: Unknown. *2. Date:* Between the end of the ninth century and before the beginning of the eleventh century (Van Hove). *3. Place:* Gaul. *4. Type:* Chronologically arranged collection of conciliar canons and decretals; most of the texts are taken from the *Collectio Hispana*. *5. Edition:* None.

6. *Manuscripts*

Montpellier, Bibliothèque Interuniversitaire, H.137, saec. XI^2, France, fol. 307^r–314^r
Palermo, Archivio della Cattedrale, 14, saec. XII, France (cited as Palermo, Biblioteca Comunale, 2.Qq.E.17)
Paris, Bibliothèque nationale, lat. 3839A, saec. XI^2, Prov. St-Aubin, Angers

Cf. the manuscripts of the *Collectio 342 capitulorum,* above

Cf. the manuscripts of the *Abbreviatio Ansegisi et Benedicti Levitae,* above

7. *Bibliography*

Fournier-Le Bras 1.311–312; Van Hove, *Prolegomena* 317

Fournier, 'Manuscrit de Montpellier' 357–389
E. Besta, 'Di una collezione canonistica palermitana', *Il Circolo Giuridico* 40 (1909) 8–21
Seckel, 'Benedictus Levita' 420–421
J. Vezin, 'Les "scriptoria" d'Angers au XIe siècle', *Positions des thèses de l'Ecole nationale des chartes* (Paris 1958)
Rambaud-Buhot, 'Corpus inédit' 271–281
Mordek, *Kirchenrecht und Reform* 118 n. 398

The Lorrainese Collection of Canonical Materials (München Clm 3851) and Their 'Additiones' ('Compilation of Worms')

1. Author: Unknown. *2. Date:* Ninth to tenth century. *3. Place:* Lorraine. *4. Type:* Collection of materials. *5. Edition:* None.

6. *Manuscripts*

München, Bayerische Staatsbibliothek, Clm 3851, saec. IX^{ex}, Eastern France, Lorraine

'Southern German' Recension
Changing the order of texts at the beginning; numerous *'Additiones'*

Dresden, Sächsische Landesbibliothek, A 157, saec. XVIII, German, cf. Hartmann, *Worms* 14–20 and MGH Capit. episc. 2.27 and 121–122, 2.159–160
Heiligenkreuz, Stiftsbibliothek, 217, saec. X^{ex}, Southeastern Germany, Prov. Bohemia-Moravia; cf. Mordek, *Bibliotheca capitularium* 158–172; MGH Capit. n.s. 1.1.93–96
München, Bayerische Staatsbibliothek, Clm 3853, saec. X^{ex}, Southern Germany, Prov. Cathedral Library of Augsburg; cf. V. Krause, 'Die Münchener Handschriften 3851.3853 mit einer Compilation von 181 Wormser Beschlüssen', NA 19 (1894) 85–139, especially 96–117; Mordek, *Bibliotheca capitularium* 287–305; MGH Capit. n.s. 1.102–104
Paris, Bibliothèque nationale, lat. 3878, saec. X^{ex}, Southern Germany, Prov. Bressanone(?) (according to H. Hoffmann), cf. Mordek, *Bibliotheca capitularium* 444–451 (one of the missing double leaves of this codex found by H. Hoffmann: Weimar, Hauptstaatsarchiv, Depos. Hardenberg Fragm. 9); MGH Capit. n.s. 1.113–115

7. *Bibliography*

Fournier-Le Bras 1.276–283 (l. 26: '287' has to be corrected to '217'); Van Hove, *Prolegomena* 319

V. Krause, 'Die Münchener Handschriften 3851.3853 mit einer Compilation von 181 Wormser Beschlüssen', NA 19 (1894) 85–139

Mordek, *Kirchenrecht und Reform* 121 n. 91; 129
Hartmann, *Worms* 13–21
Kottje, *Bußbücher Halitgars* passim
Müller, *Collectio Duodecim Partium* 277–284
R. Haggenmüller, *Die Überlieferung der Beda und Egbert zugeschriebenen Bußbücher* (Frankfurt 1991) 74–78
S. Hansen, *Die Rechtscorpora in den Handschriften Clm 3853, Heiligenkreuz 217 und Paris lat. 3878* (Master's Thesis, Tübingen 1992)
J. Müller, 'Collectio duodecim partium und Decretum Burchardi' *Proceedings San Diego* 70 n. 32

Cf. *Collectio duodecim partium*

Collectio 77 capitulorum (München Clm 3853 etc.)

1. Author: Unknown. *2. Date:* Tenth century (after 922, because c. 9 of the Council of Koblenz is cited). *3. Place:* Southern Germany. *4. Type:* Additions of series of excerpts taken from different canonical collections and penitentials, mainly from the *Epitome Hispana* and the *Collectio Dacheriana*. The first addition to 'Southern-German Recension' of the Lorrainese Collection. *5. Edition:* None.

6. Manuscripts

Heiligenkreuz, Stiftsbibliothek, 217, saec. X^{ex}, Southeastern Germany, Prov. Bohemia-Moravia, fol. 152^{v}–182^{v}; cf. Mordek, *Bibliotheca capitularium* 158–172; MGH Capit. n.s. 1.1.93–96

München, Bayerische Staatsbibliothek, Clm 3853, saec. X^{ex}, Southern Germany (Augsburg?), Prov. Cathedral Library of Augsburg, fol. 129^{r}–157^{r}, cf. V. Krause, 'Die Münchener Handschriften 3851.3853 mit einer Compilation von 181 Wormser Beschlüssen', NA 19 (1894) 85–139, especially 96–117; Mordek, *Bibliotheca capitularium* 287–305; MGH Capit. n.s. 1.102–104

Fragment

Paris, Bibliothèque nationale, lat. 3878 (and Weimar, Hauptstaatsarchiv, Depositum Hardenberg Fragm. 9), saec. X^{ex}, Southern Germany, Prov. Bressanone(?) (according to H. Hoffmann), fol. 80^{r}–89^{v}, 162^{r}–163^{r}, 90^{r}–92^{v}, 164^{r}–165^{v}, 93^{r}–95^{v}, 166^{r-v}

7. Bibliography

Fournier-Le Bras 1.277–280; Van Hove, *Prolegomena* 319; Naz, DDC 7 (1965), 1066–1067

Martínez-Díez, 'El Epítome Hispánico' 22–35
Kottje, *Bußbücher Halitgars* 25–28, 38–39 and 53–54
S. Hansen, *Die Rechtscorpora in den Handschriften Clm 3853, Heiligenkreuz 217 und Paris lat. 3878* (Master's Thesis, Tübingen 1992)
Mordek, *Bibliotheca capitularium* 158–172, 287–304, 444–451

(Pseudo-)Remedius of Chur, Collectio canonum

1. Author: Unknown. *2. Date:* Compiled during fourth quarter of the ninth century shortly after 880 and, at the latest, shortly before the Synod of Tribur (895). *3. Place:* Probably St. Gall or Reichenau. *4. Type:* Collection of excerpts from Pseudo-Isidorian material.

5. Editions

M. Goldast, *Rerum Alemannicarum Scriptores aliquot vetusti* (Frankfurt 1606, ²1661) 2.2, 119, 121–133 (according to St. Gallen 614)

J. Hartzheim, *Concilia Germaniae* 2 (Cologne 1760) 414–426 (PL 102.1093–1112)

F. Kunstmann, *Die Canonensammlung des Bischofs Remedius von Chur, aus den Handschriften der königlichen Bibliothek zu München zum erstenmale vollständig herausgegeben und kritisch erläutert* (Tübingen 1836)

John, *Collectio canonum Remedio . . . ascripta*

6. Manuscripts

For bibliographical references concerning the mss. cf. John 29–60

Freising Group of Manuscripts

Bamberg, Staatsbibliothek, Can. 9 (olim P.I.9, olim Dombibliothek C 64); saec. XI^{in}, Southern Germany, Prov. cathedral library at Bamberg, fol. $128–169^{v}$

München, Bayerische Staatsbibliothek, Clm 6241 (Fris. 41), saec. X2/2, Prov. cathedral library at Freising (olim B.F.1), a work from the scriptorium at Freising, fol. 106^{v}–141, closely related to München Clm 6245 (source for Clm 6241);

München, Bayerische Staatsbibliothek, Clm 6245 (Fris. 45), saec. IX3/4, probably from the scriptorium at Freising during the episcopate of Bishop Anno (854–875); Prov. cathedral library of Freising (olim B.K.1), codex made up of five originally independent parts of varying age, bound together during the tenth century, Pseudo-Remedius: fol. $79–124^{r}$, cf. H. Schneider, 'Eine Freisinger Synodalpredigt aus der Zeit der Ungarneinfälle (Clm 6245)', *Festschrift Fuhrmann* (1991) 96 n. 5–7

Wien, Österreichische Nationalbibliothek, lat. 2198 (olim iur. can. 99), saec. $X^{1\text{-}med}$; fol. 1–43

Other Provenance

Berlin, Staatsbibliothek Preußischer Kulturbesitz, Phill. 1764; codex consisting of three originally separate manuscripts, saec. X^{ex}, written mostly at Soissons, fol. $48–53^{v}$ and fol. 62–82

Köln, Erzbischöfliche Diözesan- und Dombibliothek, 118 (olim Darmstadt 2117), saec. IX^{ex}, Reims or surrounding area, pp. 2–33, only the second half of the collection of Pseudo-Remedius (from c. 40.15 onward) is preserved; for a discussion of B. Bischoff's opinion on the date and place of origin of this manuscript, cf. Kottje, *Bußbücher Halitgars* 29–30

St. Gallen, Stiftsbibliothek, 614, ca. 900; written in a hand characteristic of St. Gall; codex whose binding dates back to the thirteenth century (eight different parts of varying age, some of them used to be independent); the collection of Pseudo-Remedius is in Part 5, pp. 135–182; it is the text of this manuscript which was published by Goldast for the first time (this part of the codex used to be an independent manuscript)

St. Gallen, Stiftsbibliothek, 1398 a II, p. 1–12 (olim 343–354), saec. IX[ex], cf. Hoffmann-Pokorny 76 n. 39

Wolfenbüttel, Herzog August Bibliothek, Helmst. 454, written ca. 1000, Saxony (H. Hoffmann), fol. 22[v]–63 (particular form, cf. Fournier-Le Bras 1.301); cf. below *Collectio 233 capitulorum*

7. *Bibliography*

Fournier-Le Bras 1.212; Kurtscheid-Wilches 1.143; R. Naz, 'Remedius de Coire', DDC 7 (1965) 577–578

F. Knust, 'Über die Kanonensammlung des Bischofs Remedius von Chur', *Theologische Studien und Kritiken* 9 (1836) 161–170

F. Kunstmann, 'Über die Canonen Sammlung des Remedius von Chur', *Theologische Quartalschrift* 18 (1836) 57–119

H. Wasserschleben, 'Ueber die dem Remedius zugeschriebene Canonensammlung', *Kritische Jahrbücher* 3 (1838) 485–487

K. Zeumer, 'Zu den vermeintlichen Canones Remedii', ZKR 21 (1886) 40

Fournier, 'Groupe de recueils' 375

J. G. Mayer, *Geschichte des Bistums Chur* 1 (1906)

H. Fuhrmann, 'Die sogenannte Kanonessammlung des Remedius von Chur', DA 18 (1962) 231–235

Mordek, 'Herovalliana' 240 n. 97

Fuhrmann, *Einfluß und Verbreitung* 2.415–419

Kerner et al., 'Textidentifikation' 33, 40

The Freising Collection of Canonical Materials

(München Clm 6245 etc.)

1. *Author:* Unknown. 2. *Date:* Second half of the tenth century. 3. *Place:* Freising. 4. *Type:* Collection of various canonical materials. 5. *Edition:* None.

6. *Manuscripts*

Bamberg, Staatsbibliothek, Can. 9, fol. 128–232, saec.X3/3, Regensburg, fol. 128–232; cf. Krause, 'Acten' 303–305; John, *Collectio canonum Remedio . . . ascripta* 42–43; Hartmann, *Worms* 53–43; MGH Conc. 3.68 and 238; MGH Conc. 6.1.117–118.

München, Bayerische Staatsbibliothek, Clm 6241, saec. X3/3, Freising; cf. Krause, 'Acten' 292–294; John, *Collectio canonum Remedio . . . ascripta* 33–36; Mordek, *Bibliotheca capitularium* 319–321 and 976–977; MGH Capit. episc. 3.221

München, Bayerische Staatsbibliothek, Clm 6245, five continuous quires, saec. IX3/3–X[2], Freising; cf. Krause, 'Acten' 289–292; John, *Collectio canonum Remedio . . . ascripta* 30–33; Mordek, *Bibliotheca capitularium* 325–328 and 967–968

Wien, Österreichische Nationalbibliothek, lat. 2198, saec. X1/2, Freising; cf. Krause, 'Acten' 295–303; John, *Collectio canonum Remedio . . . ascripta* 36–41; Hartmann, *Worms* 53–54; MGH Conc. 3.68 and 328; MGH Conc. 6.1.146; Hoffmann-Pokorny 113–115

7. *Bibliography*

Krause, 'Acten' 281–326

N. Daniel, *Handschriften des 10. Jahrhunderts aus der Freisinger Dombibliothek* (Münchener Beiträge zur Mediävistik und Renaissance-Forschung 11; Munich 1973) 99–100

John, *Collectio canonum Remedio . . . ascripta* 30–36

Müller, *Collectio duodecim partium* 285–297

Pokorny, 'Triburer Synodalakten' 433–434, 447

Cf. *Decretum Burchardi* and *Collectio duodecim partium*

Collectio 234 capitulorum (Troyes 1979)

1. Author: Unknown. *2. Date:* Tenth century. *3. Place:* Lotharingia? *4. Type:* Composed of *Capitularia episcoporum,* other texts concerning the administration of dioceses, series of excerpts taken from the *Dacheriana* together with many single excerpts.

5. *Editions*

Only partial editions

MGH Capit. episc. 1.103–142 (Theodulf of Orléans, First Capitulary)

MGH Capit. episc. 3.169–171 (Capitula Trecensia)

6. *Manuscript*

Troyes, Bibliothèque municipale, 1979, remarkably thick manuscript, about the size of a postcard (140–145mm × 100mm), saec. XI^1, Eastern France or Western Germany, Prov. Dijon, St. Bénigne (once belonged to the library of the President of the Dijon Parliament Jean IV. Bouhier [1683–1746], shelf-mark F.14); fol. 41^v–44^r (*Capitulatio*), 158^r–210^v, 221^r–243^v

7. *Bibliography*

Fournier-Le Bras 1.272–276; R. Naz, 'Troyes (Collection du manuscrit 1979 de T.)', DDC 7 (1963) 1350–1351; Van Hove, *Prolegomena* 318; Stickler, *Historia* 1.148

De Clercq, *Législation* 2.350–352, 411–414

Mordek, *Kirchenrecht und Reform* 128–130

Kottje, *Bußbücher Halitgars* 63–65

Mordek, *Bibliotheca capitularium* 739–742

MGH Capit. n.s. 1.357–359

Collectio of Trier 1098/14

1. Author: Unknown. *2. Date:* Twelfth century. *3. Place:* Trier (St. Eucharius, St. Matthias). *4. Type:* Extracts from several systematic canonical collections dating from the ninth and tenth centuries (*Ansegis, Dacheriana,* Council of Worms [868], *Quadripartitus, Regino*). *5. Edition:* None.

6. Manuscript

Trier, Stadtbibliothek, 1098/14, saec. XII–XIII, Prov. St. Matthias, Trier, fol. 94^r–110^v

7. Bibliography

Christ, 'Überlieferung' 316
G. Kentenich, *Beschreibendes Verzeichnis der Handschriften der Stadtbibliothek zu Trier,* Part 10: *Die philologischen Handschriften* (Trier 1931) 29
Kerff, *Quadripartitus* 74–75
MGH Capit. n.s. 1.360–362

Collectio 98 capitulorum (Wien 2198 etc.)

1. Author: Unknown. *2. Date:* Tenth century, after 922. *3. Place:* Germany. *4. Type:* Influenced by Regino of Prüm (59 chapters, almost exclusively taken over from Liber II); the *Collectio sancti Emmerami Ratisbonensis* depends on it.

5. Edition

Incipit-Explicit edition: Krause, 'Acten' 297–303

6. Manuscripts

Bamberg, Staatsbibliothek, Can. 9 (P.I.9), saec. XI3/3; Regensburg; Prov. Cathedral of Bamberg, fol. 206^r–232^r
Wien, Österreichische Nationalbibliothek, lat. 2198 (Ius can. 99), saec. X^{ex}, Southern Germany, fol. 88^v–123^v

Excerpts

Stuttgart, Württembergische Landesbibliothek, HB.VI.107, saec. XI, cf. Seckel, 'Studien zu Benedictus Levita VII, Teil I', NA 34 (1909) 334 no. 6

7. Bibliography

Fournier-Le Bras 1.290, 292; Van Hove, *Prolegomena* 319; Stickler, *Historia* 1.148

Theiner, *Disquisitiones criticae* 152–154
Krause, 'Acten' 295–304
Seckel, 'Studien zu Benedictus Levita VII, Teil 1', NA 34 (1909) 334–335
John, *Collectio canonum Remedio . . . ascripta* 36–41
Hartmann, *Worms* 114

Cf. Freising Collection of canonical materials

Collectio Sancti Emmerami Ratisbonensis

(München Clm 14628)

1. *Author:* Unknown. 2. *Date:* After 922 (dependent on the *Collectio 98 capitulorum*). 3. *Place:* Regensburg (monastery of St. Emmeram). 4. *Type:* About 500 chapters of independently formulated abridgements of canons and texts from penitential books; gathered texts pertaining to the rights of the Bishop of Regensburg (who was at the same time abbot of the monastery) in all matters concerning the religious house; influenced by the *Collectio 98 capitulorum* and thus indirectly by Regino. 5. *Edition:* None.

6. *Manuscript*

München, Bayerische Staatsbibliothek, Clm 14628, saec. XI, Regensburg (?), Prov. St. Emmeram at Regensburg, fol. 1r–34v

7. *Bibliography*

Fournier-Le Bras 1.292–298; Van Hove, *Prolegomena* 319

Krause, 'Acten' 51–82, 283–326, especially 319–323
Brommer, 'Rezeption' 131 no. 44–45, 153 no. 22–23
Mordek, *Kirchenrecht und Reform* 133 n. 169
Hartmann, *Worms* 114–115
Kölzer, 'Farfenser Kanonessammlung' 96
Landau, 'Regensburg' 64–66, 71 n. 57
Kölzer, 'Mönchtum und Kirchenrecht' 136
Pokorny, 'Triburer Synodalakten' 434–435

Collectio of Salzburg, St. Peter a.IX.32

1. *Author:* Unknown. 2. *Date:* First quarter of the eleventh century. 3. *Place:* Southern Germany; making extensively use of materials from Cologne (that arrived in Salzburg during the twenties or thirties of the tenth century) and adding local texts to them. 4. *Type:* Collection of canonical materials. 5. *Edition:* None.

6. *Manuscript*

Salzburg, Bibliothek der Erzabtei St. Peter, a.IX.32 (olim X.28), saec. XI1/4, Southern Germany (Salzburg?) according to H. Hoffmann (cf. Pokorny, 'Triburer Synodalakten' 435 n. 20); cf. also MGH 6.1.98–99; fol. 117r–150r (closely related to Cologne 120)

7. *Bibliography*

Fournier-Le Bras 1.305–312

G. Phillips, 'Der Codex Salisburgensis S. Petri IX 32: Ein Beitrag zur Geschichte der vorgratianischen Rechtsquellen', *SB Vienna* 44 (1863) 437–510
Kottje, 'Salzburger Handschrift' 286–290

Kottje, *Bußbücher Halitgars* 57–58, 131–134
Zechiel-Eckes, *Cresconius* 156–160 and 337–338, 359–361
Mordek, *Bibliotheca capitularium* 644–652 (further bibliographical references on the manuscript)

Cf. Hinkmar of Laon, Pittaciolus

Collectio 4 librorum (Köln 124)

1. Author: Tenth-century canonist. *2. Date:* First half of the tenth century; soon after *Regino* (about 906) whose collection was used as a source (genuine form) but was written before the end of the tenth century (reception in Clm 3853, saec. X^{ex}) (cf. Schmitz, 'Vier-Bücher-Sammlung' 240–241). *3. Place:* Lorraine or the adjacent part of Germany (Schmitz 241). *4. Type:* Unstructured collection of canons and decretals with coherent blocks of texts. *5. Edition:* None.

6. Manuscripts

Köln, Erzbischöfliche Diözesan- und Dombibliothek, 124, saec. XI^2, Central Italy, Roman Minuscule (Romanesca), a Farfa script, cf. Schmitz, 'Vier-Bücher-Sammlung' 234 n. 7 (according to Bernhard Bischoff) and Hoffmann-Pokorny 75 n. 38

Reception
München, Bayerische Staatsbibliothek, Clm 3853, fol. 41^r–43^v (1.86, 108; 2.6, 48–50; 3.43–45, 47–48)
Vaticano, Città del, Archivio di San Pietro H.58, fol. 117^r–118^r (3.96–99; 4.38–48)

7. Bibliography

Fournier-Le Bras 1.283–290; Van Hove, *Prolegomena* 319; Stickler, *Historia* 1.148

Wasserschleben, *Beiträge* 20–28 (on the manuscript)
Hartmann, *Worms* 114
Hoffmann-Pokorny 70–76
Schmitz, 'Vier-Bücher-Sammlung' 233–255
Zechiel-Eckes, *Cresconius* 1.250–254, 296
Pokorny, 'Triburer Synodalakten' 429–511

Collectio of Milano, Ambrosiana A.58 sup.

1. Author: Unknown. *2. Date:* End of the ninth century. *3. Place:* Italy? *4. Type:* Collection of various individual texts; gathered together from quires written by various hands.

5. Editions

F. Maassen, 'Eine Rede des Papstes Hadrian II. vom Jahre 869: Die erste umfassende Benutzung der falschen Dekretalen zur Begründung der Machtfülle des römischen Stuhles', SB Vienna 72 (1872) 521–554 (partial edition)

O. Seebass, 'Ein bisher noch nicht veröffentlichtes Poenitential einer Bobbienser Handschrift der Ambrosiana', *Deutsche Zeitschrift für Kirchenrecht, 3. Folge, 6* (1896–97) 24–50 (partial edition)

C. G. Mor, *Bobbio, Pavia e gli 'Excerpta Bobiensia'* (Contributi per la storia dell'Università di Pavia; Pavia 1925) 71–114 (partial edition)

W. Hartmann, *Die Konzilien der karolingischen Teilreiche 860–874* (MGH, Concilia 4; Hannover 1998) 366–379 (same text as in Maassen)

6. *Manuscript*

Milano, Biblioteca Ambrosiana, A.58 sup., saec. IX^{ex}, Bobbio (cf. MGH Conc. 3.153)

7. *Bibliography*

Fournier-Le Bras 1.334–339 (erroneously citing it as 'G.58 inf.')

F. Maassen, 'Bobbienser Excerpte des römischen Rechts', *SB Vienna* 46 (1864) 237–241

F. Maassen, 'Eine Rede des Papstes Hadrian II. vom Jahre 869: Die erste umfassende Benutzung der falschen Dekretalen zur Begründung der Machtfülle des römischen Stuhles', SB Vienna 72 (1872) 521–554

O. Seebass, 'Ein bisher noch nicht veröffentlichtes Poenitential einer Bobbienser Handschrift der Ambrosiana', *Deutsche Zeitschrift für Kirchenrecht, 3. Folge, 6* (1896–97) 24–50

C. G. Mor, *Bobbio, Pavia e gli 'Excerpta Bobiensia'* (Contributi per la storia dell'Università di Pavia; Pavia 1925) 71–114

R. Haggenmüller, *Die Überlieferung der Beda und Egbert zugeschriebenen Bußbücher* (Frankfurt 1991) 72–73

L. Körntgen, *Studien zu den Quellen der frühmittelalterlichen Bußbücher* (Quellen und Forschungen zum Recht im Mittelalter 7; Sigmaringen 1993) 10–11

Cf. *Excerpta Bobiensia*

Collectio of Merseburg, Dombibliothek 104

1. Author: Unknown. *2. Date:* End of the ninth or beginning of the tenth century. *3. Place:* Northern Italy or Southern France. *4. Type:* Collection of materials.

5. *Editions*

P. Hinschius, *Decretales Pseudo-Isidorianae et Capitula Angilramni* (Leipzig 1863; repr. Aalen 1963) 454.35–455.2 (Pseudo-Roman Synod of Pope Julius I, following JK †196)

E. Dümmler, *Auxilius und Vulgarius: Quellen und Forschungen zur Geschichte des Papstthums im Anfange des zehnten Jahrhunderts* (Leipzig 1866) 157–161 (Councils of Rome [April 876], Rome [June 876) and Troyes [878])

R. Riedinger, ACO 2.1 (Berlin 1984) 3.1–12 (Lateran Synod 649)

H. Fuhrmann, 'Papst Nikolaus I. und die Absetzung des Erzbischofs Johann von

Ravenna', ZRG Kan. Abt. 44 (1958) 353–358 (only the introductory note of the Roman Synod of Nicholas I [Feb. 24, 861]).
W. Hartmann, *Die Konzilien der karolingischen Teilreiche 860–874* (MGH, Concilia 4; Hannover 1998) 50 (same text as in Fuhrmann)

6. *Manuscript*

Merseburg, Dombibliothek, 104, saec. IX^{ex} or X^{in}, Northern Italy or Southern France (Bobbio?) (some parallels to Milano, Ambrosiana A.58 sup.)

7. *Bibliography*

Archiv VIII (1869) 668–669
Martínez Díez, 'El Epítome Hispánico' 27–32 and passim
John, *Collectio canonum Remedio . . . ascripta* 89–92, especially 90 n. 4
MGH Conc. 3.314

Cf. *Epitome Hispana*

Collectio of Verona LXIII (61)

1. Author: Unknown. *2. Date:* End of the ninth or beginning of the tenth century. *3. Place:* Italy. *4. Type:* Collection of canonical materials, sort of handbook for the parish priests. *5. Edition:* None.

6. *Manuscript*

Verona, Biblioteca Capitolare, LXIII (61), saec. $X^{med\text{-}2/2}$

7. *Bibliography*

Fournier-Le Bras 1. 340–341; Van Hove, *Prolegomena* 315

MGH Capit. episc. 1.13
H. Mordek and G. Schmitz, 'Papst Johannes VIII. und das Konzil von Troyes (878), *Geschichtsschreibung und geistiges Leben im Mittelalter: Festschrift für Heinz Löwe,* ed. K. Hauck and H. Mordek (Cologne-Vienna 1978) 204–210
R. Haggenmüller, *Die Überlieferung der Beda und Egbert zugeschriebenen Bußbücher* (Frankfurt 1991) 110–111

Atto of Vercelli, Collectio canonum

1. Author: Atto, Bishop of Vercelli (924–about 960, died before 964). *2. Date:* Middle of tenth century. *3. Place:* Vercelli. *4. Type:* Main sources are the *Collectio Anselmo dedicata,* Theodulf of Orléans (Capitulary I) and the *Collectio Dionysiana adaucta.*

5. *Editions*

Luc d'Achery and L.-F.-J. de la Barre, *Spicilegium sive collectio veterum aliquot scripto-*

rum qui in Galliae Bibliothecis delituerant 1 (Paris ^{2}1723) 402–414 (PL 134.27–52; Mansi 19.145–264) (according to Vat. lat. 4323)
C. Buronzo del Signore, *Attonis opera* 2 (Vercelli 1768) 263–295
MGH Capit. episc. 3.243–304

6. *Manuscripts*

Vaticano, Città del, Biblioteca Apostolica Vaticana, lat. 4322, saec. X, Vercelli, fol. 69^{v}–83^{r}

Vercelli, Biblioteca Capitolare, XXXIX (40), saec. X, fol. 198ra–205rb (Buronzo used this manuscript for his edition)

Younger Copies of Vat. lat. 4322

Toledo, Archivo y Biblioteca Capitular, 8–19, saec. XVII, fol. 29^{r}–48^{r}
Vaticano, Città del, Biblioteca Apostolica Vaticana, lat. 4323, saec. XVII, fol. 15^{r}–35^{r}

7. *Bibliography*

Conrat, *Geschichte* 26; F. Bonnard, 'Atton de Verceil', DHGE 5 (1931) 191; R. Naz, 'Atton de Verceil', DDC 1 (1935) 1331–1332; A. Frugoni, DBI 4 (1962) 567–568; *Rep. font.* 2 (1967) 417–418; T. Kölzer, LMA 1 (1980) 1181

J. Schultz, *Atto von Vercelli* (Diss. Göttingen 1885)
Fournier, 'Fausses Décrétales' RHE 8 (1907) 56
G. Biscaro, 'Le origini della signoria della chiesa metropolitana di Milano sulle valli di Blenio, Leventina e Riviera, nell'Alto Ticino', *Bolletino storico della Svizzera italiana* 32 (1910) 33–43, 58–64
G. Schwartz, *Die Besetzung der Bistümer Reichsitaliens unter den sächsischen und salischen Kaisern, mit den Listen der Bischöfe (951–1122)* (Leipzig-Berlin 1913) 134–136
Manitius, *Literatur* 2.27–34
A. Fliche, *La Réforme grégorienne,* 1: *La formation des idées grégoriennes* (Louvain-Paris 1924; repr. Louvain 1966) 61–74
E. Pasteris, *Attone di Vercelli* (Milan 1925)
P. Pirri, 'Attone di Vercelli', *La Civiltà Cattolica* 88 (1927) 40
P. E. Schramm, 'Studien zu frühmittelalterlichen Aufzeichnungen über Staat und Verfassung,' ZRG Germ. Abt. 49 (1929) 180–188
R. Ordano, *Un vescovo italiano del secolo di ferro: Attone di Vercelli* (Vercelli 1948)
P. Levine, 'Historical Evidence for Calligraphic Activity in Vercelli from S. Eusebius to Atto', *Speculum* 30 (1955) 561–581
Fuhrmann, 'Pseudoisidor in Rom' 30 n. 36
S. F. Wemple, 'The Codex Holstenianus in Toledo: A Collection of Ninth, Tenth and Eleventh Century Capitularies', *Manuscripta* 13 (1969) 90–95
S. F. Wemple, 'The Canonical Resources of Atto of Vercelli (926–960),' *Traditio* 26 (1970) 335–350 (345–350: Appendix)
Fuhrmann, *Einfluß und Verbreitung* 2.317–318 n. 52
Brommer, 'Rezeption' 117–118
S. F. Wemple, *Atto of Vercelli, Church, State and Christian Society in Tenth Century Italy* (Studi e Testi 27; Rome 1979)
M. Guerra Gomez, 'En torno a los términos femeninos correspondientes a las de-

signaciones (sacerdos, episcopus, presbyter) de los sacerdotes cristianos', AnTh 2 (1988) 261–293

Landau, 'Kanonessammlungen in der Lombardei' 432

G. Cavallo, 'Libri scritti, libri letti, libri dimenticati' *Il secolo di ferro* 759–794

D. Iogna-Prat, 'L'oeuvre d'Haymon d'Auxerre. Etat de la question', *L'école carolingienne d'Auxerre de Murethach à Remi 830–908: Entretiens d'Auxerre 1989,* ed. D. Iogna-Prat, C. Jeudy and G. Lobrichon (Paris 1991) 157–179

M. Oldoni, 'Phrenesis di una letteratura solitaria', *Il secolo di ferro* 1007–1043

Cf. *Collectio Dionysiana adaucta* above

Collectio 233 capitulorum (Wolfenbüttel 454 Helmst.)

1. Author: Unknown. *2. Date:* Compiled between 964 and 1000. *3. Place:* Saxony. *4. Type:* A collection of materials rather than a fully elaborated *Collectio canonum; Collectio of Pseudo-Remedius* at the beginning; influenced by *Regino of Prüm* (57 chapters taken over from Book 1–2 and from Appendix B of a codex of the interpolated version).

5. *Editions*

Only partial editions

MGH Capit. episc. 3.185–186 (Capitula Helmstadensia)
MGH Concilia 2.1.78–79 (Roman Synod of Pope Stephan III)
MGH Epp. 4.20–29 (English Papal Legate Synod of 786)
MGH Const. 1.532–536 (Synod of Rome 964 held under Pope John XII)

6. *Manuscript*

Wolfenbüttel. Herzog August Bibliothek, Helmst. 454 (488), fol. 22^{v}–159^{v}, saec. X^{ex}; Hildesheim, Scriptorium of the Cathedral; Prov. Hildesheim, Cathedral, then St. Maria at Huysburg near Halberstadt

7. *Bibliography*

Fournier-Le Bras 1. 300–305; Van Hove, *Prolegomena* 319

Wasserschleben, *Beiträge* 29–30, 162–164, 189

O. von Heinemann, *Die Handschriften der herzoglichen Bibliothek zu Wolfenbüttel,* 1: *Die Helmstedter Handschriften* (Wolfenbüttel 1884) 1.356–357

L. Weiland, 'Zwei ungedruckte Papstbriefe aus der Kanonensammlung des sog. Ruotger von Trier' ZKR 20 (1885) 99–101

Sdralek, *Wolfenbüttler Fragmente* 86–100

John, *Collectio canonum Remedio . . . ascripta* 52–58, especially 53–54

Hartmann, *Worms* 115

MGH Conc. 6.1.60–61

R. Pokorny, 'Zwei unerkannte Bischofskapitularien des 10. Jahrhunderts', DA 35 (1979) 487–513 (especially 503–504 for bibliographical references)

E.-D. Hehl, 'Der wohlberatene Papst: Die Synode Johannes' XII. von 964', *Festschrift Zimmermann* (1991) 257–275, especially 259–260
Hoffmann-Pokorny (index 327)

Collectio Diessensis (München Clm 5541)

1. Author: Unknown. *2. Date:* About 1000 with an addition at the end taken from the *Decretum Burchardi*. *3. Place:* Germany. *4. Type:* Influenced by *Regino,* 50 chapters taken over from a codex of the interpolated version, and 32 from the *Collectio Novariensis.*

5. Edition

Incipit-Explicit-Edition by Krause, 'Acten' 305–319

6. Manuscript

München, Bayerische Staatsbibliothek, Clm 5541, between 1020 and 1050, Mainz-Trier-region, Prov. Dießen, fol. 63^r–140^v; cf. Hoffmann-Pokorny 130–131

7. Bibliography

Fournier-Le Bras 1.442–444; Van Hove, *Prolegomena* 321

M. Sdralek, 'Handschriftlich-kritische Untersuchungen über eine Gruppe von Briefen Papst Nikolaus' I.', AKKR 47 (1882) 179–184
Krause, 'Acten' 305–319
Hartmann, *Worms* 116
Hoffmann-Pokorny 70–76, 130–132
Pokorny, 'Triburer Synodalakten' 429–511

Tractatus de sacrilegiis et immunitatibus et eorum compositionibus

1. Author: Unknown. *2. Date:* Oldest manuscript dates to the end of the eleventh century (see Darmstadt below). *3. Place:* Southern Germany? *4. Type:* Canonistic treatise, especially popular in twelfth-century manuscripts from Bavaria and Austria.

5. Editions

F. J. von Schulte, 'Über drei in Prager Handschriften enthaltene Canonen-Sammlungen', SB Vienna 57 (1867) 183–194 (according to Cod. Praha VIII. H.7)
F. X. Kraus, 'Zur kirchenrechtlichen Literatur des elften Jahrhunderts', *Österreichische Vierteljahresschrift für Katholische Theologie* 8 (1869) 579–590 (according to Cod. Bernkastel-Kues 52)

6. Manuscripts

Admont, Stiftsbibliothek, 43, saec. XII^2; cf. Mordek, *Bibliotheca capitularium* 1036: treatise version

Admont, Stiftsbibliothek, 48; saec. XIII^{in}; cf. P. Weimar, *Zur Entstehung des sogenannten Tübinger Rechtsbuches und der Exceptiones legum Romanarum des Petrus* (Studien zur europäischen Rechtsgeschichte, ed. W. Wilhelm; Frankfurt 1972) 6 and 29; Mordek, *Bibliotheca capitularium* 1036: treatise version

Bernkastel-Kues, Bibliothek des St.-Nikolaus-Hospitals, 52, saec. XII, fol. 242^{v}–245^{v}; cf. Williams, *Codices Pseudo-Isidoriani* 9–10; Mordek, 'Suche' (as below, 'Bibliography') 189 n. 9; Mordek, *Bibliotheca capitularium* 1036: letter version

Darmstadt, Hessische Landes- und Hochschulbibliothek, 314, saec. XI^{ex}, Prov. Liège; cf. Mordek, *Bibliotheca capitularium* 1036: treatise version

Göttingen, Niedersächsische Staats- und Universitätsbibliothek, Theol. 92 (cf. Mordek, 'Riforma gregoriana' 106 n. 68); a. 1489 (cf. Mordek, *Bibliotheca capitularium* 1036: letter version)

Göttweig, Stiftsbibliothek, 43 (33), cf. Mordek, *Bibliotheca capitularium* 1036: treatise version

Göttweig, Stiftsbibliothek, 60 (71); Mordek, *Bibliotheca capitularium* 1036: treatise version

Göttweig, Stiftsbibliothek, 181 (88); cf. von Schulte 183 n. 2; Mordek, *Bibliotheca capitularium* 1036: treatise version

Klosterneuburg, Stiftsbibliothek, 638, saec. XII, cf. Mordek, 'Suche' 196 n. 34 and Mordek, *Bibliotheca capitularium* 1036 and 1037: abridged letter version and excerpt of the *compositio* (treatise version)

København, Kongelike Bibliotek, Gl. Kgl. Saml. 1617 4°, saec. XII^{1} (cf. *Decretum Burchardi)* Prov. St. Martin at Munich, cf. Mordek, 'Suche' 195 n. 28 and Mordek, *Bibliotheca capitularium* 1036: treatise version

München, Bayerische Staatsbibliothek, Clm 3909 (Excerpt), saec. XII (a. 138–1143), Prov. Augsburg; cf. Mordek, 'Suche' 192 n. 22 and Mordek, *Bibliotheca capitularium* 1036: abridged letter version

München, Bayerische Staatsbibliothek, Clm 9660, saec. XIII, fol. 1^{r}–4^{r} (only beginning of the *Tractatus*) cf. Mordek-Schmitz (see below) 219 n. 66 and Mordek, *Bibliotheca capitularium* 1037

München, Bayerische Staatsbibliothek, Clm 9661, saec. XII, cf. Mordek, *Bibliotheca capitularium* 1036 (abridged letter version)

München, Bayerische Staatsbibliothek, Clm 13004, saec. XII3/4 resp. 2/2 (cf. Mordek, 'Suche' 197 and Mordek, *Bibliotheca capitularium* 1036: treatise version)

München, Bayerische Staatsbibliothek, Clm 13109, saec. XII–XIII (abbreviated form without introduction and ending with Ivo's *Decretum* 3.98); cf. Mordek, *Bibliotheca capitularium* 1037: excerpts of the treatise version

München, Bayerische Staatsbibliothek, Clm 22253, saec. XII, fol. 206^{r}–213^{r} (same recension as the Göttweig manuscripts and Bernkastel-Kues 52), cf. Mordek-Schmitz 219 n. 66 and Mordek, *Bibliotheca capitularium* 1036: treatise version

Paris, Bibliothèque nationale, lat. 14833 (treatise version, cf. Mordek, *Bibliotheca capitularium* 1036)

Paris, Bibliothèque nationale, lat. 14884 (exerpts of the treatise-version; cf. Mordek, *Bibliotheca capitularium* 1037)

Paris, Bibliothèque nationale, lat. 15018 (for the last three manuscripts cf. Mordek, 'Riforma gregoriana' 106 n. 68)

Praha, Národní Knihovna Ceské Republiky, IV. B.12 (Prov. Liège), a. 1418; cf.

Williams, *Codices Pseudo-Isidoriani* 50–51 and Mordek, *Bibliotheca capitularium* 1036: letter version

Praha, Národní Knihovna Ceské Republiky, VIII. H.7, saec. XII2/2 (cf. v. Schulte, above, 'edition'); Prov. probably from St. Lambrecht, Styria; cf. Mordek, *Bibliotheca capitularium* 1036: treatise version

Salzburg, Bibliothek der Erzabtei St. Peter, a.VIII.7 (abridged version), cf. Mordek, *Bibliotheca capitularium* 1036

Vitry-le-François, Bibliothèque municipale, 18 (cf. Mordek, 'Riforma gregoriana' 106 n. 68 and Mordek, *Bibliotheca capitularium* 1036: treatise version)

Vorau, Stiftsbibliothek, 376; cf. Funk, *Catalogus Voraviensis seu codices manuscripti Bibliothecae canoniae in Vorau* (Graz 1936); Mordek, 'Suche' 195 and Mordek, *Bibliotheca capitularium* 1037: treatise version

Wien, Österreichische Nationalbibliothek, 1180, fol. 177^{v}–181^{v}, saec. XIII^{in}, Prov. Neuburg a. d. Mürz, Styria; Mordek, *Bibliotheca capitularium* 1037: treatise version

Wien, Österreichische Nationalbibliothek, 2219, saec. XII, fol. 67^{v}–78^{v}, cf. Mordek, *Bibliotheca capitularium* 1037: treatise version

Zwettl, Stiftsbibliothek, 41; saec. XII2/2; cf. St. Rössler, *Verzeichnisse der Handschriften des Stiftes Zwettl* (Vienna 1891) 318; Mordek, 'Suche' 195 (close relationship to München Clm 13109); cf. Mordek, *Bibliotheca capitularium* 1037

7. *Bibliography*

F. Maassen, 'Kleine Beiträge zur Kenntniß der Glossatorenzeit', *Jahrbuch des gemeinen deutschen Rechts* 2 (1858) 220–240, especially 231 n. 33.

F. J. von Schulte, 'Über drei in Prager Handschriften enthaltene Canonen-Sammlungen' SB Vienna 57 (1868) 182–198

H. Mordek and G. Schmitz, 'Papst Johannes VIII. und das Konzil von Troyes (878), *Geschichtsschreibung und geistiges Leben im Mittelalter: Festschrift für Heinz Löwe*, ed. K. Hauck and H. Mordek (Cologne-Vienna 1978) 186

Mordek, 'Suche' 187–200

Mordek, 'Kanonistik und gregorianische Reform' 77

Mordek, 'Riforma gregoriana' 105–106

Landau, 'Gefälschtes Recht' 38–39 n. 115 (Ivo-Appendix of the *Tractatus*)

K. Zechiel-Eckes, 'Neue Aspekte zur Geschichte Bischof Hermanns von Augsburg (1096–1133): Die Collectio Augustana, eine Rechtssammlung aus der Spätzeit des Investiturstreits', *Zeitschrift für bayerische Landesgeschichte* 57 (1994) 21–43, especially 28

Mordek, *Bibliotheca capitularium* 1035–1037

Cf. *Collectio Augustana* below and *Benedictus Levita, Collectio capitularium,* above

Collectio 9 librorum (Vat. lat. 1349)

1. Author: Unknown. *2. Date:* Compiled about 920. *3. Place:* Apparently composed in the region around Naples or Benevento. *4. Type:* Systematic collection; used the *Collectiones Hibernensis* and *Dacheriana*, the *Collectiones of Vallicelliana T.XVIII* and Penitentials.

5. Edition

A. Mai, *Spicilegium Romanum* 6 (1841) 396–472 (for an edition of the *capitulationes* of the *Collectio 9 librorum* see PL 138.397–442)

6. Manuscript

Vaticano, Città del, Biblioteca Apostolica Vaticana, lat. 1349 (on the dating of this manuscript cf. Loew-Brown, *Beneventan Script* 145); saec. XI ca. med., Southern Italy (according to Reynolds)

7. Bibliography

Maassen, *Geschichte* 885–887; Conrat, *Geschichte* 210 and 215 n. 2; Fournier-Le Bras 1.341–347; Van Hove, *Prolegomena* 232, 315; Stickler, *Historia* 1.151

Savigny, *Geschichte* 7.72–73

H. J. Schmitz, *Die Bußbücher und die Bußdisciplin der Kirche* 2 (Düsseldorf 1898, repr. Graz 1958) 210–217

Fournier, 'Recueils canoniques italiens' 124–158

I. P. Pozzi, 'Le ms. T. XVIII de la Vallicelliana et le libelle *De episcoporum transmigratione et quod non temere iudicetur regula quadraginta quattuor*', *Apollinaris* 31 (1958) 321–323

F. Patetta, 'Contributi alla storia del diritto romano nel medio evo I', BIDR 3 (1891) (repr. *Studi sulle fonti giuridiche medievali,* ed. G. Astuti [Torino 1967] 14–17)

G. Santini, *Ricerche sulle 'Exceptiones Legum Romanarum'* (Milan 1969) 190–191

M. Fornasari ed. *Collectio canonum in V libris, Libri I–III* (CCL, Continuatio mediaevalis 6, Turnhout 1970) p. xiii–xiv

Mordek, 'Herovalliana' 235 n. 82 (Bibliography!)

R. E. Reynolds, 'The *De officiis VII graduum:* Its Origins and Early Medieval Development', MS 34 (1972) 130 n. 71 (further reading)

Mordek, *Kirchenrecht und Reform* 138 including n. 185 and 187

Reynolds, 'Excerpta' 1–9

C. G. Mor, 'Per la storia del diritto romano nell'alto medio evo: Lex iustiniana e beneventana', *Scritti di storia giuridica* (Pisa 1977) 279–287

F. Kerff, 'Das Penitentiale Pseudo-Gregorii III.: Ein Zeugnis karolingischer Reformbestrebungen', ZRG Kan. Abt. 69 (1983) 731–741

Reynolds, 'Unity and Diversity' 134

L. Mahadevan, 'Überlieferung und Verbreitung des Bußbuchs *Capitula Iudiciorum*', ZRG Kan. Abt. 72 (1986) 17–75, especially 45

Landau, 'Gefälschtes Recht' 28, 37

R. E. Reynolds (ed. trad.), 'A South Italian Liturgico-Canonical Mass Commentary', MS 50 (1988) 626–670

G. Picasso, 'Il monaco', *Condizione umana e ruoli sociali nel Mezziogiorno normanno-svevo,* ed. Giosuè Musca (Bari 1991) 279–291

Zechiel-Eckes, *Cresconius* 1.248–249, 270–271, 273–274, 295–296

Mordek, *Bibliotheca capitularium* 389

Cf. *Collectio 5 librorum*

Collectio of London, British Library, Add. 16413

1. Author: Unknown. *2. Date:* Eleventh century? *3. Place:* Unknown (Southern Italy?). *4. Type:* Penitential and canonical material; isolated papal and conciliar texts, and sections drawn from other collections (cf. Mahadevan). *5. Edition:* None.

6. Manuscript

London, British Library, Addit. 16413, saec. XI^{in}, southern Italy (Beneventan script), fol. 13^{v}–18^{v}, cf. L. Mahadevan, 'Überlieferung und Verbreitung des Bußbuchs *Capitula episcoporum*', ZRG Kan. Abt. 72 (1986) 17–75, especially 24–28

7. Bibliography

R. Reynolds, 'The *De Officiis VII Graduum:* Its Origins and Early Medieval Development', MS 34 (1972) 113–151, especially 146

R. Reynolds, 'A South Italian Liturgico-Canonical Mass Commentary', MS 50 (1988) 626–670, especially 644–645

L. Böhringer, 'Zwei Fragmente der römischen Synode von 769 im Codex London, British Library, Add. 16413', *Festschrift Kottje* 93–105

Collectio of Archivio San Pietro H.58

1. Author: Unknown. *2. Date:* Around 1000. *3. Place:* Italy. *4. Type:* Mélange of collections and texts, liturgical, penitential and canonical materials, arranged from blocks of texts taken from other sources. *5. Edition:* None.

6. Manuscripts

Vaticano, Città del, Archivio di San Pietro H.58, about 1000, probably at Rome

7. Bibliography

See R. Reynolds' chapter on 'Italian Collections' to be published in this *History:* Vol. 3, *The History of Western Canon Law to 1000*

Collectio of Vat. lat. 3830

1. Author: Unknown. *2. Date:* About 1025–1050 (Fournier-Le Bras); after the pontificate of Pope Leo IX (Ryan). *3. Place:* Southern Italy? *4. Type:* Organized in blocks of texts taken from other collections. *5. Edition:* None

6. Manuscript

Vaticano, Città del, Biblioteca Apostolica Vaticana, lat. 3830, saec. XI^{med}, Central Italy

7. *Bibliography*

Fournier-Le Bras 1.453–454; Van Hove, *Prolegomena* 316; Stickler, *Historia* 154

F. Patetta, 'Contributi alla storia del diritto Romano nel Medio evo', BIDR 2 (1889) 296–299

Mor, 'Reazione al *Decretum Burchardi*' 197–206

J. J. Ryan, 'Letter of an Anonymous French Reformer to a Byzantine Official in South Italy: De simoniaca heresi (MS Vat. lat. 3830)', MS 15 (1953) 233–242

Ryan, 'Observations' 97–98

Kerff, *Quadripartitus* 69 n. 16

Reynolds, 'South Italian Collection' 278–295

M. Wojtowytsch, 'Die Kanones Heinrici regis: Bemerkungen zur römischen Synode vom Februar 1014', *Festschrift Fuhrmann* (1991) 165–166

MGH Capit. episc. 1.231–232

Cf. *Collectio 5 librorum (Vat. lat. 1339)*

Abbo of Fleury, Collectio canonum

1. Author: Abbo, Abbot of Fleury (†1004). *2. Date:* Between 988 and 996 (during the time when Hugh Capet and Robert the Pious reigned together, but more likely about 996 than 988, cf. Fournier-Le Bras 1.324 including n. 2, cf. Lot, *Etudes sur le règne de Hugues Capet* 174: conjectures 993. *3. Place:* Fleury-sur-Loire. *4. Type:* Systematically arranged collection of conciliar canons and decretals in two parts with Abbo's own comments 'ad defensionem monastici ordinis'.

5. *Editions*

Abbonis Floriacensis monasterii abbatis collectionem 52 capitulorum cum praefatione ad Ugonem Francorum regem filiumque eius Robertum, ed. Jean Mabillon, *Vetera analecta* 2 (Paris 1676) 248–348

Jean Mabillon, *Vetera analecta* (Paris ^{2}1723) 133–248 (PL 139.473–508)

RHF 10 (1760) 626–630 (excerpts)

6. *Manuscript*

Paris, Bibliothèque nationale, lat. 2400, saec. XI1/3, Prov. St-Cybard, Angoulême

7. *Bibliography*

Conrat, *Geschichte* 259–261; U. Berlière, 'Abbon de Fleury', DHGE 1 (1912) 49–51; A. Amanieu, 'Abbon', DDC (1935) 71–76; Fournier-Le Bras 1.320–330; Van Hove, *Prolegomena* 238–239, 317; 418 and 420; *Rep. font.* 2 (1967) 98–100

'S. Abbon, abbé de Fleuri', HLF 7 (Paris 1746) 159–184

Tardif, *Sources* 164

Ch. Pfister, *Etudes sur le règne de Robert le Pieux* (996–1031) (Paris 1885) 9–14

Sackur, *Cluniacenser* 1.270; 2.345–351 and 488

Manitius, *Literatur* 2.664–672

A. Van de Vyver, 'Les oeuvres inédites d'Abbon de Fleury', RB 47 (1935) 125–169

J. Adamek, *Vom römischen Endreich der mittelalterlichen Bibelerklärung* (Diss. Munich 1939) 81

Fliche, *Réforme Grégorienne* 1.47–60

J.-F. Lemariginier, 'L'exemption monastique et les origines de la réforme grégorienne', *A Cluny: Congrès scientifique: Fêtes et cérémonies liturgiques en l'honneur des saints abbés Odon et Odilon, 9–11 juillet 1949* (Dijon 1950) 302–306

P. Cousin, *Abbon de Fleury-sur-Loire: Un savant, un pasteur, un martyr à la fin du Xe siècle* (Paris 1954) 141–156

Gaudemet, 'Survivances romaines' 172 n. 86

Sprandel, *Ivo von Chartres* 52–53

A. Vidier, *L'historiographie à Saint-Benoît-sur-Loire et les miracles de Saint Benoît* (Paris 1965) 93–94; 102–111

Mordek, *Kirchenrecht und Reform* 4–5 n. 12

Motta, 'Regula Benedicti' 261–279

Kölzer, 'Mönchtum und Kirchenrecht' 135–136

M. Mostert, 'Le séjour d'Abbon de Fleury à Ramsey', BEC 144 (1986) 199–208

M. Mostert, *The Political Theology of Abbo of Fleury: A Study of the Ideas about Society and Law in the Tenth-century Monastic Reform Movement* (Middeleeuwse Studies en Bronnen 2; Hilversum 1987)

M. Mostert, 'Die Urkundenfälschungen Abbos von Fleury', *Fälschungen im Mittelalter* 4 (Diplomatische Fälschungen 2) 287–318

M. Mostert, 'The Political Ideas of Abbo of Fleury: Theory and Practice at the End of the Tenth Century', *Francia* 16.1 (1989) 85–100

M. Mostert, *The Library of Fleury: A provisional list of manuscripts* (Hilversum 1989) (cf. index)

M. Lapidge, 'Learning and Literature in Tenth-Century England', *Il secolo di ferro* 951–998

P. Jacques, *L'église et la culture en Occident, IXe–XIIe siècles, 1: La sanctification de l'ordre temporel et spirituel, 2: L'éveil évangelique et le mentalités religieuses* (Paris 1986) [Spanish translation: P. Jacques, *La iglesia y la cultura en Occidente (siglos IX–XII), 1: La sanctificación del orden temporal y espiritual, 2: El despertar evangélico y las mentalidades religiosas* (Barcelona 1988)]

D. Pingree, 'The Preceptum canonis Ptolomei', *Rencontres de cultures dans la philosophie médiévale: Traductions et traducteurs de l'antiquité tardive au XIVe siècle: Actes du colloque international de Cassino,* ed. J. Hamesse and M. Fattori (Louvain-la-Neuve-Cassino 1990) 355–375

V. Sivo, 'Nuovi studi sui trattati grammaticali mediolatini', QM 30 (1990) 267–284

M. Mostert, 'La bibliothèque de Fleury-sur-Loire', *Religion et culture autour de l'an mil: Royaume capétien et Lotharingie: Actes du colloque Hugues Capet 987–1987: La France de l'an Mil. Auxerre, 26–27 juin Metz, 11–12 septembre 1987,* ed. D. Iogna-Prat and J.-Ch. Picard (Paris 1990) 119–123

G. Giordanengo, 'Le pouvoir législatif du roi de France (XIe–XIIIe siècles): Travaux récents et hypothèses de recherche', BEC 147 (1989) 283–310, especially 292–308

F. Brunhölzl, *Geschichte der lateinischen Literatur des Mittelalters, 2: Die Zwischenzeit vom Ausgang des Karolingischen Zeitalters bis zur Mitte des 11. Jahrhunderts* (Munich 1992) 172–180 and 581–582

Siems, *Handel und Wucher* 181

H.-H. Kortüm, '*Necessitas temporis:* Zur historischen Bedingtheit des Rechtes im früheren Mittelalter', ZRG Kan. Abt. 79 (1993) 34–55

Abbo of Fleury, Epistola XIV

1. Author: Abbo, Abbot of Fleury (†1004). *2. Date:* About 995. *3. Place:* Fleury-sur-Loire. *4. Type:* Dossier of canonical, patristic and Roman law texts.

5. Edition

PL 139.440–460

6. Manuscript

London, British Library, Add. 10972, saec. XI.

7. Bibliography

A. Van de Vyver, 'Les oeuvres inédites d'Abbon de Fleury', *Revue Bénédictine* 47 (1935) 125–169

P. Cousin, *Abbon de Fleury-sur-Loire: Un savant, un pasteur, un martyr à la fin du X*[e] *siècle* (Paris 1954) 156

M. Mostert, *The Political Theology of Abbo of Fleury: A Study of the Ideas about Society and Law in the Tenth-century Monastic Reform Movement* (Middeleeuwse Studies en Bronnen 2; Hilversum 1987) 63–64

Cf. above, Abbo of Fleury, *Collectio canonum*

Odoramnus of Sens, Opusculum III

1. Author: Benedictine monk Odoramnus (ca. 985–ca. 1046). *2. Date:* Between 1022 and 1045. *3. Place:* Gaul (addressed to the abbot of Saint-Denis). *4. Type:* Collection of conciliar canons and decretals, Fathers of the Church and Roman law for the defense of monastic rights.

5. Editions

A. Mai, *Spicilegium Romanum* 9 (Rome 1839–1844) 63–67

PL 142.803–806 (only parts)

Odorannus de Sens, Opera omnia, ed. R.-H. Bautier and M. Gilles (Paris 1972) 114–133

6. Manuscripts

Vaticano, Città del, Biblioteca Apostolica Vaticana, Reg. lat. 577 (saec. XI) (autographe); Prov. Abbey of Saint-Pierre-le-Vif (Sens); cf. Bautier (as below) 29–36

Copies

Paris, Bibliothèque nationale, lat. 10000, saec. XVII

Paris, Bibliothèque nationale, lat. 13834 (only part of the collection), saec. XVI, Prov. Saint-Germain-des-Prés

7. *Bibliography*

Conrat, *Geschichte* 263; Van Hove, *Prolegomena* 317

R.-H. Bautier and M. Gilles (eds.), *Odorannus de Sens, Opera omnia* (Paris 1972) 7–28 and 50–53

Kölzer, 'Mönchtum und Kirchenrecht' 142

F. Brunhölzl, *Geschichte der lateinischen Literatur des Mittelalters 2: Die Zwischenzeit vom Ausgang des Karolingischen Zeitalters bis zur Mitte des 11. Jahrhunderts* (Munich 1992) 235–238 and 589

Collections of the Gregorian Reform Period
(From the Middle of the Eleventh Century to Gratian)

Collectio Sinemuriensis (Collectio Remensis)

1. Author: Unknown. An example of the reform initiative among the higher French clergy (cf. Fowler-Magerl, 'Vorgratianische Kanonessammlungen' 141). *2. Date:* First circulated after 1067 (Fowler-Magerl: after the Council of Reims 1049). *3. Place:* Reims. *4. Type:* Neither a systematically nor a chronologically arranged collection, but composed of different 'blocks of sources'; cf. Fowler-Magerl 125; in connection with the *Collectio 74 titulorum*. *5. Edition:* None.

6. Manuscripts

Madrid, Biblioteca Nacional, 428 (C.40), saec. XI^{ex}–XII^{in}

Orléans, Bibliothèque municipale, 306, saec. XI^{ex}–XII^{in}, Prov. Fleury

Paris, Bibliothèque nationale, lat. 18221, saec. XI2/2

Sélestat (Schlettstadt), Bibliothèque Humaniste, 13 (olim 99), saec. XI^{ex} (after 1075), Southern Germany, Constance?, Prov. St. Aurelius at Hirsau, fol. 110^{r}–205^{v}

Semur-en-Auxois, Bibliothèque municipale, 13, saec. XI^{ex}–XII^{in}

Fragment

Vaticano, Città del, Biblioteca Apostolica Vaticana, Ottobon. lat. 811, fol. 112^{r}–114^{v}

Vaticano, Città del, Biblioteca Apostolica Vaticana, Reg. lat. 453, fol. 50^{r}–55^{v} fragment of the version in manuscript Semur 13 (cf. Fowler-Magerl, 'Vorgratianische Kanonessammlungen' 146: 'Addenda')

7. Bibliography

P. Hinschius, 'Ueber Pseudo-Isidor-Handschriften und Kanonensammlungen in Spanischen Bibliotheken', ZKR 3 (1863) 122–146 especially 139–141

P. Adam, *L'humanisme à Selestat: L'école, les humanistes, la bibliothèque* (1962) (errors in the description)

H. Büttner, 'Abt Wilhelm von Hirsau und dic Entwicklung der Rechtsstellung der Reformklöster im 11. Jahrhundert', *Zeitschrift für Württembergische Landesgeschichte* 25 (1966) 321–338

Fransen, 'Trois notes' 446

Fransen, 'Manuscrits' 67–68 and *Appendice* 70–71 (passages from Hincmar)

I. S. Robinson, 'Zur Arbeitsweise Bernolds von Konstanz und seines Kreises: Untersuchungen zum Schlettstädter Codex 13', DA 34 (1978) 51–122, especially 51–82

Gilchrist, 'Reception 2' 202–203

Fowler-Magerl, 'Vorgratianische Kanonessammlungen' 124–141 (cited as *Collectio Remensis*)

Kerff, *Quadripartitus* 73

L. Fowler-Magerl, *Ordo iudiciorum vel ordo iudiciarius: Begriff und Literaturgattung* (Ius Commune, Sonderheft 19; Frankfurt 1984) 20

Gilchrist, 'Epistola Widonis' 589

Hartmann, 'Kanonessammlung' 45–64, especially 47 n. 10

Landau, 'Kanonessammlungen in der Lombardei' 450

Brett, 'Collectio Lanfranci' 169

Hartmann, 'Autoritäten' 437–438

Collectio 74 titulorum (Diversorum patrum sententie)

1. Author: Unknown. *2. Date:* Around 1050 (cf. Fournier-Le Bras 2.16), 1073–1075 (Gilchrist); Swabian Recension: about 1077 (Gilchrist). *3. Place:* Rome (a notation in three manuscripts of the Swabian Recension—Engelberg, Stuttgart, München—proves that they were brought to France by papal legates, cf. Fournier-Le Bras 2.16). *4. Type:* Systematic collection, very important for the reception of Pseudo-Isidore at the end of the eleventh century; Gregorian tendencies but with certain differences.

5. Editions

J. Cochlaeus, *Canones apostolorum, Veterum conciliorum constitutiones, Decreta pontificum antiquiora, De primatu Romanae ecclesiae, Ex tribus vetustiss. exemplaribus transscripta* (Mainz 1525)

Gilchrist, *Diversorum patrum sententie*

English Translation

The Collection in Seventy-Four Titles: A Canon Law Manual of the Gregorian Reform, translated and annotated by J. Gilchrist (Mediaeval Sources in Translation 22; Toronto 1980)

6. Manuscripts

According to Gilchrist, *Diversorum patrum sententie* xxxii–lxii, see also his extensive bibliography for the single manuscripts; cf. also Fournier, 'Manuel' 150–153

Cassino Recension

El Escorial, Real Biblioteca de San Lorenzo, L.III.19, saec. XI–XII, fol. 1^{r}–40^{v} (text ending 263.8 'dicata'): fol. 1–38^{r} (Carolingian minuscle), saec. XI and fol. 38^{v}–40^{v} (Beneventan script), saec. XII^{in}, probably written at Monte Cassino

Firenze, Biblioteca Medicea Laurenziana, Plut. XVI 15, saec. XI–XII, fol. 49^{r}–98^{r}

Firenze, Biblioteca Medicea Laurenziana, Conv. soppr. 91 (olim Badia 2685), saec. XII^{in}, Prov. Abbey of Santa Maria e Benedetto in Albarese (Grancia dell'Albarese, diocese of Savona), fol. 21^{v}–106^{v}

Monte Cassino, Archivio e Biblioteca dell'Abbazia, 522, saec. XI–XII^{in}, probably written at Monte Cassino, and always in the possession of the abbey, p. 7–179, cf. *Collectio 5 librorum*

Namur, Musée archéologique, 5, saec. XI^{ex}; probably written at St-Hubert-en-Ardennes (diocese of Liège), fol. 85ra–104rb

New Haven, Yale University, Law Library, 31, saec. XI–XII; Prov. Belgium–Northeastern France (during the fifteenth century in the Abbey of Saint-Laurent in Liège, then in Florence; in 1956 it was obtained by Yale) fol. 1^{r}–59^{r}

Wien, Österreichische Nationalbibliothek, lat. 2206 (olim Salzburg 295), saec. XII^{in}, fol. 2ra–13rb

Liège Recension

Bruxelles, Bibliothèque Royale Albert Ier, 9706–25 (van den Gheyn 1360), saec. XII^{in}, probably written in the Abbey of Saint-Laurent in Liège, fol. 30^{r}–60^{r}

El Escorial, Real Biblioteca de San Lorenzo, Z.III.19; saec. XI^{ex}, Prov. Italy, near Monte Cassino, fol. 1^{v}–74^{r}, cf. *Collectio 5 librorum*

Roma, Biblioteca Casanatense, 2010 (olim B.V.17), saec. XI^{ex} with some additions saec. XII, Prov. Farfa (expresses doubts: O. Bruguoli, 'Note sulla minuscola farfense', *Rivista di cultura classica e medioevale* 3 [1961] 332–341, especially 334, 337, 338), Reynolds: written either in Rome or Farfa; fol. 1^{r}–62^{v}, cf. *Collectio 5 librorum*

Roma, Biblioteca Vallicelliana, F.54, saec. XI^{ex}–XII^{in}, Prov. Italy, fol. 1^{r}–62^{v}, cf. *Collectio 5 librorum*

Swabian Recension

Engelberg, Stiftsbibliothek, 52 (olim I 4/2), saec. XI–XII; possibly written in the abbey of St. Blasien and from there it got to Engelberg (found 1120); fol. 5ra–39ra: 74T, fol. 39va–45ra: Swabian Appendix

St. Gallen, Stiftsbibliothek, 676, saec. XI, ca. 1080–1100, written under the supervision of Bernold of Constance whose annotations are in the manuscript; probably at Sankt Blasien or in the abbey of Allerheiligen at Schaffhausen; after that it came to St. Gall; p. 98^{a}–156^{b}: 74T; p. 156^{b}–158^{b}: Swabian Appendix; p. 174^{a}–179^{b}: *capitulatio* of the 74T; p. 259–261: continuation of the Swabian Appendix

Stuttgart, Württembergische Landesbibliothek, HB.VI.107 (olim Weingarten C 6), saec. XI^{ex}, fol. 1^{v}–43^{v}: 74T, fol. 44^{r}–52^{r}: Swabian Appendix; probably written in Constance, Sankt Blasien or Schaffhausen (fol. 111^{r}: 'Hoc est liber St. Martini' in a hand saec. XIII or XIV); perhaps it got to Weingarten in 1630 (not 1603!) (see note on fol. 1^{r})

Vaticano, Città del, Biblioteca Apostolica Vaticana, lat. 4160, saec. XI^{ex}, Prov. Italy, fol. 1^{v}–50^{r}

Wien, Österreichische Nationalbibliothek, lat. 2153, saec. XII^{in} and XIV; olim in the possession of the convent of St. Pölten (fol. 58^{v}) (14.–15. cent.); fol. 1^{r}–41^{v}: 74T, fol. 41^{v}–42^{r}: Swabian Appendix (only cc. 319, 321 and 328)

Wolfenbüttel, Herzog August Bibliothek, August 9.4. (Heinemann 2985), saec. XII (saec. XIII according to Heinemann), Prov. St. Johann Baptist and St. Blasius, Braunschweig, fol. 1ra–28rb

Further Manuscripts (according to Mordek, *Kirchenrecht und Reform* 7 n. 14)

Berlin, Staatsbibliothek Preußischer Kulturbesitz, Theol. lat. fol. 281, saec. XII, fol. 1^{r}–26^{r}, Prov. Rhineland (Prüm), cf. H. Knaus, 'Rheinische Handschriften in Berlin, 6. Folge: Der Fonds Maugérard', *Archiv für Geschichte des Buchwesens* 14 (1974) 271–272; Mordek, 'Kanonistik und gregorianische Reform' 70 n. 25

Vaticano, Città del, Biblioteca Apostolica Vaticana, Reg. lat. 818 (a. 1536), probably copy from Cod. Vat. lat. 4160 (saec. XI^{ex} or XII) (cf. Mordek, *Kirchenrecht und Reform* 258)

Fragments and Excerpts (according to Gilchrist)

Angers, Bibliothèque municipale, 278 (269), saec. X, Prov. Saint-Aubin, fol. 125^{v}–126^{r} (74T, cc. 21–23, in a saec. XI hand)

Bruxelles, Bibliothèque Royale Albert Ier, II.1147, fol. 39^{v}–45 (saec. XI^{ex}; Prov. abbey of Aulne, Hainaut) cf. Fransen, 'Trois notes' 446; Fransen, 'Manuscrits' 69

München, Bayerische Staatsbibliothek, Clm 9515, saec. IX–X, fol. 1^{v}–5^{r} (Swabian Recension, cc.1–42), fol. 1–5 is a separate fragment from 'St. Petrus in superiori Altach [= Oberaltaich]'; cf. Seibert, 'Unbekannte Überlieferung' 92

München, Bayerische Staatsbibliothek, Clm 22289, saec. XII, fol. 191^{r}–207^{v}

Stuttgart, Württembergische Landesbibliothek, Frag. 41, saec. XI, probably near Constance (Author used the Swabian Recension)

Vaticano, Città del, Biblioteca Apostolica Vaticana, lat. 4977, saec. XI–XII (in possession of A. Agustín), fol. 6^{v}–23^{v}, Excerpts from 74T (Author used the Liège-recension)

Vaticano, Città del, Biblioteca Apostolica Vaticana, Reg. lat. 1054, saec. XI, Pseudo-Isidore Class A-1, fol. 1^{r} in a different hand (saec. XII) c.39 from 74T (probably Cassino-Recension)

Zürich, Staatsarchiv, C II 17 Vr.17a, fol. 1^{r-v} (cf. Seibert, 'Unbekannte Überlieferung' 87–100: Fragment in Rheinau Cartulary)

Abridged Form (according to Gilchrist)

Firenze, Biblioteca Nazionale Centrale, Conv. soppr. B.III.1122, Prov. Northern France, fol. 1–40^{v}, critical edition announced by G. Fransen, 'Autour de la Collection en 74 Titres', RDC 25 (1975) 61–73 ('Abrégé de Florence'); cf. G. Fransen, 'Un manuscrit de Saint-Hubert en Ardennes à la Bibliothèque nationale de Florence', RB 87 (1977) 194–196 and Fransen, 'Manuscrits' 69; Gilchrist, 'Epistola Widonis' 588; Gaudemet, 'Primauté' 155–156

Later Recensions (according to Gilchrist)

Collectio of Paris, BN nouv. acq. lat. 326, saec. XI^{ex}, Prov. Saint-Denis; cf. below

Collectio of Admont, Stiftsbibliothek, 257 (saec. XII^{2}), fol. 72^{r}–87^{r}; Seibert, 'Unbekannte Überlieferung' 92 n. 23 does not take into account that these texts are excerpts; he refers to Autenrieth, 'Bernold von Konstanz' 386; cf. also Fuhrmann, 'Papst Urban II. und der Stand der Regularkanoniker', *SB Munich* 1984, 33–34 (description of the manuscript); F. Thaner, MGH Ldl 1 (Hannover 1891, repr. 1956) 472, 17–19 and NA 16 (1891) 540–543

San Daniele del Friuli, Biblioteca Civica Guarneriana, 203, saec. XI1/2 (About 1127–1133, Italy), U.-R. Blumenthal, 'Codex Guarnerius 203': A manuscript of the Collection in 74 Titles at San Daniele del Friuli', BMCL 5 (1975) 11–33 and Blumenthal, *Manuscripta* 22 (1978) 94; Kretzschmar, *Alger von Lüttich* 86–87 n. 109, 88–92, 95 n. 160. According to Gilchrist, San Daniele 203 is a later recension of the *Collection in 74 titles* and not a manuscript of the original text

Collectio of Milano, Biblioteca Ambrosiana, H.5 inf., saec. XII^{in}, Prov. near Milan, perhaps Bergamo or Brescia; critical edition: G. Picasso, *Collezioni canoniche Milanesi* 144–157

Erroneous Attribution

Tarragona, Biblioteca Publica (Provincial), 26 (44); cf. Valls-Taberner, *Estudis d'Historia juridica Catalana* (1929) 80 and Fournier-Le Bras 2.14 n. 2, is a manuscript of the *Liber Tarraconensis*

7. *Bibliography*

Fournier-Le Bras 2.14–20; Kurtscheid-Wilches 1.156–157; Van Hove, *Prolegomena* 234, 323; Stickler, *Historia* 1.167–170; P. Palazzini, *Enciclopedia Cattolica* 9 (1952) 1378; García y García, *Historia* 1.312–313; J. Gilchrist, 'Seventy-four titles, Collection of', NCE 13 (1967) 141; *Rep. font.* 3 (1970) 508–509

Theiner, *Disquisitiones criticae* 338–341

F. Thaner, 'Untersuchungen und Mittheilungen zur Quellenkunde des canonischen Rechts, 1: Die nachpseudo-Isidor'sche Sammlung des Codex 522 von Montecassino', SB Vienna 89 (1878) 601–632

Fournier, 'Manuel' 147–223, 285–290

Wretschko, *Theodosiani libri XVI*, p. ccclvii–ccclviii

Fournier, 'Collections canoniques romaines' 280–288

L. Levillain, 'Etudes sur l'abbaye de Saint Denys à l'époque mérovingienne, 3: Privilegium et immunitates ou Saint-Denis dans l'Eglise et dans l'Etat', BEC 87 (1926) 245–346, especially 299–325

G. Le Bras, 'Manuscrits canoniques', *Revue des sciences religieuses* 8 (1928) 270–273, especially 271–272 ('Le manuscrit liégeois de la *Collection en 74 titres*')

A. Michel, *Die Sentenzen des Kardinals Humbert, das erste Rechtsbuch der päpstlichen Reform* (Schriften des Reichsinstituts für ältere deutsche Geschichtskunde 7; Stuttgart 1943)

J. Haller, 'Pseudoisidors erstes Auftreten im deutschen Investiturstreit', SGreg 2 (1947) 91–101

A. Michel, 'Die folgenschweren Ideen des Kardinals Humbert und ihr Einfluß auf Gregor VII.', SGreg 1 (1947) 65–92

F. Pelster, 'Das Dekret Burkhards von Worms in einer Redaktion aus dem Beginn der Gregorianischen Reform', SGreg 1 (1947) 321–351

A. Michel, 'Pseudo-Isidor, die Sentenzen Humberts und Burkards von Worms im

Investiturstreit', SGreg 3 (1948) 149–161 (also in: ZRG Kan. Abt. 35 [1948] 329–339)
Ch. Dereine, 'L'école canonique liégeoise et la réforme grégorienne', *Annales du Congrès archéologique et historique de Tournai* (1949) 1–16
Ch. Dereine, 'L'école canonique liégoise et la réforme grégorienne', *Miscellanea Tornacensia: Annales du Congrès archéologique et historique de Tournai 1949,* 1 (1951) 80 n. 2
A. Michel, 'Humbert von Silva Candida (†1061) bei Gratian: Eine Zusammenfassung', SG 1 (1953) 83–117
P. Palazzini, 'Il diritto strumento di riforma ecclesiastica in S. Pier Damiani', *Ephemerides iuris canonici* 12 (1956) 9–58, 21–26 (cf. Reindel, DA 14, 1958, 572–573; Ryan, *Saint Peter Damiani* 14, 157, 166)
J. Gilchrist, *The Political Ideas of Cardinal Humbert of Silva Candida (1050–61) with an edition of the Diversorum Patrum Sententiae* (Unpubl. Diss., Univ. of Leeds 1957)
Autenrieth, 'Bernold von Konstanz' 375–394
Ryan, 'Observations' 99, 100
H. P. H. Jansen, 'Nieuw licht op de investituurstrijd', *Tijdschrift voor Geschiedenis* 74 (1961) 484–485
G. May, 'Die Bedeutung der pseudoisidorischen Sammlung für die Infamie im kanonischen Recht', ÖAKR 12 (1961) 87–113, 192–207
J. Bernhard, *La collection en deux livres (Cod. Vat. lat. 3832)* = RDC 12 (1962)
J. Gilchrist, 'Canon Law Aspects of the Eleventh Century Gregorian Reform Programme', JEH 13 (1962) 21–38
J. Gilchrist, 'Humbert of Silva Candida and the Political Concept of "Ecclesia",' *Journal of Religious History* 2 (1962) 13–38
O. Capitani, 'La figura del vescovo in alcune collezioni canoniche della seconda metà del secolo XI', *Vescovi e diocesi in Italia nel Medioevo, sec. IX–XIII: Atti del II convegno di storia della chiesa in Italia, Roma 5–9 sett. 1961* (Padova 1964) 161–191
J. Gilchrist, 'The Collectio of Cod. Vat. lat. 3832: A Source of the Collection in Seventy Four Titles?' *Etudes . . . Le Bras* 1.141–156
L. F. J. Meulenberg, *Der Primat der römischen Kirche im Denken und Handeln Gregors VII.* (s'-Gravenhage 1965) 14
O. Capitani, *Immunità vescovili ed ecclesiologia in età 'Pregregoriana' e 'Gregoriana': L'avvio alla 'Restaurazione'* (Biblioteca degli Studi medievali III; Spoleto 1966) 183–208
J. Gaudemet, 'Collections canoniques et primauté pontificale', RDC 16 (1966) 105–117
J. Gilchrist, 'Gregory VII and the Juristic Sources of His Ideology', SG 12 (1967) 1–37
J. Gilchrist, 'Gregory VII and the Primacy of the Roman Church', TRG 36 (1968) 123–135 (Review of: L. F. J. Meulenberg, *Der Primat der römischen Kirche im Denken und Handeln Gregors VII.*, s'-Gravenhage 1965)
Rambaud-Buhot, 'Critique' 37
H. Hoesch, *Die kanonischen Quellen im Werk Humberts von Moyenmoutier: Ein Beitrag zur Geschichte der vorgregorianischen Reform* (Forschungen zur kirchlichen Rechtsgeschichte und zum Kirchenrecht 10; Cologne-Vienna 1970)
A. Marchetto, *Episcopato e primato pontificio nelle decretali pseudoisidoriane* (Pontificia Università Lateranense; Rome 1971)

H. Fuhrmann, 'Über den Reformgeist der 74-Titel-Sammlung (Diversorum Patrum Sententiae)', *Festschrift für Hermann Heimpel zum 70. Geburtstag am 19. September 1971* (Göttingen 1972) 2.1101–1120

Gilchrist, 'Economic Policy' 400–401

R. Knox, 'Finding the Law: Developments in Canon Law during the Gregorian Reform', SGreg 9 (1972) 419–466, especially 448 (cf. *Decretum Burchardi*)

Somerville, 'Berengar' 53–75

J. Gilchrist, 'Cardinal Humbert of Silva-Candida, the Canon Law and Ecclesiastical Reform in the Eleventh Century', ZRG Kan. Abt. 58 (1972) 338–349 (Review of: H. Hoesch, *Die kanonischen Quellen im Werk Humberts von Moyenmoutier*)

Fuhrmann, *Einfluß und Verbreitung* 2.486–509

Gilchrist, 'Reception 1' 37

M. Maccarrone, 'La teologia del primato romano del secolo XI', *Le istituzioni ecclesiastiche della 'Societas christiana' dei secoli XI–XII: Papato, cardinalato ed episcopato* (Atti della quinta settimana internazionale di studio: Mendola, 26–31 agosto 1971; Pubblicazioni dell'Università Cattolica del S. Cuore, Serie terza, Scienze storiche; Miscellanea del Centro di Studi Medioevali; Milan 1974) 21–122

U.-R. Blumenthal, 'Codex Guarnerius 203. A Manuscript of the Collection in 74 Titles at San Daniele del Friuli', BMCL 5 (1975) 11–33

Brommer, 'Kirchenrechtliche Sammlungen' 88 (Bifolio Koblenz, Landeshauptarchiv, 701 no. 759,7 B, saec. XI, erroneously described as a fragment of the *Collectio 74 titulorum*; but according to Mordek, 'Kanonistik und gregorianische Reform' 66 n. 5 it is a fragment of the *Collectio 4 librorum*, see below)

G. Fransen, 'Autour de la Collection en 74 Titres', *Etudes offertes à René Metz* = RDC 25 (1975) 61–73

F. Kempf, review of Gilchrist (ed.), *Diversorum patrum sententie*, DA 31 (1975) 440–444

P. Landau, review of H. Fuhrmann, *Einfluß und Verbreitung*, ZRG Kan. Abt. 61 (1975) 377–392, esp. 387–388

Mordek, *Kirchenrecht und Reform* 7 n. 18, 124 n. 104 (partly common transmission with *Decretum Gelasianum*) 249

U.-R. Blumenthal, 'A proposito del ms. 522 dell'archivio di Monte Cassino', *Benedictina* 22 (1976) 444

John, *Collectio canonum Remedio . . . ascripta* 114–115

K.-G. Schon, 'Exzerpte aus den Akten von Chalkedon bei Pseudoisidor und in der 74-Titel-Sammlung', DA 32 (1976) 546–557

Gilchrist, 'Reception 2' 193–194

J. Gilchrist (ed.), *The Collection in Seventy Four Titles: A Canon Law Manual of the Gregorian Reform* (Mediaeval Sources in Translation 22; Toronto 1980)

Horst, *Polycarpus* passim

J. Gilchrist, 'The Collection in Four Books (4L): The Source of the Collection in Seventy Four Titles (74T)?' BMCL 11 (1981) 77–80

J. Gilchrist, 'The Relationship between the Collection in Four Books and the Collection in Seventy-Four-Titles', BMCL 12 (1982) 13–30

M. C. De Matteis, 'Tematica della povertà e problema delle *Res ecclesiae*: Notazioni ed esemplificazione campione su alcune collezioni canoniche del periodo della riforma ecclesiastica del sec. XI', BISIAM 90 (1982–1983) 177–226

Mordek, 'Systematische Kanonessammlungen' 193–194

A. Degl'Innocenti and S. Cantelli, 'La riforma gregoriana e l'Europa (Salerno, 20–25 maggio 1985)', SM 26 (1985) 483–493 (Report on the Congress)

Kretzschmar, *Alger von Lüttich* 78–99

Mordek, 'Kanonistik und gregorianische Reform' 65–66

Blumenthal, 'Fälschungen' 247–248, 254

O. Capitani, 'Da Landolfo Seniore a Landolfo Iuniore: momenti di un processo di crisi', *Atti dell' 11° Congresso internazionale di studi sull'alto medioevo: Milano e il suo territorio in età comunale (XI–XIII secolo), Milano 26–30 ottobre 1987* (Centro italiano di studi sull'alto medioevo; Spoleto 1989) 2.589–622

Seibert, 'Unbekannte Überlieferung' 87–100

Landau, Gefälschtes Recht' 33–34

A. García y García, 'Reforma gregoriana e idea de la *Militia sancti Petri* en los reinos ibéricos', SGreg 13 (1989) 241–262

J. Gilchrist, 'The Canonistic Treatment of Jews in the Latin West in the Eleventh and Early Twelfth Centuries', ZRG Kan. Abt. 75 (1989) 70–106

Landau, 'Kanonessammlungen in der Lombardei' 449–450

R. Maceratini, 'Aspetti della posizione giuridica dell'eretico in alcune opere della Riforma gregoriana', *Scritti di storia del diritto offerti dagli allievi a Domenico Maffei*, ed. M. Ascheri (Padova 1991) 1–25 (cf. review by D. Jasper, DA 49 [1993] 345)

Gaudemet, 'Primauté' 155–156

Hartmann, 'Autoritäten' 426–427, 430, 436, 441

S. Kuttner, '*Auctor noster beatus Petrus Apostolus*: Pope Agatho on the Papal Office', *Studia in Honorem A. M. Stickler* (1992) 215–224

E. Vodola, 'Sovereignty and Tabu: Evolution of the Sanction against Communication with Excommunicates, 2: Canonical Collections', *Studia in Honorem A. M. Stickler* (1992) 581–598, esp. 592–594

J. Gilchrist, 'Changing the Structure of a Canonical Collection: The Collection in Seventy-Four Titles, Four Books and the Pseudo-Isidorian Decretals', *In Iure Veritas: Studies in Canon Law in Memory of Schafer Williams*, ed. S. B. Bowman and B. E. Cody (Cincinnati 1991) 93–117

J. Gaudemet, 'La primauté pontificale dans les collections canoniques grégoriennes', *Studi in onore Luigi Prosdocimi* (1994) 1.1.59–90

Collectio 4 librorum

1. Author: Unknown. *2. Date:* Last years of the pontificate of Gregory VII (about 1080–1085); Gilchrist: shortly after 1076. *3. Place:* France. *4. Type:* Systematic collection; revision of the *Collectio 74 titulorum* with additions. *5. Edition:* None.

6. *Manuscripts*

Bergamo, Biblioteca Civica 'Angelo Mai', MA 244, saec. XII2/2; Prov. San Alessandro in Bergamo, fol. 12ra–74vb, cf. Jasper, *Papstwahldekret* 19–25

Bern, Burgerbibliothek, 314, saec. XI, Prov. west bank of the Rhine, fol. 1^{v}–43^{r}

Canterbury, Cathedral and Chapter Library, Lit. B.7, saec. XI–XII, Prov. France, fol. 1^{r}–55^{r}

Celle, Bibliothek des Oberlandesgerichts, C. 8, saec. XI^{ex}, fol. 3^r–68^v, cf. *Traditio* 14 (1958) 509 and Gilchrist, 'Manuscripts' 66 n. 13

Genève, Bibliothèque Publique et Universitaire, lat. 166, saec. XII, fol. 1^r–64^v

'S Gravenhage (Den Haag), Museum Meermanno-Westreenianum, RB 72 I 10, saec. XII

Koblenz, Landeshauptarchiv, 701, no. 759,7 B, saec. XI, bifolio; cf. Mordek, 'Kanonistik und gregorianische Reform' 66 n. 5; Brommer, 'Kirchenrechtliche Sammlungen' 88 described it as a fragment of the *Collectio 74 titulorum*

Leiden, Bibliotheek der Rijksuniversiteit, BPL 111 I, saec. XI–XII, Prov. possibly from Poitiers region, fol. 3^r–117^v

London, British Library, Add. 22286, saec. XI–XII, Prov. France, fol. 5–76^v, cf. Fransen, 'Abrégés' 165 and Jasper, *Papstwahldekret* 23 n. 80

London, British Library, Arundel 173, saec. XI (saec. XII^{in} according to Jasper, *Papstwahldekret* 23 n. 80), Prov. unknown, fol. 45^r–46^r, 79^r–123^r

Madrid, Biblioteca Nacional, 267 (olim C 144), saec. XII–XIII, Prov. Italy (Gilchrist, 'Manuscripts' 68) but saec. XII^{in}, France according to Jasper, *Papstwahldekret* 23 n. 80, cf. also G. Fransen, *Les collections canoniques* (Typologie des sources du moyen âge occidental 10; Turnhout 1973) 30; P.-I. Fransen, 'Prologue patristique' (as below) 205–215; Gilchrist, 'Economic policy' 411–413; abridged version of the *Collectio 4 librorum* on fol. 115^r–152^v, 49^r–64^v, 153^r–155^r,

Milano, Biblioteca Ambrosiana, C.51 sup., saec. XII^{in}, France, cf. Somerville, 'Berengar' 66–68; from Bourgeuil-la-Vallée; Prov. Bologna? cf. Mordek, *Bibliotheca capitularium* 241–242, fol. 9^r–19^r (*capitulatio*) and fol. 19^v–120^v (text), fol. 121^r–128^v (additions),

Paris, Bibliothèque nationale, lat. 3187, saec. XI, fol. 1–122, cf. *Catalogue général* 4 (Paris 1958) 325–330

Paris, Bibliothèque nationale, lat. 4281A, saec. XII, Prov. possibly near Poitiers, belonged to the Cistercian abbey of Beaupré in the fourteenth century, fol. 1^v–10^v *(capitulatio)* and fol. 17^v–96ra (text)

Paris, Bibliothèque nationale, lat. 4376 (discovered in 1983)

Paris, Bibliothèque nationale, lat. 9631, fol. 3^r–46^r (cf. Somerville, *Proceedings Salamanca* 40–41); according to Fransen, 'Autour de la collection en 74 titres', RDC 25 (1975) 61, oldest version of the *Collectio 4 librorum*; cf. also Mordek, 'Kanonistik und gregorianische Reform' 66 n. 5

St. Petersburg, Rossiyskaya Natsional'naya Biblioteka, F.v.II.13, saec. XII, since 1944 lost in Warsaw, fol. 23^v–29^r and 37^r–111^r; cf. A. Halban-Blumenstok, 'Die canonistischen Handschriften der kaiserlichen öffentlichen Bibliothek in Sankt Petersburg', *Deutsche Zeitschrift für Kirchenrecht*^{3} 5 (1895) 226, 287–302, described this manuscript erroneously as a Dubrowski-manuscript from Saint-Germain. Cf. Gilchrist, 'Manuscripts' 67 and Staerk, *Manuscrits Latins* 1.253–260, no. xcix who assigns it correctly to the Zaluski collection and to a date 1130–1143, cf. D. Whitelock—M. Brett—C. N. L. Brooke (eds.), *Councils and Synods with Other Documents Related to the English Church* 1.2 (Oxford 1981) 720 n. 1 and 735

Vaticano, Città del, Biblioteca Apostolica Vaticana, Reg. lat. 276, fol. 220–226, 227, 228, 229–231, 233–236, 237–240, (bifolio I: fol. 1–219 [saec. XV] and II:, fol. 220–240 [saec. XI–XII]: *Collectio 4 librorum;* cf. Fournier, 'Manuel' 147, 156 and

220; Wilmart, *Codices Reginenses latini* 2 [Vatican City 1945] 75–78), Prov. Marmoutier near Tours

Cf. Gilchrist, 'Manuscripts' 64–70 and Jasper, *Papstwahldekret* 19–33

Four different recensions according to Fransen, 'Autour de la Collection en 74 Titres', *Etudes offertes à René Metz* = RDC 25 (1975) 6

1. Paris lat. 9631 and Genève 166; gradually augmented in manuscripts Canterbury Lit. B.7, Paris lat. 3187 and Milano, Ambros. C.51 sup.
2. Paris lat. 4281A and Leiden, BPL 111 I
3. St. Petersburg, F v.II.13; and depending from this manuscript: Madrid, Biblioteca Nacional, 267 (C 144), London Arundel 173 and London Add. 22286 (excerpt)
4. (and without classification among these recensions): Bern, Burgerbibliothek 314, Vat. Reg. lat. 276

According to Jasper, *Papstwahldekret* 19–33 the manuscripts St. Petersburg, Madrid, London Arundel as well as Add. and Vat. Reg. lat. 276 depend on the Bergamo manuscript. Depending from the Leiden manuscript: Canterbury, Milano, Paris lat. 3187.

7. *Bibliography*

Fournier-Le Bras 2.235–240; Van Hove, *Prolegomena* 331; Stickler, *Historia* 1.176; R. Naz, DDC 7 (1965) 425; García y García, *Historia* 1.317.

Gerhard von Maastricht, *Historia juris ecclesiastici* (Duisburg 1676; Halle 1719) 440–442

Fournier, 'Manuel' 147–223, 285–290

A. Halban-Blumenstok, 'Die canonistischen Handschriften der kaiserlichen öffentlichen Bibliothek in St. Petersburg', ZKR 27 (1895) 287–302

Brooke, *English Church* 241

Ryan, 'Observations' 99 and 102

Gilchrist, 'Economic Policy' 411–412

Somerville, 'Berengar' 66–68

Gilchrist, 'Reception 1' 53–54

G. Fransen, 'Autour de la collection en 74 titres' RDC 25 (1975) 61–73

Mordek, *Kirchenrecht und Reform* 7 n. 18

P.-I. Fransen, 'Le Prologue patristique d'une forme de la Collection en quatre livres', *Mélanges Fransen* 1.205–215

J. Gilchrist, 'The Collection in Four Books (4L): The Source of the Collection in Seventy-Four-Titles (74T)?', BMCL 11 (1981) 77–80

J. Gilchrist, 'The Relationship between the Collection in Four Books and the Collection in Seventy-four-Titles', BMCL 12 (1982) 13–30

Kölzer, *Collectio canonum* 45–48

Gilchrist, 'Manuscripts' 64–120 (description of fifteen manuscripts)

Mordek, 'Kanonistik und gregorianische Reform' 65–66

Jasper, *Papstwahldekret* 19–33

Landau, 'Kanonessammlungen in der Lombardei' 449

J. Gilchrist, 'Changing the Structure of a Canonical Collection: The Collection in Seventy-Four Titles, Four Books and the Pseudo-Isidorian Decretals', *In Iure*

Veritas: Studies in Canon Law in Memory of Schafer Williams, ed. S. B. Bowman and B. E. Cody (Cincinnati 1991) 93–117

Gaudemet, 'Primauté' 155–156

J. Gaudemet, 'La primauté pontificale dans les collections canoniques grégoriennes', *Studi in onore Luigi Prosdocimi* (1994) 1.1.59–90

Collectio 17 librorum (Collectio S. Hilarii Pictaviensis)

1. Author: Unknown. *2. Date:* 1075–1100 (Gilchrist). *3. Place:* Poitiers (according to Tardif), sceptically: Fournier-Le Bras 2.234 (only French origin is certain). *4. Type:* Mainly excerpts from the *Decretum Burchardi* and the *Collectio 74 titulorum,* also reception of the *Abbreviatio Ansegisi et Benedicti Levitae. 5. Edition:* None.

6. Manuscripts

Berlin, Staatsbibliothek Preußischer Kulturbesitz, Phill. 1778, saec. XII, Prov. Saint-Hilaire in Poitiers, in the seventeenth century in possession of Hauteserre de Salvaison, professor of the university at Poitiers, who handed it over to the Jesuits of the Collège Louis-le-Grand; then it was transfered to the library of Sir Thomas Phillipps and finally the Royal Library of Berlin; the last leaves of this manuscript are lost; cf. Rose, *Handschriften-Verzeichnisse* 12, 194–197

Hereford, Cathedral Library, O.II.7, saec. XII^{in}, Prov. Hereford (probably written at Hereford Cathedral, where it was by saec. XII^{med}), fol. 46^{r}–150^{v}, cf. Schenkl, 'Bibliotheca patrum Latinorum Britannica' *SB Vienna* 143 (1898) 8–9 (saec. X); W. Holtzmann, *Papsturkunden in England, 2: Die kirchlichen Archive und Bibliotheken,* 1: *Berichte und Handschriftenbeschreibungen* (Abh. Göttingen, 3. Folge 14, Berlin 1935) 58; P. Brommer, 'Kurzformen' 21 n. 10; saec. XII, Brooke, *English Church* 89 and 237 (as an abridged version of the *Decretum Burchardi*), cf. Mynors-Thomson, *Catalogue of Hereford* 14

Reims, Bibliothèque municipale, 675 (olim G 528); Prov. Italy according to the *Catalogue des manuscrits de Reims,* but see also Fournier-Le Bras 2.230: France, perhaps Eastern or Northeastern France; in the fourteenth century in the possession of the Archbishop of Reims, Gui de Roye, who gave it to the chapter library

Extensive Excerpts

Bern, Burgerbibliothek, 314, saec. XI cf. H. Hagen, *Catalogus Codicum Bernensium (Bibliotheca Bongarsiana)* (1874) 323–324; Fowler-Magerl (see below) 143–144

7. Bibliography

Fournier-Le Bras 2.230–235; Van Hove, *Prolegomena* 331; Stickler, *Historia* 1.176; García y García, *Historia* 1.317.

J. Tardif, 'Une collection canonique Poitevine', RHD 21 (1897) 149–216, especially 158–159

Fournier, 'Collections canoniques issues du Décret de Burchard' 189–214

Fournier, 'Décret' 695–696

Seckel, 'Benedictus Levita' 455–460

Brooke, *English Church* 89, 92, 237
Fournier, 'Angleterre' 129–130
G. Le Bras, 'L'activité canonique à Poitiers pendant la réforme grégorienne (1049–1099)', *Mélanges offerts à René Crozet,* ed. P. Gallais and Y.-J. Riou (Poitiers 1966) 1.237–239
Reynolds, 'Turin Collection' 508–514
Gilchrist, 'Reception 1' 57
Brommer, 'Kurzformen' 19–45
Brommer, 'Rezeption' 144
Fowler-Magerl, 'Vorgratianische Kanonessammlungen' 143–144
Schmitz, 'Abbreviatio Ansegisi' 176–199, especially 191–199

Collectio (Liber) Tarraconensis

1. Author: Unknown. *2. Date:* First recension between 1080 and soon after the death of Gregory VII (Fowler-Magerl 139). Between 1085 and 1090 (Gilchrist). Second recension between 1093 and 1095? (Fowler-Magerl). *3. Place:* Poitiers, Aquitaine, Northwestern France. *4. Type:* Neither a systematically nor a chronologically arranged collection, but composed of different 'blocks of sources' (Fowler-Magerl 125). *5. Edition:* None.

6. Manuscripts

First Recension

Milano, Biblioteca Ambrosiana, D.59 sup. (soon after 1080?, incomplete in the beginning)

Paris, Bibliothèque nationale, lat. 5517, saec. XII, (Gilchrist, 'Reception 2': saec. XI) fol. 46^{v}–141^{v}; according to Gilchrist, 'Reception 2' 199–200 it contains an early version of the *Liber Tarraconensis* whose precise relation to the first and the second recension has not been established yet; but see Fowler-Magerl 142: 'first recension'; Prov. Tulle, Département Corrèze

Tarragona, Biblioteca Publica (Provincial), 26 (44); saec. XI^{ex}, Prov. Abbey of Santes Creus, Catalonia, fol. 13^{r}–157^{v}; cf. Mordek, *Kirchenrecht und Reform* 691 [Index])

Second Recension

An enlarged version of the first recension

Paris, Bibliothèque nationale, lat. 4281B

Vaticano, Città del, Biblioteca Apostolica Vaticana, lat. 6093, saec. XII (in all probability the very manuscript that Antonio Agustín got from the Cistercians of Poblet in the province of Tarragona)

7. Bibliography

Fournier-Le Bras 2.240–247; Kurtscheid-Wilches 1.165; Van Hove, *Prolegomena* 330; Stickler, *Historia* 1.176; García y García, *Historia* 1.316 including n. 67.

P. Fournier, 'Le *Liber Tarraconensis*: Etude sur une collection canonique du XIe siècle', *Mélanges Julien Havet* (Paris 1895) 259–281

Ryan, 'Observations' 99 and 102
J. J. Ryan, 'Cardinal Humbert *De s. Romana ecclesia*: Relics of Roman Byzantine Relations 1053–1054', MS 20 (1958) 206–238, especially 213
Reynolds, 'Turin Collection' 510 n. 14
Kuttner, 'Roman Manuscripts' 7–29
Gilchrist, 'Economic Policy', 413–414
Gilchrist, 'Reception 1' 55–56
Petersmann, 'Kanonistische Überlieferung' 381–382
G. Fransen, 'Autour de la collection en 74 titres', RDC 25 (1975) 61–73, especially 62
Gilchrist, 'Reception 2' 199–200
Gilchrist, 'Epistola Widonis' 588
Fowler-Magerl, 'Vorgratianische Kanonessammlungen' 139 and 142
J. N. Hillgarth and G. Silano, 'A Compilation of the Diocesan Synods of Barcelona (1354): Critical Edition and Analysis', MS 46 (1984) 78–157
R. Reynolds, 'The Ordination Rite in Medieval Spain: Hispanic, Roman, and Hybrid', *Santiago, Saint-Denis, and Saint Peter: The Reception of the Roman Liturgy in Leon-Castile in 1080*, ed. B. F. Reilly (New York 1985) 131–155, especially 143
G. Fransen, 'Appendix Seguntina, Liber Tarraconensis et Décret de Gratien', REDC 45 [1988] 31–34
Landau, 'Gefälschtes Recht' 47 n. 148
L. Orfila, 'A propósito del manuscrito 6.093 de la Biblioteca Vaticana', *Hispana Christiana* 279–302
Landau, 'Kanonessammlungen in der Lombardei' 450
J. Gaudemet, 'La primauté pontificale dans les collections canoniques grégoriennes', *Studi in onore Luigi Prosdocimi*, (1994) 1.1.59–90

Collectio Burdegalensis (Bordeaux 11 and Würzburg M.p.j.q. 2)

1. *Author:* Unknown. 2. *Date:* After 1078 (Synod of Poitiers). 3. *Place:* Aquitaine, perhaps Poitou. 4. *Type:* Combination of the *Decretum Burchardi* and the *Collectio 74 titulorum*. 5. *Edition:* None.

6. *Manuscripts*

Bordeaux, Bibliothèque municipale, 11, saec. XI^{ex} (XII according to Brommer), Prov. La Sauve in Poitou, cf. C. Couderc, *Catalogue des manuscrits de la bibliothèque de Bordeaux: Catalogue général* 23 (1894) 7–16 (contains only seven books), fol. 147^{r}–171^{v}, fragmentary, only part of a collection in 16 books, without *capitulatio*

Würzburg, Universitätsbibliothek, M.p.j.q. 2, saec. XI^{ex}–XII^{in}, Western France, Prov. from the library of Nicolaus Joseph Foucault (1643–1722); complete in 16 books; cf. Fowler-Magerl, 'Vorgratianische Kanonessammlungen' 144

7. *Bibliography*

Fournier-Le Bras 2.247–250; Van Hove, *Prolegomena* 331; Stickler, *Historia* 1.176; García y García, *Historia* 1.317

J. Tardif, 'Une collection canonique poitevine', RHD 21 (1897) 149–216
Fournier, 'Polycarpus' 55–101
Reynolds, 'Turin Collection' 508–514
Gilchrist, 'Economic Policy' 414–415
Gilchrist, 'Reception 1' 57
Petersmann, 'Kanonistische Überlieferung' 381–382
Brommer, 'Kurzformen' 42
Fowler-Magerl, 'Vorgratianische Kanonessammlungen' 144
Gilchrist, 'Monastic Forgeries' 263–287

Collectio 183 titulorum

1. Author: Supporter of the Gregorian Reform. *2. Date:* Between 1063 and 1083–1085 (Motta, 'Liber canonum' 333: Passage from the Lateran Council 1110 [cf. Blumenthal, *Early Councils* 110 n. 37] is a later addition). *3. Place:* Perhaps Northwestern Tuscany (Lucca?). *4. Type:* Systematic collection, source of the *Collectio 5 librorum* (Vat. lat. 1348), cf. Motta; makes extensive use of Pseudo-Isidore and the *Decretum Burchardi*

5. Edition

Liber canonum diuersorum sanctorum patrum siue Collectio in CLXXXIII titulos digesta, ed. J. Motta (MIC, Series B: Corpus Collectionum 7; Vatican City 1988), cf. review by J. Gaudemet, 'Notes d'histoire des collections canoniques (à propos d'une publication recente)', RHD 67 (1989) 47–53

6. Manuscripts

Firenze, Biblioteca Nazionale Centrale, Conv. soppr., A.IV.269, written after the pontificate of Paschal II (about 1120), Prov. S. Maria Novella, cf. Motta 333 (probably from Lucca, already in Prato at a very early date; the Dominican Gerardus Naso bought it for the library of his order in Santa Maria Novella in Florence, cf. fol. 227^{v}, notation of a fourteenth century hand (or from the end of the thirteenth century) cf. Fournier-Le Bras 2.152 n. 1), fol. 7^{r}–227^{v}
Firenze, Biblioteca Marucelliana, C.386, saec. XII^{in}, fol. 1^{r}–161^{r}

Revised Version
Firenze, Biblioteca Riccardiana, 3006 (3108), saec. XII^{in} (only manuscript which subdivides the collection in two books of 98 and 85 titles)

7. Bibliography

Fournier-Le Bras 2.151–155; Van Hove, *Prolegomena* 326; Stickler, *Historia* 1.176–177

Mordek, 'Handschriftenforschungen' 629–630 and n. 7
Mordek, *Kirchenrecht und Reform* 227 n. 62
G. Motta, 'I rapporti tra la Collezione canonica di S. Maria Novella e quella in Cinque Libri (Firenze, Bibl. Naz. Conv. soppr. MS A.4.268 e Bibl. Vaticana, Vat. lat. 1348)', BMCL 7 (1977) 89–94

Blumenthal, *Early Councils* 110 n. 37

U.-R. Blumenthal, 'Decrees and Decretals of Pope Paschal II in Twelfth-Century Canonical Collections', BMCL 10 (1980) 26 n. 55

M. Pogliani, 'Chiesa, diritto e ordinamento della *Societas christiana* nei secoli XI e XII (Passo Mendola, 28 agosto–2 settembre 1983)', RSCI 37 (1983) 575–587

Mordek, 'Systematische Kanonessammlungen' 193

Motta, 'Liber canonum' 331–339

J. Gaudemet, 'Notes d'histoire des collections canoniques (à propos d'une publication recente)', RHD 67 (1989) 47–53 (review of Motta's edition)

Gaudemet, 'Primauté' 137–156, especially 155–156

J. Gaudemet, 'La primauté pontificale dans les collections canoniques grégoriennes', *Studi in onore Luigi Prosdocimi* (1994) 1.1.59–90

Collectio 5 librorum (Vat. lat. 1348)

1. Author: Unknown. *2. Date:* End of the pontificate of Gregory VII (about 1083–1085). *3. Place:* Italy (Tuscany?). *4. Type:* Abridged version of the *Collectio 183 titulorum* cf. Motta, 'Liber canonum' 332.

5. Edition

List of incipits and explicits by Wolf von Glanvell (see below, 'Bibliography')

G. Motta (ed.), *Liber canonum diuersorum sanctorum patrum siue Collectio in CLXXXIII titulos digesta* (MIC, Series B: Corpus Collectionum 7; Vatican City 1988) 303–324 (Appendix) *Collectio canonum in quinque libris* (Vat. lat. 1348): List of titles and chapters

6. Manuscript

Vaticano, Città del, Biblioteca Apostolica Vaticana, lat. 1348, saec. XII^{in}, written during the pontificate of Paschal II (1099–1118) (Motta: saec. XI2/2); central Italy (cf. Mordek, *Kirchenrecht und Reform* 201 n. 529); since the Middle Ages in the convent of Santa-Maria-dei-Angeli in Florence; title: *Liber excerptus ex sententiis canonum sanctorum Patrum*, fol. 7^{v}–165^{r}

7. Bibliography

Fournier Le Bras 2.131–135; Van Hove, *Prolegomena* 325; Stickler, *Historia* 1.176

F. Arevalo, *Ad opera S. Isidori Hispalensis Prolegomena* 2.262 (PL 81.792)

V. Wolf von Glanvell, 'Die Canonessammlung des Cod. Vatican. lat. 1348' SB Vienna 136.2 (1897) 1–55

Stickler, 'Potere coattivo' 275–278

Picasso, *Collezioni canoniche Milanesi* 33

H. Hees, 'Zur Collectio quinque librorum (Cod. Vat. lat. 1348)', BMCL 4 (1974) 63–64

Mordek, *Kirchenrecht und Reform* 201 n. 529

G. Motta, 'I rapporti tra la Collezione canonica di S. Maria Novella e quella in

Cinque Libri: Firenze, Bibl. Naz. Conv. soppr. MS A.4.269 e Bibl. Vaticana, Vat. lat. 1348', BMCL 7 (1977) 89–94
Gilchrist, 'Reception 2' 206
Mordek, 'Systematische Kanonessammlungen' 193
Motta, 'Liber canonum' 332
Kuttner-Elze, *Catalogue* 1.106–108

Anselm II of Lucca, Collectio canonum

1. Author: Bishop Anselm II of Lucca († before 18 March 1086). *2. Date:* Not before 1081 (contains an extract from a letter of Gregory VII to Hermann of Metz dating from 15 March 1081); perhaps about 1083 (one of the collections used as a source was not compiled before 1083, cf. Sickel, *Das Privilegium Otto I. für die Römische Kirche vom Jahre 962* [Innsbruck 1883] and Fournier-Le Bras 2.27–28). *Recension C* probably originated in the first quarter of the twelfth century (Mordek, *Kirchenrecht und Reform* 136 n. 179 according to Fournier, 'Observations' 448–449). *3. Place:* Italy. *4. Type:* Systematic collection.

5. Editions

Angelo Mai, *Spicilegium Romanum* 6 (Rome 1832) 316–395 (*Capitulationes* of the entire collection according to manuscripts of Recension B and C) (PL 149.485–568)

F. Thaner, *Anselmi episcopi Lucensis collectio canonum, una cum collectione minore* (Innsbruck 1906–1915; repr. Aalen 1965) (incomplete edition to 11.15, based on Form A: Vat. Barb. lat. 535)

G. Motta (ed. comm.), 'La redazione A 'Aucta' della *Collectio Anselmi Episcopi Lucensis*', *Studia in Honorem A. M. Stickler* (1992) 375–449 (Manuscripts Venezia IV.55; Mantova C.II.23) (Introduction, text and *Initia canonum)*

6. Manuscripts

Still valid for the distinction of the different recensions: Fournier, 'Observations' 427–458; but now revised by Landau, 'Erweiterte Fassungen'

Recension A

Cambridge, Library of Corpus Christi College, 269, saec. XII; Italy, perhaps in England in the first half of the twelfth century; in the fifteenth century it belonged to the Cistercian abbey of Pipewell in Northamptonshire; cf. Brooke, *English Church* 91; see also M. Brett, 'The Canons of the First Lateran Council in English Manuscripts', *Proceedings Berkeley* 21 n. 27 and *Proceedings Cambridge* xxviii)

Paris, Bibliothèque nationale, lat. 12519, saec. XII

Vaticano, Città del, Biblioteca Apostolica Vaticana, lat. 1363, saec. XII

Recension A' (A 1 in Thaner)

Most widely diffused form of the collection in the first half of the twelfth century; Northern Italy, perhaps Po valley; Gratian presumably used a manuscript of this recension

Firenze, Biblioteca Medicea Laurenziana, Ashburnham 53, saec. XII, Italy

Firenze, Biblioteca Medicea Laurenziana, San Marco 499, saec. XII (end?), Central Italy, probably Tuscany, fol. 10^{v}–185^{v}, cf. Mordek, 'Handschriftenforschungen' 628 n. 6; Blumenthal, *Early Councils* 64

Graz, Universitätsbibliothek, II 351 (olim 41/43?); in 1184 it was given to the convent of Seckau

Napoli, Biblioteca Nazionale Vittorio Emanuele II, XII.A.37–39, saec. XII

Parma, Biblioteca Palatina, Parm. 976, saec. XII, cf. also Alger of Liège, below

Pisa, Biblioteca del Seminario Santa Catarina, 59 (contains only the abridged version and thus is not easy to classify)

Recension Anselm A Ven (*Motta:* 'A Aucta')

Northern Italy; competing version of A', not only of local importance, but also known outside of Northern Italy, cf. *Collectio 13 librorum* (Berlin, Savigny 3); must have originated during the eleventh century

Mantova, Biblioteca Comunale, C.II.23 (318), saec. XII^{in}, Prov. monastery of San Benedetto di Polirone at Mantova (cf. R. Brunell, *Sant'Anselmo a Mantova* [catalogue published on the occasion of the Centenario IX in 1986] 70–71) Ballerini listed it as *Codex Padirilonensis* (P. IV, cap. XIII, c. 2, 4, 6)

Venezia, Biblioteca Nazionale Marciana, lat. IV.55 (2243), saec. XII (considerable additions to Recension A), possibly from the region around Padova (belonged to Bishop Niccolà Ormaneto of Padova, cf. Kuttner, 'Roman Manuscripts' 20)

Recension Bb

Fournier classified it as a supplemented version of Form A; according to Landau a version of only local importance (restricted to Lucca and its surrounding area) without further impact; there is no evidence in favor of Fournier's assumption that this recension was used by Polycarpus, the author of the Caesaraugustana or Gratian, cf. Fournier, 'Polycarpus' 71 n. 1, Fournier, 'Caesaraugustana' 62, and Landau, 'Erweiterte Fassungen' 331–333

Vaticano, Città del, Biblioteca Apostolica Vaticana, Barb. lat. 535 (olim Barberini XI.178), saec. XII, written during the pontificate of Paschal II (cf. catalogue of popes) at Lucca (according to Fournier, 'Observations' 453 and 454) perhaps even in the famous chapter of canons of San Frediano (cf. Landau, 'Erweiterte Fassungen' 331–332); the manuscript contains only Books I–VII of the collection, cf. Ballerini, P. IV, cap. XIII, § 1 (shelf-mark 1881); M. Sarti and M. Fattorini, *De claris Archigymnasii Bononiensis Professoribus* (Bologna ^{2}1888–1896) 2.280–282; the collection itself originated after 1109 (contains the fragment of a letter by Paschal II which can be dated to 1109); the Bb version has two additions which are decretals of Alexander II, former bishop of Lucca and an uncle of Anselm's II of Lucca; cf. Landau: three texts of Urban II source of Book I–VII (following books modelled on Vat. lat. 4983), the copy made by d'Achery (Paris lat. 12450–51) which in turn became the source of the copy made by Gustav Haenel (Leipzig 3528)

Recension B (deletion of the penitential Book 11 of Recension A)

Close connection with C Recension and the origin of Vat. lat. 1364 indicate that Recension B also originated in Northern Italy

Berlin, Staatsbibliothek Preußischer Kulturbesitz, lat. fol. 597, saec. XII^{in}, cf. Gilchrist, 'The Collectio canonum of Bishop Anselm II of Lucca († 1086): Recension B of Berlin, Staatsbibliothek Preussischer Kulturbesitz Cod. 597', *Studi in onore Luigi Prosdocimi* (1994) 1.2.377–403

Vaticano, Città del, Biblioteca Apostolica Vaticana, lat. 1364, saec. XI^{ex} (after 1095, cf. Landau, 'Erweiterte Fassungen' 333 n. 51); Prov. Cluniac Priory Pontida near Bergamo, cf. G. Spinelli, 'Il Vat. lat. 1364 e l'Abbazia di Pontida', RSCI 26 (1972) 101–104

Vaticano, Città del, Biblioteca Apostolica Vaticana, lat. 6381 (ends with Ans. B XIII, 17 [Ans. A XIII, 16]); written in Nothern Italy or Southern France; cf. Gassò - Batlle, *Pelagii I Papae epistulae* l; in the sixteenth century it belonged to the auditor at the Rota and later bishop of Sarno, Luis Gomez, whence it came into the possession of Antonio Agustín (cf. Kuttner, 'Roman Manuscripts' 16 and 18–20)

Fragment

Bologna, Biblioteca Universitaria, 375; incomplete, only to Ans. 4.33, cf. L. Paolini, 'La *Collectio canonum* di Anselmo da Lucca (Codice 375 della Biblioteca Universitaria di Bologna)', *Il Carobbio* 5 (1979) 368–372 (from the private library of Prosper Lambertini [Pope Benedict XIV] to the University of Bologna)

'Recension C'

Landau, BMCL 16, 1986 (as below), however, places this version as a 'B' version, made into the distinctive 'C' version by a post-medieval scholar. Probably shortly after 1138 in Northern Italy; there is no indication that it was used by Gratian, cf. Landau

Huesca, Biblioteca Pública Provincial, 20, saec. XVI; cf. Kuttner, 'Roman Manuscripts' 13; Landau, 'Erweiterte Fassungen' 325

Vaticano, Città del, Biblioteca Apostolica Vaticana, lat. 4983, saec. XVI^{2}; copy of a manuscript saec. XII; the *Correctores Romani* used a so far untraced *vetustus codex* that belonged to Hieronymus Parisetti; on the basis of this codex Vat. lat. 4983 was made for Miguel Taxaquet, the secretary of the *Correctores;* a sixteenth-century copy combining several recensions of Anselm served as a 'working' manuscript for the *Correctores*

Vaticano, Città del, Biblioteca Apostolica Vaticana, Ottobon. lat. 224 (a. 1600), a copy of Vat. lat. 4983; cf. Mordek, 'Herovalliana' 241; Landau, 'Erweiterte Fassungen' 325

Fragment

Bern, Burgerbibliothek, 756.52, saec. XII, Italy (one leaf, Anselm II 43–45)

Fragmentary Later Copies

Paris, Bibliothèque nationale, lat. 1444, about 1600 (same size as Vat. lat. 3531) (Recension Bb)

Vaticano, Città del, Biblioteca Apostolica Vaticana, lat. 3531, saec. XVI^{ex} (Recension Bb)

Vaticano, Città del, Biblioteca Apostolica Vaticana, Reg. lat. 325, saec. XV

Other Copies

These are later copies, according to Landau, BMCL 16, 1986, 19 n. 20

Leipzig, Universitätsbibliothek, Haenel 31 (olim no. 3528), saec. XIX (copy made by Haenel) is according to Fournier, 'Observations' 430 and 455 a transcription of Paris lat. 12450–51, Bb-Recension

Paris, Bibliothèque nationale, lat. 12450–51 (olim Sangerm. 939; saec. XVII) transmits a mixed form: Books 8–13 are modelled on Vat. lat. 4983 (C Recension), Books 1–7 on Cod. Vat. Barb. lat. 535 (Bb Recension) (cf. Fournier, 'Observations' 454–455); at the end of the seventh Book (End of Paris lat. 12450) the scribe has added the additional texts of C (including the *Herovalliana*-Canon) in a cluster.

Small Excerpt

Milano, Biblioteca Ambrosiana, A.46 inf., saec. IX^{ex}, Reims, fol. 132^{r} (addition saec. XII); cf. Mordek, *Bibliotheca capitularium* 236

7. *Bibliography*

Conrat, *Geschichte* 132, 364–366; C. Mirbt, 'Anselm von Lucca', RE 1 (^{3}1896) 572–573; P. Richard, 'Anselme de Lucques', DHGE 3 (1924) 489–493; Fournier-Le Bras 2.25–37 and 192–198 (on the Bb and C Recensions); A. Amanieu, 'Anselme de Lucques (Collection d')', DDC 1 (1935) 567–578; Kurtscheid-Wilches 1.156–158; Van Hove, *Prolegomena* 235, 264, 323–324, 328; Stickler, *Historia* 1.170–172; C. Violante, DBI 3 (1961) 399–407; G. M. Fusconi, 'Anselmo II, vescovo di Lucca', *Bibliotheca Sanctorum* 2 (1962) 26–36; García y García, *Historia* 1.313–314; *Rep. font.* 2 (1967) 368–369; Th. Kölzer, 'Anselm von Lucca', LMA 1 (1980) 679–680

Ballerini, *De antiquis . . . collectionibus et collectoribus* P. IV, cap. XIII (PL 56.326–329)

Monsacrati, *Animadversiones in Decretum manuscriptum S. Anselmi episcopi Lucensis* (Rome 1821)

E. L. Richter, *Beiträge zur Kenntnis der Quellen des canonischen Rechts* (Leipzig 1834) 77

Theiner, *Disquisitiones criticae* 363–364 (PL 149.535–568)

Wasserschleben, *Beiträge* 150–158

H. Hüffer, *Beiträge zur Geschichte der Quellen des Kirchenrechts und des römischen Rechts im Mittelalter* (Münster 1862) 71 (Roman law texts contained in Anselm)

T. Sickel, *Das Privilegium Otto I. für die römische Kirche vom Jahre 962* (Innsbruck 1883) 59–61 and 77

Fournier, 'Observations' 427–458

Wretschko, *Theodosiani libri XVI* p. ccclvii

M. Massimo, *Gregor VII. im Verhältnis zu seinen Legaten* (Greifswald 1907) 32ff.

Fournier, 'Tournant' 129–180

Fournier, 'Collections canoniques romaines' 294–327, 365–395

A. Guerra and P. Guidi, *Compendio di Storia ecclesiastica Lucchese* (Lucca 1924) 150–160

A. Fliche, *La Réforme grégorienne, 2: Grégoire VII* (Louvain 1925) 389–402

P. Guidi, 'Il primicerio lucchese Bardo non è l'autore della *Vita S. Anselmi episcopi Lucensis*', *Miscellanea Lucchese di Studi Storici e Letterari in onore di Salvatore Bongi* (Lucca 1926) 11–29

Brooke, *English Church* 91 and 241

A. Fliche, *La Réforme grégorienne, 3: L'opposition antigrégorienne* (Louvain 1937) 127

R. Montanari, *La 'Collectio Canonum' di S. Anselmo di Lucca e la riforma gregoriana* (Mantova 1941)

A. Michel, *Die Sentenzen des Kardinals Humbert, das erste Rechtsbuch der päpstlichen Reform* (Schriften des Reichsinstituts für ältere deutsche Geschichtskunde [MGH] 7; Stuttgart 1943)

A. Fliche, 'La valeur historique de la collection canonique d'Anselme de Lucques', *Miscellanea historica in honorem Alberti de Meyer* 1 (Louvain-Brussels 1946) 348–455

L. Simeoni, 'Il contributo della contessa Matilde al papato nella lotta per le investiture', SGreg 1 (1947) 353–372

S. Kuttner, 'Liber canonicus: A Note on *Dictatus Papae* c. 17', SGreg 2 (1947) 388 n. 7

Stickler, 'Potere coattivo' 235–285

Ch. Dereine, 'Le problème de la vie commune chez les canonistes d'Anselme de Lucques à Gratien', SGreg 3 (Rome 1948) 287–298

M. Giusti, 'Le canoniche della città e diocesi di Lucca al tempo della riforma gregoriana', SGreg 3 (Rome 1948) 321–367

U. Tibaldi, *S. Anselmo vescovo di Lucca e patrone di Mantova* (Mantua 1955) ('worthless' according to Fuhrmann, *Einfluß und Verbreitung* 2.509, n. 226)

G. B. Borino, 'Il monacato e l'investitura di Anselmo vescovo di Lucca', SGreg 5 (1956) 361–374

Gossman, *Urban II* 38–41

J. Bernhard, *La collection en deux livres (Cod. Vat. lat. 3832),* 1: *La forme primitive de la collection en deux livres, source de la collection en 74 Titres et de la collection d'Anselme de Lucques* 1–2, RDC 12 (1962) 1–601

Sprandel, *Ivo von Chartres* 53–54, 57–58, 63–64, 70–71

A. Stickler, *Salesianum* 25 (1963) 502–503

R. Amiet, 'Une *Admonitio Synodalis* de l'époque carolingienne', MS 26 (1964) 15 n. 1 (Cod. Vat. Reg. lat. 325 [saec. XVI] not a copy of the Barberinus, but a tradition of its own)

E. Pasztor, 'Sacerdozio e regno nella *Vita Anselmi episcopi Lucensis',* AHP 2 (1964) 91–115

J. Gilchrist, 'The Collection of Cod. Vat. lat. 3832: A source of the Collection in Seventy four Titles?' *Etudes . . . Le Bras* 1.141–156

E. Pásztor, 'Motivi dell'ecclesiologia di Anselmo di Lucca: In margine a un sermone inedita', *Bulletino dell'Istituto storico italiano per il medioevo* 77 (1965) 45–101 (on Bruxelles lat. 18644–52 and the 'Sermo Anselmi episcopi de charitate')

M. L. Corsi, 'Note sulla famiglia da Baggio (secoli IX–XIII)', *Raccolta di studi in memoria di G. Soranzo* (1968) 166–206

Rambaud-Buhot, 'Critique' 5–62, especially 40–42

Mordek, 'Herovalliana' 241

Kuttner, 'Roman Manuscripts' 13–23 (III. Anselm of Lucca: the Manuscripts of the *Correctores Romani* and of Antonio Agustín) (repr. Kuttner, *Medieval Councils, Decretals and Collections of Canon Law* [London 1980] no. 11)

Mordek, 'Handschriftenforschungen' 628 including n. 6

W. Wattenbach and R. Holtzmann, *Deutschlands Geschichtsquellen im Mittelalter* 3, ed. F.-J. Schmale (Darmstadt 1971) 857–858

W. Berschin, *Bonizo von Sutri: Leben und Werk* (Beiträge zur Geschichte und Quellenkunde des Mittelalters 2; Berlin-New York 1972); Italian translation: *Bonizone di Sutri: La vita e le opere,* trans. A. Tabarroni (Centro Italiano di Studi sull'Alto Medioevo; Spoleto 1992)

Gilchrist, 'Economic Policy' 401–403

R. Knox, 'Finding the Law: Developments in Canon Law during the Gregorian Reform', SG 9 (1972) 419–466

Kuttner, 'Turning point' 55–85

A. Nitschke, 'Das Verständnis für Gregors Reformen im 11. Jahrhundert', SGreg 9 (1972) 143–166

G. Spinelli, 'Il Vat. lat. 1364 e l'Abbazia di Pontida', RSCI 26 (1972) 101–104

J. Ziese, *Historische Beweisführung in Streitschriften des Investiturstreites* (Münchener Beiträge zur Mediävistik und Renaissance-Forschung; Munich 1972) 18–95

H. Fuhrmann, 'Das Reformpapsttum und die Rechtswissenschaft', *Investiturstreit und Reichsverfassung,* ed. J. Fleckenstein (Vorträge und Forschungen 17; Sigmaringen 1973) 175–203

Fuhrmann, *Einfluß und Verbreitung* 2.509–522

Gilchrist, 'Reception 1' 37–38

R. H. Rough, *The Reformist Illuminations in the Gospels of Matilda, Countess of Tuscany: A Study in the Art of the Age of Gregory VII* (The Hague 1973) 27–33

H. Schwarzmeier, *Lucca und das Reich im 11. Jahrhundert* (Tübingen 1973) 400–412

Petersmann, 'Kanonistische Überlieferung' 368–369, 374–378

Brommer, 'Rezeption' 113–160

G. Kreuzer, *Die Honoriusfrage im Mittelalter und in der Neuzeit* (Päpste und Papsttum 8; Stuttgart 1975)

Mordek, *Kirchenrecht und Reform* 136 n. 179, 137 n. 182, 184 including n. 411 and 412

U.-R. Blumenthal, 'Paschalian Additions in Manuscripts of the Collectio canonum of Anselm of Lucca', *Manuscripta* 20 (1976) 3–4

U.-R. Blumenthal, 'Some Notes on Papal Policies at Guastalla, 1106', SG 19 (1976) 59–78

Blumenthal, *Early Councils* 57–59, 65–68, 132–133

L. Paolini, 'La *Collectio canonum* di Anselmo da Lucca: (Codice 375 della Biblioteca Universitaria di Bologna)', *Il Carrobbio* 5 (Bologna 1979) 368–372

Gilchrist, 'Reception 2' 195–196 (on Cod. Firenze, Ashburnham 53)

Horst, *Polycarpus* 45–46 (on Rec. Bb)

R. Somerville, 'Anselm of Lucca and Wibert of Ravenna', BMCL 10 (1980) 1–13 (repr. *Papacy, Councils and Canon Law in the 11th–12th Centuries* [Aldershot 1990])

M. C. De Matteis, 'Tematica della povertà e problema delle *Res ecclesiae*: Notazioni ed esemplificazione campione su alcune collezioni canoniche del periodo della riforma ecclesiastica del sec. XI', BISIAM 90 (1982–1983) 177–226

P. Landau, 'Neue Forschungen zu vorgratianischen Kanonessammlungen und den Quellen des gratianischen Dekrets', *Ius commune* 11 (1984) 1–29

P. J. Payer, *Sex and the Penitentials: The Development of a Sexual Code 550–1150* (Toronto 1984)

M. Brett, 'The Canons of the First Lateran Council in English Manuscripts', *Proceedings Berkeley* 13–28, especially 21, n. 27

G. Folliet, 'Une collection anonyme *Pro causa injustae excommunicationis* des VIIe–VIIIe siècles', *Miscellanea di studi agostiniani: Studi in onore di P. Agostino Trapè* (Rome 1985) 295–308

C. Märtl, 'Zur Überlieferung des Liber contra Wibertum Anselms von Lucca', DA 41 (1985) 192–202 (cf. Somerville, 1980)

Mordek, 'Systematische Kanonessammlungen' 195 including n. 53

R. Pescaglini Monti, 'Le dipendenze polironiane in diocesi di Lucca', *L'Italia nel quadro dell'espansione europea del monachesimo cluniacense: Atti del convegno internazionale di Storia medioevale, Pescia, 26–28 novembre 1981*, ed. C. Violante, A. Spicciani and G. Spinelli (Cesena 1985) 143–172

Mordek, 'Kanonistik und gregorianische Reform' 70

Mordek, 'Riforma gregoriana' 95 including n. 25

P. Landau, 'Die Rezension C der Sammlung des Anselm von Lucca', BMCL 16 (1986) 17–54

J.-M. Salgado, 'La maternité spirituelle de la Sainte Vierge chez les Pères durant les quatre premiers siècles, du Ve au VIIIe siècle, dans la vie de l'Eglise du IXe au XIe siècle', *Divinitas* 30 (1986) 53–77, 120–160, 240–270

Picasso, 'Reformatio Ecclesiae' 70–88

Jasper, *Papstwahldekret* 52–53

S. Cantelli, 'Le preghiere a Maria di Anselmo da Lucca', *Sant'Anselmo, Mantova* 291–299

C. D. Fonseca, 'La memoria gregoriana di Anselmo da Lucca', *Sant'Anselmo, Mantova* 15–25

G. Fornasari, 'S. Anselmo e il problema della *caritas*',*Sant'Anselmo, Mantova* 301–312

P. Golinelli, 'Dall'agiografia alla storia: Le *Vitae* di sant'Anselmo di Lucca', *Sant'-Anselmo, Mantova* 27–62

Landau, 'Erweiterte Fassungen' 323–338 (Italian translation: P. Landau, 'Intorno alle redazioni più ampie del XII secolo della raccolta di canoni di Anselmo da Lucca', *Sant'Anselmo, Mantova* 339–348)

E. Pásztor, 'Lotta per le investiture e *ius belli:* La posizione di Anselmo di Lucca', *Sant'Anselmo, Mantova* 375–421

G. Picasso, 'La *Collectio canonum* di Anselmo nella storia delle collezioni canoniche', *Sant'Anselmo, Mantova* 313–321

P. Piva, 'Chiesa dei canonici o seconda cattedrale? Anselmo da Lucca e la chiesa di S. Paolo in Mantova', *Sant'Anselmo, Mantova* 137–158

R. Signorini, 'Per la storia della salma di sant'Anselmo e delle sue traslazioni', *Sant'Anselmo, Mantova* 97–118

M. Vaini, 'Sant'Anselmo nella vita religiosa e culturale di Mantova', *Sant'Anselmo, Mantova* 63–79

Blumenthal, 'Fälschungen' 242

J. Gaudemet, 'Le deuxième concile de Nicée (787) dans les Collections canoniques occidentales', AHC 20 (1988) 287–288

P. Golinelli, 'Una agiografia di lotta: Le *Vitae* di s. Anselmo da Lucca', *'Indiscreta sanctitas': Studi sui rapporti tra culti, poteri e società nel pieno Medioevo* (Rome 1988) 117–155

Landau, 'Gefälschtes Recht' 34–35, 44 (on Recensions Bb and C), 47 n. 147

G. Motta (ed.), *Liber canonum diversorum sanctorum patrum sive Collectio in CLXXXIII titulos digesta* (Vatican City 1988)

C. Piacitelli, 'Milano e il suo territorio in età comunale (sec. XI–XIII)' RSCI 42 (1988) 245–255

P. Skubiszewski, 'Une vision monastique de l'Eglise au XIIe siècle: A propos d'un livre récent sur les peintures murales de Prüfening', CCM 31 (1988) 361–376

Landau, 'Kanonessammlungen in der Lombardei' 447–478

R. Bellini, 'Anselmo da Lucca nella storiografia degli ultimi quarant'anni', *Benedictina* 37 (1990) 317–362 (from Stickler to the conference in Mantova)

P. Golinelli, 'Sulla successione a Gregorio VII: Matilde di Canossa e la sconfitta del riformismo intransigente', *Studi in onore Ovidio Capitani*, ed. M. C. De Matteis (Bologna 1990) 68–86

P. Landau, 'Frei und Unfrei in der Kanonistik des 12. und 13. Jahrhunderts am Beispiel der Ordination der Unfreien', *Die abendländische Freiheit vom 10. zum 14. Jahrhundert: Der Wirkungszusammenhang von Idee und Wirklichkeit im europäischen Vergleich*, ed. J. Fried (Sigmaringen 1991) 177–196

W. Berschin, 'Die publizistische Reaktion auf den Tod Gregors VII. (nach fünf oberitalienischen Streitschriften)', SGreg 14 (1991) 121–135

J. Gaudemet, 'L'ordre du monde vu par un canoniste à la fin du XIe siècle' (Anselme de Lucque, Collectio Canonum, L.I.CH. 71 à 89)', PerDer 25 (1991) 59–71

J. Gaudemet, 'Le serment dans le droit canonique médiéval', *Le serment*, ed. R. Verdier (Paris 1991) 2.63–75

R. Maceratini, 'Aspetti della posizione giuridica dell'eretico in alcune opere della Riforma gregoriana', *Scritti di storia del diritto offerti dagli allievi a Domenico Maffei*, ed. M. Ascheri (Padova 1991) 1–25 (cf. review by D. Jasper, DA 49 [1993] 345)

K. G. Cushing, *Anselm of Lucca, Reform and the Canon Law, c.1046–1086 : The Beginnings of Systematization* (Diss. Oxford Univ. 1991)

U.-R. Blumenthal, 'An episcopal handbook from twelfth-century Southern Italy: Codex Rome, Bibl. Vallicelliana F.54/III', *Studia in Honorem A. M. Stickler* (1992) 13–24

H. E. J. Cowdrey, 'Canon Law and the First Crusade', *The Horns of Hattin: Proceedings of the Second Conference of the Society for the Study of the Crusades and the Latin East, Jerusalem and Haifa, 2–6 July 1987*, ed. B. Z. Kedar (Jerusalem-London 1992) 41–48

G. Fransen, 'Anselme de Lucques canoniste?' *Sant'Anselmo vescovo* 143–155

Gaudemet, 'Primauté' 155–156

Hartmann, 'Autoritäten' 427, 431, 434, 439–440

H. Keller, 'Le origini sociali e famigliari del vescovo Anselmo', *Sant'Anselmo vescovo* 27–50

E. Pásztor, 'La *Vita* anonima di Anselmo di Lucca. Una rilettura', *Sant'Anselmo vescovo* 207–222

Landau, 'Vorgratianische Kanonessammlungen bei den Dekretisten' 93–116

G. Motta, 'La Redaziona A 'aucta' della *Collectio Anselmi episcopi Lucensis*', *Studia in Honorem A. M. Stickler* (1992) 375–449 (Introduction, text and Initia canonum)

A. Spicciani, 'L'episcopato lucchese di Anselmo II da Baggio', *Sant'Anselmo vescovo* 65–112

E. Vodola, 'Sovereignty and Tabu: Evolution of the Sanction against Communication with Excommunicates, 2: Canonical Collections, *Studia in Honorem A. M. Stickler* (1992) 581–598, especially 594–595

Zechiel-Eckes, *Cresconius* 1.285–290

H. Zimmermann, 'Anselm II. zwischen Gregor VII., Mathilde von Canossa und Heinrich IV.', *Sant'Anselmo vescovo* 129–142

G. Motta, 'Monachesimo e funzioni sacerdotali in una testimonianza del secolo XI', *Medioevo e latinità in memoria di Ezio Franceschini*, ed. A. Ambrosini, M. Ferrari, C. Leonardi, G. Picasso, M. Regoliosi and P. Zerbi (Milan 1993) 303–324

R. Savigni, 'La signoria vescovile lucchese tra XI e XII secolo: Consolidamente patrimoniale e primi rapporti con la classe dirigente cittadina', *Aevum* 67 (1993) 333–367

J. Gilchrist, 'The Collectio canonum of Bishop Anselm II of Lucca (†1086): Recension B of Berlin, Staatsbibliothek Preußischer Kulturbesitz Cod. 597', *Studi in onore Luigi Prosdocimi* (1994) 1.2.377–403

P. Landau, 'Wandel und Kontinuität' 215–233

K. Zechiel-Eckes, 'Eine Mailänder Redaktion der Kirchenrechtssammlung Bischof Anselms II. von Lucca (1073–1086)', ZRG Kan. Abt. 81 (1995) 130–147

J. Gaudemet, 'La primauté pontificale dans les collections canoniques grégoriennes', *Studi in onore Luigi Prosdocimi* (1994) 1.1.59–90

R. Somerville, 'A Textual Link between Canterbury and Lucca in the Early Twelfth Century?' *Studi in onore Luigi Prosdocimi* (1994) 1.2.405–415

Collectio 13 librorum (Berlin, Savigny 3)

1. Author: Unknown. *2. Date:* Last decade of the eleventh century (about 1090–1100). *3. Place:* Poitiers? (cf. Fournier-Le Bras 2.238). *4. Type:* Unstructured collection; excerpts taken from earlier collections. Main sources: Anselm of Lucca (Recension Ans. A Ven., cf. Landau, 'Erweiterte Fassungen' 330) and *Decretum Burchardi*. *5. Edition:* None.

6. Manuscript

Berlin, Staatsbibliothek Preußischer Kulturbesitz, Savigny 3, saec. XII, cf. Theiner, *Disquisitiones criticae* 183–186; E. Friedberg (ed.), *Corpus iuris canonici* 1 (Leipzig 1879) lxxv; in possession of Hauteserre de Salvaison (†1658), brother of the famous canonist Dadin de Salvaison; Sirmond purchased it for the library of the Collège Clermont

7. Bibliography

Fournier-Le Bras 2.251–259 (according to Gilchrist erroneous identification of the *capitula*); Van Hove, *Prolegomena* 331; Stickler, *Historia* 1.187; García y García, *Historia* 1.322

Theiner, *Über Ivo's vermeintliches Decret* 58–61 (= *Disquisitiones criticae* 184–186)

Savigny, *Geschichte* 2.298

Fournier, 'Décret' 697

G. Le Bras, 'L'activité canonique à Poitiers pendant la réforme grégorienne (1049–1099)', *Mélanges offerts à René Crozet*, ed. P. Gallais and Y.-J. Riou, 1 (Poitiers 1966) 237–239

Gossman, *Urban II* 93

J. J. Ryan, 'The Legatine Excommunication of Patriarch Michael Cerularius (1054) and a New Document from the First Crusade Epoch', SG 14 (1967) 15–49, especially 23–24

Reynolds, 'Turin Collection' 508–514

Gilchrist, 'Reception 1' 58–60

Petersmann, 'Kanonistische Überlieferung' 377

Fowler-Magerl, 'Vorgratianische Kanonessammlungen' 140

Landau, 'Erweiterte Fassungen' 329–330

Landau, 'Kirchweihe' 225–240

Collectio 2 librorum (Vat. lat. 3832)

1. *Author:* Unknown. 2. *Date:* About 1085 (Gilchrist). 3. *Place:* Rome, under Gregorian influence (Gilchrist). 4. *Type:* Unstructured collection.

5. Edition

J. Bernhard, *La Collection en deux livres (Cod. Vat. lat. 3832), I: La forme primitive de la collection en deux livres, source de la collection en 74 Titres et de la collection d'Anselme de Lucques.* 1–2 RDC 12 (1962) 1–601 (cf. review by Stickler, *Salesianum* 25, 1963, 502–503)

6. Manuscript

Vaticano, Città del, Biblioteca Apostolica Vaticana, lat. 3832, saec. XI^{ex}–XII^{in}, Italy (Dobschütz, *Decretum Gelasianum* 168: Germany), fol. 1–99^{v}

7. Bibliography

Fournier-Le Bras 2.127–131; Van Hove, *Prolegomena* 325; Stickler, *Historia* 1.175; García y García, *Historia* 1.315

Ryan, 'Observations' 96

Gossman, *Urban II* 18–19

J. Gilchrist, 'The Collection of Cod. Vat. lat. 3832: A Source of the Collection in Seventy Four Titles?' *Etudes . . . Le Bras* 1.141–156

J. J. Ryan, 'Bernold of Constance and an Anonymous Libellus de Lite: *De Romani Pontificis Potestate Universas Ecclesias Ordinandi*', AHP 4 (1966) 9–24

J. J. Ryan, 'The Legatine Excommunication of Patriarch Michael Cerularius (1054) and a New Document from the First Crusade Epoch', SG 14 (1967) 13–50, especially 26–28

Gilchrist, 'Economic Policy' 404

Gilchrist, 'Reception 1' 43

Gilchrist, 'Epistola Widonis' 590

Gaudemet, 'Primauté' 155–156

J. Gaudemet, 'La primauté pontificale dans les collections canoniques grégoriennes', *Studi in onore Luigi Prosdocimi* (1994) 1.1.59–90

Collectio 8 partium (Assisi CL 227)

1. Author: Unknown. *2. Date:* At the beginning of the pontificate of Pope Paschal II, after 1100. *3. Place:* Italy. *4. Type:* Mainly excerpts taken from decretals; some small parts of the *Decretum Burchardi* or derivated collections. *5. Edition:* None.

6. Manuscript

Assisi, Biblioteca Comunale, CL 227, saec. XII

7. Bibliography

Fournier-Le Bras 2.167–169; Van Hove, *Prolegomena* 327 ('Collectio Assisiensis'); Stickler, *Historia* 1.187; García y García, *Historia* 1.322

F. Ehrle, 'Zu Bethmanns Notizen über die Handschriften von St. Francesco in Assisi', *Archiv für Literatur- und Kirchengeschichte des Mittelalters* 1 (1885) 470–508, especially 477–481

Fournier, 'Collections canoniques issues du Décret de Burchard' 189–214

Ryan, 'Observations' 96

Gilchrist, 'Economic Policy' 408–409

Gilchrist, 'Epistola Widonis' 585

Hartmann, 'Kanonessammlung' 47 n. 10

Deusdedit, Collectio canonum

1. Author: Deusdedit, cardinal presbyter of SS. Apostolorum in Eudoxia (today: S. Pietro in Vincoli); (†1098–1099 as a monk at Tulle). *2. Date:* Completed in 1087 (in the preface, he dedicated it to Pope Victor III whose pontificate lasted from 9 May until 16 September, 1087), not before 1081, however, because the *Collectio canonum* contains a letter of Gregory VII from the same year; probably written between 1083 and 1087, as a passage of the *Collectio* alludes to the election of the Abbot Gebizo of Saint Alexis in Rome to the episcopal see of Cesena which took place in 1083 (cf. E. Stevenson, *Osservazioni* 95 [of the separate edition] and Sickel, *Das Privilegium Otto I. für die Römische Kirche vom Jahre 962* [Innsbruck 1883] 78, Fournier-Le Bras 2.40–41). *3. Place:* Rome. *4. Type:* Systematic collection in four parts

5. Editions

Pio Martinucci, *Deusdedit presbyteri cardinalis tituli Apostolorum in Eudoxia collectio canonum e codice Vaticano edita*, Venice 1869 (on the basis of manuscript Vat. lat. 3833)

Die Kanonessammlung des Kardinals Deusdedit, ed. V. Wolf von Glanvell (Paderborn 1905; repr. Aalen 1967)

6. Manuscripts

Complete Manuscripts

Milano, Biblioteca Ambrosiana, C.288 inf., not long before 1616 (copy of Vat. lat. 3833)

Vaticano, Città del, Biblioteca Apostolica Vaticana, lat. 3833, saec. XII^{in} (written 1099–1118), Italy, Prov. San Pietro in Vincoli, only complete medieval manuscript, cf. Fournier-Le Bras 2.39, cf. also the arguments of H. Steinacker, 'Deusdedithandschrift' 113–114, who tries to demonstrate that the manuscript was written in Southeastern France (Provence), sceptical about this, Fournier-Le Bras 2.39 n. 1

Fragments and Excerpts

Cambrai, Bibliothèque municipale, 554 (olim 512), saec. XII2/2, fol. 120–126: chapters 184–186, 188–239, 241–251, 253–262, 264–279 of the third book of Deusdedit's collection

Paris, Bibliothèque nationale, lat. 1458 (codex is a composite), saec. XII2/2, for quite a long time it belonged to the library of the Dominican friars in Valence; fol. 242–261^{v}, fragments, cf. Mordek, *Bibliotheca capitularium* 412–414

Roma, Biblioteca Casanatense, 2010 (olim B.V.17), saec. XI^{ex}, Farfa, fol. 93^{v}–102 (cf. above, *Collectio 74 titulorum*)

Roma, Biblioteca Vallicelliana, C.19, saec. XVI, fol. 85–88, excerpts

Roma, Biblioteca Vallicelliana, C.24, saec. XVI^{ex}–XVII^{in}, fol. 194–197, excerpts

Vaticano, Città del, Archivio di San Pietro C.118, saec. XII (probably 1125–1130), written in Italy, fol. 123–124, chapters 262–281 of the first book of Deusdedit's canonical collection

Vaticano, Città del, Biblioteca Apostolica Vaticana, lat. 1984, saec. XII, fol 196^{v}–200, fragments

Vaticano, Città del, Biblioteca Apostolica Vaticana, lat. 8486, saec. XIII, contains chapters 184–186, 188–285 and a part of Chapter 286 of the third book as well as Chapter 1,420–425, 427 of Book IV of Deusdedit's collection; for this manuscript P. Fabre, *Étude sur le Liber censuum de l'Église Romaine* (Paris 1892) 189–200 (claims that Vat. lat. 8486 was the original of the *Liber censuum*)

Vaticano, Città del, Biblioteca Apostolica Vaticana, Ottobon. lat. 3057, saec. XII, about 1185 (by 1339 in the sacristy of the Franciscan convent at Assisi), chapters of Deusdedit's collection at fol. 130–134^{v}, 136, 136^{v}, fol. 134^{v}, 135, fol. 146, fol. 146^{v}–147, fol. 136, fol. 137

Vaticano, Città del, Biblioteca Apostolica Vaticana, Ottobon. lat. 3139, saec. XVII, fol. 88–91: Deusdedit's prologue, fol. 92–107: table of contents by Deusdedit (in inverted order)

Further Manuscripts

These manuscripts of the *Liber censuum* contain the aforementioned chapters of Deusdedit's canonical collection

Bologna, Biblioteca Universitaria, 477, saec. XVII^{in}

Catania (from S. Nicolò d'Arena), saec. XVIII

Cheltenham, Phillipps Collection, 5368, saec. XVIII

Firenze, Biblioteca Riccardiana, 228, saec. XIII2/4 (1228–1236, completed in March 1431)

Firenze, Biblioteca Riccardiana, 229, saec. XIV^{ex} (1388)
Napoli, Biblioteca Nazionale Vittorio Emanuele II, Brancaccianus II. E. 10, saec. XVII (copy of Napoli V.H.63)
Napoli, Biblioteca Nazionale Vittorio Emanuele II, V.H.63, saec. XVI^{ex}
Paris, Bibliothèque nationale, lat. 4188, saec. XV
Roma, Biblioteca dell'Accademia Nazionale dei Lincei, Corsin. 249, 250 and 245, 246, saec. XVII^{ex}
Roma, Biblioteca dell'Accademia Nazionale dei Lincei, Corsin. 1041, saec. XVII^{ex}
Roma, Biblioteca Vallicelliana, I.48, saec. XVI
Vaticano, Città del, Archivio di San Pietro, Arm. XV no. 1, saec. XIII^{ex}
Vaticano, Città del, Archivio di San Pietro, Arm. XV no. 2, saec. XVII
Vaticano, Città del, Archivio di San Pietro, Arm. XXXV no. 18, saec. XV^{1}
Vaticano, Città del, Biblioteca Apostolica Vaticana, lat. 6223, saec. XVI
Vaticano, Città del, Biblioteca Apostolica Vaticana, Barb. XXXIII 34, saec. XVII
Vaticano, Città del, Biblioteca Apostolica Vaticana, Barb. XLII 100, saec. XVII
Venezia, Biblioteca Nazionale Marciana, Cl. XIV no. DIII, saec. XV

The Codices Vat. Ottobon. lat. 3078 and 3082 also share material with the canonical collection of Deusdedit (writings of the Cardinal d'Aragon, Nikolaus Roselli, d. 1362), saec. XIV^{ex}

7. *Bibliography*

C. Mirbt, 'Deusdedit', RE ^{3}4 (1898) 581–583; Conrat, *Geschichte* 367–369; G. Bareille, 'Deusdedit', DThC 4 (1924) 647–651; Fournier-Le Bras 2.37–53; Kurtscheid-Wilches 1.159–160; Van Hove, *Prolegomena* 233, 235, 264, 324, 325; Lefebvre, 'Deusdedit', DDC 4 (1949) 1186–1191; Stickler, *Historia* 1.172–174; Stickler, 'Deusdedit', LThK^{2} 3 (1959) 260; J. J. Ryan, 'Deusdedit, collection of', NCE 4 (1967) 823; García y García, *Historia* 1.314; H. Van de Wouw, 'Deusdedit', LMA 3 (1986) 739–740

Ballerini, *De antiquis . . . collectionibus et collectoribus* P. IV, cap. XIV (PL 56.330–338)
Savigny, *Geschichte* 2.299
T. Sickel, *Das Privilegium Otto I. für die römische Kirche vom Jahre 962* (Innsbruck 1883) 61–64 and 77
S. Löwenfeld, 'Die Canonsammlung des Cardinals Deusdedit und das Register Gregors VII.', NA 10 (1885) 309–329
E. Stevenson, 'Osservazioni sulla Collectio canonum di Deusdedit', *Archivio della R. Società Romana di Storia patria* 8 (1885) 381–398 (on Vat. lat. 3833)
H. Fitting, 'Über die Stellen des römischen Rechtes in einer Streitschrift des Cardinales Deusdedit', ZRG Rom. Abt. 9 (1888) 376–381
P. Scheffer Boichorst, 'Die Sammlung des Kardinals Deusdedit und die Schenkung der Gräfin Mathilde', MIÖG 11 (1890) 119–121
P. Fabre, *Etude sur le 'Liber censuum' de l'Eglise romaine* (Bibliothèque des Ecoles françaises d'Athènes et de Rome; Paris 1892) 10 (Ottobonianus 3057)
E. Sackur, 'Der Dictatus papae und die Canonsammlung des Deusdedit', NA 18 (1893) 137–153
Steinacker, 'Deusdedithandschrift' 113–144
E. Hirsch, 'Leben und Werke des Kardinals Deusdedit', AKKR 85 (1905) 706–718

Wretschko, *Theodosiani libri XVI*, p. ccclvii
E. Hirsch, 'Der Simoniebegriff und eine angebliche Erweiterung desselben im 11. Jahrhundert', AKKR 86 (1906) 3–19
E. Hirsch, 'Die Auffassung der simonistischen und schismatischen Weihen im 11. Jahrhundert, besonders bei Kardinal Deusdedit', AKKR 87 (1907) 25–70
E. Hirsch, 'Kardinal Deusdedits Stellung zur Laieninvestitur' AKKR 88 (1908) 34–49
E. Hirsch, 'Die rechtliche Stellung der römischen Kirche und des Papstes nach Kardinal Deusdedit', AKKR 88 (1908) 595–624
E. Perels, 'Die Briefe Papst Nikolaus' I.', NA 37 (1912) 535–586; NA 39 (1914) 45–153
W. Peitz, *Das Originalregister Gregors VII. im Vatikanischen Archiv (Reg. Vat. 2) nebst Beiträgen zur Kenntnis der Originalregister Innocenz' III. und Honorius' III. (Reg. Vat. 4–11)* (SB Vienna 165.5; Vienna 1911) 133–146 and 246–258 (on Vat. lat. 3833) and 'Exkurs II' 258–265 (on the edition by Wolf von Glanvell)
Fournier, 'Collections canoniques romaines' 327–395
K. Hofmann, *Der 'Dictatus papae' Gregors VII.: Eine rechtsgeschichtliche Erklärung* (Paderborn 1933)
H.-W. Klewitz, 'Die Entstehung des Kardinalkollegiums', ZRG Kan. Abt. 25 (1936) 115–221, repr. Klewitz, *Reformpapsttum und Kardinalkolleg* (Darmstadt 1957) 9–134, especially 67–68 and 75
W. Holtzmann, 'Kardinal Deusdedit als Dichter', HJB 57 (1937) 217–232
S. Kuttner, 'Cardinalis: The History of a Canonical Concept', *Traditio* 3 (1945) 129–214 (repr. Kuttner, *The History of Ideas and Doctrines of Canon Law in the Middle Ages*, London 1980, no. IX)
S. Kuttner, 'Liber canonicus: A Note on the *Dictatus Papae* c. 17', SGreg 2 (1947) 387–401
Stickler, 'Potere coattivo' 275
J. J. Ryan, 'Cardinal Humbert *De s. Romana ecclesia*: Relics of Roman-Byzantine Relations 1053–1054' MS 20 (1958) 206–238
M. Ríos Fernández, 'La *Collectio Canonum* del Cardenal Deusdedit y el *Dictatus Papae*', *Compostellanum* 5.3 (1960) 181–212
H. Hoffmann, 'Der Kalender des Leo Marsicanus' DA 21 (1965) 82–149, especially 94 and 134 n. 39 (restricts the date of Deusdedit's death to 1098–99 [March 2])
Rambaud-Buhot, 'Critique' 42–46
Kuttner, 'Roman Manuscripts' 7–29
R. Schieffer, 'Tomus Gregorii papae: Bemerkungen zur Diskussion um das Register Gregors VII.' AfD 17 (1971) 169–184
Gilchrist, 'Economic Policy' 403
Kuttner, 'Turning point' 55–85
H. Mordek, 'Proprie auctoritates apostolice sedis: Ein zweiter Dictatus papae Gregors VII?' DA 28 (1972) 105–132
Fuhrmann, *Einfluß und Verbreitung* 2.522–533
Gilchrist, 'Reception 1' 38–43
Petersmann, 'Kanonistische Überlieferung' 368–369, 374–377
R. Hüls, *Kardinäle, Klerus und Kirchen Roms 1049–1130* (BDHI 48; Tübingen 1977) 114

Blumenthal, *Early Councils* 126

I. S. Robinson, *Authority and Resistance in the Investiture Contest: The Polemical Literature of the Eleventh Century* (Manchester 1978)

R. Somerville, 'Anselm of Lucca and Wibert of Ravenna', BMCL 10 (1980) 1–13

Gilchrist, 'Epistola Widonis' 586

S. Kuttner, 'Universal Pope or Servant of God's Servants: The Canonists, Papal Titles, and Innocent III', RDC 32 (1981) 109–149, especially 113–114

H. Fuhrmann, 'Pseudoisidor, Otto von Ostia (Urban II.) und der Zitatenkampf von Gerstungen (1085)', ZRG Kan. Abt. 68 (1982) 52–69

M. C. De Matteis, 'Tematica della povertà e problema delle *Res ecclesiae*: Notazioni ed esemplificazione campione su alcune collezioni canoniche del periodo della riforma ecclesiastica del sec. XI', BISIAM 90 (1982–1983) 177–226

H. E. J. Cowdrey, *The Age of Abbot Desiderius, Montecassino, the Papacy and the Normans in the Eleventh and Early Twelfth Centuries* (Oxford 1983) 99–102 and 158–160

H. Fuhrmann, 'Kritischer Sinn und unkritische Haltung: Vorgratianische Einwände zu Pseudo-Clemens-Briefen', *Festschrift Kempf* (1983) 81–95

T. Montenecchi Palazzi, 'Cencius camerarius et la formation du *Liber censuum* del 1192', MEFR 96 (1984) 49–93

Mordek, 'Kanonistik und gregorianische Reform' 69

J. H. Van Engen, 'Observations on *De consecratione*', *Proceedings Berkeley* 309–320

Jasper, *Papstwahldekret* 54–57 and passim

Hartmann, 'Kanonessammlung' 45–64

Blumenthal, 'Fälschungen' 241–262

Landau, 'Gefälschtes Recht' 36

J. Gaudemet, 'Le droit romain dans la *Collectio Canonum* du Cardinal Deusdedit', *Etudes Metman* (1988) 155–165

P. Skubiszewski, 'Une vision monastique de l'Eglise au XIIe siècle: A propos d'un livre récent sur les peintures murales de Prüfening', CCM 31 (1988) 361–376

G. Fransen, 'Textes grégoriens dans un manuscrit espagnol', ZRG Kan. Abt. 75 (1989) 58–69

Landau, 'Kanonessammlungen in der Lombardei' 448

A. Thanner, *Papst Honorius I. (625–638)* (St. Ottilien 1989) (cf. the very critical review by Jasper, DA 47 [1991], 677–678)

W. Kurze, 'Notizen zu den Päpsten Johannes VII., Gregor III. und Benedikt III. in der Kanonessammlung des Kardinals Deusdedit', QF 70 (1990) 23–45

R. Maceratini, 'Aspetti della posizione giuridica dell'eretico in alcune opere della Riforma gregoriana', *Scritti di storia del diritto offerti dagli allievi a Domenico Maffei*, ed. M. Ascheri (Padova 1991) 1–25 (cf. review by D. Jasper, DA 49 [1993] 345)

U.-R. Blumenthal, 'Rom in der Kanonistik', *Festschrift Elze* (1992) 29–45

U.-R. Blumenthal, 'An Episcopal Handbook from Twelfth-Century Southern Italy: Codex Rome, Bibl. Vallicelliana F.54/III', *Studia in Honorem A. M. Stickler* (1992) 13–24

Brett, 'Collections attributed to Ivo' 35–36

Gaudemet, 'Primauté' 155–156

Hartmann, 'Autoritäten' 427, 431–432, 439–440, 443

Landau, 'Kirchweihe' 225–240
A. M. Piredda, 'La Sardegna in Vaticano (Città del Vaticano 19 novembre 1991–31 gennaio 1992)', *Sandalion* 15 (1992) 179–185
E. Vodola, 'Sovereignty and Tabu: Evolution of the Sanction against Communication with Excommunicates, 2: Canonical Collections', *Studia in Honorem A. M. Stickler* (1992) 581–598, especially 595–597
G. Picasso, 'Motivi ecclesiologici nella *Collectio canonum* del cardinale Deusdedit: I testi di san Cipriano', *Medioevo e Latinità: in Memoria di Ezio Franceschini,* ed. A. Ambrosini, M. Ferrari, C. Leonardi, G. Picasso, M. Regoliosi, and P. Zerbi (Milan 1993) 403–415

Atto of San Marco, Breviarium

1. Author: Atto, Cardinal presbyter of S. Marco at Rome, Bishop-elect of Milan. *2. Date:* About 1075, certainly before 1084. *3. Place:* Rome. *4. Type:* Smaller collection for the use of the clerics of S. Marco in Rome

5. Editions

Attonis cardinalis presbyteri Capitulare seu Breviarium canonum, ex Codice Vaticano, ed. Angelo Mai, *Scriptorum veterum nova collectio e Vaticanis codicibus edita* VI.2 (Rome 1832) 60–102 (cf. Ryan, 'Observations' 98–99)
PL 134.27–52

6. Manuscripts

Toledo, Archivo y Biblioteca Capitular, 8–19, saec. XVII, a copy made by Lucas Holste (†1661) ('Codex Holstenianus', cf. Wemple, below, 'Bibliography')
Vaticano, Città del, Biblioteca Apostolica Vaticana, lat. 586, saec. XI

7. Bibliography

Fournier-Le Bras 2.20–25; Fliche, 'Atton, archevêque de Milan', DHGE 5 (1931) 184–185; R. Naz, 'Atton de Saint Marc ou de Milan', DDC 1 (1935) 1330–1331; Kurtscheid-Wilches 1.157; Van Hove, *Prolegomena* 323; Stickler, *Historia* 1.166–167; R. Abbondanza, 'Attone', DBI 4 (1962) 564–565; García y García, *Historia* 1.311; J. J. Ryan, 'Atto (Collection of)', NCE 1 (1967) 1031–1032

A. Solmi, *Stato e Chiesa secondo gli scritti politici da Carlomagno fino al concordato di Worms* (Modena 1901) 181 n. 3
Fournier, 'Collections canoniques romaines' 288–294
F. Pelster, 'Das Dekret Burkhards von Worms in einer Redaktion aus dem Beginn der gregorianischen Reform (Cod. Vat. lat. 3809 and Clm 4570)', SGreg 1 (Rome 1947) 321–351 (on the prologue)
Stickler, 'Potere coattivo' 275
Ryan, 'Observations' 98–99
K. Ganzer, *Die Entwicklung des auswärtigen Kardinalats im hohen Mittelalter* (Tübingen 1963) 37–38

R. Kottje, 'Zu Geschichte und Inhalt einer rheinischen Handschrift in der Vatikanischen Bibliothek', RQ 59 (1964) 86 n. 33
Rambaud-Buhot, 'Critique' 39–40
S. F. Wemple, 'The Codex Holstenianus in Toledo: A Collection of Ninth, Tenth and Eleventh Century Capitularies', *Manuscripta* 13 (1969) 90–95
Fuhrmann, *Einfluß und Verbreitung* 2.529–532
Gilchrist, 'Reception 1' 37
Mordek, 'Kanonistik und gregorianische Reform' 67–68
Picasso, 'Reformatio ecclesiae' 70–88
Landau, 'Gefälschtes Recht' 34 including n. 98
Hartmann, 'Autoritäten' 430–431

Bonizo of Sutri, Liber de vita christiana

1. Author: Bishop Bonizo of Sutri († ca. 1095), one of the most ardent followers of Gregory VII. *2. Date:* Between 1089 and 1095 (during this period Bonizo was in central Italy because he had been exiled from his episcopal see of Piacenza); no allusions to the councils held at Piacenza and Clermont in 1095, cf. Perels, 'Einleitung' p. xxi and Fournier-Le Bras 2.146. *3. Place:* Central Italy (see above). *4. Type:* Systematic collection.

5. Editions

'Ex libris Decreti Bonizonis Episcopi excerpta', ed. A. Mai, *Nova Patrum biblioteca* 7.3 (Rome 1845) 1–75
Bonizonis Liber de vita christiana, ed. E. Perels (Texte zur Geschichte des römischen und kanonischen Rechts im Mittelalter 1; Berlin 1930)

6. Manuscripts

Brescia, Archivio e Biblioteca Capitolare, sine num., saec. XII (possibly written as late as about 1150), Prov. Italy (probably Lombardy), fol. 1–131
Firenze, Biblioteca Medicea Laurenziana, Plut. XXIII 5, saec. XII2/4 (possibly written as late as about 1150), Prov. Franciscan convent of Santa Croce at Florence, fol. 91–182^{v} (fragment)
Mantova, Biblioteca Comunale, D.III.13 (439) from San Benedetto di Polirone, ca. saec. XII^{med} (between 1142 and ca. 1152), cf. G. Miccoli, 'Un nuovo manoscritto del *Liber de vita christiana* di Bonizone di Sutri', SM 7 (1966) 371–398
Mantova, Biblioteca Comunale, D.IV.6 (452), saec. XV, cf. Berschin, *Scriptorium* 41 (1987) 87–90
München, Bayerische Staatsbibliothek, Clm 11504 (Polling. 204), saec. XVIII, copy of the manuscript from Brescia
Paris, Bibliothèque nationale, lat. 12391 (olim 921, 650), copy made for d'Achery based on Firenze, XXIII 5, saec. XII, cf. Berschin, *Scriptorium* 41 (1987) 87–90
Vaticano, Città del, Biblioteca Apostolica Vaticana, Ross. lat. 226 (olim Rossianus VIII, 165 of the library of the Jesuit college in Vienna-Lainz), saec. XII (about 1130 according to Perels), Prov. unknown (Italy, according to Berschin, *Bonizo* 57); fol. 1–83^{v}

Erroneously Taken for a Manuscript of Bonizo's *'Liber de vita christiana'*

Wien, Österreichische Nationalbibliothek, lat. 2186 (iur. can. 80), saec. XII (cf. Perels NA 39, 95–97; the manuscript contains a canonical collection in seven books which draws heavily on Bonizo's *Liber de vita christiana* and begins with a fragment of the *Liber de vita christiana*, cf. Berschin, *Bonizo* 25 and below, *Collectio 7 librorum* (Vat. lat. 1346 etc.)

Incomplete

Toronto, Bergendal Collection, 79 (olim Heythrop College [Oxfordshire] Z 105 BON). Cf. I. S. Robinson, 'A Manuscript of the *Liber de vita christiana* of Bonizo of Sutri', BMCL 3 (1973) 135–139

7. *Bibliography*

Conrat, *Geschichte* 369–370; C. Mirbt, 'Bonizo', RE ^{3}3 (1897) 311–313; Fournier-Le Bras 2.139–150; L. Jadin, 'Bonizo de Sutri', DHGE 9 (1937) 994–998; J. Pétrau-Gay, 'Bonizo', DDC 2 (1937) 951–956; Kurtscheid-Wilches 1.161; Van Hove, *Prolegomena* 233, 235, 264, 326 n. 1; Stickler, *Historia* 1.174–175; F. Caraffa, 'Bonizone', *Bibliotheca Sanctorum* 3 (1963) 339–340; García y García, *Historia* 1.314–315; *Rep. font.* 2 (1967) 559–560; G. Miccoli, 'Bonizone' DBI 12 (1970) 246–259; W. Goez, 'Bonizo', LMA 2 (1983) 424–425

Ballerini, *De antiquis . . . collectionibus et collectoribus* P. IV, cap. XV (PL 56.338–342)

E. Steindorff, *Jahrbücher des deutschen Reiches unter Heinrich III.* 1 (Leipzig 1874; repr. Darmstadt 1963) 457–463; 2 (Leipzig 1891; repr. Darmstadt 1963) 473–479

H. Lehmgrübner, *Benzo von Alba: Ein Verfechter der kaiserlichen Staatsidee unter Heinrich IV: Sein Leben und der sogenannte Panegyrikus* (Historische Untersuchungen 6; Berlin 1887) 129–151

C. Mirbt, *Die Publizistik im Zeitalter Gregors VII.* (Leipzig 1894) 42–44

A. Dulac, 'Bonizo: Le libellus de sacramentis et le Decretum', *Revue d'histoire et de littérature religieuses*, n. s. 3 (1912) 230–239

G. Schwartz, *Die Besetzung der Bistümer Reichsitaliens unter den sächsischen und salischen Kaisern* (Leipzig 1913)

E. Perels, 'Die Briefe Papst Nikolaus' I., Teil II', NA 39 (1914) 43–153, especially 90–95

P. Fournier, 'Bonizo de Sutri, Urbain II et la Comtesse Mathilde, d'après le *Liber de vita christiana* de Bonizo', BEC 76 (1915) 265–298

P. Fournier, 'Les sources canoniques du *Liber de vita christiana* de Bonizo de Sutri', BEC 78 (1917), 117–134

E. Perels, Introduction to his edition (cf. above), p. xi–xxxiii

U. Lewald, *An der Schwelle der Scholastik: Bonizo von Sutri und das Kirchenrecht seiner Tage* (Weimar 1938)

U. Lewald, 'Das Eherecht in Bonizos von Sutri Liber de Vita Christiana', ZRG Kan. Abt. 27 (1938) 560–598

E. Nasalli Rocca di Corneliano, 'Osservazioni su Bonizone vescovo di Sutri e di Piacenza come canonista', SGreg 2 (1947) 151–162

G. Miccoli, 'Un nuovo manoscritto del *Liber de vita christiana* di Bonizone di Sutri', SM 7 (1966) 371–398 (manuscript Mantova 439 from San Benedetto di Polirone); cf. review by W. Berschin, DA 23 (1967) 215

L. Gatto, *Bonizone di Sutri e il suo 'Liber ad amicum': Richerche sull'età gregoriana* (Collana di saggi e ricerche 2; Pescara 1968)

L. Gatto, 'Il problema delle elezione simoniache nel Liber ad amicum di Bonizone da Sutri', *Chiesa e riforma* 137–167

L. Gatto, 'Matilde di Canossa nel Liber ad amicum di Bonizone da Sutri', *Studi Matildici: Atti e memorie del II Convegno di Studi Matildici, Modena-Reggio E., 1–3 maggio 1970* (Deputazione di Storia Patria per le antiche provincie modenesi: Biblioteca n.s. 16; Modena 1971) 307–325

W. Berschin, *Bonizo von Sutri: Leben und Werk* (Beiträge zur Geschichte und Quellenkunde des Mittelalters 2; Berlin-New York 1972); Italian translation: *Bonizone di Sutri: La vita e le opere*, trans. A. Tabarroni (Centro Italiano di Studi sull'Alto Medioevo; Spoleto 1992)

C. Villa, 'Due antiche biblioteche bresciane: I cataloghi della Cattedrale e di San Giovanni de Foris', *Italia Medioevale e Umanistica* 15 (1972) 63–97

Gilchrist, 'Economic Policy' 405–406

Fuhrmann, *Einfluß und Verbreitung* 2.534–541

Gilchrist, 'Reception 1' 44

I. S. Robinson, 'A Manuscript of the *Liber de vita christiana* of Bonizo of Sutri', BMCL 3 (1973) 135–139

Mordek, *Kirchenrecht und Reform* 61 n. 100 and 184 n. 412

H. Schadt, 'Eine neue Handschrift von Bonizo von Sutris Konsanguinitätstraktat und ihre Darstellungen', BMCL 6 (1976) 72–75

Hartmann, *Worms* 113

W. Berschin, 'Herrscher, Richter, Ritter, Frauen: die Laienstände nach Bonizo', *Love and Marriage in the Twelfth Century*, ed. W. van Hoecke and A. Walkenhuysen (Mediaevalia Lovaniensia 1.8; Louvain 1981) 116–129

Motta, 'Regula Benedicti' 261–279

H. Schadt, *Die Darstellungen der Arbores Consanguinitatis und der Arbores Affinitatis* (Tübingen 1982) especially 124–127

M. C. De Matteis, 'Tematica della povertà e problema delle *Res ecclesiae*: Notazioni ed esemplificazione campione su alcune collezioni canoniche del periodo della riforma ecclesiastica del sec. XI', BISIAM 90 (1982–1983) 177–226

G. Folliet, 'Une collection anonyme *Pro causa iniustae excommunicationis* des VIIe–VIIIe siècles', *Miscellanea di studi agostiniani: Studi in onore di P. Agostino Trapè* (Rome 1985) 295–308

Mordek, 'Systematische Kanonessammlungen' 19

J. H. Van Engen, 'Observations on *De consecratione*', *Proceedings Berkeley* 309–320

Jasper, *Papstwahldekret* 74–78

W. Berschin, 'Zwei neue Bonizo-Handschriften', *Scriptorium* 41 (1987) 87–90

W. Berschin, 'Bonizone da Sutri e lo stato di vita laicale: Il codice Mantova 439', *Sant'Anselmo, Mantova* 281–290

M. Heim, 'Zisterziensische Kreuzzugs-Ideologie in der *Gral-Queste* des *Prosa-Lancelot*', SMGBOZ 99 (1988) 133–182

C. Piacitelli, 'Milano e il suo territorio in età comunale (sec. XI–XIII) (Milano 26–30 ottobre 1987)', RSCI 42 (1988) 245–255

M. D'Acunto, 'Il prefetto urbano Cencio di Giovanni Tignoso nelle fonti del suo tempo', BISIAM 95 (1989) 1–44

W. Berschin, 'Die publizistische Reaktion auf den Tod Gregors VII. (nach fünf oberitalienischen Streitschriften)', SGreg 14 (1991) 121–135
O. Capitani, 'Sondaggio sulla terminologia militare in Urbano II', SM 31 (1990) 1–25
J. Laudage, 'Gregor VII. und die *Electio Canonica'*, SGreg 14 (1991) 83–101
Gaudemet, 'Primauté' 155–156
Hartmann, 'Autoritäten' 432–435, 442–443
C. Violante, 'La pataria e la *militia Dei* nelle fonti e nella realtà', *'Militia Christi' e Crociata nei secoli XI–XIII: Atti della undecima Settimana internazionale di studio, Mendola, 28 agosto–1° settembre 1989* (Milan 1992) 103–127

Collectio Britannica

1. Author: Unknown. *2. Date:* About 1090 or shortly afterwards. *3. Place:* Northern France (Somerville, *Urban II* 13–14). *4. Type:* Collection of papal letters, Roman law and patristic excerpts.

5. Editions

P. Ewald, 'Die Papstbriefe der Brittischen Sammlung' NA 5 (1880) 275–414, 503–596
A. von Hirsch-Gereuth, MGH Epp. 5 (Berlin 1899) 585–614
R. Somerville, with the collaboration of S. Kuttner, *Pope Urban II, the Collectio Britannica and the Council of Melfi (1089)* (Oxford 1996) Editions and translations of all the materials related to Urban II

6. Manuscript

London, British Library, Add. 8873, saec. XII^{in}

7. Bibliography

M. Conrat, *Geschichte* 345–347, 351–354, 370–372; Fournier-Le Bras 2.10–14, 155–163; P. Lemercier, 'Brittannica (collectio)' DDC 2 (1937) 1115–1117; Kurtscheid-Wilches 1.162; Van Hove, *Prolegomena* 326; Stickler, *Historia* 1.175; García y García, *Historia* 1.315 including n. 63

P. Ewald, 'Die Papstbriefe der Brittischen Sammlung' NA 5 (1880) 275–414 and 503–596
S. Loewenfeld, *Epistolae Romanorum Pontificum ineditae* (Leipzig 1885)
M. Conrat (Cohn), *Der Pandekten- und Institutionenauszug der Brittischen Decretalensammlung: Quellen des Ivo* (Berlin 1887)
Mor, 'Digesto' 631–647, 679–692
W. Ullmann, *'Nos si aliquid incompetenter* . . . Some Observations on the Register Fragments of Leo IV in the *Collectio Britannica'*,*Ephemerides iuris canonici* 9 (1953) 3–11 (repr. *The Church and the Law in the Earlier Middle Ages: Selected Essays*, London 1975, no. vii)
Gossman, *Urban II* 19–32

Kuttner, 'Turning point' 53–85

T. Schmidt, *Alexander II. und die römische Reformgruppe seiner Zeit* (Päpste und Papsttum 11; Stuttgart 1977) 224–226

W. Ullmann, *Gelasius I. (492–496): Das Papsttum an der Wende der Spätantike zum Mittelalter* (Päpste und Papsttum 18; Stuttgart 1981) 218 n. 3 and 225–226

Gilchrist, 'Epistola Widonis' 586 n. 31

R. Somerville, 'Mercy and Justice in the Early Months of Urban II's Pontificate', *Chiesa, diritto e ordinamento* 138–158

Mordek, 'Kanonistik und gregorianische Reform' 73

R. Somerville, 'The Letters of Pope Urban II in the *Collectio Britannica*', *Proceedings Cambridge* 103–114

Landau, 'Gefälschtes Recht' 40–42

H. Löwe, 'Consensus–consessus: Ein Nachtrag im Streit um Methodius', DA 46 (1990) 507–515

G. Constable and R. Somerville, 'The Papal Bulls for the Chapter of St. Antonin in Rouergue in the Eleventh and Twelfth Centuries', *Speculum* 67 (1992) 827–864

A. Thanner, *Papst Honorius I. (625–638)* (Studien zur Theologie und Geschichte; St. Ottilien 1989); cf. the critical review by Jasper, DA 47 (1991) 677–678

Brett, 'Collections attributed to Ivo' 27–46

Siems, *Handel und Wucher* 292, 295, 302

R. Somerville, 'Edmond Bishop and his Transcription of the *Collectio Britannica*', *Studia in Honorem A. M. Stickler* (1992) 535–548

P. Landau, 'Wandel und Kontinuität' 221–229

R. Somerville with the collaboration of S. Kuttner, *Pope Urban II, The Collectio Britannica and the Council of Melfi (1089)* (Oxford 1996)

Excerptiones Egberti

1. Author: Unknown. Erroneously attributed to Archbishop Egbert of York. Some manuscripts mention a certain Huscarius (Levita Huscarius). *2. Date:* Eleventh century. *3. Place:* Southern England. *4. Type:* Unstructured collection of conciliar canons, some decretals and excerpts from the Fathers of the Church; it was compiled for the practical use of a bishop in the everyday administration of his diocese; extensive use of the fourth book of the Carolingian *Quadripartitus* (see above)

5. Editions

H. Spelman (ed.), *Concilia, Decreta, Leges, Constitutiones, in re ecclesiarum orbis britannici* 1 (London 1639) 258–275 *(Editio princeps)*

B. Thorpe (ed.), *Ancient Laws and Institutes of England* (London 1840) 2.97–127 (based on London, Cotton Nero A.I)

PL 89.377–400

R. A. Aronstam (ed.), *The Latin Canonical Tradition in Late Anglo-Saxon England: The Excerptiones Egberti* (Diss. Columbia Univ.; New York 1974) 55–129

6. *Manuscripts*

First Recension

Cambridge, Library of Corpus Christi College, 190, saec. XI^{med}, Exeter, cf. N. R. Ker, *A Catalogue of Manuscripts containing Anglo-Saxon* (Oxford 1957) 70–73

London, British Library, Cotton Nero A.I, saec. XI^{in}, time of Bishop Wulfstan I, Worcester or York, fol. 127v1–154r18, cf. H. R. Loyn (ed.), *A Wulfstan Manuscript containing Institutes, Laws and Homilies, British Museum Cotton Nero A.I* (Early English Manuscripts in Facsimile 17; Copenhagen 1971)

Second Recension

Cambridge, Library of Corpus Christi College, 265, saec. XI$^{in\text{-}med}$, Worcester

Oxford, Bodleian Library, Barlow 37, saec. XII^{ex} or XIII^{in}, England, cf. Sauer (as below) 345; fol. 1^{r}–7^{r}, 120 texts from the *Excerptiones Egberti*, close connection with Cambridge 265

Rouen, Bibliothèque municipale, 1382 (U.109), saec. XI, Normandy or England

Fragment

Oxford, Bodleian Library, Junius 121, saec. XI3/4, Worcester

7. *Bibliography*

Fournier-Le Bras 1.316–320; Stickler, *Historia* 1.149; García y García, *Historia* 304 n. 43 (French collection)

Ballerini, *De antiquis . . . collectionibus et collectoribus* P. IV, Cap. VI, c. 6 (PL 56.300–302)

M. Bateson, 'A Worcester Cathedral Book of Ecclesiastical Collections, made c. 1000 A.D.', EHR 10 (1895) 712–731

K. Jost, *Wulfstanstudien* (Berne 1950)

H. R. Loyn (ed.), *A Wulfstan Manuscript* (cf. above 'Manuscripts') 13–54 (introduction), especially 17 and 49–52

R. A. Aronstam, 'Recovering Hucarius: A Historiographical Study in Early English Canon Law', BMCL 5 (1975) 117–122

Mordek, *Kirchenrecht und Reform* 120 n. 86

H. Sauer, 'Zur Überlieferung und Anlage von Erzbischof Wulfstans *Handbuch*', DA 36 (1980) 341–384

Kerff, *Quadripartitus* 72–73

Mordek, 'Karolingische Kapitularien' 42 and n. 95

Siems, *Handel und Wucher* 674 n. 722

MGH Capit. n.s. 1.362–366

Collectio Lanfranci

1. *Author:* Unknown. Lanfranc, Prior of Bec, later Abbot of Saint-Etienne at Caen and finally Archbishop of Canterbury (†1089), certainly brought a copy from Bec for use at Canterbury, and so ensured its dissemination. 2. *Date:* Second half of the eleventh century (after 1059); cf. Brooke, *English Church* 65. 3. *Place:* Bec-Canterbury. 4. *Type:* Chronologically arranged collection of decretals and conciliar canons;

an only slightly abridged edition of the long form of the Pseudo-Isidorian Decretals.
5. Edition: None.

6. *Manuscripts*

In many manuscripts it circulated under the title *Excerpta ex decretis Romanorum Pontificum* (Hinschius, *Decretales Pseudoisidorianae* lxxiv–lxxvi; Van Hove 337 n. 1); S. Williams, *Codices Pseudo-Isidoriani* 77–82, listed sixteen manuscripts of the *Collectio Lanfranci* as Excerpta 1–16 of Pseudo-Isidore.

Complete Manuscripts

Cambridge, Library of Corpus Christi College, 130, saec. XI–XII (Williams, Excerpta no. 3)

Cambridge, Library of Peterhouse College (now kept at the University Library), 74, saec. XI^{ex}, Prov. St. Cuthbert's, Durham, a donation by William of St. Carileph to the library of Durham cathedral (cf. Brooke); (Williams, Excerpta no. 2)

Cambridge, Library of Trinity College, B.16.44 (405), saec. XI, Prov. Bec, maybe Lanfranc's own copy, Script. Bec (probably during the 1060s), archetype of the *Collectio Lanfranci*, abridged version of the long form (contains a notice of purchase in Lanfranc's own hand); (Williams, Excerpta no. 1)

Chartres, Bibliothèque municipale, 409 (424), saec. XIV, destroyed in 1944 (Williams, Excerpta no. 41)

Hereford, Cathedral Library, O.IV.5 and P.II.8, saec. XII^1, written in an English hand, copy of Hereford O.VIII.8, Prov. Hereford Cathedral (Williams, Excerpta no. 6), cf. Mynors-Thomson, *Catalogue of Hereford* 27 and 77–78

Hereford, Cathedral Library, O.VIII.8 , saec. XI^{ex}, written in a French hand, Prov. Hereford Cathedral (Williams, Excerpta no. 5), Mynors-Thomson, *Catalogue of Hereford* 57

Lincoln, Cathedral Chapter Library, 161, saec. XII^{in}, written in an English hand, made at and for Lincoln Cathedral, fol. 4^r–250^v (Williams, Excerpta no. 9), cf. Thomson, *Catalogue of Lincoln* 130

London, British Library, Cotton Claudius D.IX, saec. XI–XII (Williams, Excerpta no. 4)

London, British Library, Cotton Claudius E.V, saec. XII, cf. Schieffer, *Investiturverbot* 209

London, British Library, Royal 9.B.XII, saec. XII^1, Prov. Worcester (Williams, Excerpta no. 8)

London, British Library, Royal 11.D.IV, saec. XV (cf. Schieffer, *Investiturverbot* 209)

London, British Library, Royal 11.D.VIII, saec. XII, Prov. Gloucester Abbey (Williams, Excerpta no. 10)

Paris, Bibliothèque nationale, lat. 1563, saec. XV (Williams, Excerpta no. 11)

Salisbury, Library of the Cathedral Church, 78, saec. XI–XII, Prov. Salisbury (Williams, Excerpta no. 7), cf. T. Webber, *Scribes and Scholars* (1992) 132–138

Decretals Only

Exeter, Cathedral Library, 3512, saec. XII^{in}, Exeter; was originally bound with Oxford, Bodleian Library, Bodley 810, although they were written at different times by different scribes (cf. Mordek 473; Schieffer, *Investiturverbot* 209; see Oxford manuscript immediately below)

Paris, Bibliothèque Nationale, lat. 3856, saec. XII, Prov. Normandy (Williams, Excerpta no. 14)

Rouen, Bibliothèque municipale, 701 (E.78), saec. XII, Prov. Abbey of Jumièges (Williams, Excerpta no. 12)

Rouen, Bibliothèque municipale, 703 (E.23), saec. XII, Prov. Abbey of Jumièges, but perhaps not written there; incomplete, the missing ending may be identical with the first quire of Rouen, Bibliothèque municipale, 1408 (saec. XII, from Jumièges) cf. Schieffer, *Investiturverbot* 65 n. 81 (Williams, Excerpta no. 13)

Councils Only

Oxford Bodleian Library, Bodley 810, saec. XI^{ex}, Prov. Exeter Cathedral (Williams, Excerpta no. 15) cf. also above Exeter 3512

Fragments

Lincoln, Cathedral Chapter Library, 106, saec. XI^{ex}, probably of Norman origin but possibly written in England, fol. 5^{r}–21^{v} (Williams, Excerpta no. 17), cf. Thomson, *Catalogue of Lincoln* 79–80

London, British Library, Harley 633, saec. XII^{2}, Northern England (Williams, Excerpta no. 19)

Oxford, Bodleian Library, Rawlinson A.433, saec. XII, Prov. Waltham Abbey (Williams Excerpta no. 18)

Paris, Bibliothèque nationale, lat. 1458, saec. XII, fol. 96^{r}–103^{r}, last part of a copy of the decretals compiled in the *Collectio Lanfranci*, cf. Somerville, 'A Parisian fragment of the Collectio Lanfranci', BMCL 16 (1986) 87–89

Paris, Bibliothèque nationale, nouv. acq. lat. 2657, fol. 7, saec. XI–XII (cf. BEC 136, 1978, 284)

Rouen, Bibliothèque municipale, 1408 (Y.109), saec. XII (cf. above, Rouen 703, and Schieffer, *Investiturverbot* 210)

Vaticano, Città del, Biblioteca Apostolica Vaticana, Reg. lat. 1044, saec. XII, Prov. St. Pierre de la Couture (Diocese of Le Mans), fol. 1–71^{v}; contains only decretals (dating from a very early period), cf. Schieffer, *Investiturverbot* 65 n. 81. Perhaps excerpt from the *Collectio Lanfranci* or from an unidentified version of the *Collectio Lanfranci* (Williams, Excerpta no. 16)

Abridged Versions

Durham, Cathedral Library, B.IV.18, saec. XII (about 1125), Prov. Christ Church, Canterbury (*Canterbury abbreviation* with additions from the letters of Gregory I; cf. Brett, 'Collectio Lanfranci' 161 with n. 14); (Williams, Excerpta no. 20)

Hereford, Cathedral Library O.II.7, saec. XII^{in}, Prov. Hereford (probably written at Hereford Cathedral, where it was by saec. XII$^{med.}$, fol. 1–11, cf. Brooke, *English Church* 237–238, cf. Mynors-Thomson, *Catalogue of Hereford* 14

Lincoln, Cathedral Chapter Library, 193, saec. XII$^{med.}$, England, fol. 159^{r}–205^{r}, cf. Thomson, *Catalogue of Lincoln* 154–155 (who describes it as a modified version of Ivo's *Decretum*)

London, Lambeth Palace Library, 351, saec. XII, Prov. Christ Church, Canterbury, affinity to Durham B.IV.18 cf. Fuhrmann, *Einfluß und Verbreitung* 1.169 n. 61 (Williams, Excerpta no. 21)

Cf. below, *Collectio of Oxford, Bodley 561*

7. *Bibliography*

H. Böhmer, 'Lanfrank' RE ^{3}11 (1902) 249–255; E. Amann and A. Gaudel, 'Lanfranc', DThC 8 (1925) 2558–2570; Fournier-Le Bras 2.227–230 and 365; Van Hove, *Prolegomena* 241, 336; G. Dolezalek, 'Lanfrancus', HRG 2 (1978) 1604–1605; M. T. Gibson, 'Lanfranc', LMA 5.8 (1991) 1684–1686

H. Böhmer, *Kirche und Staat in England und in der Normandie im XI. und XII. Jahrhundert* (Leipzig 1899)

H. Böhmer, *Die Fälschungen Erzbischof Lanfranks von Canterbury* (Studien zur Geschichte der Theologie und der Kirche 8.1; Leipzig 1902)

E. Longuemare, *L'Eglise et la conquête de l'Angleterre: Lanfranc moine bénédictin, conseiller politique de Guillaume le Conquérant* (Caen 1902)

N. Tamassia, 'Lanfranco, arcivescovo di Canterbery e la scuola Pavese', *Mélanges Fitting* 2 (Montpellier 1907–1908) 189–201

E. Hora, 'Zur Ehrenrettung Lanfranks, des Erzbischofs von Canterbury', *Theologische Quartalschrift* 111 (1930) 288–319

Brooke, *English Church*

A. J. Macdonald, 'The Eadmer and the Canterbury Privileges', JTS 32 (1931) 39–55

G. Le Bras, 'Les collections canoniques en Angleterre après la Conquête normande', RHD, 4e sér. 11 (1932) 144–153

Fournier, 'Angleterre' 129–134

Mor, 'Recezione' 301

W. Holtzmann, 'Zur Geschichte des Investiturstreites', NA 50 (1935) 246–319, especially 253, 261

R. R. Darlington, 'Ecclesiastical Reform in the Late Old English Period', EHR 51 (1936) 385–428, especially 411–412 (on the collections of canon law)

S. Williams, 'The Pseudo-Isidorian Problem Today', *Speculum* 29 (1954) 702–707

N. F. Cantor, *Church, Kingship and Lay Investiture in England 1089–1135* (Princeton 1958)

F. Barlow, 'A View of Archbishop Lanfranc', JEH 16 (1965) 163–177

P. Riché, 'Enseignement du droit en Gaule aux VIe–XIe siècles', IRMAE I.5.b (Milan 1965)

W. Ullmann, 'On the Influence of Geoffrey of Monmouth in English History', *Speculum historiale: Festschrift Johannes Spörl* (Freiburg-Munich 1965) 259 n. 14

D. J. A. Matthew, *The Norman Conquest* (London 1966) 175–176

C. N. L. Brooke, 'Archbishop Lanfranc, the English Bishops, and the Council of London of 1075', *Collectanea Stephan Kuttner* 2 (=SG 12, 1967) 40–59

J. De Montclos, *Lanfranc et Bérenger: La controverse eucharistique du XIe siècle* (Etudes et Documents 37; Louvain 1971) cf. review by Somerville, *Speculum* 50 (1975) 106–108

S. Williams, *Codices Pseudo-Isidoriani* 77–82 (*Collectio Lanfranci* as the Excerpta 1–16 of Pseudo-Isidore)

M. Richter, 'Archbishop Lanfranc and the Canterbury Primacy—Some Suggestions', *Downside Review* 90 (1972) 110–118

Somerville, 'Berengar' 55–75

R. Somerville, 'Lanfranc's Canonical Collection and Exeter', BIHR 45 (1972) 303–306 (very useful summary of the results of the latest research)

Fuhrmann, *Einfluß und Verbreitung* 1.47, 229–232, 2.419–422

Petersmann, 'Kanonistische Überlieferung' 383

D. R. Bates, 'The Character and Career of Odo, Bishop of Bayeux (1049–50–1097)', *Speculum* 50 (1975) 1–20

P. Landau, Review of Fuhrmann, *Einfluß und Verbreitung*, ZRG Kan. Abt. 61 (1975) 377–392, especially 384

D. Sheerin, 'Some Observations on the Date of Lanfranc's *Decreta*', *Studia monastica* 17 (1975) 13–27

J. Yver, 'Le droit romain en Normandie (avant 1500)', IRMAE 5.4.a (Milan 1976)

M. T. Gibson, *Lanfranc of Bec* (Oxford 1978)

A. Gouron, 'La science juridique française aux XIe et XIIe siècles: diffusion du droit de Justinien et influences canoniques jusqu'à Gratien', IRMAE 1.4.d-e (Milan 1978) 11–13

Richter, 'Stufen' 25–27 (Eton College 97)

R. M. Thomson, 'William of Malmesbury's Edition of the *Liber pontificalis*', AHP 16 (1978) 106 n. 67, 107 n. 72 (Eton College 97 and Cotton Claudius E.V.)

F. Barlow, *The English Church 1066–1154* (London-New York 1979) 146

M. Richter, *Canterbury Professions* (1979)

H. Fuhrmann, 'Reflections on the Principles of Editing Texts: The Pseudo-Isidorian Decretals as an Example', BMCL 11 (1981) 1–7

Schieffer, *Investiturverbot* 65 n. 81 and 209–210

K. Christensen, 'The Schafer Williams Papers at the Institute of Medieval Canon Law', BMCL 16 (1986) 101–104

R. Somerville, 'A Parisian Fragment of the Collectio Lanfranci', BMCL 16 (1986) 87–89 (on Paris lat. 1458; very useful for the identification of the manuscripts)

B. C. Brasington, '*Non veni Corinthum:* Ivo of Chartres, Lanfranc and 2 Corinthians 1.16–17, 23', BMCL 21 (1991) 1–9

M. Brett, 'The Collectio Lanfranci and its Competitors', *Intellectual Life in the Middle Ages: Essays Presented to Margaret Gibson,* ed. L. Smith and B. Ward (London 1992) 157–174

R. Grégoire, 'Il diritto monastico elaborato nei "Decreta" di Lanfranco', *Lanfranco di Pavia et l'Europa del secolo XI,* ed. G. D'Onofrio (Italia sacra: Studi e documenti di storia ecclesiastica 51; Roma 1993) 117–129

M. Philpott, *Archbishop Lanfranc and Canon Law* (Diss. Oxford Univ. 1993)

M. Philpott, 'Lanfranc's Canonical Collection and the Law of the Church', *Lanfranco di Pavia et l'Europa del secolo XI,* ed. G. D'Onofrio (Italia sacra: Studi e documenti di storia ecclesiastica 51; Roma 1993) 131–147

G. Picasso, 'Lanfranco e la riforma gregoriana', *Lanfranco di Pavia et l'Europa del secolo XI*, ed. G. D'Onofrio (Italia sacra: Studi e documenti di storia ecclesiastica 51; Roma 1993) 425–438

M. Gullick, 'The Scribes of the Durham Cantor's Book (Durham, Dean and Chapter Library, MS B.IV.24) and the Durham Martyrology Scribe', *Anglo-Norman Durham 1093–1193,* ed. D. Rollason, M. Harvey, and M. Prestwich (Woodbridge 1994) 93–109

M. Philpott, 'The *De iniusta vexacione Willelmi episcopi I* and Canon Law in Anglo-Norman Durham', *Anglo-Norman Durham 1093–1193,* ed. D. Rollason, M. Harvey, and M. Prestwich (Woodbridge 1994) 125–137

Ivo of Chartres, Collectio tripartita

1. Author: Probably Bishop Ivo of Chartres (ca. 1040 to 1115–1117), a student of Lanfranc of Bec, together with Anselm, the later Archbishop of Canterbury; provost of the canons regular at Saint-Quentin in Beauvais; he became Bishop of Chartres in 1091; On the biography of Ivo of Chartres cf. Fournier, 'Yves de Chartres et le droit canonique' 51–98, 384–405; on the authorship of Ivo of Chartres (discussing the *Tripartita, Decretum*, and *Panormia*) cf. Fournier-Le Bras 2.99–105. *2. Date: Collection A* (= Parts 1 and 2): about 1093 or 1094 (Fournier-Le Bras 2.64). *Collection B* (= Part 3): in the last years of the eleventh century. Both parts *(Collections A* and *B*) were probably united by the end of the eleventh century (no manuscript has survived that contains only one of the two parts cf. Fournier-Le Bras 2.66). Fuhrmann believes that the entire collection dated to 1091–1096 (cf. Fuhrmann, *Einfluß und Verbreitung* 2.544) *3. Place:* Chartres? *4. Type:* Chronologically arranged collection of decretals and conciliar canons (Form A is a source of Ivo's *Decretum*). At first a bipartite work, it was later augmented with a third part by adding excerpts from the *Decretum* which was written later (Form B) (First Part: excerpts from papal decretals, especially Pseudo-Isidore, from Clement to Urban II; Second Part: conciliar canons; Third Part: excerpts of the *Decretum*). For some time, Form A and Form B seem to have existed independently of one another. It is striking, however, that all manuscripts containing the complete *Tripartita* A include some texts of the *Tripartita* B; after the two parts had been united (earlier form), the whole text was revised (comprehensive rubrics, separate *capitulationes* for each section and one or two new canons) in a later version (Theiner, Wasserschleben, Fournier).

5. Edition

Theiner, *Disquisitiones criticae* 154–155 (only *prefatio* according to Berlin Hamilton 345)

6. Manuscripts

Cf. Fournier, 'Collections canoniques attribuées à Yves de Chartres' 646–649

Admont, Stiftsbibliothek, 162, saec. XII; cf. Sdralek, *Wolfenbüttler Fragmente* 16–17; later version

Alençon, Bibliothèque municipale, 135, saec. XII^{1}; Prov. St. Evroult, cf. Schulte, 'Iter Gallicum' 454–456); greatly abridged to 1.43, then full length; earlier version

Berkeley, University of California, Law Library, Robbins 102, saec. XII^{in} cf. M. Brett, 'The Berkeley Tripartita', BMCL 16 (1986) 89–91; (to 2.19.14), perhaps the lost manuscript from Lambach; later version

Berlin, Staatsbibliothek Preußischer Kulturbesitz, 197, saec. XII (?) ('Liber monasterii beatae Virginis Mariae in lacu'), Prov. Maria Laach; later version (used by Theiner)

Berlin, Staatsbibliothek Preußischer Kulturbesitz, Hamilton 345; saec. XII^{med} (?); on the Italian origin of this codex cf. Boese, *Sammlung Hamilton* 166–167; Hinschius, 'Die kanonistischen Handschriften der Hamiltonschen Sammlung',

ZKG 6 (1884) 239–242 dates the manuscript to saec. XIII; according to Landau ('Kanonessammlungen in der Lombardei' 451 n. 104) it needs further paleographical investigation; earlier version

Cambridge, Library of Gonville and Caius College, 393 (455) (to 3.28.10); earlier version

Gniezno (Gnesen), Archiwum Archidiecezjalne i Biblioteka Kapitulna, 25, saec. XII

København, Kongelike Bibliotek, Thott 555 4°, saec. XII^{1} (Brett, 'Collections attributed to Ivo' 32 n. 22: beginning at 2.28.38; earlier version)

Kraków, Archiwum Kapitulny Metropolitalnej Krakowskiej, sine num. (84?), saec. XII, on the manuscripts of Gniezno (Gnesen) and Kraków, cf. Fuhrmann, *Einfluß und Verbreitung* 3.777 n. 9 (with full bibliography); later version (?)

Lambach, Bibliothek des Benediktinerstifts, 107, saec. XII; cf. Sdralek 16–17 (incomplete), not among the abbey's manuscripts; perhaps identical with the manuscript at Berkeley (information from M. Brett)

München, Bayerische Staatsbibliothek, Clm 12603, saec. XIII, Prov. St. Pankraz at Ranshofen; later version

Olomouc (Olmütz), Kapitulni Knihovna (now: Státni vedecké knihovna, Universitni knihovna) 205, saec. XII^{1} (about 1130–1140); cf. T. Reuter, 'Zur Anerkennung Papst Innocenz II.', DA 39, 1983, 395–396; later version

Oxford, Bodleian Library, d'Orville 46 (both manuscripts listed in Brooke); written in an Anglo-Norman hand of saec. XII^{med}; cf. Brett, 'Collections attributed to Ivo' 32 n. 22: 1.5.4.–20.32; earlier version

Oxford, Bodleian Library, 561; cf. Brett, 'Collections attributed to Ivo' 32 n. 22: only 3.29.8–283A; earlier version (fragment)

Paris, Bibliothèque nationale, lat. 3858, saec. XII^{1}, Prov. Troyes; earlier version

Paris, Bibliothèque nationale, lat. 3858A, saec. XII^{1}, written at Fécamp, cf. B. Branch, 'Willermus peccator et les manuscrits de Fécamp', CCM 26 (1983) 195–207; later version

Paris, Bibliothèque nationale, lat. 3858B, saec. XII^{2}, Prov. Le Mans (?) cf. Fournier, 'Collections canoniques attribuées à Yves de Chartres' 647 including n. 1; later version

Paris, Bibliothèque nationale, lat. 4282, saec. XII^{2}; earlier version

Paris, Bibliothèque nationale, lat. 13656, saec. XII, cf. Fournier, 'Collections canoniques attribuées à Yves de Chartres' 647; Brett, 'Collections attributed to Ivo' 32 n. 22: first few leaves are illegible; earlier version

Vaticano, Città del, Biblioteca Apostolica Vaticana, Reg. lat. 973, saec. XII^{2}, written in France (the manuscript was used by both Ballerini and Theiner); later version written in France

Wien, Österreichische Nationalbibliothek, lat. 982 (theol. 335), saec. XII, fol. 116–133, incomplete; later version

Wolfenbüttel, Herzog August Bibliothek, Helmst. 180 (207), saec. XIII^{in} (?); later version but many readings are closer to the earlier version

Zürich, Zentralbibliothek, Car. C 42, saec. XII, Prov. Zürich ('Ecclesie sanctorum Felicis et Regule prepositure Thuricensis') fol. 1^{r}–173^{r}, cf. Mohlberg, *Mittelalterliche Handschriften der Zentralbibliothek Zürich*, 1.2: *Handschriften der Stiftsbibliothek* (Zurich 1932) 103 no. 250; later version

Fragments

Berlin, Staatsbibliothek Preußischer Kulturbesitz, Fragm. 123, saec. XII[1], cf. G. Dolezalek, 'Seckels Handschriftenfragmente', *Ius commune* 4 (1972) 294–297, especially 297 n. 13

Frankfurt (Main), Max-Planck-Institut für Europäische Rechtsgeschichte, 3, cf. G. Dolezalek, 'Seckels Handschriftenfragmente', *Ius commune* 4 (1972) 294–297, especially 296–297

Extracts

Admont, Stiftsbibliothek, 43 and 48; *Tripartita* B, XXIX, cc. 1–284; later version; cf. W. Stelzer, *Gelehrtes Recht in Österreich* (MIÖG Ergänzungsband 26; 1982)

7. *Bibliography*

1. On Ivo of Chartres in General

Conrat, *Geschichte* 378–390; G. Le Bras, 'Mariage' DThC 9 (1926) 2138–2139; Kurtscheid-Wilches 1.162–165; *Vies des Saints* 5 (1947) 400–407; E. Amann and L. Guizard, 'Yves de Chartres', DThC 15.2 (1950) 3625–3640; L. Chevailler, 'Yves de Chartres', DDC 7 (1965) 1641–1666; M. Noirot, *Bibliotheca Sanctorum* 7 (1966) 994–997; P. Landau, 'Ivo von Chartres (ca. 1040–1115)', TRE 16 (1987) 422–427 (Bibliography); A. Becker, 'Ivo von Chartres', LMA 5.4 (1990) 839–840

Ballerini, *De antiquis . . . collectionibus et collectoribus* P. IV, cap. XVI (PL 56.342–346)

Savigny, *Geschichte* 2.303–318, 494–499

Wasserschleben, *Beiträge* 47–77

G. Oesterle, 'Ivonis Carnutensis epistolae incognitae', *Archivio di diritto ecclesiastico* 2 (1840) 56–63, 205–217

J. R. Menu, *Recherches et nouvelles études critiques sur les recueils canoniques attribués à Yves de Chartres* (Paris 1880)

Dombrowski, *Ivo Bischof von Chartres: Sein Leben und seine Werke* (Breslau 1881)

A. Foucault, *Essai sur Yves de Chartres d'après sa correspondance* (Chartres 1883)

Th. Sickel, *Das Privilegium Otto I. für die römische Kirche vom Jahre 962* (Innsbruck 1883) 59

L. Merlet, *Lettres de saint Yves évêque de Chartres traduites et annotées* (Chartres 1885)

A. Sieber, *Bischof Ivo von Chartres und seine Stellung zu den kirchenpolitischen Fragen seiner Zeit* (Königsberg 1885)

M. Conrat (Cohn), *Der Pandekten- und Institutionenauszug der brittischen Dekretalensammlung: Quelle des Ivo* (Berlin 1887)

A. Esmein, 'La question des investitures dans les lettres d'Yves de Chartres', *Bibliothèque de l'Ecole des hautes études, section religieuse* 1 (Paris 1889) 139–178

C. Mirbt, *Die Publizistik im Zeitalter Gregors VII.* (Leipzig 1894) 512–514

M. A. Stiegler, 'Dispensation und Dispensationswesen in ihrer geschichtlichen Entwicklung dargestellt vom IX. Jahrhundert bis auf Gratian, XII. Kap.' AKKR 77 (1897) 542–551 (repr. Stiegler, *Dispensation, Dispensationswesen und Dispensationsrecht im Kirchenrecht* 1 [Mainz 1901])

A. Scharnagl, *Der Begriff der Investitur in den Quellen und in der Literatur des Investiturstreites* (Kirchenrechtliche Abhandlungen 56; Stuttgart 1908) 80–88

M. Grabmann, *Geschichte der scholastischen Methode* 1 (Freiburg 1909) 243–246

P. L. Schmidt, *Der hl. Ivo, Bischof von Chartres* (Studien und Mitteilungen aus dem kirchengeschichtlichen Seminar der theologischen Fakultät der kaiserlich-königlichen Universität in Wien, Heft 7; Vienna 1911)

F. P. Bliemetzrieder, 'Zu den Schriften Ivos von Chartres (†1116)' *SB Vienna* 182.6 (1917) 3–40

Fournier, 'Tournant' 129–180

L. Fischer, 'Ivo von Chartres, der Erneuerer der vita canonica in Frankreich', *Festgabe Alois Knoepfler* (Freiburg 1917) 67–88

S. Grelewski, *La réaction contre les ordalies depuis le IXe siécle jusqu'au Décret de Gratien: Agobard archevêque de Lyon et Yves évêque de Chartres* (Rennes 1924)

J. Brys, 'De Dispensatione in Iure Canonico', *Dissertationes ad gradum magistri in facultate theologica* 2.14 (1925) 46–51

A. Esmein and R. Génestal, *Le mariage en droit canonique* 1–2 (Paris ²1929–1935)

Brooke, *English Church* 242–245

J. J. Juglas, 'Yves de Chartres et la question des investitures', *Mélanges Albert Dufourcq* (Paris 1932) 57–72

P. David, *Un disciple d'Yves de Chartres en Pologne: Galon de Paris et le droit canonique* (Société polonaise d'histoire; Warsaw 1933)

Mor, 'Digesto' 633–638, 690–692

F. P. Bliemetzrieder, 'Paul Fournier und das literarische Werk Ivos von Chartres', AKKR 115 (1935) 53–91

L. Ott, *Untersuchungen zur theologischen Briefliteratur der Frühscholastik* (BGPhMA 34; Münster 1937) 26–33

J. Leclercq, 'La collection des lettres d'Yves de Chartres', RB 56 (1945–46) 108–125

J. De Ghellinck, *Le mouvement théologique au XIIe siècle* (Bruges ²1948) 115–155

J. Leclercq (ed.), *Yves de Chartres. Correspondance* 1 *(1090–1098)* (Paris 1949) (to letter no. 70)

A. Fliche, *La Réforme grégorienne et la Reconquête chrétienne (1057–1125)* (Histoire de l'église 8; Paris 1950)

A. Becker, *Studien zum Investiturproblem in Frankreich* (Saarbrücken 1955)

G. B. Borino, 'Ivo Magister Scholarum Ecclesiae Carnotensis', SGreg 5 (1956) 375–381

Gassò-Batlle, *Pelagii I papae epistulae*

J. Rambaud-Buhot, 'Le décret de Gratien et le droit romain: Influence d'Yves de Chartres', RHD, 4e sér. 35 (1957) 290–300

N. F. Cantor, *Church, Kingship and Lay Investiture in England 1089–1135* (Princeton 1958, repr. 1969) 202–216

H. Hoffmann, 'Ivo von Chartres und die Lösung des Investiturproblems', DA 15 (1959) 393–440

S. Kuttner, 'Harmony from Dissonance: an Interpretation of Medieval Canon Law', *Wimmer Lecture* 10 (1960) 1–16 (repr. *The History of Ideas and Doctrines of Canon Law in the Middle Ages* (Collected Studies Series 113; Aldershot ²1992) no. 1

E. Pellegrin, 'Notes sur quelques manuscrits de sermons, provenant de Fleury-sur-Loire', *Bibliothèques retrouvées: Manuscrits, bibliothèques et bibliophiles du Moyen Age et de la Renaissance: Recueil d'Etudes publiées de 1938 à 1985* (Paris 1988) 211–231 (first published in: *Bulletin d'information de l'Institut de recherche et d'histoire des textes* 10, 1961, 7–27)

R. Sprandel, 'Ivo von Chartres und die moderne Doktrin *Nulla poena sine lege*',

ZRG Kan. Abt. 47 (1961) 95–108 (on this, cf. Fuhrmann, *Einfluß und Verbreitung* 2.561 n. 373)

Sprandel, *Ivo von Chartres*

R. Sprandel, 'Über das Problem neuen Rechts im früheren Mittelalter', ZRG Kan. Abt. 48 (1962) 117–137

F.-L. Ganshof, 'Note sur deux textes de droit canonique dans le *Liber Floridus*', *Etudes . . . Le Bras* 1.99–115

B. Jacqueline, 'Yves de Chartres et Saint Bernard, *Etudes . . . Le Bras* 1.179–184

E. Pellegrin, 'Bernard Collot et les manuscrits du collège de Fortet', *Bibliothèques retrouvées: Manuscrits, bibliothèques et bibliophiles du Moyen Age et de la Renaissance. Recueil d'Etudes publiées de 1938 à 1985* (Paris 1988) 101–104 (first published in BEC 123, 1965, 196–199)

Rambaud-Buhot, 'Critique' 47–53

H. M. Klinkenberg, 'Die Theorie der Veränderbarkeit des Rechtes im frühen und hohen Mittelalter', MM 6 (1969) 157–188

Kuttner, 'Turning point' 53–85

Fuhrmann, *Einfluß und Verbreitung* 2.542–544

Brommer, 'Fragmente' 228–233

W. Hartmann, 'Beziehungen des Normannischen Anonymus zu frühscholastischen Bildungszentren', DA 31 (1975) 108–153

R. Reynolds, 'Ivonian opuscula on the ecclesiastical offices', SG 20 (1976) 309–322

T. Schmidt, *Alexander II. (1061–1073) und die römische Reformgruppe seiner Zeit* (Päpste und Papsttum 11; Stuttgart 1977) 226–227

M. Gibson, *Lanfranc of Bec* (Oxford 1978) (expresses doubts about the suggestion that Ivo had been a pupil of Lanfranc but cf. Bliemetzrieder's observations, which have merit)

T. Doran, *Canon Law in the Twelfth Century: The Views of Bernold of Constance, Ivo of Chartres and Alger of Liège* (Excerpta ex dissertatione ad Doctoratum in Facultate Juris Canonici Pontificiae Universitatis Gregorianae; Rome 1979)

Kerff, *Quadripartitus* passim

J. A. Brundage, 'St. Anselm, Ivo of Chartres, and the Ideology of the First Crusade', *Les mutations socio-culturelles au tournant des XIe–XIIe siècles: Etudes Anselmiennes (IVe session) . . . 1982* (Paris 1984) 175–187

P. J. Payer, *Sex and the Penitentials: The Development of a Sexual Code 550–1150* (Toronto 1984)

G. Folliet, 'Une collection anonyme *Pro causa iniustae excommunicationis* des VIIe–VIIIe siècles', *Miscellanea di studi agostiniani. Studi in onore di P. Agostino Trapè* (Rome 1985) 295–308

Mordek, 'Systematische Kanonessammlungen' 195–196

J. H. Van Engen, 'Observations on *De consecratione*',*Proceedings Berkeley* 309–320

R. Sprandel, 'Ivo von Chartres und die Aufwertung einer weltlichen Kultur im Investiturstreit', *Höfische Literatur, Hofgesellschaft, Höfische Lebensformen um 1200*, ed. by G. Kaiser and J.-D. Müller (Düsseldorf 1986) 57–65

J. Gaudemet, 'L'apport d'Augustin à la doctrine médiévale du mariage', *Augustinianum* 27 (1987) 559–570

S. Kuttner and W. Hartmann, 'A New Version of Pope John VIII's Decree on Sacrilege (Council of Troyes, 878)', BMCL 17 (1987) 1–32

F. Lotter, 'Zur Ausbildung eines kirchlichen Judenrechts bei Burchard von Worms und Ivo von Chartres', *Antisemitismus und jüdische Geschichte: Studien zu Ehren von Herbert A. Strauss*, ed. R. Erb and M. Schmidt (Berlin 1987) 69–96

G. Motta, 'I codici canonistici di Polirone', *Sant'Anselmo, Mantova* 349–374

L. K. Barker, *History, Reform and Law in the Work of Ivo of Chartres* (Diss. Chapel Hill, North Carolina 1988)

J. Gaudemet, 'Le deuxième concile de Nicée (787) dans les Collections canoniques occidentales', AHC 20 (1988) 287–288

Landau, 'Gefälschtes Recht' 38–39

G. Schoovaerts, 'L'amour et le mariage selon les lettres d'Yves de Chartres', *Studia Canonica* 22 (1988) 205–225

M. M. Sheehan, 'Theory and Practice: Marriage of the Unfree and the Poor in Medieval Society', MS 50 (1988) 457–487

G. Fransen, *La préface d'Yves de Chartres: Essai de traduction* (Strasbourg 1989) with a short preface by J. Schlick. (The translation will be revised after the publication of B. Brasington's critical edition)

G. Giordanengo, 'Le pouvoir législatif du roi de France (XIe–XIIIe siècles): Travaux récents et hypothèses de recherche', BEC 147 (1989) 283–310, especially 292–308

A. Placanica, 'La concezione della donna nella dottrina di alcuni teologi scolastici', *Seminari sassaresi* IV (Sassari 1989) 105–127

B. C. Brasington, '*Non veni Corinthum:* Ivo of Chartres, Lanfranc and 2 Corinthians 1.16–17, 23', BMCL 21 (1991) 1–9

B. C. Brasington, 'Zur Rezeption des Prologs Ivos von Chartres in Süddeutschland', DA 47 (1991) 167–174

J. Gaudemet, 'Le serment dans le droit canonique médiéval', *Le serment*, ed. R. Verdier (Paris 1991) 2.63–75

P. Landau, 'Frei und Unfrei in der Kanonistik des 12. und 13. Jahrhunderts am Beispiel der Ordination der Unfreien', *Die abendländische Freiheit vom 10. zum 14. Jahrhundert: Der Wirkungszusammenhang von Idee und Wirklichkeit im europäischen Vergleich*, ed. J. Fried (Sigmaringen 1991) 177–196

R. Maceratini, 'Aspetti della posizione giuridica dell'eretico in alcune opere della Riforma gregoriana', *Scritti di storia del diritto offerti dagli allievi a Domenico Maffei*, ed. M. Ascheri (Padova 1991) 1–25 (cf. review by D. Jasper, DA 49 [1993] 345)

Hartmann, 'Autoritäten' 436–437, 443–446

G. Fornasari, 'Urbano II e la riforma della Chiesa nel secolo XI ovvero la riforma nella *dispensatio*', *Studi in onore Luigi Prosdocimi* (1994) 1.91–110

Landau, 'Kirchweihe' 225–240

P. Landau, 'Wandel und Kontinuität' 215–233

2. On the *Collectio tripartita*

Conrat, *Geschichte* 388–390; Fournier-Le Bras 2.58–68, 99–114; Kurtscheid-Wilches 1.163–164; Van Hove, *Prolegomena* 240, 331–332; Stickler, *Historia* 1.180–181; García y García, *Historia* 1.319

Fournier, 'Collections canoniques attribuées à Yves de Chartres', 646–698 and 312–326

Fournier, 'Yves de Chartres et le droit canonique' 51–98, 384–405, especially 393–395 (in an abridged version presented at: Fribourg/Switzerland: *Compte rendu du quatrième Congrès scientifique international des catholiques tenu à Fribourg, Suisse 1898: Section des sciences historiques* 216ff.)

E. Perels, 'Die Briefe Papst Nikolaus' I. (Teil II)', NA 39 (1914) 43–153

P. David, *Un disciple d'Yves de Chartres en Pologne: Galon de Paris* (VIIe Congrès International des Sciences Historiques; Warsaw 1933)

J. (von) Sawicki, 'Die Entwicklung der Kirchenrechtswissenschaft in Polen', ÖAKR 9 (1958) 262

W. Sawicki, 'W plyw niektórych praw obcych na ustrój prawny panstwa pierwszych Piastów (Influence de quelques sources étrangères sur le droit polonais aux XIe et XIIe s.; with summary in French)', *Annales Universitatis Mariae Curie–Sklodowska, Sectio* G, 11.2 (1964) 31ff. (augmented version of an earlier study published in the same periodical (9, 1961, 295ff.) about the manuscripts at Kraków and Gniezno which represent the *Collectio tripartita* in Poland)

G. Dolezalek, 'Seckels Handschriftenfragmente', *Ius Commune* 4 (1972) 294–297 (cf. above, 'Manuscripts')

Gilchrist, 'Economic Policy' 415–416

Fuhrmann, *Einfluß und Verbreitung* 2.378 n. 62, 542–552 and 3.777

Gilchrist, 'Reception 1' 64

Petersmann, 'Kanonistische Überlieferung' 383–384, 386–389

R. Reynolds, 'Basil and the Early Medieval Latin Canonical Collections', *Basil of Caeserea, Christian, humanist, ascetic* (Toronto 1981) 513–532 (especially 530 on the *Tripartita* as a source for Basil-Texts in the *Decretum Gratiani*)

Kerff, *Quadripartitus* 74

Landau, 'Dekret' 33–34 (texts of the *Decretum* in the Collection B of the *Tripartita*)

M. Brett, 'The Berkeley Tripartita', BMCL 16 (1986) 89–91

Landau, 'Kanonessammlungen in der Lombardei' 451

Brett, 'Collections attributed to Ivo' 27–46

Brett, 'Collectio Lanfranci' 163–165

U.-R. Blumenthal, 'An episcopal handbook from twelfth-century Southern Italy: Codex Rome, Bibl. Vallicelliana F.54/III', *Studia in Honorem A. M. Stickler* (1992) 13–24

Landau, 'Vorgratianische Kanonessammlungen bei den Dekretisten' 93–116

Landau, 'Eheschließung' 460–461

Ivo of Chartres, Decretum

1. Author: Ivo of Chartres, see above *Collectio tripartita. 2. Date:* Probably after 1093 (used letters of Urban II; none of the fragments for which a precise date could be established, belongs to the period after 1093). The date given by Patetta (after 1096 because of a council held at Nîmes in 1096) cannot be correct, because the Council of Nîmes is actually a forgery, cf. Kuttner-Somerville 175–189. Brett: After 1095, even a date after 1099 cannot be excluded (cf. Brett, 'Collections attributed to Ivo' 44). *3. Place:* Chartres (cf. Fournier-Le Bras 2.83). *4. Type:* A very comprehensive, systematically arranged collection in 17 parts

5. Editions

Editio princeps: Jean Dumoulin (Molineaeus, van der Meulen), *Decretum D. Ivonis episcopi Carnutensis, septem ac decem tomis sive partibus constans, scriptum quidem ante annos quadringentos quinquaginta, sed antehac numquam in lucem aeditum, nunc autem primum divulgatur* (Louvain 1541). On the basis of a certain *Codex Coloniensis* (cf. Landau, 'Dekret' 14–17 and 27–30)

Jean Fronteau (Paris 1647) (on the basis of the manuscript from Saint-Victor, today's Paris lat. 14315)

PL 161.59–1022 (Reprint of Fronteau's edition)

6. Manuscripts

Cf. Landau, 'Dekret' 8–30

Complete manuscripts of the *Decretum Ivonis*

Landau distinguishes between a 'French' and an 'English' group

1. 'French group'

Paris, Bibliothèque nationale, lat. 14315, saec. XII^{in}, Prov. Saint-Victor, cf. Landau, 'Dekret' 8–9, 18–23

Vaticano, Città del, Biblioteca Apostolica Vaticana, lat. 1357, saec. XII, Prov. France, cf. Landau, 'Dekret' 9, 18–23

2. 'English group'

Cambridge, Library of Corpus Christi College, 19, saec. XII, Canterbury (written probably between 1127 and 1130), Prov. Canterbury, Cathedral Library, cf. Landau, 'Dekret' 9–10, 23–24

London, British Library, Royal 11.D.VII, saec. XII, Prov. Lincoln, Cathedral Library, cf. Landau, 'Dekret' 10, 23–24

3. Lost manuscripts

'Vienna Manuscript' (mentioned in Theiner, *Über Ivo's vermeintliches Decret* 46–47); it has not been identified so far: cf. Landau, 'Dekret' 13–14

Codex Coloniensis, cf. above, 'Edition'

Incomplete Manuscripts

Paris, Bibliothèque nationale, lat. 3874 (*Colbertinus*), saec. XII, the last (XVII.) part is missing, cf. Landau, 'Dekret' 10–11 including n. 29 and 24, related to the 'French group'

Sigüenza, Archivo de la Catedral, 61, cf. G. Fransen, 'Manuscrits canoniques (1140–1234) conservés en Espagne (II)', RHE 49 (1954) 152–153, n. 5 and G. Fransen, 'Varia ex manuscriptis', *Traditio* 21 (1965) 516, cf. also Landau, 'Dekret' 12–13, 26–27

Vaticano, Città del, Biblioteca Apostolica Vaticana, Pal. lat. 587, saec. XII, perhaps written in Germany, excerpt and fragment (breaking off after the VI. Part, to 6.432), cf. Landau, 'Dekret' 11–12 including n. 36 and 25–26, related with the 'English group'

Fragments

Koblenz, Landeshauptarchiv, 701, no. 759,35, probably saec. XII^1, Rhineland, three single leaves, Prov. Koblenz, cf. Brommer, 'Unbekannte Fragmente einer Dekrethandschrift Ivos von Chartres', *Francia* 5 (1977) 753–755

Nassau, Archiv der Freiherren vom Stein, sine num., one leave, probably saec. XII^1, Rhineland, cf. also Brommer (as above)

Straubing, Stadtarchiv, Grundbuch St. Nikola (1631), covering folio, and Salbuch St. Nikola (1631), covering folio, s.n., two leaves (*Decretum* 5.73–5.80 and 5.132–137), saec. XII^{in}, Northern France; cf. R. Deutinger, 'Neue Handschriftenfragmente zum Dekret Ivos von Chartres', DA 51 (1995) 539–546

Excerpts

The first four are all the same excerpt; on the manuscripts of this excerpt, cf. Fournier, 'Collections canoniques attribuées à Yves de Chartres' 412–413; on the contents, cf. Theiner, *Über Ivo's vermeintliches Decret* 55–58; F. P. Bliemetzrieder, 'Zu den Schriften Ivos von Chartres [d. 1116]', *SB Vienna* 182 (1917) 81–86; see also Landau, 'Dekret' 32

Leipzig, Universitätsbibliothek, 955.9

London, British Library, Harley 3090, saec. XII

Roma, Biblioteca dell'Accademia Nazionale dei Lincei, Corsin. 1808, saec. XII

Wien, Österreichische Nationalbibliothek, lat. 2196

Paris, Bibliothèque nationale, lat. 4809, fol. 314^r–393^v, cf. Landau, 'Dekret' 32 including n. 94 (according to Fournier: '14809', cf. Brommer, 'Kurzformen' 21 n. 11)

Paris, Bibliothèque de l'Arsenal, 713, saec. XII–XIII, Prov. Saint-Victor at Paris, not a genuine abridged version of the *Decretum* but mainly chapters of the *Decretum* which have been augmented by adding other texts, especially texts from the *Panormia* (cf. Landau, 'Dekret' 33)

Leiden, Bibliotheek der Rijksuniversiteit, BPL 184, fol. 1^v–41^r (extracts)

7. *Bibliography*

On Ivo of Chartres in general cf. above, *Collectio tripartita*

On the Decretum (see also below, *Panormia*): Conrat, *Geschichte* 378–383; Fournier-Le Bras 2.67–85; 99–114; Kurtscheid-Wilches 1.164 and 165; Van Hove, *Prolegomena* 240, 264, 298, 331–332; Stickler, *Historia* 1. 181–182; G. Lepointe, 'Du Moulin (Jean)', DDC 5 (1953) 67–70; García y García, *Historia* 1.319–320

D. Blondel, *Pseudo-Isidorus et Turrianus vapulantes* (Geneva 1628)

Ballerini, *De antiquis . . . collectionibus et collectoribus* P. IV cap. XVI § 9 (PL 56.342–346)

Theiner, *Ueber Ivo's vermeintliches Decret*

P. Ewald, 'Die Papstbriefe der Brittischen Sammlung', NA 5 (1879–80) 277–414 and 501–596

M. Conrat, *Der Pandekten- und Institutionenauszug der Brittischen Dekretalensammlung: Quelle des Ivo* (Berlin 1887) [on the sources of Roman law in the *Decretum*]

Fournier, 'Collections canoniques attribuées à Yves de Chartres' 26–77 and 312–326

Fournier, 'Yves de Chartres et le droit canonique' 395–396

Wretschko, *Theodosiani libri XVI*, p. cccxlv–ccclviii
M. Tangl, 'Studien zur Neuausgabe der Bonifatius-Briefe II', NA 41 (1919) 23–101, especially 94–98 (on the sources of the *Decretum*)
Gassò-Batlle, *Pelagii I papae epistulae* p. xliii–xlv
Sprandel, *Ivo von Chartes* 52–85
J. Gaudemet, 'Collections canoniques et primauté pontificale', RDC 16 (1966) 105–117 (overrates the Pseudo-Isidorian contribution to the section of the *Decretum* dealing with papal primacy)
Fuhrmann, *Einfluß und Verbreitung* 2.544–554
Gilchrist, 'Reception 1' 61–62
Brommer, 'Kurzformen' 21 including n. 11
John, *Collectio canonum Remedio . . . ascripta* 115–116
P. Brommer, 'Unbekannte Fragmente einer Dekrethandschrift Ivos von Chartres', *Francia* 5 (1977) 753–755 (consists of covers kept at the Landeshauptarchiv Koblenz and in the Freiherr-vom-Stein Archiv at Nassau)
Hartmann, *Worms* 113
Motta, 'Regula Benedicti' 261–279
Landau, 'Dekret' 1–44
Blumenthal, 'Fälschungen' 250
Landau, 'Gefälschtes Recht' 38
P. Leisching, 'Consuetudo und ratio im Dekret und der Panormia des Bischof Ivo von Chartres', ZRG Kan. Abt. 74 (1988) 535–542
M. M. Sheehan, 'Theory and Practice: Marriage of the Unfree and the Poor in Medieval Society', MS 50 (1988) 457–487
J. Gilchrist, 'The Canonistic Treatment of Jews in the Latin West in the Eleventh and Early Twelfth Centuries', ZRG Kan. Abt. 75 (1989) 70–106
Landau, 'Kanonessammlungen in der Lombardei' 451
B. C. Brasington, 'A Note on Johannes Molinaeus, Editor of Ivo of Chartres' Decretum', BMCL 20 (1990) 74–77
Brett, 'Collections attributed to Ivo' 27–46
Brett, 'Collectio Lanfranci' 163–165, 168
Gaudemet, 'Primauté' 155–156
Landau, 'Vorgratianische Kanonessammlungen bei den Dekretisten' 93–116
R. Somerville, 'A Textual Link between Canterbury and Lucca in the Early Twelfth Century?' *Studi in onore Luigi Prosdocimi* (1994) 1.2.405–415

Ivo of Chartres, Panormia

1. *Author:* Ivo of Chartres. 2. *Date:* Not before 1095 (about 1094–1095), because the *Panormia* depends on the *Decretum*; the *Panormia,* however, contains neither any canons of Council of Clermont nor any documents which can be dated to the last years of the pontificate of Urban II; therefore, it has to be concluded that the *Panormia* was also compiled around 1094, i.e. very shortly after the *Decretum* (Fournier-Le Bras 2.95–97); Sprandel thinks that it is quite likely that a longer period of time elapsed between the compilation of the *Decretum* and the *Panormia* (cf. Sprandel, *Ivo von Chartres* 73 n. 61); cf. approving this view, Fuhrmann, *Einfluß und Verbreitung* 2.560 n. 372; but cf. Landau, TRE 16 (1987) 423: 'Fournier's dating must

be maintained'; according to Brett after 1095. *3. Place:* Chartres. *4. Type:* A manual with a wide circulation; a revision of the *Decretum* that reduced its size.

5. Editions

Sebastian Brant (Basel 1499)
Melchior de Vosmédian (Louvain 1557)
Vosmédian's edition was reprinted in PL 161.1041–1344

6. Manuscripts

Very numerous. The list that follows is taken from Brommer, 'Fragmente' 232 n. 13 and supplemented by Landau, 'Rubriken und Inskriptionen' (as below) 48–49 (manuscripts of the *Panormia* at the Bayerische Staatsbibliothek München)

Admont, Stiftsbibliothek, 257, saec. XII, fol. 1^r–66^v (with omissions and additional chapters)
Admont, Stiftsbibliothek, 541, cf. Brasington DA 47 (1991) 173
Angers, Bibliothèque municipale, 369, saec. XII^1, St-Aubin
Avranches, Bibliothèque municipale, 147, saec. XII
Bamberg, Staatsbibliothek, Can. 90, cf. Brasington, DA 47 (1991) 173
Berlin, Staatsbibliothek Preußischer Kulturbesitz, 613 lat. 8° 51
Berlin, Staatsbibliothek Preußischer Kulturbesitz, 614 lat. 4°982
Berlin, Staatsbibliothek Preußischer Kulturbesitz, Savigny 13
Bern, Burgerbibliothek, 422, saec. XII
Bruxelles, Bibliothèque Royale Albert Ier, 1817–2501, saec. XII, Prov. Louvain, Jesuite College
Burgo de Osma, Biblioteca de la Santa Iglesia Catedral, 8, saec. XII^2; Prov. France, fol. 8^r–162^v; *Appendix Seguntina,* cf. Fransen, 'Appendix Seguntina, Liber Tarraconensis et Décret de Gratien', REDC 45 (1988) 31–34
Cambridge, Library of Pembroke College, 103, saec. XIII, England
Cambridge, University Library, Ff.IV.41 (1284), saec. XII–XIII, Prov. Durham (saec. XV)
Cambridge, University Library, Ii.IV.28 (1825), saec. XII^{ex}, Prov. England
Clongowes Wood College, Naas (Ireland), sine num. saec. XIII^1, Prov. Fountains
Douai, Bibliothèque municipale, 584, saec. XII, Anchin
Edinburgh, National Library of Scotland, Adv. 18.8.6, saec. XII–XIII
Einsiedeln, Stiftsbibliothek, 196, saec. XII
El Escorial, Real Biblioteca de San Lorenzo, D.III.14, saec. XII, Prov. A. Agustín ('abridged version')
Engelberg, Stiftsbibliothek, 56, saec. XII^{ex}, fol. 1–102^v
Engelberg, Stiftsbibliothek, 57, saec. XIII
Evreux, Bibliothèque municipale, 25L, saec. XII^2, Prov. Lyre
Firenze, Biblioteca Medicea Laurenziana, San Marco 487, cf. Brasington, DA 47 (1991) 174
Firenze, Biblioteca Nazionale Centrale, Conv. soppr. G.1, Prov. Vallombrosa
Ghent (Gand), Centrale Bibliotheek der Rijksuniversiteit (Bibliothèque Universitaire), 140, after 1128, St. Peter, Ghent

Ghent (Gand), Centrale Bibliotheek der Rijksuniversiteit (Bibliothèque Universitaire), 505, saec. XIII, Cambron

Graz, Universitätsbibliothek, 327, saec. XII, Prov. Neuberg

Hereford, Cathedral Library, O.VI.13 , saec. XII^{1}, Prov. Hereford by 1300, cf. Mynors-Thomson, *Catalogue of Hereford* 45

Jena, Thüringer Universitäts- und Landesbibliothek, El. q. 2, saec. XII^{1}, Prov. Mildenfart near Weida (OPraem)

Klosterneuburg, Stiftsbibliothek, 638/1, cf. Brasington, DA 47 (1991) 174

København, Kongelike Bibliotek, Thott 158 fol., saec. XII, France

København, Kongelike Bibliotek, Thott 555.4^{o}

Köln, Historisches Archiv, W 142, cf. Brasington, DA 47 (1991) 174

Lincoln, Cathedral Chapter Library, 192, saec. XII^{in}, written by a French hand, Prov. France, owned by the Celestines of Marcoussis (dioc. Paris) in the 15th century, fol. 2^{r}–101^{r}, cf. Thomson, *Catalogue of Lincoln* 154

London, British Library, Add. 11440, saec. XII^{2}, fol. 73–112 ('abridged version')

London, British Library, Add. 17513, saec. XIII^{ex}, Prov. Arras (?)

London, British Library, Add. 18371, saec. XIII^{ex}, Prov. Fiecht, fol. 3^{r}–129^{r}

London, British Library, Addit. 22802, saec. XII, Prov. S. Maria, Belcastro ('abridged version')

London, British Library, Arundel 252, saec. XIII, Prov. Newburgh, fol. 1^{r}–94^{v}

London, British Library, Cotton Vitellius A.III, saec. XII, fol. 1^{r}–110^{v} (incomplete, quire missing)

London, British Library, Egerton 749, saec. XII

London, British Library, Royal 7.B.V, saec. XIII, Prov. London Carmelites (saec. XV), fol. 1^{r}–122^{r}

London, British Library, Royal 11.B.XIII, saec. XIII, Prov. Chester, fol. 1^{r}–67^{r}

Luxembourg, Bibliothèque nationale, 49, saec. XIII^{1}, Orval, fol. 49^{r}–109^{v} (1–4.105 only)

Madrid, Biblioteca Nacional, 6302 (R 127)

Mantova, Biblioteca Comunale, B.II.21 (198), saec. XII, Prov. Polirone

Modena, Biblioteca Estense, XIII.F.28

Monte Cassino, Archivio e Biblioteca dell'Abbazia, 215 Z, saec. XIII, p. 2–263

München, Bayerische Staatsbibliothek, Clm 2593; Prov. Aldersbach (to Pan. 8.136 on fol.155^{r})

München, Bayerische Staatsbibliothek, Clm 4545, saec. XII$^{med.}$(?), Prov. Benediktbeuern (to Pan. 8.136)

München, Bayerische Staatsbibliothek, Clm 6354, Prov. Freising (contains complete version of the *Panormia* to Pan. 8.136)

München, Bayerische Staatsbibliothek, Clm 11316, saec. XII–XIII, Prov. St. Salvator, Polling (to Pan. 8.134)

München, Bayerische Staatsbibliothek, Clm 17099, saec. XII^{2}, Prov. Schäftlarn (to Pan. 8.136)

München, Bayerische Staatsbibliothek, Clm 17100, Prov. Schäftlarn (to Pan. 8.136) fol. 166^{r}–236^{v}

München, Bayerische Staatsbibliothek, Clm 22289, Prov. Windberg; fol. 117–151 (abridged version of the *Panormia;* text beginning at fol. 117^{r} with Pan. 1.9)

München, Bayerische Staatsbibliothek, Clm 28223, Prov. Kaisheim (to Pan. 8.134;

four more chapters were added in a different hand later; another scribe added the chapters Pan. 8.135, 136; not listed in the catalogue)

München, Bayerische Staatsbibliothek, Clm 29172, Prov. St. Mang at Stadtamhof near Regensburg; cf. Landau, 'Regensburg' 73 n. 81

Orléans, Bibliothèque municipale, 222 (194), saec. XII, Prov. Fleury, p. 1–78

Oxford, Bodleian Library, Bodley 388, saec. XIII^{1}, Prov. Worksop

Oxford, Bodleian Library, Lat. misc. d.74, saec. XII$^{med.}$ (? or later), France, Prov. Chester Franciscans

Oxford, Bodleian Library, Laud. 226

Oxford, Bodleian Library, Laud. misc. 547, saec. XII (?), Germany

Oxford, Jesus College, C.26, saec. XII, Prov. Cirencester, fol. 5–191

Oxford, Jesus College, C.50, saec. XII^{ex}

Oxford, St. John's College, C. 125, saec. XII, to chap. 7.37, followed by Burchard 7 and 8 to 33 med.

Paris, Bibliothèque de l'Arsenal, 713 (11 B.L.), saec. XII–XIII

Paris, Bibliothèque Mazarine, 1286 (1203), saec. XII–XIII, Prov. Val-Notre-Dame

Paris, Bibliothèque nationale, lat. 2472, saec. XII, Prov. Colbert, known to Baluze

Paris, Bibliothèque nationale, lat. 2703, saec. XII, Prov. Colbert, fol. 17–104^{v}

Paris, Bibliothèque nationale, lat. 3348, saec. XII^{2}

Paris, Bibliothèque nationale, lat. 3864, saec. XIII, cf. Petersmann (as below)

Paris, Bibliothèque nationale, lat. 3865, saec. XII^{2}, Prov. St-Amand

Paris, Bibliothèque nationale, lat. 3866

Paris, Bibliothèque nationale, lat. 3867, saec. XII^{2}

Paris, Bibliothèque nationale, lat. 3868

Paris, Bibliothèque nationale, lat. 3869, saec. XII^{2}

Paris, Bibliothèque nationale, lat. 3869A, saec. XIII

Paris, Bibliothèque nationale, lat. 3870, saec. XIII or saec. XII^{med}

Paris, Bibliothèque nationale, lat. 3871

Paris, Bibliothèque nationale, lat. 3872, saec. XII^{2}, Prov. Italy

Paris, Bibliothèque nationale, lat. 3873

Paris, Bibliothèque nationale, lat. 3874 (erroneously identified; it is a manuscript of Ivo's *Decretum*)

Paris, Bibliothèque nationale, lat. 4284, saec. XIII, cf. Petersmann (as below)

Paris, Bibliothèque nationale, lat. 4285, saec. XII^{ex} (?), Northern France

Paris, Bibliothèque nationale, lat. 4286

Paris, Bibliothèque nationale, lat. 4890 (erroneously identified according to Mordek, 'Kanonistik und gregorianische Reform' 71 n. 29)

Paris, Bibliothèque nationale, lat. 10742

Paris, Bibliothèque nationale, lat. 13660

Paris, Bibliothèque nationale, lat. 14315 (erroneously identified; it is a manuscript of Ivo's *Decretum*)

Paris, Bibliothèque nationale, lat. 14994, Prov. St-Victor

Paris, Bibliothèque nationale, lat. 14995, saec. XII, Prov. St-Victor

Paris, Bibliothèque nationale, lat. 17526, saec. XII, Prov. Notre-Dame

Paris, Bibliothèque nationale, lat. 18222, saec. XII$^{med.}$, Northern France?

Parma, Biblioteca Palatina, V.22

Philadelphia, University of Pennsylvania, lat. 58, saec. XII, France, cf. Brasington, DA 47 (1991) 174

Roma, Biblioteca dell'Accademia Nazionale dei Lincei, Corsin. 1365
Roma, Biblioteca Nazionale Centrale, Sessor. LXIV (2086), saec. XIII (?), Prov. S. Croce
Roma, Biblioteca S. Croce, 64
Roma, Biblioteca Vallicelliana, B.77
Roma, Biblioteca Vallicelliana, C.20
Rouen, Bibliothèque municipale, 705 (A.330), saec. XII–XIII, Prov. St-Evroult-St-Ouen
Saint-Omer, Bibliothèque municipale, 360, saec. XV, Prov. St-Bertin
Saint-Omer, Bibliothèque municipale, 364, saec. XII^2, Prov. St-Bertin
Saint-Omer, Bibliothèque municipale, 381, saec. XIII, Prov. St-Bertin
Salzburg, Bibliothek der Erzabtei St. Peter, a.VIII.15, saec. $XII^{med.}$
Sankt Paul im Lavanttal, Stiftsbibliothek, 22/1, Prov. St. Blasien, cf. Brasington, DA 47 (1991) 174
Sigüenza, Archivo de la Catedral, 5 (207); *Appendix Seguntina,* cf. Fransen, 'Appendix Seguntina, Liber Tarraconensis et Décret de Gratien', REDC 45 (1988) 31–34
Sigüenza, Archivo de la Catedral, 75; *Appendix Seguntina,* cf. Fransen, 'Appendix Seguntina, Liber Tarraconensis et Décret de Gratien', REDC 45 (1988) 31–34
Sigüenza, Archivo de la Catedral, 110
St. Petersburg, Rossiyskaya Natsional'naya Biblioteka, Ermit. lat. 25, saec. XI, Prov. Weissenau
Strasbourg, Bibliothèque nationale et universitaire, 108, saec. XI^{ex}–XII, cf. Munier, 'Panormie' (as below) 348 n. 4
Tarragona, Biblioteca Publica (Provincial), 92, G. Fransen, 'Varia ex manuscriptis', *Traditio* 21 (1965) 517
Torino, Biblioteca Nazionale Universitaria, D.V.19, saec. XII, analysed by E. Seckel, NA 20 (1895) 323–327 (excerpt)
Torino, Biblioteca Nazionale Universitaria, E.V.16 (756), saec. XIII
Trier, Stadtbibliothek, 909, saec. XIII, Eberhardshausen, fol. 1–70
Trier, Stadtbibliothek, 910, saec. XII, St. Matthias, fol. 1–126
Troyes, Bibliothèque municipale, 480, saec. XII, Clairvaux
Troyes, Bibliothèque municipale, 1293, saec. XII, Clairvaux
Troyes, Bibliothèque municipale, 1328, saec. XII, Clairvaux
Troyes, Bibliothèque municipale, 1519, saec. XII, Clairvaux
Utrecht, Bibliotheek der Rijksuniversiteit, 621, saec. XIII–XIV, Charterhouse of Utrecht
Vaticano, Città del, Archivio di San Pietro G.19, cf. Brasington, DA 47 (1991) 174
Vaticano, Città del, Archivio di San Pietro G.19bis. saec. XII^{ex}, Italy, cf. Brasington, DA 47 (1991) 174
Vaticano, Città del, Biblioteca Apostolica Vaticana, lat. 1358, saec. XII (?), Germany, fol. 5^v–113
Vaticano, Città del, Biblioteca Apostolica Vaticana, lat. 1359, saec. XII or later, Avignon
Vaticano, Città del, Biblioteca Apostolica Vaticana, lat. 1360, saec. XII, fol. $1–87^v$, cf. Märtl, 'Investiturprivilegien' (as below) especially 35
Vaticano, Città del, Biblioteca Apostolica Vaticana, lat. 1362, saec. XII, Prov. S.

Maria in Crescenzago near Milan, cf. Landau, 'Kanonessammlungen in der Lombardei' 452 n. 109
Vaticano, Città del, Biblioteca Apostolica Vaticana, lat. 1363
Vaticano, Città del, Biblioteca Apostolica Vaticana, lat. 5002, cf. Märtl, 'Investiturprivilegien' (as below) 35
Vaticano, Città del, Biblioteca Apostolica Vaticana, lat. 7152, saec. XVII
Vaticano, Città del, Biblioteca Apostolica Vaticana, Barb. lat. 502
Vaticano, Città del, Biblioteca Apostolica Vaticana, Barb. lat. 534
Vaticano, Città del, Biblioteca Apostolica Vaticana, Ottobon. lat. 164
Vaticano, Città del, Biblioteca Apostolica Vaticana, Reg. lat. 340, saec. XII[2], Northern France, fol. 1–156; seems to be a 'working' manuscript, cf. G. Fransen, 'La tradition manuscrite de la Panormie d'Yves de Chartres', *Proceedings San Diego* 25
Vaticano, Città del, Biblioteca Apostolica Vaticana, Reg. lat. 972, cf. Märtl, 'Investiturprivilegien' (as below) 35
Vaticano, Città del, Biblioteca Apostolica Vaticana, Reg. lat. 991, saec. XII[1], Northern Germany/Poland?
Vendôme, Bibliothèque municipale, 160, saec. XII
Venezia, Biblioteca Nazionale Marciana, lat. IV.41 (293)
Venezia, Biblioteca Nazionale Marciana, lat. IV.51, saec. XIII (?), Franciscans of SS. Giovanni e Paolo, cf. Landau, ZRG Kan. Abt. 67 (1981) 84
Venezia, Biblioteca Nazionale Marciana, San Marco 12
Vich, Archivo Capitular, 145
Wien, Österreichische Nationalbibliothek, lat. 986
Wien, Österreichische Nationalbibliothek, lat. 2192, saec. XII, cf. Märtl, 'Investiturprivilegien' 36
Wien, Österreichische Nationalbibliothek, lat. 2200
Wien, Österreichische Nationalbibliothek, lat. 2212, saec. XIII (?)
Wien, Österreichische Nationalbibliothek, lat. 5130
Zwettl, Stiftsbibliothek, 231, saec. XII[2], fol. 118[v]–211

Fragments

Amiens, Bibliothèque municipale, Fonds Lescalopier 10, fol. 2
Graz, Universitätsbibliothek, 887
Koblenz, Landeshauptarchiv, 701, no. 759,7, cf. Brommer, 'Kirchenrechtliche Sammlungen' 86–89
Marburg, Hessisches Staatsarchiv, Hr 9 fasc. 4, saec. XIII (fragment of Book VII), cf. Brommer, 'Fragmente' 231–232
Paris, Bibliothèque nationale, lat. 14135
Pisa, Biblioteca del Seminario Santa Catarina, 53, cf. Somerville, *Decreta Claromontensia* 95

Excerpts

Auxerre, Bibliothèque municipale, 39, saec. XII, Prov. cathedral of Sens

See also the manuscripts of the Prologue in B. C. Brasington, 'Zur Rezeption des Prologs Ivos von Chartres in Süddeutschland', DA 47 (1991) 167–174, especially 173–174: 'Anhang: Überlieferung des Prologs Ivos von Chartres': A list of 173 manuscripts of the *Prologue;* cf. also *Proceedings San Diego* 3–22

7. *Bibliography*

On Ivo of Chartres in general cf. above, *Collectio tripartita*

On the *Panormia*: Conrat, *Geschichte* 383–385; Fournier-Le Bras 2.85–105 and 105–114; Kurtscheid-Wilches 1.164; Van Hove, *Prolegomena* 331–332; Stickler, *Historia* 1.182–183; García y García, *Historia* 1.318–320

J. Doujat, *Praenotionum canonicarum liber* V (Venice 1769) 259–263 (exact comparison of the subject index of the *Decretum* with that of the *Panormia*)

Wasserschleben, *Beiträge* 61–77

R. Stintzing, *Geschichte der populären Literatur des römisch-kanonischen Rechts in Deutschland am Ende des fünfzehnten und im Anfang des sechzehnten Jahrhunderts* (Leipzig 1867; repr. Aalen 1959) 458–459 (on Brant's edition)

Tardif, *Sources* 171 (on the relationship of *Decretum* and *Panormia*)

Fournier, 'Collections canoniques attribuées à Yves de Chartres' 293–312 and 312–326

Fournier, 'Yves de Chartres et le droit canonique' 396–398

A. Vetulani, 'Le Décret de Gratien et les premiers décrétistes à la lumière d'une source nouvelle', SG 7 (1959) 309–313

H. Wagnon, 'L'Université de Louvain et les éditions de textes et anciens commentaires de droit canonique', *Congrès de droit canonique médiéval: Louvain et Bruxelles, 22–26 juillet 1958* (Louvain 1959) 13–24 (on Vosmédian's edition; contrary to Wagnon's assertion, the edition of V. was not based on two English manuscripts but on the edition of Sebastian Brant dating from 1499)

Sprandel, *Ivo von Chartres* 52–85

G. Fransen, 'Varia ex manuscriptis', *Traditio* 21 (1965) 516

J. Rambaud-Buhot, 'Les sommaires de la Panormie et l'édition de Melchior de Vosmédian', *Traditio* 23 (1967) 534–536

C. Munier, 'Pour une édition de la *Panormie* d'Ive de Chartres', *Revue des sciences religieuses* (Strasbourg 1969) 347–358 (repr. *Vie conciliaire et collections canoniques en Occident, IVe–XIIe siècles* [London 1987] no. XIV) (on Strasbourg 108)

R. Somerville, 'Two Notes on Scotland and the Medieval Papacy', *Innes Review* 23 (1972) 149–151

Fuhrmann, *Einfluß und Verbreitung* 2.554–562

Gilchrist, 'Reception 1' 63

Brommer, 'Fragmente' 232 including n. 13 (a provisional list of the *Panormia*-manuscripts)

Petersmann, 'Kanonistische Überlieferung' 383–385, 386–389

Brommer, 'Kirchenrechtliche Sammlungen' 86–89

Gilchrist, 'Reception 2' 192, 194

P. Landau, 'Die Rubriken und Inskriptionen von Ivos Panormie: Die Ausgabe Sebastian Brants im Vergleich zu der Loewener Edition des Melchior de Vosmédian und der Ausgabe von Migne', BMCL 12 (1982) 31–49

Landau, 'Dekret' 3–4, 34 (texts of the *Decretum* taken over into the *Panormia*)

Mordek, 'Kanonistik und gregorianische Reform' 70–71

G. Fransen, 'La tradition manuscrite de la Panormie d'Yves de Chartres', BMCL 17 (1987) 91–95

C. Märtl, 'Die Kanonistische Überlieferung der falschen Investiturprivilegien (Ivo, *Panormia* 8.135 and 136: D.63 c.22)', BMCL 17 (1987) 31–44

G. Fransen, 'Appendix Seguntina, Liber Tarraconensis et Décret de Gratien', REDC 45 (1988) 31–34

P. Leisching, 'Consuetudo und ratio im Dekret und der Panormia des Bischof Ivo von Chartres', ZRG Kan. Abt. 74 (1988) 535–542

J. Gilchrist, 'The Canonistic Treatment of Jews in the Latin West in the Eleventh and Early Twelfth Centuries', ZRG Kan. Abt. 75 (1989) 70–106

Landau, 'Kanonessammlungen in der Lombardei' 451–453

B. C. Brasington, 'Zur Rezeption des Prologs Ivos von Chartres in Süddeutschland', DA 47 (1991), 167–174 (173–174: Appendix: transmission of the Prologue of Ivo of Chartres)

B. C. Brasington, 'The Prologue of Ivo of Chartres: A Fresh Consideration of the Manuscripts', *Proceedings San Diego* 3–22

Brett, 'Collections attributed to Ivo' 27–46

G. Fransen, 'La tradition manuscrite de la Panormie d'Yves de Chartres', *Proceedings San Diego* 23–25 (demands a distinction between the manuscripts of the Panormie and those of the Panormie augmentée)

Hartmann, 'Autoritäten' 437

Gaudemet, 'Primauté' 155–156

S. Kuttner, 'Marbod of Rennes on the *Ordo iudiciorum' Nachrichten der Akademie der Wissenschaften in Göttingen, phil.-hist. Klasse* (1992) 3–6

G. Motta, 'La cultura canonistica di San Bernardo', *San Bernardo e l'Italia: Atti del Convegno di Studi, Milano, 24–26 maggio 1990*, ed. P. Zierbi (Milan 1993) 131–139

Landau, 'Eheschließung' 458–459

Collectio Caesaraugustana

1. *Author:* A member of the Gregorian Reform party. 2. *Date:* Any date between 1108 and 1140 is possible, but a date after 1120 is more probable. 3. *Place:* Northern Spain, Aquitaine or Burgundy; Eastern Pyrenees? 4. *Type:* Systematic collection; its most important direct sources are the collections of Anselm of Lucca, Deusdedit and Ivo of Chartres (*Decretum* and *Collectio Tripartita*), it exerted a considerable influence on the *Decretum Gratiani*; drew heavily on a collection very close to Paris, Bibl. de l'Arsenal 713, fol. 117^r–192^v. 5. *Edition:* None.

6. *Manuscripts*

First Recension

Madrid, Biblioteca Nacional (mentioned by Tarré, *Positions des thèses de l'Ecole des Chartes,* 1927, 134; cf. Fournier-Le Bras 2.270 and n. 1)

Paris, Bibliothèque Nationale, lat. 3875, saec. XII (lacks Books XIV–XV)

Salamanca, Biblioteca Universitaria, 81, saec. XV, fragmentary (book 1.1–54, book 2.11–12, 14–16), fol. 288^r–297^r, cf. García y García, 'Canonistica Hispanica (III)', *Traditio* 26 (1970) 457

Vaticano, Città del, Biblioteca Apostolica Vaticana, lat. 535 (olim Bibl. Barberini 2864, subsequently XVI, 104; incorrect shelfmark listed in Fournier-Le Bras and Van Hove; cf. Vat. Barb. lat. 897)

Vaticano, Città del, Biblioteca Apostolica Vaticana, lat. 4976

Second Recension

Paris, Bibliothèque nationale, lat. 3876, saec. XII[1] (1143–1144), Southern France?

Salamanca, Biblioteca Universitaria, 2664, saec. XV (='lost' manuscript of the Carthusian monastery of Aulae Dei near Saragossa)

Vaticano, Città del, Biblioteca Apostolica Vaticana, Barb. lat. 897 (olim Bibl. Barberini 2864, subsequently XVI, 104) (copy of Salamanca 2664)

Vaticano, Città del, Biblioteca Apostolica Vaticana, lat. 5715, saec. XII[1], shortly after 1143, fol. 1ra–126ra (perhaps a copy of Paris lat. 3876)

Third Recension

Barcelona, Archivo de la Corona de Aragón, San Cugat 63, saec. XII[1], shortly after 1143; cf. Fowler-Magerl 144; cf. also F. X. Miquel Rosell, 'Católeg dels llibres manuscrits de la Biblioteca del Monestir de Sant Cugat del Vallès existents a l'Arxiu de la Corona d'Aragó', *Butlletí de la Biblioteca de Catalunya* 8 (Barcelona 1937) 7–154, especially 108–110; F. Valls y Taberner, *Estudis d'historia juridica catalona* (Barcelona 1929) 82–83

7. *Bibliography*

Conrat, *Geschichte* 390–392; Fournier-Le Bras 2.269–284; R. Naz, 'Caesaraugustana (collectio)', DDC 2 (1937) 1188–1191; Kurtscheid-Wilches 1.165; Van Hove, *Prolegomena* 241, 333, 421; Stickler, *Historia* 1.184–185; García y García, *Historia* 1.320–321; García y García, 'Caesaraugustana collectio', LMA 2 (1983) 1359

A. Agustín, *De emendatione Gratiani dialogorum libri duo* I, dial. V, xi, xvi and passim

Ballerini, *De antiquis . . . collectionibus et collectoribus* P. IV, cap. XVIII, § 11 (PL 56.352)

Savigny, *Geschichte* 2.299–300

Theiner, *Disquisitiones criticae* 356–359

J. Flach, *Etudes critiques sur l'histoire du droit romain au moyen âge avec textes inédits* (Paris 1890) 285–286

Fournier, 'Collections canoniques attribuées à Yves de Chartres' 416–426

Wretschko, *Theodosiani libri XVI*, p. cccxlviii

Fournier, 'Caesaraugustana' 53–79

C. G. Mor, 'I testi di diritto Giustinianeo nelle due redazioni della collezione canonica Cesaraugustana' *Studi in onore di Francesco Scaduto* 2 (Florence 1936) 417–437

Gassò-Batlle, *Pelagii I Papae epistulae* 25–26

Ryan, 'Observations' 100

Gossman, *Urban II* 62–67

G. Santini, 'Richerche sulle "*Exceptiones Legum Romanarum*": Contributo alla storia dei *libri legales* e delle scuole giuridiche di età preirneriana' (Milan 1969) 85–92

Kuttner, 'Roman Manuscripts' 7–29

Gilchrist, 'Reception 1' 65–66

Petersmann, 'Kanonistische Überlieferung' 383, 385, 386–389

Brommer, 'Rezeption' 135–136

Mordek, *Kirchenrecht und Reform* 139 n. 188

Blumenthal, *Early Councils* 104 (details about JL 6613 corrected by Fowler-Magerl, 'Vorgratianische Kanonessammlungen' 145)

A. Gouron, 'La Science juridique française aux XIe et XIIe siècles: Diffusion du droit de Justinien et influences canoniques jusqu'à Gratien', IRMAE I.4.d-e (Milan 1978) 42–43
Gilchrist, 'Reception 2' 193 and 207–209
Fowler-Magerl, 'Vorgratianische Kanonessammlungen' 144–146
Landau, 'Dekret' 35
E. Tejero, 'El matrimonio en la *Collectio Caesaraugustana*', *Proceedings Cambridge* 115–134
E. Tejero, '*Ratio* y jerarquia de fuentes canónicas en la *Caesaraugustana*', *Hispania Christiana* 303–322
Landau, 'Kirchweihe' 225–240

Collectio 9 librorum (Ghent 235 and Wolfenbüttel, Gud. lat. 212)

1. Author: Jean de Warneton, Bishop of Thérouanne (1099–1130) according to J. M. De Smet (see also Waelkens-Van den Auweele, 'Codex Gandavensis' 139). *2. Date:* Between 1096–1100 with additions dating from 1120 reflecting the Gregorian Reform. Book I–VIII before the Council of Clermont (1095), Book IX after the Council of Clermont (Waelkens-Van den Auweele, 'Codex Gandavensis' 132). *3. Place:* Ecclesiastical province of Reims, perhaps Thérouanne (cf. Sdralek, Fournier-Le Bras). *4. Type:* Used *Collectio of the Ms. Arras 425* as a source; the assertion made by Fournier-Le Bras, that the *Collectio tripartita* of Ivo of Chartres had been used as a source, is without foundation according to Brett, 'Collectio Lanfranci' 169 n. 47. *5. Edition:* None.

6. Manuscripts

Ghent (Gand), Centrale Bibliotheek der Rijksuniversiteit (Bibliothèque Universitaire), 235, about 1100, Prov. St. Pierre-au-Mont-Blandin (Gand), cf. Waelkens-Van den Auweele, 'Codex Gandavensis' 124–125
Wolfenbüttel, Herzog August Bibliothek, Gud. lat. 212 (Heinemann 4517), saec. XII^{2}, Prov. Saint-Germain-des-Prés, fol. 1^{r}–48^{r}

7. Bibliography

Fournier-Le Bras 2.285–296 and 55–114 (on Ivo of Chartres); Van Hove, *Prolegomena* 333–334

Sdralek, *Wolfenbüttler Fragmente* 3–86
J. M. De Smet, *De heilige Jan van Waasten en de Gregorianische hervorming in het bisdom Terwaan* (Louvain 1943; mémoire de licence dactylographié; K.U. Leuven, Centrale Bibliotheek, LV 4022, see also Waelkens-Van den Auweele)
Gossman, *Urban II* 68–77
Somerville, *Decreta Claromontensia* 56–57, 60
Petersmann, 'Kanonistische Überlieferung' 387
Blumenthal, *Early Councils* 86, 103, 105, 109, 114
Gilchrist, 'Reception 2' 209–211

Waelkens-Van den Auweele, 'Codex Gandavensis' 115–153
Brett, 'Collectio Lanfranci' 169

Cf. also *Collectio of Arras 425*

Collectio 10 partium

1. Author: French canonist, possibly Hildebert of Lavardin (Bishop of Le Mans, Archbishop of Tours, d. 1133); cf. Theiner, *Disquisitiones criticae* 165–166; Fournier-Le Bras 2.302–306). Gautier de Thérouanne (according to De Smet, cf. Van Hove and Waelkens-Van den Auweele). *2. Date:* 1123 or shortly afterwards. *3. Place:* Ecclesiastical province of Reims or at Le Mans. *4. Type:* Revised version of the *Collectio 9 librorum*, depends heavily on the *Panormia* of Ivo of Chartres (cf. Waelkens-Van den Auweele, 'Codex Gandavensis' 123)

5. Editions

Only *Prefatio*

Theiner, *Disquisitiones criticae* 166–168 (based on Wien 2178)
Rose, *Handschriften-Verzeichnisse* 1.205–212 (based on Berlin Phill. 1746)

6. Manuscripts

Berlin, Staatsbibliothek Preußischer Kulturbesitz, Phill. 1746, saec. XII, cf. Rose, *Handschriften-Verzeichnisse* 1.205–212, no. 95; manuscript of French origin which used to belong to the library of the Collège de Clermont at Paris
Cambridge, Library of Corpus Christi College, 94, saec. XIII, Prov. Canterbury, according to Brooke
Firenze, Biblioteca Nazionale Centrale, Conv. soppr., D.II.1476 (SS. Annunziata)
Paris, Bibliothèque nationale, lat. 10743, saec. XII^1, Prov. Evreux, Cathedral
Paris, Bibliothèque nationale, lat. 14145, Prov. Saint-Germain-des-Prés (only plan of the collection excluding the tenth part, the *Capitulatio* and the first seven chapters of this part, cf. Fournier-Le Bras 2.297)
Wien, Österreichische Nationalbibliothek, lat. 2178 (Iur. can. 91) saec. XII

7. Bibliography

H. Böhmer, 'Hildebert von Lavardin', RE ^{3}8 (1900) 67–71; J. Besse, 'Hildebert de Lavardin', DThC 6 (1925) 2466–2468; Fournier-Le Bras 2.296–306; Van Hove, *Prolegomena* 333 n. 8 and 334 n. 2

Ballerini, *De antiquis . . . collectionibus et collectoribus* P. IV, cap. XVIII, c. 14 (PL 56.353–354)
Theiner, *Disquisitiones criticae* 165–171
Fournier, 'Collections canoniques attribuées à Yves de Chartres' 433–442
A. Dieudonné, *Hildebert de Lavardin: Évêque du Mans, Archévêque de Tours (1056–1133): sa vie, ses lettres* (Paris 1898)
F. Barth, *Hildebert von Lavardin (1056–1133) und das kirchliche Stellenbesetzungsrecht* (Stuttgart 1906, repr. Amsterdam 1965)

R. Somerville, 'The Council of Beauvais 1114', *Traditio* 24 (1968) 493–503, especially 498–501
Petersmann, 'Kanonistische Überlieferung' 385–386, 386–389
Blumenthal, *Early Councils* 19
Gilchrist, 'Reception 2' 200–202
Waelkens-Van den Auweele, 'Codex Gandavensis' 122 n. 44
R. Somerville, 'The Councils of Pope Calixtus II and the Collection in Ten Parts', BMCL 11 (1981) 80–86

Haimo, Summa Decretorum

1. Author: Aimon (Haimon) de Bazoches (Bishop of Châlons-sur-Marne, †1153). *2. Date:* Probably between 1130 and 1135. *3. Place:* France, Châlons-sur-Marne. *4. Type:* An abridged version of the *Collectio 10 partium* (and not of the *Panormia*).

5. Editions

Only *Prefatio*

Theiner, *Disquisitiones criticae* 180–182
Rose, *Handschriften-Verzeichnisse* 1.210

6. Manuscripts

München, Bayerische Staatsbibliothek, Clm 2594 (Aldersbach 64); saec. XII–XIII
Oxford, Bodleian Library, Laud. misc. 218 (D. 82), saec. XII
Paris, Bibliothèque nationale, lat. 4286, Prov. Saint-Martin de Tournai, saec. XII
Paris, Bibliothèque nationale, lat. 4377, Prov. Colbert; saec. XII

7. Bibliography

P. Fournier, 'Aimon de Bazoches' DHGE 1 (1912) 1191; Fournier-Le Bras 2.306–308; A. Lambert, 'Bazoches (Aimon de)' DDC 2 (1937) 266–267 (contains errors); Van Hove, *Prolegomena* 334; Stickler, *Historia* 1.186

Theiner, *Disquisitiones criticae* 180–182
HLF 12 (1869) 426–428
Fournier, 'Collections canoniques attribuées à Yves de Chartres' 442–444
Somerville, *Decreta Claromontensia* 136–138
Petersmann, 'Kanonistische Überlieferung' 388 and 389
R. Reynolds, 'Marginalia on a Tenth-Century Text on the Ecclesiastical Offices', *Essays in Honor of Stephan Kuttner* (1977) 121–122
R. Reynolds, 'The *Isidorian* Epistula ad Leudefredum: An Early Medieval Epitome of the Clerical Duties', MS 41 (1979) 252–330, especially 302–303

Collectio Farfensis

1. Author: Gregory of Catino. *2. Date:* End of the eleventh century; Books I and II between 23 May 1099 (last entry of Gregory in the *Regestum* of Farfa) and about the middle of September 1100; the two remaining books only slightly later. *3. Place:* Farfa. *4. Type:* Collection defending monastic rights; main source: Pseudo-Isidore.

5. Editions

Il Regesto di Farfa compilato da Gregorio di Catino, ed. I. Giorgi and U. Balzani, 1–5 (Biblioteca della Società romana di storia patria; Rome 1879–1914)

Kölzer, *Collectio canonum;* cf. reviews by M. Bertram, RSCI 38 (1983) 217–221; J. Gaudemet, RHD, 4ᵉ sér. 61 (1983) 419–420

6. Manuscript

Vaticano, Città del, Biblioteca Apostolica Vaticana, lat. 8487 (probably the archetype of the *Collectio Farfensis*) (XI3/4, Farfa)

7. Bibliography

Conrat, *Geschichte* 215; Fournier-Le Bras 2.118–121; Van Hove, *Prolegomena* 316; Stickler, *Historia* 1.160

I. Giorgi, *Archivio della R. Società Romana di storia patria* 2 (1879) 426

F. Patetta, 'Contributi alla storia del diritto romano nel medio evo', BIDR 4 (1891) 249–286

P. Fournier, 'La Collezione canonica del Regesto di Farfa', *Archivio della Reale Società romana di storia patria* 27 (1894) 285–301

P. Fournier, 'Influence' 42

Fournier, 'Recueils canoniques italiens' 204–205

I. Schuster, *L'imperiale abbazia di Farfa* (Rome 1921)

H. Zielinski, *Studien zu den spoletinischen 'Privaturkunden' des 8. Jahrhunderts und ihrer Überlieferung im Regestum Farfense* (BDHI 39; Tübingen 1972) 99–103 (about Todinus)

H. Hees, 'Die Collectio Farfensis', BMCL 3 (1973) 11–49; cf. the review by D. Jasper, DA 30 (1974) 249

B. S. Pedeaux, *The Canonical Collection of the Farfa Register* (Rice University Ph. D., Ann Arbor, Xerox University Microfilms 1976) cf. the announcement in *Speculum* 50 (1975) 178; DissA (1976–77) 2350

Kölzer, 'Farfenser Kanonessammlung' 94–100

Th. Kölzer, 'Farfenser Auszüge aus der *Sammlung der Vatikanischen Handschrift*', BMCL 12 (1982) 1–12

Kölzer, 'Mönchtum und Kirchenrecht' 134–135

Gilchrist, 'Monastic Forgeries' 280

Mordek, 'Systematische Kanonessammlungen' 198

Reynolds, 'South Italian Collection' 280–281

Collectio 7 librorum (Torino D.IV.33)

1. Author: Unknown. *2. Date:* About 1100 (newest texts are from the Council of Piacenza; no texts dating from the period of Paschal II, cf. Fournier-Le Bras 2.167).

3. Place: Italy (Fournier-Le Bras 2.167); Poitou (Southwestern France) according to Reynolds; Fowler-Magerl 144: it could as well have originated in Nothern Italy. *4. Type:* Combination of the *Decretum Burchardi* with the *Collectio 74 titulorum. 5. Edition:* None.

6. Manuscript

Torino, Biblioteca Nazionale Universitaria, D.IV.33, saec. XII^{in}

7. Bibliography

Fournier-Le Bras 2.163–167; Van Hove, *Prolegomena* 327; Stickler, *Historia* 1.187; R. Naz, 'Turin (collection de)', DDC 7 (1965) 1351; García y García, *Historia* 1.322

Fournier, 'Manuel' 147–223, 285–290
Fournier, 'Collections canoniques issues du Décret de Burchard' 208–213
Ryan, 'Observations' 96
Gossman, *Urban II* 32
Reynolds, 'Turin Collection' 508–514 (*Collectio 7 librorum* of French not of Italian origin)
Gilchrist, 'Economic Policy' 407
Brommer, 'Kurzformen' 42
Gilchrist, 'Reception 1' 44–45
Petersmann, 'Kanonistische Überlieferung' 381–382
Brommer, 'Rezeption' 139–140
Mordek, *Kirchenrecht und Reform* 137–138 n. 183 (discussing Reynolds' thesis) and 226 n. 56 (on JK †868)
H. Mordek and G. Schmitz, 'Johannes VIII. und das Konzil von Troyes (878)', *Geschichtsschreibung und geistiges Leben im Mittelalter: Festschrift für Heinz Löwe zum 65. Geburtstag*, ed. K. Hauck and H. Mordek (Cologne-Vienna 1978) 188
Gilchrist, 'Epistola Widonis' 589
Fowler-Magerl, 'Vorgratianische Kanonessammlungen' 144
Hartmann, 'Kanonessammlung' 46–47
Landau, 'Kanonessammlungen in der Lombardei' 450
Landau, 'Kirchweihe' 225–240
D. Jasper, review of R. Weigand ('Zusätzliche *Paleae* in fünf Dekrethandschriften', ZRG Kan. Abt. 78, 1992, 65–120) in: DA 48 (1992) 693

Polycarpus, Collectio canonum

1. Author: Gregory, cardinal presbyter of S. Grisogono (last mentioned 15 Feb. 1113; died between February 1113 and June 1114; according to H. W. Klewitz, 'Die Entstehung des Kardinalkollegiums', ZRG Kan. Abt. 56 [1936] 212, he died on 21 Nov. 1113). *2. Date:* By 1113 at the latest, not before 1104 (dedication to Diego Gelmirez, Bishop of Compostella, on whom the pallium was bestowed through a papal letter dating 31 Oct. 1104; cf. Fournier-Le Bras 2.170–171: 1104–1106. Shortly after 1111 but before 1113 (Gilchrist). *3. Place:* Rome. *4. Type:* Systematic collection, source of the *Collectio 7 librorum* (Vat. lat. 1346)

5. Edition

Excerpts Only

A. Mai, *Nova bibliotheca Patrum* (Rome 1852–1888) 7.3 (PL 56.346) 1–76
(A complete edition is in preparation by H. Fuhrmann based on C. Erdmann's materials)

6. Manuscripts

Cf. Fournier, 'Polycarpus' 58–60 and Horst, *Polycarpus* 11–13 (based on Erdmann's papers)

Italian-German Manuscript Group

Firenze, Biblioteca Nazionale Centrale, Conv. soppr. B.IV.559, saec. XII, Prov. Camaldoli

Firenze, Biblioteca Riccardiana, 258, saec. XII, incomplete, Prov. Italy (in the first part the Greek and African councils of the *Hispana* are transmitted, cf. Mordek, *Kirchenrecht und Reform* 251)

Madrid, Biblioteca Nacionale, 7127, saec. XII, Prov. presumably Rome (cf. Le Bras, *Revue des Sciences religieuses* 8, 1928, 272); according to Erdmann the most ancient and the most important manuscript (Horst, *Polycarpus* 11)

Sub-Group of Italian-German Manuscripts

Firenze, Biblioteca Medicea Laurenziana, Strozzi 27, saec. XII^{in}, Prov. Switzerland, Italy or Germany

Köln, Erzbischöfliche Diözesan- und Dombibliothek, 126 (olim Darmstadt 2125), saec. XII, presumably from Germany, incomplete

French Manuscript Group

Carpentras, Bibliothèque Inguimbertine, 169, saec. XII

Salamanca, Biblioteca Universitaria, 2348, saec. XII^2, Prov. Maguelone (Southern France)?, cf. F. M. Rodriguez, 'Tres manuscritos del siglo XII con colecciones canónicas', *Analecta sacra Tarraconensia* 32 (1959) 10ff.

Vaticano, Città del, Biblioteca Apostolica Vaticana, lat. 1354, saec. XII

Vaticano, Città del, Biblioteca Apostolica Vaticana, lat. 3530 (Sixteenth-century copy of Vat. lat. 1354)

Vaticano, Città del, Biblioteca Apostolica Vaticana, Reg. lat. 1026, saec. XIII^{in}

Sub-Group of French Manuscripts

Paris, Bibliothèque nationale, lat. 3881, saec. XII^{ex}

Vaticano, Città del, Biblioteca Apostolica Vaticana, Reg. lat. 987, saec. XIII^{in}

Later Recension (so-called second recension of *Polycarpus*)

Probably shortly after 1120 in Rome; according to Fournier, the author of this expansion of *Polycarpus* worked at the Roman curia or in its surroundings, cf. Landau, 'Gefälschtes Recht' 44

Paris, Bibliothèque nationale, lat. 3882, saec. XIV^{ex}, possibly from Provence or adjacent regions (copy of a manuscript saec. XII)

Manuscripts erroneously classified as Polycarp-manuscripts

Burgo de Osma, Biblioteca de la Santa Iglesia Catedral, 8, saec. XIII (?), Prov. France, fol. 162^{v}–182^{v}: excerpts; cf. T. Rojo Orcajo, 'Catálogo descriptivo de los códices en la Santa Iglesia Catedral de Burgo de Osma', *Boletin de la Real Academia de la Historia* 94 (1929) 655–792 and 95 (1929) 152–314, esp. 94 (1929) 710–715

Firenze, Biblioteca Marucelliana, C. 386 (*Collectio 183 titulorum*, cf. Mordek, 'Handschriftenforschungen' 629 n. 7 and above)

Firenze, Biblioteca Nazionale Centrale, Conv. soppr., C.I.2777 (Badia Fiorentina), saec. XII, according to a note in the catalogue and the shelf-mark on its back, it is described as a *Polycarpus*, but actually contains an excerpt from Burchard's *Decretum* with some additions (cf. Mordek, 'Handschriftenforschungen' 629 n. 7 and 642)

Vaticano, Città del, Biblioteca Apostolica Vaticana, Reg. lat. 1039

7. *Bibliography*

Conrat, *Geschichte* 374–375; Fournier-Le Bras 2.169–185; Kurtscheid-Wilches 1.161–162; Van Hove, *Prolegomena* 327; Stickler, *Historia* 1.178–179; Naz, DDC 7, 18–20; A. Bride, 'Grégoire', *Catholicisme* 5 (1962) 268; García y García, *Historia* 1.318; G. May, 'Polycarpus', NCE 11 (1967) 536; G. Fransen, 'Grégoire, cardinal diacre de S.- Chrysogone (†1113)', DHGE 21 (1986) 1455–1456

Ballerini, *De antiquis . . . collectionibus et collectoribus* P. IV, cap. XVII (PL 56.346–348)

Theiner, *Disquisitiones criticae* 341–354

H. Hüffer, *Beiträge zur Geschichte der Quellen des Kirchenrechts, 2: Zur Geschichte des römischen Rechts im Mittelalter insbesondere über die Rechtssammlung Polykarpus und ihre dem römischen Recht entnommenen Bestandtheile* (Münster 1862) 67–109

F.-J. Schulte, 'Ueber drei in Prager Handschriften enthaltene Canonen-Sammlungen', SB Vienna 57, 1867 (1868) 175–182

H. Hüffer, *Beiträge zur Geschichte der vorgratianischen Kirchenrechtsquellen* (1869) 86–109

Fournier, 'Collection canonique italienne' 209–233, 343–438, 400–409

Fournier, 'Polycarpus' 55–101

G. Le Bras, 'Manuscrits canoniques', *Revue des sciences religieuses* 8 (1928) 270–273

Mor, 'Digesto' 672–675, 693–694

H.-W. Klewitz, 'Die Entstehung des Kardinalkollegiums', ZRG Kan. Abt. 25 (1936) 212

Gossman, *Urban II* 32–34

H. Fuhrmann, 'Zwei Papstbriefe aus der Überlieferung der Rechtssammlung *Polycarpus*', *Aus Reichsgeschichte und Nordischer Geschichte*, ed. H. Fuhrmann, H. E. Mayer and K. Wriedt (Kieler Historische Studien 16; Stuttgart 1972) 131–140

Kuttner, 'Turning point' 55–85

Gilchrist, 'Economic Policy' 409

Gilchrist, 'Reception 1' 46–47

Petersmann, 'Kanonistische Überlieferung' 378–380

Gilchrist, 'Reception 2' 194

Horst, *Polycarpus* passim

J. Gilchrist, 'The *Polycarpus,*' ZRG Kan. Abt. 68 (1982) 441–452 (Review of Horst, *Polycarpus*)

G. Motta, 'Nuove identificazioni nella collezione canonica detta *Polycarpus*', *Aevum* 57 (1983) 232–244
A. Degl'Innocenti and S. Cantelli, 'La riforma gregoriana e l'Europa (Salerno, 20–25 maggio 1985)', SM 26 (1985) 483–493
Mordek, 'Systematische Kanonessammlungen' 195
J. Arrieta, 'Polycarpus, Liber I', DissA 48 (1987–1988) 250
Landau, 'Gefälschtes Recht' 42–46 (also on *Polycarp II* in Paris lat. 3882: 47 n. 147)
A. García y García, 'Reforma gregoriana e idea de la *Militia sancti Petri* en los reinos ibéricos', SGreg 13 (1989) 241–262
Landau, 'Vorgratianische Kanonessammlungen bei den Dekretisten' 93–116

Collectio 7 librorum (Vat. lat. 1346 etc.)

1. Author: Unknown. A supporter of the Gregorian Reform, who is very much opposed to lay investiture (Fournier-Le Bras 2.190–191). *2. Date:* Between 1112 and 1120. *3. Place:* Compiled in central Italy, perhaps at Rome or in the region surrounding it. *4. Type:* Systematically arranged collection (titles are preceded by short summaries). *5. Edition:* None.

6. Manuscripts

Cortona, Biblioteca Comunale e dell'Accademia Etrusca, 43, saec. XII[1]; this manuscript is closely related with Wien 2186

Vaticano, Città del, Biblioteca Apostolica Vaticana, lat. 1346, saec. XII^{in}, Prov. Rome? cf. Kuttner-Elze, *Catalogue* 1.100–103, fol. 21^{v}–166^{r}; Theiner, *Disquisitiones criticae* 345–355

Wien, Österreichische Nationalbibliothek, lat. 2186, saec. XII, Prov. Italy, cf. Thaner, *SB Vienna* 89 (1878) 603; to then it was generally taken for a manuscript of Bonizo, because the manuscript began with a fragment of the *Liber de vita christiana* of Bonizo; cf. Pertz, *Archiv* 10 (1851) 488

7. Bibliography

Fournier-Le Bras 2.185–192; Van Hove, *Prolegomena* 328; Stickler, *Historia* 1.187

Theiner, *Disquisitiones criticae* 345–355
Gossman, *Urban II* 35–38
Mordek, *Kirchenrecht und Reform* 140 including n. 196
Blumenthal, *Early Councils* 52, 104–106, 109, 111, 112
Gilchrist, 'Reception 2' 205–206

Collectio 3 librorum (Pistoia C.135, Vat. lat. 3831)

1. Author: A Roman canonist, a supporter of the Reform movement in the period of Paschal II (cf. Fournier-Le Bras 2.202–203). *2. Date:* About 1112, but certainly not before that date (contains excerpts from the *Liber de honore Ecclesiae* of Placidus of Nonantola written near the end of the year 1111), cf. Fournier-Le Bras 2.202;

Gilchrist, 'Reception 1' 47; after 1113 and before 1123 (Gilchrist). First recension between 1118 and 1123. *Place:* Rome, central Italy. Northern Italy (cf. Jasper). *4. Type:* Systematically arranged collection; each title is preceded by a short summary. *5. Edition:* None. (Announced by G. Picasso, cf. BMCL 2 [1972] 4)

6. Manuscripts

Pistoia, Archivio Capitolare del Duomo, C. 135 (olim 109), saec. XII$^{1\text{-med}}$, begun in 1119 and completed about 1123, it probably belonged to the cathedral chapter of Pistoia since the Middle Ages; cf. L. Chiapelli, 'I manoscritti giuridici di Pistoia con testi e documenti inediti', *Archivo Giuridico* 34 (1885) 245ff.; E. B. Garrison, *Studies in History of Mediaeval Italian Painting* 3.1 (Florence 1957) 39; H. Mordek, 'Proprie auctoritates apostolice sedis: Ein zweiter Dictatus papae Gregors VII.?' DA 28 (1972) 110–111 n. 24; Schieffer, *Investiturverbot* 70–71; Motta, 'Osservazioni' (as below) 50ff. (also for Vat. lat. 3831)

Vaticano, Città del, Biblioteca Apostolica Vaticana, lat. 3831, saec. XII1/2, belonged to the church of Sidon in Syria, it later was obtained by the papal library, at which it has been kept since the second half of the fourteenth century, cf. Fournier-Le Bras 2.198–199; about 1150 according to Gilchrist

7. Bibliography

Fournier-Le Bras 2.179, 198–203, 205; Van Hove, *Prolegomena* 328; Stickler, *Historia* 1.179; García y García, *Historia* 1.318

Chiappelli, 'I manoscritti giuridici di Pistoia', *Archivio Giuridico* 34 (1885) 201–275, 35 (1886) 61–110, especially 34 (1885) 245–257

Fournier, 'Manuel' 215

Fournier, 'Collection canonique italienne' 343–438

A. Solmi, *Stato e Chiesa secondo gli scritti politici da Carlomagno fino al concordato di Worms* (Modena 1901) 186 n. 1

A. Vetulani, 'Gratien et le droit romain', RHD, 4e sér. 25 (1946–1947) 35, 37

Munier, *Sources patristiques* 133 including n. 73

Gossman, *Urban II* 41–44

S. Kuttner, 'Urban II and Gratian', *Traditio* 24 (1968) 504–505

S. Kuttner, 'Urbano II, Placido da Nonantola e Graziano', *Annali della Facoltà di Giurisprudenza di Genova* 9 (1970) 1–3

J. H. Erickson, 'The Collection in Three Books and Gratian's Decretum', BMCL 2 (1972) 67–75

Gilchrist, 'Economic Policy' 409–410

Gilchrist, 'Reception 1' 47–48

H. Mordek, '*Dictatus papae e Proprie auctoritates Apostolice Sedis:* Intorno all'idea del primato pontificio di Gregorio VII', RSCI 28 (1974) 1–22

Mordek, *Kirchenrecht und Reform* 140 n. 197

G. Motta, 'Testi di sant'Ambrogio nella Collezione canonica dei Tre Libri e nel Decreto di Graziano', *Ambrosius episcopus: Atti del convegno internazionale di studi ambrosiani nel XVI centenario dell'elevazione di S. Ambrogio alla cattedra episcopale, Milano 2–7 dicembre 1974,* ed. G. Lazzati (Milan 1976) 2.82–93

G. Picasso, 'Testi Canonistici nel Liber de Honore Ecclesiae di Placido di Nonantola', SG 20 (1976) 289–308
G. Motta, 'A proposito dei testi di Origene nel Decreto di Graziano', RB 88 (1978) 315–320
G. Motta, 'Osservazioni intorno alla Collezione Canonica in tre libri (MSS C. 135 Archivio Capitolare di Pistoia e Vat. lat. 3831)', *Proceedings Salamanca* 51–65
Hartmann, *Worms* 116
P. Landau, 'Neue Forschungen zu den vorgratianischen Kanonessammlungen und den Quellen des gratianischen Dekrets', *Ius Commune* 11 (1981) 23–25
Mordek, 'Systematische Kanonessammlungen' 196
Gilchrist, 'Monastic Forgeries' 278
Landau, *Officium* 66 and 72
Landau, 'Vorgratianische Kanonessammlungen bei den Dekretisten' 93–116
D. Jasper, 'Eine neue Handschrift des Liber de honore ecclesiae des Placidus von Nonantola', DA 48 (1992) 537–550, especially 547–550

Collectio 9 librorum (Archivio S. Pietro C.118 etc.)

1. Author: Unknown. *2. Date:* About 1123 (Canon of the First Lateran Council of 1123 'De conjugiis' is not an addition; on the other hand later texts such as Canon 4 of the Second Lateran Council of 1139 and the *Libellus accusationis* dating from the period of Pope Eugene III [1145–1153] can clearly be identified as additions according to Fournier-Le Bras 2.208). Gilchrist believes that it was compiled about 1125. *3. Place:* Italy (Rome?). *4. Type:* Augmented version of the *Collectio trium librorum* (Vat. lat. 3831 and Pistoia C. 135). *5. Edition:* None.

6. *Manuscripts*

Berlin, Staatsbibliothek Preußischer Kulturbesitz, lat. fol. 552, saec. XIII^{in} (Johanna Petersmann, Tübingen, cf. Mordek, *Kirchenrecht und Reform* 140 n. 197)
Vaticano, Città del, Archivio di San Pietro C.118, saec. XII, Rome

7. *Bibliography*

Fournier-Le Bras 2.203–208; Van Hove, *Prolegomena* 240, 328; Stickler, *Historia* 1.179; García y García, *Historia* 1.318

Theiner, *Disquisitiones criticae* 383–397
Fournier, 'Collection canonique italienne 343–438
Gossman, *Urban II* 44–47
A. Riesco Terrero, 'Aportación de las colecciones canónicas de los siglos XI y XII a la legislación de beneficencia', *Ius Canonicum* 8 (1968) 399–470
J. Erickson, 'The Collection in Three Books and Gratian's Decretum', BMCL 2 (1972) 67–76
Gilchrist, 'Reception 1' 49–51
Brommer, 'Rezeption' 113–160
Mordek, *Kirchenrecht und Reform* 140 n. 197
G. Motta, 'Osservazioni intorno alla collezione canonica in tre libri (MSS C. 135

Archivio Capitolare di Pistoia e Vat. lat. 3831), *Proceedings Salamanca* 51–65, especially 62–65

Landau, 'Vorgratianische Kanonessammlungen bei den Dekretisten' 93–116

Alger of Liège, Liber de misericordia et iustitia

1. Author: Alger, a canon of Liège, after 1121 a monk at Cluny, d. about 1131. *2. Date:* Between 1095 and 1121 (cf. Kretzschmar, *Alger von Lüttich* 27–30: cannot be dated more exactly). *3. Place:* Liège. *4. Type:* A first attempt to establish a canonical concordance.

5. Editions

Martène and Durand, *Thesaursus novus anecdotorum* 5 (Paris 1717) 1022–1138 (based on Troyes 443)

PL 180.857–968

R. Kretzschmar, *Alger von Lüttichs Traktat 'De misericordia et iustitia': Ein kanonistischer Konkordanzversuch aus der Zeit des Investiturstreits: Untersuchungen und Edition* (Quellen und Forschungen zum Recht im Mittelalter 2; Sigmaringen 1985)

6. Manuscripts

Bruxelles, Bibliothèque Royale Albert Ier, 10611–14, saec. XVI^{in}, Prov. Saint-Laurent at Liège (a. 1530); fol. 3ra–57rb, cf. Kretzschmar, *Alger von Lüttich* 158–161

Cambrai, Bibliothèque municipale, 562, saec. XII^{2}, Northern France, fol. 2ra–79ra, cf. Kretzschmar, *Alger von Lüttich* 161–163

Parma, Biblioteca Palatina, Parm. 976, ca. saec. XII^{ex}; written in Italy, fol. 231^{v}–240^{v} (excerpt), cf. Kretzschmar, *Alger von Lüttich* 165–168 and Brasington, DA 47 (1991) 172

Troyes, Bibliothèque municipale, 443, saec. XII, written in Northern France, Prov. Clairvaux, fol. 2va–69rb (Martène's edition is based on this manuscript); cf. Kretzschmar, *Alger von Lüttich* 164–165

Abridged Version

Wien, Österreichische Nationalbibliothek, lat. 2177, saec. XII, Prov. Heiligenkreuz; cf. B. C. Brasington, 'Zur Rezeption des Prologs Ivos von Chartres', DA 47 (1991) 171–173

7. Bibliography

A. Amanieu, 'Alger de Liège', DDC 1 (1935), 390–403, especially 393–400; Fournier-Le Bras 2.340–344; Kurtscheid-Wilches 1.165–166; Van Hove, *Prolegomena* 334, 344, 421; Stickler, *Historia* 1.192–193; García y García, *Historia* 1.323; L. Ott, 'Alger v. Lüttich', LMA 1 (1980) 410–411

M. Grabmann, *Die Geschichte der scholastischen Methode* 2 (Freiburg 1911; repr. Graz 1957) 520–521

G. Le Bras, 'Le Liber de misericordia et justicia d'Alger de Liège', *Nouvelle* RHD 45 (1921) 80–118

G. Le Bras, 'Alger de Liège et Gratien', *Revue des sciences philosophiques et théologiques* 20 (1931) 5–26
S. Kuttner, 'Zur Frage der theologischen Vorlagen Gratians', ZRG Kan. Abt. 23 (1934) 244 n. 2
L. Brigué, *Alger de Liège, un théologien de l'eucharistie au début du XIIe siècle* (Paris 1936)
J. De Ghellinck, *Le mouvement théologique du XIIe siècle* (Bruges ²1948)
C. Dereine, 'L'école canonique liégeoise et la réforme grégorienne', *Miscellanea Tornacensia: Annales du Congrès archéologique et historique de Tournai 1949* (1951) 79–94
Gilchrist, 'Reception 1' 66
T. Doran, *Canon Law in the Twelfth Century: The Views of Bernold of Constance, Ivo of Chartres and Alger of Liège* (Excerpta ex dissertatione ad Doctoratum in Facultate Juris Canonici Pontificiae Universitatis Gregorianae; Rome 1979)
Kretzschmar, *Alger von Lüttich*
F. Merzbacher, 'Alger von Lüttich und das kanonische Recht', ZRG Kan. Abt. 66 (1980) 230–260 (repr. *Recht-Staat-Kirche: Ausgewählte Aufsätze*, ed. G. Köbler, H. Drüppel and D. Willoweit [Vienna-Cologne-Graz 1989] 588–618)
Mordek, 'Systematische Kanonessammlungen' 197
Mordek, 'Kanonistik und gregorianische Reform' 77–78
M. L. Arduini, 'Considerazioni sul Liber III del *De misericordia et iustitia* e del *De sacramentis* di Algero di Liegi: Ipotesi interpretativa', *Proceedings Cambridge* 171–195
R. Maceratini, 'Aspetti della posizione giuridica dell'eretico in alcune opere della Riforma gregoriana', *Scritti di storia del diritto offerti dagli allievi a Domenico Maffei*, ed. M. Ascheri (Padova 1991) 1–25 (cf. review by D. Jasper, DA 49 [1993] 345)
Hartmann, 'Autoritäten' 438

Sententiae Magistri A.

1. *Author:* Alger of Liège? (cf. Hüffer, as below, 1–66, but this is rather unlikely according to Amanieu, Le Bras, Fournier-Le Bras, Van Hove); Albericus of Reims (but cf. Uruszczak), Ailmerus of Canterbury (†1130) at least in its earliest recension (cf. Reinhardt, 1975). 2. *Date:* First half of the twelfth century (after Ivo's *Panormia* and before Gratian's *Decretum*). 3. *Place:* Northern France. 4. *Type:* Systematic collection (conciliar canons and decretals); is a source of the *Collectio of Milano, Ambrosiana I 145 inf.* (see below).

5. *Editions*

H. J. F. Reinhardt, *Die Ehelehre der Schule des Anselm von Laon* (BGPhMA, N.F. 14; Münster 1974) 125–263 (Only partial edition of the marriage treatise)
P. Maas, *The Liber Sententiarum Magistri A.: Its Place amidst the Sentences and Collections of the First Half of the 12th Century* (Middeleeuwse Studies 11; Nijmegen 1995)

6. *Manuscripts*

Cambridge, University Library, Ii.IV.19, saec. XII1/2, England
Firenze, Biblioteca Medicea Laurenziana, V 7, saec. XII3/4, Florence
München, Bayerische Staatsbibliothek, Clm 12668, saec. XII–XIII
Oxford, Bodleian Library, Lat. Douce 89, saec. XII–XIII
Paris, Bibliothèque nationale, lat. 2878, saec. XII–XIII
Paris, Bibliothèque nationale, lat. 3881, saec. XII1/2, Southern France or Northern Spain
Troyes, Bibliothèque municipale, 1180, saec. XII1/2, Clairvaux
Troyes, Bibliothèque municipale, 1317, saec. XII–XIII, Clairvaux
Vaticano, Città del, Biblioteca Apostolica Vaticana, lat. 4361, saec. XII
Zürich, Zentralbibliothek, C.111, saec. XII1/2 and XIII

Partial Texts

Bamberg, Staatsbibliothek, Can. 10 (P.I.4)
Milano, Biblioteca Ambrosiana, I.145 inf., ca. a. 1140
Valenciennes, Bibliothèque municipale, 177, saec. XII1/2
Vaticano, Città del, Biblioteca Apostolica Vaticana, lat. 4931, saec. XIII
Vaticano, Città del, Biblioteca Apostolica Vaticana, Ottobon. lat. 943, saec. XVII

7. *Bibliography*

A. Amanieu, 'Alger de Liège', DDC 1 (1935), 390–403, especially 400–403; Fournier-Le Bras 2.329–332; Van Hove, *Prolegomena* 335

H. Hüffer, 'Über Algerus von Lüttich und einen noch ungedruckten Liber sententiarum, der wahrscheinlich von ihm verfaßt und von Gratian benutzt worden ist' *Beiträge zur Geschichte der Quellen des Kirchenrechts und des römischen Rechts im Mittelalter* 1 (Münster 1862, repr. Aalen 1965) 1–66

G. Le Bras, 'Alger de Liège et Gratien', *Revue des sciences philosophiques et théologiques* 20 (1931) 5–26

F. Stegmüller, *Repertorium Commentariorum in sententias Petri Lombardi* 1: *Textus* (Würzburg 1947) 374

N. Häring, 'The *Sententiae Magistri A* (Vat. Ms Lat. 4361) and the School of Laon', MS 17 (1955) 1–45

Coquin, 'Sort' 193–224

P. H. J. T. Maas, *Vorbereidende studies voor het uitgeven van het Liber Sententiarum Magistri A* (Diss. Nijmegen 1969)

H. J. F. Reinhardt, 'Literarkritische und theologiegeschichtliche Studie zu den Sententiae Magistri A. und deren Prolog *Ad iustitiam credere debemus*', *Archives d'histoire doctrinale et littéraire du moyen âge* 36 (1969) 23–56

H. J. F. Reinhardt, *Die Ehelehre der Schule des Anselm von Laon: Eine theologie- und kirchenrechtsgeschichtliche Untersuchung zu den Ehetexten der frühen Pariser Schule des 12. Jahrhunderts; im Anhang: Edition des Ehetraktats der Sententie Magistri A.* (Beiträge zur Geschichte der Philosophie und Theologie des Mittelalters NF 14; Münster 1974)

H. J. F. Reinhardt, 'Die Identität der Sententiae Magistri A. mit den Compilationes Ailmeri und die Frage nach dem Autor dieser frühscholastischen Sentenzensammlung', *Theologie und Philosophie* 50 (1975) 381–403

Mordek, 'Systematische Kanonessammlungen' 198

P. Landau, 'Gratian und die Sententiae Magistri A', *Festschrift Kottje* (1991) 311–326

W. Uruszczak, 'Maître A. et Gauthier de Mortagne, deux lettrés français au XIIe siècle', *Recueil de mémoires et travaux publiés par la Société d'histoire du droit et des institutions des anciens pays de droit écrit* (Montpellier) 15 (1991) 121–131 (refuses to accept the current opinion that Magister A. has to be identified with Albericus of Reims)

Collections of Local Importance

Collectio of Firenze, Laur. IV sin. 4

1. Author: Unknown. *2. Date:* Mid-eleventh century. *3. Place:* Italy? *4. Type:* Unstructured collection. Used the *Collectio 5 librorum* (Vat. lat. 1339) and the *Decretum Burchardi* as sources. *5. Edition:* None.

6. Manuscript

Firenze, Biblioteca Medicea Laurenziana, IV sin. 4, saec. XI, Italy?

7. Bibliography

Fournier-Le Bras 1.445–446; Van Hove, *Prolegomena* 316

Fournier, 'Recueils canoniques italiens' 192–194
Fournier, 'Influence' 68
E. Seckel, 'Zu den Acten der Triburer Synode 895: Zweite Abhandlung', NA 20 (1895) 318–322
Brommer, 'Bischöfliche Gesetzgebung' 35 n. 219
MGH Capit. episc. 1.14, 34, 82
Zechiel-Eckes, *Cresconius* 1.281–285, 296

Collectio of Verona LXIV

1. Author: A contemporary of the Gregorian Reform, who was not influenced by it in any way (cf. Fournier-Le Bras 2.118). *2. Date:* Middle of the eleventh century (cf. Landau 77). *3. Place:* Northern Italy? (used Pseudo-Isidore in the Form A-2). *4. Type:* Drew upon *Pseudo-Isidore, Epitome Hispana, Decretum Burchardi, Cresconius,* and others arranged in blocks; special interest in procedure, especially suits against bishops (Landau).

5. Edition

Only list of Incipit-Explicit by Landau, 'Collectio Veronensis' (as below) 89–115 (including identification of texts)

6. Manuscript

Verona, Biblioteca Capitolare, LXIV (olim 62), saec. XI, Verona? fol. 20^{v}–100^{r}

7. Bibliography

Fournier-Le Bras 1.218–220 and 2.116–118; Van Hove, *Prolegomena* 316

P. Landau, 'Die Collectio Veronensis', ZRG Kan. Abt. 67 (1981) 75–120
Mordek, 'Riforma Gregoriana' 101 n. 47
Landau, 'Kanonessammlungen in der Lombardei' 431
Zechiel-Eckes, *Cresconius* 1.277–281
J. Gaudemet, 'La primauté pontificale dans les collections canoniques grégoriennes', *Studi in onore Luigi Prosdocimi* (1994) 1.1.59–90

Collectio Palermitana (Panormitana)

1. Author: Unknown. *2. Date:* Second half of the eleventh century. *3. Place:* Italy. *4. Type:* Unstructured collection with very different parts. *5. Edition:* None.

6. *Manuscript*

Palermo, Archivio de la Cattedrale, 14; the second part of the manuscript contains a Gregorian collection (beginning at c. 129); Enrico Besta (as below) supposes that the now-lost archetype originated in the region around Chartres, where it was compiled shortly before the canonical collections of Ivo. Fournier-Le Bras accept this hypothesis only for the first part, cf. Fournier-Le Bras 2.150–151

7. *Bibliography*

Fournier-Le Bras 2.150–151; Van Hove, *Prolegomena* 326 n. 2 ('Collectio Panormitana')

E. Besta. 'Di una collezione canonistica palermitana', *Circolo giuridico* 40 (1909) 8–21
Rambaud-Buhot, 'Corpus inédit' 271–281

Collectio Riccardiana

1. Author: Unknown. A supporter of the Gregorian reform movement who tried to vindicate it by collecting old texts that had long been known in Italy; he used new texts rather reluctantly and cautiously; the principal texts of the Reform movement are missing; Fournier-Le Bras 2.124. *2. Date:* During the time of the Gregorian Reform. *3. Place:* Italy. *4. Type:* Unstructured collection. Main source is the *Collectio 5 librorum*. *5. Edition:* None.

6. *Manuscript*

Firenze, Biblioteca Riccardiana, 300, saec. XII1/4, central Italy, cf. Mordek, *Kirchenrecht und Reform* 199 n. 188

7. *Bibliography*

Fournier-Le Bras 2.121–124; Van Hove, *Prolegomena* 316

Lami, *Catalogus codicum manuscriptorum qui in bibliotheca Riccardiana Florentiae adservantur* (Livorno 1756)

J. Merkel, 'Über die Bibliothek des Cistercienserklosters S. Croce di Gerusalemme in Rom', NA 1 (1876) 576–579
E. Seckel, 'Zu den Akten de Triburer Synode 895, Zweite Abhandlung', NA 20 (1894) 313–314
Fournier, 'Influence' 43 (extract)
Fournier, 'Recueils canoniques italiens' 200–201
Mordek, *Kirchenrecht und Reform* 139 n. 188
Reynolds, 'South Italian Collection' 278–295

Collectio Ashburnhamensis (Firenze, Ashburnham 1554)

1. Author: Unknown monk at a Benedictine monastery near Rome cf. Fournier-Le Bras 2.138. *2. Date:* During the pontificate of Pope Gregory VII; about 1085. *3. Place:* Italy, a Benedictine monastery near Rome. *4. Type:* Attempted to complete the *Collectio 74 titulorum;* first part: rather systematically arranged, second part: mostly conciliar canons in almost chronological order. *5. Edition:* None.

6. *Manuscript*

Firenze, Biblioteca Medicea Laurenziana, Ashburnham 1554, saec. XII1/4 (during the pontificate of Pope Calixtus II), in an Italian hand, later additions written in a French hand

7. *Bibliography*

Fournier-Le Bras 2.135–139; Van Hove, *Prolegomena* 325; Stickler, *Historia* 1.175; García y García, *Historia* 1.316 with n. 65

Gilchrist, 'Economic Policy' 405
Gilchrist, 'Reception 1' 44
Mordek, *Kirchenrecht und Reform* 251 (African conciliar canons in the manuscript Firenze Ashburnham 1554, fol. 99^{v}–119^{v})

Collectio of Paris nouv. acq. lat. 326

1. Author: Unknown. *2. Date:* About 1085. *3. Place:* St. Denis, France? *4. Type:* Newly arranged form of the *Collectio 74 titulorum*. *5. Edition:* None.

6. *Manuscript*

Paris, Bibliothèque nationale, nouv. acq. lat. 326, saec. XI^{ex}, ca. 1085, Prov. Saint-Denis; later bound with the Cartulary of Saint-Denis. On the manuscript see Fuhrmann, *Einfluß und Verbreitung* 2.490–491 n. 81

7. *Bibliography*

Fournier-Le Bras 2.14 n. 2 (erroneously attributed to the *Collectio 74 titulorum*).

J. Gilchrist, 'Gregory VII and the Primacy of the Roman Church', TRG 36 (1968) 123–135, especially 124–127

Gilchrist, 'Economic Policy' 410–411
Gilchrist, *Diversorum patrum sententie* xxvi
Gilchrist, 'Reception 1' 53
Kölzer, 'Mönchtum und Kirchenrecht' 135

Collectio of Arras 425

1. Author: Unknown. *2. Date:* Last quarter of the eleventh century, about 1100, after 1078. *3. Place:* Flanders, Northern France, ecclesiastical province of Reims (Arras?). *4. Type:* Source of the *Collectio 9 librorum* of Cod. Wolfenbüttel, Gud. 212. *5. Edition:* None.

6. Manuscript

Arras, Bibliothèque municipale, 425, saec. XII, Prov. Arras, library of the cathedral chapter (fragmentary)

7. Bibliography

Fournier-Le Bras 2.259–260; Van Hove, *Prolegomena* 333 including n. 8; Stickler, *Historia* 1.185

Brommer, 'Rezeption' 127–128
Waelkens-Van den Auweele, 'Codex Gandavensis' 139–153
Gilchrist, 'Monastic Forgeries' 266
Brett, 'Collectio Lanfranci' 169

Collectio of Cambridge, Corpus Christi College 442

1. Author: Unknown. *2. Date:* About 1100 (not earlier). *3. Place:* Probably Northern France. *4. Type:* Bewildering attempt to construct a new canonical collection. Its most important source was a long version of Pseudo-Isidore containing more texts than the *Collectio Lanfranci*. *5. Edition:* None.

6. Manuscript

Cambridge, Corpus Christi College, 442, saec. XII^{in}, English manuscript of unknown provenance (written in a Northern French hand)

7. Bibliography

Brett, 'Collectio Lanfranci' 169–170

Collectio of Monte Cassino 216

1. Author: Unknown. *2. Date:* Not earlier than the last quarter of the eleventh century (contains a text of Gregory VII), cf. Fournier-Le Bras 2.125. *3. Place:* Montecassino. *4. Type:* Combination of excerpts from the *Collectio 5 librorum* and Book XIX of the *Decretum Burchardi*. *5. Edition:* None.

6. *Manuscript*

Monte Cassino, Archivio e Biblioteca dell'Abbazia, 216; saec. XII^{ex}, Southern Italy (Reynolds)

7. *Bibliography*

Fournier-Le Bras 2.124–125; Van Hove, *Prolegomena* 316

Theiner, *Disquisitiones criticae* 305–307
Fournier, 'Recueils canoniques italiens' 95–213
Mor, 'Reazione al *Decretum Burchardi*' 197–206
Reynolds, 'South Italian Collection' 278–295

Collectio of Vat. lat. 4977

1. Author: Unknown. *2. Date:* By the end of the eleventh century during the pontificate of Pope Urban II at the earliest (Fournier-Le Bras 2.127). *3. Place:* Unknown. *4. Type:* Partly derived from the pre-Gregorian *Collectio 5 librorum* (cf. Kuttner, 'Roman Manuscripts' 7). *5. Edition:* None.

6. *Manuscript*

Vaticano, Città del, Biblioteca Apostolica Vaticana, lat. 4977, saec. XI^{ex}–XII^{in}, beginning at fol. 24 (to fol. 23: fragment of the *Collectio 74 titulorum* according to Fournier; according to Kuttner the fragment is written on fol. 6^{v}–23^{v} and contains only cc. 1–129 of the *Collectio 74 titulorum*, as Gilchrist confirmed); Vat. lat. 4977 belongs to the Roman manuscripts from the library of A. Agustín, cf. Kuttner, 'Roman Manuscripts' 7 including n. 4

7. *Bibliography*

Fournier-Le Bras 2.125–127; Stickler, *Historia* 1.160

Fournier, 'Manuel' 150
Fournier, 'Influence' 41 (extract)
Fournier, 'Recueils canoniques italiens' 205–206
Gossman, *Urban II* 18
Kuttner, 'Roman Manuscripts' 7
Gilchrist, *Diversorum patrum sententie* 160 n. 8
Reynolds, 'South Italian Collection' 278–295

Collectio of Celle, Oberlandesgericht C. 8

1. Author: Unknown. *2. Date:* Late eleventh century. *3. Place:* Unknown. *4. Type:* Perhaps identical with the collection described by Gerhard of Maastricht in his *Historia iuris ecclesiastici* (Duisburg 1676) 441–443 (cf. Gilchrist, 'Economic Policy' 412 n. 91). *5. Edition:* None.

6. *Manuscript*

Celle, Bibliothek des Oberlandesgerichts, C. 8, saec. XI^{ex}, fol. 3^{r}–68^{v} (abridged form of the *Collectio 3 librorum* with additions taken from the *Decretum Burchardi*)

7. *Bibliography*

S. Kuttner, 'News of Canonical Collections before Gratian', *Traditio* 14 (1958) 509
Gilchrist, 'Economic Policy' 412–413
Gilchrist, 'Reception 1' 54

Collectio of Madrid 11548

1. Author: Unknown. *2. Date:* By the end of the eleventh century. *3. Place:* Aquitaine (cf. Fransen). *4. Type:* There is a connection with the *Liber Tarraconensis* (cf. Fransen), the first part of the collection taken from the *Collectio Dionysio-Hadriana*. *5. Edition:* None.

6. *Manuscript*

Madrid, Biblioteca Nacional, 11548 (olim Ee 106), saec. XI^{ex}, fol. 1–13, 1 unnumbered fol., fol. 14–68; Prov. Aquitaine

7. *Bibliography*

García y García, *Historia* 1.322

G. Fransen, 'Une collection canonique de la fin du XIe siécle', RDC 10–11 (1960–1961) 136–156
Fuhrmann, *Einfluß und Verbreitung* 2.404, 414
Gilchrist, 'Reception 2' 198
Gilchrist, 'Epistola Widonis' 586–587
Mordek, *Kirchenrecht und Reform* 248

Collectio of Brugge (Bruges) 99

1. Author: Unknown. *2. Date:* Towards the end of eleventh century? *3. Place:* Unknown. *4. Type:* Excerpts of Pseudo-Isidore, *prefationes* of the *Collectio tripartita*. *5. Edition:* None.

6. *Manuscripts*

Brugge (Bruges), Stedelijke Bibliotheek (Bibliothèque de la Ville), 99, saec. XII^{in}, Prov. the Cistercian Abbey of Ter Duinen; fol. 63–82, cf. A. de Poorter, *Catalogue des manuscrits de la bibliothèque publique de la ville de Bruges* (Catalogue général des manuscrits des bibliothèques de Belgique 2; Gembloux - Paris 1934) 123; cf. also Fournier, RHE 26 (1930) 611; Brooke 93 and Fuhrmann, *Ein-*

fluß und Verbreitung 2.412 n. 6; it has been incorrectly regarded as a copy of Ivo's *Tripartita*; cf. now Brett, 'Collections attributed to Ivo' 39–40 n. 41

London, British Library, Cotton Cleopatra C.VIII, fol. 64–91; cf. R. Pokorny, 'Eine Kurzform der Konzilskanones von Trosly (909)', DA 42 (1986) 122–128, cf. Brett, 'Collections attributed to Ivo' 39–40 n. 41

7. *Bibliography*

Fournier-Le Bras 2.58 n.2

Theiner, *Disquisitiones criticae* 178
Fournier, 'Collections canoniques attribuées à Yves de Chartres' 411
Fournier, 'Yves de Chartres et le droit canonique' 399
Brooke, *English Church* 93–94, 243
Brett, 'Collections attributed to Ivo' 39–41 including n. 41

Collectio of Roma, Vallicelliana F.92

1. Author: Unknown. *2. Date:* Eleventh century. *3. Place:* Italy. *4. Type:* A miscellaneous codex of canonical texts. *5. Edition:* None.

6. *Manuscript*

Roma, Biblioteca Vallicelliana, F.92, saec. XI^{ex}, Sant'Eutizio in Val Castoriana near Norcia

7. *Bibliography*

Fournier-Le Bras 1.446–447; Van Hove, *Prolegomena* 316

H. Wasserschleben (ed.), *Die Bußordnungen der abendländischen Kirche* (Halle 1851; repr. Graz 1958) 682–688
Fournier, 'Influence' 40 ('extrait')
Fournier, 'Groupe de recueils' 345–402
Fournier, 'Recueils canoniques italiens' 205–206
Landau, 'Gefälschtes Recht' 37 n. 110
Reynolds, 'South Italian Collection' 278–295

Collectio of Barcelona 944

1. Author: Unknown. *2. Date:* Eleventh century. *3. Place:* Pyrenées. *4. Type:* Chronologically arranged collection of conciliar canons and of some decretals. Main source is the *Collectio Hispana*. 'Colección no gregoriana, fiel a la tradicion', Martínez Díez 224.

5. *Edition*

G. Martínez Díez, 'Una colección canónica pirenaica del siglo XI', *Miscelánea Comillas* 38 (1962) 225–270

6. *Manuscript*

Barcelona, Biblioteca Central de la Diputación Provincial, 944, saec. XI^{ex}, Ripoll, fol. 131^{r}–180^{v}

7. *Bibliography*

G. Martínez Díez, 'Una colección canónica pirenaica del siglo XI', *Miscelánea Comillas* 38 (1962) 211–224

R. Reynolds, 'Marginalia on a tenth-century text on the ecclesiastical offices', *Essays in Honor of Stephan Kuttner* (1977) 118 including n. 30

A. García y García, 'En torno a la canonistica portuguesa medieval', *Iglesia, sociedad y derecho* (Bibliotheca Salmanticensis Estudios 74; Salamanca 1985) 13–27

A. García y García, 'Del derecho canónico visigótico del derecho comun medieval', *Iglesia, sociedad y derecho* (Bibliotheca Salmanticensis Estudios 74; Salamanca 1985) 29–76

Collectio Barberiniana

1. Author: Unknown. *2. Date:* Work on this collection began between 1050 and 1073, it was augmented from 1078 to 1080 and completed between 1081 and 1120 (Gilchrist, 'Reception 2' 204); the additions contain 'typical Gregorian material' (García y García). *3. Place:* Tuscany? (Lucca). *4. Type:* A very elaborately composed collection; it uses the texts as arguments to support its line of reasoning very much in the manner of a treatise.

5. *Edition*

M. Fornasari, 'Collectio canonum Barberiniana', *Apollinaris: Commentarius Iuris Canonici* 36 (1963) 127–141 [Analysis] and 214–297 [Edition] (also published as a separate volume Rome-Florence 1964); cf. *Traditio* 20 (1974) 517

6. *Manuscript*

Vaticano, Città del, Biblioteca Apostolica Vaticana, Barb. lat. 538 (XI.181), saec. XI–XII; Tuscany, probably Lucca according to García y García

7. *Bibliography*

García y García, *Historia* 316 including n. 66

Fornasari, *Osservatore Romano* (Jan. 4, 1963, p. 5)

Fornasari (cf. above, 'Edition')

Kuttner, *Traditio* 19 (1963) 536–537

G. Fransen, 'Principes d'édition des collections canoniques', RHE 66 (1971) 130

Fuhrmann, *Einfluß und Verbreitung* 2.529 including n. 281 (for some texts there must be an intermediate source which they share with Deusdedit)

Fowler-Magerl, 'Vorgratianische Kanonessammlungen' 132–137

Gilchrist, 'Reception 2' 204–205

Mordek, 'Systematische Kanonessammlungen' 197

Collectio of Paris, Sainte-Geneviève 166

1. Author: Unknown. *2. Date:* Probably end of the eleventh century, or beginning of the twelfth century (Fournier-Le Bras 2.268). *3. Place:* France, perhaps Paris. *4. Type:* Systematic collection. The first part relies heavily on the *Decretum Ivonis* and the following ones on the *Decretum Burchardi* (Fournier). *5. Edition:* None.

6. Manuscript

Paris, Bibliothèque Sainte-Geneviève, 166, saec. XII, France?

7. Bibliography

Fournier-Le Bras 2.265–268; Van Hove, *Prolegomena* 333

Theiner, *Disquisitiones criticae* 186–187
A. Blumenstok, 'Die Canonensammlung der Bibliothek St. Geneviève in Paris', AKKR 65 (1891) 150–153
Fournier, 'Collections canoniques attribuées à Yves de Chartres', BEC 58 (1897) 426–430
Fournier, 'Collections canoniques issues du Décret de Burchard' 203–204
Brommer, 'Kurzformen' 42
Landau, 'Dekret' 35 (close connection with the French manuscripts of the *Decretum Ivonis*)

Collectio of Torino, E.V.44

1. Author: Unknown. *2. Date:* Between late eleventh and early twelfth century (about 1100). *3. Place:* Italy. *4. Type:* Unstructured mass of conciliar, papal and patristic texts, an extract from the collection of Deusdedit, a great number of adulterated or forged texts. *5. Edition:* None.

6. Manuscript

Torino, Biblioteca Nazionale Universitaria, E.V.44 (903), saec. XII

7. Bibliography

Fournier-Le Bras 2.218–222; R. Naz, 'Turin (Collection de)', DDC 7 (1965) 1351–1352

J. v. Pflugk-Harttung, 'Eine große Fälschung von Canones', ZKR 19 (1884) 361–372
Fuhrmann, *Einfluß und Verbreitung* 1.140 n. 9
Mordek, *Kirchenrecht und Reform* 141–143
Gilchrist, 'Reception 2' 203–204
Landau, 'Gefälschtes Recht' 42

Collectio of Milano, Ambrosiana M.11

1. Author: Unknown. Italian author under French influence; he borrows from the *Decretum Ivonis* and quotes a letter of Hinkmar's of Reims at full length (Fournier-Le Bras 2.224). *2. Date:* About 1100 (Fowler-Magerl 140) or 1130–1139 (Picasso). *3. Place:* Northern Italy; perhaps from the chapter of San Ambrogio at Milan. *4. Type:* Local collection of excerpts taken from the *Decretum Burchardi,* the *Collectio 74 titulorum* and Ivo of Chartres.

5. Edition

Picasso, *Collezioni canoniche Milanesi* 37–80: only Incipits and Explicits

6. Manuscript

Milano, Archivio Capitolare de la Basilica Ambrosiana, M.11, saec. XII1/2, cf. Mordek, *Kirchenrecht und Reform* 121 n. 91

7. Bibliography

Fournier-Le Bras 2.222–224; Van Hove, *Prolegomena* 329

V. Foffano, 'Descrizione paleografica del cod. M.11 dell'Archivio della Basilica di S. Ambrogio di Milano: Decretales de sacerdotio', *La vita comune del clero nei secoli XI e XII: Atti della Settimana di Studio, Mendola, settembre 1959* (Milan 1962) 2.48–69, especially 64

H. Fuhrmann, DA 27 (1971) 581–583 (review of Picasso, as above)

Gilchrist, 'Reception 1' 51

Picasso, 'Identificazioni' 139–141

Fowler-Magerl, 'Vorgratianische Kanonessammlungen' 140

Landau, 'Kanonessammlungen in der Lombardei' 448–449, 452 including n. 107

Collectio of Roma, Vallicelliana F.54

1. Author: Unknown. *2. Date:* Eleventh century. *3. Place:* Unknown. *4. Type:* Collection that groups its material by topics. *5. Edition:* None.

6. Manuscript

Roma, Biblioteca Vallicelliana, F.54, Part I and II, saec. XI^{ex}, Southern Italy, Beneventan; Part III (fol. 170^{r}–226^{r}) originally a separate codex

Kuttner, 'Roman Manuscripts' 23–25, gives the contents as follows:

Part I: fol. 1–130^{r}, saec. XI: *Collectio 74 titulorum* (fol. 1–62^{r}) and another collection of conciliar and patristic canons (fol. 62^{v}–130), including the so-called apocryphal council of the 'Pope Sylvester' which was edited in 1886 by Charles Poisnel on the basis of this manuscript (fol. 103^{v}–111^{r})

Part II: fol. 131^{r}–169^{v} in Beneventan script saec. XI–XII, principally penitential texts based on the *Collectio 5 librorum* (beginning at fol. 158^{v}–169^{r}) the rubrics of conciliar canons are headed *hera* instead of *capitulum;* on the possible influence of the *Herovalliana* on the *Poenitentiale Vallicellianum primum* in this manuscript, cf. Mordek, *Kirchenrecht und Reform* 131 n. 154; fol. 169 written in a different hand (saec. XII, no longer Beneventan) entry: Lateran Council held by Paschal II from 7, March, 1110, cc. 1–4, then the Lateran Council held by Calixtus II (1123) c. 9 (vulg. 5) was entered in yet another, but still a Beneventan hand

Part III: fol. 170^{r}–226^{r}, saec. XII, canonical collection which does not have any formal division by *tituli;* contains letters and councils of eleventh-century popes; sources: Burchard of Worms, Deusdedit, Ivo of Chartres

7. Bibliography

Fournier-Le Bras 1.444–445; Van Hove, *Prolegomena* 316

Fournier, 'Influence' 38 (extract)
Fournier, 'Groupe de recueils' 345–402
Fournier, 'Recueils canoniques italiens' 205–206
Kuttner, 'Roman Manuscripts' 24–25
Kuttner, 'Corrigendum', BMCL 2 (1972) 5
Gilchrist, 'Reception 1' 52–53 including n. 21
Reynolds, 'South Italian Collection' 278–295
U.-R. Blumenthal, 'An Episcopal Handbook from Twelfth-Century Southern Italy: Codex Rome, Bibl. Vallicelliana F. 54/III', *Studia in Honorem A. M. Stickler* (1992) 13–24

Collectio Pragensis

1. Author: Unknown. *2. Date:* During the pontificate of Paschal II. *3. Place:* 'Ex Styria oriunda' (Van Hove 328). Gouron argues for Provence. *4. Type:* Compilation modelled on the first recension of the *Polycarpus*; between 1123 and 1154, supplemented by drawing on the *Collectio tripartita* and the *Decretum* of Ivo of Chartres

5. Edition

J. F. Schulte, 'Über drei in Prager Handschriften enthaltene Canonen-Sammlungen', SB Vienna 57 (1868) 175–221

6. Manuscripts

Praha, Národní Knihovna Ceské Republiky, VIII. H.7, saec. XII^{2}, probably from St. Lambrecht, Styria

Second Recension
Only partial transmission

München, Bayerische Staatsbibliothek, Clm 13109, Prov. Prüfening, later at Regensburg, fol. 1ra–19va, cf. Mordek, 'Suche' 192 n. 23

7. *Bibliography*

Conrat, *Geschichte* 498–499 ('Gaul'); Fournier-Le Bras 2.180; Van Hove, *Prolegomena* 328; Stickler, *Historia* 1.188

C. G. Mor, *Scritti giuridici preirneriani, fonti delle 'Exceptiones legum romanarum', Libro di Ashburnham, Libro di Tubinga, Libro di Graz* (Milan 1935) 257–260

Brommer, 'Rezeption' 129

A. Gouron, 'Sur la collection en 294 chapitres (manuscript Prague Univ. VIII.H.7)', *Annales de la Faculté de Droit* (Université de Bordeaux I, Centre d'Etudes et de Recherches d'histoire institutionelle et régionale 2; 1978) 95–106

G. B. Ladner, 'Eine Prager Bildnis-Zeichnung Innocenz' III. und die Collectio Pragensis', *Images and Ideas in the Middle Ages: Selected Studies in History and Art* 1 (Raccolta di Studi e Testi 155; Rome 1983) 367–376

Mordek, 'Suche' 188 n. 6, 190, 192 n. 23

Collectio of Pisa, Santa Catarina 59

1. Author: Unknown. *2. Date:* Beginning of the twelfth century. *3. Place:* Pisa. *4. Type:* Abridged version of Recension A' of Anselm's *Collectio canonum.* *5. Edition:* None.

6. *Manuscript*

Pisa, Biblioteca del Seminario Santa Catarina, 59, saec. XII^{in}, fol. 1–16

7. *Bibliography*

G. Miccoli, 'Un florilegio sulla dignità e i diritti del monachesimo (Cod. Pis. S. Cat. 59, ff.1–16)', *Bullettino storico pisano* 33–35 (1964–1965) 117–129

Gilchrist, *Diversorum patrum sententie* p. xl–xli (points out the similarity between this manuscript and a Collectio of Firenze, Biblioteca Medicea Laurenziana, Conv. soppr. 91; Mordek identified the section for Gilchrist)

Kölzer, 'Mönchtum und Kirchenrecht' 136

Collectio of Köln, W 199

1. Author: Unknown. *2. Date:* First decades of the twelfth century. *3. Place:* Unknown. *4. Type:* Revision of a chronologically arranged collection into a systematically arranged collection. *5. Edition:* None.

6. *Manuscript*

Köln, Historisches Archiv, W 199, saec. XII (not before 1130–1139), Prov. Knechtsteden (near Cologne)

7. *Bibliography*

Petersmann, 'Kanonistische Überlieferung' 383, 385, 386–389, especially 447–449

Collectio of Paris, Arsenal 721

1. Author: Unknown. *2. Date:* About 1110. *3. Place:* France, possibly from the region around Paris, cf. Fournier-Le Bras 2.264. *4. Type:* A combination of the *Decretum Burchardi* with Pseudo-Isidore. *5. Edition:* None.

6. Manuscript

Paris, Bibliothèque de l'Arsenal, 721 (15.J.L.), saec. XII, Prov. Saint-Victor at Paris, fol. 170ff. (according to Gilchrist, 'Reception 1' 60: 'fol. 165^{r} seqq.')

7. Bibliography

Fournier-Le Bras 2.261–265; Van Hove, *Prolegomena* 331; Stickler, *Historia* 1.187; García y García, *Historia* 1.322

Fournier, 'Collections canoniques issues du Décret de Burchard' 199–203
Gilchrist, 'Economic Policy' 415
Brommer, 'Kurzformen' 42
Gilchrist, 'Reception 1' 60–61
Schneider, MGH *Ordines* 131

Collectio of Vat. lat. 3829

1. Author: Unknown, cf. Fournier-Le Bras 2.217. *2. Date:* During the pontificate of Gelasius II (1118–1119); does not contain texts after Pope Paschal II (†1118). *3. Place:* Northern Italy. *4. Type:* Chronologically arranged collection of decretals. *5. Edition:* None.

6. Manuscript

Vaticano, Città del, Biblioteca Apostolica Vaticana, lat. 3829, saec. XII^{ex}–XIII^{in} (cf. Hinschius, *Decretales pseudoisidorianae,* lxxvi and Williams, *Codices Pseudo-Isidoriani* 87–88, Excerpta 28, cf. above, Pseudo-Isidorus Mercator, Decretals)

7. Bibliography

Fournier-Le Bras 2.210–218; Van Hove, *Prolegomena* 328; Stickler, *Historia* 1.188

P. Fournier, 'Une forme particulière des Fausses Décrétales d'après un manuscrit de la Grande-Chartreuse', BEC 49 (1888) 325–349, especially 329–330
Gossman, *Urban II* 47–48
Kuttner, 'Roman Manuscripts' 21–22
Williams, *Codices Pseudo-Isidoriani* 87–88
Gilchrist, 'Reception 1' 48–49

Collectio Beneventana

1. Author: Unknown. A monk of S. Sofia at Benevento. *2. Date:* 1119. *3. Place:* Benevento. *4. Type:* Systematic collection. *5. Edition:* None.

6. *Manuscript*

Vaticano, Città del, Biblioteca Apostolica Vaticana, lat. 4939, saec. XII^{in}, Southern Italy

7. *Bibliography*

García y García, *Historia* 1.316–317

O. Bertolini, 'La collezione canonica beneventana del Vat. lat. 4939', *Collectanea Vaticana in honorem Anselmi M. Card. Albareda* 1 (Studi e Testi 219; Vatican City 1962) 119–137; repr. *Scritti scelti di storia medioevale* 2 (Pubblicazioni dell'Istituto di Storia della facoltà di lettere dell'Università degli Studi di Pisa 2; Livorno 1969) 771–789

Fuhrmann, *Einfluß und Verbreitung* 2.507

Kölzer, 'Farfenser Kanonessammlung' 96

Kölzer, 'Mönchtum und Kirchenrecht' 135

A. Degl'Innocenti and S. Cantelli, 'La riforma gregoriana e l'Europa' (Salerno, 20–25 maggio 1985)', SM 26 (1985) 483–493

Mordek, 'Systematische Kanonessammlungen' 198

Reynolds, 'South Italian Collection' 278–295

Collectio Gaddiana

1. Author: Unknown. *2. Date:* Probably dates from the time of Pope Calixtus II (1119–1124), not earlier (Fournier-Le Bras 2.210). *3. Place:* Italy. *4. Type:* Series of isolated texts mostly from the *Decretum Burchardi*, but also from the *Collectio 74 titulorum* and other sources. *5. Edition:* None.

6. *Manuscript*

Firenze, Biblioteca Medicea Laurenziana, Plut. LXXXIX, sup. 32, saec. XII1/2

7. *Bibliography*

Fournier-Le Bras 2.209–210; Van Hove, *Prolegomena* 328

Mordek, *Kirchenrecht und Reform* 140 n. 195

Collectio Augustana

1. Author: Unknown. *2. Date:* Between 1106 (Synod of Guastalla) and 1140, probably about 1110–1120. *3. Place:* Augsburg. *4. Type:* Systematic collection. A comprehensive collection for use as manual by the bishop. Regino's *Libri duo* and the *Decretum Burchardi* as main sources.

5. *Edition*

H. J. Schmitz (ed.), *Die Bußbücher und die Bußdisciplin der Kirche* 1 (Mainz 1883) 737–741 (text of Clm 3909, fol. 24^{r}–26^{v}); only the beginning of the collection

6. *Manuscripts*

Klosterneuburg, Stiftsbibliothek, 638, saec. XII3/3, written at Klosterneuberg, fol. 191–198, cf. Zechiel-Eckes (as below) 23–24

München, Bayerische Staatsbibliothek, Clm 3909, between 1138 and 1143, Augsburg; Prov. Augsburg, fol. 24^{r}–42^{v}, cf. Zechiel-Eckes (as below) 22

München, Bayerische Staatsbibliothek, Clm 9661, saec. XII3/4, probably Southern or Southeastern Germany, Prov. Oberaltaich, fol. 53^{r}–60^{v}

7. *Bibliography*

Mordek, 'Suche' 196 (for the Klosterneuburg manuscript)

K. Zechiel-Eckes, 'Neue Aspekte zur Geschichte Bischof Hermanns von Augsburg (1096–1133): Die Collectio Augustana, eine Rechtssammlung aus der Spätzeit des Investiturstreits', *Zeitschrift für bayerische Landesgeschichte* 57 (1994) 21–43

Collectio Catalaunensis I

1. Author: Unknown. *2. Date:* About 1125 or 1130. *3. Place:* Châlons-sur-Marne *4. Type:* Systematic collection. *5. Edition:* None.

6. *Manuscript*

Châlons-sur-Marne, Bibliothèque municipale, 47, saec. XII1/2; Prov. Saint-Pierre, Châlons-sur-Marne

7. *Bibliography*

Fournier-Le Bras 2.308–311; Van Hove, *Prolegomena* 334; Stickler, *Historia* 1.186

Fournier, 'Collections canoniques attribuées à Yves de Chartres' 624–640

Gossman, *Urban II* 77–78

Gilchrist, 'Reception 2' 195

Collectio Catalaunensis II

1. Author: Unknown. *2. Date:* Between 1130 and 1140. *3. Place:* Châlons-sur-Marne. *4. Type:* Systematic collection. Main sources: *Collectio tripartita, Collectio 10 partium* and *Collectio Catalaunensis I*. *5. Edition:* None.

6. *Manuscript*

Châlons-sur-Marne, Bibliothèque municipale, 75, saec. XII, Prov. St-Pierre, Châlons-sur-Marne

7. *Bibliography*

Fournier-Le Bras 2.311–313; Van Hove, *Prolegomena* 334; Stickler, *Historia* 1.186

Fournier, 'Collections canoniques attribuées à Yves de Chartres' 624–650
Gossman, *Urban II* 78–88
Petersmann, 'Kanonistische Überlieferung' 383, 386–389
Brommer, 'Rezeption' 136

The Canonical Dossier of Leipzig, Universitätsbibliothek, 276

1. Author: Unknown. *2. Date:* About 1120–1139. *3. Place:* Northern Italy. *4. Type:* Collection focusing on the rights of monks; there are parallels to the second recension of *Polycarpus* (Vat. lat. 3882) in its subject matter; closely related to the Collectio of Vat. lat. 1361. *5. Edition:* None.

6. *Manuscript*

Leipzig, Universitätsbibliothek, 276, saec. XII

7. *Bibliography*

R. Helssig, *Katalog der lateinischen und deutschen Handschriften der UniversitätsBibliothek zu Leipzig,* 1: *Die theologischen Handschriften* (Leipzig 1926–1935) 400–405, MS 276, fol. 70^r–82^v
F. S. Paxton, 'A Canonical Dossier on Monastic Rights in Leipzig Universitätsbibliothek MS 276', BMCL 15 (1985) 1–17
Landau, 'Gefälschtes Recht' 46

Collectio of Vat. lat. 1361

1. Author: Unknown. *2. Date:* About 1135. *3. Place:* Italy, monastery near Bergamo (cf. Kuttner, BMCL 1, 1971, 13). *4. Type:* Principally taken from Anselm of Lucca (Recension A'), but also influenced by Ivo's *Panormia* (a rare instance of the use of the *Panormia* in Italy); much monastic material; opposed to the canons regular. *5. Edition:* None.

6. *Manuscript*

Vaticano, Città del, Biblioteca Apostolica Vaticana, lat. 1361, saec. XII[1], between 1133 (coronation of Lothar II at Rome mentioned on the first leaf) and 1137 (death of Lothar II)

7. *Bibliography*

Fournier-Le Bras 2.225–226; Van Hove, *Prolegomena* 329; Stickler, *Historia* 1.187.

Fournier, 'Collections canoniques attribuées à Yves de Chartres' 430–433, 674
Fournier, 'Yves de Chartres et le droit canonique' 400 n. 1
Fournier, 'Observations' 430, 456–458
Gossman, *Urban II* 89–93

Kuttner-Somerville 178
Kuttner, 'Roman Manuscripts' 9–13
Petersmann, 'Kanonistische Überlieferung' 388–389
Blumenthal, *Early Councils* 68–71
Gilchrist, 'Reception 2' 206–207
Kölzer, 'Mönchtum und Kirchenrecht' 137
F. S. Paxton, 'A canonical Dossier on Monastic Rights in Leipzig Universitätsbibliothek MS 276', BMCL 15 (1985) 1–17, especially 16
Kuttner-Elze, *Catalogue* 1.133–134
Landau, 'Erweiterte Fassungen' 328
Landau, 'Gefälschtes Recht' 44, 47 n. 147
Landau, 'Kanonessammlungen in der Lombardei' 448

Collectio of Milano, Ambrosiana I.145 inf.

1. *Author:* Unknown. 2. *Date:* About 1140 (Picasso), cf. Fowler-Magerl 140–141: End of the eleventh century (the latest canons dating from the time of Urban II). 3. *Place:* Milan? 4. *Type:* Local collection of excerpts taken from the *Decretum Burchardi,* the *Collectio 74 titulorum* and Ivo of Chartres.

5. Edition

Picasso, *Collezioni canoniche Milanesi* 81–143: only Incipits and Explicits

6. Manuscript

Milano, Biblioteca Ambrosiana, I.145 inf., saec. XII^{med}

Excerpt

München, Bayerische Staatsbibliothek, Clm 16086 (from the library of St. Nikolaus in Passau), cf. Fowler-Magerl, 'Vorgratianische Kanonessammlungen' 140–141

7. Bibliography

Picasso, *Collezioni canoniche Milanesi* 17–18, 20–23 and 81–143
Fuhrmann, DA 27 (1971) 581–583 (review of Picasso with additional information)
Gilchrist, 'Reception 1' 52
Picasso, 'Identificazioni' 139–141
Fowler-Magerl, 'Vorgratianische Kanonessammlungen' 140–141
Landau, 'Kanonessammlungen in der Lombardei' 447 n. 88 and 452 including n. 107

Collectio of Milano, Ambrosiana H.5 inf.

1. *Author:* Unknown. 2. *Date:* About 1140. 3. *Place:* Region around Bergamo or Brescia. 4. *Type:* Local collection of excerpts taken from the *Decretum Burchardi,* the *Collectio 74 titulorum* and Ivo of Chartres

5. *Edition*

Picasso, *Collezioni canoniche Milanesi* 144–157: only Incipits and Explicits

6. *Manuscript*

Milano, Biblioteca Ambrosiana, H.5 inf., fol. 56^{v}–66^{r}, saec. XII

7. *Bibliography*

C. Dereine, 'La prétendue Règle de Grégoire VII pour Chanoines réguliers', RB 71 (1961) 108–118, especially 109–110
Picasso, *Collezioni canoniche Milanesi* 18–19, 23–24, 144–157
Fuhrmann, DA 27 (1971) 581–583 (important additional information)
Gilchrist, 'Reception 1' 52
Picasso, 'Identificazioni' 139–141
Landau, 'Kanonessammlungen in der Lombardei' 449

Collectio of Roma, Vallicelliana B.89

1. Author: Unknown. *2. Date:* Twelfth century. *3. Place:* Possibly Southern France, Poitiers; shares the same sources as the *Collectio 7 librorum of Torino D.IV.33*? cf. Hartmann, 'Kanonessammlung' 47. *4. Type:* Probably compiled gradually as a collection of excerpts. Main source is the *Collectio Sinemuriensis* cf. above. *5. Edition:* None.

6. *Manuscript*

Roma, Biblioteca Vallicelliana, B.89, saec. XII

7. *Bibliography*

P. Kehr, 'Papsturkunden in Rom: Die römischen Bibliotheken III', *Nachr. Akad. Göttingen 1903,* 125; repr. Kehr, *Papsturkunden in Italien: Reiseberichte zur Italia Pontificia* 4: *(1903–1911)* (Vatican City 1977) 125
Gilchrist, 'Reception 1' 61
Hartmann, 'Kanonessammlung' 45–64

Collectio of Paris lat. 13658

1. Author: 2. Date: Twelfth century. *3. Place:* Unknown. *4. Type:* A collection of 305 chapters that is based on a rearranged recension of the *Collectio 74 titulorum*. *5. Edition:* None.

6. *Manuscript*

Paris, Bibliothèque nationale, lat. 13658, saec. XII, from Saint-Germain-des-Prés; Prov. Chezal-Benoît

7. *Bibliography*

Fournier, 'Manuel' 218–219
Gilchrist, 'Reception 1' 61
G. Fransen, 'Autour de la collection en 74 Titres', RDC 25 (1975 = *Etudes offertes à René Metz* 1) 61–73, 65–66
Fransen, 'Manuscrits' 69

Collectio of Oxford, Bodley 561

1. *Author:* Unknown. 2. *Date:* Twelfth century. 3. *Place:* France? 4. *Type:* About half of the material derives from the *Tripartita* (provides evidence for the origins of *Tripartita* B); further source: Pseudo-Isidore (long form). 5. *Edition:* None.

6. *Manuscript*

Oxford, Bodleian Library, Bodley 561, saec. XII^{in}, fol. 7–37, cf. also above, *Collectio Lanfranci*

7. *Bibliography*

R. Reynolds, 'The 'Isidorian' *Epistula ad Leudefredum:* An Early Medieval Epitome of the Clerical Duties', MS 41 (1979) 252–330, especially 300–301

Indices

Index of Manuscripts

Index of Collections

CPSIA information can be obtained at www.ICGtesting.com
Printed in the USA
BVOW03s0907120514

353083BV00001B/1/P

9 780813 221908